MULTIMEDIA
DEMYSTIFIED

Sponsored by Apple Computer, Inc.
Multimedia Business Development Group, New Media Division
for the Apple Multimedia Program

NEW MEDIA

MULTIMEDIA
DEMYSTIFIED

A Guide to the World of Multimedia from Apple Computer, Inc.

Endicott College
Beverly, Mass. 01915

RANDOM HOUSE
ELECTRONIC PUBLISHING
New York

NEW MEDIA

Multimedia Demystified

Sponsored by Apple Computer, Inc., Multimedia Business Development Group,
New Media Division for the Apple Multimedia Program

Copyright © 1994 by Apple Computer, Inc. All rights reserved.

ƒ Color by Parker-Fields Ltd.

Originally produced by **vivid** studios

Published in the United States by Random House, Inc., New York, and simultaneously in Canada by Random House of Canada, Limited.

Manufactured in the United States of America.

0 9 8 7 6 5 4 3 2

ISBN 0-679-75603-5

QA
76.575
.A66
1994

New York   Toronto   London   Sydney   Auckland

Senior Editor

Randy Haykin, Apple Computer, Inc.

vivid studios

Managing Editor	J. Sterling Hutto
Creative Director	Nathan Shedroff
Associate Managing Editors	Eileen LaPorte, Apple Computer, Inc. Dana De Puy Morgan
Research and Writing	Mark Beaulieu Chris Okon
Additional Writing	Nathan Shedroff Ken Fromm J. Sterling Hutto Randy Haykin, Apple Computer, Inc. Henri Poole
Editors	Ken Fromm Nathan Shedroff
Technical Editor	Henri Poole
Illustrations	Nathan Shedroff Kathleen Egge
Photography	Jim Cottle
Layout	J. Sterling Hutto Ken Fromm Nathan Shedroff Henri Poole
Cover (First Edition)	Patty Richmond, Apple Computer, Inc.
Cover (Second Edition)	Nancy Cutler, HyperMedia Communications, Inc.

vivid studios
A multimedia production studio.
510 Third Street, Suite 420, Box 7
San Francisco, CA 94107-1814

TEL 415/512-7200
FAX 415/512-7202
NET info@vivid.com
LINK vivid
www: hpttp://groundzero.vivid.com/kaboom

Editorial Board

Rita Brennan, *Apple Computer, Inc.*
Jeffrey Davis, *Lumen Production Company*
Abbe Don, *Kaleida Labs*
Steve Franzese, *Apple Computer, Inc.*
David Grabel, *Apple Computer, Inc.*
Bill Hanson, *Apple Computer, Inc.*
Maury Haykin, *The Haykin Group*
Dr. Kristina Hooper-Woolsey*, *Apple Computer, Inc.*
Hal Josephson, *The 3DO Company*
Duncan Kennedy, *Apple Computer, Inc.*
David Krathwohl, *Apple Computer, Inc.*
Brenda Laurel, *Interval Research*
Greg Memo, *Apple Computer, Inc.*
Tyler Peppel, *Aborescence*
Pam Sansbury*, *AGI*
Jill Sarnoff*, *Apple Computer, Inc.*
Phil Schiller
Barry Schuler, *Medior*
Kirk Shorte, *Apple Computer, Inc.*
Martha Steffen, *Apple Computer, Inc.*
Oliver Thompson, *Apple Computer, Inc.*
Vicki Vance, *Apple Computer, Inc.*

Special Thanks

Beatrice Blatteis
Satjiv Chahil, *Apple Computer, Inc.*
Leslie Fithian*, *Apple Computer, Inc.*
Kristine Hansen
Cody Harrington, *Cody Film*
Ken Hawk
Heintzelman's Bookstore, *Los Altos, CA*
Cathy Hess*, *Apple Computer, Inc.*
Nick Keefe, *BMR*
Kenneth Jones
Wendy Mattson
Trish Mayers, *Magnum Design*
Brooks McChesney, *Hands On Technology*
S. Joy Mountford*, *Apple Computer, Inc.*
Sandra Mueller, *The Voyager Company*
Christine Perey
Bill Rollinson
Roy Stringer, *Interactive Designs, Ltd.*

Extra thanks for going beyond the call of duty.

Contents

There are many roles in the multimedia process. We've grouped the most common into 12 categories that define the most important division of responsibilities. If you want to get involved in the multimedia industry, these overviews will show you where your skills are needed in the development process.

If you need to hire someone with the skills described in any of these roles, this section will help you identify who these people are and how to find them. It will also give you an understanding of their backgrounds and experiences.

There are many types of multimedia projects. We've grouped the most common into 12 categories that describe what the major issues and concerns are and any differences in the overall process.

If you know what kind of project you want to create (or want to explore the possibilities), this section is a good place to start. It provides a different view of the book based on the perspective from a particular project.

This book is organized around the process of creating and developing multimedia projects and products. This process is a prototypical one and not every section or concern applies to every project. However, most multimedia projects do follow a similar process.

MULTIMEDIA
DEMYSTIFIED

Sponsored by Apple Computer, Inc.
Multimedia Business Development Group, New Media Division
for the Apple Multimedia Program

NEW MEDIA

Dear Multimedia Developer,

Hardly a day goes by without a newspaper headline heralding the excitement and the viability of the multimedia marketplace. According to InfoTech, CD-ROM title revenue in 1993 grew by 149 percent to $9 billion and is projected to reach $125 billion in 1999.

By year end 1994, Apple Computer will have sold over three million CD-ROM drives, building a critical mass of CD-ROM-based multimedia-capable computer systems. Apple is committed to the establishment and growth of emerging new media markets. This determination is illustrated by the introduction of the Apple Multimedia Program, cross-platform authoring and playback solutions, media-rich system software upgrades, and initiatives for title publishing, distribution, and marketing.

In a recent survey, Dataquest found that new media developers recognized the Macintosh as the premier multimedia development platform by two to one. The introduction of Power Macintosh further strengthens Apple's leadership providing unprecedented performance to multimedia developers.

Multimedia Demystified: A Guide to the World of Multimedia from Apple Computer, Inc. is an example of Apple's commitment to provide resources for developing and distributing successful multimedia products. We created it specifically for current and aspiring new media pioneers, providing information on how to manage the development roles, projects, and process, including interviews of producers and case studies of products.

The future of multimedia begins with you—the developer. Your titles, tools, and ideas will create the demand that will continue to build the market and satisfy the rising expectations of consumers. Apple looks forward to an exciting future, continuing its leading role as an innovator of multimedia technologies, expanding its new media market support, and providing its most important partner—the developer community—with the resources necessary to succeed.

Sincerely,

Satjiv S. Chahil
Vice President and General Manager
New Media Division
Apple Computer, Inc.

NEW MEDIA

Introduction

Multimedia is really not such a new medium, but rather old individual media that have come to life together in new formats on new devices and for new personal uses. There are many lessons that the print world, story telling, music and film production can offer about how to make multimedia work as a unified interactive experience. This book enhances those lessons by bringing together some powerful examples and experiences from a host of viewpoints that are very compelling and useful to help shape this new medium.

— S. Joy Mountford, Manager, Apple Design Center

Multimedia enhances the way people work, learn, play, and most importantly, communicate.

Multimedia is growing up and finally gaining some respect! That "0 billion $ market" saw a turning point in 1992 when most of the largest players in personal computing and consumer electronics — Apple®, IBM, Microsoft, SONY, Tandy, Dell, Sega, Nintendo — began spending large budgets to advertise and market multimedia products and equipment. Many of the multimedia software tools, vendors, and title developers have even begun to turn a profit.

The fact that you are reading this book means you are probably already involved with multimedia in some way. Many of you may just be getting started in developing multimedia as an extension to your existing work, such as desktop publishing, software development, or consulting. You're anxious to get involved in the revolution and share in the opportunities this revolution will produce. If you're ready to jump in and start doing great things, *Multimedia Demystified: A Guide to the World of Multimedia from Apple Computer, Inc.* is for you.

Some of you may have been involved in this growing industry for years and want to strengthen your skills in a specific area. Or perhaps you want to learn about new areas where your skills can be applied. Dive in! This book will present new ideas on how to capitalize on your skills and develop new ones.

Others of you may just now be getting involved. You've watched the industry develop and have thought about joining in when the time is right. Based on many indications, there may be no better time than now. This book will help you overcome the steep learning curve involved in multimedia production.

Still others — vendors, distributors, and **information providers** in publishing, music, art, and education — are on the periphery of the multimedia industry. This book can help you understand the issues facing the multimedia developers you work with and give you numerous ideas on how to enhance your business.

Watch for a Digital Boom...

Something extraordinary is happening on a global scale. Five mega-industries — personal computing, consumer electronics, publishing, entertainment, and telecommunications — are converging. By the year 2000, each of these industries could independently represent nearly **one trillion dollars** in size.

Rarely before has the world seen a merging of different disciplines like this one. For the first time, they will all use a common format. By the year 2000, raw content and information for each one of these industries will be available in digital formats, stored in bits and bytes. Almost everything we see on TV, read in print, view at the theater, and receive over wires or airwaves

The Information Industry in 1971: Separate and Parochial

Services

Mail & Courier Services | TELEX, E-Mail, & Mailgrams | International, Long Distance, and Local Telephone Services

Teletext | Broadcast Networks

Distribution

FM Subcarriers | Cable Networks

Professional & Consulting Services

Videotext

Information Vendors

News Services

Photo Agencies | Advertising Services

Mobile & Paging Services

Telecommunications

Telephone Switching Equipment

PABXs

Telephones

Mainframes | Transaction Processors

Minicomputers | **Computers** | Custom Software

Terminals

Dedicated Word Processors

Publishing Media

Directories
Catalogs
Film, TV, & Video
Records & Casettes
Newspapers
Newsletters
Magazines & Journals
Books

Point of Sale

Cash Registers | Printers

Typewriters | **Office Equipment** | Copiers

Dictation Equipment | Microfilm

File Cabinets | Business Forms
Paper

Televisions | Video Games

Radios & Receivers | **Consumer Electronics**

Tape Decks & Phonographs

Products

containers | transport | translate | transform | present | content will be easily accessible and available anywhere, at any time. We're looking at a **digital boom**!

One of the great challenges with this incredible array of digital information is to provide **interfaces ▶ 32, 131, 209** and **searching mechanisms ▶ 141,162** that allow people to sift this information. Multimedia represents intuitive and realistic ways for people to sort through this digital web—to present this "content" to consumers who are not programmers or "digital scientists." It also represents ways for people to customize their interaction with the digital world so that the information they receive through their senses makes the most sense to them—be it aural, visual, tactile, kinetic, or a combination of these. Think of multimedia as an enhancement to the way people communicate.

Multimedia Defined

Everyone has his or her own impression of what multimedia is. Some think of it as a slide show set to music, others see it is an interactive retail kiosk, still others believe it is a video game at home on a TV screen. In fact, with the coming of the "digital boom," multimedia may look like ALL of these. There is no right or wrong definition—it is a continuum of applications and technologies that allow for a wide range of experiences.

In its most basic definition, multimedia can be thought of as applications that bring together multiple types of media: text, illustrations, photos, sounds, voice, animations, and video. A combination of three or more of these with some measure of user interactivity is usually thought of as **multimedia computing**. Although multimedia can span a wide range of platforms and devices, this book concerns itself with multimedia computing on desktop or portable devices, which are used in specific customer applications.

The power and promise of multimedia is that it gives control to the end user. Once content in various media forms is combined, it can be made **interactive**. Users can begin to navigate and choose relevant

information for themselves. Behind this power of choice stands another major trend—customization for both the user and developer. Digital information allows today's multimedia developers to reach individual consumers with specific, tailored content. Multimedia is at the heart of this trendization with interfaces and options that allow consumers to interactively control the content they want to view.

Since there are so many definitions and examples of multimedia, it may be helpful to view the possibilities on a continuum of complexity and types of **interactivity ▶ 95, 113, 128**. At one end of the spectrum are the simplest and least interactive projects that make use of only two or three types of media. Early videotext or children's computer games using 8-bit color graphics are two examples of these.

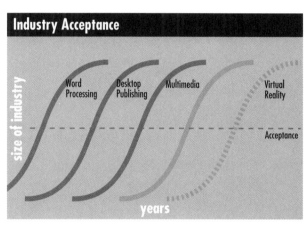

Industry Acceptance

size of industry

Word Processing — Desktop Publishing — Multimedia — Virtual Reality

Acceptance

years

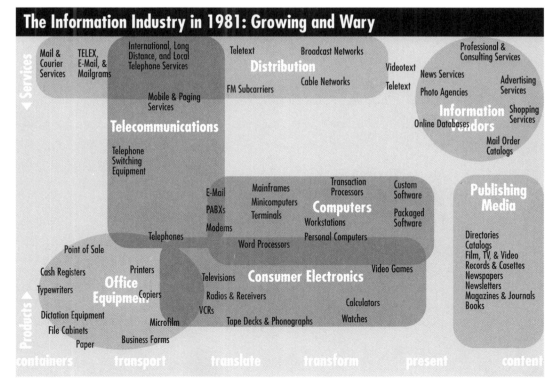

The Information Industry in 1981: Growing and Wary

◀ Services

Mail & Courier Services · TELEX, E-Mail, & Mailgrams · International, Long Distance, and Local Telephone Services · Teletext · **Distribution** · Broadcast Networks · Videotext · Professional & Consulting Services

FM Subcarriers · Cable Networks · Teletext · News Services · Advertising Services · Photo Agencies

Mobile & Paging Services

Telecommunications · **Information Vendors** · Online Databases · Shopping Services · Mail Order Catalogs

Telephone Switching Equipment

E-Mail · Mainframes · Transaction Processors · Custom Software · **Publishing Media**

PABXs · Minicomputers · **Computers** · Packaged Software

Modems · Terminals · Workstations · Directories · Catalogs · Film, TV, & Video · Records & Casettes · Newspapers · Newsletters · Magazines & Journals · Books

Telephones · Personal Computers

Word Processors

Point of Sale · Video Games

Cash Registers · Printers · Televisions · **Consumer Electronics**

Typewriters · **Office Equipment** · Copiers · Radios & Receivers · Calculators

VCRs

Dictation Equipment · Microfilm · Tape Decks & Phonographs · Watches

File Cabinets · Business Forms

Paper

Products ▶

containers · transport · translate · transform · present · content

The whole focus of the industry in the late 1970s was the business of making computers do things. It was all technology and programming. Then the Macintosh® computer came along and popularized the graphical user interface. All of a sudden, the computer changed from being 100% code and all technology to 80% code and 20% graphics. Graphic design and user interface metaphors were part of the mix. It wasn't just a matter of writing code, you had to have artists to make drawings. This spawned a number of applications that took advantage of the incorporation of graphics in programming—desktop publishing and presentations, for example.

Now we are at a point where we are incorporating all these dynamic media and developing content. The whole ratio flops around. The graphics and dynamic media become 80% and the programming is 20%. The accumulation of content is the critical piece of the puzzle.

—Barry Schuler, Medior

At the other end are the highly engaging, highly interactive, and **adaptive projects** ▶ 51, 95. These applications may be displayed on a computer screen, TV screen, or in a theater environment, but they all have one thing in common: Users are highly engaged, in control, and almost "surrounded" with multiple media. For example, a training product for the U.S. Air Force might teach pilots how to fly using multiple media to simulate "real-world" flight. Such a system might reconfigure itself to the user's reactions and information.

One area thought by many to be the ultimate form of multimedia is **virtual reality** ▶ 121,158, a computer environment so realistic and so interactive that the user's senses interpret images as real. The technology to fully accomplish this "suspension of disbelief" may not be as many years away as once thought. The power of today's simple video games to engage children is so tremendous, imagine the power of multimedia when taken to this extreme definition.

Different Markets and Different Processes

The multimedia industry today is comprised of numerous applications of multimedia across many different markets. In 1992, after a study of over 25 multimedia research reports, Apple categorized multimedia applications into six major solution classifications.

These six general market **solutions** allow us to view the full spectrum of multimedia projects or products for multimedia developers. These classifications cut across market boundaries, such as home, business, education, and government. The wide variety of both **casual multimedia** ▶ 92 and **for-profit** solutions suggests opportunities in both the private and public sectors. The classifications can never be exact, since there are many areas of overlap between these segments. For example, an interactive brochure for a travel agency might be viewed both as an information management tool, like a kiosk, and as a communications and sales presentation tool for the travel agent.

Every month, new classes of applications emerge. With the arrival of portable multimedia devices in 1993, even more revolutionary applications are sure to emerge. Portability from one location to another will enable people to take their multimedia with them and use the information anywhere at any time. Portability from one platform to another (for example from desktop computer to handheld consumer electronic device) will enable new uses of multimedia.

Perhaps the most important question to ask is, what justifies the use of multimedia for various applications? Is it the level of control that it delivers to the user? Is it the presentation of material in new and informative ways? Is it the ability to captivate and engage the user? Is it that multimedia saves time, resources, travel, or other costs? Is it that the brain absorbs and retains more

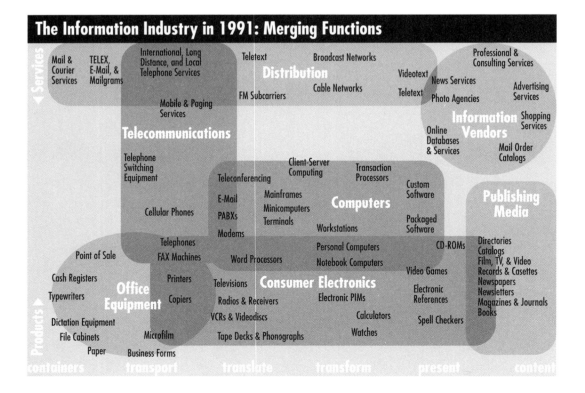

The Information Industry in 1991: Merging Functions

information when the information is presented in multiple formats?

Each solution brings different challenges. This book captures the many possibilities for multimedia usage by looking at the differences in development process as you move from one solution area to another. For example, the steps in the process of developing a consumer multimedia CD-ROM for children are in some ways the same, but in many ways different from the steps in developing an interactive kiosk application for the large business market.

Multimedia developers can save enormous amounts of time by understanding the steps, technologies, and skills necessary to complete each stage of the development process. After reading this book, you will be in a better position to develop and successfully apply solutions for every stage of the multimedia development process.

Yet there are also fundamental differences between the traditional software developers for personal computing and the emerging class of multimedia developers and producers. Today's multimedia developers have a much shorter time-to-market and development cycle. They must rely on more diverse teams of artists, producers, and technical programmers. They also tend to produce one-time products or "multimedia titles" with much longer life cycles than the traditional software developer. The role of the **artist** ▶ 24 and **designer** ▶ 32 in laying out the interface and aesthetics of each project is a critical element of multimedia development, an element less emphasized in traditional software development. This book explores this theme in detail.

Multimedia Industry Participants

Who will profit from the opportunities brought about by the merging of these various industries? The pioneers who are working on today's multimedia projects and products will be in a good position to exploit the advances of future technologies. Are you one of the pioneers or will you wait until the industry has taken off?

In many ways, watching the **digital boom** is like watching the rebirth of the software industry of the 1980s. Back then, software developers had to discover and learn new ways to manipulate digital data. They had to invent new roles, new paradigms, new interfaces, and new forms of interaction. Now the baton is being passed to multimedia developers. New processes, new products, and new techniques on shoestring budgets and with pioneering spirit are all part of today's environment.

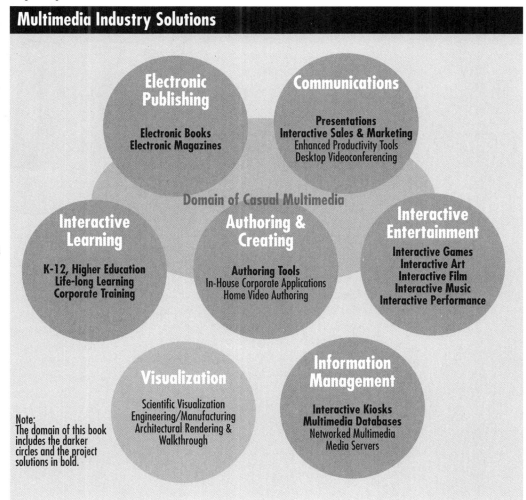

Multimedia Industry Solutions

Electronic Publishing
Electronic Books
Electronic Magazines

Communications
Presentations
Interactive Sales & Marketing
Enhanced Productivity Tools
Desktop Videoconferencing

Domain of Casual Multimedia

Interactive Learning
K-12, Higher Education
Life-long Learning
Corporate Training

Authoring & Creating
Authoring Tools
In-House Corporate Applications
Home Video Authoring

Interactive Entertainment
Interactive Games
Interactive Art
Interactive Film
Interactive Music
Interactive Performance

Visualization
Scientific Visualization
Engineering/Manufacturing
Architectural Rendering &
Walkthrough

Information Management
Interactive Kiosks
Multimedia Databases
Networked Multimedia
Media Servers

Note:
The domain of this book includes the darker circles and the project solutions in bold.

A Guide to the World of Multimedia from Apple Computer, Inc.

Multimedia projects can employ teams with as many as 30 different roles contributing to a project. The model for multimedia development may be more comparable to a **Hollywood production studio** ▶ **64** than it is to the **software development model** ▶ **64.** Many new people are trying to learn new skills and manage complex environments involving both artists and developers. One challenge is managing these diverse variables to produce successful multimedia products. This book explores this theme as well.

Why This Book?

This book was developed for the new media pioneers (current or aspiring multimedia developers). In mid-1992, Apple questioned over 500 multimedia developers to survey their needs. The response clearly indicated a need for information from Apple—not just hardware and code-level support, but also tools to help integrate content, design products, manage diverse creative teams, and produce products. Multimedia developers need good cutting-edge information on how to manage the entire development process, from start to finish, for all kinds of multimedia. They need to be guided through the resources available in the industry. This book represents a strong start in providing that information.

Multimedia Demystified: A Guide for Multimedia Developers from Apple Computer, Inc. is for anyone who is developing projects or products that take advantage of the merging of the five mega-industries. This book explores a finite number of key projects and product types. There will likely be many more created in the coming years. We have only begun to see the first stages in the merging of the five mega-industries and the birth of multimedia. You, the reader, are a direct participant in shaping the future of multimedia.

The purpose of this book is to demystify the processes that go into making multimedia projects and products. This embodies the same underlying approach that Apple takes in designing its computers, consumer electronics, and software: Make it simple to understand and simple to use. *Multimedia Demystified: A Guide for Multimedia Developers from Apple Computer, Inc.* is designed to introduce newcomers to multimedia as well as to allow more experienced multimedia developers to "double-click" on their specific areas of interest. This book is not only exciting introductory reading but also a useful and comprehensive reference.

This Book's Contents

Much of what is available on the projects, processes, actions, and principles in the multimedia industry resides in the minds of those who have walked down these paths. A large part of the book was developed by interviewing current multimedia developers to find out how they have approached and moved from an initial spark to a completed product. This book includes many interviews and case studies of multimedia producers who have faced—and overcome—real challenges.

Three important themes are covered in this book—process, roles, and projects. **Process** ▶ **91** is the primary theme. Most of the book covers the central process of all multimedia projects by describing and illustrating each stage of the process in depth. The secondary themes are **roles** ▶ **10** and **projects** ▶ **34**. Although not covered explicitly, they are interwoven throughout the text and design of the book. Icons indicate the roles or projects that are especially pertinent to specific topics.

A series of content indexes in the book also accesses information from the point of view of skills and abilities. The Roles Index helps describe the skills needed for various types of multimedia projects and how to find talent for each role in the process. The Projects Index helps define the different domains of multimedia and different processes within each domain.

It is the human component, or role that each team member plays in the development of a multimedia project, that ultimately defines the success of a project. This book looks at both the simple and complex ways of organizing and motivating a team to accomplish the many tasks needed to create a successful multimedia work.

A Call to Arms

Although there are many multimedia developers creating products these days, their numbers are small when you consider the digital boom of trillion-dollar industries. There is PLENTY of room for many more players and individual styles. Will you be part of the revolution? We invite you to flip the page and join us.

How to Use This Book

Icons at the top of left-hand pages indicate the different roles associated with the information on these pages.

This book is process oriented, taking you from the beginning, organizing steps of a project through prototyping, production, testing, and distribution. The navigation bars at the top of each page tell you the page number and project phase.

The text has been written to clearly explain the often complex terms and processes in the multimedia industry. Industry "buzz words" are explained both when used and in the combined Glossary/Index at the end of the book.

Twelve basic project types are described in 12 special two-page spreads following the roles indexes. Use these spreads as summaries of some of the key differences between different kinds of projects and as guides to the rest of the book from the perspective of these projects.

The book has been color coded to help visually identify each section.

Margin notes, box stories, and quotes from industry professionals provide related and expanded information from different points of view.

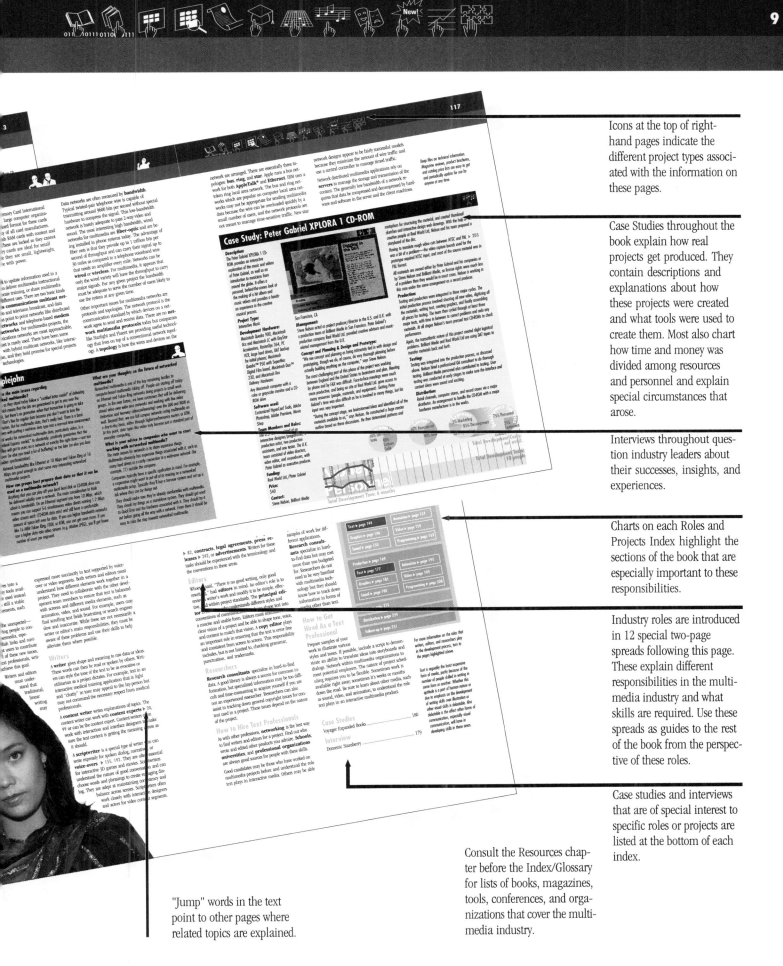

Icons at the top of right-hand pages indicate the different project types associated with the information on these pages.

Case Studies throughout the book explain how real projects get produced. They contain descriptions and explanations about how these projects were created and what tools were used to create them. Most also chart how time and money was divided among resources and personnel and explain special circumstances that arose.

Interviews throughout question industry leaders about their successes, insights, and experiences.

Charts on each Roles and Projects Index highlight the sections of the book that are especially important to these responsibilities.

Industry roles are introduced in 12 special two-page spreads following this page. These explain different responsibilities in the multimedia industry and what skills are required. Use these spreads as guides to the rest of the book from the perspective of these roles.

Case studies and interviews that are of special interest to specific roles or projects are listed at the bottom of each index.

Consult the Resources chapter before the Index/Glossary for lists of books, magazines, tools, conferences, and organizations that cover the multimedia industry.

"Jump" words in the text point to other pages where related topics are explained.

Audience

When you see this icon at the top of a page, it signifies a topic in the text with specific relevance to audience issues.

According to computer market researcher firms, as of April 1994, 11.4 million CD-ROM drives are in active use.

Each type of project is likely to appeal to a different audience and channel of distribution. Traditional media and subject matter have their loyal followings. Readers have their books and magazines, movie-goers have films, and music fans buy CDs and cassettes. In many cases multimedia appeals to the same audiences along traditional lines of interest. Multimedia, however, expands the media through new interaction, offering greater depth and providing added materials. For example, dictionaries can be searched instantly or an action game about sports can provide multiple camera views as well as player and team information. The challenges in these cases are to convince customers of the added value and to deliver the products to them in forms they can use on suitable **delivery media** ▶ **108, 230** and **delivery platforms** ▶ **118**.

Custom Audiences

Multimedia projects are typically directed to either a custom or a **mass-market audience**. The **custom** audience has very specific characteristics and interests. Products are often designed specifically for these needs. Custom audiences can be **business** clients or **employees** or students in an educational project. Examples of products for custom audiences are multimedia databases, corporate training, presentations, pre-visualizations, demo disks, and

kiosks. When working for a client, both the client and the client's audience must be satisfied. In building kiosks, for example, designers study the kinds of information audiences are interested in and the average amount of time they are willing to spend at a booth.

The highly focused nature and the limited or targeted distribution of most custom projects can make identifying a custom audience easier than a mass-market audience. The challenge in this case is meeting their **specific needs**. The constraints provided by a custom audience make the success or failure of an approach more measurable. How well a project succeeds in helping the audience learn may be much easier to gauge with a custom corporate training program than with an electronic storybook for children.

Consumers

Consumer markets for multimedia products are challenging to identify. Large consumer markets often do not grow when a technology is still under development. Added to this is the fact that multimedia standards and equipment at the moment do not match many of the consumer electronic **standards** or **price points**. The consumer audience is putting demands on computer equipment that are only beginning to be met. For digital video, they expect television standards. For audio, they want CD-quality sound. Consumers expect products to have an entertainment value and be inexpensive, simple to use, and indestructible. They want convenience and predictability. Added to this, the nature of interaction and the appropriate forms of presentation are still being developed. All this adds up to a fractured picture of platforms, publishers, distributors, retailers, and customers.

Despite the difficulty, many **developers** and **publishers** ▶ **62, 236** are looking closely at their intended markets from a variety of angles to help with decisions about content, design, and distribution. For example, audience age plays a significant role in the look and complexity of interactive games and educational titles. Knowing what a child can handle or expects influences the content and design. Most state or county **school boards** ▶ **44** have guidelines concerning content and appearance of educational materials. Many government departments have regulations about security or special file formats. Screen size and other technology issues can also play an important role.

Different **cultures** ▶ **96** and **languages** of audiences should also be considered in the design, support, and distribution. For example, supporting a Japanese version may require a text-handling system that can accommodate non-Roman languages. Fortunately, several operating systems are moving or have moved in that direction, taking care of many of the implementation issues. Supporting people with **disabilities** ▶ **97** may also impact the design of a product.

Audiences not only use multimedia products, they sometimes help design and test them. During the multimedia development process, the issue of the targeted audience is involved in almost every step, with the possible exception of production. As part of a marketing **focus group** ▶ **106**, they provide responses for product design considerations. If a **participatory design** ▶ **139** approach is used in the prototype stage, representatives from the potential audience play a critical role in giving new products their definition by responding to mock-ups. They may also provide responses to **test marketing** ▶ **224**. Finally, audience opinions and reactions to the product can be used to provide the basis for following versions of a product.

Other Audiences

Other audiences are equally as important as the end-user audience because they help shape the final audience. These audiences include mail-order houses, distributors, retailers, and the press. **Distributors** and **retailers** act as intermediaries between a publisher

and the end-user, buying product from a publisher and selling it to a customer at a higher price. **Press sources** ▶ **242** include newspapers, magazines, newsletters, television stations, and, to some extent, books. A few sources such as *NewMedia* magazine and the newsletter *Digital Media* specifically cover the multimedia industry, but other computer, business, and general interest sources are featuring more and more stories on multimedia issues and products.

Approaching these audiences at the appropriate times in the development of a project is an important consideration. Many distributors and magazines have policies against ordering or reporting on products that are not shipping. Almost all are discouraged by poorly packaged and presented materials. They are also more apt to carry or cover a product that has an existing market demand than a new product unknown to their customers or audience.

Distribution channels ▶ **237** form an important pathway to the consumer, but the sale of products to a distributor is not the final sale. The final sale is the transaction between the retailer and the end-user, but much of the responsibility for sales still falls on the publisher and its ability to create the demand for a product.

Case Studies

Interviews

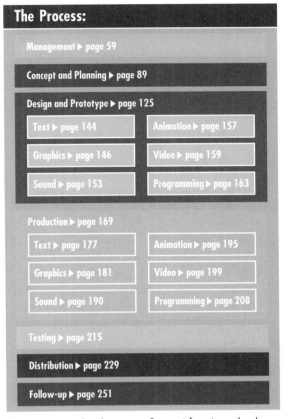

The Process:

For more information on the roles an audience plays in the development process, turn to the pages highlighted above.

In 1992, 27 computer companies announced CPUs with built-in CD-ROMs.

At least three electronic book titles have sold 100,000 or more copies—Compton's Multimedia Encyclopedia, Icom Simulations' Sherlock Holmes, and National Geographic's Mammals Encyclopedia.

Clients

When you see this icon at the top of a page, it signifies a topic in the text with specific relevance to client relations.

A **client** *is a person or company that commissions a piece of work from an outside and independent group. A* **production house** *is a group that designs and creates a product commonly under the sponsorship and direction of a client. A* **publisher** *is typically the group that sponsors the product, owns the copyright, is liable for the content, and responsible for setting up the distribution channels. Some publishers have* **affiliated label** *programs. The main publisher provides the distribution channel and affiliates handle development.*

While some multimedia projects are created directly for the marketplace, others are created for clients under specific direction. Clients fund and sponsor multimedia producers to build specific products. Rather than acquiring equipment and hiring people internally, the client commissions the production company to design an interactive project based on either new or repurposed client content. Although some clients can sponsor mass-market products, most fund projects for one-time use or internal purposes.

The clients interested in distributing mass-market products are typically **publishers ▶ 62, 236**. Some fund complete projects in exchange for marketing and/or partial rights. Others have their own multimedia staff and equipment and are capable of taking a working prototype and producing, packaging, and distributing the final work. A mature publishing market does not yet exist as it does in the print, music, and film industries. Affiliated label programs blur the line between publisher and production house.

A large amount of multimedia business falls to custom projects commissioned by clients. Clients are motivated to bring a project quickly to market with low costs. The client typically provides content, thematic direction, and a background of their audience. Many play a large role in shaping a project but the range of collaboration can vary widely. Some clients can specify a completed project while others work closely throughout all stages and major decisions, helping to craft the project as it goes through the development process.

Contracts and Proposals

A client/contractor relationship can follow an informal process where the two parties get together and work out a contract without any preliminaries, or it can follow a more formal bidding process with a **request for proposals** (RFP) and **proposals ▶ 82**. A request for proposals is usually developed by the client. It outlines the goals and requirements of a project. RFPs are commonly sent out to a number of firms with the understanding that parties interested in bidding will submit a proposal in response. A proposal is a formal document that outlines the relationship between the client and contractor, containing a description of the work to be performed and the terms and conditions of the bid. In many cases, a proposal can function as a contract. In others, a contract is drawn up using the proposal as a guideline.

To establish a successful working arrangement between client and contractor, a number of issues should be resolved at the beginning of the relationship. It begins with having a written **contract**. This document should include the amount and terms of payment and a definitive endpoint of the project (containing a list of deliverables, the handling of change orders, royalties, etc.). It should also include the resolution of copyright issues, credits, and responsibilities for content, liability, testing, and support. Problems deemed insignificant at the beginning of a project have a way of magnifying in importance and creating misunderstanding and conflict. Resolving them up front clears the way for focusing primarily on development of the project. For projects whose scope and contents are unknown at the beginning, build checkpoints into a contract that establish conditions for each successive phase of development.

Process

Depending on the strength of a project concept, a production house can work with the client to refine the purpose **▶ 93**, **goals**, **audiences ▶ 95**, and **delivery media ▶ 108, 230** and **platforms ▶ 118**. Once these items are resolved, the identification of content and development of interaction and interface models can proceed. **Storyboards ▶ 123, 136**, followed by a prototype, act as important checkpoints in refining the organization, design, and media interaction before the expensive process of production begins. Each decision that gets finalized earlier in the process saves time, money, and aggravation at a later point. The **assembly and integration of content** is followed by testing and then integration. **Maintenance ▶ 253** and **support ▶ 255** may follow with responsibility typically falling on the client unless stated otherwise in the contract. Any distribution issues are also usually handled by the client.

How a Client Finds Multimedia Production Groups

One of the first steps is to develop a good idea of what is wanted. Existing project models can help target the particular project solution in mind. The range of projects is wide and the skill sets between them are not necessarily compatible. For example, the skills for producing an interactive storybook for children may not translate to the production of a public information kiosk in a shopping mall. Knowing the type of project can help in qualifying potential production houses. If the type of project is not readily known, then consider hiring a consultant with a wide knowledge of the industry to help decide. (A consultant may also help decide if a multimedia project is appropriate in the first place.)

Another valuable piece of information is knowing the amount of **existing content ▶ 101**. Assembling pre-existing training materials, such as course outlines and video tapes, can help a production house develop better estimates of scope, time, and cost. A thorough description of the **audience** will also give the production house more information to work with.

Once the type of project is known, contact **production companies** who have experience making similar projects. Computer trade shows or multimedia-specific periodicals may provide leads. The industry at the moment is relatively tight-knit. If a firm does not have the time or the skill sets to work on a project, they may be able to recommend others that do. Experienced **project managers ▶ 16, 66** can be good sources of information. Ask them how various products are made, how much they cost, and what the company is like that produced them. Another source to consider are **multimedia directories** that list companies, services, and products. Apple provides a list of some multimedia developers on AppleLink as well.

When contacting a group, examine their **portfolio** and see if their style and skills match the intended project. Determine their production strengths—some are great at designing interfaces, others handle content creatively, and still others have strong animation, video, or audio skills. Inquire about the schedules and budgets for previous projects. Some firms may do great work but miss important deadlines, while others may make deadlines but turn out inadequate results. Availability may be an issue as the number of potential projects increase at a rate faster than the increase in experienced production teams. Check references and ask others in the industry.

How to Find Clients

Just as a client tries to identify the type of project in mind, a production house should identify the type of projects that match its skills and capabilities. A production house may receive a lot of interesting offers. It can pay to think a little ahead of time about direction and focus to avoid being seduced by lucrative but risky proposals.

The number one concern for most clients is to work with a firm that has **experience**. Having well-designed collateral materials on hand, such as business cards and letterhead as well as a portfolio (hopefully containing several completed works) will help project a **professional image**. Accompanying this information should be examples of project plans and comparisons of estimated and actual production costs and times.

A production house can actively search for clients or make themselves available for potential clients to contact or both. The first strategy means researching industries and locating the decision makers within organizations. The second strategy means publicizing a firm's capabilities either through friends and developers or more formally through press releases and directories.

Case Study

Lockheed Waste Management 142

Interviews

Peter Mitchell 70-71

Mark Schlichting and Todd Power 96

Barry Schuler 63

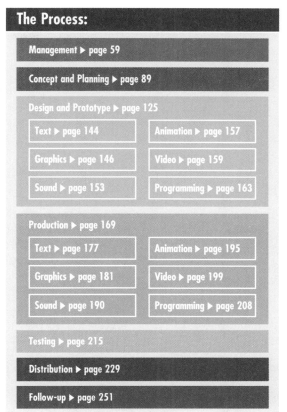

The Process:

Management ▶ page 59

Concept and Planning ▶ page 89

Design and Prototype ▶ page 125
- Text ▶ page 144
- Animation ▶ page 157
- Graphics ▶ page 146
- Video ▶ page 159
- Sound ▶ page 153
- Programming ▶ page 163

Production ▶ page 169
- Text ▶ page 177
- Animation ▶ page 195
- Graphics ▶ page 181
- Video ▶ page 199
- Sound ▶ page 190
- Programming ▶ page 208

Testing ▶ page 215

Distribution ▶ page 229

Follow-up ▶ page 251

For more information on the roles clients play in the development process, turn to the pages highlighted above.

Some areas of the United States are developing large talent pools in multimedia. One such area is called "multimedia gulch" in the South of Market warehouse district of San Francisco. The city has over 38 multimedia companies and its proximity to Silicon Valley provides an abundance of talented and skilled artists and developers. In December 1992, the San Francisco Board of Supervisors adopted a statement of intent to promote the city as the global capital of multimedia. The resolution calls for zoning laws to facilitate high-bandwidth telecommunication lines; support for a center equipped with interactive titles, hardware and software, and conference areas; and partial sponsorship of an annual Interactive Media Festival.

Business and Legal Professionals

When you see this icon at the top of a page, it signifies a topic in the text with specific relevance to business or legal professionals.

Business and law often often play meaningful roles in multimedia companies; however, not all companies need an array of business or legal resources. Where it is most helpful is in small companies that have plans to grow. A small consulting business or production house may not need complex accounting and inventory systems. But companies that want to create several titles or work on several projects at once often have a need to bring in specialists to put in systems or procedures to free others to create and develop. Developers may also need legal help, for example, when signing publishing agreements or content licensing agreements.

One of the biggest advantages to bringing in business and legal experts, **full-time** or on a **consulting basis**, is that it is a relatively less expensive way to gain **experience**. (As compared to alternatives such as learning from mistakes.) Many times it can help to have someone who knows the right questions to ask and the right procedures to follow, especially in areas outside the domain of the project team. Another advantage to working with experienced professionals is that they can add weight and credibility in the eyes of clients and distributors. For example, using an agent to negotiate a deal with a publisher, like many authors and actors do, may result in a quicker, easier, and better deal for a developer.

Business Professionals

Business professionals can include presidents, operating officers, financial advisors—in short, anyone who is involved in maintaining a viable business. One of the principal roles of a business manager is to make sure a company is profitable. This responsibility can range from raising funds on a corporate or project basis or ensuring that sales are sufficient, to supporting the continued operation of a company. Many multimedia companies see a direct relationship between managing items such as funding, costs, and inventory effectively and having the freedom to create the projects they want to create.

Developing a CD-ROM title can cost anywhere from $25,000 to $1,000,000, depending on the amount of content and the level of interaction (not including mastering and manufacturing charges). Locating and managing money for developing a project is not an easy task. Financial aspects common to almost all multimedia businesses and projects include budgets and cash flow. A **budget** ▶ 67 is an estimate of the money needed to complete a product or function. Experience provides many of the initial estimates in a project, with research in the earlier stages helping to fill in more exact numbers. **Cash flow** ▶ 74 is the financial input and output of an organization measured over time. A budget lists expenses while revenue projections provide estimates of expected income. The combination of these mapped against time provides a picture of the cash flow. Managing money effectively does not only mean having enough money to create a product, it also means having the money at the right time in the process. Good financial managers have experience in accounting, project finances, and handling inventory (if this is an issue). They should also understand tax, employee, and accounts payable and receivable issues.

Legal Professionals

Legal professionals can provide advice and information on **intellectual property** ▶ 104, **licensing**, and **contract issues**, as well as on general corporate matters and employee or contractor issues. One of the biggest concerns in multimedia at the moment is the issue of **copyrights** and intellectual property protection. The relatively unique situation of multimedia, where one film clip can comprise only a fraction of the entire content, poses new challenges when securing permissions and licensing content owned by others. Some projects have been delayed or significantly altered because of these problems. Having people knowledgeable not only in the law, but in the law as it applies to multimedia, can help ensure the success of many projects.

Large companies commonly have their own **legal counsel** or staff, but many use outside resources for litigation, patent filings, and other special legal work. Small companies often use outside legal advice. Many firms can reduce their legal expenses by becoming more aware of legal issues. This can include preparing standard employee, contractor, and client agreements and putting simple procedures in place, such as getting model releases at the time of a photo or video shoot. At the same time, production houses should consider building relationships with knowledgeable law firms or hiring legal professionals to periodically review general practices.

How to Hire Business or Legal Professionals

Knowledge of the multimedia industry is a benefit for business people, but experience in a related industry, such as book or software publishing or filmmaking, can make up for a lack of experience in multimedia. Look for people who have worked for companies of comparative size, as well as the size you wish to grow to within the next few years. It can help to have people on hand who have already gone through similar stages of growth in a company. Also look for someone with the ability to listen. A valuable skill for a business or legal person is to take general principles in their fields and apply them to specific concerns in multimedia.

A lawyer or legal professional should preferably have experience in multimedia and **intellectual property issues** as well as industry conventions, such as **royalty rates** and **payment terms**.

Finding people will depend on what they are needed for and how long they are needed. Searching for full-time employees may be harder than using an accounting firm or a law firm. Many of these firms that serve the computer and software industries are beginning to

expand into multimedia. Find out who other multimedia companies use and then find out who their competitors are. This can provide a number of firms from which to choose.

How to Get Hired As a Business or Legal Professional

Many multimedia companies may not have the need or the desire to hire business or legal people on a full-time basis. Consider approaching a firm with the idea of consulting in return for small up-front fees and equity, a percentage of royalties, or a commission on signing a deal. Show how your skills will translate into more sales, more products, greater freedom, or other benefits that go along with being a profitable company. Show an understanding of multimedia and a willingness to learn, and try to understand the motivations of the people in the company.

Find companies by looking in industry magazines and books, or attending conferences and trade shows. To get exposure, write articles or give talks at user group meetings or conferences on issues in business or law as they relate to multimedia.

Case Studies

Ben & Jerry's Ice Cream Statistical Process Control ... 84

Voices of the 30s 176

Interviews

Peter Mitchell 70-71

Steve Nelson 86

Minoo Saboori and Matthew London 80

Joe Sparks 247

The Process:

Management ▶ page 59

Concept and Planning ▶ page 89

Design and Prototype ▶ page 125

Text ▶ page 144	Animation ▶ page 157
Graphics ▶ page 146	Video ▶ page 159
Sound ▶ page 153	Programming ▶ page 163

Production ▶ page 169

Text ▶ page 177	Animation ▶ page 195
Graphics ▶ page 181	Video ▶ page 199
Sound ▶ page 190	Programming ▶ page 208

Testing ▶ page 215

Distribution ▶ page 229

Follow-up ▶ page 251

For more information on the roles the business or legal professional plays in the development process, turn to the pages highlighted above.

Project Managers

When you see this icon at the top of a page, it signifies a topic in the text with specific relevance to project managers.

A point stressed by many developers and production houses is the role that good management plays in successful multimedia projects. Executive producers, project managers, and creative directors may be roles played by a single person or by three separate people. Looking at the roles from a film industry perspective, an executive producer is someone who signs deals and helps arrange the financing. The project manager is the film producer, controlling the people, logistics, and resources. The creative director is the film director, responsible for the vision and creative aspects of the project. All of these people need to "know multimedia" to some extent—not necessarily at the level of a production person, but conversant enough in the tools, technology, people, and markets to quickly arrive at decisions in the face of uncertain information.

Executive Producers

An **executive producer** is usually tied to the business side of an organization and spends time putting together deals and helping to arrange financing. In larger organizations, they may be called **vice presidents of development**. On smaller projects and in smaller firms, the project manager essentially assumes the role of executive producer, handling the up-front work with a client or upper management, as well as the creation and production of a finished product.

Project Managers

The **project manager ▶ 66** is probably one of the most critical roles to fill for any project. Project managers bear the ultimate responsibility for the success or failure of projects. They coordinate the project budget, schedule, and resources. When played out properly, this role may seem to the untrained eye to be invisible. As with any profession, though, the performer who makes it appear easy is often working with a precision unparalleled by the amateur.

Budget skills and scheduling knowledge are essential when dealing with the client and with other managers on a project. Good managers decide how much it affects the bottom line to shoot five more minutes of video or put in two new program features. They know what happens when one team member gets sick for a week. They know how it affects the budget and the other team members, and they can shift priorities and responsibilities so it does not cause a disaster. Most of these skills come about only with **experience**. Managers need to learn from past projects so that they have a better understanding of future ones.

With this knowledge of budgets and schedules comes the responsibility of translating this information into project proposals that can be sold profitably to clients and internal management. **Proposals ▶ 82** for custom projects are a combination of industry practices blended with individual nuances. Project managers not only need to know the cost and implications of each item. They also need to negotiate an agreement that is of fair value to both parties.

Understanding people is important to all managers but it can be paramount to those who manage creative people. A good multimedia project manager knows how to **motivate people**, recognizing that some people need encouragement and praise while others need prodding and challenging. An experienced manager will recognize the types and know the right way to approach them. Managers must be perceptive of personality conflicts, and know how to defuse and avoid them. They must also understand the collaborative process and be willing to put their own egos aside. A good manager accepts blame but passes credit on to the other team members.

Creative Directors

The **creative director** is a type of project manager whose responsibility is to maintain a **consistent design** ▶ 128 and a consistent interaction model. A substantial portion of the personnel on large projects may be managed by the creative director. These may include designers, writers, editors, artists, animators, musicians, and possibly programmers. The creative director establishes and monitors the **standards** ▶ 167 and **styles** of the individual efforts and the integrated work.

A creative director has to be careful not to overmanage or stifle the creative process of the team. Some creative managers are skilled artists in their own right, and tend to push their ideas onto others. This approach may work, but it can also drive wedges into teams, causing them to fall apart. Successful creative directors provide clear direction and high expectations but know that some of the best work comes from providing **creative freedom**. They also know that ideas become good ideas only after a lot of collaboration and rework.

Above all, the two traits that are most needed by project managers and creative directors are **ambition** and **confidence**. The price for innovation is criticism, a price that any creative spirit must be willing to pay. The drive to create coupled with the confidence to continue will produce great works where others would have failed or never even tried.

How to Hire Project Managers

Look for experience, management skills, and knowledge of putting together a multimedia piece. They do not need to be experts at every task but they should know what is possible and what type of person best fits the job. Having managed previous projects can often translate into significantly lower costs and shorter schedules. One estimate in the industry is that the second and third projects can cost up to one-third as much as the first. Part of that savings is attributable to creating reusable tools and templates but most is due to overcoming the steep learning curve in multimedia projects.

How to Get Hired As a Project Manager

Prior experience managing projects is almost a prime requisite. One way to build up this experience is to perform a variety of roles in the relatively controlled environment of an established company. Another way is to bring together artists and others to create a multimedia piece with little outside influence. Expect to break even or lose money doing it this way but expect to learn enough to hopefully translate into successful projects in the future. A number of aspiring directors in Hollywood in recent years have begun a trend of going outside established channels and putting together films independently. Many of the same things are happening today in the multimedia industry.

Case Studies

Voices of the 30s 176

Voyager Expanded Books 180

Interviews

Rosalyn Bugg 122

Peter Mitchell 70-71

Steve Nelson 86

Minoo Saboori and Matthew London 80

Joe Sparks 65, 247

The Process:

Management ▶ page 59

Concept and Planning ▶ page 89

Design and Prototype ▶ page 125

Text ▶ page 144	Animation ▶ page 157
Graphics ▶ page 146	Video ▶ page 159
Sound ▶ page 153	Programming ▶ page 163

Production ▶ page 169

Text ▶ page 177	Animation ▶ page 195
Graphics ▶ page 181	Video ▶ page 199
Sound ▶ page 190	Programming ▶ page 208

Testing ▶ page 215

Distribution ▶ page 229

Follow-up ▶ page 251

For more information on the roles the project manager plays in the development process, turn to the pages highlighted above.

Marketing and Sales Managers

When you see this icon at the top of a page, it signifies a topic in the text with specific relevance to marketing and sales managers.

Innovative and flexible **marketing ▶ 85, 241, sales ▶ 81, 245,** and **distribution strategies ▶ 230, 236** can provide a competitive advantage in the rapidly changing marketplace of multimedia. Keeping balance in the midst of ever-evolving technology, broadening audiences, and converging industries are often compared to surfing, where the skilled surfers search out and ride the largest waves while the unprepared shy away and settle for the ones left behind. Aggressive companies make use of their marketing and sales people throughout a project, relying heavily on their skills in planning as well as in preparation for distribution.

Some multimedia production companies may have less of a need for marketing and sales than others. Firms that contract to other companies may only need sales skills to help develop clients and manage the relationship. Others that are using publishers or affiliated labels may need sales experience only in signing the original agreements. In small companies, the marketing and sales groups can be the same, even to the point where the same person also happens to be the project manager. In larger companies, the marketing and sales departments are commonly separate.

Marketing and sales complement each other. Where **marketing** addresses a broader spectrum of messages and demographics, **sales** identifies the commitments involved in an individual purchase. Where marketing builds on overall strategy, sales uses specific tactics to move from initial contact to final

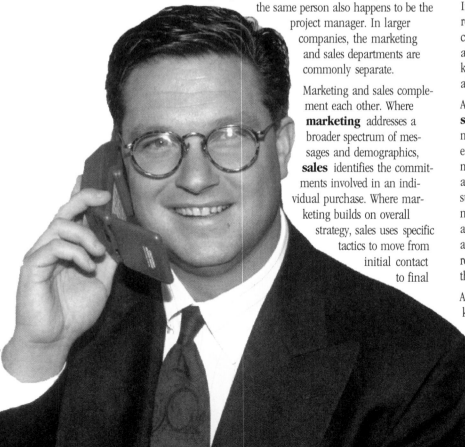

close. Both contribute to distribution, that is, getting the product into a client's or customer's hands. Marketing strategies initiate and control the distribution channels. Sales controls the interactions at each juncture from client to developer and from developer to customer. Both use general principles and apply them to the nuances of an industry such as multimedia.

Marketing Managers

A **marketing manager** helps identify **potential markets ▶ 106** and finds the common ground between what a potential audience wants and what is technically possible. They challenge a development team to create a product that has benefits for customers, not just a set of well-designed and laid-out features. A marketing manager also helps determine a product's **price** by mediating between the cost of production and the value to potential customers. Marketing managers must make decisions in the face of direct competition and indirect forces.

In a custom project, the project manager may fill the role of marketing manager, setting the expectations, communicating the project's progress, and delivering it at its completion. For a mass-market product, the marketing manager manages external communications about the product and its capabilities.

A marketing manager needs **good communication skills** and tools. The primary role of the marketing manager is that of a bridge or liaison between the client and developer or between the developer and the marketplace. The marketing manager communicates to an external audience with **marketing tools ▶ 241,** such as press releases, brochures, and advertising. Internally, they should be knowledgeable of the capabilities and skills of the members of the project team. Frequent and informal interaction with the project team will help reduce the friction between marketing and development that is common in many companies.

Another strength of a good marketing manager is the knowledge of a wide range of distribution and marketing options. The methods of delivering products to customers are changing as rapidly as the technology behind the products. Just as a developer or artist has to stay in tune with new tools and procedures, a marketing manager must also be aware of new strategies and practices in their particular industry, as well as other industries.

Sales Managers

The role of the **sales manager** ▶ 249 is to set up the structure for finding, coordinating, and rewarding sales people. Sales managers may not actively initiate and sign agreements but they need to provide the people who do with the resources and training to do their jobs. These resources include sales materials, such as brochures, selling guides, and product demonstration templates. Sales people should also have access to information on prospective clients. In a small company, the role of the marketing and sales manager may be filled by the same person because of the small number of distribution channels.

Sales People

Unlike development, the sales operations never have a definitive end. Sales can occur anywhere in the multimedia process. At the beginning of a project, sales may mean arranging a deal with a client. Near the end, it may mean selling products to retailers and customers. With the start of a new quarter the count is set back to zero and the pressure to reach a quota begins anew. An individual sale follows the cycle of prospecting, qualifying, meeting, closing, and following up.

Good **sales people** ▶ 249 allocate their time, their most precious resource, efficiently. They do this by making sure prospective clients have the budget, authority, and desire to reach an agreement. Successful sales people also sign agreements with an eye towards generating future business. The time and emotional cost of closing a sale are so high that creating repeat business is a cost-saving strategy.

How to Hire Marketing or Sales Managers

Experience and **success** are probably two of the best indications of good marketing and sales people. Other indicators are the ability to listen and a healthy amount of confidence. Good marketing and sales people require more than just the ability to paint a pretty picture for a customer. They require the ability to take input from users, distributors, media people, and customers and form plans and responses that meet the needs of these groups in beneficial ways. Confidence is needed both to project a positive image and to help handle the large percentage of rejections common in sales.

Both marketing and sales skills can be difficult and expensive to learn on the job. Marketing people that have worked for larger companies in the multimedia industry are good resources. They may have knowledge of multimedia-specific concerns and experience in setting up distribution channels. For sales people, knowledge of the industry may not be as important (although knowledge of related industries, such as book or software publishing, will help), but some form of sales training or experience can be critical.

How to Get Hired As a Marketing or Sales Manager

For someone looking to get hired, the ability to document past successes coupled with knowledge of a company, the industry, and its competitors can open many doors. Enthusiasm for the company, its product line, and its charter will also help. But before reaching this point, a marketing or sales person might have to get experience by filling roles in lower positions in marketing or sales and working up to higher levels of responsibility. For example, an inside sales position may eventually lead to outside sales and then to a sales manager position.

Case Studies

Interviews

The Process:

For more information on the roles marketing and sales managers play in the development process, turn to the pages highlighted above.

Content Experts

When you see this icon at the top of a page, it signifies a topic in the text with specific relevance to content experts.

Liability for the accuracy of data is important. That's why you use experts. . . . If you work with the best people, no one is going to dispute them, at least not in a major way.
—Roy Stringer, Interactivity Designer, Theseus *medical database*

Content ▶ 101, 127, 223 includes the text, video, audio, and illustrations that convey the subject matter of a multimedia product. A **content expert** ▶ 99 is someone who knows a subject area intimately and can help a project team find and select materials for a multimedia product. Content experts come from all walks of life: teachers, historians, amateur researchers, or anyone who can speak with knowledge and authority about a subject. Content experts bring depth, credibility, and accuracy to the presentation of a subject.

Disciplines such as filming documentaries, publishing books, or writing corporate white papers rely heavily on content experts. A content expert for a video about bicycle maintenance might be an accomplished bicycle mechanic. A content expert for a book on stand-up comedy may be an experienced comedian. Content experts for a children's game may be children as well as child psychologists. The content expert helps with accuracy, authenticity, and scope of the material used to represent a subject. Content experts not only have knowledge, they can explain what they know to others.

Content experts can contribute to multimedia applications in several ways. They can help create the content, in a sense, acting as a writer or author of a piece, or just advise a project manager and consult on the organization and accuracy of the subject matter. For example, a corporate training program about customer service can draw on the expertise of the company's customer service representatives. A project to build an on-demand help system can enlist technical support personnel to help create and manage content. UCLA music professor Robert Winter was the primary content expert/writer for Voyager's *Ludwig van Beethoven: Symphony No. 9 CD Companion*, a five-part interactive HyperCard program that presents the music, score, historical background, and an explanation of the symphony. Winter guided the content preparation of the piece, provided commentary and interpretations, and worked with programmers to build the framework for interaction.

Content experts should be able to work well with others and see how different elements contribute to the big picture of a project. Good content experts have something to show for their **expertise**. Perhaps they have written a book, created art, conducted presentations, or taught a subject in a high school or university. They could be amateur hobbyists who have spent evenings or weekends researching or collecting information and material.

Many multimedia projects are born from the enthusiasm of a content expert. Nikki Yokokura is a Japanese language teacher who wanted to develop an interactive training program to introduce the language and the culture of Japan to native English speakers. She created a simple model of a training program in HyperCard and soon discovered that she needed programming and design assistance to expand the product. She maintained her enthusiasm and commitment for the project by playing the role of the primary content expert. The product matured to a point where it is now marketed by The Voyager Company as *Exotic Japan*.

If an expert is not available, a **content researcher** can collect information from different sources, such as literature, historical media, interviews, and other materials. The content researcher must not only be able to select appropriate content for the subject and purpose of the multimedia project but also evaluate the **validity of sources**. A good content researcher is like a good reporter who thinks critically, investigates different leads, and assembles information in a meaningful and appropriate way.

Content can be original, recycled, licensed, or in the public domain. For example, a composer can provide an original score or a clip-art service can provide copyright-free images for a fee. A film producer can grant permission to use a plot idea or a government agency can provide access to its files. Interaction with a **content provider** ranges from negotiating business and licensing contracts, to requesting information or materials from individuals or groups.

Information sources are as varied as the kinds of subjects possible for multimedia projects. A good place to get a grounding in a subject area is the library. Magazines and trade journals are useful for finding names of potential content experts, as are special topic conferences and seminars. Educators are another good source of information about current knowledge and research in a subject area.

How to Hire Content Experts

Content experts for specialized subject areas can be found at universities, businesses, publications, or a site of activity for the subject area. Check the credentials of a content expert. Items to look for can include academic degrees, letters of references, press reports, or published works. An important thing when working with any content source is to have a clear definition of a project's purpose and the experience it intends to create. The interface designer, programmer, and project manager need to collaborate with content professionals to select and use materials in the project. Besides having specific knowledge in an area, a good content expert

should be able to explain difficult concepts in understandable terms and be open to exploring new avenues for getting information across.

How to Get Hired As a Content Expert

Content experts can sometimes inspire new products. A person with knowledge in a field may develop an idea as fully as possible and then search for the talent necessary to turn it into a multimedia project. For example, an art history teacher may present ideas about an interactive art education program in a proposal to a publishing company. Individuals with research skills might apply for jobs in publishing companies that will be creating new multimedia titles in different subject areas. Content providers, if not contacted directly, can promote their services through mail-order catalogs and through organizations such as the WPA Film Library, an organization which provides select newsreel footage. Another route is to actively promote their knowledge by sending samples to television talk shows, media contacts, and multimedia production houses.

Case Studies

Interview

The Process:

Management ▶ page 59

Concept and Planning ▶ page 89

Design and Prototype ▶ page 125

Text ▶ page 144	Animation ▶ page 157
Graphics ▶ page 146	Video ▶ page 159
Sound ▶ page 153	Programming ▶ page 163

Production ▶ page 169

Text ▶ page 177	Animation ▶ page 195
Graphics ▶ page 181	Video ▶ page 199
Sound ▶ page 190	Programming ▶ page 208

Testing ▶ page 215

Distribution ▶ page 229

Follow-up ▶ page 251

For more information on the roles content experts play in the development process, turn to the pages highlighted above.

The Research Department in Los Angeles, founded by Chris Darryn, provides research to organizations, especially the entertainment industry. They have access to countless news items, publications, scientific journals, and other sources through several online databases and charge fees for each research item. They have fulfilled many research requests for films and TV shows ranging from how to build an atomic bomb for a Saturday Night Live skit about Saddam Hussein to the latest in bulletproof school clothes for a morning talk show.

Writers, Editors, and Researchers

When you see this icon at the top of a page, it signifies a topic in the text with specific relevance to writers, editors, and researchers.

And though many believe that interactive multimedia, with its emphasis on pictures and sound, will kill what little desire our children still have for books, others argue that multimedia will not finish off the printed word unless we let it. It has been proven over and over again that children will read books if we provide them with the books they want to read.

—Denise Caruso, former editor of Digital Media *(now at Friday Holdings), in* Utne Reader, Jan/Feb 1993

Long before electronic media, descriptive writing was the chief means of communicating experiences to a wide audience. With multimedia, text moves into a bigger arena. Words are no longer the only tools available to describe content. An image can be used instead and replace a page or two of text. Text is still a viable medium, but it must work with other elements, such as sound and pictures.

Multimedia introduces an element of the unexpected— **interactivity ▶ 95, 113, 128**, allowing people to control their own path and *explore*. Hypermedia, especially, gives users the power to establish links and navigate at will. A product might prompt users to contribute their own material. Throughout all of these new issues, text must communicate well. As text professionals, writers and editors work together to achieve this goal.

Writers and editors must understand that traditional, linear writing may

not be appropriate. Long detailed passages may not work on notebook-size screens. Ideas may need to be expressed more succinctly in text supported by voice-over or video segments. Both writers and editors must understand how different elements work together in a project. They need to collaborate with the other development team members to ensure that text is balanced with screens and different media elements, such as animation, video, and sound. For example, users may find scrolling text fields frustrating or search engines slow and inaccurate. While these are not necessarily a writer or editor's main responsibilities, they must be aware of these problems and use their skills to help alleviate them where possible.

Writers

A **writer** gives shape and meaning to raw data or ideas. These words can then be read or spoken by others. Writers can style the tone of the text to be as evocative or utilitarian as a project dictates. For example, text in an interactive medical training application that is light and "chatty" in tone may appeal to the lay-person but may not command the necessary respect from medical professionals.

A **content writer** writes explanations of topics. The content writer can work with **content experts ▶ 20, 99** or can be the content expert. Content writers often work with interaction and interface designers to make sure the text content is getting the meaning across as it should.

A **scriptwriter** is a special type of writer who can write expressly for spoken dialog, narratives, or **voice-overs ▶ 155, 192**. They are often essential for interactive 3D games and movies. Scriptwriters understand the nature of good conversation and can choose words and phrasings to create engaging dialog. They are adept at maintaining consistency and balance across scenes. Scriptwriters often work closely with interaction designers and actors for video content segments.

Writers may also be needed to generate or edit any necessary **documentation** ▶ 212, 254, **proposals** ▶ 82, **contracts**, **legal agreements**, **press releases** ▶ 242, or **advertisements**. Writers for these tasks should be experienced with the terminology and the conventions in these areas.

Editors

Whoever said, "There is no good writing, only good rewriting," had **editors** in mind. An editor's role is to review a writer's work and modify it to be simple, effective, and within project standards. The **principal editor** is someone who understands different styles and conventions of communication and can shape text into a concise and usable form. Editors must maintain a clear vision of a project and be able to shape tone, voice, and content to match that vision. A **copy editor** plays an important role in ensuring that the text is error-free and consistent from screen to screen. This responsibility includes, but is not limited to, checking grammar, punctuation, and trademarks.

Researchers

Research consultants specialize in hard-to-find data. A good library is always a source for common information, but specialized information may be too difficult and time-consuming to acquire yourself if you are not an experienced researcher. Researchers can also assist in tracking down general copyright issues for content used in a project. These issues depend on the nature of the project.

How to Hire Text Professionals

As with other professions, **networking** is the best way to find writers and editors for a project. Find out who wrote and edited other products you admire. **Schools**, **universities**, and **professional organizations** are always good sources for people with these skills.

Good candidates may be those who have worked on multimedia projects before and understand the role text plays in interactive media. Others may be able to gain that knowledge quickly. Ask to see samples of work for different applications. **Research consultants** specialize in hard-to-find data but may cost more than you budgeted for. Researchers do not need to be very familiar with multimedia technology but they should know how to track down information in forms of media other than text.

How to Get Hired As a Text Professional

Prepare samples of your work to illustrate various styles and tones. If possible, include a script to demonstrate an ability to translate ideas into storyboards and dialogs. Network within multimedia organizations to meet potential employers. The nature of project scheduling requires you to be flexible. Sometimes work is available right away; sometimes it's weeks or months down the road. Be sure to learn about other media, such as sound, video, and animation, to understand the role text plays in an interactive multimedia product.

Case Studies

Voyager Expanded Books 180

Interview

Domenic Stansberry 179

The Process:

Management ▶ page 59

Concept and Planning ▶ page 89

Design and Prototype ▶ page 125

Text ▶ page 144	Animation ▶ page 157
Graphics ▶ page 146	Video ▶ page 159
Sound ▶ page 153	Programming ▶ page 163

Production ▶ page 169

Text ▶ page 177	Animation ▶ page 195
Graphics ▶ page 181	Video ▶ page 199
Sound ▶ page 190	Programming ▶ page 208

Testing ▶ page 215

Distribution ▶ page 229

Follow-up ▶ page 251

For more information on the roles that writers, editors, and researchers play in the development process, turn to the pages highlighted above.

Text is arguably the least expensive form of media, partly because of the number of people skilled in writing in some form or another. Whether this aptitude is a part of human nature or due to emphasis on the development of writing skills over illustration or other visual skills is debatable. Also debatable is the effect other forms of communication, especially visual communication, will have in developing skills in these areas.

Graphics Professionals

When you see this icon at the top of a page, it signifies a topic in the text with specific relevance to graphic professionals.

Get a designer in from day one to figure out your visual schema, typeface, and some basic ground rules, but also build in flexibility. The reason for getting a graphic designer is that the general public is very discerning about good-quality images. We have an eye for good-quality design on paper, which is culturally expected. On television, we're used to seeing information presented beautifully. If multimedia isn't as good or better, people aren't going to spend time on it because their eye will become bored. It's not a conscious thing. They will just lose interest because they will want to see something more interesting.

— Roy Stringer, Interactivity Designer, Theseus medical database

Graphic skills are essential to all multimedia projects. They are needed to create pictures and the layout and visual design of the electronic product. They may also be involved in designing packaging, documentation, and supplemental print materials. **Photographs** ▶ 157, 185 and **illustrations** ▶ 149, 181 add meaning and create understanding in ways that text or sound cannot. However, imagery must balance other media. For example, the mood of a picture should work with the mood established by music.

Graphic Designer

A **graphic designer** lays out screens, designs icons and symbols, establishes type specs and color schemes, and decides on the overall visual balance of elements. Many of the graphic design tasks, such as screen design, font selection, and image sizing, are completed in the prototype stage and do not carry over into production. An information designer can look through content with the graphic designer to organize and present information in a navigable system.

Illustrator

An **illustrator** creates drawings, diagrams, charts, maps, and cartoons. An illustrator draws idealized or realistic images of people, objects, places, ideas, processes, or concepts. Illustrations can be especially useful when photographic representation presents too much information or is not sufficient in detail or clarity. Medical illustration is an example where a drawing can represent components or features with a style and precision that photographs are not able to convey. Illustrations can use a variety of drawing styles and media effects.

Photographer

Photographs can be the main focus of a multimedia project or play a supporting role. Digital photographs may appear in any type of project, including catalogs, presentations, kiosks, electronic photo essays, and picture databases. Photographs presented in a series are frequently used to create interactive stories. Photographers can now get their work digitized by a photofinishing service by having film converted to **Photo CD** ▶ 112, 188 format. One of the photographer's greatest technical skills is the ability to record the light of a subject. Photographers should also be able to get along and communicate with all kinds of subjects, from children to celebrities.

Scanning and Image Processing Specialists

By working with scanners and image processing programs, **scanning** and **image processing specialists** ▶ 151, 188 can digitize drawings and photographs to create the digital formats often required by a computer system. Technical responsibilities for these roles include creating storage size, resolution, and quality standards. A photofinishing service can replace scanning by converting slides or negatives into a Photo CD format, but some type of image processing may still be necessary to clean up or enhance the images. Special **filters** ▶ 189, 206 and techniques can be used to create new interpretations and styles of digital imagery. Image processing can also be used to fix flaws in lighting, color balance, or contrast, and clean up speckling or other stray images.

How to Hire Graphics Professionals

Start by identifying the project's stylistic needs and estimated project size (such as number of screens, scenes, or elements). If a **style** has been determined, then show examples to see if candidates can work in it. Designers may understand the audience and know what works better than the people who hire or manage them.

Some photographers and illustrators specialize in a specific subject matter, anything from people to food, caricatures to maps. When hiring a photographer, consider local talent in an art department or working freelance for local newspapers or magazines. Consider contacting a photo agency or directory. Ask personnel in camera shops to recommend people.

Spend time looking at portfolios. Look for a **range** of subject matter and ability that matches the style of the project. Look for examples that display a consistent, skilled technique. Ask candidates how they plan and execute assignments. Ask if they have access to needed equipment—especially photographers. All these questions build up a picture of capabilities and resources. Having previously published works may not be critical but knowledge and skill will be.

Speed, though, is sometimes more important than creative ability. Try to get an idea of how long it takes a person to produce a particular piece. Great work done two months late may not be worth the aggravation. Familiarity with computers is also a bonus. Illustrations and photographs need to be in digital form in order to operate in an interactive environment. Constraints such as low screen resolution or bit depth may make it necessary to change an image or drawing after digitizing it. Having the same person create the image and retouch it will eliminate possible destructive alterations.

How to Get Hired As a Graphics Professional

Be conversant in the tools of the trade, including image processing tools of the "electronic darkroom," scanning techniques, and painting and drawing software. Build a

portfolio that contains a wide variety of subjects, black-and-white work and color, or different stylistic variations of the same image. Include demos or screen shots of actual electronic pieces. Point out any versatility and knowledge you may have with digital media.

Most illustrators and photographers must usually start small and work their way up to more prominent roles and responsibilities. Working on multimedia projects is no different in this regard. The advantage, though, lies with the person who is conversant with digital techniques and is adept at connecting with other forms of media. Attend multimedia and professional conferences and meetings to generate leads about multimedia projects, producers, and project managers. Approach multimedia production houses, publishers, and consultants in order to present a portfolio. The size of the portfolio should depend on the timing of their current or future projects. Someone actively looking for assistance will want to see an extensive portfolio. Someone else may only need a sample to keep on file should an opportunity arise.

Case Studies

Four Footed Friends 102

Kai's Power Tools 100

Interview

Kenneth Jones 182

Wayne Williams 152

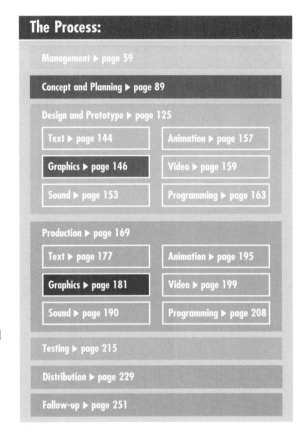

The Process:

Management ▶ page 59

Concept and Planning ▶ page 89

Design and Prototype ▶ page 125

Text ▶ page 144 Animation ▶ page 157

Graphics ▶ page 146 Video ▶ page 159

Sound ▶ page 153 Programming ▶ page 163

Production ▶ page 169

Text ▶ page 177 Animation ▶ page 195

Graphics ▶ page 181 Video ▶ page 199

Sound ▶ page 190 Programming ▶ page 208

Testing ▶ page 215

Distribution ▶ page 229

Follow-up ▶ page 251

For more information on the roles graphic professionals play in the development process, turn to the pages highlighted above.

Sound Professionals

When you see this icon at the top of a page, it signifies a topic in the text with specific relevance to sound professionals.

Sound provides the author a direct line of communication through dialog and narration, an emotional palette with music, and an enriched palette of effects and design elements.
—Jim McKee, Sound Producer, Earwax Productions

Sound design ▶ 153, 190 is integral to multimedia production, providing a distinct level of communication. Sound can communicate while other things are happening. Voice-overs and historical speeches can convey meaning and emotion in a completely different way than displayed text. Good sound professionals can make a big difference to any project. They should not be overlooked when animation or video is added.

Audio professionals contribute primarily to the production stage of a project, although sound designers may be involved in the early planning. Production of good sound in the multimedia development process involves an awareness of how sound fits into the entire design scheme, the nature of the audience, and the location of the multimedia experience. (Kiosks in public places have far different sound requirements and constraints than an interactive music title may have.) Using sound in a project also brings up issues of the behavior of the delivery platform, the budget of the project, and whether existing material is available for processing or must be generated anew.

Sound must first be recorded. Production may require musicians, sound effects engineers, and voice talent. Material may also be obtained from existing sources such as client audiotapes, films, or historical speeches. In any case, audio material must be converted to digital format, balanced correctly or "sweetened," and incorporated into the final piece. Sound is usually designed for interactive pieces in ways that let a user interrupt the sound at any point. The more interactive a product is, the more challenging the sound design might be to permit new combinations.

Sound Designers and Researchers

Sound designers are artists responsible for creating a continuous **soundscape**, creating tension or emotion where needed. Sound is probably the least expensive way to set mood and establish emotion. Sound designers are able to rework sound tracks with special **digital sound processors ▶ 121, 193**, as well as mix and balance sound levels into one sonic experience that fits with the rest of the media and interactions in a project. **Sound researchers** are needed to explore sound and music libraries for appropriate sounds. They can also help clear up licensing issues with copyrighted materials.

Musicians and Voice Talent

Musicians are often needed to create tracks for **background music ▶ 154** and scores for interactive games and movies. They also are an integral part of interactive musical performances given in auditoriums or other public places. CD-Audio discs can be extended with multimedia in the form of accompanying diskettes. CD-quality sound can also be integrated into interactive CD-ROM products. In these cases, musicians may be the primary focus of a project. They may have existing works on the market. A multimedia product might consist of a repurposing of this work, enriched with text, pictures, video, and other nonmusical elements.

MIDI ▶ 155, 192 is a popular format for recording, playing, and creating music, since some computers now have built-in MIDI processing capabilities and many instruments can provide MIDI output.

Voice talent is used for supplying dialog, narrating **voice-overs**, creating cartoon voices for characters and objects, and translating products for foreign markets. The quality or beauty of a voice may not be as important in some cases as the ability to convey emotion. Many TV and movie actors provide voice-overs for animated features, commercials, and documentaries. The quality of their voice does not set them apart as much as their delivery.

Audio Engineers

Audio engineers record voice, sound effects, and background ambient sounds. They also help record interviews and support the sound track for video production. When sound is used with videotaping (especially with multicamera shoots), it is critical that the sound be of good quality. All too often, background noise in video or audio makes speech or featured sounds difficult to understand. This problem can be avoided by having an audio engineer take full responsibility for making good source recordings. Good microphones and sound recording techniques are the mark of a good audio engineer.

How to Hire Sound Professionals

Go to a small **recording studio** (there are several in most major cities), tell them what you want to do, and see if they are interested or know someone who is. You should know what you want. Sound engineers are often associated with television facilities as well. These can be good places to find competent **freelance engineers**.

Professional sound designers have a rich repertoire of knowledge and a fine sense for using sound. Listening to **demo tapes** ▶ 155 is one way to get to know the

work of an artist or engineer. Voice work should show clear diction, energy, and range of intonation. An especially good conference at which to meet electronic musicians is CyberArts, held every fall in Pasadena, California.

How to Get Hired As a Sound Professional

Sound professionals should produce demo tapes or demo CDs that show a range of music or sound work. Sound designers should produce "before" and "after" tapes that highlight their capabilities and knowledge. Consider collaborating with graphic designers or animators to produce music or sound for a multimedia demo to showcase abilities. Networking, attending conferences, and joining professional organizations like the Audio Engineering Society can generate contacts and leads.

Case Studies

Peter Gabriel XPLORA 1 CD-ROM 117

Total Distortion 222

Interviews

Jim McKee 156

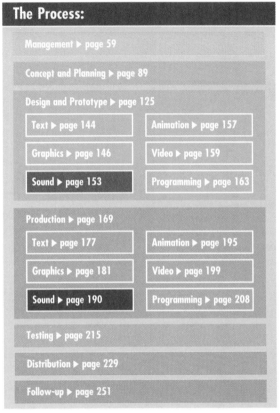

The Process:

Management ▶ page 59

Concept and Planning ▶ page 89

Design and Prototype ▶ page 125

Text ▶ page 144   Animation ▶ page 157

Graphics ▶ page 146   Video ▶ page 159

Sound ▶ page 153   Programming ▶ page 163

Production ▶ page 169

Text ▶ page 177   Animation ▶ page 195

Graphics ▶ page 181   Video ▶ page 199

Sound ▶ page 190   Programming ▶ page 208

Testing ▶ page 215

Distribution ▶ page 229

Follow-up ▶ page 251

For more information on the role sound professionals play in the development process, turn to the pages highlighted above.

Studies have shown that good sound quality is often more important than good video quality. People consistently believe that a TV with better sound quality actually has a better picture than one with poorer sound even though the two picture tubes are the same.

Animators

When you see this icon at the top of a page, it signifies a topic in the text with specific relevance to animators.

Animation ▶ 157, 195 is a common element in many multimedia projects. It is the creation of moving illustrations that help users visualize a process, idea, or abstract concept in a way that is not easily communicated through words or single pictures. Animation may be the only affordable way to show something, compared to the expense of video. Any type of product—kiosks, electronic books, and games—can use animations but they should be appropriate for both the content and the style of the product.

An **animator** uses the illusion of movement and depth to present active ideas about processes. A good animator has the ability to plan animations, understand storyboards, sketch ideas, and work with designers. They must work within limitations of time and technology as well as within the demands of the content and audience. Good ones are adept at understanding abstractions as well as following through with patient detail.

Animators must build animations to work within the context of the whole product and other media, such as sound and text. Animated characters often need voices, objects may need sounds, or whole scenes may need music. As a result, animators

frequently work with **musicians** ▶ 26, 153, 190, **sound engineers**, and **voice talent** to bring together the right combination of pictures and sound.

The best animators have **solid drawing skills** and are sensitive to the nuances of creating movement. They are artists, trained in the tools of their trade, which include color theory, life drawing, and composition. In addition, they are adept at working with software tools and technologies.

An animator's responsibilities begin in the prototype stage when variations of elements or characters are drawn, matched with different voices, and set in various backgrounds. Sometimes the project prototype is itself one big animation or simulation of how the product will work. The project concept is put into animated form using available computer technology. Storyboards for animations are developed in the design stage and finished in the production stage. Animators are used extensively in the production stages of a project but may also be required to work in the design and prototype state where styles and limitations are set.

Animators usually specialize in either two-dimensional (2D) or three-dimensional (3D) forms because the two types are very different. 2D animation is an evolution of traditional cel or character animation. While 2D animation does not have to look cartoonish, styles vary much more than with 3D animation. 3D animation tends to be much more realistic in style.

2D Animators

2D animators may still use traditional tools, such as sketchbook, pencil, or tracing paper, to draw characters and scenes and scan these into a computer to add color, texture, and motion. The 2D animator works frame by frame creating the illusion of space and the characters and objects that inhabit it. Other tools of the 2D computer animator are scanners, image processors, and 2D animation applications.

3D Animators

3D animation presents objects and scenes in three-dimensional space, rendered by computer technology. 3D animators use **modeling programs** to create an environment of geometries and objects. They then use **animation/rendering programs** that calculate perspective, lighting, texture, volume, movement, and other realistic features. Objects can be made to move around in the space and follow paths. A great deal of processing power is needed for 3D rendering.

Compared to the 2D animator who may work with both paper and the computer, the 3D animator works almost exclusively with computer animation programs. The knowledge of a filmmaker or set designer can be useful to animators who must plan the effects of lighting, the placement of characters, the movement across the stage, or the position of a camera.

How to Hire Animators

Before hiring an animator, have a strong idea of a project's concept and audience and determine if animation is really necessary to convey the concept. Sometimes, simple illustrations or video are more effective and affordable.

An animator's **style** contributes much to the look and feel of an entire project. A style that works well for a children's book may not carry over into a corporate presentation. Collect samples of animation styles, from television commercials or other productions, that illustrate the desired style of the product.

To find good animators, research who produced the animations in existing products and obtain recommendations from other developers and project managers. Many animators prefer to work on a freelance basis. Those whose work you admire may be available to work independently. Local colleges and universities that offer animation programs may also recommend candidates. The roster of SIGGRAPH, the ACM special interest group for computer graphics, also contains names of accomplished animators.

When interviewing an animator, determine the extent of their knowledge and experience with computer tools and with working on a multimedia team. An excellent animator may be reluctant to work within the existing limitations of digital media. When reviewing someone's

portfolio, determine the time, effort, and cost required to generate special sequences. Special animations may exceed the budget and time limits of a project. Before negotiating work with an animator, the project manager should use the animator's estimates to fine-tune the project tasks and schedule. Bringing an animator on board without a clear idea of the work to be done can be costly.

How to Get Hired As an Animator

Understand both traditional and newer methods of animation. Learn at least one common computer animation tool well—an especially important skill for 3D animators. Build a **portfolio** of animations for different applications, such as charts, spinning logos, children's characters, or process diagrams. Include select **storyboards ▶ 123, 136** that show how animations evolved during development and be able to explain the time, cost, and effort involved in each sequence.

Since animation skills are relatively scarce compared to other media, actively promoting one's skills can lead to many contacts and jobs. Sending out small pamphlets, postcards, or other materials may not provide responses immediately but they may provide responses in the future from people who keep them on file. Hooking up with several producers and project managers can also help.

Case Studies

IslandTrapper Demonstration Disk 196

Total Distortion 222

Interviews

Lucia Grossberger Morales 158

Kenneth Jones 182

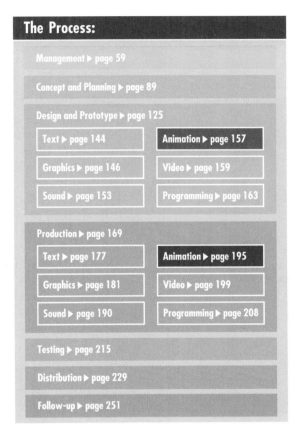

The Process:

Management ▶ page 59

Concept and Planning ▶ page 89

Design and Prototype ▶ page 125

Text ▶ page 144	Animation ▶ page 157
Graphics ▶ page 146	Video ▶ page 159
Sound ▶ page 153	Programming ▶ page 163

Production ▶ page 169

Text ▶ page 177	Animation ▶ page 195
Graphics ▶ page 181	Video ▶ page 199
Sound ▶ page 190	Programming ▶ page 208

Testing ▶ page 215

Distribution ▶ page 229

Follow-up ▶ page 251

For more information on the role animators play in the development process, turn to the pages highlighted above.

Video Professionals

When you see this icon at the top of a page, it signifies a topic in the text with specific relevance to video professionals.

Video ▶ 159, 199 is a powerful and versatile medium. Videos can present intimate views, on-the-scene reports, or interviews with personalities. Video production can be one of the most expensive undertakings in a multimedia project and requires special planning and coordination of people and equipment. People using digital video technology are aware that it is undergoing tremendous change—especially with traditional video production equipment, such as editing and processing tools.

The effort to produce a video from script to final edit involves several roles. In **preproduction**, writers, directors, location staff, and producers are needed. In **production**, camera, sound, and lighting people, stage managers, and actors are needed. In **postproduction**, sound and video editors become necessary.

Traditional roles in video carry over into multimedia productions. One individual

often performs several roles. Researchers check video and film archives and may also work as editors. **Videographers** handle the camera, lights, and sometimes record the sound. Quality sound can make a large difference in the outcome of a video production, so it is worthwhile having a sound professional take responsibility for recording sound. Sound recording, though, is commonly directed by the video crew.

For large productions, the task of making the video can be handled by a **production company** with someone from the multimedia team assuming the role of producer. For smaller projects, the multimedia team might handle the entire process of producing video. They will need to develop a **script** and **storyboard** ▶ 123, 136, arrange to use all necessary video, audio, and lighting equipment, and line up locations and talent. They may shoot video and sound on **location** or in a **studio**. An editor may digitize the video as well as the audio tape and then edit and mix the content. To incorporate the video into an interactive format, the editor and director might work closely with an interface designer. Video, like other elements of multimedia production, must be balanced in the context of the total production.

When shooting video for multimedia, the director follows a script which is sometimes backed up by a storyboard. A multimedia script that is geared for interactivity is usually not strictly sequential. In a sense, users will be creating their own "edits" with each interactive choice. Although ideographers and filmmakers normally shoot materials out of sequence, they have a sense of the order of the shots. The order is different in interactive production. Interactive motion sequences can be reordered by the viewer, and this takes a kind of self-contained modular shooting style.

Many multimedia projects still use **videodisc** ▶ 112 technology that stores video in analog form. These projects include kiosks and many interactive education titles. When following computer digital movie standards like **QuickTime™** ▶ 153, 208, the director, videographer, and programmer must be aware of the storage limits of digitized data. It is important to know about compression techniques and hardware configurations.

One way to finish making high-quality professional video using computers is to have the multimedia editor work off-line with a postproduction service bureau or "post house." **Post houses** produce professionally finished video. Many are now organized to digitize source video and audio that can be edited off-line with a digital film editing program. The **off-line editor** ▶ 205 uses an editing package on a standard computer to organize and trim the sequences, arrange transitions, and add titles. The program generates an **edit decision list** (EDL) identifying all the edited changes to the source media. The post house uses the EDL to reassemble the source video and audio materials on professional equipment to produce a single finished videotape. The editor can bring this tape to the interface designer and programmer for insertion in the multimedia production.

How to Hire Video Professionals

Producing good video requires someone who not only is skilled in the use of video and audio equipment but can also develop a concept with a production team. Look for individuals who have demonstrated talent, teamwork, and patience. Plan to spend time looking at a videographer's tapes and their original storyboards. Discuss professional concerns about tools of the trade—details about cameras, digitizers, compression tradeoffs, sound synchronization, and editing software. When working in multimedia, the videographer needs to know the eventual context of the material. Some project managers strongly suggest spending preliminary time with videographers and orienting them to the project concept and process. The increased cost of video makes it especially critical to create a common understanding as early as possible.

For larger productions, professional experience may be essential. Hiring a video production company to do all the work may be a wise decision. This route involves interviewing a representative of the company, looking at their finished pieces, and understanding their fee requirements.

How to Get Hired As a Video Professional

If inexperienced, volunteer with the idea that there is a lot to learn. Novices may be able to work in an apprentice role. For professionals, having your own equipment can be a big asset. Show videotapes or finished digital movies and if you are a videographer, show camera work. **Traditional film and video skills** are honored, but it helps to have an awareness of interactive design. If you are an editor, explain how your approach to the video and audio elements is apparent in the work you show. If the work is to be edited and stored digitally in the final production piece, editors should be "digitally aware" and know the capabilities and limits of digital tools. Traditional videographers can make a successful transition into multimedia production by understanding the limitations and potential of computer interactivity. Spend some time growing new skills by learning new tools.

Case Studies

Greg LeMond's Bicycle Adventure 238

Theseus Cervical Cytology Multimedia Package 164

Interview

Nicole Leduc 161

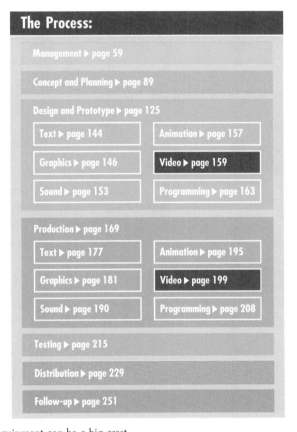

The Process:

Management ▶ page 59

Concept and Planning ▶ page 89

Design and Prototype ▶ page 125

Text ▶ page 144

Animation ▶ page 157

Graphics ▶ page 146

Video ▶ page 159

Sound ▶ page 153

Programming ▶ page 163

Production ▶ page 169

Text ▶ page 177

Animation ▶ page 195

Graphics ▶ page 181

Video ▶ page 199

Sound ▶ page 190

Programming ▶ page 208

Testing ▶ page 215

Distribution ▶ page 229

Follow-up ▶ page 251

For more information on the role video professionals play in the development process, turn to the pages highlighted above.

Many hardware and software manufacturers are partnering to create complete video production solutions. For example, the Apple Professional Video Production Solution designed around the Radius VideoVision Studio card allows users to capture, edit, manipulate, and output full-screen, industrial-quality video from the desktop. Radius' VideoVision Studio video card provides full-motion, full-screen video at 640x480 resolution at 30 frames per second with 60 fields per frame. The package is targeted at independent video producers, training departments, and multimedia designers and producers.

Information Designers, Interface Designers, and Programmers

When you see this icon at the top of a page, it signifies a topic in the text with specific relevance to information designers, interface designers, or programmers.

User interaction is a central issue of game design. Interaction is doing things for fun. Sometimes you make the game harder to use just for fun. If you pull down a menu item to destroy a plane, that wouldn't be fun. Make users search, challenge them. In a game, people love to do ordinary things—opening a door, turning on a faucet, dragging cups. To figure out how to do things in the computer game draws the most surprising responses. To want to have an effect is very human.

—Joe Sparks, Game Designer, Pop Rocket

A multimedia project can have great content, but without organized access to information and a clear, usable, and attractive interface, it may not find much use. Good **information** and **interface design** span all project types. To get a person to use a kiosk, an interactive game, an electronic book, or an interactive tutorial, a design team must work with other artists to produce a design that is inviting, easy to navigate, provides access to anticipated information, and is generally fun to use.

Unlike conventional media that is built to be experienced in a linear manner, multimedia applications can take off in whatever direction the user chooses. This aspect is a key design challenge for a design team. For example, in navigating content, a set of interactive maps might be designed by the interface designer to have a common graphic style, spatial orientation, and set of buttons for the user. The interaction design may involve visual navigational cues to leave on visited screens, audio transitions intended to move from one place randomly to another, and special animated guides to list options for exploring content.

In small projects, the information designer, interface designer, and graphic designer are often the same person, with this crossover being useful in creating a cohesive product. In the multimedia process, information designers, interface designers, and programmers take the primary responsibility for developing the project prototype. The information designer looks at the content base and organizes its presentation in ways that meet the goals and purposes of a project. Information and interface designers finish most of their work when a prototype is accepted. Programmers then go on to implement the design. Programmers also help optimize user access, media loading, and technical performance on each delivery system.

Information Designers

An **information designer** ▶ **129** is someone who is versed in different ways of **organizing information**. Information design looks a level above visual depictions to abstract orderings. The organization of information in many products is often taken for granted. For example, the organization of words in a dictionary is almost always alphabetical; the orientation of a map in the U.S. and in Europe is almost always with north at the top. New and enriching revelations can arise by organizing information in nontraditional or more pronounced ways. **Multiple** "**views**" of information chosen at the discretion of the user can also bring out patterns in ways that are unique to an individual.

Interface Designers

A good **interface designer** ▶ **131** is someone skilled in both visual presentation and interaction skills in the electronic domain. An interface designer uses layout, typography, map design, color, and graphics to communicate information in an electronic domain. They also build in ways for users to interact and control a product. This requires an under-standing of the nature of the product and its audience. It also means using the tools and conventions available to allow easy access to all product elements. Interface designers work closely with programmers to get response times, user feedback, and transitions to work smoothly. Good interfaces and interaction schemes often go unnoticed. If people are spending more time trying to figure out how to work an interface than reading or entering text or looking at images or videos, then something is wrong.

Programmers

It is almost always necessary in multimedia development to have someone with programming skills on the team. The multimedia **programmer ▶ 139, 163, 170, 208** often finds a much shorter development cycle for multimedia projects than traditional software development. This is largely because many basic multimedia tools already exist and provide most of the functionality required by multimedia projects. Programmers typically script for an **authoring system ▶ 139, 208** although some developers choose to create their own tools and **engines** to tailor the production process to the needs of the project. They will sometimes write special subroutines to automate some of a project's more repetitive tasks, check errors, resolve version changes, track the status of different elements, or automate building and testing of the final product.

How to Hire Information Designers, Interface Designers, or Programmers

Information design is not a relatively well-known term in comparison to graphic design or interface design, but many from these two latter fields are skilled at organizing information. The best ones are consciously aware of and experienced in organizing content in optimal ways. When hiring an information designer, look for different organizations of information in various projects and ask why each was specifically chosen. Explain the type of project, the goals, and the materials available. After hiring, allow some creative freedom and measure results in terms of the project goal.

Since interface design assignments generally last only through prototyping, these people may be more readily available than a project manager or programmer. Some have spent years working in labs investigating user interface issues. Inquire who designed popular multimedia applications. Designers should be adept at visualizing end results. This skill should be apparent by comparing storyboards or initial versions and prototypes with finished work.

Most multimedia programming assignments require a scripting programmer familiar with authoring software. Programmers that are software engineers are best suited

to system-level work and are useful in large-scale projects. The ideal candidates understand both the computer and audio/visual aspects of multimedia projects. They understand the combined roles of user interface design, programming, and artistic content required to build interactive media. Experience with different media is a plus. Ask to see samples of work from different applications. Ask about their approach to design and examples of how they produced projects while on a team.

How to Get Hired As an Information Designer, Interface Designer, or Programmer

Be ready to show **designs**, **prototypes ▶ 136**, and **finished work**. If you are not already a part of a team, work up some prototypes that would illustrate a design style.

Programmers should be prepared to show **source code** printouts and have knowledge of the strengths and weaknesses of authoring tools and development environments. Programmers should also have technical knowledge of operating systems, their multimedia extensions, and programming utilities.

Case Studies

Four Footed Friends 102

We Make Memories/Share With Me a Story 138

Interviews

Sally Ann Applin 209

Michael Arent 134-135

Dan Backus 210

Dr. Kristina Hooper-Woolsey 92

The Process:

Management ▶ page 59

Concept and Planning ▶ page 89

Design and Prototype ▶ page 125

Text ▶ page 144	Animation ▶ page 157
Graphics ▶ page 146	Video ▶ page 159
Sound ▶ page 153	Programming ▶ page 163

Production ▶ page 169

Text ▶ page 177	Animation ▶ page 195
Graphics ▶ page 181	Video ▶ page 199
Sound ▶ page 190	Programming ▶ page 208

Testing ▶ page 215

Distribution ▶ page 229

Follow-up ▶ page 251

For more information on the role programmers and interface professionals play in the development process, turn to the pages highlighted above.

A good organization to belong to is SIGCHI—Special Interest Group on Computer Human Interface, a subchapter of the Association for Computer Machinery. They hold an annual conference where you can read publications, attend workshops, and view exhibits that cover art, industry, and science. Educational courses on interactive media design and multimedia issues are also worth investigating.

Electronic Books

When you see this icon at the top of a page, it signifies a topic in the text with specific relevance to electronic books.

Electronic books extend the printed word into a digital domain. They offer not only text, illustrations, and photos but add sound, video, and animation, providing access and understanding not available with printed books. They offer a far greater storage capacity as well as the ability to quickly search and retrieve text and other elements.

Electronic books, like printed books, can be developed for many markets—adult, professional, corporate, educational, children's, to name a few. They can range from fiction to reference books, from poetry to student manuals. Some books are rich with video clips and spoken text, while are others are simply compact digitized versions of printed books that come on **diskettes** ▶ **113** or **CD-ROMs** ▶ **109, 231**.

Electronic books can serve to repurpose existing content into a digital form, but more importantly, they offer a forum for redefining the nature of publishing and subsequent interpretation of published materials. The linearity of a printed book is no longer a constraint. Instead, it becomes a single option for a reader who has the power to navigate at will through the hypermedia world of an

electronic book. The ability to combine different media and create new paths of navigation is already challenging the traditional published forms such as novels, reference books, children's stories, even atlases.

Electronic versions of existing printed materials are a popular electronic book form and one that many consider the primary definition of an electronic book. The Voyager Company with its Expanded Books series, for example, publishes electronic versions of popular print books specifically for Apple PowerBook™ computers. *Alice's Adventures in Wonderland,* Michael Crichton's *Jurassic Park,* and Douglas Adams' *Hitchhikers Guide to the Galaxy* are a few of the selections in this series. To follow a philosophy of remaining true to an author's style, Voyager does not embellish original text and graphics with sound or animation unless the author agrees. To simplify and standardize production of the books, Voyager has created a toolkit that handles much of the text formatting and pagination in addition to providing a robust search engine. Voyager uses the toolkit for its own production needs but also sells it in retail channels as the *Expanded Book Toolkit.* Many publishers can use toolkits such as this to produce simple to moderately complex electronic versions of their print-based books. The toolkits even give "amateurs" enough guidance and functionality for the casual generation of their own projects.

Traditional children's storybooks in print form present text and graphics, some with the added thrill of pop-up pictures. But often the stories in a book go beyond the printed page as a child begins to develop questions about characters, scenery, and mysteries, such as where does the sun hide when it rains and what makes the moon come out during the day. Electronic books can encourage a child's natural curiosity to ask questions and explore topics by providing explanations that are rich with animations, color pictures, sounds, and spoken text. Examples of interactive children's books are Brøderbund Software's Living Books series, such as *Just Grandma and Me*, *Arthur's Teacher Trouble,* and *The Rabbit and the Hare,* as well as *Macmillan's Multimedia Dictionary for Children* and Storybook Software's *Four Footed Friends.*

An electronic companion can also augment the experience of a printed book, as in the case of *From Alice to Ocean,* the story of Robyn Davidson's

7 1/2-month journey on camelback across the Australian outback. A beautiful full-color book of photographs by Rick Smolan, with written narration by Davidson, is packaged with two CD-ROMs, one interactive and the other in Photo CD format. These CD-ROMs expand the story of the journey by providing video, animation, music, spoken narration, and hundreds of additional photographs not included in the hardbound book.

A typical 200-page printed book can expand to up to 700 "pages" in electronic form. A "page" in electronic form typically means a screen full of information. A reader commonly "flips" pages by triggering a screen element to change the contents of the screen. The more critical areas involved in publishing electronic books are design, production, and distribution. An electronic book should be compelling enough to warrant its purchase over a standard printed book. The content and design of a title should make it easy to use and provide more information and be more entertaining than a printed book. Otherwise, most people may not be willing to pay more for an electronic version when they can just as easily buy a printed version.

The cost and complexity of producing a title will vary according to the size and sophistication of the title. A book without animations and video will cost far less to produce than a book with them. A primary need is a delivery vehicle or **authoring tool** ▶ **99, 139** that displays screens and buttons or other control elements and provides basic capabilities like turning pages, creating bookmarks, and searching text.

Once an engine or delivery vehicle is readied, a production team then integrates the content, in some cases in a similar manner to page layout in desktop publishing. The text in an electronic book is flowed into position along with graphics and photos. If the text is not already in digital form, a **scanner** and **optical character recognition (OCR)** ▶ **145, 178** software can help convert it. Scanners and image-manipulation programs can also help convert graphics and photos into digital forms needed for storage and display. If sounds, animations, and movies are included, they are also put into position at this point, commonly appearing as graphical elements with controls that trigger the sound or video to play.

The proliferation of electronic books at the moment is hindered in part because of nonstandard CD-ROM

delivery platforms ▶ **114, 118** and systems. The next few years will likely show the emergence of a few dominant platforms, making it easier for publishers to decide what platforms to support. Another current problem is the lack of definitive retail channels for multimedia titles. Some marketing specialists feel that the first **channels** ▶ **237** to embrace CD-ROM titles will be mail order (the number one outlet currently), followed by computer and consumer electronics stores, audio/video stores, and finally bookstores.

A person wishing to create a multimedia title either as a content expert or as a production house can approach a **publisher** or **affiliated label** ▶ **236** to handle the marketing, sales, and distribution of a title as well as the packaging and possibly even funding concerns. Another alternative is to **self-publish**, which entails handling everything from initial concept, design, production, and testing to mastering, replication, and distribution. A prominent point among many title developers is that the publishing and distribution outlook is rapidly evolving. Although electronic book publishing borrows heavily from book and software publishing, it is also charting its own course.

Case Studies

Interviews

The Process:

Management ▶ page 59

Concept and Planning ▶ page 89

Design and Prototype ▶ page 125

Text ▶ page 144	Animation ▶ page 157
Graphics ▶ page 146	Video ▶ page 159
Sound ▶ page 153	Programming ▶ page 163

Production ▶ page 169

Text ▶ page 177	Animation ▶ page 195
Graphics ▶ page 181	Video ▶ page 199
Sound ▶ page 190	Programming ▶ page 208

Testing ▶ page 215

Distribution ▶ page 229

Follow-up ▶ page 251

Turn to the above pages for information on the stages of development.

The AppleCD Multimedia Kit For Macintosh and the Multimedia Kit for PCs bring you all the benefits of multimedia by offering a complete CD-ROM playback environment to enhance your Macintosh or PC-compatible computer. These kits include the latest Apple CD-ROM player, AppleDesign Powered Speakers, and headphones. Also included are all the necessary cables and connections (including a 16-bit sound card with the PC Kit), and five free CD-ROM titles.

Electronic Magazines

When you see this icon at the top of a page, it signifies a topic in the text with specific relevance to electronic magazines.

A magazine is a collection of stories, photographs, illustrations, essays, and advertisements packaged and distributed in a regular and periodic form to a general or specific audience. Traditional printed magazines cater to a range of interests such as general news (*Time*), outdoor sports (*Field & Stream*), women's fashions (*Vogue*), and just about everything else. Electronic magazines extend the magazine concept into the digital domain by allowing the inclusion of sounds, animation, video clips, an information database, and other elements of an interactive interface. Because of the use of multiple media, electronic magazines also borrow from conventions of broadcast media such as

television or radio. To many, electronic magazines reflect a convergence of print and broadcast media. Electronic magazines can be distributed through CD-ROMs, diskettes, or computer networks, as well as future technologies for transmitting digital media such as **interactive television** ▶ 121.

To compete with sophisticated print and broadcast outlets, electronic magazines must not only satisfy the consumer's expectations of visual appeal and timely information, they should also provide an experience not available through print, such as **interactivity** ▶ 95 or **multiple viewpoints** ▶ 130. An example of this direction was created by Warner New Media and *Time* magazine who collaborated to create *Desert Storm: The War in the Persian Gulf,* an interactive CD-ROM compilation of correspondents' reports, eyewitness accounts, photographs, audio recordings, maps, charts, research, and documents.

Newsweek magazine has plans to produce a quarterly CD-ROM magazine, dubbed Newsweek Interactive, that will cover original presentations of issues such as the environment and the family. It will play initially on Sony Corporation's CD-ROM Multimedia Player, quickly followed by versions that support other multimedia platforms. The CD-ROMs will mix text with photographs, video, and animation along with voice-overs provided by Newsweek correspondents to explore the subject matter.

Some electronic magazines are being sold and distributed on a subscription basis to individuals who have the appropriate delivery hardware, usually CD-ROM players. Because this market is still in the "early adopter" ▶ 106 stage, electronic magazines have yet to cater to diverse and esoteric audience interests. *Verbum Interactive* is a CD-ROM magazine that presents

A few of the current electronic magazines are published on a monthly or quarterly schedule and cost around $100 for a yearly subscription. These include Nautilus and Newsweek Interactive.

diverse information on computer and art issues. It features animations and interactive multimedia works, video clips, feature stories, musical excerpts, advertisements, and other elements for an audience comprised primarily of technical enthusiasts.

Another CD-ROM magazine available on a subscription basis is *Nautilus,* which includes development tips, stories, advertisements, articles, and miscellaneous information, also aimed at computer developers and enthusiasts. *Nautilus* functions as an information service in which the content (stories, news, MIDI sound files, pictures, and computer programs) is prepared separately from different search and display engines. Separating the content from the engine simplifies multiplatform production and distribution.

One experiment with networking as a means of distributing an electronic magazine was the *News Navigator* system produced by Apple Computer for EDUCOM '90, an educational conference. The *News Navigator* was a daily interactive magazine that made current CNN news video clips, still graphics, and text available over a network to conference attendees. Each day's installment was produced with a combination of QuickTime, network software, and HyperCard technologies the day and night before delivery. Every morning, the daily issue of the "magazine" was transmitted via Ethernet to kiosks in the conference area and nearby hotels. People could select news stories at will and view the accompanying video clips. Although constrained by limitations in available network and compression technology, the *News Navigator* provided a sneak preview of the future of network-distributed electronic magazines.

The production of an electronic magazine is not much different from that of an electronic book except that most tasks must be **repeated with each issue**. Most electronic magazines have a consistent format to establish an identifiable style and to optimize production. This "**shell**" or **template** ▶ 170, 211 not only presents a characteristic appearance but also provides a standard way to add, index, and navigate materials on a repeating basis. The emphasis on production tasks is often a principal concern in the design of the shell and the frequency of issues. The current state of tools may not be good enough to allow for frequent production of issues. Daily, weekly, and possibly even monthly issues

may be difficult to provide at the moment without a heavy investment in custom tools and equipment.

Materials can come from various sources, not all of which may be in digital form. Audiotapes, printed text, and photographs may have to be digitized before they can be included. Diversity of source materials and the need for consistency demand clear production standards when assembling content.

Another challenge in publishing electronic magazines, aside from technology and production, may be adapting the revenue stream of the print-based magazines and broadcast TV to an electronic form. Most magazines obtain two-thirds to three-quarters or more of their **revenue from advertising**. A few magazines feature the reverse revenue scheme, with some funded 100% by subscriptions, but their circulations are small compared to their advertising-driven counterparts. The majority of television and radio stations also derive most of their revenues from advertising. It is possible that some electronic magazines can be funded entirely by subscriptions, but many will likely need advertising to offset high production and distribution costs. Some plans for advertisements in current magazines include interactive ads for cars and other products that require larger purchasing decisions. How much subscriptions will cost, what form advertising will take, and how much it will cost are all issues that are still evolving.

Case Study

Interview

The Process:

Management ▶ page 59

Concept and Planning ▶ page 89

Design and Prototype ▶ page 125

Text ▶ page 144	Animation ▶ page 157
Graphics ▶ page 146	Video ▶ page 159
Sound ▶ page 153	Programming ▶ page 163

Production ▶ page 169

Text ▶ page 177	Animation ▶ page 195
Graphics ▶ page 181	Video ▶ page 199
Sound ▶ page 190	Programming ▶ page 208

Testing ▶ page 215

Distribution ▶ page 229

Follow-up ▶ page 251

Turn to the above pages for information on the stages of development.

One publisher of an electronic magazine has decided to ignore any advertising or subscription concerns for now and plans to give it away. The release of Hypertexture is anticipated in the first quarter of 1993, first as a Macintosh-only CD-ROM followed later by DOS versions. The multimedia magazine will contain art, music, criticism, and political activism and is supported by a mix of grants and donations. For more information, write to: Hypertexture, PO Box 7266, Boulder, CO 80306-7266

Kiosks

When you see this icon at the top of a page, it signifies a topic in the text with specific relevance to kiosks.

Work completed for a kiosk can often be reapplied to other multimedia applications. For example, the California Academy of Sciences conducted an exhibit called Life Through Time *that was presented on nine kiosks, each running a program called* LIFEMap, *designed by the San Francisco multimedia firm Arborescence. The kiosk content, composed of digitized photographs, color illustrations, and speech, was reused and reformatted for a related CD-ROM title that is now distributed and sold commercially. This repurposing of content provides an additional source of revenue for the museum.*

*An **attraction loop** is an introductory visual that provides an inviting and directed backdrop for beginning an interactive session. Action and colors are common elements, though sound is cautioned against because of the possible interference with people working nearby.*

Kiosks are public installations designed to make information accessible to many people. Poster-plastered concrete and wood kiosks have appeared for decades on street corners throughout Europe. Today, many multimedia kiosks (computers housed in attractive shells) are found in corporate lobbies, hospital waiting rooms, museums, shopping malls, checkout lines, airline terminals, rental car agencies, and other public and semipublic spaces. A multimedia kiosk can provide and even collect information, promote business, and show and distribute products.

Kiosks address two basic needs. They convey information to many people in a consistent way and they make its access appealing and useful. Kiosks allow people to search for information at their own pace and "ask questions" without imposing on others. A user can request directions again and again and the kiosk will reply in a consistent manner, whereas a person might tire of repeating the same information and answering the same questions. The key to a successful kiosk is a highly usable interface understandable by a wide variety of people.

Spatial Data Architects, a San Francisco multimedia production company, has created several kiosks for Ziff-Davis and *MacUser* magazine for use at tradeshows they attend throughout the year. All kiosks run on Macintosh computers accessing hard drives for presentation materials. One of the kiosks is a public relations piece that runs on a 19-inch monitor. It makes extensive use of photos, animations, voice-over, and music to provide information on ZD Labs, a division of the Ziff-Davis Publishing Company, the publisher of *MacUser* magazine. Another kiosk runs on a 12-inch screen and contains two separate presentations, *Which Mac Should I Buy?* and *1500 MacUser Product Ratings*. This kiosk adapts to user input on intended uses to recommend appropriate Macintosh hardware and software solutions. A third kiosk, created for the 1993 MACWORLD tradeshow, incorporates a bar-code scanner to help coordinate the give-away of over 1500 products during the tradeshow. It relies heavily on animations, photographs, and a database to display the products, record entrants, and select winners.

A sophisticated **network ▶ 116** of kiosks might involve a dozen kiosks stationed throughout an area, such as a shopping mall, and networked to a single server. These kiosks could provide store locations, general news, and consumer information, such as product availability and comparative descriptions. Some can be designed to receive nightly updates from merchants and advertisers.

Costs can range from $10,000 for a single-site kiosk on standard equipment to over $1,000,000 for a networked, multiple-unit system. Prices vary with the degree of quality, time, media and content complexity, hardware components, number of stations, and maintenance required. A mid-

range kiosk might showcase a company's products and capabilities using extensive full-color animations and video, while a simpler kiosk might be based on an interactive HyperCard stack using text, graphics, and a few simple animations. Special hardware or the use of video may increase the cost dramatically.

Most kiosks are custom-built for a particular **client** ▶ 81 and a particular **environment** ▶ 98. As a result, clear communication between the client and production house is critical to creating a kiosk that performs its function on schedule and under budget. Other tasks involve finding the right level of information and assembling the necessary hardware to fit the function and the design. An information kiosk in a museum will likely have a different function and therefore different information and technology than a point of sale kiosk in a grocery store or a travel kiosk in a rental car agency. Arriving at appropriate design decisions will likely require in-depth **market research** ▶ 106 into traffic flow, buying patterns, and information needs. A production house may benefit from having some type of marketing knowledge or expertise on hand to help interpret this research into design decisions.

Two rules of thumb mentioned by many developers are to keep the interface simple and to provide prompt feedback. The **organization of the information** ▶ 129 and the **design of the interface** ▶ 131 is important, since much of the audience may not be familiar with computers and may not have a lot of time to try to figure out how a system works. Most kiosks feature an attraction loop that invites people to use the system, and they keep the number of options and the number of "hops" or branches of information to a minimum.

A common hardware component in most kiosks is a **touchscreen** interface, an alternative to a keyboard and mouse. It allows people to easily interact with a kiosk by physically touching selections on the screen. Rarely do public kiosks feature keyboards because of the difficulty and time involved in keying in requests. Another component may be a videodisc player to show video segments. These analog players are more prone to breakdowns and more expensive to update than using digital video with video compression boards, but they are still a common choice for many developers. Other components may include credit card readers, bar scanners, printers, or other types of input and output

devices. The booth that houses the equipment also needs to be tailored to the environment. It should look good, have appropriate lighting, signs, and instructions and be durable and secure enough to protect the equipment housed in the booth.

The custom nature of kiosks, the frequency of use, and the hardware components often make support and **maintenance** ▶ 253 a big issue. Monitors may need to be replaced because of burn-in. Videodisc players, credit card readers, or printers may need maintenance or replacement because of wear. Kiosks may need backup equipment on site for most components, as well as people trained in both routine and special maintainence. Maintenance not only applies to the physical components but also to the information and content provided by a kiosk. Kiosks that contain outdated or incorrect content may be more of a disservice than an aid.

Any organization that has a need to present consistent information with minimal effort to a large number of people in a public or semipublic area is a prospect for a custom-built kiosk. These institutions include federal, state, and city government offices, museums, exhibition companies, schools and universities, retailers, and manufacturers.

Case Studies

Interviews

The Process:

Turn to the above pages for information on the stages of development.

The Ordnance Survey in Great Britain, the English counterpart to the U.S. Census Bureau and U.S. Geological Survey, is moving forward aggressively to acquire and publish digital map information of Great Britain. They are developing map kiosks for installation throughout the country, featuring almost nightly updates of information to provide convenient and low-cost maps.

Multimedia Databases

When you see this icon at the top of a page, it signifies a topic in the text with specific relevance to multimedia databases.

A database is an organized set of data that provides a scheme or approach for storing and accessing information. Databases traditionally store data that represent text or numbers. However, this is rapidly changing as multimedia becomes more prominent on the desktop. Three principal types of databases are flat-file, relational, and object-oriented. **Flat-file databases** are common for simple organization of information such as address books and mailing lists. **Relational databases** allow for more sophisticated searches, retrievals, and ordering of information. They are commonly used in large organizations to manage orders, inventory, and other types of transaction processing. **Object-oriented databases** are relatively new and offer many of the advantages of relational databases while allowing greater customization for handling different types of data. Important issues in databases, especially large and distributed databases, are storage, integrity, and security.

Multimedia databases can include various media, such as audio, video, graphics, or animations. Because these media can be efficiently stored, reused, and distributed in digital form, multimedia databases are attractive options for many organizations. One database developed with multiple media in mind is Aldus Fetch, a multiuser, mixed-media cataloging, browsing, and retrieval tool that can index clip art, photo images, presentations, QuickTime movies, sounds, and other elements. Multimedia developers and database designers can use this database (or other more traditional databases that support nontext data types) to create custom implementations that fit into standalone single-user environments or are distributed over networks.

Uses of multimedia databases include **advertising, product planning, electronic catalogs, business directories, executive information systems**, and **on-demand help systems**. Multimedia database projects often begin with a useful custom prototype that grows into a full-scale production and publishing system.

Other areas offering great potential are the **travel, real estate, insurance, criminal justice**, and **medical industries**. A medical multimedia database, for example, might contain patient information, such as name, address, age, and insurance, and medical history as well as medical data, such as X-rays, MRI scans, EKGs, and other nontext information all stored in digital format. Several implementations currently exist in many of these industries and many more are in development.

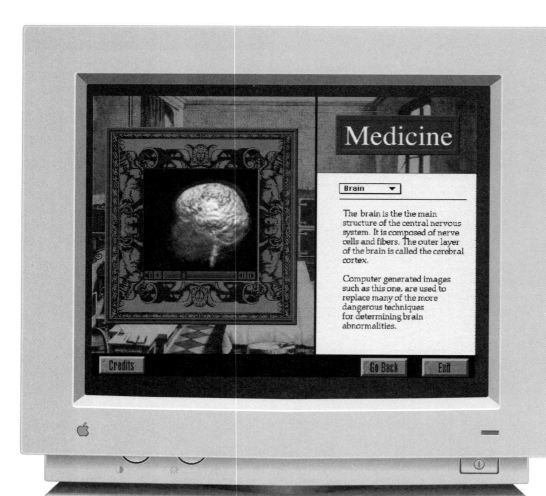

The requirements of multimedia databases for optimized organization, storage, and retrieval are being addressed by advanced database technologies such as media servers. Media servers are centralized **file servers** designed to house various media types and facilitate distributed access. An example of an application using media server technology is a corporate training program in which high-quality video, audio, and other media are quickly supplied to client terminals on a network.

Multimedia databases raise special concerns for those involved with creating and managing database systems. These concerns often go much farther than many other types of multimedia projects because of their size, timing requirements, and distributed nature. They include **storage and retrieval, networking, data formats, system performance,** and **visualization issues**. A single picture can take up thousands of bytes of storage. Video, animation, and other dynamic media can also demand large storage resources. During playback of time-based media across a network, information must arrive on time and in order, a constraint not typically found in conventional networked databases. (Archiving issues such as backup media and version tracking are important concerns in large and more complicated databases.) These storage concerns extend into transmitting and displaying dynamic media, especially in a networked environment.

A current challenge to maintaining database integrity is the lack of standards among many media types. Whereas text and numbers are commonly represented in ASCII format (a format recognized by almost all systems or applications), movies, sounds, animations, and to some extent graphic formats are only recently moving towards standards recognizable by many systems. These concerns will lessen as standards and filters or translation capabilities develop. In the meantime, they are a fundamental concern for anyone planning to incorporate nonstandard data into current databases across multiple platforms and servers.

The visualization, access, and presentation qualities of information contained in a multimedia database are quickly evolving. In many current systems, the graphics, sound, video and other nontext media supplement text. The principle access method is through text **queries** usually using keywords to describe the nontext elements. This approach might be common in an insurance-claims database, for example, where pictures of car damage would be attached to a claim. Access to the photographs would be through the record but not through the photographs themselves. Some more sophisticated databases support thumbnail views and other orderings of images. In the future, systems may allow direct access routes to nontext media. One example is where a researcher might want to identify all flood zones contained in Los Angeles County using a spatial access method to frame the query. Another example is where a doctor might want to locate all current and past patients that exhibit certain readings on tests stored as sampled wave forms.

Solutions to creating better access methods may come about through research into graphical queries and advancements in **natural language** and **image processing**. One possible interface technique is a software **agent** ▶ 133, which is a process or program conditionally triggered to perform specialized functions like the coordination of data elements. A database designer might include an animated agent to help users find information they need. Prototypes are being developed to allow richer and faster access to ordinary information, possibly resulting in interactive television guides or electronic yellow pages, for example.

Case Studies

Theseus Cervical Cytology Multimedia Package 164

Voices of the 30s 176

We Make Memories/Share With Me a Story 138

Interviews

Doug Camplejohn 116

Wayne Williams 152

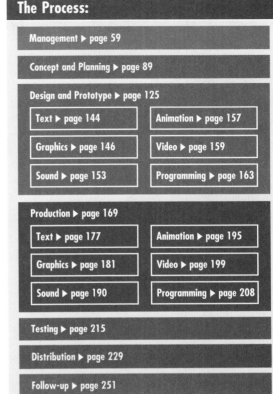

The Process:

Management ▶ page 59

Concept and Planning ▶ page 89

Design and Prototype ▶ page 125

Text ▶ page 144	Animation ▶ page 157
Graphics ▶ page 146	Video ▶ page 159
Sound ▶ page 153	Programming ▶ page 163

Production ▶ page 169

Text ▶ page 177	Animation ▶ page 195
Graphics ▶ page 181	Video ▶ page 199
Sound ▶ page 190	Programming ▶ page 208

Testing ▶ page 215

Distribution ▶ page 229

Follow-up ▶ page 251

Turn to the above pages for information on the stages of development.

*The growth of **object-oriented databases** dovetails nicely into the creation of multimedia databases. Using basic data types and tools, database designers can create sophisticated implementations that handle the multiple demands of text, graphics, sound, animations, and video. For example, a designer could create an image data type that would contain image data as well as routines for compressing, decompressing, and filtering the data in a manner specific to a particular use, such as medical imaging or satellite reconnaissance.*

Multimedia databases represent the convergence of advancements in artificial intelligence, operating systems, database studies, telecommunications, and other disciplines. Many in the industry point to them as pivotal components in helping to define and evolve the future of information management.

Corporate Training

When you see this icon at the top of a page, it signifies a topic in the text with specific relevance to corporate training.

Every company has a need to train its employees on a wide range of subjects, from personnel policy to equipment maintenance. Training has always presented the challenge of providing up-to-date, consistent, and useful information quickly and efficiently to a large number of people. Training personnel must design, prepare, and maintain course material and present it repeatedly to various sets of employees, many of whom may be at remote sites. Studies have shown that interactive learning environments, such as hands-on tutorials, under the guidance of instructors are more helpful to students. They provide experiences that are not afforded by reading textbooks or watching videotapes; they can be spontaneous and entertaining.

In an attempt to augment the power and reach of direct interaction, many companies have turned to **computer-based training** (CBT) methods. CBT allows students to learn a topic at their own pace through a series of computer screens. Initially text-based, CBT systems became early implementations of interactive videodisc technology laying the groundwork for advances in multimedia **corporate training**. As authoring tools and hardware have become increasingly accessible, more and more companies are turning to interactive multimedia as a corporate training option.

Interactive training commonly performs three principle functions: supporting **in-class training**, providing **individual instruction materials**, and facilitating **on-demand/just-in-time training**. Implementations can range from standalone videodisc programs on corporate policies, to fully adaptive network products where individuals can contribute materials and ideas. For example, a CD-ROM program that provides interactive training for machine maintenance may include a schematic interface that allows employees to point to a problem area and obtain instructions for repair. Videodiscs have also been designed to teach on-the-spot skills. In one medical training application, students must make life and death decisions in simulated emergency situations.

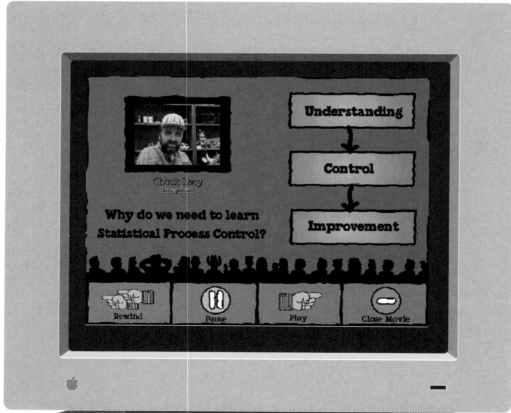

Some companies may be able to create in-house multimedia training materials, but many others need to contract to outside production houses, at least initially, until they acquire the necessary knowledge and tools. Many corporate trainers begin projects by outlining course materials and assembling visual aids. Existing training materials and courses often provide the basis for new interactive multimedia training projects. If existing procedures are still relevant and materials are still in reasonable condition, a project can be planned to convert these materials into digital forms, supplementing them with new materials, such as video or audio clips, where necessary. The creation of new materials will require the use of professionals in the appropriate areas.

Once appropriate content material is collected, training developers use **storyboards** ▶ **123, 136** to demonstrate key interaction screens of the planned system. Some multimedia **authoring tools** ▶ **139** are specifically designed to simplify the development of corporate training materials. They provide a general set of diagrammatic tools to organize and arrange lessons and simplify the addition of media, such as video or sound. Testing routines are also provided. A good package will also include procedures for updating materials.

Corporate personnel involved in these projects include training and technical individuals, possibly sales and marketing, as well as content experts and test participants. Roles from the multimedia production team include an interaction designer, writers, programmers, and a project manager. Various media production personnel may also be needed if new content needs to be developed.

Once corporate training is established, the material might be used for other purposes. For example, the content can be put into a kiosk for on-demand help. Some materials can be organized and shipped on CD-ROMs to support field operations. For example, the Apple Desktop Seminar on QuickTime CD-ROM explains QuickTime concepts by using interactive movies, narration, and quizzes. Originally developed by Apple's

USA training department for internal use, Apple now offers the CD-ROM through retail channels.

Multimedia training can lighten the load on training departments and circulate current procedures and information effectively within an organization. The cost savings for corporate training comes when a consistent "**shell**" and interaction scheme are established that allows material to be added and updated as needed. Training applications based on a design template can be tailored to different requirements. Additional savings are realized through the reduced cost of sending employees to remote training centers. Increased productivity from using consistent practices is an ultimate benefit of good training.

Producing in-house interactive multimedia training requires an investment in time, equipment, and personnel. Depending on the scope of the training project, many training managers may choose to contract outside help to develop these programs because of time, budget, and resource limitations. As with desktop publishing, however, newer advances in multimedia technology are giving training managers more options to design and produce training programs in-house.

Case Studies

Ben & Jerry's Ice Cream Statistical Process Control .. 84

EyeLearn 218

Ultrasound Equipment Acceptance Testing 204

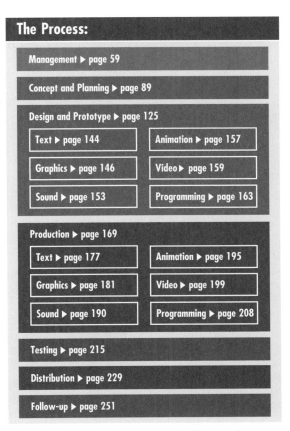

The Process:

Management ▶ page 59

Concept and Planning ▶ page 89

Design and Prototype ▶ page 125

Text ▶ page 144	Animation ▶ page 157
Graphics ▶ page 146	Video ▶ page 159
Sound ▶ page 153	Programming ▶ page 163

Production ▶ page 169

Text ▶ page 177	Animation ▶ page 195
Graphics ▶ page 181	Video ▶ page 199
Sound ▶ page 190	Programming ▶ page 208

Testing ▶ page 215

Distribution ▶ page 229

Follow-up ▶ page 251

Turn to the above pages for information on the stages of development.

The Apple Desktop Seminar Toolkit includes tools that allow users to create seminars without having to program. Authors can assemble QuickTime movies and fill in information in a series of templates linked to a course outline. The toolkit helps authors organize content and synchronize multimedia components as well as prepare multiple choice quizzes to help users test their comprehension. The toolkit also includes information on how to build seminars and tips on instructional methods and content organization. It can be ordered from an authorized Apple reseller or by phoning 800/850-2442.

Interactive Education

When you see this icon at the top of a page, it signifies a topic in the text with specific relevance to interactive education.

As new technology becomes desirable, new public policy questions become more urgent. The issue of creating a division in learning between the technically literate and the technically illiterate is a concern for many people. Many private or suburban schools are able to afford modern equipment and training materials while many inner-city public schools are not. This schism to some extent has always been around. Many fear that the consequences of having such a broad dichotomy in technical literacy, though, will have far greater consequences than previously as society places more and more emphasis on technology and information processing.

October 1992 marked the first time in California state history that schools spent textbook money on nonprint curriculum. Five of eight programs selected for the elementary science program contained videodisc materials.

The best education comes from experience. For years, innovative teachers have been reaching for ways to enhance the learning experience of their students through field trips, lab exercises, demonstrations, and hands-on activities. Teachers were early explorers of using multiple media in the classroom by combining movies, filmstrips, audio recordings, illustrations, and narrative to present subject matter. (What adult does not recall the days of the audio/visual assistant, the garbled soundtracks, the film flapping at the end of the reel, and the frantic call for lights?)

Now, rapidly evolving multimedia technologies are creating more options for education. Interactive education can cover a broad domain of topics. Identifiable markets include preschool or in-house education, K-12, and higher education (colleges and universities). Products and projects can range from interactive storybooks for children, like The Learning Company's *Reader Rabbit,* to a workbook-like product like WINGS for Learning's *Voices of the 30s,* which contains excerpts, photos, speeches, and other resources as well as activities for students to do. Other possibilities include interactive versions of high school and college textbooks. Topics that are getting a significant amount of coverage include math, science, social studies, history, and languages.

Computers, video cameras, scanners, editing equipment, and tape recorders are more common and accessible than they were even five years ago. These components, in combination with authoring tools and multimedia toolkits, let teachers, students, and publishers combine familiar media in new ways, rewarding self-paced exploration and fostering new possibilities for group interaction and collaboration. An essay on racial tensions in the 1960s is a single form of expression. Combining that essay with video clips and photographs of riots in Detroit or the Freedom Marches in the deep South finds its way deeper into one's soul. Similarly, in an interactive chemistry program, students can learn principles of molecular structure at their own pace by exploring and building different molecules, guided along the way by text, narration, or video instruction.

Interactive education offers great possibilities for group collaboration and learning by encouraging the development of problem-solving abilities through interaction, visualization, and play. At the 1992 SIGGRAPH convention in Chicago, a special workshop was set up called SigKids in which local schoolchildren participated in collaborative activities enabled by a central computer model. The Nueva school in Hillsborough, California, under the direction of educator Ann McCormack, uses computer and multimedia technology as a springboard for collaborative learning among at-risk youth. Another experiment in experiential learning using newer technology is the Journey School in Soquel, California, in which students learn about different topics by working directly with experienced individuals and using interactive technology to interpret their understanding. Interactive multimedia contributes to the possibilities of experiential education, a far cry from rote learning.

At least initially, the majority of products are falling closer to electronic textbooks as most publishers begin producing electronic materials that resemble their analog counterparts. The similarity in product definition to an electronic book does not necessarily mean that an electronic book will function as an educational title to be sold to school systems or universities. Many educational titles will be sold successfully to a general audience, but the product needs and sales channels to educational institutions are different enough to invalidate many assumptions made for a mass-market product, assumptions such as content, buying patterns, price, and platforms. Teachers often need **resource guides** to course materials showing teachers how to teach lessons using the materials. They are standard requirements in textbook publishing and the need for them may apply to electronic materials. Teachers may also need ways to evaluate student performance, such as quizzes and tests, using them not just to test comprehension but to provide mechanisms for grading and evaluation.

The **sales channels** ▶ 240 into educational markets are also different, highlighted by cyclical buying patterns, longer sales cycles, and direct sales forces. Broadly speaking, new products in college-level textbook publishing must be ready in early winter for use in the fall of the next year. Sales representatives need them to show to professors who are selecting course materials. (At the K-12 level, product development cycles are often keyed to deadlines set by large states such as California, Texas, and New York.) Decisions are made from January to June, purchases in the summer, and payment to publishers in September. Publishers in turn pay royalties to their authors three months later in December. These long timelines mean educational publishing can be a game of "delayed gratification," but offering potentially large payoffs in some cases. Texas, for instance, recently spent more than $100 million on a textbook reading program. The difficulty of publishing for an education market versus a consumer audience is marked by the fact that most book publishers do not publish for both categories, at least not from the same division of a company. Only a few organizations are able to reconcile the differences and be successful in both markets.

Some obstacles to incorporating multimedia into schools are equipment cost, lack of standards, multiple platforms, and multiple devices to install, learn, and maintain. Most **K-12 schools** do not have a lot of money and college costs have risen, leaving students with less money to spend on purchasing course materials. Knowledge and market research in the education markets can help provide realistic design and sales expectations, as well as identify the proper publishers, selling strategies, or sales channels. It is important to decide on appropriate platforms and factor in necessary lifetimes of products. For example, many states have big adoption cycles where products must have a lifetime of

five to seven years at the elementary to high school level (two to four years at the university level). Many textbook publishers still have to guarantee prices for five years. This practice is beginning to change, but long timeline thinking for "fixed" product purchases is something that any educational publisher will have to contend with.

But technology, tools, and materials are evolving to where they may be within reach of most schools. Computers that ship with onboard CD-ROM drives are but one example of affordable and accessible technology. As these configurations become more popular, teachers and school systems may be more willing to explore the potential of interactive education. Many states are opening up their adoption listings to multimedia products and more and more teachers are realizing how different media shape experiences and views of the world. They believe incorporating multimedia into educational curricula will encourage new ways of participating, strengthen students **visual and language skills**, and build critical reasoning abilities. Many talented people believe revolutionary change can occur in this area and are working hard at making this change a reality.

Case Studies

EyeLearn 218

Ultrasound Equipment Acceptance Testing 204

Voices of the 30s 176

Interviews

Dr. Kristina Hooper-Woolsey 92

Mark Schlichting and Todd Power 96

Joe Sparks 247

The Process:

Management ▶ page 59

Concept and Planning ▶ page 89

Design and Prototype ▶ page 125

Text ▶ page 144 | Animation ▶ page 157

Graphics ▶ page 146 | Video ▶ page 159

Sound ▶ page 153 | Programming ▶ page 163

Production ▶ page 169

Text ▶ page 177 | Animation ▶ page 195

Graphics ▶ page 181 | Video ▶ page 199

Sound ▶ page 190 | Programming ▶ page 208

Testing ▶ page 215

Distribution ▶ page 229

Follow-up ▶ page 251

Turn to the above pages for information on the stages of development.

At the el-hi level (elementary-high school), many states have special requirements for educational materials. Books may have to be bound a certain way. If it's not a supplement, your offering must cover all course topics according to published guidelines (available through a state's Department of Education). Not producing or packaging them in these ways can disqualify you from further consideration. As a developer, you should be prepared to show how your product/service provides greater benefits than traditional-media publications. The age of "gee-whiz" is over.

— Nick Keefe, BMR, a company in Corte Madera, CA that creates and packages textbooks and multimedia products for educational publishers.

Interactive Games

When you see this icon at the top of a page, it signifies a topic in the text with specific relevance to interactive games.

Any activity that entertains or amuses can conceivably be called a game. As a result, the category of electronic games can be relatively broad. Common types include electronic board games, 3D sport or adventure games, and interactive movies featuring control over characters and story lines. Interactive games already form a large and lucrative market, shipping on a variety of delivery media, including diskettes, game cartridges and CD-ROMs. Each delivery media brings with it advantages and limitations that are reflected in part by the types of games that can be produced and the audiences for whom they are written.

Nintendo and Sega dominate the consumer game player market by offering game cartridges that plug into inexpensive players with remote controls. Com-

bined sales for these firms' fiscal year 1992 surpassed $5.5 billion. More recent products delivered on a CD-ROM will run on Macintosh or PC platforms. Examples of this type include Reactor's *Spaceship Warlock*, *Iron Helix*, and Pop Rocket's *Total Distortion*. Interactive game sequences are also added to other multimedia products. For example, games are sometimes added to interactive music CDs to test listening skills and musical knowledge in humorous ways. Several of the Voyager classical music titles featuring Robert Winter, contain contestant game sequences that prompt for the identification of music scores or instrument types.

Electronic games can be based on a key premise or paradigm that appeals to a particular audience. For some, combat and sports seem common themes. Others feature medieval fantasies with magic and fortune-telling, historic simulations with time travel, and futuristic worlds with space travel. A growing interest of some people is for the development of more games that de-emphasize violence and competition and reward imagination and collaboration. A category called *edutainment* covers products that both inform and amuse. For example, a game called *Sim City* lets players create cities that develop and grow over time. It offers a fun and rewarding understanding of both successful and unsuccessful city planning.

You've got to get a good idea, of course. You've got to come up with something. Do some sketches, some testing.... After you get your first idea, sit down and try to make an ad. What points would you highlight? What things would you show? Then start to fill that out and try to think of all the activities. Don't let any one thing in your prototype phase, your sketching, or your planning phase overshadow the rest. If you really want to do lots of music or you really want to do lots of animation or 3D modeling or some special feature, make sure that your zeal for that particular feature doesn't override the actual fun or value of the product. You can go so whole hog on one thing that you end up with something that's lopsided. You want to round things out, especially in entertainment games.

— Joe Sparks, Game Designer, Pop Rocket

Most developers create games that require high performance for retrieval, display, and interaction, such as futuristic 3D adventure games. Some rely on off-the-shelf authoring systems as both a prototyping and delivery tool, while others create their own proprietary engines to control the interaction and visual display. *Spaceship Warlock* is an example of the first approach. It was built using a standard multimedia authoring tool but makes use of high-quality sound and faster routines for CD-ROM data retrieval. The interactive game/movie *Lunicus,* published by CyberSoft, relies on proprietary applications and routines for controlling "cyber puppets" and interactive movie sequences.

The development process for a typical CD-ROM-based adventure game takes between nine months and a year to complete. Such games usually require heavy use of scriptwriters, programmers, animators, and musicians.

Many game design concepts take about a month to work out, with the development of scripts, characters, props, backdrops, and game rules occurring at this time. The concept and the style are often determined by studying or researching the targeted audience. The topics and the level of sophistication are determined by the audience's expectations, the amount of manipulation, type and amount of sounds, style and sophistication of animation, and overall length and complexity.

A prototype typically follows, which attempts to balance sections, features, scenes, animations, and characters. Some projects benefit from independent, modular pieces that can be tested separately as they are built. Prototyping also helps create **production standards** ▶ 167, 173 that can make it easier to handle issues of consistency with characters and their actions and words.

Interactive games have more advanced outlets of distribution than many other areas of multimedia. They appear in stores and catalogs outside of the computer realm and in the general **consumer market**. Many developers prefer to use publishers and affiliated labels to market and distribute their products so that they can spend time creating more games rather than working with distribution and sales issues. **Royalty rates** for a developer can range between 2% and 12.5% of the retail price. The wide range in the figures indicates that rates are highly negotiable and dependent on the product, the production costs, the

development team, and their track record. Some developers recommend developing a game as far as possible without outside help to better negotiate with a **publisher** or **affiliated label** ▶ 236. Publishers who have great confidence in a developer or production house may be more willing to agree to a deal. Developers who have successfully produced titles are usually in a much easier position than someone just entering the field. A good relationship between publisher and developer is also important, sometimes even more so than a particular royalty rate.

Improvements in technology will likely pave the way for faster and more realistic game and movie sequences. These advancements touch on the hardware and system level in the areas of CD-ROM, 3D rendering, and display technologies. Such advancements should also bring improvements in graphic and animation tools that would allow easier creation of scenes and characters. Also noted by some game designers is the need for more artificial intelligence in games to provide more random and natural interaction. Instead of a character following a set pattern of one or several behaviors, a character or object may become more cognizant of and adaptive to its surroundings and current situation.

Case Study

Total Distortion 222

Interviews

Todd Power and Matthew Schlichting 96

Joe Sparks 247

The Process:

Management ▶ page 59

Concept and Planning ▶ page 89

Design and Prototype ▶ page 125

Text ▶ page 144	Animation ▶ page 157
Graphics ▶ page 146	Video ▶ page 159
Sound ▶ page 153	Programming ▶ page 163

Production ▶ page 169

Text ▶ page 177	Animation ▶ page 195
Graphics ▶ page 181	Video ▶ page 199
Sound ▶ page 190	Programming ▶ page 208

Testing ▶ page 215

Distribution ▶ page 229

Follow-up ▶ page 251

Turn to the above pages for information on the stages of development.

Concepts and materials for games can come from a variety of sources. Steven Speilberg has reportedly shot extra footage of his movie Jurassic Park for use in an interactive 3D video game. (The film is about dinosaurs.) Edison Brothers Entertainment plans to release in late 1993 virtual reality games based on the Star Trek: The Next Generation television series. Plans are to place the games in shopping malls, providing a new alternative to the quarter-driven joystick video games of years past. Interactive comic books are also in the works for the Alien, Predator, Terminator, and Indiana Jones movies.

Interactive Music

When you see this icon at the top of a page, it signifies a topic in the text with specific relevance to interactive music.

The compact disc industry started when Philips and Sony introduced the Compact Disc Digital Audio Standard, commonly known as the **Red Book** ▶ 110. The Red Book describes the **Audio Compact Disc (CD)** that you find in music stores today. It is the foundation on which all the other CD standards are built. Because audio discs are manufactured per the Red Book standard, all audio compact discs will play in any audio compact disc player. This interchangeability has been a major factor in the growth of the CD music industry.

— James R. Fricks, Compact Disc Terminology, available from Disc Manufacturing, Inc., 800/433-DISC

MIDI ▶ 155, 193 is a digital format for communicating musical instructions between instruments. It can be added to multimedia performances, control MIDI instruments or synthesizers and is used to create, play, or teach music. It is compact enough to store performances on diskettes.

Interactive music is the presentation of a musical performance with other media and information so that the listener can develop alternative or enhanced interpretations. Some products ship as a consumer audio CD disc accompanied by an interactive application contained on a diskette. Others are delivered on CD-ROM discs with the entire content interwoven in an interactive format. Interactive music is often distinguished from other interactive forms by its focused development on "titles" and the potential distribution channel offered by music stores.

With an interactive music product, a listener can play music selections, summon a music critic, and view text and graphic information about a musical piece, style, or period. Interactive music can be extremely engaging for any fan of a featured composer, musician, or group. Comprising a new kind of liner notes found formerly on LP albums and audio CDs, interactive music titles can now provide photographs of the artist, videos of a performance, bilingual translations of the lyrics (the libretto of an opera, for example), music scores, computer generated music, biographical information, general music theory, explanations of symbolism, and other critical interpretations.

The first form of products contain musical performances on audio CD discs (the type of CD found in music stores). The majority of CD-ROM drives can play these types of CDs. A program running on the computer controls the CD in the CD-ROM drive, offering interactive control of the musical sequences. The controlling program also contains the extra materials and commentary. The second form of products contain the music and accompanying materials integrated on one or more CD-ROMs. The extra materials and commentary of both types are often produced under the direction of a **content expert** ▶ 20, 99, well-versed in the knowledge and history of the pieces.

One example of interactive music is *The Magic Flute*, produced by Warner New Media, filling three CD-ROM discs with both HyperCard stacks and commentary by Roger Englander, the television producer of Leonard Bernstein's Young People's Concerts. Another example, *Ludwig Van Beethoven, Symphony No. 9*, part of the Voyager CD Companion Series, provides enriching commentary by UCLA music professor Robert Winter. It is an especially good example of full-featured interactive music using a conventional audio CD disc.

The pioneers of interactive music titles originally worked with classical music forms, but all types of music are receiving attention these days. A Swiss/Italian production, *Montreux Jazz Festival 6-21 July 1990* from Montreux Sounds SA, combines sound, jazz biographies, photographs, and videos controlled by a HyperCard browser. The presentation was used at the 1992 TED3 conference as a background for Quincy Jones' commentary on the world of jazz.

Possible spinoffs of interactive music are **multimedia databases** ▶ 40 of audio CD title samples, similar to font CD-ROMs that allow users to browse through font catalogs and purchase them by phone (obtaining a "key" in the process that "unlocks" the font on the CD-ROM). The particulars of **audio catalogs** would differ because of the larger size of audio data but the idea is similar. An audio catalog on CD-ROM might allow interactive control to samples of songs, albums, and artists

supplemented by commentary and other materials mentioned previously. Ordering by phone with next-day delivery of the selected CDs may offer an informed and convenient way to select and purchase music.

When interactive music is combined in a **performance** setting, it can be an interactive art form, a form separate from title development. The MIDI ball (Musical Instrument Digital Interface), for example, pioneered by the San Francisco band D'Cuckoo, allows audiences of their performances to create music and participate in the performance. Similar to a giant beach ball, the MIDI ball is batted about by a crowd and triggers changes in the characteristics of the music according to the movement of the ball.

The design and production of most interactive music titles are not too different from an electronic book or magazine. Because much of the emphasis in interactive music is on sound, though, some of the content issues are more pronounced. One issue is the importance of obtaining the highest-quality sound from the original assets and then filtering as needed to match the media constraints and delivery platforms. New formats and technologies will likely increase storage capacities and playback capabilities. Having the best recordings on hand will reduce the expense of resampling the materials.

Copyrights and **intellectual property** rights are an important concern in any multimedia product, and are equally so with music. The proliferation of music on radio and TV, its use in commercials, the practice of taping on audio cassettes, and the music sampling common in rap and other music forms has created a more pronounced tendency, in some respects, toward using recorded music in other works of art. According to copyright law, though, using copyrighted musical pieces without permission may infringe on the rights of the copyright owner. This is a significant concern for any publisher. Most experienced multimedia producers go to great lengths to either obtain the necessary permissions or create original materials.

When creating original music, one of the biggest expenses is obtaining high-quality **voice recordings** ▶ 155, 192, a task that usually requires professional studio equipment and expertise. (Voice recordings cannot be created or stored using MIDI technology. It

is often integrated as sampled data combined with MIDI sequences.) Time in a recording studio is expensive and finding voice talent that matches the style needed for a project can be challenging. **Background music** ▶ 154, 192 is less difficult to obtain. Most forms can be generated by musicians, many of whom have their own equipment.

Once the music is recorded, it is integrated into a multimedia project. During prototyping, many developers use placeholders for many of the musical sequences and include a few finished clips to ensure that playback is feasible. (The slower retrieval rates of the earliest CD-ROM players caused many developers to preload sound sequences to reduce the delay in response.) During production, the music is edited and mixed. It is also tested for synchronization, queuing, and triggering.

A number of developers are prototyping and introducing new interactive music CD-ROMs. They are playing with multiple performances and video sessions to provide point-of-view music variations, user-programmable mixes, MIDI play-along patches, and combinations with other interesting media. The rapid increase of interactive music titles and the growing distribution channels in music stores and catalogs make interactive music a significant and early multimedia entry in the consumer market.

Case Study

Peter Gabriel XPLORA 1 CD-ROM 117

Interviews

Steve Nelson 86

Joe Sparks 247

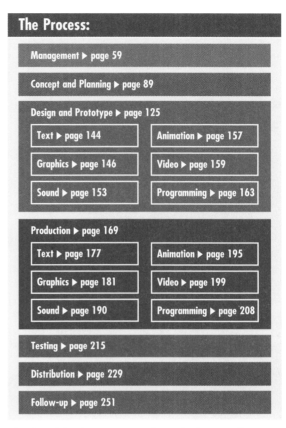

The Process:

Management ▶ page 59

Concept and Planning ▶ page 89

Design and Prototype ▶ page 125
Text ▶ page 144 / Animation ▶ page 157
Graphics ▶ page 146 / Video ▶ page 159
Sound ▶ page 153 / Programming ▶ page 163

Production ▶ page 169
Text ▶ page 177 / Animation ▶ page 195
Graphics ▶ page 181 / Video ▶ page 199
Sound ▶ page 190 / Programming ▶ page 208

Testing ▶ page 215

Distribution ▶ page 229

Follow-up ▶ page 251

Turn to the above pages for information on the stages of development.

The track type defined in the Red Book standard is:
- *CD-Audio for audio music*

The track types defined in the Yellow Book standard are:
- *CD-ROM Mode 1, for computer data*
- *CD-ROM Mode 2, for compressed audio data, and video/picture data*

The track type defined by CD-ROM/ XA is:
- *CD-ROM Mode 2, XA Format, for computer data, compressed audio data, and video/picture data*

Interactive Art and Performance

When you see this icon at the top of a page, it signifies a topic in the text with specific relevance to interactive art and performance.

Over the past 13 years, I've been working collaboratively with composers, programmers, robotics engineers, photo montage artists, and a wide variety of performers, opera singers, and dancers. Multimedia artists have developed interactive processes to enable live performers to appear within projected and animated environments. A flow of images is projected from the audience like a movie film, but onto a three-dimensional screen structure that can support the weight of live performers, rather than onto a two-dimensional movie screen that can display recorded performances only.

Imagine a movie screen that is sucked back, or alternately, extends out to the audience. The environments, locales, and effects are all projected onto the screen in actual 3D, while the performers enter, exit, and dissolve right before the spectators' very eyes. It creates a stunning, magical effect.

— George Coates, Technologies for the 21st Century, On Multimedia

"First the impulse, then the form. That's the way art works," says Mark Petrakis, one of a growing community of artists who are exploring new forms of expression through digital media. Although "art" defies concrete definition, it includes all the ways in which human beings follow their impulses to creatively express personal messages and statements in an endless universe of form.

Interactive digital artists balance technology with creative expression as they strive, as Petrakis says, "to escape the desktop, invoke the body, and bring the interface off the screen and into three dimensions, real-time and gesture driven." Interactive artists are exploring the domains of art works, film, animation, and performance to define new canvasses and spaces for personal and collaborative expression.

Interactive films and videos allow people to control views of an environment or object and thus explore new spaces and experience different perspectives. The 1992 QuickTime Movie Festival winner, *The Other Side of Town*, presents a video story about a woman who

meets different characters, a bag lady or a diner waiter, for example, while trying to find her way around an unknown neighborhood. By clicking on the video image of each character, the viewer experiences the story from that character's perspective.

Visual artists and animators exploring the canvas of digital media often see the computer as a collaborator in the creation process. The computer's ability to generate images with different filters and algorithms opens new doors that an artist can use to enter and explore new forms of expression. David Em, Rebecca Allen, Marjorie Franklin, Beverly Reiser, and Gary Winnick are a few artists whose work enters new forms that result from balancing an awareness of technology with personal artistic expression. Em uses the computer canvas to create new worlds of color, light, and shapes. Allen, who teaches animation at UCLA, fuses real-world and computer-generated imagery together in her haunting animations about human relationships. Franklin (also a programmer) and Reiser have both created works with the program *Mandala* in which people use their bodies to interact on an electronic stage with computer-generated video imagery. Winnick, experienced as a game designer for Lucas-Films, creates interactive collaborative networks such as *Habitat* that bring people together in a spirit of fun and creativity.

Another form of personal expression is performance and theater art, which has always been an interactive medium. With computer technology, however, actors can move through 3D holographic space to computer-generated music as in *The Architecture of Catastrophic Change* or *The Desert Music*, two productions by George Coates Performance Works of San Francisco. Dancers can translate movements into electronic sounds and musicians can translate galactic light waves into music. Digital equipment such as MIDI instruments and Macintosh computers have become as integral to these types of performances as the lighting, sound system, and stage itself.

CD-ROM technology can enable a new kind of interactive exhibition/portfolio that includes an artist's work, biography, narrative, and other references. Pedro Meyer's *I Photograph to Remember* is a moving CD-ROM interactive presentation of photographs Meyer took of his parents, accompanied by bilingual narration and overlaid with gentle, poignant music.

An exciting direction of adaptive, interactive art is what Abbe Don calls "co-creation," in which viewers participate in and contribute to an art piece. Don explores new media to create environments for personal storytelling. While her piece *We Make Memories* is a personal collection of her family's experiences, *Share With Me a Story* allows people in an installation to digitize their own family photographs and record their own oral stories into a shared "family album." Storytelling is a universal model for human interaction and artists like Don are only beginning to explore its potential in the technological realm.

The production process and the distribution channels are as equally hard to define as the form itself. (This condition may, in fact, be part of the definition of art.) In some cases, interactive art may reflect electronic books or interactive education pieces. In these cases, they may be sold in mail order catalogs and in CD-ROM bins next to electronic book and music titles. In other cases, they may be shown in galleries or auditoriums, much as art, theater, and films are shown, retaining the shared aspect so common to art. In the future, art performances could possibly be shown to world-wide audiences over interactive networks, allowing viewers opportunities to participate, just as people

in attendance can trigger changes in the music by batting around a MIDI ball.

Digital technology extends people's ability to interact with each other by freeing them from the limits of time and space. It can create new collaborative art forms, which is the premise for public digital art locations, such as the Electronic Cafe International in Santa Monica, California. The "Cafe" stands for **C**omputer **A**ccess **f**or **E**veryone and is a space for developing new artistic genres and alternative technical systems that engage both the performing arts and public participation in highly sophisticated and interactive telecommunications environments. Networking is a technology that allows people from different physical locations to contribute their expressions and build an art piece. "Networking is a form of sculpture," says Anna Couey. She is the organizer of "cyberart galleries," including Art Com on the WELL, where artists use computer networks to create and distribute art. Couey, who is also a weaver, sees diverse and unpredictable human interaction as threads that are "woven" into new and beautiful forms.

Artists are pioneering the digital frontier. Annual events such as CyberArts, organizations like SIGGRAPH and YLEM, and the increasing emergence of cyberart galleries everywhere serve as evidence of their influence on shaping the multimedia aesthetic.

Case Study

We Make Memories/Share with Me a Story 138

Interview

Lucia Grossberger Morales 158

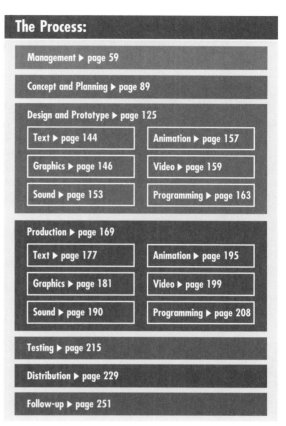

The Process:

Management ▶ page 59

Concept and Planning ▶ page 89

Design and Prototype ▶ page 125

Text ▶ page 144	Animation ▶ page 157
Graphics ▶ page 146	Video ▶ page 159
Sound ▶ page 153	Programming ▶ page 163

Production ▶ page 169

Text ▶ page 177	Animation ▶ page 195
Graphics ▶ page 181	Video ▶ page 199
Sound ▶ page 190	Programming ▶ page 208

Testing ▶ page 215

Distribution ▶ page 229

Follow-up ▶ page 251

Turn to the above pages for information on the stages of development.

*Co-creation is where the author or artist creates a product that lets the user add or create additional materials. It is another term for an **adaptive interaction model** ▶ 95.*

Interactive art pieces have already embraced the political realm. Projects such as HarshWordsForJesse, SimBush, and BushWacked have artistically voiced their creator's feelings about political issues and governmental policies.

Interactive Sales and Marketing

When you see this icon at the top of a page, it signifies a topic in the text with specific relevance to interactive sales and marketing products.

Two important items to include in all demos and advertisements are contact and purchasing information.

Almost all electronic marketing materials share a common purpose—to increase the awareness and sales of a product or products. Common categories include demonstration disks, advertisements, and electronic catalogs. The purpose of a demo is to sell, inform, and educate a user about a product (typically a software product) while the purpose of an advertisement is to sell any product—whether it is related to computers or not. Both demos and advertisements are often distributed freely or used at trade conferences. They also show up in kiosks and are likely to appear in many electronic magazines. Electronic interactive catalogs are beginning to appear and their distribution and pricing are still fluctuating.

Demos

Demo disks can give people a sneak preview of a new product's functionality, illustrate features of an existing product, and provide a vivid overview of a product line. Demo disks are popular sales tools that provide information in response to inquiries about a product. Demo disks can also accompany press releases to illustrate features described in text.

Lotus created a demo disk featuring an animated magician that showed Lotus 1-2-3's features and capabilities. The magician helps the user navigate through the various segments of the demo. Stratus Software, developers of a 3D animation package called StrataVision 3d, created an instructional and entertaining demo disk of their rendering application. Users not only learn about the product features but get a quick course on the principles of 3D modeling and rendering.

Advertisements

A multimedia advertisement takes advantage of the power of combined media and interactivity to encourage customers to learn about, and ultimately purchase, a product or service. Multimedia advertisements can be distributed on traditional media such as diskettes, but show great potential for distribution over networks, cable transmissions, and online facilities such as Compuserve or America Online. A multimedia advertisement should make it easy for the consumer to understand the concept quickly and take action on a decision to buy. An online advertisement, for example, could include an icon that prompts a customer to complete an order form that is sent automatically to a central collection service when completed. Today's cable television shopping channels with their dial-in access are evolving into interactive advertisements that are headed straight for the home.

Catalogs

A catalog is a collection of materials on different products and brands organized and presented in a manner that promotes and facilitates orders from customers. An electronic catalog can use interaction and multiple media types to provide a more

convincing product than print-based catalogs or cable shopping networks. Several electronic catalogs already exist for ordering applications, typefaces, stock photos, images, and sounds. Most of these contain the actual products on the CD. A customer typically calls up a telephone number listed on the CD-ROM, provides a credit card number, and obtains an digital code to unlock the product from the CD-ROM and copy it to their hard disk. While other industries may not have the advantage of this type of "one-stop shopping," the use of different media types may make for compelling products. Record companies could combine sound, pictures, and text to provide a better idea of what an artist or group sounds like. A travel company could provide a CD-ROM listing several different destinations and packages. A real estate firm or multiple listing bureau could press CD-ROMs listing available houses allowing interactive control over specifications, interior and exterior pictures, floor plans, and the surrounding neighborhood. While the potential is large, electronic catalogs may not be appropriate at the moment for many industries. Potential customers may not have access to computers or they may find that browsing through a catalog on a computer and looking at low resolution photos is not the same as sitting on the couch, tea in hand, and thumbing through a well-designed and produced four-color print catalog.

Design Issues

Demos and advertisements should present a simple message. If a demo or advertisement contains too much information or too many functions, people may be too impatient or intimidated to buy the complete product. In some sense, a sales piece should lead a customer in revealing only the amount of information they can reasonably understand. **The interface should be simple, intuitive, and fun**. A potential customer who is frustrated by a demo disk or catalog will hardly want the product or products it promotes. They may instead just reformat the diskette for other uses or toss the CD-ROM away. The content can be developed by anticipating people's questions about the product such as what it can do, how people would use it, what they need to install it, how it compares to similar products, and where they can get more information. **Contact and purchasing information** are two important items to include in almost all sales and marketing materials. This information can be an **address**,

phone number, **email address**, **order form**, **list of retailers**, and even a map or series of maps showing **store locations**. Any information or element that reduces the number of steps a potential customer must go through in order to purchase a product increases the potential for more sales.

Demos and advertisements are usually distributed on 3.5 in. **diskettes** because it is the most common delivery medium, inexpensive, and easy to replicate and distribute in large quantities. Some vendors create demos or catalogs on CD-ROMs which can carry more information. For example, Sony has market tested **bilingual CD-ROMs** that work as instruction and sales information covering their large set of new consumer devices. This approach has its advantages but it will limit the audience to those who have the appropriate CD-ROM drives.

Concerns about **delivery media** ▶ 108, 230 raise concerns about **delivery platforms** ▶ 118. Most products should be designed to run on a wide range of computers which demand rigorous testing of all configurations. Diskettes or CD-ROMs should be readily available and clearly labeled for each compatible platform. Delivery platforms should be chosen to communicate the product's sales or marketing message to the widest possible audience.

Multimedia is already expanding the way businesses can interact with customers. Demo disks and advertisements are early examples of what is possible in the years to come. They point the way to electronic catalogs that can offer interactive control over purchasing decisions.

Case Study

IslandTrapper Demonstration Disk 196

The Process:

Management ▶ page 59

Concept and Planning ▶ page 89

Design and Prototype ▶ page 125

Text ▶ page 144	Animation ▶ page 157
Graphics ▶ page 146	Video ▶ page 159
Sound ▶ page 153	Programming ▶ page 163

Production ▶ page 169

Text ▶ page 177	Animation ▶ page 195
Graphics ▶ page 181	Video ▶ page 199
Sound ▶ page 190	Programming ▶ page 208

Testing ▶ page 215

Distribution ▶ page 229

Follow-up ▶ page 251

Turn to the above pages for information on the stages of development.

Apple's En Passant product is an example of a new category of multimedia project: interactive shopping CD-ROMs. It includes photos, prices, and contact information for name-brand products from companies such as Land's End, Williams-Sonoma, and Tiffany & Co. This pilot CD was sent to over 30,000 users in early 1994 as part of a market test program.

*The challenge in designing any sales piece is to mediate between offering too little information and too much. Too little may not capture a customer's attention. Too much can detract from the **sales process** ▶ 246*

Presentations and Communications

When you see this icon at the top of a page, it signifies a topic in the text with specific relevance to multimedia presentations and communications.

Presentations are common events in any organization. They can help illustrate ideas to a group of people in an auditorium as well as demonstrate a product to a client in a small conference room. The traditional, stand-by model for a presentation is a step-by-step slide show of bullet-pointed text and graphics panels, perhaps with an accompanying video. Multimedia, however, gives new options to presenters by letting them combine animation, sound, QuickTime movies, and graphics into an interactive interface that can go beyond linear access to information. Many computer-based presentation tools have added capabilities to include QuickTime elements.

Well-designed multimedia presentations get the attention of an audience and improve retention of the ideas at a **recall rate often two to three times that of static presentations**. A presentation about the need to improve customer service with video and voice clips of actual customers may be more likely to persuade a manager to take action than a verbal explanation (provided the media elements are produced well).

The form of a presentation can include a one-to-one presentation, a one-to-many presentation often in an auditorium, or a videoconferencing session. A multimedia presentation using Apple computers helped Atlanta become the site of the 1996 Olympics. In another example, multimedia developer Roy Stringer developed a multimedia presentation for the city of Manchester, England to help pitch the city as a site for the 2000 Olympics. Stringer's presentation lets the viewer visualize how the facilities, service, security, and entertainment would be handled for the Olympics.

With the increased use of portable computers like the Apple PowerBook, **portable presentations** are becoming more common. The power of a portable presentation is that it can be used anytime, anywhere. Unplanned meetings with potential clients can win business with a convincing interactive presentation in the hip pocket. The cost and size of projection devices for auditoriums are also dropping

dramatically. Color projection panels, about the size of a notebook computer, plug into a computer's video port and sit on top of an overhead projector, using its light source and magnification to project on to a screen. They can be purchased for under $10,000 or rented from some resellers.

Simple multimedia presentations can be made with in-house, end-user tools such as Aldus Persuasion, which can incorporate QuickTime movies. More sophisticated presentations may need more robust **authoring systems** ▶ 139 such as MacroMind Director. In many of these cases, the work may need to be contracted to an experienced production firm. Their knowledge and use of existing templates and resources can help produce a compelling piece in an affordable and timely manner. One thing to keep in mind in planning and designing presentations is the amount of time it takes to produce multimedia against how long it takes to present it. This production-to-presentation averages about 60:1, with every hour of production time resulting in about one minute of general multimedia presentation. The ratio increases for high-end presentations with a large amount of original illustration, video, and animation. Digital video may be very effective but usually requires high quality production. The need for a multimedia presentation should be measured heavily against its production cost.

Creating effective multimedia presentations takes practice and a sense for **information design** ▶ 129 can be useful. The nature of the content, the purpose of the presentation, and the attitude of the audience influence the choice of media. For example, a presentation for a new kind of software tool can take on different forms. It could include bullet points on slides, show simulated use of solving a real problem with overlaid animated cartoon guides, or provide video testimonials where speakers explain the value of the software tool. In some cases, the most highly "produced" presentation may not be the best. For example, in many legal cases, rougher animation sequences seem to influence a jury more than more realistic renderings. Finding designers and project managers experienced not only in

the technical aspects of putting a presentation together, but in the audience considerations, is one of the more important steps.

The presentation should supplement but not replace the speaker; otherwise, a videotape may be more appropriate. The level of interactivity of the presentation depends on the comfort level of the speaker. Some prefer to proceed through a series of slides in a prepared sequence, while others move freely around the presentation following the flow of discussion. The presentation should be designed to give the speaker the needed control for navigation. An important thing to remember about any presentation is the **environment** ▶ 98, 221 in which it will be conducted. A presentation for a large **audience** can be designed to take advantage of room acoustics and video broadcasting equipment. The text and graphics in the presentation should be visible at a distance. The presentation should be rehearsed to ensure that all components are available, functioning, and synchronized. A presentation that attempts to showcase a client's colorful new product selection will fail if the wrong video card is installed at show time.

The principle goal of presentations is to make a statement to a specific audience. The combination of multimedia and inexpensive and portable display technology provides a quiver of options for accomplishing this objective.

Case Study

Lockheed Waste Management 142

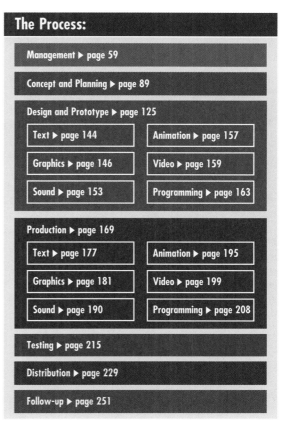

The Process:

Management ▶ page 59

Concept and Planning ▶ page 89

Design and Prototype ▶ page 125

Text ▶ page 144	Animation ▶ page 157
Graphics ▶ page 146	Video ▶ page 159
Sound ▶ page 153	Programming ▶ page 163

Production ▶ page 169

Text ▶ page 177	Animation ▶ page 195
Graphics ▶ page 181	Video ▶ page 199
Sound ▶ page 190	Programming ▶ page 208

Testing ▶ page 215

Distribution ▶ page 229

Follow-up ▶ page 251

Turn to the above pages for information on the stages of development.

Productivity and Authoring Tools

When you see this icon at the top of a page, it signifies a topic in the text with specific relevance to authoring tools.

Anything worth doing over and over until your brain gets numb is worth building a macro to do faster.
— Brooks Cole, President, Mindsphere

There are some great tools out there, but none of them are good enough.
— Anonymous

Much of the focus of multimedia is on the creation of specific projects like kiosks or demo disks or the development of titles such as electronic books or electronic music titles. This focus on "content" products does not address how multimedia fits into many of the existing software applications such as spreadsheets, project management, and e-mail applications. Publishers of these productivity tools may wish to add support for using mixed-media types. Also left unspecified are the differences between creating titles and creating tools. One type of tool is an end-user application that lets an individual or team easily create a multimedia presentation from raw source materials to final presentation. It is similar to the page-layout application that lets many people create publishable-quality work. A related category is authoring tools, templates, and production tools.

Productivity Tools

Most of the software applications on the market can be considered **productivity tools**. At the moment, most information about using the application is conveyed through text, icons, and other graphical elements, as well as with written documentation. In addition, many support as input only text, graphics, and photos, excluding time-based information such as sound, animation, or video. In the future, though, productivity tools may include multimedia as either supplements to learning an application or additional elements to incorporate into a document to communicate or convey additional meaning.

End-User Tools

End-user tools are tools that are explicitly designed to let the lay-person create multimedia presentations and works. A number of authoring tools exist, but they typically require experience with the tools and with design issues. An end-user tool is something that is higher up on the scale of ease-of-use and guidance. An example of an end-user presentation tool is Aldus Persuasion which supports QuickTime capabilities.

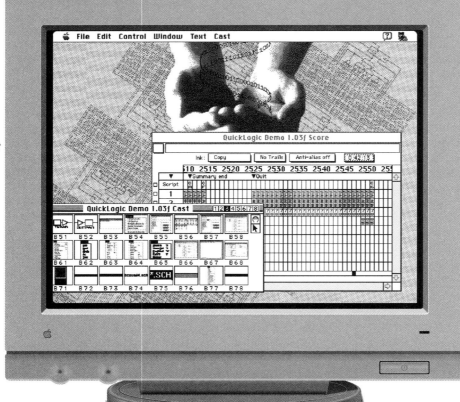

This application lowers the threshhold by giving many people access to incorporating a variety of media. Aldus Fetch is another example. People can use this application to store mixed-media catalogs containing standard Macintosh graphic file formats (PICT, EPS, TIFF, Photo CD, etc.) as well as QuickTime movies, sounds, and several proprietary application formats.

Authoring Tools

An **authoring tool** ▶ 139 facilitates and standardizes the creation and development of a multimedia project. A component of some authoring tools is a template. A **template** ▶ 170 is a standard arrangement of media types that allows them to be easily added, changed, and moved in an established process. Many developers will spend months developing an authoring tool that will save production time in future jobs. To format and prepare text for its Expanded Books series, The Voyager Company devised special tools for continued production of its books. Reinventing the wheel with each book would have drained time and resources. Voyager now markets this toolkit, called the Expanded Book Toolkit, to the public.

A related type of tool is one that helps manage the complexity or improve the efficiency of production tasks. Whereas an authoring tool or template forms a backbone for a multimedia piece, **production tools** help in the tasks that go into its creation. This is similar to using prefabricated construction to help form the structure of a house while using power drills, electric hammers, and forklifts during the construction. Multimedia production involves several iterative processes, such as digitizing video clips, converting file formats, enhancing images, and checking for format and typographical errors. To save time as well as sanity, many developers have developed tools that automate these types of processes. Production tools can become valuable property that can be marketed or bartered for other products and services. For example, a developer who has invented a tool to speed up the process of sound conversion and identification may swap the tool with another developer who has devised a proprietary compression algorithm. Tools that automate processes also lighten the demands of testing. For example, many developers create a simple script that goes through a HyperCard or SuperCard stack and tests for locked or unlocked text fields.

Creating and selling tools, though, can be much different from creating multimedia titles or working on custom products. The issues of providing **documentation**, **supporting customers**, and **creating new versions** may be magnified many times over. The **targeted markets**, **pricing issues**, and **distribution channels** are also much different from those of title development. One risk with creating system-level tools is that new versions of operating systems or applications may incorporate the same functions a set of tools provide. And in an emerging market, the task of improving tools to keep pace with capabilities can be a big obligation.

Development tools can be developed for in-house use, passed around to friends on an informal basis, or given away openly as "freeware." They can also be distributed as "shareware" products, where developers release fully enabled versions and rely on people using the product to voluntarily send money to the developer. It may also be possible to sell tools to a software publisher for a flat fee, or a percentage of royalties, or both. The support and market issues are usually lower with these options than they are with self-publishing. Anybody who hopes to sell tools in a retail environment should look closely at the software industry so that they understand the amount of time and support needed to successfully sell tools.

A trend in multimedia is toward the democratization of the technology through easy-to-use and widely available end-user, authoring, and productivity tools. Tools designed to help the range of multimedia contributors—from the average consumer to the professional production team—will help define the success of the industry.

Case Studies

The Process:

Management ▶ page 59

Concept and Planning ▶ page 89

Design and Prototype ▶ page 125

Text ▶ page 144	Animation ▶ page 157
Graphics ▶ page 146	Video ▶ page 159
Sound ▶ page 153	Programming ▶ page 163

Production ▶ page 169

Text ▶ page 177	Animation ▶ page 195
Graphics ▶ page 181	Video ▶ page 199
Sound ▶ page 190	Programming ▶ page 208

Testing ▶ page 215

Distribution ▶ page 229

Follow-up ▶ page 251

Turn to the above pages for information on the stages of development.

Hardware and software bundles are an easy way to create a complete editing suite for creating interactive multimedia products. For example, the Apple Media Authoring Solution consists of hardware products and software tools such as the SuperMac DigitalFilm and ThunderStorm Acceleration cards, Apple Media Tool, Adobe Premiere, Adobe Photoshop, Macromedia Director, and Macromedia MacroModel. These products and tools allow developers to use animation, 3-D modeling, special video effects, and object-oriented authoring tools to create CD-ROM titles, multimedia presentations, video kiosks, and games for Macintosh and Windows computers.

Management

Management

If you were to travel the wide world of multimedia, you would come upon a number of interesting and inspiring multimedia projects. You would see how they are made and you would speak with the individuals who make them. Along the way, you would find a single, significant lesson that would resonate through your mind. That single lesson would be that almost all of the truly great multimedia projects have a well-balanced sense of management.

Experienced multimedia developers are surprised at how many new developers underestimate the importance of good **management**. They tell stories about brilliant, compelling multimedia projects that failed because of confusion due to poor communication, burn-out due to poor motivation and pacing, budget missteps, lawsuits over copyright issues, lemons due to limited user testing, personality conflicts resulting in products left undone, shabby work due to poor understanding of technology, and beautiful but useless projects, with little or no compelling content. All of these problems can be placed at the feet of management. Luck always plays a role in the success or failure of a product, but many of the cases above are not controlled by luck. More frequent and truthful communication, more realistic estimates of time and money, and a better understanding of the marketplace, technology, and development process may well have made the difference in many of these failed projects.

In a sense, management is a form of navigation. Whether a project is a small custom application or a large-scale commercial venture, whether the vessel is the *African Queen* or the Starship *Enterprise*, certain principles can help chart a course, maintain direction, work with a crew, and deal with challenges in order to reach the destination. In addition, a pioneer spirit, some common sense and flexibility, a realistic perspective, a willingness to learn and unlearn, and a sense of humor will help. Managing multimedia projects is challenging because it means navigating the

Questions managers should continually ask themselves:
- *Is our process a good one?*
- *Could we do things differently?*
- *Is anything missing?*
—Brooks McChesney, Co-founder, Hands On Technology

apparent chaos of new and emerging markets, evolving content issues, unbalanced pricing models, and new technology, all without getting lost. Challenging—but not impossible.

Two categories of management are commonly seen in multimedia today. The first is **business management** ▶ 14 which is the handling of the day-to-day operation and growth of a company. The second is **project management** ▶ 16 which entails the coordination of the creation of a specific project. In some instances, business management is already defined. For example, a team may already exist within a larger organization where budgets, direction, and operations are already determined. In other cases, having a good business model and way of operating can be the difference between creating one project and then closing shop or going on to do many more.

Business Management

Business management is the overall set of actions and operations that implement and sustain the identity, operation, and growth of a company. It is different from project management in that it encompasses how all projects fit into the image, direction, and revenue of a company. Business management addresses the top-level issues that project management takes as assumptions. Many of the principles may be the same but the scopes of the two are widely different.

Developing a Charter

Many multimedia companies work hard on focusing their energies and activities. They do this by developing and refining a **charter**, sometimes called a business definition or a **mission statement**. A clear charter can help define and constrain the products and services that a company offers. For example, a company that states that its mission is to make great interactive education titles about social and environmental issues for children would not get in the business of producing corporate multimedia training programs. They may have the skills and resources to do so but it would violate principles and goals they collectively agreed upon.

A charter can be developed by questions such as, "What does the company do?" or "How would you define the business in one paragraph?" It can be specific, listing the types of products or services offered, or goal-oriented, such as becoming one of the largest electronic book publishers. It can even be figurative. For example, the publishers of *Wired*, a new technology magazine, describe the magazine as the "Rolling Stone of technology" and a "Vanity Fair for propeller heads." The issue is not how the charter is reflected but how well it reflects the goals of the company. If the charter is at odds with many of the beliefs of the people in the company then this may be the first indication that something is wrong.

Setting up some type of structure beforehand for deciding the types of projects a team takes on can help keep a company focused. Otherwise the direction and prospects can change according to circumstances not according to desires, goals, and markets. People can sometimes get seduced by a few successes and begin working on different projects or with different motivations than originally planned. Changing direction is not the danger. Working in a disorganized fashion, though, can be.

Developing a Framework

Another component that is related to a charter is a **framework** for operating the company. A framework lists the **priorities** of an organization, giving people a way of supporting the charter in the face of conflicting, new, or uncertain circumstances. Frameworks can be put into place on a company-wide level or for specific issues like individual projects. For example, if the schedule of a project is critical due to a trade show or limited market window, then that would make *time* a priority over the feature set and the content. If the development team wants to include consulting, the framework would say that it is acceptable only if it does not slip the schedule. A working framework can help answer questions and make decisions at the time and place they occur instead of putting them off or moving them up the chain of command.

Defining Skills and Capabilities

Defining the **skills** and **capabilities** of a company or project team is another step that often goes hand in hand with formulating goals. This step involves an honest

assessment of what the people in a company or on a project team already know and do, and what they want to know and do. It is balanced with an awareness that there is always room to learn and improve. This can be done either by gaining expertise or collaborating with others. For example, someone who is an excellent programmer may have great ideas for an interactive game but may have neither the patience nor the desire to deal with issues like planning, marketing, or distributing a product. On the other hand, a marketing professional may know how to measure audiences but be confused by options and trends in technology. An honest assessment of skills and capabilities upfront can allow for planning to fill upcoming needs. Some projects run out of time, money, and nerves when trying to bluff on this point. The producers realize too late down the line that they got into more than they bargained for.

An informal approach is to simply look at the activities that people gravitate towards. A team that is constantly developing prototypes and never taking them to finished products may need help going to the next step. Or, maybe their focus should be just developing the concepts and designs of products for others. A writer who prefers writing new material to revising old copy, may signal the need to hire an editor to refine text. An honest assessment will show the strengths of an organization. It will also show the places for improvement or for bringing in outside parties.

Creating a Business Plan

For better or worse, many young companies skip writing a **business plan**. They just pick a name for the company and start developing a product. Investors or potential partners, though, will likely want to see a business plan before investing in or joining the company. A **business plan gives a clear and exhaustive picture of the objectives of a company.** It also shows how a company plans to get there. It lists finances, markets, products, distribution channels, and key employees. Other plans, such as marketing plans and project plans, often fall out of topics and areas presented in this plan.

An important purpose of a business plan is not to show to outside parties, but to serve as an internal contract to all the parties inside an organization. It provides another way of looking at the objectives and goals of a company. A good way to create a business plan is to look at those of others for topics and organizational structure. Then, develop the plan to reflect the unique situation of the company, products, market, and industry.

Elements likely to change in the multimedia industry in the next few years:

- *Hardware platforms*
- *Software systems*
- *Delivery media*
- *Product categories*
- *Authoring tools*
- *Production tools*
- *Funding sources*
- *Copyright issues*
- *Licensing issues*
- *Pricing models*
- *Distribution channels*
- *Everything else*

VCs view business plans as a contract. Entrepreneurs who view their business plans as a mere selling document will live to regret it. CEOs who raise capital using hockey stick projections, and then fail to deliver the results, should not be surprised when their investors decide to change captains in the middle of the journey.

— David T. Gleba, President, VentureOne, in "CEO Survival," Upside, September 1992

The point in which I am different from most inventors is that I have, besides the usual inventor's make-up, a bump of practicality as a sort of appendix, the sense of the business, money value of an invention. Oh, no, I didn't have it naturally. It was pounded into me by some pretty hard knocks.

— Thomas A. Edison

INC.: Is that how you see your job, as the communicator of the strategy?

CARLZON: Yes, I suppose so. My job is not to make business; my job is to ensure that other people can make business.

INC.: OK, but you must have to keep your message fairly simple if you want to get it across on that scale.

CARLZON: Oh, definitely. I want to keep it simple. I say, "We want to be the preferred airline for the frequent business traveler." It can't be misunderstood. If you start to give goals that can be misunderstood, you have to begin again.

INC.: Don't you worry that such a goal leaves too much room for interpretation?

CARLZON: Well, you must provide a framework in which people can act. For example, we have said that our first priority is safety, second is punctuality, and third is other services. So, if you risk flight safety by leaving on time, you have acted outside the framework of your authority. The same is true if you don't leave on time because you are missing two catering boxes of meat. That's what I mean by framework. you give people a framework, and within the framework you let people act.

—Jan Carlzon, President of Scandinavian Airlines System Group, "The Art of Loving," Inc. magazine, May 1989

HyperBole is dedicated to publishing original works of interactive fiction and art and literature which will continue to futher the digital domain. We learn as we go. We do cutting edge work of interactive art and fiction which are designed to open up our minds further to the industry...and open up wider channels of the way the industry is developing....The way we do stories is that we don't say, "That's never been done before. We can't do it." We say instead. "That's never been done before. How can we do it?"

— Halle Eavelyn, Director of Marketing and Evangelism, HyperBole Studios

Developing a Business Model

A **business model** places a company in the context of other companies and other industries. It also helps in targeting both internal and external activities and relationships. Each industry has its own models that are continually evolving as new technologies change production and distribution factors and as new movements occur in a society.

The industries in which multimedia has its roots all help to define possible models. The print industry uses the divisions of author, publisher, and distributor. The software industry has evolved away from sole authors and into in-house development teams, generally working with a publisher-distributor relationship. The film and TV industries have evolved a little differently. The first films were single-angle renditions of stage plays. The first television shows were extensions of radio programs. But beyond the terminology of the production houses, movie studios, and theaters, lies the general structure of a creator, a publisher, and a distributor.

The **creator** or **production house** initiates the concept and develops the product. It may be an individual, a small group, or a large team. The **publisher ▶ 236** finances, packages, and markets the product. The **distributor ▶ 239** manages the flow of the product from publisher to customer. The distribution may be direct or several levels deep, and often involves a number of different companies and outlets. Many multimedia projects have these divisions with the added element of a content provider.

A number of services or sub-categories support these three principal activities including writing (song, screen, or technical writing), search firms or talent agencies, design houses, printers, and duplication houses. Industries and companies are constantly redefining the borders and the tasks within each category. Some companies are highly integrated and cover the range from the initial idea to the end distribution. Others play a single role over multiple products.

A good example of this content provider, producer, and publisher arrangement is the multimedia CD-ROM title *LIFEMap*, produced by Arborescence in San Francisco. *LIFEMap* was developed under a business arrangement between the producer (Arborescence), the content provider (California Academy of Sciences), and a publisher (Time-Warner). The Academy provided scientific content to Arborescence who then designed and produced a CD-ROM. Time-Warner advanced money for production in exchange for marketing rights to carry the product.

This type of interaction creates several possibilities for a working relationship. For example, consultants often work on a project basis for multimedia producers who

license content from various sources. Publishers, in turn, fund, license, or purchase the completed multimedia title from the producer for sale through distribution channels. Sometimes, producers and content owners form joint ventures. At this early stage in the industry, each project can involve different interactions with each one creating a new blend of ideas and results.

The advantage of following an established model is that it provides a ready-made structure for running a business and producing a project. Using a model from the publishing, film, or software industries can offer insights on funding a project, coordinating, paying and motivating project members, ensuring quality, and meeting deadlines and budgets. One disadvantage to following a pre-existing model is determining when to abandon it for more creative approaches. The way to produce a project for one discipline may not match the complexities of producing multimedia—a process that

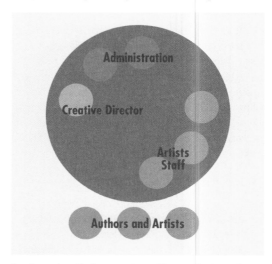

has been described as creating a film, producing software, publishing a book, and then some.

Publishing

A **publishing model,** borrowed from print media such as books, magazines, and newspapers, may be useful for looking at the production of products such as electronic books and magazines. In fact, many CD-ROM projects are **repurposed works ▶ 101, 175, 257,** using existing printed works and converting them to digital, interactive formats to be experienced with the aid of a computer device.

In this model, a chief editor in a multimedia firm signs contracts with authors to produce finished works. Editors organize and transform the work and then producers and designers place it in electronic from. Authors may decide to retain the copyright to the work but may also transfer it to the publisher, either for a set time or indefinitely. A publisher may pay a percentage of the

Interview: Barry Schuler

What is the business philosophy of Medior?
By the end of the 1990s, the focus of the software industry will change from hardware to content. We at Medior want to be really well positioned as a company to take advantage of this "boom" when it comes. In order to do this, we had to look at today's business opportunities.

We want to focus on the profit-making opportunities today, rather than spend a two-year development cycle making something for some market that will hopefully exist when we are done. There is no question that there is a cottage industry of "multimedia content developers"—primarily making multimedia presentations, very lightweight multimedia information systems, kiosks, and so on.

When we looked at how to get into the multimedia market, we decided not to merely treat it as a service business. We asked how we could evolve *service products* out of it. Focusing on custom development opportunities and productizing them, we want to build a company that has what it needs to score the content win in the future. That involves talent, technology, and a systems approach to the marketplace. It does come down to talent: talented people who know the tools, who have good tools to work with, and who can make content. That's what we've been doing.

If you look at traditional media and its content you see people have interests and product loyalties. What brings people to use multimedia?
The biggest question mark that hangs over multimedia content today is "What is the value added of this medium?" I believe this industry is very, very early in the development of the value-added elements. We take magazines and slap them on a CD-ROM ▶ 109. The value of the CD is that you can have 100 magazines in one place. You can have a search engine to get the articles. Although this is better than having a stack of magazines on a shelf with an index supplement, I do not consider that a CD-ROM offers a lot of value added. If that is the best we can do, than multimedia will not become mainstream. The biggest challenge facing us as developers today is how to make this medium do things—provide an experience, provide a space—that no other medium can.

What limits your business in making a multimedia mass market product?
There are two issues—the platform and the format. The resolution of what the multimedia platform will be, who will provide it, and how it will be positioned will make the "VHS-Betamax" war look like a picnic. Everybody is scrambling to own that particular piece of technology. The consumer electronics people, computer people, and even the phone people want it. Without really knowing what "it" is, everybody wants it. Everybody sees the brass ring, but this is not today's reality. Let the major computer, consumer electronic manufacturers, and phone companies bash their heads in. Let them take the next five years to decide what the delivery platforms are going to be.

Formats are another issue. If you look at consumer electronic models, it generally takes about ten years for a new format such as CD-Audio ▶ 48, 110 to become mass-market product. The problem is that we have not established a multimedia format yet, and it will take another ten years to create the market.

If we are still establishing formats and platforms that will suit computer, communications industries, and the Japanese, what do we still need to get it right?
It depends on how big your goals are. For mass-market products, the single most important component is the development environment. The delivery piece of the puzzle is much easier than the development piece. Again, if you look at the history of development environments we've moved from code-based systems in the '70s, to graphical-interface based systems of the '80s, to media based systems of the '90s. Building a state-of-the-art interactive CD-ROM today is more complex than making a movie. All of the nuances of making a movie are there.

To be able to show the value added and the compelling use of the medium, there must be tools to help create really good content that people will want to do things with. The widget that they use to view it, whether it is a phone, a CD, handheld, or hooked into their TVs, is completely irrelevant.

Content will drive delivery?
It has to. It's irrelevant to postulate what these appliances are going to be. The content transcends it all. It completely transcends the platform. The trick here is to figure out how to create a new pervasive medium that will provide an experience and do things that no other medium will do. Acquire the content and build the content, make this happen, then we can make it work on whatever platform is there.

How do you identify a market and build product for it?
Medior is going to focus on the money-making opportunities today, and these are in producing industrial and commercial content. In the custom development project, you use the tools to solve real business problems today. We are building the talent and technology base that applies to any type content.

While the platform issue is being resolved, our talent base will be portable. The new machines will be faster and better and the media problems like video will be solved.

And Medior's business model?
We work in the Hollywood production model. We treat projects as units. Each unit has producers, line managers, and a crew. The Hollywood model is also glued to the service company model in which we have an account executive who works with the client.

How do you recommend solutions to your clients?
The very first phase of any proposal we write is needs analysis. Clients usually don't know what can be done. The biggest part of our business is understanding the tools and how they apply to a client's practical problems. We also look at the appliance, the front-end, who is going to interact with it, and how they are going to interact. Finally, we determine how a system will be maintained.

Let's say a paint manufacturer comes to you and wants to put a kiosk ▶ 38 in every hardware store. They want to update information on a monthly basis. Someone is going to have to fulfill the delivery of that information. You have to think about who will be maintaining a system when you select a platform. This is why the systems integration has to be folded into the company structure. For large system bids, you need to structure your deal to include the CPU vendor and large national service organizations. We will also help them write the business plan and form the revenue model.

Barry Schuler, president of Medior Incorporated, a multimedia system integrator and content developer based in the San Francisco Bay Area, talks about new evolving business models for multimedia production companies.

*New multimedia models are emerging such as one called the title brewery. A **title brewery** is a centralized and shared facility that provides the environment, methodology, equipment, software, and personnel needed to simultaneously produce several multimedia CD-ROM titles. This is similar to a commune or co-op and is the first of many hybrids likely to develop in the industry. The structure and financial arrangements vary between participants.*

Management cannot make people work together. It can only create an environment that allows people to work together.

Although management books can offer valuable lessons, many aspects of management cannot be developed by reading from a book. Learning how to communicate clearly, motivate team members, plan ahead, and react well to new events are best developed through practice, including both successes and failures.

gross sales to the author, distributing the risk and the reward evenly between the author and publisher.

Frequently, a publishing project begins by accepting a writer's proposal and paying an advance fee that is subtracted from royalties paid later. Authors are treated as **independent contractors** and often have little control over how their work is implemented once they deliver it. Authors with a "name" (those who are known and recognized in the market), however, can command larger royalties and a bit more control if their previous works are successful and the publisher has confidence in their vision.

Production may be handled by employees of the publisher or free-lance workers who come in on a project-by-project basis. These contributors are paid a salary or fee for their work but hardly ever share in royalties, and even then, only if the producer or illustrator is well-known. Marketing, sales, and distribution are controlled by the publisher. People in these positions usually handle a collection of titles and are commonly full-time employees paid a salary and possibly a commission on sales.

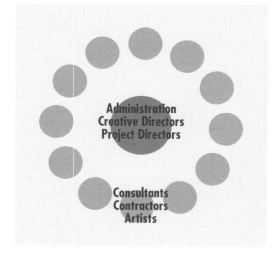

Movie Studio

The **movie studio model** differs mainly in the number of "staff" versus the number of part-time or free-lance contributors. In this model, a multimedia company or "movie studio" consists of a small, tight group of mostly managers, administrators, executive producers, sales and marketing people, and some creative directors. Almost all specialized jobs like videography, sound and image processing, editing, and programming are handled by contractors who work on a project-by-project basis. Depending on the fees they are paid and their skill-level, these contractors may receive royalties on their portion of the overall project. These projects are usually mass-market products but they do not necessarily have to be.

Contractors ▶ 76, especially interface designers and programmers, may retain rights to the materials they create (if only limited ones). These rights define whether code, concepts, or content can be used (in whole or in part) by these contractors for other projects. Rights, fees, and royalties are all variables in the compensation equation. Limited rights and no royalties will require higher fees to attract skilled, creative workers. The absence of high fees can still attract great contributors if compensation includes royalties and the retention of rights to work produced.

The advantages of this model include flexibility, efficiency, and freedom. The **production house** can maintain a fairly low overhead using full-time employees to handle corporate and administrative issues while expanding and contracting as needed for various projects. This allows the studio to respond better to changing market and economic forces. Contractors also benefit because they can choose which projects they wish to work on and can manage their own time. They can take time off between projects simply by not accepting work.

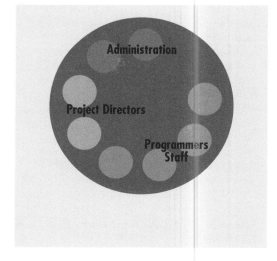

Software Development

The areas where the movie studio model can break down are with issues like supporting multiple platforms and releasing new versions. "One-shot" products like most books or movies do not need much technical maintenance or support. Software products, however, do need maintenance and support and so the "talent" (programmers) is usually kept around full-time to maintain current versions and develop future ones. Therefore, a **software development model** can fit certain parts of the multimedia process as well as system integration aspects associated with some custom projects.

Developing a software application usually requires a team of people knowledgeable both in computers and in the subject matter of the application. It also requires testing and support people. A highly structured process moves from initial design to production, testing, duplication, and then distribution. Existing applications or modules are sometimes purchased from outside developers but typically only at or near completion.

Software development provides a structured way to create, test, and deliver a product. The steps from initial concept to final delivery are similar to the ones presented as the prototypical multimedia production process in this book. The software production model also has similarities to how technology is integrated into current business practices. Multimedia is not always a shrink-wrapped product. This means that many custom projects are created by analyzing the needs of a business and recommending solutions. This analysis may differ from **system integration** in the software industry only in the types of hardware and software solutions provided. With client approval, integrators in both industries assemble teams that design, develop, test, and integrate the system into an existing business structure. "System integrators practice digital midwifery to bring multimedia into the world," explains developer Kate Rain of Kate Rain Creations, "crossing the bridge between systems and organizations."

Work Environments

Many multimedia developers see the way they work as a departure from traditional hierarchical work. A "virtual corporation" is made possible in part by the fixed duration of a project, by its nature, and by technology that allows for distributed work environments. The fact that most multimedia projects have definitive start and end

points allows for a direct allocation of resources to a project. When the project is done, many of the resources are freed for other projects. Once the message and type of work are known by the project members, many of the team members can break off and work independently on separate elements. They can do this work without a whole lot of interaction with others. The third component that allows for creative and collaborative work is the **infrastructure** that includes personal and laptop computers, fax machines, modems, and e-mail. Having these tools available lets each person and each team craft an environment and way of working that meets their needs and desires. Recognizing and accommodating personal styles can produce a large jump in productivity and motivation.

Project Management

Project management plays a role from the initial concept of the product to its eventual production and distribution. It involves understanding how to finance the project, establish a budget, construct contracts, structure a team, handle customer and client relations, hit deadlines, plan distribution and a whole array of other aspects of a project. **Project management** is the act of estimating and coordinating **finances ▶ 71**, **people ▶ 74**, and **resources ▶ 79** to produce a specific project as a series of processes. Project management involves organizing artists, programmers, interface designers, and content experts into an operating team. It also involves overseeing **legal issues ▶ 104**, and, in some cases, **client acquisition ▶ 81** and **contact** and, possibly, **marketing ▶ 85, 241** and **sales ▶ 245** efforts.

*The term **virtual corporation** describes the dynamic and temporary interaction of people with outstanding specialized skills who are involved only for the duration of a project. It is a way of getting the best people to contribute without shouldering the weight of full-time personnel issues. The advantage to such a structure is that the individuals imprint their style on the project and are free to move on to others.*

Understanding the development process increases the chance of bringing a multimedia project into existence but it will not solve every problem along the way. Many projects fall into a rut of constant meetings without ever producing the work that is placed on the schedule. The work of updating the schedule and managing the meetings can end up taking the place of getting actual work done. The development process gives a framework, but only hard work and dedication can provide a finished product.

Interview: Joe Sparks

How do you organize and account for all the pieces?
In many ways, you have to be a librarian. You have to have ways of naming things that are consistent to you . . . to what you are thinking. You have to come up with something that works. Inform all of your team how it is going to work. Everyone has to stick with it no matter what. Begin with early things you are starting to find out. Tell everyone we are going to name all of the dialogues using the first two letters of the character's name followed by a one; make these data sheets that are followed by the number of the line; and tell everyone to stick to it. But it goes further than that. You want to come up with names for things. There are good techniques to establish early and stick with. Say I have this animation, we're going to use several of these like this and what we're going to do here is a process that has to happen on every frame. These events happen here, there, and everywhere, and they affect all these parts at the beginning. So, I will sit down and do a few tests with a few samples and determine what is the best image processing, masking, clipping,

storing, naming, filing—all the different things that you are going to do to this image before it actually ends up in the product as a final image. Usually these images go through all sorts of steps from the 3D package, maybe generating texture files that went into it, 24-bit versions, cropped alpha channel versions, the eighth version. There are all these different versions and different names. You have to keep all of those around until you are sure you're done because you might have to go back and step back into it. So, a lot of planning involves how to "library" all of this material, the process that happens to it all along the way, and where it all goes and is organized on the many magneto-optic drives. A lot of it is really boring stuff but it's very important. On this project right now we have some ten or twelve 600 MB optical cards, about thirty 45 MB cards, endless floppies, two 600 MB hard drives, and a 100 MB hard drive. We have lots of hard drives and cards all over the place. It's a nightmare if you start getting lazy about keeping an iron fist over all of your files to go into the production.

Joe Sparks is an interactive game designer and runs a multimedia game design company, Pop Rocket in San Francisco, CA.

I've noticed that it is extraordinarily difficult after a really good idea has emerged to recall exactly what was the project that gave birth to it. Certainly, it is never the case that one person suddenly had a brilliant idea, which is then accepted by everyone in that original, untouched form. The really good idea is always traceable back quite a long way, often to a not very good idea which sparked off another idea that was only slightly better, which somebody else misunderstood in such a way that they then said something which was really interesting.... That's actually why I have always worked with a writing partner, because I'm convinced that I get to better ideas than I'd ever do on my own.

— *John Cleese, former member of the Monte Python troupe, quoted by Michael Schrage in* Share Minds: The New Technologies of Collaboration

Teach your [content] experts
▶ 20, 99 *as much as you can about what you can do for them. Have them work with you to come up with all the best things to produce. Get them very involved in the production. Let them have the final say on the content. They will feel totally responsible and committed to the project. The two pathologists I work with on the Theseus project really believe that they are making this thing, and they're right. All I'm doing is empowering them, and this is absolutely crucial. It's not like in the movies where the director is in total control. I simply regard myself as a facilitator to build the product.*

— *Roy Stringer, Interactivity Designer, Theseus medical database*

Calculate the time it would take to complete a task under optimal conditions and then triple it. That's how long it is going to take.

— *Henri Poole, **vivid** studios*

Development Process

Every creative process follows a general pattern that moves from early conceptualization to final realization. The details within each step and the extent of each stage will differ with the media or use but the overall process should be the same. A formal structure for the process shows six stages: **concept and planning**, **design and prototype**, **production**, **testing**, **distribution**, and **follow-up**. In print publishing, the concept and planning and design and prototype stages may be so closely linked that there is no clear distinction between the two. Copy-editing forms the bulk of the testing, and printing and delivery to book distributors or bookstores makes up the distribution. Film-making or music-making may have the same blurring of the lines but by viewing the process in these discrete steps, the timing, tasks, and roles that are needed can be seen more easily.

Depending on a company's role, the responsibility for any phase or part of a phase may fall to other parties. Using the book publishing example, the author is typically involved in only the concept, design, and production stages whereas the publisher is usually involved in all six. In addition, many of the stages may overlap or even happen at the same time. For example, distribution arrangements for an electronic book on CD-ROM can be planned while the product is still being prototyped. Testing may begin on some parts of the product while others are still being built.

Project teams in multimedia have different ways of following the process, depending on the project organization, type of product, and team dynamics. Some multimedia developers of small teams may hardly write anything down yet they still follow a plan that is shared verbally with everyone involved on a daily basis. Large multimedia production teams may formally publish their progress with a process flowchart that informs team members and clients about the steps in the development process.

One key to working with any process is to build in **iteration** ▶ 216. Things are typically never done correctly the first time. This could be passed off as inexperience or miscommunication but is more often due to new ideas developing that are better than the old ones. The first step for people involved is to recognize this as part of the nature of a project, a part that is a necessary good. A bad first draft or prototype can be too easily dismissed as a horrible failure if it is off from the expected mark. But expecting the first attempt to be somewhat off, and planning for two or three more before moving

on, turns an unmitigated failure into just another step in the process.

This means integrating iterations into budgets and schedules. Testing and checking assumptions along the way, bringing in others and listening to their opinions, editing and re-editing, and evaluating whether it is appropriate to go on to the next step—all are important parts of coordinating an interactive and creative process.

Importance of the Project Manager Role

Fundamentally, project management in multimedia is similar to other kinds of project management. The distinguishing feature of multimedia management is the need to orchestrate different technologies, skills, personalities, resources, and opportunities in a marketplace that is evolving and changing every day. Multimedia draws on the diverse talents of artists and technicians alike—two groups that may not share compatible world views and working styles. This diversity can lead to incredible dynamics, positive and negative, and calls for someone to step in and make things run smoothly, much as a conductor works with an orchestra. This person is commonly called the **project manager** ▶ 16. Depending on the size of the project, the project manager may also carry out multiple duties, from designing and prototyping to marketing and testing. In fact, many successful multimedia developers state that the balance of creativity and management has helped them succeed.

Just as the key to a successful restaurant, good food notwithstanding, is location, the key to successful projects, good ideas notwithstanding, is management. A great idea and enough money to develop the idea are important, but the key to getting it done is the person or people who help define and manage expectations, schedules, costs, people, and resources. The idea that good management is key to a project should not be too strange. The key to a good political administration is not in the policies or the programs but in how they are presented and implemented. Projects may succeed despite good management, just as some children will grow up to be good persons despite lousy environments, but the easiest way to guarantee success is to find a good manager.

This does not mean that a production team needs to hire a business or project manager. But it does mean that someone has to take the responsibility. One step in managing a project is to establish a **goal** ▶ 93; a second step is to develop a **team** ▶ 74 of people to meet that goal and a third is to provide the team with the **resources** ▶ 74 they need. Whether the project consists of one person

wearing a lot of hats or a large team of specialists, a project manager will find that knowledge of people and the development process are important tools for surviving and thriving on the multimedia frontier.

Learning How to Manage

Where does someone learn how to manage? Many of the variables and responsibilities involved in managing a project can be listed, but the way to move forward and motivate others is not something that can be taught in school or read in a book. For the most part, management skills are learned by interacting with people and events, which is something that most people do frequently in the normal course of their lives. Organizing a team to run a crisis hot-line can provide as much insight as leading a project team for a previous product. Good managers recognize effective ways of communicating with others, understand the steps in a particular process, and practice them in a consistent and focused manner.

Good managers integrate these elements as part of their own personal style. Some people make the mistake of putting on a management hat and becoming something they are not. They confuse managing with making decisions. In most cases, managing is *reaching* decisions and attaining goals, regardless of who makes them or achieves them.

Project Plan

Every multimedia project has a project plan. On small projects, it can be held in the minds of the team members or be as simple as a one-page statement of budgets, tasks, responsibilities, and schedules. On larger projects, it can be as complex and intricate as a dependency tracking chart, generated with project planning software and approved by managers from different departments. A **project plan** is an approach to solving a problem. A well-formed and well-stated plan helps all parties follow the same direction so that no momentum is lost even, if the project manager is not around.

A project plan identifies the activities, responsibilities, and schedules that will thread throughout the process. It is like a blueprint for building a house. Where a blueprint shows the framework and the locations of all the electrical outlets and doors and hinges

for subcontractors to put in place, a project plan shows all the pieces of the product for programmers, illustrators, videographers, and others to work on. The project plan is a point of reference that should be used throughout a project. It should expand and change as the project expands and changes.

The initial plans can have conservative or **worst-case estimates**. They should be updated after the design and prototype stage when more information is known to represent as accurate a plan as possible.

Managing a multimedia project involves managing a number of variables, but three of the most important ones, besides people, are time, costs, and quality. The delivery media and platform, and production tools follow closely behind. Knowing how these three principal elements rank in comparison with each other can help make decisions clearer when plans or schedules change.

Estimating Budgets, Schedules, and Roles

With or without hard constraints, once a particular project begins, the job of estimating the schedule, budget, and roles then comes into play. A **schedule** help describes how long resources need to be committed to the project. It also outlines when certain tasks in the project can begin, such as setting up production and testing resources or preparing for the project launch. A **budget** provides the basis for funding sources or client negotiations. Estimating **roles ▶ 74** helps in the preparation for staffing a project. Defining the roles will help decide what type of people to hire and how many.

Rough estimates are fine initially, but as the concept and design become more refined, they should be turned into solid dates, numbers, and tasks. The rough estimates may show that a particular project will cost more in time, effort, expense, and nerves than it will bring in return. Or, it may show that the project can go beyond the client's expectations and build future business.

The time and costs for developing and completing a project are difficult to estimate but it helps to be as **realistic** as possible. Many times, someone who is eager to close a deal with a client makes the mistake of underestimating the work it will take to fulfill the agreement. The result can be damaged because the trust and worth of the product team will be

Be sure the changes you make are affordable and worthwhile. Ponder them beforehand, take your best shot, then move on. Having regrets later about changing or not changing things takes too much energy.

— Kristina Hooper-Woolsey, Distinguished Scientist, Apple Computer

The project plan should include the following items at some level of detail:

- Concept
- Marketing
- Budget
- Schedule
- Content
- Features
- Delivery platform
- Delivery media
- Production tools
- Roles
- People
- Resources
- Legal issues
- Testing
- Sales and distribution

People working on multimedia projects can never have too much:

- Talent, both creative and managerial
- Hardware, mostly in the form of data storage capacity
- Time, to prototype, build, and thoroughly test ideas

— Christine Perey

Show respect for a vendor's time by knowing everything needed for an estimate ahead of time and by explaining the purpose of the estimate. You can waste a lot of a vendor's time by having them develop a formal estimate where a rough estimate would do.

*A **time-and-materials basis** typically means an hourly rate plus reimbursible materials. A **fixed-price contract** means a single dollar value for a project. Estimates need to be much more precise for a fixed-dollar contract.*

tarnished, despite the quality of the finished product. A negative image is hard to reverse in a client's mind, and it will be much harder to work on other projects in the future. One saving grace is that once a project gets done, if it meets or exceeds expectations, many of the trials and delays are often forgotten. Just as the body has the intrinsic ability to forget pain, people and groups seem to have the same ability to forget conflicts and delays—provided the end result is worthwhile.

Sources for Estimates

Estimating is a skill based on **experience.** A veteran multimedia developer who specializes in a certain area will be able to build reliable estimates based on past projects. A potential danger when working from experience, though, is to use the **original estimates** from past projects and not the **actual values** ▶ 252. Not bothering to calculate final budgets and schedules can mean using the wrong estimates time and time again. Another mistake is not treating each project with a fresh slate to accommodate changes in technology and processes. For example, the experience of producing an interactive tutorial with videodisc technology is similar to, but not exactly like, producing the same tutorial with QuickTime for a CD-ROM. Using QuickTime brings additional concerns of digitization, frame rate, window size, and optimization.

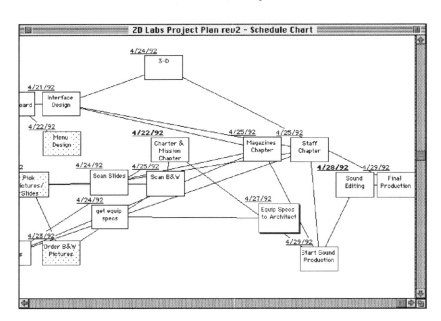

Another good resource of information is from **other developers, contractors, vendors**, and **experts**. If you are not sure about a task or a cost, you might ask someone who has done it already. For an example, if you

need an estimate for a 10-second 3D animated sequence, you can go directly to an animator. (They may not only give you the estimate but may ask to perform the job.) If you need a price on mastering or manufacturing charges for CD-ROMs, call up several disc manufacturers to get quick estimates. Provided you know the particulars about a job, this route may be faster and more accurate than researching the information in a book or trade journal. (Especially in areas where costs are dropping dramatically.) Asking a lawyer for an estimate of the time needed to put together a licensing agreement might show that allocating two weeks to get the rights to certain video clips might actually be a six month process from original contact to final signature.

Ways of Estimating

Creating High and Low Estimates

One useful approach to estimating is to make **high** and **low** estimates that reflect a range between the best and worst case scenarios. For example, how long would it take to gather source material if everything were at the fingertips and in perfectly usable condition? Compare that with the time needed in the worst case to generate and process everything from scratch. A reasonable figure will lie somewhere in that range. Presenting these estimates to the design team or to the client will also help move the expectations to a common ground.

Constraining Some Elements

Another technique is to **constrain some variables** and see how the other numbers come out. Even without an exact due date, picking one to play with and then working through the costs and content will give enough information to know if the timeframe is realistic. Adjusting it as needed will help work through the variables iteratively to find a good balance. This is not unlike trying to graph an algebraic equation. Putting in numbers for x provides values for y. Plotting these points gives a good feel for the shape of the actual line or curve, provided enough points are used to reflect the complexity of the equation.

Working from Different Angles

Working through an estimate from **different angles** is another way to flush out inconsistencies. Working through a schedule from front to the back and then switching and working from back to front will challenge unrealistic assumptions that might be made if only one direction were used. The temptation to allocate tasks to the time remaining is all too real. For example, allocating two weeks for testing is a decision made time after time, even though the time might realistically take a month.

Dividing into Units

Another common approach is to divide the project into **units** and gather as much information as possible for that unit. An example is to count all the media elements and tasks and multiply them by size, cost, and frequency. Breaking down elements discretely and then building back up to total estimates checks the validity of "ball-park" figures. Throwing out a rough number and not checking it can be dangerous move. Using an estimate of $1,000 for 20 animations would quickly prove wrong when considering that each one alone would cost around $400. Multiplying that figure by the 20 needed would show that up to $8,000 would be needed for the animations. Going on a rough figure without checking may result in sudden shortages of content or money somewhere in production.

Putting in a Safety Margin

Once some estimates have been developed, a good rule of thumb for inexperienced producers is to **build in a safety margin** by multiplying the estimates by a certain factor. Depending on the length of the task and the number of unknowns, the safety margin can be anywhere from 20% to 300%. Only half in jest, some developers suggest arriving at a figure (time or cost), doubling it, and then doubling it again to get a real expectation of when a project will be done or how much it will cost. This suggestion helps to factor in elements often excluded in preliminary estimates. These include the time to get financing, develop a concept, get tools running, handle computer problems, obtain permissions, or test a few more times.

Including Overhead

Overhead is the cost of doing business that is not directly attributable to a specific project. It includes the costs for such items as taxes, business cards, equipment, rent, insurance, telephones, e-mail, supplies, and travel. Overhead is often factored into an estimate by including it as a percentage or an hourly or daily rate. Rarely is it called out as a specific value in a proposal. Direct reimbursibles may be, however. If a client is located out of the state or country, then a higher proportion should be allocated for long distance phone, fax, and express mail charges (provided none of these are included as directly **reimbursable costs ▶ 82** in an agreement). Independent contractors hired on a project basis should also include their overhead in their rates. Otherwise, a programmer or image processing specialist, for example, may end up making a lot of money but not enough to cover equipment, software, or training materials.

Fixed-Price Contracts

The estimates on **fixed-price contracts** need to be much more solid at the outset than estimates for self-published products or projects billed at a scheduled rate. A fixed-price contract is a contract with a set dollar amount for performing certain tasks. Clients generally prefer fixed-priced contracts over time-and-material contracts because they are easier to budget and they put a relative cap on the cost. One advantage for production houses in this type of contract is that it leaves more room to increase profit margins by managing tasks efficiently and coming in under the budget. An experienced and talented firm may not gain as much using a time-and-materials contract because they can typically perform tasks in much less time than a less experienced firm. A time-and-materials contract may not capitalize on the experience and knowledge of the firm.

A disadvantage of fixing the cost at the onset is the risk taken in estimating the cost. The contractor must perform at the agreed-upon price, regardless of the costs incurred. The client is not obligated to pay anything unless the developer delivers that which has been agreed upon. Problems can arise if the estimates are too low or the client's objectives are too vague. Successful fixed-price contracts result from precise and specific definitions of the work to be performed as well as expertise in making estimates.

A guideline for building a fixed-priced contract is to create a **pricing sheet**. A pricing sheet is a detailed breakdown of costs including all the sections listed above. The purpose of the pricing sheet is to document a claim for the project price. The client usually sees only the total figures, although some government agencies require detailed breakdown of all costs. A pricing sheet can serve as a reference tool for both parties.

One way of creating a pricing sheet is to break down all costs according to **roles ▶ 74**. This can be done with the use of a spreadsheet. The first step is to figure out the roles needed on a project. Roles can include a project manager and a creative director, designers, programmers, animators, and video, sound, and content people. The next step is to calculate the time needed for each role and then assign a market rate for each role. An animator, for example, may cost anywhere from $60-$150 an hour, an illustrator $30-$100. The range of rates is difficult to list because it depends on the type of role and the skill-level and duration needed. Estimating the costs this way builds the overhead and profit into the hourly rates.

If I'm working with someone like an animator or designer that is notoriously late, as a producer, I have to know that. I have to factor that in. I also have to set a lot of interim milestones and hedge my bets by giving them earlier dates.
*— Henri Poole, **vivid** studios*

Clearly stated responsibilities and deliverables in the contract are especially needed for fixed-price contracts. If the project costs change substantially due to changes in the project goals, the contract will help define which features should be considered new work.

Other Considerations

Do not forget the time needed to research and license any content. If the content is supplied from the client, include a clause in the contract that makes them responsible for gathering the appropriate permissions. Also, consider testing a separate cost from production. Testing often gets squeezed when placed into the production budget.

Interview: Peter Mitchell

Peter Mitchell is the managing director of a multimedia production company called Big Animated Digital Productions (BAD) in Sydney, Australia. He has been extensively involved with such enterprises as Apple Computer, Inc., Telecom Australia, and the Commonwealth Bank. He believes strongly in safeguarding the proprietary issues raised in the production of multimedia and is very much in favor of using contract agreements to prevent unauthorized use of specifically created software.

What is one of the most important things to know about multimedia development?

Running a multimedia production company efficiently requires various essential ingredients. Safeguarding your rights is of paramount importance and can involve extensive contract preparation, depending on the type of project. It boils down to the parties involved in a production negotiating their specified terms, documenting them formally, and— most importantly—executing a contract.

Considering the growth of this industry it is not unreasonable to assume that many large projects are in place. Unless developers have protected their interests under a signed contract, the potential for hardship is almost guaranteed. You could work hard for nine months, often under taxing conditions, and produce a really first class job. But if you did not sign a contract with anybody at the beginning, you could wind up in court saying "I did that, I know I did this," and the judge will say, "But you did not have a contract." The **contract** ▶ 81 is more important than the storyboard or anything. If you fail to clearly define the agreed-upon terms and such of a project then you could find yourself in dispute with your client. If you have not made necessary allowances for contingencies then you leave yourself legitimately exposed. The business world can be very harsh—especially where large sums of money are involved—and little provision is made for ethics and morals. Intentions are always well meant but "legal escape" due to scant regard for contracts can result in enormous financial loss.

If you have never done a contract for a large chunk of multimedia before, then a lot of questions will pop up. Who owns the graphics? Who owns the sound? Who did the interface design? Is the design itself copyrightable? Remember, stipulate your terms and performance conditions and get your client to agree in writing. Draw up a contract, however costly it seems.

What type of contract exists in the multimedia development business?

Well, this is what happened on one job. We were working on a large project and thought we should draw up a contract. The **client** ▶ 12, 81 was interested and we had been in a situation previously which proved rather costly, so we all sat down and discussed what to include in this contract. We borrowed ideas from other arrangements we had in place and started to design a contract specifically suited to the new job we were working on. A week went by. We were still working on the contract. We were still going through it up to 20 pages of legal banter later. We could have just briefed our lawyers to prepare the document for us, but legal costs of this nature can become very expensive. Eventually

we worked it all out and sent a copy off to our lawyer just to make sure we were not making any fatal mistakes. We finally presented it to our client who said, "We never thought of this! We had better give this to our legal department." It takes another three and a half weeks to come up with their version of the contract. You go over that and meanwhile, two months have gone past and more time has been spent writing the contract than the time it actually takes to complete the project. For example, a job valued at ten thousand dollars should only take two or three weeks, but you can not commence it until all the contract implications are sorted out. This could become a major financial problem for a lot of small multimedia companies unless they have a well-prepared document that covers their proprietary rights. Having the right code or fabulous graphics, animation, and interface design will stand for little if the "business side" is ignored, and that is a side that not many developers address.

If you are a three-person company developing a $50,000 project and your contract doesn't provide sufficient protection, your client can come to you at the end of the job and say, "I really hate it. I am not going to pay you for it. I don't care about how many hours you have put into it, I don't like it. It is not the color that my wife likes" or something like that. Every good intention on your part as the developer means absolutely nothing if you have not previously identified the conditions under which the parties are bound to perform. The contract should be designed so that the expected outcome is described and agreed to at the beginning of the project. At milestone points along the way client and developer can review progress and address whatever criteria have been defined.

Another problem arises if either you, the developer, or the company you are contracting to goes bankrupt. You end up with all of these ifs, buts, and maybes. You could go to court and face a wall of problems, all of which could have been avoided with a detailed contract. . . . Already in the multimedia business (and I do not want to mention any names or projects) I have heard of some severe cases where people have lost their fee and the project itself because they were not covered up front. There seems to be quite a tendency for creative people (this happens in music and film circles too) to say "Hey, we're friends! We have been working together!" There are no "friends" in business. Get a contract organized and make sure all parties who are bound by it actually sign it.

If you were to come up with key points that should go into a contract, what would they be?

Apart from the legal and technical input, the fundamental points that should be identified in the contract are first, nominated ownership of copyright, content, and the rights to reproduce the content, and secondly,

When project scopes are ill-defined, consider putting clauses into fixed-priced contracts that revisit task breakdowns and costs. The clauses can allow for cost revisions if the scope of the project has changed. Also build into contracts the time needed to calculate costs and schedules. This can be done directly or as part of the overhead charge.

Finances

Funding is the process of finding sources of capital to develop your product. Many experienced developers and **business managers** ▶ 14 view funding as one of the more critical aspects to a project or business. Their first course of action is not to build the prototype but to secure the money that will pay for all the stages in the

Despite the sources shown here, financing multimedia projects does not follow a solid model. At the moment, the picture is patchy and idiosyncratic.

under what circumstances. Consider the following. You come to me as the owner of a fashion shop chain across America and require a database for cataloging clothes. I will sign an agreement that the rights to the software ONLY in the area of retail clothing belong to you. It means that I can take that shell, go to a lawnmower manufacturer, sell the shell to them, and put lawnmower and not clothes information in it.

You do not want me to sell the shell to your clothing competitors, and you do not care about lawnmowers, so you might make a deal with me that you have exclusive rights to that software in that particular industry sector. This means that if you have paid me a million dollars to make that piece of software, you might say "I want to own it outright. I want the rights to sell its use to the lawnmower company. I want to do this, I want to do that." And I say, okay I will sell you the exclusive rights to it for 5 million dollars. You can have it for one million dollars in the fashion industry, or five million dollars everywhere, because it could be worth another four million dollars to me to sell it myself. It boils down to the key issues of who owns what. Because you pay me to write some code for you, does it mean that I own the code or does it mean you own the code? I wrote it. You just asked for it. But you paid the money. So who owns it? I will tell you who owns it: whoever is specified in the contract as the owner.

Would it be similar if you digitized some movies for a kiosk and they took those and used them in presentations and brochures?

Once again, you would need the legal backup. If the database project I did for your chain of clothing stores required a substantial amount of scanned images, you as the client might decide that they would make a great animated game. You could take all my hard work, get my code, change it a little bit, collect all the graphics I've made, and release another CD. It has nothing to do with clothes shops, which is what you paid for, but it would fall back to that contract. You may have the right to use it in the clothing shop but you do not have the right to make a game of it provided this was stipulated in the contract. I cannot stress how important it is to outline the various scenarios that may arise from a project and the need to express who has the right to do what. Here's some sound advice for developers confident of their ability to deliver: decide on what your expectations are and how they will complement the needs of your client, and clearly define the outcome. At the end of the day you contract to produce something specific for your client. Documented in simple terms, the client's entitlement has been previously identified under this contract and quite frankly this is the controlling platform or stage, the rules that the game's played by. End of story.

What if the project is going along, and it becomes necessary to revise the contract?

Revision of contracts can only apply by agreement between the parties. What the developer should be doing initially is providing a clause in the original contract that stipulates any probable causes for revision, which party bears the costs, etc. There is fundamentally no problem with making alterations to production contracts PROVIDED THAT developer and client agree on whatever changes are required and the overall purpose of this complements the nature of the project. Significant contract amendments can sometimes destroy the essence of the original intentions of the parties, so prudent consideration is very important when contemplating changes to any contract. Tread carefully. We had a situation develop where some proposed amendments, which were essentially agreed to without exposing the full ramifications, turned the project into a mere shadow of its former intended size. We entered into protracted negotiations that never identified the increased costs of the additional work (among other things). The result was that we had to perform extra tasks for free, a surefire recipe for commercial suicide.

Have you ever been burned? Or have you heard stories of others being burned?

There have been several situations where I wished I'd thought more about a contract. I've seen people whom I would consider to be reliable, honest, and trustworthy do an about-face when being challenged by their peers. "Who authorized this budget? Why are we paying all of this money to have this happen? Well, it was *his* idea," and they'll point the finger. For a period of time these people are totally in support and then all of a sudden if they have had the finger pointed at them, they will point it straight at you in an attempt to pass the blame. At one particular meeting I was fortunate to have my lawyer there to restrain me from strangling my client because of accusations made that turned out to be quite incorrect. What stopped that problem from going to court was the contract. Thankfully, the contract clearly supported our position and the client was prevented from causing any problems. You have to take care of the contractual terms up front and it isn't always easy to do so. Good business is all about getting the deal signed, delivering the project, and receiving the reward.

Having the right code or fabulous graphics, animation, and interface design will stand for little if the "business side" is ignored, and that is a side that not many developers address.

— Peter Mitchell

Three things to know when looking for financing:

- *How much money is needed (include marketing and distribution costs if not using a publisher or affiliated label).*
- *The value of the product, company, or technology.*
- *The standard practices and nuances of different funding sources.*

process, including the prototype. Other developers prefer to take the risk of finding funding down the road and begin the project as if money is a foregone concern.

Many **sources of financing** exist for multimedia projects, each with its own advantages and risks. These include self-funding, loans, grants, angels, venture capital, and project funding. Each offers its own tradeoffs. A **bank loan** may allow funds for equipment or facilities but may require substantial collateral as backup. Competition for **grants** is intense and the application and approval process can take months. Grant funds can also be unpredictable from year to year, the victim of economic fluctuations. **Publishers ▶ 12, 236** can lend much financial muscle to product development as well as distribution, but lack of knowledge of terms and conditions can lead to accepting too much of the risk and too little of the reward. **Venture capital** can provide capital, but at the risk of altering the direction of a company or a product in order to achieve a high enough return to satisfy their investors.

The sources of financing vary with the degree of perceived risk. The more risk or unknown elements in a project, the greater the reward a potential investor will expect. Three items are essential before starting a

not understand the clauses and exceptions in a contract. A little knowledge of the process, some clear thinking and good communication can make financing a routine stop along the way to doing a project.

Self-Funding

Using personal funds or lines of credit, or those of family members and friends is a common way to fund a business or project. The money may be in return for equity in the company or a percentage of royalty on the project. It may also be considered a loan payable at a certain interest rate. One of the advantages of **self-funding** is that most of the control of the project still resides in the hands of the production house. Relatives and friends are less demanding about direction and operation than more sophisticated investors. Resources that might be spent overseeing the investors can be spent growing the business and the project. These funds can also be much easier and quicker to obtain.

At the same time, self-funding is a risky prospect and can be a source of anguish if a project fails. Most people know that the success rate of new restaurants is very small, but few are aware that the success rate of startup companies is also small. (One estimate puts it at a third.) Developers, brimming with high hopes and dreams, can project these onto people close to them. Sophisticated investors understand the risks involved; family and friends may not. To them, a company or project that fails would not be written off as a bad investment, as it would be to the sophisticated investor; but as a broken obligation to a pot of gold. Developers owe it to themselves and to any family or friends to present the plans and risks just as they would to a professional investor. As in the case of a loosely defined contract, if all goes well, nothing happens. If it does not, things can get pretty messy. Another disadvantage is that the amount of money raised may not be enough to cover all the costs incurred in a project. Other sources of funding or revenue may be needed.

Some developers use their own funds to take a project as far as possible and then look for other sources of financing. The benefit here is that there is more to show to convince a publisher or investor. The value of a product usually increases the farther along it is.

search for funding. The first is to know the costs of the project, including a breakdown into different components and the times the costs are due. The second is to come up with a conservative but fair estimate of the value of the product, technology, or company. The last part is knowing the different types of financing and the expectations that go along with them. An inexperienced developer can end up "selling their soul" because they either underestimated the value of the idea, did not present their case well enough, or did

Loans

A **bank loan** can supplement self-funding but may require a commitment of collateral to the lending institution. Unless a company has a successful track record or has built a strong relationship with a bank, the process to get a loan may be long and arduous and in most cases, unsuccessful. Banking institutions are by nature very conservative and typically do not lend without having hard assets to back the loan. Banks making real estate loans have land, housing, or commercial developments to cover a potential default or bankruptcy of the borrower. Creative works rarely have value unless the product is successful. An existing relationship and a good track record may open up a small line of credit covered by equipment and other hard assets in the firm. The amount is not likely to be sufficient to cover the costs of an entire project.

Grants

A **grant** is similar to a loan in that the application and selection processes can often take many months. Unlike a loan, however, a grant does not need to be paid back. Grants are provided by government agencies, non-profit organizations, corporations, and other institutions. They often fund research, education, art, and other activities that are seen as promoting a public or corporate good. An example might be a grant by an environmental group to produce an education multimedia CD-ROM on endangered species. Another grant might come from a hardware or software manufacturer to show off the capabilities of a new platform, application, or extension. One of the advantages of grants is that once the decision is made based on the proposal, the details of the implementation are often left up to the production team. The disadvantages are the length and uncertainty of the process. Also, grants rarely cover budget overruns. In some cases, grants may be contingent on the placement of the entire work, including the underlying technology, in the public domain.

An area of concern with grants is that the motivation for the grant be different than the motivation of the project team. The project team may think they have free reign to produce an innovative and inspiring project, whereas the granting organization might be looking for a useful and utilitarian tool.

Angels

An **angel** is a term for a person in a position of financial or organizational power who shares the project vision and wants to help bring it into existence. Angels are also known as patrons. Some angels may grant funds with few strings attached while others may expect some form of payment in return for the financing. Angels typically exhibit a great deal of trust. More often than not, a publisher or production house comes upon an angel by chance, either as some type of casual encounter or by the angel initiating the contact. This type of funding may be

rare in the general business world, but in an industry as dynamic, artistic, and invigorating as multimedia it may be more common.

Venture Capital

Venture capitalists are professional investors whose primary objective is to provide financial footing in high risk ventures in exchange for a high rate of return. This typically means some form of equity stake in the company. **Venture capital** is a source of funding that brings with it large possibilities and potentially large liabilities. The plus side includes large sums of money and management experience. The down side can include a dated or conservative viewpoint of emerging technologies and an increased influence or control over a company's direction. Not all venture capitalists will share the same vision of the company, market, or product. The company may be asked to make compromises for the sake of being more marketable in a quicker time frame.

Any entrepreneur or multimedia developer thinking about pursuing venture capital should know how venture capital firms work and their motivations. Venture capital firms raise money from private individuals, corporations, insurance companies, and pension funds. These funds may include their personal funds but only at nominal amounts compared to money from the outside investors. The size of the funds can range from a couple hundred million dollars to over a billion dollars. A venture capitalist firm's first responsibility is to insure a high rate of return to their investors. Their secondary goals may include many of the same visions and goals of the entrepreneurs who come to them. Their main decisions, though, may still be determined by actions that only support the first goal.

Venture capital firms often take an active role in managing a company by acquiring seats on the board or a significant stake in the company—even to the point of having a controlling interest. In order for them to realize a high rate of return on their investment, they view it as almost mandatory that a company go public, or in other words, that the company offers stock to the public. This buys out their equity at a much higher price than they paid for it. While the money from **initial public offerings** (IPOs) has created many personal fortunes and provided a lot of capital for growing businesses, the overhead, influences, and operation of a public company are much different than in a private one. Many companies developing multimedia products see it as a disadvantage to take on venture capital and go public because it transfers too much control into other people's hands.

One possible avenue for funding is a Small Business Administration (SBA) loan but a lot of time and effort may be needed to go through the application process.

*Just as a good lawyer can be helpful for working through the legal aspects of a multimedia project, an agent can be helpful when looking at the finances. Information provided by an **agent, accountant**, or **financial consultant** ▶ 14 with knowledge in valuing products or negotiating contracts can more than pay for itself with a better advance or royalty with a publisher, or a better valuation with a venture capitalist.*

Good VCs have typically been through the wars themselves. They've got the gray hairs. They can contribute something. Ideally, when the startup team runs into something they've never met before, the VC's already been there and knows what to do. He can find the right people, make the right phone call, or use his connections to get answers the company could never get.

— Roger Borovoy, former venture capitalist in "Mission Improbable" by Michael S. Malone, Upside, September 1992

Let me propose a new relationship between creative arts ensembles and the emerging technology industry. I would replace the current Research and Development wings or experimental divisions existing in the flow charts of most corporations today with something resembling the university/industry relationship that has proved effective in the sciences. It would work as follows:

Ensembles of creative artists would be assembled as non-profit tax-exempt companies. Their mission would be to explore creative applications for emerging technology and to exhibit, perform, or otherwise present publicly the results of their creative work. Corporations would endow rather than hire or contract for these ensembles, with direct grants of funds and equipment, to freely develop creative applications of available technology.

The artists would not be employees of the corporation, but the corporation would reserve proprietary licensing rights to all applications and technology developed. The non-profit arts ensembles would reserve a royalty on future income derived from products or applications developed through their work, and retain the rights to use material and hardware free of cost. The artists would be employees of the non-profit ensemble, and would be salaried through the usual arts funding channels supplemented by royalties derived from successful discoveries developed in this arts/industry relationship. This model has some precedent in the relationship between Yamaha and the CCRMA Institute at Stanford, but is far from reaching anything approaching industry-wide trials.

This relationship frees the artists from the pressure of short-term corporate goals found in current R&D division structures. Insofar as an environment of stress or anxiety is limiting to true creative endeavor, this approach should increase productivity.

— George Coates, Technologies for the 21st Century, On Multimedia

The size of the funds means that most venture capitalists will not fund companies under a million dollars, although some seed funds will consider smaller investments. Historically, the targeted return for venture capital has been 35%. In the late 80s, the actual returns were as little as 5%, so many have scaled back their targets to 20-25%. The need for them to achieve this targeted return means that they have to manage their money and resources as effectively as possible. This often means cutting out smaller deals. One way around this is to approach the partners in venture capital firms to invest as private investors. While they may not be willing to invest small amounts of the fund, they may be willing to invest some of their personal funds, provided they have a great deal of trust and knowledge in a project and its team.

Project Funding

A general definition of project funding is that it is money provided to cover costs that occur on a specific product. Many of the categories listed above with the exception of venture capital can fall under this topic. The money can come from a client in response to a proposal. It can be an advance from a publisher to produce a title. Or it can come from a group of **private investors** in exchange for a royalty on sales. This type of funding is common in book, music, and film publishing and may become a common form of funding in the multimedia industry as well. (In the movie industry in the last few years, several deals of around $500 million have been put together to cover the costs of producing a set of films. The funds are put up by public or private investors in return for a certain payout, based on an interest rate or on a percentage of net sales.)

The advantage of project funding is that it parallels the allocation of resources. Just as talent and content can be given royalties instead of or on top of cash, investors can be paid in a similar manner. The disadvantage is that some investors, especially those from a venture capital or technology background, may not be used to this form of funding and may expect to receive equity in a company instead of royalties on a project. They also may have unrealistic or unsupportable expectations of a royalty rate. Demanding a royalty rate of 40% would make a project all but untenable. This type of funding may also mean conceding some rights to a product and its components. For example, in a project financed by a client or publisher, the copyright to the work may have to be signed over as a contingency on an agreement.

Cash Flow

One part of financing a project is to come up with the funds to produce it. An equally important part is managing the money over the course of the project. Maintaining the **cash flow** on a project means having the cash on hand at any point during development (and afterwards) to pay for taxes, expenses, equipment, and salaries. Managing the cash flow of a company, especially an under-financed one, can be a difficult task. The best tool to help manage cash flow is a budget. A number of accounting applications can help in the preparation, but few can provide any of the detailed information that would make it relevant or useful. The criteria needed in determining a budget include the amount and the point in the process where each cost is likely to occur. Some of this information does not become known until later in the project, but good management means building in good estimates and leaving enough room for unexpected costs or overruns.

People

Developer Peter Mitchell compares a good multimedia project team to a good jazz band, where multiple talents work together to create a synergistic rendition of the concept. Multimedia projects by nature are exercises in collaboration. Project managers need to know something about every step of the process but should be realistic about where to bring in other people to fill out the project team. On a small project, a one-person team may have the capabilities to develop the concept, write the code, research the content, create the illustrations and images, coordinate the testing, and run the marketing and sales. In many cases, though, a project will need other people—even other companies—to handle many of these responsibilities.

Responsibilities and Roles

The first step in filling out a project team is to figure out the different responsibilities that come into play in a multimedia project. The next step is to assign roles to those responsibilities. **Responsibilities** are single tasks. **Roles** ▶ 10 are collections of tasks that fit into logical orderings. For example, managing the creative aspects of a project is a collection of many responsibilities. That collection is the role of the creative director. The roles parallel the jobs that need to be done. They define the skills needed and, to some extent, the duration they are needed.

The next step is to match existing personnel to some of the roles, recognizing that some individuals may be able to wear many hats. One danger in this step is to allocate too many responsibilities to people, ignoring the scheduling conflicts that some roles entail. Having a programmer set up some of the distribution channels may not only be a poor allocation of skills but an unrealistic expectation due to the way the two activities conflict in the schedule.

Finding Team Members

Many of the people that are in multimedia are independent contractors and work free-lance on many jobs throughout the year. One of the easiest ways to find people for a project is to consider friends and acquaintances in the industry. Project managers, in the course of doing business, should build an informal list of people to contact in the event of an opportunity. A chance meeting with a writer or animator at a trade show or product launch party may not turn into anything right away. A year down the road, though, a project may come along where those skills can be used.

Another good source for qualified people can be found by asking other developers. **Personal references** and detailed descriptions can provide the next best thing to having worked with a person on a previous project or knowing them on a personal level.

Interviews and project profiles in multimedia trade magazines may also contain names of people to contact. If a professional animator would cost too much for a project with simple animations, a local college with courses in multimedia or animation may be an alternative resource.

For general names and contacts, **resource directories** can provide listings of individuals with specific expertise such as videographers, animators, graphic designers, photographers, and others. One drawback with this approach is that it may be hard to find professionals who are comfortable producing work in a multimedia context.

Multimedia developer Michael Antman, when asked how he found talented people for his projects, made a reference to the movie *Field of Dreams*. "If you build it, they will come," he said, meaning that if the seed of a project prototype is challenging and worthwhile, talented people who see it will want to contribute. Finding good people may be just a matter of publicizing the project through friends, developers, and others in the industry and waiting for the phone calls and resumes from interested parties.

For many small developers, the need for wider expertise can lead to **skills bartering**, a collaborative means of getting work done. A 3D animator can contribute their skills to a programmer, for example, who in turn would do programming for the animator on another project.

Tasks handled in this manner should be small and manageable because they may be done on the side of larger, paying projects. The tendency may be to put these bartered-jobs at a lesser priority. If a task is too large, it may become difficult to motivate the other person. The inability to get the deliverables could jeopardize an entire project.

Qualifying Team Members

Other industries such as sports and entertainment attach big differences to people in talented positions. A .350 hitter in baseball is worth far more than a .100 hitter and is often paid accordingly. Paying a little more for qualified people may hurt at the beginning but can be worth it in the end. Look for and properly reward the best people for jobs that require high levels of responsibility or creativity. Some general guidelines to go by can provide different viewpoints on people and bring new pertinent information forward.

Skill Level

The first piece of information that people usually look at is the **skill level**. A portfolio or personal reference from someone you trust may provide enough information to tell whether a person may be able to perform the required task. The skill-level should match the level planned for the project. If routine illustrations are needed and there is already a fair amount of work developed, then a topnotch illustrator may not be needed. If, however, the illustrations form an important component of the piece and the style is not known, then a skilled illustrator may be needed to explore options and arrive at an appropriate style.

Adaptability

One consideration when dealing with creative people is how well a person will **adapt** to the style and people in a project. A person who has a set way of writing may not be able to write in the manner requested. A programmer used to developing games may not be able to convert to writing database front-end products. A creative but very strong-willed person may do innovative work but in an inflexible way that cannot mold to the other media elements.

At the same time, obnoxious or stubborn people can sometimes be critical to a team. For whatever the reason, they can challenge the status quo and push for different ways of doing things.

Speed

Related to skill but often overlooked in the emphasis on portfolios or past experience are the intangibles such as **speed** and **dedication**. A person who does award-winning animations but is often two to three months late may not be the right person for a project on a tight

Knowing beforehand the skills and the type of person you need will help you know when you have found the right person. A good deal of sampling can be eliminated if there is a reasonably good description of the time, money, and skills allocated or needed for each role.

When you get into multimedia you may discover things you don't have a clue about. You'll want to look for people who do what you do, only much, much better. You need to be competent in all areas, a professional generalist. Then you go out and get specialists. You can communicate with all of the specialists because you know what they're doing. If your ego gets in the way, tough.
— Scott Billups, Film and Video Director, Viz-Net

Multimedia is breeding skilled generalists rather than narrow specialists. If you can fill in moment to moment as either chief, cook, or bottlewasher, you'll make a better multimedia person.

My advice to new multimedia artists is to master PhotoShop and other tools that are written to grow with the industry. Beyond that, learn voraciously because today's mainstay tools will be tomorrow's moaners and groaners.

— Brooks Cole, President, Mindsphere

Gather together the best team you can; people are your main resource in any project.

— Kristina Hooper-Woolsey, Distinguished Scientist, Apple Computer

schedule. On the other hand, a person just out of college who shows up on the doorstep with a few demos in hand may end up working out perfectly.

Digital Awareness

In multimedia, an important aspect echoed by many experienced developers is that a person needs to be **digitally aware**. This means understanding the nature of digital media and possessing a pioneer spirit to discover new processes and master new tools. Knowledge of how to use sound or video effectively is important. It does not do as much good, however, if that knowledge cannot be transferred into a digital project with its vast array of processes, applications, file formats, and media constraints. For example, a graphic designer who has earned a well-known reputation in traditional print media may not be familiar enough with computer-based tools and may need extensive training and hand-holding. If things do not work out and they freeze in frustration or even fear in front of the monitor, this can put the project at risk. Someone who has experience with both ends may be able to do the job faster and more completely than having a non-technical person work with a technical assistant.

Related to this idea is finding people who have their own equipment. Most sound, video, and animation people will have their own equipment but others such as writers, editors, content experts, or ex-illustrators, may not. Although equipment may be easy to get ahold of, it is one more task in running a project. If everything else is equal between two candidates, but one candidate has their own equipment and the other does not, it might make more sense to go with the first.

It is almost never possible to find the perfect person for a job and many times the decision comes down to balancing a series of tradeoffs. One guideline that can help is to trust your intuition about a person. Any doubts about a person at the outset will be magnified many times over in the course of working together. Many projects run into trouble because of unresolvable disagreements between team members. Going on general impressions can be a good course of action in the face of conflicting or unknown information. Another consideration is the knowledge that some teaching and learning can occur throughout the course of the project. Patience, instruction, and good communication can turn raw talent into a skilled professional over a period of several months.

Hiring Employees and Contractors

A relationship between the company producing a project and a member of the project can be an **employer-employee** relationship or an **employer-contractor** relationship. An employee is someone who is hired by the firm. A contractor is someone who works independently, either for themselves or a separate company. Contractors typically work on a fixed-term basis where employees work on an indefinite basis.

One advantage of a contracting arrangement is that it can be more flexible than an employee relationship. A company can form and then dissolve project teams much more easily when they consist primarily of contractors. The overhead and payroll can be reduced substantially if no projects are in the works. Tax and employment regulations are also less of a burden for using contractors. Many multimedia production companies consist of a small number of full-time employees and a variable number of contractors. The issue of hiring or contracting people can be complex enough to consider seeking advice from lawyers, accountants, or other knowledgeable people in this area.

Keeping Good People

Retaining people throughout a project and using them on other projects is important because of the large overhead and costs associated with finding good people. Some of this can be done by signing fair contracts and setting clear expectations. Listening to team members and helping them meet their own goals can also make for a solid relationship.

A big concern for many creative people working on a project is to have a strong feeling of creative input or "ownership." Two ways of doing this are to give them **responsibility** and **credit**. Telling people how to do their jobs or pushing them aside may get a task done, but the relationship and future work may suffer. If the heart is not in a job, the work may not turn out very well. Putting them down in front of others, or not crediting them, also devalues their effort and skills, and can sometimes hurt worse than paying them an inferior wage.

Signing Employment Contracts

Contracts are legal documents which set forth the rights and obligations of each party. Simply put, contracts are tools to communicate expectations, limitations, ownership rights, and conditions of payment—all in terms that are clear and understandable to both parties. Both parties should talk through the details and their implications before a contract is signed. In addition, the signing of a contract should occur before *any* work is performed.

A verbal agreement may be sufficient if both parties agree, the project goes well, and the scope of the project is relatively small, but this is taking a big risk. Problems invariably happen with verbal agreements if there are differences about the deliverables. (Certain types of verbal agreements may not be enforceable in every state.) With a written contract, to settle any disagreements, results can be compared with the deliverables listed in the contract. With a verbal contract, memories are the only things that can be used to recreate the deliverables. Just as witnesses to an auto accident invariably give different versions of the event, witnesses to a verbal agreement often give different accounts of the contract. Differences do not need to be malicious in order to create distrust and conflict.

Each side should be knowledgeable of the definitions, clauses, and common arrangements in the industry. Many experienced professionals such as videographers, animators, scanning specialists, writers, and programmers have their own contracts and use these as a basis for negotiation. Employers may refer to their contracts as "standard contracts," and so having a "standard contract" of their own lets experienced developers counter this move. Some elements are more negotiable than others. These include terms of payment, copyright ownership, and reimbursables.

Some clauses may be needed to address uncertainty in the work performed. Because it is difficult to come up with exact estimates at early stages in the project, a contract might include a statement that addresses special conditions encountered during production. For example, an initial estimate to digitize sound from source tape may be too low once it is discovered that the quality of the source material is inadequate for production. Additional work would then be

needed from the sound engineer to clean up the source, meaning extra hours beyond the contracted amount. A simple clause that would provide for an hourly rate for any work that falls outside a contract might cover this possibility quickly and with little squabbling.

Rewarding Team Members

The types and forms of rewarding people working on projects vary greatly. One reason for this is because the multimedia industry is new and emerging. Another is because it is made up of small, poorly financed startups as well as larger less modest companies. And still another is because it borrows heavily from book, film and software publishing industries. In addition, the skill and knowledge levels needed for multimedia production put qualified people in great demand. As a result, both companies and skilled professionals often need to explore different payment options in order to come up with a solution that fits both parties.

Salaries

For employees, the most common form of payment is a **salary**. The advantage of paying salaries are that they are fixed-costs and can be budgeted easily. Employees in many fast growing companies often get incentives or **bonuses** such as **stock options**. Stock options are common in many industries such as the computer, software, and bio-technology. A vesting period is commonly used to provide an incentive for people to stay with the company.

The IRS sometimes reclassifies independent contractors as employees, forcing employers to pay withholding taxes for the contractors. Ways to help ensure your independent contractors are considered as such:

- *Do not be their sole client.*
- *Suggest they work under a business name.*
- *Do not pay their income and Social Security taxes.*
- *Do not provide them with medical, retirement, and other benefits.*
- *Have them work off-site.*
- *Let them control their own hours and other aspects of their environment.*

4 Steps to Fostering Creativity:

1. Trust your people.

Over-management and over-control are guaranteed to stifle creativity. Delineate priorities, articulate a clear sense of direction and provide support, but otherwise stay out of the way. Let them determine the best way to do their jobs. . . . If you don't trust them to be responsible, competent and creative, you cannot possibly expect them to do great things.

2. Permit people to ask tough questions and challenge the status quo.

Uncreative environments value conformity more than insight or accomplishment. Encourage people to ask "dumb questions," to challenge assumptions and to go contrary to common wisdom. If they ask piercing questions and make penetrating observations that make you uncomfortable, you're probably doing something right. Above all, never punish people for speaking the truth, even if the truth is painful.

3. Allow for mistakes or failures.

One of the biggest stumbling blocks to corporate creativity is that there is often no freedom to fail. And to make it worse, the rewards for taking a risk and succeeding can be minimal compared to the consequences of failing. Remember, it is from mistakes and failures that much learning and, eventually, major breakthroughs emerge.

4. Match freedom with stiff expectations and high standards.

If you are going to take the riskier path of a free and creative environment, you should correspondingly expect greater long-term rewards. That is, after all, the purpose. In a truly creative environment, people work really hard.

— James C. Collins, co-author of BEYOND ENTREPRENEURSHIP: Turning Your Business into an Enduring Great Company

A vesting period is a length of time over which a larger percentage of the options become available. Common vesting periods in the software industry are between 3 to 5 years. Larger stock options are typically awarded to higher-skilled employees and those hired at the outset. (Granting options is usually contingent on plans for a company to go public.)

Hourly/Daily Rates

An hourly or daily rate is often used to pay both employees and contractors, in unskilled and in highly skilled positions. In the movie industry, many of the production workers that work on the set behind the cameras are paid an hourly or daily wage. In multimedia, interface designers, graphic artists, animators, image processors and other creative talent often bill by the hour. For small jobs, an hourly rate reduces the need to come up with hard estimates and a solid list of deliverables. They are also often easier to negotiate. A disadvantage, especially with larger jobs, may be the difficulty in constraining the work. The more a person works, the more they are paid, regardless of the quality or speed of the work. People paid on an hourly basis may also have less incentive to improve their productivity.

Other Types of Rates

A variation of the hourly or daily rate is to charge a rate for each particular element in the deliverable, such as a word or illustration. Writers for magazines are often paid by the word. Illustrators and animators are often paid by the illustration or animation. An advantage is that more skilled professionals can often produce the work at a faster rate than lesser skilled workers. This gives experienced people a higher profit margin. A disadvantage is that without clear communication of style and complexity, many revisions can be made and lots of time spent before producing work that is acceptable to the client.

Fixed-Price Contracts

A **fixed-price contract** on work by a contractor provides a good way to budget a task and focus the work. A disadvantage of using fixed-price contracts is the difficulty in estimating the work accurately. Another difficulty is making sure the deliverables match the expectations.

Royalties

Another form of payment is through the use of **royalties** on the revenues of a product. Royalties are commonly allocated to highly skilled people on the project. In a film, this can be the leading actors and director. With a book or recording, it can be the author or musicians. Payment can be structured in the form of an **advance** on the royalty followed by quarterly, semi-annually, or yearly payments for the life of the product. Limiting payments to a

period of time or set of version numbers is also common, especially in software publishing. Royalties are not usually paid until the advance has been covered. Contracts can be written to make the advance refundable or not refundable in the event of a cancelled contract or unacceptable work.

Royalties are also used in cases where payment cannot be made until after a project is complete and in distribution. Many start-ups and under-financed companies use royalties because they do not have the funds on hand to pay standard rates. They also offer great incentives to people working on a project, possibly under tight deadlines and with limited resources.

A form of royalty is a commission. Commissions are used in sales to motivate sales people. Sales people who sell beyond their quota usually receive a certain percentage of the sales over the quota. The commission can vary from 5–15% depending on the product and type of sale.

Setting Expectations

Setting clear **expectations** ▶ 127 begins with the work contract and continues through the length of the project. Clearly stated goals and deadlines give people something to strive for or decline based on their capabilities and schedules. People tend to respond to structured expectations. They need and want to know where the boundaries are, what the goals are, and what the acceptable minimum results are. In short, what must be expected of them and when.

A good way of making the deliverables clear is to **create the expectations together**. Even if the idea or concept is clear in the mind of the creative director or project manager, it can be beneficial to help the other party arrive at these conclusions. Framing the boundaries and then letting the other party develop the details gives the other party a sense of independence and creative input.

One useful guideline is to phrase the expectations in a combination of forms such as with **adjectives, examples**, and **limits**. Adjectives can provide a sense of the tone or style of the work. Using terms like "sophisticated," "vibrant," or "warm" can give a clear picture to a graphic designer creating a logo. Words like "technical," "evocative," or "mystic" can help a writer. Examples can provide a visual clue to the style and tone in mind. Handing over an article, book, illustration, screenshot, or similar copy and describing how the work should compare can challenge the assumptions that words alone might create. Solid limits such as the number of hours, words, pages, screens, or some other measure of magnitude should back up definitions expectations. Stating that no more than 20 hours should be spent creating an attraction loop for a kiosk can frame the amount of work from another viewpoint than a comment on the tone and emotion would. Exploring the boundaries from a number of different angles can box the deliverables into what they are and what they are not.

After all is said and done, even if the expectations seem clear, it often helps to restate the expectations with no previous assumptions. Blocking out previous images can prevent the details from getting lost due to false assumptions.

Resources

Resources include **equipment** and **materials** needed to complete a project. A substantial amount of equipment is commonly needed for the average multimedia project. It should be included in either budget plans or proposals. If a proposal requires equipment or software that the project does not have, then the cost of these resources should be factored into the proposal. All or a portion of it can be added in to the total project cost or it can be called out directly as a reimbursible. Even if the project team already has the equipment, project managers should include some cost of equipment in the project cost.

The types of equipment needed can be for business or production uses. Business equipment includes telephones, fax machines, copiers, postage meters, even disk duplicators or shrink-wrap machines. Desks, chairs, file cabinets, bookcases, lights, and dividers can also be loosely defined as business equipment. **Production equipment** ▶ 173 can include computers, disk drives, printers, scanners, video cameras, lights, sound boards, microphones, and speakers. The **delivery platform** ▶ 118 and any peripheral equipment should also be included.

The amount of time each piece is needed and the length of time it is needed can differ from component to component. Computers may be needed throughout the process but a video camera may only be needed for the prototype and the production stages. The equipment can be obtained by borrowing, renting, or buying. The least expensive or fastest option should be explored if money or time are issues. Two frequent comments mentioned by multi-

media developers are to plan equipment needs far in advance and to get the best equipment available.

Borrowing

Borrowing equipment is one of the first options to explore. Equipment can be borrowed from relatives, friends, clients, even equipment manufacturers themselves. If a sound processing board is needed for only a few weeks, try borrowing one from another developer that has one but is not using it at the moment. An idle computer in a home office can be used during production when additional machines are needed. Equipment manufacturers are another option. A project team working on a charitable or highly-visible project may approach companies and ask for loaner equipment. Companies often have equipment set aside for these purposes. It may be just a matter of asking the appropriate person or group. However, beware of using hardware or software still in beta form in the production phase. Problematic or faulty hardware or software could seriously impact productivity.

Leasing

Leasing ▶ 173 equipment is also an option — especially equipment used only during a set period of production. Computer equipment is not like a house or a piece of art. It does not appreciate with time. Instead, it loses value—fast. Taking into account the pace of technology along with some tax issues, a good case can be argued for leasing.

Purchasing

The last option is **purchasing**. Most computer makers and many peripheral manufacturers have developer programs where equipment can be purchased at substantial discounts. Another way to negotiate discounts is with multiple volume purchases. For this reason, group purchases together whenever possible or combine your order with other developers or individuals to qualify for volume purchases.

Another consideration in managing resources is matching equipment with the types of activities needed during a project. Having enough equipment per person is not enough. The equipment must be suitable for the activity it will be used for. An older computer with less memory may be appropriate for writing or editing but would seriously hamper photo retouching. Something as simple as adding RAM or VRAM can make an existing computer capable of performing

Price and performance aside, warranties are another issue to consider when equipment shopping.

When purchasing new equipment, be sure to check the lead time and availability if it is in high demand.

high-end activity or significantly improve performance for existing tasks. The cumulative time savings when calculated over the entire development process may more than pay for the upgrade.

Software

The **software** needed to run a business or complete a project is usually not considered when putting together a budget. Worse yet, these resources are often pirated or distributed across multiple machines in conflict with licensing agreements on the applications or copyright

laws. Efforts should be made to periodically check machines and purchase applications, utilities, fonts, and other software resources that have found their way onto machines and into use.

Materials

Materials can include anything from film, negatives, Photo CDs, diskettes, cartridge disks, paper—in short, anything that does not fall under equipment or supplies used in the normal course of business. If the project is being done for a client or publisher, either include a

Interview: Minoo Saboori and Matthew London

Minoo Saboori and Matthew London together formed Eden Interactive, an innovative content-producing company located in San Francisco. Their first title, Greg LeMond's Bicycle Adventure, has been widely distributed through different retail channels.

What is Eden Interactive's mission?
Eden Interactive is not a one-title company; we are going to create a variety of titles. The thing that makes it work between us (Minoo Saboori and Matthew London) is that we come from the same value base. We want to create titles that show life as a journey, titles that will allow people to look at and explore themselves.

Eden Interactive was founded to provide a new means of exploration and reflection, for the largest possible audience, using the non-linear capabilities of interactive multimedia technology.

We have three main objectives:

- To create premium quality, entertaining, and educational interactive multimedia titles which will leave the world a better place than when we found it.

- To set the standard in the multimedia industry for profitability.

- To foster a working environment which will attract people of the highest creative talent, initiative, and integrity.

You've mentioned before the importance of getting the best tools for development. How do you know what is "best"?
ML: You've got to spend a lot of time researching.

MS: Matthew is relentless in getting people to answer questions and give the information he needs. You find out information from unexpected sources, for example, the company in southern California who processed our Photo CDs let us know about a few tools we never would have heard about. We went out and bought them, or got prereleased versions. Leasing equipment is also a good option. It preserves cash flow, and as the technology moves forward, we're in a position to trade stuff in.

Six months ago we were doing things that weren't possible a year before, and three months ago we were doing things not possible six months ago.

How did you finance the project?
MS: Matthew and I both left well-paying jobs to start Eden Interactive. We are a bootstrap organization. We've topped off credit cards, used up savings, received help from family and friends, and basically did everything we could to keep our autonomy. We lived and worked in a one-bedroom apartment and concentrated on getting the best equipment for development.

We've done a lot of bargaining, a lot of trading.

How do you get a product to market and make it look good?
ML: We found a good designer. He designed our logo, a simple leaf from the tree of knowledge. He also designed our package.

MS: We concentrate on the things we do and know well, which are content creation and tools. We would rather leave the things we don't know that much about, such as manufacturing, to companies that do.

As for selecting distribution channels, we realized that there is a glut of products in the software channel. We are a content-driven company. There are people who are interested in bikes who shop at computer stores, but there are also computer owners who shop at bike shops. We decided to go after the content-specific user to break ground in those channels. We wanted to forge our own channels such as bike retailers, direct mail, and mailing lists for bicycle-related events. Also, when we contacted Famous Cycling Videos to get rights to use their videos, they asked us if we wanted to be included in their catalog.

How do you find people to work with?
ML: If you're doing something that's really cutting edge and exciting, people are going to want to help out. They'll want to get involved. If you're a startup and can't afford to pay people, they'll want to do it because they want to be associated with the project.

This industry requires specific, sophisticated skill sets. Even though we want to maximize profits we don't want to create a huge company. We would like to bring on people for projects. The advantage is that you can get a wide range of skills and expertise.

ML: Things are new. You need people with vision to take whatever dimension you are working in and extrapolate into other dimensions. You need people who are flexible and who are willing to do things differently from what they're used to in order to get their work into the new format.

MS: We want people who understand content as well as technology.

Do you have any general advice for multimedia developers?
ML: Great rewards can come from not pounding the table and not operating under the traditional modus operandi of corporate America. We intentionally avoided that and it has paid off tremendously. We have allowed things to happen in the time they needed to happen.

MS: Be clear about who you are, be clear about whom you're dealing with and give things time to develop.

clause in the contract to reimburse production materials or factor them into the project bid, allowing considerable flexibility. These items can add significantly to a project cost in ways that are not readily apparent. Not accounting for materials can cut into profit margins.

Other Considerations

One area not to overlook is the need to keep pace with current technology. A person with experience in videodisc technology may not consider other alternatives provided by the combination of **QuickTime ▶ 153, 208** and **CD-ROM ▶ 109, 231**. Not knowing about different technologies or platforms may mean inadvertently ignoring screen constraints, different input devices, or other technical issues. Trade shows, user groups, trade periodicals, and talking to developers are good ways to keep ahead of current technologies. At the other end of the spectrum is the danger of being too seduced by technology, watching the budget expand and the office space contract as the latest equipment is added to the office. Purchases should be based on needs and not infatuation.

Legal Concerns

One of the most frequently mentioned aspects of multimedia development is licensing content. Several factors make this issue difficult. These include tracking down copyright owners, explaining how materials will be used, and dealing with unexpected licensing fees. Many experienced developers go to great lengths to either obtain permissions for anything that is not theirs or they create their own original content. The permissions or **licensing fees** necessary can only be determined in concert with knowing the content and technology associated with a project. The legal aspects in licensing content are included in the concept and planning section, since this is where content and technology are most often determined.

Other legal areas besides licensing content are important to anyone trying to run a business. These include establishing a business, finding sources of funding, working with clients, hiring people, and dealing with publishers or distributors. If you have doubts about any type of legal issue, you should consult a lawyer, legal consultant, or other expert in the field. Just a few of the legal areas involved in creating a multimedia product can include:

- Drafting contracts
- Licensing content or technology
- Applying for and asserting trademarks, copyrights, or patents
- Securing sources of funding
- Establishing a business
- Hiring employees or contractors
- Purchasing or leasing office space

Working with Clients

One of the ways to fund a project or to produce revenues for a company is to perform work for another company in exchange for direct compensation, royalties, or equity in the company. Client work brings with it issues that include writing proposals, managing client relationships, meeting contractual obligations, and trading away portions of creative control and/or copyrights. A company or project team should have a clear understanding of its direction before taking this route.

A **proposal** is the formal document that outlines the relationship between **client ▶ 12, 230** and contractor, the terms and the deliverables. A well-written and defined proposal is the foundation for a smooth relationship, provided the deliverables are on time and meet the specification. A poorly written proposal creates room for misunderstanding and problems. A good proposal is backed by extensive research and preparation. It starts with identifying and researching potential clients.

In some cases, a proposal and **contract** are viewed as the same: a single document signed by both parties defining contractual obligations. In others, a proposal is a preliminary document that outlines an agreement. The two parties then draw up a contract that states the proposal in more formal language, often with the help of lawyers. Developers with several projects under their belts often have a standard format for a proposal that they use on subsequent jobs. This preparation saves time and preserves consistency across projects.

Finding a Client

A company can find clients by directly soliciting them or by making it possible for other companies to contact them. The names of potential clients and the people to contact can be found by talking to friends and associates, reading newspapers or magazines, or going to trade shows. The second approach can occur either by specifically calling out for clients through advertising or other means, or by good fortune. An example of this might be someone seeing a previous work on the market or hearing about the company and calling out of the blue.

Beware of performing work for a client without any signed or stated agreements. Negotiating after the fact is a situation that often creates problems in a working relationship. Also, work already performed is usually valued much less than work not yet performed.

Be careful that you identify the decision maker and develop a relationship with that person. When it is time to make a final decision, there may be political and budget battles and you need to be prepared.
— *Glenn Corey, Apple Computer, Inc.*

General information to research about a client:
- *Type of business or service*
- *Management*
- *Financials*
- *Products*
- *History*
- *Number of employees and offices*
- *Industry Issues*
- *Competitors*

Multimedia information:
- *View and knowledge of technologies involved*
- *Types of computers/operating systems/networks*
- *Types of projects in industry*

Perspectives:
- *Are they risk-takers?*
- *Have they worked with outside contractors before?*
- *Do they give contractors lots of freedom?*
- *How do they handle copyright, credit, and royalty issues?*

People to ask:
- *Past and present employees*
- *Contractors*
- *Press contacts*
- *Industry Analysts*
- *Customers*

*Decision makers are people that can directly influence the progress and sale of a project. Finding and building relationships with them gain internal supporters to help move a project along. **Roadblocks** are people that can spoil or upset a deal. Identifying who they are allows the chance to develop strategies to counter their objections.*

The thing to I do when I sit down with a client, friend, or whoever, is to talk about things developers typically do. I'll say we can either work on a fixed-price contract or time and materials. We're usually interested in some type of royalty. We want copyrights to certain parts of the work, we want credits in the materials, etc. You can save a lot of time talking about these things right away. If they've got a policy of not putting credits on a package, we probably won't do it. It's important to us that our work gets valued.

You paint the picture early. I think it's important to create some solid expectations rather than to try and slip stuff in later on. Some developers hold back information. They want to get the client/sponsor hooked. Personally I don't think that's a good tactic. I'd much rather be upfront. But that's the way a few people work.

*— Henri Poole, **vivid** studios*

Researching the Background of the Client

Once a client has been identified, the next step is usually do some research on them. The principal reason to research a client is to **qualify ▶ 246** them. This means making sure they have sufficient funds and motivation to seriously consider a project. A lot of people may be just kicking the tires and looking for information. Time, money, and resources can be spent talking to these companies, only to realize weeks later that they have no intention of funding a project. More promising clients can get pushed aside because there are not enough resources to handle them. It is important to find out through direct questions or any other means how serious a company is in doing a project. The information can form a picture of how fast or how slow to proceed, how much money may be involved, and how long a project may last.

Proposals

Request for Proposal (RFP)

Some companies require that a formal statement be prepared that outlines the project. This formal statement is often referred to as the **Request for Proposal (RFP)** and is distributed to other companies for them to develop a proposal to bid on the project. The format of the RFP typically includes the definition of the current situation, the statement of a need, and preliminary budgetary requirements. The RFP may be open to all but commonly it is offered to only a handful of companies.

Companies that first introduce ideas for projects to these types of clients are in the position to help write the RFP. One risk in helping to prepare an RFP for a client is that the client can easily turn the work over to someone else or decide to do the project themselves. Not only has the project been lost, but any time and effort spent developing the RFP is not usually recoverable.

Writing a Proposal

Experienced developers agree that the failure to establish clear communication among parties is a key reason multimedia ventures collapse, regardless of how great a component or product may be. In its finished form, a proposal describes expectations and deliverables on both sides. A proposal is not so much a reactive device to use to determine fault should something go wrong, but a proactive measure to start and keep the project at equilibrium between the client and the contractor.

A verbal proposal or agreement can be tempting. It often eliminates discussion of important topics like money,

royalties, copyrights and length of work. Instead, it allows parties on both sides to concentrate on making great things. Unfortunately, a few weeks may go by and the same questions that were ignored earlier can keep coming to the front. The questions often get brushed aside with the reasoning that the answers are obvious. Only when the issues are brought up several weeks later does the obvious no longer seem obvious. If an agreement is difficult to put into writing, it can be an indication that something is wrong with the agreement in the first place.

A list of some of the possible clauses or issues in a proposal or contract is shown below. All items in a contract are negotiable, some more than others.

Deliverables

The deliverables should be as clearly defined as possible including the steps needed for signoff. Changes often arise during a project, and unless the deliverables are clearly stated, it can be difficult to decide whether they are additional or part of the original deal. This clause can also contain collateral materials such as documentation or training materials.

Deadlines

This clause defines the **schedule ▶ 67** and due dates of work and payment.

Payment

Payment can be in a number of forms. It can be done on a time-and-materials basis, a fixed-priced contract, or other forms. The timing of the payments can also vary. Payments can be half upfront and half upon delivery. They can also be in thirds or on any other schedule decided by the two parties. Shorter contracts may have easier terms and less frequent payment phases.

Royalty Fee

Royalty fees are commonly paid to contractors, but only under certain circumstances. Elements that will determine whether royalties are possible include the size of the market for the product, the amount of responsibility in its development, and the reputation of the production house. The royalty rate can range from 1% to 25% and can be tied to the gross or net sales of the product.

Reimbursed Costs

This clause lists any costs incurred by the contractor that are to be reimbursed to the contractor. The cost of licensing content can be called out here or in a separate clause. Reimbursibles may include travel expenses, phone and other communication charges, mastering and replication costs (prototype and delivery) as well as many others.

Corrections

This clause usually spells out the duration of responsibility for errors in a product introduced by the contractor. Projects where work from different organizations is tightly integrated may need a clear distinction of what constitutes an error.

Changes

Modifying the goals or scope of a project during development is common, thus there should be a well-defined way to accommodate the costs associated with these changes. Changes in fees and deliverables can be negotiated at the time of change in any manner that is agreeable to both parties (usually on a time-and-materials basis or with an additional fixed-price charge).

Copyright Ownership

The **ownership** ▶ 104 of a completed product, as well as its elements, is often as important as the amount of money or royalty involved in a contract. This clause can also control the rights to create or use derivative works subsequently created from the original products.

Credits

How credits for the contractor appear in a product or its documentation can be an important part of a contract. This clause can also cover credits in derivative works.

Demo Rights/Copies

This clause can provide the right to show work to future clients or include elements in company materials. It also can include the number of copies to be given to the contractor.

Content

The responsibility for collecting permissions for existing materials or new content can be outlined in this clause. It can also include who covers the cost for licensing content.

Indemnification

An indemnification clause might hold the contractor liable for assuring the ownership of the designs, content, or technology produced by the contractor.

Training/Support

Any **training** or **support** ▶ 253 responsibilities can be outlined here.

Presenting the Proposal

A proposal can be handed over to a client or publisher through the mail or delivery, but a better approach is to present the proposal in person. A personal meeting allows time to restate assumptions taken in preparing the proposal and touch on potential problem areas. Handing over a proposal with little explanation may be appropriate for a simple proposal or one that has been prepared with close cooperation with the client. For most cases, though, a personal introduction might build a warmer relationship and cover any disagreements better than any amount of writing could convey.

Negotiations

Negotiations ▶ 246 are an ongoing part of most relationships. Some people see negotiations as one side bidding high and the other bidding low and then haggling to meet in the middle. In reality, negotiation is often an attempt to balance different needs or differing views of value. In some cases, the different parties have a different motivation or expectation. Negotiating in this case is part understanding each other's position and part reaching a common ground that satisfies both party's needs.

The case with different views of value can be seen with an author looking for a larger royalty or an investor looking for a larger share of equity in a startup. Negotiating in this case means supporting a value with industry information, cost breakdowns, and other calculations, and then arriving at an equitable solution. The difference may be in a lack of understanding in the costs associated with a project.

For example, an author asking for 20% royalty of a multimedia product may not understand that text comprises only 30% of the content, with the remaining content made up from movies, sounds, and animations. The book, recording, film, and software industries allocate approximately 15-30% of the revenues for the development of a product. With this model, assigning 20% of the revenues for a third of the content would be inappropriate. By using a figure of 15% for content and 5% for the delivery engine (custom-built or off-the-shelf), a more realistic percentage for the text content would be 4.5%. Breaking down the other costs involved in a project can turn a disagreement into a simple misunderstanding.

Another example is handling a client who protests a fee. Coming down in price just because the client protests may not be a wise decision if the estimates are solid. In this case, a reduction in fee might be tied to a reduction in service or content. For example, a client may protest an item for professional videography, saying that they could do it with a camcorder. Illustrating how professional video affects the perception of quality for a product and showing side-by-side examples from different sources would allow the client to make a tradeoff between quality *and* price, and not just price. Solid estimates with varying tradeoffs provides ways to accommodate clients when disagreements arise. Clients should also do their own research on costs and use their own figures to analyze the bid.

If you have no track record, it is hard to get support. You need to have something to show to people, even if it's a short video clip or a black and white HyperCard demo on a Mac. You can't just show a page in a textbook. You need something that shows what you can do. Most people who are in positions to fund or accept multimedia projects do not have good **visualization skills** ▶ 122, 136 *You can get a lot further a lot faster with a simple prototype. It doesn't have to be perfect, but it has to be onscreen.*

— Abbe Don, Artist and Interface Designer

Performing work in exchange for equipment, software, office space, or service is a form of payment not uncommon in the multimedia industry. Bartering happens on projects between developers themselves and between developers and clients. One warning when bartering is to be clear about the deliverables and obligations on both sides. Treat the contract as you would any other. Otherwise, it can be a time-sink or an area for contention.

The job for the Australia Post Office was a success because the client knew enough of what they wanted to lay down guidelines. This restrained us enough to ensure that the product fit into the category that they wanted. But it also allowed us enough creative freedom for us to be able to go and do it right.

— Peter Mitchell, Big Animated Digital Productions

Case Study: Ben & Jerry's

Description:
This interactive training project presents key points of Ben & Jerry's corporate approach to Statistical Process Control or SPC. The program is comprised of a series of HyperCard stacks, with each stack providing instructions to guide the student through the modules. Ben & Jerry's management personnel appear as "QuickTime agents" to explain statistical concepts.

Project Type:
Corporate Training

Development Hardware:
Macintosh IIfx, Macintosh Quadra™ 950, Radius VideoVision

Delivery Hardware:
Macintosh IIsi or Macintosh Centris™ 610, 600 MB hard disks, 80MB internal drive, high-resolution RGB monitor, 16-bit Ethernet, trackball

Software Used:
MacroMind Director, HyperCard, DiVA VideoShop, ADDmotion 2.0 from Motion Works Inc., QuickTime, resource sounds, and QuickTime sounds. A network relational database was used to keep track of progress. At Ease™ was used for file security.

Price:
Not for sale

Contact:
Rik Dryfoos, G.U.I. Guy
Ben & Jerry's Homemade, INC.
Waterbury, VT

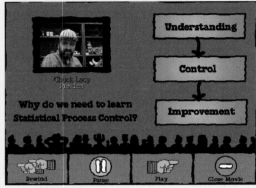

Image courtesy of Ben & Jerry's Homemade, INC.

Concept and Planning:
This project evolved from the work Rik Dryfoos and Joe Wilkins did on the "Rik & Joe Show," a public access kiosk for the company's Waterbury Plant. The problem was that the kiosk's popularity, combined with limited space in the lobby, produced traffic problems. "The kiosk was 'back-burnered' and Ben Cohen suggested that rather than abandon the whole thing, we adapt the technology for in-house use," says Dryfoos. "I knew that training was fertile ground for an interactivity project, so…we started."

Ben & Jerry's had tried working with an outside firm to develop corporate training for Quality Assurance functions. An important consideration was the corporate look and feel; "If it's not fun, why do it?" an informal motto from company co-founder Jerry Greenfield.

Two specialized in-house fonts, one similar to American Typewriter and the other like the chunky lettering on Ben & Jerry's product packaging, were used for the screens.

Design and Prototype:
Dryfoos emphasizes the importance of thorough design. It is important to map out processes and the design for interactivity before production. "The more time you can spend storyboarding before you sit down at the computer, the better off you'll be when it comes to production," he says.

It was a special challenge to educate and entertain people who knew the content very well. Also, the size of video images was not as important as the balanced integration of different media on the screen. "The biggest challenge was teaching people about the dynamic page layout, how it is different from working with an overhead projector," says Dryfoos. The design also specified a built-in mechanism for tracking students' progress.

Production:
Dryfoos worked with Mary Kamm, Director of Quality, to identify and collect content. He digitized and colorized the overhead transparencies she had been using for training and adapted them for the dynamic screen. He also worked with the corporate art department to obtain stock illustrations that were incorporated into the project.

Testing:
User testing revealed that overuse of "talking heads" was unappealing, resulting in redesigning dozens of screens to make them more pleasing. A trackball was chosen as the input device because it proved to be easier to use than a mouse.

A train-the-trainer program was launched to encourage wider acceptance and use and to measure effectiveness of training.

Distribution:
The master is backed up to DAT, both on and off site. The software is copied to the external drives at Dryfoos's desk. The hardware is delivered to each of the five sites and set up individually. The five sites each have one Macintosh IIsi or Centris 610 computer to deliver the training. Ethernet is used to monitor and update the program and to access the main database of names (students) and progress markers.

Programming: 90% Off-the-shelf tools, 10% Custom Code

Content: 20% Repurposed, 80% New

Expenses: Marketing Expenses not. app. Operations Expenses not app.

Development Expense: 70% Personnel, 30% Content
(Equipment not app.)

Total Development Costs: approx. $15,000

Total Development Team: 2 people

Money
Personnel
Delivery
Total Development Time: 6 months

Marketing and Sales

Marketing and sales are the forces within a company which define products and markets, and deliver a company's product to clients or customers. Great marketing and sales are crucial to most successful companies. No matter how innovative or refined a company's products are, if the product cannot get to the customer, then the company is not likely to survive. Publishers and affiliated labels handle many, but not all, of the responsibilities of marketing and sales.

Sales

Sales ▶ 17, 245 includes the set of actions involved in moving goods from producers to consumers. Sales, though, is not limited to this definition. Aspects of sales occur throughout the process of creating a multimedia project. They may not be titled as "sales," per se, but they include negotiating with clients, publishers, investors, disc manufacturers, or distributors. Arranging licensing agreements with content providers contains many elements of sales. Sales can even mean giving demos to end-users and editors.

The sales role might be performed by a lone developer, by the project manager, or by a separate sales organization. Sales responsibilities are shared at one time or another by many throughout an organization. A common misconception is that sales or deals "just happen." More often than not, agreements are signed only after several rounds of negotiations and reassurances. To get to that agreement often takes knowledge of the sales process. This process has stages just like the development process. These stages include identifying, qualifying, negotiation, close, and support.

Marketing

Marketing ▶ 18, 241 concentrates on long-term issues that affect the direction of a company and its sales. Elements of marketing include, but are not limited to, classifying products, determining features, setting prices, handling external communication, managing distribution, and overseeing sales. In many small companies, marketing responsibilities may not be called out directly. Instead they may fit alongside project management and development. In larger companies, marketing often takes a more formal role with its own organizational structure and procedures.

Early Marketing Components
Classifying Products

Classifying products can help a company understand its products and decide how it prices, distributes, advertises—in short, how it creates a market for a product. One question to ask about a product is if it is a **specialty** or a **commodity** product. If a product is viewed as a commodity it can easily be replaced by other products on the market. One goal of marketing is to position the product as a specialty which has no competitors. Specialty products should have value and discernible benefits over competitors' products, making it easier and more profitable to sell.

The process by which a product is made special is called **differentiation ▶ 107, 224**. Everyone within an organization can have a hand in making a distinction between their products and those of other companies. It should be an issue in the creation, production, and support of a product, not just an element that appears in advertisements and sales demos.

Differences are commonly spoken in terms of **features** in the form of faster response time, more interesting content, superior technology, or better service. Features are only features, though, and are not impressive unless they are represented in terms of how they benefit the customer. **Benefits** should be related to some concept of reducing time, cost, or risk or increasing enjoyment, meaning, or perception. A simple example would be saying that 24-bit color makes images more engaging than 8-bit color and, thus, keeps the students' attention longer. Another example is that professionally prepared sound gives a higher perception of quality to the product featured in an interactive advertisement.

Another way of classifying work is by whether it is a **product** or **service**. Each activity usually has some element of both. An electronic magazine is a product but it has some component of service to it, such as consistent availability and timely delivery. Products are more tangible and identifiable to people. They usually know what they are buying. Services are more abstract with the benefit not always apparent. If products are made-to-order for each customer, then they have a high component of service to them. If products are shrink-wrapped and move through the distribution channel, then they are more product-based. Services may have a higher price and a longer sales cycle. The sales support may be greater due to the greater contact that typically occurs with a company in a service arrangement.

This section is only a primer. Some of these issues are interwoven into many places in the book—in particular, in the market research and distribution sections. Also, the reference section contains a list of books on these topics.

Many of the issues, concerns, and principles of sales and marketing are the same in many industries. The people, approaches, and time-frames, however, are likely to vary.

Elements of Marketing:
- *Researching the industry*
- *Researching the audience*
- *Researching the competition*
- *Participating in product design*
- *Establishing the pricing*
- *Coordinating packaging*
- *Managing distribution channels*
- *Coordinating advertising*
- *Handling public relations*
- *Investigating international markets*

Elements of Sales:
- *Identifying, qualifying, and negotiating with clients, publishers, or affiliated labels*
- *Negotiating with printers, duplicators, or disc manufacturers*
- *Negotiating with content providers*
- *Managing client relationships*
- *Identifying, qualifying, and closing direct sales*
- *Giving demos to end-users, editors, and others*

Interview: Steve Nelson

Steve Nelson is president of Brilliant Media, a multimedia consulting and production firm based in San Francisco, CA. Brilliant Media is working on several projects at the moment including a CD-ROM for Peter Gabriel and in-house projects for several movie studios. Steve acts as designer and director and hires production programmers, artists, and testers as needed.

Do you produce primarily CD-ROMs?
I've done a mix of CD-ROMs and in-house corporate systems and kiosks. I am currently working with Warner Bros. and Walt Disney Studios on in-house multimedia projects. The first one is a system for Warner that involves digital video and other multimedia components in conjunction with a relational database. It helps them market movies and analyze the industry. For Disney, I'm helping with the interface design for an animation production system and working on multimedia information systems for their home video division.

How did the Peter Gabriel CD-ROM project come about?
Over a year ago I started thinking about what might work well with multimedia and the first thing that came to mind was MTV. I thought about doing a prototype of an "MTV on a disk." Eventually this evolved into the Peter Gabriel project, which focuses on the individual artist rather than a single music video.

To me, Peter Gabriel seemed to be a good choice. He's an artist who's interested in new technology. He's involved with many causes such as Amnesty International and world music. The demographics of people who like his music tend to be similar to those of Macintosh owners.

To illustrate my concept, I built a simple prototype on the Mac and showed it around to different people. Eventually I met Peter Gabriel and his manager. It turned out they were very interested in doing this sort of thing and over the past months we've worked together to make the CD-ROM project happen.

How do you deal with licensing issues?
In general, it's important to have a good lawyer. If you approach people who have rights to a movie you want to use but who have no interest in multimedia, either you won't get anything from them or you might get an OK price. Acquiring rights can be a long drawn out process. There are little or no pricing guidelines yet for how one would pay for fees and materials for use in multimedia.

Another thing about multimedia is that there's so much material that goes into each individual piece. You have to worry about licensing photographs, text, videos, sound clips, and all kinds of things.

That could be a full time job for someone.
If you have a company that does this, you really need to have a full-time coordinator to handle licensing and materials acquisition.

Is this why many developers make their own material?
Absolutely, for many reasons. It's often easier to create your own material than go through the whole licensing process. It's also more profitable because you don't have to pay out royalties. My strategy has been to go directly to people who own the content. A problem is that these people often don't have the money to make the project happen.

Or perhaps it's out of their control, because of contractual commitments?
That's also very true. Peter Gabriel is an exception in that he owns everything he does. But most directors or musicians do not own their material. The rights are held by the record company or studio. Artists don't have control unless they make arrangements with the company.

How do you plan to publish and distribute the CD-ROM?
We are going through one of the established publishers/distributors such as Brøderbund, Compton's, or Warner New Media. We will establish a distribution deal as an affiliated label.

Besides working with a publisher, what are some other avenues for funding?
Venture capitalists ▶ 73 or a **grant** ▶ 73 could work. I think that for today, the corporate market is the most lucrative. With a corporate contract, you'll get paid on a regular schedule and you're not dependent on the marketplace. You don't have to worry about which platform to develop on.

How do you see multimedia markets taking shape in the next few years?
It will take the shape of anything you can think of: magazines, ESPN, the Entertainment Channel, PBS-style documentaries, music disks, and games. Ultimately, there will be players out there that can do fancier and fancier things, and we'll see whole new genres spring up.

Education will be big market for multimedia. The problem there, again, is with players. Schools need players they can afford.

The lack of reliable standards is also a problem. None of this is going to really take off until there is some sort of standard out there. As with the VHS-Beta tape wars, something will have to win out.

What about tools for creating titles?
I have been very productive with available tools. I use HyperCard and with it have developed a shell called Digital Montage, which is like a PageMaker for multimedia. It lets me arrange different media elements as if for a magazine page. It frees me from doing all of the repetitive HyperCard programming I would normally have to do. I can very quickly create demos and prototypes, as well as shorten development time on finished products.

There's a problem with the fact that many creative people don't know how to program and that many of the tools out there are awkward or too inflexible to use. Many of the titles out there right now are done by programmers and computer "techie" types. Some of them have wonderful taste and aesthetic abilities and do great jobs but for the most part they are not designers.

Any general advice for multimedia developers?
Just do it. Do a **prototype** ▶ 136—get your hands on it and make things. With my prototype, I got all kinds of business just because I took the initiative to do something that hadn't been done before. I had an idea of what I wanted it to look like and put it together. Now the Peter Gabriel project is happening. The Warner Bros., Disney, and many other projects all came about in great part because of some well-done demos, as did a teaching contract with the American Film Institute. Get out there, even if you haven't set up a deal yet. Do something. Things will come of it.

Many markets start out first as a service market and then move into both a service and a product market. Multimedia is developing into this stage with products that cover both spectrums. A number of companies are building custom kiosks and sales presentations while others are producing and retailing standard products such as electronic books and interactive games. Determining where a product lies in this spectrum helps determine the best way to allocate resources and market the product. Selling a multimedia product as opposed to consulting carries different needs. A few include the audience and its use of technology, production costs, delivery platforms and costs, and many others. The market or distribution channels may not be as mature as needed to support some types of products.

Determining Features

Determining the content and features of a multimedia product is a fine balance between what can be done with existing and future product elements and what the market wants to see. Technology research and development input provides one component. **Market research** ▶ 106 commonly provides another. The marketing input associated with a product typically helps manage a list of product elements that make up a product. This list is often developed with the emphasis on the elements that can **benefit** an audience. Too often content or features are added with little thought to how the audience might use them or how they affect the integrity of the product. Using market research to measure the value of a product element provides a way to compare it against the cost of including it.

Setting Prices

Pricing strategy is sometimes addressed only after a product has been developed and is ready for distribution. A poor or confusing pricing strategy can make or break a product and company. Two extremes in pricing are cost-pricing and value-pricing. Cost-pricing calculates the amount of money it takes to produce and supply the market including overhead and profit. For

example, a CD-ROM that costs $15 to build (including design, content, programming, and replication) and $10 to sell would need to have a price of over $25 to produce a profit. In value-pricing, the value provided to the customers who use the product determines the cost of the product. If a customer could save $300 a year using the product, the price in this model would be one lower than $300.

In reality, the most likely price lies somewhere in between. These two amounts are important to know but any price will likely be a composite of these two approaches with the addition of other factors. Some developers never calculate the total cost associated with a product and end up pricing it too low. The symptoms of this are great sales but little money left over after expenses and overhead are paid. Without cost information, any resulting price is just guesswork. On the other end of the spectrum, many companies begin by successfully pricing on value but fail to adapt to a different strategy when lower-priced competitors enter the market.

Pricing never occurs in a vacuum. Other opportunities for people to spend their money figure into the pricing equation. With these variables also come strategies such as building up market share or maximizing profit margins. Pricing is never an easy task, especially in a changing and growing market with lots of products and many competitors. A company or an industry usually arrives at common price only after much trial and error and fluctuation. And even then, new competitors and new forces arrive that constantly throw prices into disarray.

Other Marketing Responsibilities

The marketing role has responsibilities throughout the development process. Initially, the role helps research the market and define the product. Soon after, the emphasis changes to supporting the product in the marketplace once production is complete (provided a publisher or affiliated label is not used). A few of the primary tasks at this point include managing the distribution channels and controlling advertising and public relations efforts.

Rules for pricing from Marketing in Emerging Companies, Robert Davis and F. Gordon Smith:

1. *Service is worth money to most customers.*

2. *Price is a function of value or benefits, not the cost.*

3. *The purpose of the marketing strategy is to avoid competing solely on the basis of price.*

4. *If you do compete on price make sure you have the most efficient manufacturing and production facilities.*

5. *With innovative products you should be aggressive on pricing and on "me too" products you should be prepared for price erosion.*

6. *Demand is much less elastic than usually thought, owing primarily to inertia and to personal relationships.*

7. *Inexperienced managers tend to underprice.*

8. *Price is usually a less important consideration than might be supposed. Buyers want quality, dependability, assurance of service, technical advice, and attention before they want minimum price.*

If there is any mystery to multimedia, it is the multiple issues and numerous components that must be controlled. Project management involves taking stock of the available and possible resources — time, money, people, equipment — and arranging them in a balance so that the original idea can move smoothly to finished form.

Management Tips

- **Planning is essential.**
- **Give a little more than what you promised.**
- **Do not overpromise and underdeliver.**
- **Research the market and the tools continually.**
- **Get the design solid before going on to production.**
- **Reach a decision and then move on.**
- **Obtain permissions and licenses for content early.**
- **Have fun.**

Concept and Planning

Concept and Planning

Every form of multimedia—kiosks, electronic books, interactive art, demo disks, interactive games, or presentations—begins with an idea or concept. Together with a plan, this concept defines a project. In a sense, a multimedia project is a journey with the concept forming the vision of the destination and the plan acting as the map.

All the looks and feels haven't been seen or felt.
— Ted Nelson

The most important part of assembling a working team is to establish an interdisciplinary team, with expertise in the critical content and production areas. The two team roles most often forgotten are those of user and visualizer. A team should have the ultimate end-user available to participate in the design process to steer and remind the team of their real needs and the visual thinker to facilitate storyboarding the look and feel of the interactions.

— S. Joy Mountford, Manager, Apple Design Center

The **concept** provides an answer to the question, "What does this project do?" It embodies the type of project and the content. For example, the concept for WINGS for Learning's *Voices of the 30s* is an interactive tool for learning about the 1930s for high school students. Concepts can be imaginative, risky, and pioneering, or they can be practical, conservative, and utilitarian. Anyone can think of a concept — a family friend, a client, a designer or artist, a salesperson or marketing manager, a programmer or content expert—and anyone can help refine it. Whatever the source, the concept is often a simple statement that becomes a driving force throughout the life of a multimedia project.

Strong concepts are carried to realization in other industries and arts. In the film industry, for example, the concept for a movie can be an original idea about "man's past and future life in space and the discovery of higher intelligence in the universe," as Arthur C. Clarke described the concept behind *2001: A Space Odyssey*. The concept for *West Side Story* is often expressed as an inner city version of *Romeo and Juliet*. The concept of Time-Life's CD-ROM title *Desert Storm: The War in the Persian Gulf* is a chronological story of the war using rich interactive media. The title uses the calendar of the war as a general interface to speeches, news wire transcripts, maps of the regions, color photos, and other materials. The organization and rich content, along with the unique effects of multimedia technology, create an engaging tool for learning and understanding an event that affected many people's lives.

The function of **planning** ▶ 16 is to make the realization of the concept as straightforward as possible. Some of the first comments mentioned by multimedia developers when asked what they could have done better with a project include starting the permissions process for

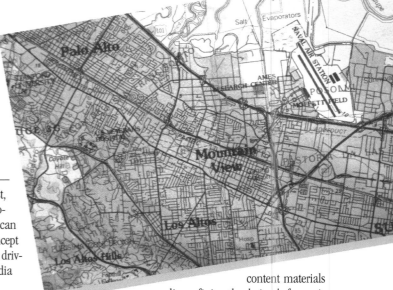

content materials earlier, refining the design before going into production, obtaining the finances, and exploring the distribution options at the beginning of a project instead of at the moment of need—in short, addressing issues earlier and to a more refined degree than was done. Planning will not solve all the issues and it will not guarantee success but it does give a project better possibilities.

The concept and planning stage is a time of asking such key questions as: What is the purpose and what are the major themes or messages? Who are the people that can make it happen? Who is the audience? What resources will it take? What are the legal, market, and technical implications? The answers to these questions will vary but the underlying goal of the concept and planning stage is the same—to give shape to the idea so that it can be communicated, developed, and then delivered to an audience.

Project Types

The list of multimedia **projects** ▶ 34 is hard to define because it is continually evolving. The twelve projects listed below, along with their expanded descriptions at the beginning of the book, provide some direction in choosing the form of expression. Each category has many variations and many products can fall into more than one category. These categories may not provide all the answers needed to form a concept, but when defining a product, it often helps to define what it is not. Having an existing framework makes this definition easier.

- Electronic Books
- Electronic Magazines
- Kiosks
- Multimedia Databases
- Corporate Training
- Interactive Education
- Interactive Games
- Interactive Music
- Interactive Art and Performance
- Interactive Sales and Marketing
- Presentations and Communications
- Productivity and Authoring Tools

Development Process

Each project has different dependencies but, by and large, addressing issues within some type of framework can help focus efforts and complete tasks at the right point in time. The prototypical process for developing multimedia looks like the following:

Development Process

Concept and Planning
Defining a project and putting resources in place

Design and Prototype
Proving the ideas

Production
Building the project

Testing
Making sure it works correctly

Distribution
Getting the product to end-users

Follow-up
Refining and growing the market

This order is chronological but some steps in each stage will need to be performed earlier, like researching publishing and distribution options or finding equipment for production and testing. Part of defining priorities and schedules comes from experience. One guideline, though, is similar to the one for estimating: double or triple initial estimates. Find out the issues beforehand and address them twice as early as you think they need to be addressed.

Project Scope

Multimedia projects range in scope. A presentation for a corporate sales force differs greatly from an interactive book. One way to classify projects is whether they are custom projects or mass-market products. The differences include the size of audience, number of contributors, method of distribution, form of payment, sales and marketing practices, promotion, and testing requirements.

A **custom project** ▶ 12, 230 is one that fulfills a specific need within a specific context. In-house business presentations, on-site kiosks, tutorials, front-ends to corporate databases, interactive art installations, and product demonstrations are all examples of custom projects. In a business arrangement, a particular client commissions the project to fulfill a perceived need. The client usually funds the project and defines the audience, delivery platform, budget, materials, and schedule. The developer and client negotiate terms and conditions such as ownership, resources, installation, and support. The client will have a rough idea of the concept, but the producer or consultant will often need to work with the client to determine the final and detailed concept as well as the means to deliver it. Some custom projects such as art installations or classroom learning aids may not have "clients" in the business sense but they would have something similar in the form of "sponsors."

Clients for custom projects usually handle some stages of the multimedia process. For example, the client may have a specific concept already in mind, arrange for the distribution of the product, or manage their own internal training and support. There is often less guesswork with custom projects when it comes to determining the audience, delivery platform, or duration of the project. On the other hand, sometimes the needs and expectations of what the client wants may be at odds with those of the audience. If this is the case, balancing these ends will pose a challenge for any project team.

A **mass-market product** ▶ 231, also commonly referred to as a commercial, third-party, or shrink-wrapped product, attempts to reach large audiences through sales, promotions, and extensive distribution channels. Electronic books, magazines, and games are all examples of mass-market products. There are many unknown variables when developing and producing a project for the mass market. For example, the target audience is often hard to define, especially in an emerging industry with rapidly changing technologies and capabilities. With many mass-market multimedia products, a production company (be it a lone developer or an established electronic publishing company) typically determines the concept, finds financing, acquires staff and equipment, plans the project, and determines whether to use a **publisher** ▶ 236 or **self-publish** ▶ 236 it and distribute the product on their own. Producing multimedia for the mass market demands a willingness

Questions for defining the framework for a project:

- *What are you making?*
  (Forms the concept)
- *What is it for?*
  (Defines the purpose)
- *What do you want to say?*
  (Shapes the messages)
- *Is multimedia appropriate?*
  (Questions the approach)

Solidifying a proposal with a client can take place near the end of the Concept and Planning stage once the scope, delivery media, platforms, and other issues are more refined. Staged billing phases can take place for large or ill-defined projects.

to take risks with ideas, markets, technology, and methods. It demands resources to acquire content and develop, package, and distribute the product. It also requires flexibility to explore new opportunities for sales in a constantly changing marketplace.

Project Champions

An individual may believe so strongly in a vision that he or she will take a personal, active interest in a project that promotes that vision. Such a person is a project or product champion, a valuable ally for any development team. A **project champion** can be anyone who sees the big picture and drives the vision to fruition. Champions make things happen.

Mickey Hart of the Grateful Dead championed the project of introducing the music of Tibetan monks to the United States and increased public awareness of

Interview: Dr. Kristina Hooper-Woolsey

Dr. Woolsey is currently a Distinguished Scientist at Apple Computer, Inc. where her responsibility is to consider future opportunities in the ubiquitous use of media-rich computing, particularly in the educational arena. Formerly she was Director of the Apple Multimedia Lab (1987-1992), where she played a pioneering role in the introduction of multimedia possibilities in computing environments. In this role, she served as Executive Producer and Director on a range of products, including Interactive NOVA: Animal Pathfinders, Visual Almanac®, Life Story, and Voices of the 30s. She also initiated and managed a wide range of prototype developments with a range of collaborators, including the National Geographic Society, LucasFilm, Ltd., the Smithsonian, the Audubon Society, WGBH, and BBC-Interactive.

Dr. Woolsey has a Ph.D. in Cognitive Science from UCSD and an A.B. in Psychology from Stanford. She was a faculty member at UCSC and a Visiting Faculty Member at the Architecture Machine Group at MIT. Prior to joining Apple Computer, Inc. in 1985 she was Director of Research at Atari.

What will it take to make multimedia accessible to everyone?

There are a number of ways in which multimedia computing is becoming more and more accessible. For one thing, schools, museums, and other public facilities are providing general access to multimedia materials. For another, reasonably priced basic multimedia hardware is now a reality rather than a dream, and prices continue to plummet as quality increases. Finally, a wide range of different businesses are entering into the multimedia arena, offering a range of titles and tools that allow entertaining experiences and convenient personal multimedia construction. Five years ago multimedia was still in research labs. Today a person can quite easily find easy-to-use materials to enter multimedia computing on their own. In five more years it will be pretty ordinary, and we will all be looking for the next great thing!

Define "casual multimedia."

At the Multimedia Lab we have used the term **casual multimedia** to refer to the everyday use of media in a computer environment. Media-rich computing should be as widespread and in as general use as pencils and paper, and computer tools should allow media to move from the selective use by the "high priests and priestesses" in our culture to a widely available two-way communication resource. Casual multimedia requires very different kinds of tools than professional multimedia productions and very different skills. It should be possible to produce materials in hours rather than days or years, for example, and non-media professionals, including kids, should be able to use the tools without much explicit training.

What do people do already that will prepare them for the multimedia experience?

There are two basic multimedia experiences. The first is to explore the publications made by others. Much like one reads a book or views a movie, one can now browse through movies and sounds and text on some topic in a multimedia title. Except for learning how to click a mouse and set up equipment (which is getting easier and easier), this is quite a direct and familiar task for everyone. The second experience is to use media in general communications: casual multimedia. People are less experienced in this arena. Few people currently use multimedia to express their ideas, nor do they feel a gap because of a lack of visual and auditory tools in making their arguments. Tools are now becoming available which will provide access to many media, but many of us will require quite extensive design experience to really incorporate media into our thinking and expression. Some people currently in the design fields have related experience already, and will surely provide leadership in this arena.

How will multimedia change the nature of the teacher-student relationship (if at all)?

Multimedia computing allows both students and teachers to have materials available "from the world" that is not typically available, including classic speeches, pictures of far-away places, microscopic images, dramatic reenactments, etc. These materials, coupled with the basic computing environments, can allow teachers and students to become full partners in exploring the world of ideas and events.

And yet multimedia computing, as provocative as it is, is only a very small part of schooling and educational environments, and so much of the student-teacher relationship is established by other things, like trust, and comfort, and monetary resources. However, often its newness can make it very compelling in breaking established routines, and in this sense offers a great opportunity in many arenas well outside the direct computing arena, by providing an arena for safe collaboration, for example.

What is your vision of the K-12 classroom in the year 2000? (only seven years away...)

Classrooms in the year 2000 will be quite similar to today's classrooms. Some will be great thriving environments for learning, others will be boring places that everyone wants to get out of.

If we are lucky, however, technology will be able to break some of the bothersome ruts of the past. It can allow very active involved learning to be located in places in which it is not a natural part of the environment. And it can allow connections for kids in isolated boring environments with more exciting and engaging environments.

Interestingly, whether or not this will happen at any large scale is not a technological issue: current technologies are quite effective in assisting in education. Even simple word processors can make major differences in learning, and multimedia provides support for thinking that has heretofore been isolated in our imaginations or in small scale lab experiments.

The challenge in the next years is to provide some solid social infrastructure that can allow these technologies to accomplish their potential. If this occurs then more K-12 environments can be places of joyful learning, and electronic technologies can become everyday accompaniments to this process.

Tibet. Francis Ford Coppola championed the movie *Apocalypse Now* through many months of filming in the 1970s. His trials and efforts are documented by his wife in the movie, *The Heart of Darkness*. Japanese teacher Nikki Yokokura did not rest until she completed her vision of using interactive media to teach students about Japanese language and culture. After years of experimenting with different prototypes and enduring frustration with limited technology and resources, she persisted in championing her cause. Eventually her idea was adopted by The Voyager Company and is now sold as the CD-ROM title *Exotic Japan*.

A project champion believes that with vision, anything is possible. Without a driving force, projects can stall or get lost in an endless cycle of revisions that have no purpose. One successful multimedia producer talks about speaking things into existence. Belief or faith in something will often make it real. This means that if you get enough people talking about something, they start visualizing and believing it will happen. Once this takes place, it is just a matter of getting them the resources they need and staying out of their way.

Custom projects need champions on both the client's side and the production house's. In a client's organization, the project champion can be anyone who has the vision, drive, and political savvy to negotiate the approval, funding, and resources for a project. This is also the person who will continue to back its progression from rough concept to reality, with all the incomplete steps, designs, and visualizations in between.

The Idea Behind the Concept

Ideas for multimedia projects can come from pure inspiration or from conclusions drawn from in-depth market research. An idea can be expressed in a brief description such as a "children's interactive dictionary" or a more specific statement based on a market need such as "my client wants a faster, useful, and more interesting way to transmit product announcements and information from headquarters into the field." An idea can be a cultural vision or a social solution such as "addressing the needs of at-risk youths in inner cities in learning how to reach mainstream career opportunities," or have roots in practicality, such as "an electronic catalog of automobile parts."

One way to generate ideas is to begin with something that interests you intensely. Look at what other people are doing to get ideas about what works and what does not. Is there anything you want to say or demonstrate

about a subject? Ask yourself how multimedia could possibly improve an existing situation. Could interactive media make it more exciting, informative, entertaining, or artistic? For example, a diesel tractor mechanic in a shop environment might find computer animated simulations of assembling fuel pumps more useful than paper copies of exploded parts diagrams. Hospital waiting room patients might want to use an interactive kiosk that describes medical procedures. People might be more likely to question the Warren Report on JFK's assassination with an interactive disc combining spoken experiences, transcriptions, and images than by just reading a book. Without an idea and purpose, multimedia for its own sake will speak to no one.

People think of ideas in different ways. Experienced multimedia producers can imagine how a product would look within seconds of the inspirational light bulb going off. Others will need to compare elements of existing models and even consult professionals before an idea takes shape. Multimedia and related industries produce a lot of literature with which you can develop ideas: conferences, industry trade shows, magazines, seminars, and classes. Many schools are exploring multimedia possibilities through their own particular specialty whether it is film, art, design, music, education, business, or computer science. Multimedia is a tool of communication much like a fountain pen, paint brush, telephone, or radio. What is done with this tool is in the hands of the developers and artists.

Purpose

Many projects often begin development without a clear, widely understood purpose. Defining a **purpose** simply answers the question, "Why are we doing this project?" Is the main purpose to educate, inform, illustrate, or entertain? Is it to make someone laugh, get angry, write their congressperson, keep them excited, or bring them to tears?

The Illuminated Books series produced by AND Communications are designed with one main purpose in mind—to create an interactive environment that helps individuals learn language arts. Although there are wide possibilities for creating books, the focus on language arts adds the most value to the experience, according to Allen DeBevoise, AND's president. One volume explores Dr. Martin Luther King's *Letter from a Birmingham Jail* in which Dr. King speaks the letter accompanied by powerful images of the racial discrimination he was protesting. A second volume features Alfred Lord Tennyson's *Ulysses* and enhances the poet's artistry

When asked why some people want only the best and why they cannot be content with just good, computer pioneer Steve Jobs once replied, "We get to create only a few things in this life. We really have such a short time here; some of us just want to make it count."

A project's purpose should be supported by business, marketing, and technical justifications.

With the realization of multimedia: the user's role is beginning to change from being one of viewer of interruptible linear sequences to one more actively engaged with the content, as an active particpant, and hopefully will evolve to one more of a creator able to enjoy personal individual experiences.
—S. Joy Mountford, Manager, Apple Design Center

New technologies are often described with the vocabulary of previous technologies as in the case of the horseless carriage, automatic teller, wireless telegraph, and talking movie. Uses of multimedia may at first be described by what they resemble to be eventually replaced by new names.

The clearer you are about your goal when you begin a multimedia production, the less likely you are to be distracted by all the wondrous options and daunting obstacles along the way.

— Kristina Hooper-Woolsey, Distinguished Scientist, Apple Computer

with language, imagery, and narrative interpretations. The third is William Shakespeare's *Hamlet*. It presents this play as a fountainhead for the numerous dramatic interpretations over the years. By interacting with the Illuminated Books, students can explore and experience language and how affecting and powerful it can be.

Although a multimedia project comprises multiple components, all of which contribute to the whole, the purpose of the particular project should be clear and useful. Otherwise, the project will lose balance and appeal, like a discordant jazz session where the drummer is dramatic, the saxophone player soulful, and the

piano joyful. The chaotic effect might be interesting at first but can ultimately frustrate or bore an audience.

Messages

In the process of refining a concept, one of the steps is to evaluate the content and choose the media that will best communicate the **messages** of the multimedia experience. This answers the question of what you want to say. What are the themes or major points? Some messages persuade and inspire in a memorable way. Others instruct or clarify a difficult or complex topic. If the message is that a topic is still in debate, for example, consider using multiple points of view in opposing ways. In designing a multimedia presentation, state the messages up front and support them throughout the presentation, or leave the message unstated until the final screen brings the previous materials into dramatic and succinct focus. Communicating to an audience involves many techniques of storytelling and is often refined only through practice and experience. The points or themes that lie behind the story, though, can be prepared by anyone.

The Why Behind the Why

When developing a multimedia product—especially one for a client—think about the why behind the why, that is, the basic reason for performing a task. As an example, a client from the petroleum industry may want to include online visual images with dossiers of the company's top executives. Upon further investigation you may find that what the client really wants is a way of communicating corporate information for all employees and not just the top executives. Clients can often be too close to their own business to understand their own needs clearly. Or even if clients do understand their needs well, they may not be able to communicate them effectively. They may not have the expertise in the area that they assume, or at least not the experience dealing with multimedia issues. Thinking beyond the surface of the initial requests can prevent projects from getting turned on their heads months later when clients finally realize what they really want.

Thinking a Level Above the Project

A distinguishing feature in multimedia project design and development is the potential reusability of information. The video clips, sound effects, animation sequences, text documents, and other items that will be collected and digitized for a current project can possibly be used again for other projects. Information gathered for a stand-alone kiosk, for example, might be recrafted into a CD-ROM title for mass-market sale and distribution. Design and build with future products and other uses of content in mind. Stay aware of new markets and technologies and consider other creative and lucrative

Understanding the Audience

Understanding the audience better helped Marney Morris of the interactive multimedia design firm Animatrix design a highly successful kiosk. Her firm was commissioned to build a kiosk for a California Trout Fisherman (Caltrout) conference with a broad definition, namely, to provide information about fish and fishing. The team members in their approach to the project thought about what users would want to see. The first question was, "Who is the audience?" The answer, of course, was fishermen, professional fishermen in particular who as a group are typically patient, knowledgeable, and persistent people. The next question was, "What do they think about?" The answer was easy: fish and fish breeds, and fishing activities, techniques, and equipment. The answer to the next question, "What would lure the fishermen to use the kiosk?" was again...fish, specifically trout. If this example seems too simple, that is precisely the point. Interactive multimedia design is brief, simple, and engaging without underestimating the audience. The kiosk drew lines of fishermen who waited for their turn to catch trout from an animated online stream. After catching a fish, the fisherman had to name the fish correctly to get information about the characteristics and habits of the breed.

Interactivity Matrix

©1992 Johnathan Steuer

high											
		Gibson's "sim-stim"						Gibson's "Cyberspace"	Bradbury's Veldt nursery		
	3D films in Odorama	*Star Tours*	Heilig's Sensorama						Star Trek's Holodeck		
	Pirates of the Caribbean	3D films									
		films	broadcast HDTV						goggles/ gloves/ headphones VR		
			broadcast TV	home shopping club	pay per view TV	VCRs	interactive TV	interactive laserdiscs	tele-conferences	goggles/ gloves VR	
vividness	museum diarama	CDs						karoke		video games	
	projected slides	View Master			voice mail						
	sculpture	photograph				answering machine		telephone	conference calls	CB radio	
	paintings				FAX						
	books	newspaper	letters	newswire	e-mail	BBSs	UNIX "talk"	real time electronic conferencing	MUDs		
					telegraph						
low					interactivity					high	

possibilities. Consider methods or systems that can be put into place now which provide new capabilities and future expandability.

Is Multimedia Appropriate?

Part of the concept and planning phase is an honest evaluation of multimedia's capabilities. In some cases, it may be best to generate a standard VHS videotape or other conventional medium to reach the target audience. Project teams should seriously consider whether multimedia improves the experience of the user over other media. If a product offers no interaction or is a straight repurposing of existing content it may not succeed as a multimedia product.

Level of Interactivity

Projects can range from simple passive presentations to fully interactive experiences. Each piece of content should support the desired experience. Projects that have little, if any, interactivity run a high risk of not engaging the audience and not selling well—especially if a project is an adaptation of existing content. Sometimes, interactivity is the only compelling reason to purchase the electronic version instead of the book, audio tape, or videotape. The greater the **level of interactivity**, that is, the greater the audience involvement and control, the greater the effort required to design and produce a multimedia product. The level of interactivity also gauges complexity when estimating project duration and cost. Levels of interactivity include passive, interactive, or adaptive.

Passive multimedia are presented in a linear manner like a slide show or videotape. Users do not interact except to perform basic actions of control such as starting or stopping. Passive media are much easier to produce but significantly less interesting and less compelling to use.

Interactive multimedia allow users to control the action and chart a personal course through the content. Multiple media types are brought together, often in a synchronized manner. There are many different levels of interactivity. An electronic book with hypertext jumps and topic searching is on the lower end. One that configures its presentation style, rearranges its content, or provides real-time simulations is on the other. Games tend to be highly interactive, for example.

Adaptive multimedia ▶ 51 are at the highest level of interactivity. They allow users to enter their own content and control how it is used. This content can be original text, illustrations, sound, video, commentary on content already in the project, or a new sequence or arrangement of the existing content. The user may be expected to add voice, provide text input, create graphics, or appear in a video. All of this input then becomes part of the product.

These projects are often the most difficult to produce since they must handle and organize almost anything the user throws at them. Examples of products with this level of interactivity include teleconferencing, some multimedia databases, and electronic workbooks.

Many times, more interactive projects can be repurposed into less interactive products. The poems of people who participated in an interactive poetry writing workshop application, for example, can be compiled into a simple electronic book (the reverse is also possible). A further consideration for interactivity is whether the product is designed for a single individual or group interaction. Groups of users require different interfaces and interactions to satisfy the richer dynamic of shared experiences. A product, for instance, may have to respond to events from different users simultaneously.

Target Audience

It is difficult to develop the purpose of a multimedia project without a sense of who will be using the product and why it would appeal to them. A product should have a **target audience** ▶ 106, those people for whom the multimedia product is intended. For interactive art, music, film pieces, or forms of self-expression, it is sometimes difficult to identify the audience exactly

Personal computers, systems, and software have been designed predominantly by and for white males (or Japanese males in some cases). It should not surprise us that these things are not universally attractive, well understood, or well used by people of differing ages, genders, or cultural affiliations. Even something as seemingly benign and "universal" as the desktop metaphor means nothing to people who do not use desks—nor should it. I think we are beginning to see in more compelling ways that difference and diversity are vital to healthy cultures and a healthy species, and that our technologies should accommodate and celebrate the uniqueness of individuals and groups who use them. Where technology is successfully appropriated, these impulses emerge immediately. New communities are formed and new tapestries are woven. Watching such things happen is a good way to learn about accommodating diversity in design.

— Brenda Laurel, Researcher, Interval Research

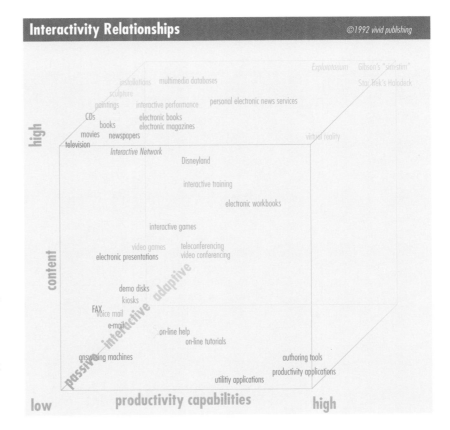

Interactivity Relationships ©1992 vivid publishing

In these cases, it may be easier to think of the experience. This is often too risky a proposition for mass-market products. If the audience is not considered, the result may be a product that is so vague and discontinuous that it has no meaning for anyone. Product designers need to stay in touch with their audience and provide useful content and interaction. As one child exclaimed after watching a fast-paced and colorful multimedia math educational title, "There's nothing left for *me* to do!" The experience was a light show, not an interactive learning opportunity for children.

Get the background details of the audience such as range of age, gender, and nationality. If you are working for a **client** ▶ 12 the client will most likely have an idea of the specific audience, for example, medical doctors, business professionals, or computer enthusiasts. For the mass market, a broad base exists of general consumers such as hobbyists, children, or the channel-surfing "couch potato." Try to characterize the audience's culture through beliefs, habits, and preferences. Meet some prospective customers and get to know them. Try to visualize the people who would be using the product and imagine their needs and desires. It may even help to visualize a single person and consider the subject or content they are interested in. What do they do now that would draw them into the subject? What do they already know? What are their interests and attitudes? What kind of experience does the subject hold for them? Would they use the product in a public lobby, a classroom, a laboratory, a car, or from a living room chair? Designing products comes from observation, inspiration, experience, and a genuine concern to give people something of value.

Designing for Others (Localization)

Multinational products often need to be "localized." **Localization** ▶ 142, 145, 150, 157 is the process of translating the native-specific content and interaction experience of a software product to a particular culture. For example, Brøderbund's *Just Grandma and Me* supports several languages and has even been used as a language primer for foreigners who have moved to the United States from other countries. In starting up the CD-ROM, the reader can click on English, Japanese, or Spanish and read the text while having it spoken to them in the appropriate language.

Interview: Mark Schlichting and Todd Power

Mark Schlichting is the creator and designer of Brøderbund's "Living Books," a series of CD-ROM-based interactive stories for children. Just Grandma and Me and Arthur's Teacher Trouble are two current titles, with more in production. Todd Power is the Product Manager for Brøderbund's Living Books. Together, Mark and Todd discuss how they learn about the audience for their product.

TP: Mark Schlichting has designed a product that is geared toward [children] about three years and up. This product must be as easy as possible for everyone to use. Living Books are designed to provide instantaneous positive feedback to users who have a big appetite for learning.

To test concepts, we met with teachers and kids in different groups. We would then watch which gags—little things that happen on screen—worked with the kids.

MS: To develop an idea for a new design I balance what teachers need with what kids want. I always trust my own intuition about what works. Yes, I do use some educational research data as background information, but if something we try out does not make me laugh or feel good I probably won't use it.

TP: I tend to distrust design processes that rely too much on quantitative research. I trust the qualitative process of watching kids interact with the product.

MS: I was a Nintendo-guilty parent. I watched my kids play the games and saw there was a great deal of critical thinking skills being used in game environments with no content. Living Books are designed to make use of the natural draw that kids—and adults—feel for interactive games with real content.

TP: Traditional learning is too often devoid of experience. Mark took his feelings about how effective Nintendo was and applied them to his ideas about creating products that would satisfy the needs of educators and parents to help kids grow. We get letters from teachers who describe the curricula they build around Living Books such as Just Grandma and Me. Students respond to the "what-if" element of the stories.

One reality is that kids learn differently at different ages. A five-year-old learns differently from a kid who is 12. In developing products, there is not something that cuts across the board. What we have found is that 4, 5, or 6 year-olds learn the most from Living Books, although anyone can enjoy them, even adults. The product also works well for ESL (English as a Second Language) children and those who may be learning impaired.

MS: What we do know is that learning goes up exponentially when the senses are engaged. With Living Books, the kids are in control. They can travel at their own pace. And they can have fun and learn at the same time.

Multimedia localization considers how language, interactivity, text, images, and sounds will be interpreted by multiple cultures. **Language ▶ 178** is the most obvious element that must be changed to reach a native audience but it is not the only one. Imagery and visual symbols usually cross borders more easily than the printed or spoken word but not all elements will be relevant to diverse cultures. By planning early for eventual localization, designers can prepare to translate their project to many different cultures.

In the process of localizing an application, the culture for which you tailor its user interface is called the **target culture**. Sometimes only minor changes are required to adapt an application to its target culture. For example, a graphics program developed in the United States might become acceptable in Great Britain with little more modification than changing the word *color* to *colour*. In this case, you may be able to avoid the whole localization process, as well as the problems of stocking and updating different versions of the product, by designing the original to be culturally neutral—that is, by eliminating those characteristics that stamp it as U.S. or British. This approach is called **generalization**. Software can be generalized in many ways, such as by careful choice of language, by substituting abstract symbols for words or pictures, or by removing nonessential features if they are culturally or linguistically specific.

Localized design is not an afterthought. An animated character who is entertaining to one group of people may be irrelevant or even offensive to another. In the *Macmillan's Multimedia Dictionary for Children* an interactive animated agent named "Zak" appears as a simple red square who makes funny faces and appropriate sounds. According to producer Wendy Richmond, Zak was designed to have no race, gender, age, or economic status and can thus appeal to the kid in everyone.

To be complete, a localized product requires marketing plans directed toward the native culture. The cost of doing business in a foreign country requires financial analysis. **International copyright** and **licensing issues ▶ 104** also have be researched.

Designing for Disability

Computers hold tremendous promise for people with **disabilities ▶ 153** but all too often they can become obstacles in themselves. **A good human interface goal is to make the interface accessible to everyone.** Designers should consider those with hearing or sight impairments or limited motor skills. This can lead to thinking about motor and sensory requirements, text legibility, color choice, interaction speed,

Apple's Localization Guidelines

Not all localization decisions are simple to make. Apple's Localization Guidelines *discusses ways to address audience diversity through design. Here are some examples:*

- **Foreign pronunciations** *must be accurate and require native speakers who are current in their language. The choice of male or female narrator can have significantly different meanings in cultures that regard **gender** as a matter of social privilege.*

- *Formats for times, dates, numbers, weights and measures, money, addresses, and phone numbers differ widely from culture to culture.*

- *The ways that people order their **given and family names** vary, as well as the names they use to address one another under **casual or formal circumstances**.*

- *Different cultures use different traditional names for **"generic persons"**—the French equivalent of the U.S. generic person "John Smith" is "Pierre Dupont," for example.*

*In addition, **writing systems** throughout the world are surprisingly varied. From the viewpoint of software design each one can be defined by three characteristics: single-byte vs. double-byte, unidirectional vs. mixed-directional, and contextual vs. noncontextual.*

Single-byte vs. double-byte: *Most writing systems (such as the Roman script you are reading now) use fewer than 255 characters meaning that their character sets can be encoded with one byte of memory. Others such as Chinese use thousands of characters and require two bytes.*

Unidirectional vs. mixed-directional: *Letters, numbers, and symbols written from left to right in the Roman script are often inserted into text composed in other writing systems. If the enclosing text is also written from left to right, the combined result is unidirectional; if the enclosing text is written from right to left, the result is mixed-directional.*

Contextual vs. noncontextual: *In some writing systems, the form or position of a character may depend on the presence or value of nearby characters. In Arabic, for example, every character is displayed or printed in up to four forms, depending on whether it is the initial character of a word, an internal or medial character, a final character, or a free-standing character.*

- **Leave room on the screen** *for each natural language string to expand up to three times the length and twice the height of its English version.*

- **Leave room in text strings** *in resources or other internal storage areas in a system, authoring tool, or programming resource that may impose limits. This gives translators the flexibility they need to write translations that do not exceed these limits.*

- *Be careful with procedures or scripts that insert **user entries** or other **unpredictable words** into natural language strings. The syntax rules of some languages make it difficult to insert an arbitrary word into a fixed sentence without knowing the word's linguistic characteristics— for example, its gender.*

- *Watch out for **abbreviations**, **acronyms**, and **mnemonic shortcuts**.*

- *Use **terminology** that is consistent with other software localized for the same language. Standard Apple terminology is described in Apple's Style Guide, available from the Apple Programmers and Developers Association (APDA®).*

Images and visual symbols *will cross more borders than the printed or spoken word. For example, many symbols are now internationally interchangeable such as those found in airports. Software graphics include pictures, icons, screen layouts, and other nonverbal elements of the application's presentation. When designing graphics for worldwide software, remember these factors:*

- **Ordinary objects,** *particularly those not marketed worldwide, **may look different** in different cultures. Beware of icons that are intended to depict such things as telephones, mailboxes, traffic signals, and so on. What looks familiar to you may be unrecognizable to someone else.*

- *Certain images may evoke **unexpected reactions** in another culture. They may be thought to bring bad luck, be considered vulgar, or symbolize unrelated ideas. Colors and even the number of objects in a group may have meanings that obscure or contradict the message you are trying to convey. If possible, have graphic designers from the target culture look at your icons and displays. If this kind of professional review is not practical, then try to stay with simple layouts and depictions of everyday objects that are used in the same form all over the world.*

Apple supports generalization by providing facilities in the system software that can partially localize Macintosh applications as they run. When an application calls the International Utilities Package, for example, the local Macintosh system provides date and number formats, sorting routines, text processing methods, and parsing algorithms that are designed to be correct for the user's language and culture.

and choice of input device. Sometimes, modifications made for disadvantaged people can improve the product for all users. For example, changing the type size can offer unexpected rewards like improving the visibility for everyone.

Even without conscious thought, designs can create unexpected advantages for some users. Mark Schlichting and Todd Power of Brøderbund cite cases where the playful interactivity of Living Books like *Just Grandma and Me* have helped children with head injuries relearn motor and language skills at their own pace.

Designing for the Project's Environment

The characteristics of the **environment** ▶ 221 where the multimedia project will be used may have some impact on a project. The location, lighting, and ambient sound are all elements that can affect a design. A public installation is quite different from home use. A public site may be able to use better quality equipment than most consumers can afford but will also require more durability and protection from weather or theft. Printing, though, may not be an option for reasons of security or maintenance.

Kiosk Environment Issues

Sound
*The ambient noise, foot traffic noise, and nearby sound sources like air conditioners are all elements that will affect the ability of a user to hear sounds from a **kiosk** ▶ 38. A designer needs to take these into account to determine volume levels and how much sound to use. Another issue is the impact sound from a kiosk will have on the environment. Some places like commercial shopping areas may be noisy and more accommodating to sound. In other places like museums or libraries, sound may be obtrusive. In these cases, kiosks may need to be placed in special areas or provided with headphones.*

Lighting
Glare on the screen can adversely affect the visibility of any displayed information. Kiosks should not be placed in direct sunlight and the ambient light should be at a readable level. Just as the impact of the sound on the environment needs to be taken into account so does the impact of the graphics. If a room has green undertones then it may be distracting to have a kiosk with a blazing red display. Also, displays are commonly designed to attract people but they may take away from the environment if they are so busy as to annoy.

Security
Security can include anything from the security of a kiosk, any of its components, or the information in the kiosk to the security of the user while using the kiosk. Lighting, access, and positioning are considerations that will affect security issues.

Designing for Reuse

Looking only at the proposed concept can cut short the value of the original effort. A project could have a second or third edition if the first is a success. The content and product can also be **leveraged** into separated content, tools, engines, or versions for other platforms or markets. Thinking about these possibilities when conceiving or designing a product can help make these goals easier to achieve. Leveraging existing work will lower costs of creating other products or versions although this may not be desirable if it extends the original development time too far.

Designing to build a project for **reuse** ▶ 257 means taking extra time to put data in a reusable format and writing software that is portable. A reusable approach organizes digital data so that it can be retrieved accurately and quickly. The time and effort spent on acquiring and organizing information the first time can be offset by future reuse of the materials. For example, you might consider recording sound with good stereo microphones even though the first project uses average computer speakers. In a later project the recordings could be used again at a higher quality for a product on a CD-ROM.

The disadvantage of a reusable approach is that it takes extra time, equipment, and materials. Considering the cost of storing digital data, it might be better to keep information in its original state until needed. In addition, not all information is reusable. Content may become outdated or irrelevant. Some information projects have a defined structure that may not permit easy restructuring. What may serve the purpose of a science and research market may not be very interesting to a mass market.

Content

Consider licensing or selling the **content** ▶ 101 you create. Investigate the market possibilities for reusing content you own. For example, the content from a kiosk might be restructured for a CD-ROM. If this is planned out carefully, only a small amount of conversion may be necessary since the material is already in a digital format. However, consider the characteristics of the new delivery medium. In the kiosk example, the differences in access times between CD-ROM and hard drives may require additional interaction design or postproduction.

Tools

The **tools** ▶ 57, 226 that are used to build the project can be generalized to accelerate the creation of similar projects. These tools can be kept proprietary or sold in the market. Arborescence, a San Francisco production company, has grouped all of its production tools into a package called Kiosk which the company uses for internal projects whereas The Voyager Company is selling its *Expanded Book Toolkit* to others who wish to create elec- tronic books. While a comprehensive tool package can aid repeat work, these tools must be general enough to allow many possibilities. They require the work of skilled **programmers** ▶ 32 and additional testing for compatibility and ease of use. They will also require support and maintenance.

Engines

Stripping the project of all content can create a **template** or **engine** ▶ 139 complete with interface and programming into which other content can be poured and other products created. The idea of templates is not unique to multimedia. Desktop publishing, television sitcoms, movies, and books commonly use templates to conserve development time. A template can save production time and contribute to a consistent look and feel for a series of products. Templates provide a specific navigation design, and so a template may work for one experience or audience but fail for another.

Other Platforms

Consider moving a multimedia product to other **platforms** ▶ 118. While this may allow access to additional users, it is no small effort because the development and delivery environments are all unique. Sound, color, text, screen size, and timing of interaction all vary from platform to platform. Each platform has distinct strengths, weaknesses, and capabilities. Identifying these differences is essential to determining the feasibility of making an effective product that works on a target platform. Porting a product (transferring it from one platform to another) is especially difficult. If multi-platform is a goal at the start, a safer strategy is to use a multi-platform development environment.

Other Markets

Consider other audiences that might be interested in your product. For example, a product aimed at teaching beginning reading skills to first graders may also be successful at teaching English as a second language. A consumer electronic book might also be used to teach the same topic in an education or training setting. Determine how to reach other markets by considering their needs and competition in the same way the first market was researched. Adapting a product for another market can be as simple as changing the packaging or as complex as adding new features or modifying the content.

Content Experts

Enthusiastic **content experts** ▶ 20, 177 drive many multimedia projects. The multimedia title *Exotic Japan* is based on the knowledge of a Japanese language teacher and her desire to easily teach Japanese language and culture. *Ludwig Van Beethoven: Symphony No. 9 CD Companion* is based on the knowledge of a classical music professor. Almost any field such as medical science, astronomy, music, and art can be a basis from which a title can develop with the aid of a knowledgeable and energetic expert in that field. This individual (sometimes it is a team or panel) provides knowledge, experience, and judgment in the acquisition, organization, and presentation of the content.

Anyone who has a passion and knowledge of a subject can potentially fill this role. Teachers, mathematicians, researchers, car mechanics, doctors, and others can contribute their knowledge. Content experts can be consultants brought in to advise the direction or they can be the driving force behind it. They can even be featured in the project itself if they are recognized experts or celebrities. Different experts can add depth, controversy, or balance. Two experts who disagree on the same content can collect materials that support **opposing opinions** ▶ 133.

A multifaceted project appeals to multiple viewpoints and experiences simultaneously. A good movie is able to reach all classes and kinds of people. A Michelangelo sculpture like the Pieta conveys passion and reverence and provides religious and personal symbolism. It is beautiful for the devoted, the common, the wealthy, and the poor. A good multimedia project appeals to both the passenger and the explorer in everyone. When building the prototype, consider the ability to convey multiple readings and multiple layers of meaning.

Multimedia developer Roy Stringer, who developed the *Theseus* medical database for John Moores University in Liverpool, England, worked closely with cytologists. He provided them with tools for creating images of cell samples and relied on their professional expertise. They urged him to recreate "focus pulls," the experience of looking through a microscope at different points of focus, a practice students go through in learning how to read a sample. Stringer listened to this and used QuickTime sequences to illustrate these focus pulls. This created an experience that Stringer admits he would not have considered on his own. Only someone skilled in the subject

matter, in this case the cytologists, could have seen the possibility of presenting the content in this manner.

Content experts can research text, narrate critiques, provide diagrams, offer descriptions, oversee historical music or visuals, approve video, and direct animations. Any content that falls into an expert's domain can be influenced by that expert, although the mechanics of creating the content such as video production or image processing may lie beyond the expert's experience. In some cases they collaborate with designers or programmers to learn tools to let them create actual content elements.

Case Study: Kai's Power Tools

Description:
KPT or Kai's Power Tools is an outgrowth of the earlier graphics editor work of Kai Krause who has been working in the field for over 10 years. Kai became an expert in the advanced use of Adobe Photoshop and has published a large set of tips for the product on America OnLine. The KPT tools are special image processing filters and generators designed for illustrators. In some cases it "fixes" certain effects found in Adobe Photoshop and in others it creates new ones. These 24-bit color tools work with programs like Adobe Photoshop, Painter by Fractal Designs, Inc., PixelPaint, Canvas, and Infini-D.

Project Type:
Productivity Tool

Development Hardware:
Macintosh Quadra™ 950, Macintosh Quadra 700, Macintosh IIci, extra displays, color scanners, and high end color printers.

Delivery Hardware:
Any Macintosh that runs Adobe Photoshop with a color monitor

Software Used:
Symantec THINK C and Adobe PhotoShop

Team Members and Roles:
Kai Krause, Architect and Interface Designer; Ben Weiss and Dean Dauger, Software Engineers

Funding:
Private

Price:
$149

Concept and Planning:
One month of work

Design and Prototype:
2-3 weeks in design and prototype

Production:
Most of the time was spent adding and refining new effects.

Testing:
Testing at beta sites was extensive (about 100 sites).

Distribution:
Distributed through retail channels and general distributors.

Quotes from John Wilczak, Business Manager:
Programmers should use a two page display. The ability to see more code and be able to edit multiple files enhances productivity tremendously.

When making tools for the market, begin first with your audience then look for standards to develop around.

Quotes from Kai Krause, Architect and Interface Designer:
The concept behind the tools I make come from two places. First, in working with existing tools, you see their limits right away. In some sense, you can be driven by the faults and shortcomings of these tools. Second, there is something new, a vision of things I want to see. When you are making new things, you have to take a minimal fallback position and then a blue-sky position. When you think of these two extremes and then take into account your resources, money, people, delivery platform and so on you will design something in between.

In interface design, you should always think minimally. Design something for people so they can have a two second experience, a two minute experience, a two hour experience, and a two month experience.

Programming
100% Custom Code

Content
(Not app.)

Expenses
Marketing Expenses not. avail.
Operations Expenses not avail.

Development Expenses
(not avail.)

Total Development Costs: approx. $250,000

Total Development Team: 4 people

Total Development Time: 7 months

Content

Simply stated, content is any material that provides information to the user of a multimedia project. Content comprises different media (text, graphics, animation, sound, video) that are collected, prepared, and organized to communicate a message to the user. Many projects begin with a body of **existing content**—often raw materials to be mined and crafted into suitable forms. At the onset of a project, most production houses take stock of content that is already available either in the client's hands or their own. They assess the digital quality of the material and then organize it so that they can identify where **new content** is needed.

Existing Content

Existing materials bring the advantages of availability, authenticity, and familiarity. Although the quality of existing materials may be behind the times stylistically or technically, they may be more effective than slickly-produced recreations or reenactments. The disadvantages to **repurposing** are the time and cost needed to handle licensing issues and the effort involved in preparing the material for use in electronic products.

Many projects involve **conversion of existing materials** ▶ 175 such as training videotapes, banks of slides, drawers of product concept illustrations, or file drawers of lecture tapes. Such data may be confidential and require special system administration release procedures. Information about data structures, naming conventions, storage regions, and access codes may be needed. Assistance in reformatting may be required. In any case, project managers or designers should ask for the materials in the form and order that are the easiest to use.

Content experts, artists, and designers should carefully check any content for **quality**, **accuracy**, and **currency** before considering it for the project. Obtain the most current work possible from the original source materials. Product literature may be outdated. Photocopies of previously photocopied illustrations may be too poor in quality to use. Grainy color photographs may lose even more resolution after scanning. In some cases, there is no other choice except to make the most of available materials of poor quality. For example, a client might provide photographs that are overexposed and barely usable. A designer or digital image processor may be able to salvage the photos or at least convert the overexposed images into simple line drawings or high-contrast stylized images.

Be sure to check if any materials need licensing approval. If you rely heavily on existing content, be sure to secure the rights to use it before you design a project around the materials.

New Content

Many projects require **new content** ▶ 175. For example, an information kiosk about AIDS for a health center might include on-the-street interviews with neighborhood youths along with interviews of medical professionals. These can be recorded and assembled with other materials such as medical reports, statistics, and illustrations. The advantages to creating original materials are ownership and control. There are fewer copyright issues with original content. Creating your own material gives you full control over production quality and the options of using the same material in other ways.

Creating original materials demands an investment in time, people, and equipment. Experts such as scriptwriters, audio technicians, and videographers are costly, as is the equipment for high-quality production. Another consideration is authenticity. Even a professionally staged and filmed modern simulation of a typical 1950s scene will likely have a different feel than existing footage from that era.

Organizing Content

Most project teams organize content in a flexible and useful way. Some developers group each piece by media type (photographs, animations, video clips, or interviews) and assign unique identifiers. Maintaining some sort of database, even a spreadsheet, helps organize the **inventory** of content not only for the current project but for subsequent projects that may make use of the same material. Preliminary organization of content allows anyone on the team to locate raw material before it is enhanced, cropped, digitized, and otherwise modified through several iterations of design, prototyping, and testing. It should always be possible to go back to the **source** or "asset" as it is sometimes called.

Comparing Media

The choice of which media to use is influenced by an understanding of the characteristics of each medium as well as the project's design goals. For example, animation excels at portraying visual change and motion but may not be appropriate for presenting realism or detail. A few spoken words, a single picture, or a bar of music may convey the same idea better. Consider each medium when determining how to present a particular piece of information. The obvious choice is often less effective than something never considered before.

The process of repurposing materials demands a labor-intensive effort to scan and process the different elements. Each media conversion process involves calibration of the various conversion devices across the sample range and variety of materials. In the prototype stage, project teams should convert a sampling of the full range of materials, noting the time it takes to convert the test material. This information can be used later to estimate the volume of work for all the materials. After this work, the quality may prove to be substandard requiring the creation of new materials.

When The Voyager Company made the electronic book Jurassic Park, they added pictures and sounds of dinosaurs to give the reader a better sense of the animals described in the book. They checked with the original author, Michael Crichton, to make sure the selections were appropriate.

Keep files on sources for licensing content. Just as market and technical information can be invaluable, instant access to content sources can be helpful when performing research for other content or when additional content is needed in a bind.

Central team members, such as product managers, creative directors, and producers, need a basic understanding of the subject area. Otherwise, great ideas can quickly be reduced to pat answers and trivial presentations.

For example, **videotext** experiments of the late 1970s and 1980s failed primarily because people hated reading long bodies of text on television screens. Videotext designers had assumed that since text was appropriate for books, it was just as appropriate for the screen. The average consumer, however, preferred to have information spoken to them as in radio.

Sometimes, a picture can instantly communicate something complex or rich to an audience. But a

single word can conjure a unique vision for each person. Each person has a personal interpretation, yet partakes of the general meaning. Each user responds from their own vantage point and may interpret content differently. They also may be more adept with different forms. While most users are experienced with text (as long as they can read), some may have trouble interpreting graphs, charts, or diagrams. Most people are comfortable with speech although few are conversant

When planning multimedia projects, always ask, "What value is added with this medium? What is the compelling use of these media?"
—Barry Schuler, President, Medior

Case Study: Four Footed Friends

Description:
Four Footed Friends is an interactive storybook for children aged 3 to 8. It is an collection of rhymes about animals that let children learn and explore.

Project Type:
Electronic Book

Development Hardware:
Macintosh and a Windows Multimedia PC, Wacom Tablet, VideoSpigot board, color scanner, Audiomedia from Digidesign Inc., and MacRecorder

Delivery Hardware:
Macintosh and Window's Multimedia MPC

Software Used:
MacroMind Director, MacroModel, Macromedia Three-D, Swivel 3D Professional, QuickTime, Adobe Photoshop, Adobe Premiere, and Painter from Fractal Designs, Inc.

Team Members and Roles:
Bill Rollinson, Project Manager; Cathy Clarke, Creative Director; Grant Livera, 3D Artist; plus three additional contractors.

Funding:
Private

Price:
$49.95

Contact:
Bill Rollinson
T/Maker
Mountain View, CA

Concept and Planning:
One of the primary concerns of the Concept and Planning stage was the development of a template interface for all other titles. The purpose of this is to streamline future production processes. There was also additional thought given to the characters to make them marketable and have longevity. These characters were created initially in a 2D format by a traditional artist and then transformed into 3D computer models for animation.

Design and Prototype:
The project team spent extra time and consideration storyboarding all parts of a story on paper. The stories were then prototyped on to the computer for user testing.

Production:
The team used QuickTime for multiple language selections and then created 3D 8-bit color animations that perform well on low-end machines. During the entire development process, CD-ROM was the target delivery media. Floppy distribution was set as an intermediate goal for the short term. Special care was give to the development to produce the highest quality graphic images and sound.

Testing:
Beta sites were chosen to best represent the target audience. Preschools and kindergarten beta sites were set up and a parent questionnaire was distributed.

Distribution:
The product is distributed through typical consumer software channels.

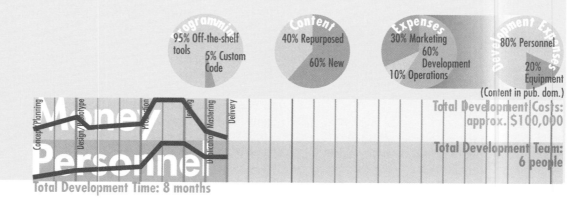

95% Off-the-shelf tools   5% Custom Code

40% Repurposed   60% New

30% Marketing   60% Development   10% Operations

80% Personnel   20% Equipment
(Content in pub. dom.)

Total Development Costs: approx. $100,000

Total Development Team: 6 people

Total Development Time: 8 months

outside of a limited number of languages or set range of vocabulary.

Besides differences in conveying meaning, media forms have different characteristics according to time, storage space, and participation. **Time** refers to the time it takes to experience a media element as well as the time it takes to prepare it. **Storage space ▶ 109** refers to the space needed to store or deliver a media element as well as the space to produce it. **Participation** refers to the user's ability to add or modify the media form as well as the effort involved in allowing it.

Time

One distinction of a medium's strength is its use of time. How long does it take to convey an idea and how much time does it take to create the media element? A single still image or series of images can communicate in a flash but a more suspenseful reaction may be desired. Text or time-based media may provide this by expanding the time of conveyance. In other cases, it may be faster to read text than to hear it spoken. Imagine having all the menu items described by the waiter instead of reading them on the menu.

Storage Space

Another distinction of a medium's strength is its use of space. How much space is required to deliver as well as produce an element? A well-drawn map can replace pages of text, sets of tables, and minutes of explanation. Well-drawn pictures can replace large amounts of descriptive text. Brief speech can be full of imagery. Even with the over 600MB available on CD-ROMs, most projects will still run into limits with the amount of content and need to make trade-offs based on storage capacity. Some video segments may have to be replaced by pictures and sound. Projects distributed on diskettes or over networks may be constrained and have to resort to less content or smaller forms of media.

Participation

The third distinction of a medium's strength is its capacity for generating participatory experiences. Reading text in a book or magazine is a personal experience that puts large demands on a reader's imagination. While film and video are fixed experiences with little **interaction ▶ 95**, they can allow us to participate in a more emotional manner. The questions at the end of a lecture or presentation allow audience members to take more control of the information they want. Conversations are one of the more interactive forms of communication because all people involved are actively sharing, interpreting, and changing the content as well as the direction of the conversation.

Combining Media

While you sort out different media, remember that all the senses work together. Music videos constantly interweave imagery and music, sometimes matching the pacing of imagery with the rhythm of the music, sometimes fighting it in counterpoint. Combining media makes stronger impressions. Voice-overs can support or elaborate on a picture. Retention rates in online systems increase when both spoken and written messages appear. Crafting multisensory messages can create richer, more effective communication.

Content can come from personal testimony, existing documentation, public records, news reports, television shows, audio interviews, historical documents, and the like. The choice of source influences how the user experiences the content. Content experts and the project design team work together to select the most appropriate sources for a particular project. This is driven largely by the vision and concept for a project

The Illuminated Book *Letter from a Birmingham Jail* is based on the words of Dr. Martin Luther King in a letter he wrote decrying racial injustice. The content experts and design team at AND Communications who produced the Illuminated Book deliberated over the many ways to convey Dr. King's meaning. Should they show the text of the actual letter? Should they depict Dr. King giving a speech? Should they have historians discuss the letter for its social impact? The decision was made to present a powerful sequence of images from stock news footage and photographs depicting instances of racial discrimination and dissension, with Dr. King's voice reading the letter. The team decided that the content spoke for itself; it needed no additional interpretation or expert commentary.

Try out different approaches and consider different sources. For example, in designing an interactive medical information resource for home use, you might use a recorded video of a doctor to present this information. While some users might enjoy the human interaction, others may be more intimidated than if they were to access the data directly and more anonymously. You might present actual medical data in a clinical, impartial format similar to a medical dictionary. Stripping information of any personality might be less engaging but some users might view the content as more **impartial**, more **accurate**, or even more **credible**. Another approach could use the **point of view ▶ 133** of a peer, another person who shares the same experience as the user and who is searching for similar information. These different points of view can affect a user's experience.

*Marshall McLuhan provided some early insights into the inventory of effects that media provide through comparisons of mass media. A stream of books in the 1960s established his reputation for controversial insights into the effects of mass media. The central parts of McLuhan's studies are found in two books, **The Medium Is the Massage** and **Understanding Media**. In The Medium Is the Massage, strong graphics and typography present a view of how the human senses are amplified and connected, just as all electronic media are connecting the global village. In Understanding Media, he compares and contrasts the mass media of the 60s including transportation, clothing, clocks, photography, comics, games, telegraph, telephone, movies, radio, television, money, and weapons. McLuhan repeats a general theme that all the senses interact and balance each other in human perception. The change in one sense affects the prominence of the others. For example, lower light levels enhance the senses of taste and hearing. In the extreme case, blind people develop remarkable senses of hearing, touch, smell, and taste. McLuhan argued that mass media change the nature of society's senses and understanding.*

One way to evaluate the origin of content is to include more than one point of view and test their effects. Someone who experiences an event tells a different story than someone who causes it to happen. Who is to be believed and why? Remember that the source and point of view can be more important than the media used to represent it.

Graphical excellence is that which gives to the viewer the greatest number of ideas in the shortest time with the least ink in the smallest space.
— Edward Tufte

Legal Issues in the Production of Multimedia

The following article is excerpted from presentations given by the author to the American Intellectual Property Law Association (January, 1992); the State Bar of California Annual Meeting (October, 1992); the Santa Clara County Bar Association (March, 1993); and the International QuickTime Multimedia Conference (March, 1993). The opinions set forth in the article are those of the author. Readers should contact their own legal counsel for opinions or advice pertaining to individual fact situations.

Typical multimedia CD-ROM products may contain hundreds of different materials—software engines and applications that work "behind the scenes" to drive the product, software demonstrations—both active and disabled, written documentation, graphics, animation, video clips, photographic stills, music and interviews.

When multimedia product consists entirely of internally created documents, supported by internally created software, there are few, if any, legal ramifications to consider. When the multimedia product exceeds these internal bounds there are legal issues which must be addressed.

To give you an example of the potential enormity of the legal issues involved in producing multimedia programs, let's imagine that Liz & Wally, Inc. is a small company that wants to produce a multimedia CD-ROM product on the plays and times of William Shakespeare, called "If You Knew Willy Like I Knew Willy."

Liz & Wally want the CD-ROM package to contain operating system software, programming software, and a myriad of application software programs to support graphics, sound and animation; copies of historical documentation from Elizabethan England; articles from contemporary scholars; portions of films of Shakespeare plays— for example, Sir Laurence Olivier as Hamlet or Mel Gibson as Hamlet— or maybe both Sir Laurence Olivier and Mel Gibson in side by side clips to compare acting styles; the late Richard Burton doing a dramatic reading; an interactive question and answer section for student participation; a drawing program to enable students to create their own costumes and sets; and finally, the latest recording of Elizabethan music performed by the Royal London Philharmonic Orchestra.

Liz & Wally want to know what, if anything, do they need to do to legally produce, manufacture and distribute "If You Knew Willy Like I Knew Willy."

The primary legal issues to which I will refer are those in the intellectual property area and the related tort issues of invasion of privacy and the right of publicity.

Recent technological advancements have made the VCR, document scanner, CD player, and audio and video cassette editors standard equipment of many— if not most— corporate marketing and communications departments. Thus the possibilities for misuse of copyrighted or other proprietary materials are rife—unless corporate boundaries are set and properly communicated to the production people.

Most multimedia programs consist of hundreds of different items. Some will be specifically created in-house for the multimedia project while others may be public domain or third party proprietary materials.

In-house materials are more easily dealt with—corporate employees should ideally sign employment agreements that specifically state that materials created by the employee during the scope of the employee's business are owned by the employer, while contractors or consultants employed on a project basis should execute consultant agreements that expressly assign all rights to the materials created for the project— and which license pre-existing works used to create the original works— to the corporate author.

Public domain and third party proprietary materials are not as easily dealt with. Public domain materials may not be what they appear to be. For example, while Shakespeare's play Hamlet is itself in the public

domain, the Franco Zeffirelli film of the same name is under copyright. A recording of Richard Burton doing the "To be or not to be" soliloquy requires permission from the owner of the copyright in the recording itself, and possibly permission from Mr. Burton's estate— under the state-law-based right of publicity— to use his resonant (and highly recognizable) voice.

An historical document on Elizabethan England may be in the public domain, but a contemporary dissertation on the historical document is protected. Use of the dissertation, in whole or in part, will require permission of the copyright owner.

Similarly, while the likeness of William Shakespeare is not protected, the artist's rendering used in the project may be copyrighted. And, certainly, photographs or video clips of both Sir Laurence Olivier and Mel Gibson are protected by copyright, while their individual likenesses are independently protected under the state law right of publicity.

Inclusion of third party software either "upfront" or behind the scenes, as well as illustrations, photographs and references on packaging and documentation, may involve issues of patent, trade secret and trademark, as well as copyright law.

It is important to be aware of the layers of the multimedia project in order to uncover all potential proprietary materials the producer may wish to include, and verify that all public domain material is in fact legally unprotected and that all proprietary material is properly licensed.

Intellectual property rights and publicity/privacy issues love to play hide-and-seek—you need to be alert to issues lurking beneath the surface.

Suppose you are a computer company doing a series of "success stories" on some of your small business clients to show potential customers that other companies similar to theirs have used your product to great advantage and increased profit. ("Success stories" are vignettes consisting of video interviews with the principals of the client company, illustrated with the materials produced with your product.)

Let's say you want to showcase a small advertising agency, a start-up entertainment magazine publisher, and a local graphic artist.

The ad agency landed a big corporate client using your computer to create an animated storyboard that eventually turned out to be a famous commercial with a big name movie star. The magazine publisher just distributed its first issue—written, printed and illustrated in-house with your products. The graphic artist created the jacket cover for the latest number one album from the hottest rock group in England.

The ad agency says you can use the storyboard in your success story. Can you? Does the ad agency own the storyboard or does the corporate account? Can the ad agency speak for the corporate account—and provide you with sufficient written proof of its authority to let you use the storyboard? Take a look at the storyboard—does the animated actor bear any resemblance to the actor who actually did the commercial? Even if the ad agency has the corporate account's permission to let you use the storyboard, does the corporate account have the right to let you use the actor's name or likeness?

In this case, you may well have to obtain the permission of the ad agency, the corporate account and the actor to use the storyboard without running afoul of the copyright or right-of-publicity laws.

The magazine publisher wants you to use a full shot of the cover of the new magazine, featuring a photograph of a famous rock star. Can you? The publisher owns the copyright in the magazine and presumably can use the cover photograph to promote sales of the magazine itself— does the publisher have the right to let you use the rock star to promote your products?

The graphic artist is shown explaining how the album jacket illustration was created with your company's new graphics software, while the album plays in the background. In this case it is unlikely that the artist has any rights to the music, so you need to go directly to the record producer (or the Harry Fox Agency or ASCAP or BMI) or even the rock group, to get permission for the synchronization rights to play the album in the background— depending on who has the rights— to license you to reproduce and use the album soundtrack.

The foregoing examples are typical of the legal issues involved in the production of corporate multimedia.

Addressing the Legal Issues

There are two ideal solutions. The first is to use only materials you already own. The second is to acquire the copyrighted material outright. Once you own the material it is yours to do with as you please—with a few caveats. Most countries allow the assignment of all rights to copyrighted materials, either individually or in their entirety. However, there are a few countries that consider moral rights to be inalienable and thus non-assignable with the original copyrights. In that case, my suggestion is to check with the original copyright owner before you embark on extensive changes to the original work or plan to use it in ways that might be considered morally questionable. You also need to consider whether the proposed use might be deemed libelous or defamatory.

When you do not own the third party proprietary material and cannot acquire the rights by assignment, you need to obtain licenses or other permissions before you can use it in your multimedia product. And please do not make the common mistake of assuming that because the material has been used in a previous multimedia project it is licensed for use in a subsequent project unless you know the copyright owner has given your company an unlimited site-license (in the case of software) or unlimited permission to use the copyrighted material (i.e., video, cartoons, music).

It is imperative to check the terms and conditions of previous license agreements before you redistribute or take excerpts from a prior multimedia project. The original license may not cover your new plans.

Types of Licenses and Permissions

Now let's look at the various types of licenses and permissions you will generally come across in putting together a multimedia product.

Software Agreements: Software may be proprietary and contain patented or copyrighted material, in which case you will need a license from the owner to include it in the multimedia project. Software engines that drive the multimedia program usually need to be licensed as fully operational software; software applications that are included

for demonstration purposes may be licensed either as fully operational or in disabled form (disabled in this sense means the program is incapable of being downloaded from the CD-ROM to a hard drive or won't print or perform usual tasks). Software that has been site-licensed to your company for internal use by employees may need to be re-licensed for the multimedia project if the proposed distribution is outside the scope of the original site-license.

Be scrupulous about "public domain software"— true public domain software is non-proprietary and may be duplicated and distributed by third parties at will. However, software that is labeled "public domain" may in fact contain additional materials such as music or graphics that are proprietary to a third party. Be sure to carefully review any public domain software that your client may wish to include in the project.

Copyright Permissions and Releases: Depending on the desires of the parties and the nature and extent of the proposed use of the copyrighted material, a comprehensive license agreement may not be necessary. A permission letter or release form signed by the copyright owner that includes the terms of the permitted use may suffice. Permission letters and release forms are generally acceptable for non-edited use of graphics (including trademarks, logos and software icons that will be used to identify the products of the source of a referenced product), cartoons, charts, photographs, illustrations, music or movie or video clips.

Personal Model Releases: State law prohibits the use of a person's name or likeness for commercial purposes without the individual's written consent. Accordingly, all persons whose name or likeness will be used in a multimedia project that is to be commercially distributed or whose purpose is to promote the sale of your company's products (even if it will not itself be "sold") should sign a model release form. References to corporate clients may involve interviews with corporate personnel or visual references to the company's offices or plant. Such references may actually violate a confidentiality provision in an intercompany agreement or otherwise engender bad feelings if prior permission is not obtained. It is wise to require releases executed by an officer of that company and from any individual employees of the company who will be identifiable in the multimedia project.

Trademark Agreements: Depending on your proposed use of third party proprietary materials (such as software), you may find that your multimedia project is actually a distribution source. Perhaps you want to use the logos or trademarks of such proprietary materials on your packaging or promotional literature. To the extent you become a link in the trademark owner's distribution chain, or if there is a likelihood that your proposed use of the third party trademark may appear to create a sponsorship of your multimedia product by the trademark owner, you may also need to obtain a trademark license — rather than a permission letter or release — from the trademark owner.

— Jill Robin Sarnoff, Senior Trademark and Copyright Counsel
Apple Computer, Inc., ©1992 APPLE COMPUTER, INC.

Market Research

Know thy user — for they are not you.
— Linda Jacobson, Editor, CyberArts:
Exploring Art and Technology

Effective **market research** ▶ **18, 224** helps a project manager, marketing team, or design team understand an audience's needs and desires, problems and concerns. Deciding whether a project is worth pursuing may depend

on discovering a number of issues such as what delivery technologies are most popular, what pricing is possible, what distribution schemes are plausible, and most importantly, what customers want and expect. Researching a market can open up a number of options for implementing a project. For example, Eden Interactive chose an authoring system with a powerful proprietary compression scheme that allowed them to distribute their product on diskettes instead of CD-ROM. This increased the potential market for their product, *Greg LeMond's Bicycle Adventure,* because of the large installed base of PC and Macintosh users without CD-ROMs.

Some developers are successful just by acting on assumptions about market and audience needs for a product. But market research can help improve the chances by supporting or defeating these assumptions. Market research determines the size and location of a market, analyzes the cost of production, and surveys the competing alternatives. For newly defined markets, definitive information on audiences is difficult to get. Much of what serves to fill the gap in the absence of recognizable sources is personal contact with users, distributors, members of the press, vendors, and other developers. Telephoning or visiting people or conducting focus groups can often provide many more direct and applicable answers than reading an article or viewing a table or graph. When trying to get information from personal sources, it is important to refrain from asking leading questions or showing biases. Otherwise, their answers may not give a true reflection of the market.

Multimedia Industry Newsletters:

Converge
Bi-monthly
Multi-Facet Communications, Inc.
Sunnyvale, CA 408/749-0549

Digital Media: A Seybold Report
Bi-weekly
Seybold Publications
Media, PA 215/565-6864

Multimedia Business Report
Bi-weekly
SIMBA Information, Inc.
Wilton, CT 203/834-0033

Multimedia Week
Weekly
Phillips Business Information, Inc.
Potomac, MD 301/340-2100

Market Segments

Market research analyzes products and their audience or **market segments**. It uncovers information about the people who make up an audience such as how many there are, what they do, what they need, and what they like. Segments are specific audience groups that have common characteristics such as interest, age, or gender. In multimedia, there is not much clear market segmentation. History, however, can provide useful comparisons. **Markets for new technologies evolve in roughly three stages: early, middle, and late.** Deciding how to identify and appeal to segments can impact the content, design, technology and distribution approaches taken with a product.

Multimedia markets are primarily new and have few precedents. The people that make up early markets are called **early adopters**. These people commonly look to technology for advantages and personal interest. One attractive segment of the early adopter market for multimedia is the computer audience, a small, technically sophisticated group. Computer owners are characteristically early adopters who take chances with new technologies including multimedia. These people are looking for something more to do with their computers. Although early adopters often feel that technology for technology's sake is reason enough to buy in, they are also attracted to good content and high standards.

A second segment of the early adopter multimedia market is the **subject audience**, people who care about a specific topic and are willing to purchase the necessary equipment to use this content. For example, Nintendo proved that people will buy proprietary hardware to play interactive games if the games are exciting enough. The middle market segment for multimedia includes the business market. The **business market** offers great potential because these customers are used to investing time and money into other forms of technology if there is promise of added value, improved productivity, and increased sales.

The later market is the **consumer market** and is only now beginning to form. This market demands inexpensive, standard, and easy-to-use products (both hardware and titles). This often requires competitors to agree on standards of equipment, technology, or interaction. The large consumer market hesitates to invest in what it perceives to be a fleeting or temporary technology. Consumers who already have a closet full of 8-track tapes or Betamax VCRs will hesitate to buy technology that has not yet proven its general appeal. Although the bulk of the consumer market is largely out of reach until multimedia players arrive, it is somewhat accessible through the **business**, **home office**, or **education markets**. For example, parents often buy hardware and software for their children that is identical to what the children use in school. Also, products that allow users to integrate video, audio, and graphics for business presentations may find an audience among consumers who want to create multimedia family movies.

Focus Groups

A useful market research tool is a focus group. A **focus group** is a formal gathering of people who represent a segment of the potential audience. The purpose of a focus group is to present different solutions and scenarios and gauge the reaction from the focus group participants. This compares project assumptions with real world feedback. Running a focus group requires preparation. A small team of observers is often organized to take notes and record user responses. They may use tape recorders or video cameras. A script is commonly prepared along with mock-ups and materials to help fuel the focus session. During the meeting, the focus group leader typically asks questions to develop general reactions. The information from these sessions can help justify the concept and refine the design.

Focus groups are notoriously difficult to conduct accurately because the potential for influencing the group members and eliciting biased views is so high. Also, when reviewing the data, it is easy to discount unwanted comments and reactions or read more into them than seems favorable.

Competition

The multimedia marketplace is growing rapidly with more and more products entering the arena. An important component of market research is investigating competing products. This includes researching their product as well as their market. Such things as their installed base, audience characteristics, and distributors can be as useful as the authoring tool they use and their navigation scheme. Examining competitive projects and their capabilities is the key to **differentiation** ▶ 87. Differentiation emphasizes the elements that set a product apart from the rest. For example, an electronic magazine could be differentiated by design, interaction, or content as well as through creative distribution strategies, advertising arrangements, or packaging solutions.

Even if there are no existing multimedia competitors, there are sure to be existing **non-multimedia competitors**. In fact, this is one of the biggest challenges of multimedia development—to create a product that adds more value to an experience than can be provided by a traditional solution. For example, an electronic book not only competes with other electronic books but also with printed books and magazines and all of the traditions, rituals, and expectations buyers have for

these materials. The design or distribution of an electronic book should ideally provide readers with experiences they cannot get with printed materials.

Where to Look for Marketing Information

Market research in multimedia can often be overwhelming at first because of the complexity and rapid change in the industry. It can be difficult to certify the quality of numbers, figures, rates, and other quantitative information. Added to this is that most of the information is soon outdated in six months as new products, pricing strategies, distribution options, and other changes take place.

To manage this complexity, find good sources such as industry newsletters and developer programs. Even though subscriptions for newsletters can cost several hundred dollars, they can be well worth the effort insofar as providing relevant and timely knowledge and reducing levels of information anxiety. In addition, **marketing research firms** can produce accurate and highly specific materials. Researching firms commonly operate on a consulting basis, researching only the subject matter the client is interested in.

Other good sources are people in the industry. Networking within the multimedia community can yield important information about business, markets, legal issues, and technology. Because this industry is an intersection of many industries, it is a rich world of experience, knowledge, and skills. Many people in multimedia are often willing to share information because of the large number of opportunities and wide range for growth. Many feel that collaboration and cooperation are fundamental to the development of the industry.

First, our team looked at the multimedia software that was available on the market today. Second, we talked to parents who owned computers and parents who were thinking of buying computers in the future. Finally, we visited a preschool and watched how the teachers told stories and how the children reacted.

Perhaps more important than the technical data we gathered, was the information we received from parents and their children. Kids want to be in control. Parents want their kids to learn, but most of the time television and videos end up as the medium of choice. Interactive software has the ability to entertain kids (like TV), while at the same time teaching them. There also is a common perception that a computer is a tool for learning. Reading and books are also an important part of a child's early years. Why not reinforce the importance of reading and books with a technology that can compete with television for a child's interest?

We wanted to do more than just put a book on the computer. We wanted to add value above and beyond a traditional book. Our ultimate goal was to do things that you just couldn't do with paper and ink.

— *Bill Rollinson, T/Maker*

Positioning Strategy

*Developing a **positioning strategy** is a three-step process. To start with, a company must have a good understanding of itself—its strengths and weaknesses, its goals and dreams. Top managers should have a coherent vision of the culture and goals of the company. If different managers have widely different visions, the company never will be able to develop a solid positioning strategy.*

*Second, the company needs to understand the market environment. That is trickier than it might seem. Most companies gather statistics about customer behavior. Then, they make decisions based on the market data. This quantitative approach is quite satisfying to numbers-happy MBAs. In most cases, however, it obscures reality. Instead, companies should use more qualitative approaches to understanding the environment. Marketing managers must develop an intuitive feel for the market. Rather than gather numbers, **companies should listen to customers' needs, problems, frustrations, and desires**. Customer comments won't translate into graphs, but the company that listens to them will come to a better understanding of customers and the marketplace.*

Finally, the company must use this information to decide on a positioning strategy. There is no single formula for deciding on a strategy. Just as the world is filled with a tremendous variety of technologies and products, so too is it filled with a variety of positioning strategies. Every company must find its own road to success.

— *Regis McKenna, CEO, Regis McKenna, Inc. in Relationship Marketing*

Sources for Market Research:

- *Customers*
- *Other developers*
- *Industry studies*
- *Multimedia newsletters (Digital Media)*
- *Computer and multimedia magazines (MacWeek, PC Week, NewMedia)*
- *Business publications (Wall Street Journal, The New York Times, Forbes, Business Week)*
- *Trade shows (MACWORLD, Seybold)*
- *Trade associations (SIGGRAPH)*
- *Electronic bulletin boards/online services (AppleLink, Compuserve, America Online)*
- *Developer programs (Apple Multimedia Program)*
- *Developer conferences (Apple QuickTime Conference)*

But by far the most enlightening information can come from potential **customers**. All the data in the world is often not as useful as a few comments by members of a target audience. Finding out their needs and desires, problems and concerns can lead to better product designs and positioning strategies.

Technical Research

Market research and **technical research** are closely related and often difficult to separate. In some sense, much of the market is about who has what device and how many of them they have. Technical considerations influence and constrain many design aspects such as the amount of content and its display or playback capabilities. The rapidly changing costs and turn-around times for CD-ROM duplication will affect the price of most CD-ROM titles. Technical research can lead to answers in a number of areas like delivery and development platforms, CD-ROM formats and standards, compression schemes ▶ **153, 206**, and authoring tools ▶ **139**. This research will not only provide information on how to create a product, it will provide information on how to create a product that is better, cheaper, and more useful than anything else available.

In researching videodisc characteristics for a project, Glenn Corey, formerly of Lumen Productions, discovered that the long seek times (the time it takes the player to find the correct spot on the disc) created unacceptable transitions between screens. He tested several alternatives and, armed with the knowledge of the timing characteristics, devised a method of using animations that hide the visual transitions and provide a continuous experience for the viewer.

Development Media

The storage media used for prototyping and production is often not the same media used for delivery. Most developers use hard drives and cartridges when developing a product and a variety of other storage media to send to premastering service bureaus and disc manufacturers. They often use cartridges, CD-Rs, and tapes for archiving and backup and Photo CD, DAT, and videotape for content-specific production work.

Many of these storage types are impractical for use as delivery media because of their high cost or special purpose. The focus during development is on creating the project and so this concern is not really an issue. But using development media can be misleading, especially in terms of timing and storage capacity. Developers need to be careful not to mistake performance and capabilities on development media from that of the final delivery medium. Another issue is with testing. All projects need to be tested thoroughly on the media they will be distributed on. This is especially true for CD-ROM because of the number of steps in the duplication process but it also has importance for all other types of storage media and project types. For example, a multimedia presentation should be tested on its delivery media to make sure that any extensions or resources are available.

Delivery Media

Knowing both the merits and limits of various storage media characteristics is helpful when deciding on a specific distribution and **delivery media** ▶ **230** such as diskette, CD-ROM, or videodisc. Some are inexpensive, some are fast, some have a large storage capacity, some are not writable. Each has a special mix of reasons for use but one of the overriding issues, however, is how many people use or are likely to use a given storage media. The market is often determined by the number of drives in use capable of playing that media or the number of drives that will be in use in the near future.

Although select media can be used for both development and delivery, it is more common to have one medium for development and another for delivery. For example, you might build a multimedia project on a hard drive but distribute it on a CD-ROM. For a multimedia presentation, you may deliver it on a cartridge disk.

Custom Projects

Media appropriate to the custom market is frequently based on the kinds of machines the client has available, is able to obtain, and willing to maintain. Examples of media used in custom projects are CD-ROMs to distribute multimedia to an outside sales force, hard drives or videodiscs running inside kiosks, and cartridges used for multimedia presentations.

Some custom projects take a hybrid approach and use different media for the same project. A mall-based kiosk might have a monthly CD-ROM update as well as use a network to provide daily updates and record user responses by writing to a hard drive. One type of delivery media may be used as a transfer mechanism while others are used for operation because it is either faster, more stable, or is writable.

Mass-Market Products

In the software mass-market industry, diskettes are clearly the most popular means of distribution but CD-ROM distribution is quickly becoming more popular. (Distribution on CD-ROM of system software and technical information for developers has long been popular for many platforms.) Third-party software applications containing instructional movies, templates, and other collateral materials have started to appear on CD-ROMs in place of diskettes. Applications are also starting to appear together on a CD-ROM in an encoded format that can be decoded by making a phone call, placing an order, and receiving a special identification number to "unlock" the application from the disc.

Pros and Cons of Delivery Media

The choice of which delivery media to use for a project should be based on the most effective way to reach an audience. If the audience does not already have a bias for one kind of equipment on which to play the media, then consider the formal issues of installed base, storage capacity, speed, economy, and recordability for each media type.

Installed Base—The choice of delivery media is many times governed by its popularity. Almost everyone has a diskette drive and can play diskettes, but not everyone has a CD-ROM drive. To reach as many people as possible, you may distribute on diskettes but also offer a CD-ROM version to appeal to existing drive owners as well as the people purchasing new computer models that have built-in CD-ROM drives. When researching the installed base, pay attention to configurations, peripherals, extensions, and other components besides the base platform or drive category. For example, the number of CD-ROM drives that are dual-speed or offer multi-session drives is far smaller than the total number of drives in the marketplace.

Storage Capacity—A vital consideration for the multimedia project is the amount of required storage for all the content and software that must fit on the delivery media. Video and sound files require a lot of storage. A multimedia project that fills one CD-ROM would take well over 400 standard diskettes. Few software applications ship on more than 5 diskettes. Requiring end-users to install many more than this may be an unreasonable request. Sizing all media and software early will help you estimate whether you can get by with a moderate storage requirement. For large projects, especially those that are audio- and video-based, the storage estimate should also address what compression technology can be used to get further savings.

Speed—Playing interactive video, sound, and large picture files requires a fast delivery speed. Hard-drive and memory-based systems are the fastest. CD-ROM is adequate for most projects, although highly interactive projects may show some limitations. CD-ROM drive technology is rapidly improving, though, and performance concerns may be less important than they were before.

Economy—Memory is fast but it is also the most expensive medium. The most economical form of delivery media measured in cost per megabyte of storage is CD-ROM. Its large capacity and common availability makes it a popular multimedia delivery medium. Diskettes are the cheapest medium per unit price and store a little over a megabyte in their current form. The diskette is ideal for mailing a demo and for producing low volumes with fast turnarounds.

Recordability—Applications which require updating or recorded user input require a writable medium. While most delivery media are writable, some like CD-ROM are not. Others like tape are writable but take too long to update. Sometimes the strategy is to provide a hybrid media solution. A title may be delivered in CD-ROM but be designed to dedicate files on a hard drive or some other writable storage for personal modification. The new magnetic-optical formats appear to have many of the advantages of CD-ROM plus the ability for revision.

CD-ROM

CD-ROM ▶ 231 (Compact Disc-Read Only Memory) is a powerful delivery medium. It has a tremendous advantage over other media because it offers a massive storage capacity in a stable format for a low reproduction cost. A CD-ROM has the capacity to store all types of digital information in ways that allow interactive control over this information. One disc can hold over 600MB of data and can be reproduced at a cost of $1-2 per disc in volume (not including premastering and mastering charges). The quantities for reproduction can range from 50 to tens of thousands.

CD-ROM can be used for many multimedia projects, especially those with high-definition sound or projects delivering a large volume of media. However, if the

What we found [during our market research] was that the majority of multimedia content was being written for future machines. Our design philosophy was to create content that was efficient on today's computers, but was a solid foundation for the machines of the future. We were determined to keep our software simple, elegant, and fast on low-end machines. We cut out all of the fat possible and added things as they made sense. For example, we decided early on to deliver both on floppy disks (to be loaded on a hard-drive) and CD-ROM, because a number of the parents we talked to didn't have a CD-ROM drive. This didn't mean that we thought the CD-ROM market was not important—we did, but the majority of today's market are without CD-ROM drives and are not ready to rush out and buy new equipment. Our challenge was to deliver the CD-ROM "look and feel" in a format that could be played-back with existing hardware.

— Bill Rollinson, T/Maker

The amount of music that an audio CD can hold was arbitrarily chosen to match the length of Hebert Von Karajan's interpretation of Beethoven's Ninth Symphony.

Estimates from various sources for the number of CD-ROM drives in the marketplace range from 2.5 million to 5.5 million. Getting solid numbers on what systems they are hooked up to and how they are used can be difficult.

A common remark made by many developers is the need for more storage space during design and production. Original sources or "assets," trial images and movies, prototypes, demos, backup copies and other forms of data can quickly fill up a developer's available capacity. Experienced developers usually have extremely large hard drives for production and premastering work and use cartridges, CD-Rs, or tapes for archiving and backup.

project is highly interactive, then look closely at CD-ROM performance and data access speeds during prototype testing. For projects involving user input the fact that CD-ROM is not a writable medium can introduce complexities. Once the data is encoded it cannot be changed or updated. Therefore a CD-ROM cannot be used like a hard drive or diskette.

One of the problems with CD-ROM in the mass market is that there are a large number of differing data formats. Even though each disc is physically identical, the way the data is stored on each disc varies with each format. Some CD-ROM players support only certain CD-ROM formats. For consumers, this can be more confusing than the wars over videotape between Betamax and VHS.

CD-ROM Drives

Most existing CD-ROM drives operate with relatively slow access times and transfer rates compared to computer hard drives. The **access time** is how long it takes to find and return data. The access time of an average CD-ROM is 300 milliseconds, while the access time for a hard drive is about 10-20 milliseconds. The **transfer rate** is the amount of data that is passed in a second. The transfer rate for CD-ROM is about 150 kilobytes per second, rooted in the technology designed to play a steady stream of digital CD music. (The transfer rate needed for non-compressed full-screen full-motion video is approximately 30MB/sec.) New dual-speed drives help improve performance issues by providing up

to 300KB per second transfer rates. This can make a big difference in the playback of digital movies. It is important to prototype and test CD-ROM movies in user testing phases and with clients to confirm acceptability.

Red Book

The compact disc industry started in 1982 when Sony and Philips created the Compact Disc Digital Audio Standard commonly known as the **Red Book** ▶ 48. This format describes the CDs found in music stores and is the foundation for the other compact disc formats. One disc can hold up to 74 minutes of stereo music using Pulse Code Modulation (PCM) to compress two stereo channels into over 600MB of space. The Red Book organizes the audio into one or more tracks with each track normally being one song. The tracks are further divided into sectors with a fixed size and duration.

Yellow Book

The **Yellow Book** CD-ROM standard, also published by Sony and Philips, defines the physical format for storing computer data on a CD-ROM disc. Yellow Book takes the basic Red Book definition and defines two new track types—**computer data** and **compressed audio** or **video/picture data**. The second type or mode is an extremely rare form. The format also adds better error correction (necessary for computer data) and better random access capabilities.

When a CD has CD-ROM tracks and CD-Audio tracks, it is called a **Mixed Mode** disc. Unfortunately, data cannot be read while sound is being played, so computer applications must use Mixed Mode in a staged manner. To get around these limits and to obtain synchronization of multiple tracks, an interleaved style was added in the form of the CD-ROM/XA standard.

CD-ROM/XA (CD-ROM eXtended Architecture) was proposed by Philips, Sony, and Microsoft in 1988 as an extension to Yellow Book. This specification extends Yellow Book and adds the interesting ideas from the Green Book (CD-I), notably **interleaved audio**. Before this time, audio was confined to one track at a time. Interleaved audio allows the sound to be divided and intermixed with other content. Actually any media can be interleaved and synchronized with the computer code coming from the disc. The CD-ROM/XA drive needs special hardware to separate the channels. When it does, it gives the appearance of simultaneous synchronized media. Not only does CD-ROM/XA allow for intermixed sound, but it also provides various levels of fidelity and compression. CD-ROM/XA uses a more efficient technique of audio compression than the Red Book, allowing 4-8 times more audio on the same disc.

CD-ROM Formats

Red Book - CD-Audio
Yellow Book - CD-ROM, CD-ROM/XA
Green Book - CD-I
Orange Book - CD-MO, CD-R (proposed)

The reasons for having different CD-ROM formats are part historical, part political, and part technical. CDs were initially made for music. Red Book, that first standard, proved insufficient for computer data because of limited error correction capabilities and other technical aspects, which led to the creation of the Yellow Book. Other "books" and standards such as ISO 9660 provided additional capabilities for platforms, file systems, and certain media, particularly interleaved data. Derivations or extensions to ISO 9660 allow support for native file systems such as Unix, Macintosh, MS-DOS, and DVI.

Another CD-ROM format in the works is known as the Frankfurt specification, also called ECMA 168 from the European Computer Manufacturers Association. This format promises to offer equal facilities for Unix, Macintosh, OS/2, and Windows NT file systems. In conjunction with the Orange Book, Frankfurt will support the update capabilities needed to create multiple sessions. This combination will define a standard CD-R format as well as to provide a richer CD-ROM format to support better cross-platform computer characteristics.

To obtain the specifications for Red Book, Yellow Book, or ISO 9660 contact ANSI, 212/642-4900. The Green Book specification can be obtained from the American CD-I Association, 213/444-6619. Both are listed in the Resources section.

Green Book

The **Green Book** CD-ROM standard was introduced by Philips in 1986 and is the basis for a special format called **Compact Disc Interactive** or **CD-I**. Although CD-I using the Green Book standard is a general CD-ROM format, all CD-I titles to date require a CD-I player where the data must be read back by a special operating system called OS/9. A CD-I system consists of a stand-alone player connected to a TV set. The CD-I market is limited by the special CD-I development environment and the relatively small number of manufacturers of CD-I players. A unique part of the Green Book standard is the specification for **interleaved data** which is the mixing of pictures, sounds, and movies, and programming them into one track on a disc. Interleaving is one way to make sure that data in the same track is synchronized, a problem with Yellow Book CD-ROM.

CD-Bridge Disc

A bridge CD-ROM can run in either a CD-ROM drive or a CD-I drive. The **CD-Bridge Disc** specification defines a way to put additional information in a CD-ROM/XA track. This format lets a CD-I player read a CD-I application from the disc. An example of a bridge disc is the Photo CD format from Kodak.

Orange Book

The recently published **Orange Book** standard defines a new writable CD-ROM format. Part 1 of the standard covers the new magneto-optical which is completely revisable. Part 2 covers CD-R (Compact Disc Recordable) for compact disc write-once media that defines the multi-session format that allows for incremental updates to the media. Ordinary CD-ROM drives cannot write to CD-R media and can only play the first session on a multi-session disc.

Other Formats

At the beginning of 1993 there were over a dozen proprietary CD-ROM formats. Although the major ones are discussed, the other formats of mention include CD+G, CD+MIDI, CDTV from Commodore, Sega, and Nintendo, and Video Information System (VIS) from Tandy.

ISO 9660

While the Yellow Book standard provided a low-level definition to encode bits on an optical disc, it was necessary to provide some degree of standard organization so that computer systems could read them in an operating-system-independent manner. This general file system for CD-ROM encoding was first proposed in 1985 and called the High Sierra format. This proposal was modified slightly to become the **ISO 9660** file system recognized by the International Standards Organization. ISO 9660 standardizes such things as directory, sub-directories, and the length of filenames and the characters that can be used in them. It looks most like an MS-DOS file system in design, largely due to the significant part Microsoft played in defining the standard.

Many operating system vendors have added their own extensions to this standard. Apple created a variation of ISO 9660 which supports subtleties of the Hierarchical File System, especially the Macintosh icons and resources. This extension is needed to get the standard Macintosh file conventions to work from a CD-ROM. Microsoft supplies the MSCDEX.EXE extension for an MS-DOS or Windows CD-ROM and Unix has the Rock Ridge format that allows long filenames, permissions, and symbolic links. Some, but not all, of these variations can be read as regular ISO 9660 compliant images on systems other than their native systems. Some Macintosh developers supply both HFS and ISO 9660 partitions on the same disc allowing them to be read in their native formats by both Macintosh computers and PCs.

CD-R

Compact Disc Recordable ▶ 175, 180, 232
(CD-R) is a storage technology that has some of the same uses as its optical competitors WORM and MO but it allows data to be stored in a CD-ROM format. (It is also called Compact Disc Write Once or CD-WO.) CD-R drives, also called CD-ROM recorders, are expensive and cumbersome to use but the prices are rapidly dropping.

One useful property of the ISO 9660 standard format is that data can be accessed by multiple platforms from the same disc. Macintosh, Windows, and UNIX can all read ISO 9660. This does not ensure that all data can be used by all platforms, but it does mean that these platforms will have access to the data. If the disc contains an executable program then it will only run on the operating system the program was written for. A disc can be created that will contain multiple executable files, each one applicable to a different operating system.

Most Macintosh developers ship a CD-ROM Mode 1 disc with an HFS or ISO 9660 file structure.

The discs look similar in size to a CD-ROM (a CD-ROM has a silver bottom, a CD-R is typically gold) but the CD-R is made differently to accommodate recording onto the disc. CD-R is used in the premastering process for CD-ROMs to generate a check disc and is also used for archival purposes by some multimedia developers with CD-ROM recorders.

A "one-off" or "check disc" is a CD-R disc created by a CD-ROM recorder. The price of CD-ROM recorders are dropping rapidly and are impacting the CD-ROM publishing industry in some of the same ways that low-cost laser printers impacted the desktop publishing industry many years ago.

Photo CD

Photo CD ▶ 188 is a system from Kodak introduced in 1992 for digitizing negatives and slides and storing them in a CD-ROM format. Consumers can view the images on the disc on a television with a Kodak Photo CD player or a Philips CD-I player. Because they are derived in part from the CD-ROM/XA format, Photo CDs can be read by CD-ROM drives (provided the system software can read an ISO image in the XA format). The difference from CD-ROM/XA is that Photo CD permits the writing of further material at the end of the disc. (Photo CD uses a write-once compact disc that allows photos to be appended at later points in time.) This **multi-session** capability requires a multi-session CD-ROM drive to read all sessions. Some XA drives can be upgraded to be multi-session drives by replacing a chip. Without the chip, older drives can only read the first session of data that was recorded on the disc.

Kodak developed the Photo CD system as a standard for digital photography. Images

recorded on Photo CD have a Kodak encoding for resolution and color. There are five Photo CD formats. A **Master** format Photo CD can store roughly 100 pictures in five different resolutions. The Master format is the only format available at the time of the printing of this book. The other formats include: **Portfolio** for holding up to 800 images at video resolution, **Catalog** for holding up to 6,000 images and allowing branching from menu screens, **Pro** for accommodating sizes other than 35mm, and **Medical** for holding X-rays and digital data from CT or MR scanners.

Kodak provides the service that converts photos and digitizes them to a Master disc. Anyone can bring undeveloped print, slide, or transparency film to photo finishers that offer the service and have the pictures transferred to a Photo CD disc. Multimedia developers use this as an inexpensive means of storing digital pictures during production.

Videodisc

Videodiscs are a widely used delivery media in educational markets. A videodisc is a large optical disc that stores data (usually sound and video) in **analog** form. Because the data is analog, videodiscs can store much more movie data than CD-ROM although it is not in a form that can be easily used with a computer. In many computer installations, a videodisc player typically shows the videodisc material on a dedicated display, separate from the computer screen display. One option is to use a video overlay board and route the playback to the computer screen.

The Visual Almanac
An Interactive Multimedia Kit

Videodisc

Videodiscs are two-sided. Most players require the disc to be ejected and manually turned over to access the data on the other side. A videodisc can store up to 60 minutes of **NTSC video** ▶ 203 and stereo sound. Videodisc comes in two formats: constant angular velocity (CAV) and constant linear velocity (CLV). CAV can be used for interactive videodisc and CLV can be used for simple linear media such as consumer movie videodiscs. Only CAV will let you perform such functions as random access, still frame, and variable speed. CAV discs play frames on a spiral track from the center of the disc out spinning at 1800 revolutions per minute. The industry standard videodisc format LaserVision is used in commercial and most interactive videodisc systems.

Videodisc formats can be recorded for players providing four levels of interactivity. **Level 1** allows linear play of videodisc information and uses no computer control information. It is the easiest to produce but has no interactivity. **Level 2** allows branched play of videodisc information and also uses no computer control information. Branched instructions for viewers are stored in audio channel 2 and all command control is mastered with the disc. **Level 3** is the common interactive **multimedia videodisc** format. Only the audio and video signals are recorded on the disc which means a computer with the appropriate software is required to control it. Any software changes can be made separately and do not involve remastering the videodisc. To optimize seek time and play, commonly used videodisc segments should be stored at the center of the disc. **Level 4** allows for the storage of both data and computer information on the videodisc. These types of discs are the most difficult to debug, because of the way in which program instructions are stored.

A recent format for videodisc that provides data in addition to video and audio is called LD-ROM. **LD-ROM** is likened to CD-ROM, in that it can store any digital information such as executable programs, text, graphics, sounds, and movies.

Diskette

The **diskette** is one of the more common and least expensive formats to distribute data, especially in the software industry. The small storage capacity and slower access speed make the diskettes in use today impractical for anything but transfer and delivery media for small multimedia projects. Rather than run a program from a diskette, the practice is to copy material from the diskette and run it from a hard drive. There are a few different types of diskettes: **double-density**, **high-density**, and **extended- density** diskettes. The most common diskette for the Macintosh at the printing of this book is a double-sided double-density 3.5in. diskette which stores approximately 1.2MB of data. Unlike ISO 9660 CD-ROMs which use a operating-system-independent file format, diskettes must be **formatted** for a particular operating and file system. Utility programs and system extensions, though, provide the access capabilities to diskettes formatted under non-native systems.

Advantages of diskettes are that they are used in almost every computer, portable, and easy to send by mail. They are also inexpensive and easy to duplicate. They do not need extensive premastering and mastering processes like CD-ROM. A small quantity of diskettes can be duplicated and labeled in-house cheaply and quickly. Unfortunately, diskettes are slow and wear out in time, and since most multimedia makes use of large amounts of data, their use may be limited to select projects.

For more information about Photo CD, call Eastman Kodak Company at 800/235-6325 (CD-KODAK).

Hard Drive

Hard drives are permanently installed media with fast access and potentially large capacities. These capacities commonly run from 20MB to 1000MB. They are used extensively for multimedia development and are sometimes part of custom multimedia installations like kiosks. The hard drive gives the best performance of any storage media except computer memory. They store their data on magnetic oxide coated aluminum disks that spin at high speeds.

One of the risks with hard drives, because of their large size and prominence in development and not because they are necessarily unstable, is the loss of data due to hard-disk crashes or users inadvertently destroying files. It is critical to **backup data ▶ 175** and have a means of restoring all data and programs should the drive fail or other unexpected occurences take place. Although this is the case with all storage media, the issue is more pronounced with hard drives.

To play large format high resolution movies, hard drives can be combined and synchronized in arrangements called disk arrays. A **disk array** is an arrangement of hard drives with a special disk controller and dedicated microprocessor to stream video at speeds up

to 200MB per second compared to a normal SCSI transfer of 10MB per second. Apple refers to this high-speed architecture as QuickRing which provides fast data transfer for NuBus-based Macintosh computers. The new Apple architecture connects modified NuBus cards and a microprocessor. Disk array technology enables fast high-volume throughput enabling high-end video applications in multimedia, HDTV, and graphics acceleration of complex imagery.

Cartridge

Removable **cartridges** store data and run on special cartridge disk drives. A cartridge is a sealed disc that can be inserted and removed much like a diskette. Cartridge drives run almost as fast as a hard drive and cartridges can store as much data as a common hard drive. Cartridges are used heavily in desktop publishing to exchange materials with service bureaus and in multimedia for the delivery of custom projects such as presentations. They are not a mass market media. Cartridges are fairly reliable and come in 44, 88, and 150MB capacities. The newer 88MB drives can write to 44MB cartridges whereas earlier ones could not. This limited the popularity of the larger drive because the 44MB cartridges were still in wide use.

Magneto-Optical (MO)

Removable **magneto-optical discs** are efficient writable storage for large volumes of data. They are similar in operation to the cartridge drive. They are a little slower compared to hard drives, although MO performance is rapidly improving with each generation of design. These drives are ideal for making digital film and have the size of a CD-ROM, but the discs are far more expensive than CD-ROMs. MOs are rapidly replacing WORM for archival purposes in the computer industry. Because this is a **writable** optical media, it has potential for general purpose use for all kinds of multimedia projects.

MiniDisc (MD)

Sony introduced the **MiniDisc**, a small, writable, and durable MO disc, for consumer music in 1992. Although MD stores only 128MB of data, it is able to hold as much music as an audio CD (over 600MB) by using a decompression technology to play back a highly compressed digital sample. Pre-recorded MDs are being sold at about the same price as CD-Audio discs. MiniDisc might

become a useful multimedia format in the near future since you can record your own material on a small, portable, durable, and affordable optical medium. But as of 1992, the only pressing plant is in Japan, which currently limits the commercial distribution potential.

WORM

WORM is a Write Once/Read Many storage format. Standard 5.5 in. WORM cartridges can store from 300 to 650MB depending on the format. It is a professional archiving medium only, not appropriate for distribution. One problem with WORM media is that it must be recorded and played back on the same WORM drive, so this media is limited to local archiving.

Floptical

A **floptical** is a 3.5in. magnetic disc, much like a diskette, that uses an optical guidance system to be able to store about 20MB of data, far more than a conventional diskette. Flopticals operate faster than diskettes but not as fast as cartridges or hard drives. While they are efficient, they are not yet widely used and are therefore not a useful delivery medium. Most floptical drives will read conventional diskettes.

DAT & 8mm Tape

Digital Audio Tape (DAT) was developed initially for sound recording and file backup. It is used now for computer storage in multimedia development. Both

DAT and **8mm** digital tapes are limited in terms of interactive playback capabilities because of their sequential access. Tapes have to wind and rewind to access different portions, making access times extremely long. Both are cost-effective ways, however, to store large volumes of data. They can be used either for archiving or for transferring data to a premastering service (provided the premastering service supports them). The size of a DAT tape is about 2 by 3 inches and it holds approximately 1.3 gigabytes of data. A 8mm tape is slightly larger but holds 2.5-5 gigabytes of data.

Flash RAM Card

Flash RAM (random access memory) cards, sometimes called PC Cards, are lightweight, thick credit card-sized storage devices that use little power and have extremely fast performance. Since they have no spinning disc or moving parts they are durable and have few technical problems. When applications play from flash memory they are almost as fast as conventional memory. If data is written to them, however, they are about as slow as a hard drive or even a diskette. Flash memories are nonvolatile which means that the data is secure even when the power is turned off. Conventional RAM forgets everything stored in it when the power is turned off. Most flash RAM cards include a small battery to operate the circuitry. The current generation of cards can hold up to 20MB with 65MB capacities expected in a few years.

Media Comparison Table

Medium	Capacity (MB)	Cost ($/MB)	Access Speed (ms)	Use
HD Diskette	1.4	$0.70	2000	Transfer/Delivery
ED Diskette	2.8	$0.70	2000	Transfer/Delivery
Floptical	20	$1.00	1000	Transfer/Custom Delivery
Hard Drive	40-1000	$5.00-1.50	10-20	Production/Custom Delivery
Cartridge	44/88	$1.40/$1.00	15-30	Production/Custom Delivery
CD-ROM	600	$0.003	300	Delivery/Archival (CD-R)
3.5 in Magneto-Optical	128/660	$0.50	40	Production
5.25 in Magneto-Optical	660	$0.25	90	Production
WORM	300-650	$0.15	1200	Archival
DAT	1300	$0.01	long/variable	Archival
Flash Memory	20	$30.00	1	Future Delivery

Sources for Technology Research:

- Other developers
- Computer and multimedia magazines (MacUser, Byte, NewMedia)
- Trade magazines (CD-ROM Professional, Videography)
- User Groups
- Vendor literature (product brochures, price lists)
- Trade shows (MACWORLD, Seybold)
- Conferences (SIGGRAPH, CyberArts)
- Developer programs (Apple Multimedia Program)
- Developer conferences (Apple QuickTime Conference)
- Trade Associations (ANSI, American CD-I Association)
- University programs (multimedia studies, film and video studies)

The Personal Computer Memory Card International Association (**PCMCIA**), a large computer organization, establishes the standard format for these cards and ensures compatibility of all card manufactures. **Publish cards** are flash RAM cards with content and applications provided. These are locked so they cannot be overwritten. Memory cards are ideal for small portable devices since they are small, lightweight, fast, and conservative with power.

Networks

Networks are used to update information used in a kiosk installation, to deliver multimedia instructional materials for corporate training, or share multimedia storage for many different uses. There are two basic kinds of networks: **mass communications multicast networks** like radio and television broadcast, and data communications point to point networks like distributed **local area networks** and telephone-based **modem connected networks**. For multimedia projects, the data communications networks are most approachable, while broadcast is rarely used. There have been some experiments with hybrid multicast networks, like interactive television, and they hold promise for special projects and future technologies.

Data networks are often measured by **bandwidth**. Typical twisted-pair telephone wire is capable of tranmitting around 9600 bits per second without special hardware to compress the signal. This low-bandwidth network is barely adequate to pass 2-way video and sound. The most interesting high bandwidth, wired networks for multimedia are **fiber-optic** and are being installed in phone systems today. The advantage of fiber nets is that they provide up to 1 trillion bits per second of throughput and can carry their signal up to 30 miles as compared to a telephone voiceband wire that needs an amplifier every mile. Networks can be **wired** or **wireless**. For multimedia, it appears that only the wired variety will have the throughput to carry major signals. For any given project the bandwidth must be adequate to serve the number of users likely to use the system at any given time.

Other important issues for multimedia networks are protocols and topologies. The network protocol is the communication standard by which devices on a network agree to send and receive data. There are no **network multimedia protocols** today but companies like Starlight and Fluent are providing useful technology that lives on top of a conventional network topology. A **topology** is how the wires and devices on the

Interview: Doug Camplejohn

Doug Camplejohn is the manager of product strategy at Starlight Networks in Mountain View, CA. Starlight Networks, Inc. provides a video networking system which consists of video application server software and desktop-based video network interface software. Camplejohn, who was part of the first QuickTime team at Apple Computer, discusses the present and future of networked multimedia computing.

What are the main issues regarding networked multimedia?
Networks as they stand today follow a "certified letter model" of delivering data, which means that the bits are guaranteed to get to you over the network, but there's no guarantee when that transaction is going to take place. That's fine for regular data because you don't want to lose the information. But for multimedia data, that's really bad. There is a basic problem with putting a real-time data type into a non-real time environment.

What works for networked multimedia data, particularly video, is a "Federal Express model," to absolutely, positively guarantee that the video will get to users on a network at exactly the right time—not too soon (or else you need a lot of buffering) or too late (or else you lose video synchronization).

Network bandwidths like Ethernet at 10 Mbps and Token Ring at 16 Mbps are good enough to start some very interesting networked multimedia projects.

How can groups best prepare their data so that it can be used on a multimedia network?
Anything that you can play off your local hard disk or CD-ROM drive can be delivered reliably over a network. The main consideration to think about is bandwidth. On an Ethernet segment you have 10 Mbps, which means you can support 5-6 simultaneous video clients running 1.2 Mbps video stream each (CD-ROM data rate) and still have a comfortable amount of space left over for data. If you use higher bandwidth networks like 16 MBit Token Ring, FDDI, or ATM, you can get even more. If you use a higher data rate video stream (e.g. Motion JPEG), you'll get fewer number of users per segment.

What are your thoughts on the future of networked multimedia?
Networked multimedia is one of the key remaining hurdles to computer-based multimedia taking off. People are starting off today on Ethernet and Token Ring networks doing projects in small work groups. In the near future, we have customers that will be delivering stored video over wide area networks and working with live video (television and two-way videoconferencing) over the LAN and WAN as well. Beyond that, we see full campus networks using multimedia on a day-to-day basis, either through higher-performance routers or ATM. At this point, data types like video truly become just a standard part of everyday computing.

What is your advice to companies who want to start working with networked multimedia?
The main reason for networks is to share expensive things. Multimedia obviously has expensive things associated with it, such as many hard drives or a costly connection to a wide-area network (for example, T1) outside the company.

Companies typically have a specific application in mind. For example, a corporation might want to put all of its training on a networked multimedia setup. Typically they'll buy a ten-user system and set up a lab where they can try things out.

They should make sure they're already comfortable with multimedia. They should try things on a standalone system. They should get used to QuickTime and the hardware associated with it. They should try it out before going all the way with a network. From there it should be easy to take the step towards networked multimedia.

network are arranged. There are essentially three topologies: **bus**, **ring**, and **star**. Apple runs a bus network for both **AppleTalk®** and **Ethernet**. IBM uses a token ring local area network. The bus and ring networks which are popular on computer local area networks may not be appropriate for sending multimedia data because the wire can be overloaded quickly by a small number of users, and the network protocols are not meant to manage time-sensitive traffic. New star

network designs appear to be fairly successful models because they minimize the amount of wire traffic and use a central controller to manage timed traffic.

Network distributed multimedia applications rely on **servers** to manage the storage and transmission of the content. The generally low bandwidth of a network requires that data be compressed and decompressed by hardware and software in the server and the client machines.

Keep files on technical information. Magazine reviews, product brochures, and catalog price lists are easy to get and periodically update for use by anyone at any time.

Case Study: Peter Gabriel XPLORA 1 CD-ROM

Description:
The Peter Gabriel XPLORA 1 CD-ROM provides an interactive exploration of the music and videos of Peter Gabriel, as well as an introduction to musicians from around the globe. It offers a personal, behind-the-scenes look at the making of a hit album and music videos and provides a hands-on experience in the creative musical process.

Project Type:
Interactive Music

Development Hardware:
Macintosh Quadra 900, Macintosh IIcx and Macintosh LC with DayStar Accelerators, RasterOps 364, PC VCR, large hard drives, DAT backup for initial phases; Macintosh Quadra™ 950 with SuperMac Digital Film board, Macintosh Duo™ 230, and Macintosh IIvx Delivery Hardware:

Any Macintosh computer with a color or grayscale monitor and a CD-ROM drive

Software used:
Customized HyperCard Tools, Adobe Photoshop, Adobe Premiere, Movie Shop

Team Members and Roles:
The U.S. team consisted of an interactive designer/programmer; a production artist, two production assistants, and one tester. The U.K. team consisted of video directors, video editor, and co-producers, with Peter Gabriel as executive producer.

Funding:
Real World Ltd./Peter Gabriel

Price:
$40

Contact:
Steve Nelson, Brilliant Media

San Francisco, CA

Management:
Steve Nelson acted as project producer/director in the U.S. and U.K. with a production team at Brilliant Media in San Francisco. Peter Gabriel's production company Real World Ltd. provided creative advisors and music-related management from the U.K.

Concept and Planning & Design and Prototype:
"We see concept and planning as being intimately tied in with design and prototyping, though we do, of course, do very thorough planning before actually building anything on the computer," says Steve Nelson.

The most challenging part of this phase of the project was working between England and the United States to brainstorm and plan. Meeting by phone and by FAX was difficult. Face-to-face meetings were much more productive, and being on site at Real World Ltd. gave access to many resources (people, materials, and equipment). Getting Peter Gabriel's time was also difficult as he is involved in many things, but his input was very important.

"During the concept stage, we brainstormed ideas and identified all of the materials available to us," says Nelson. He constructed a huge master outline based on these discussions. He then determined patterns and

metaphors for structuring the material, and created thumbnail sketches and interactive design web drawings. With the help of the creative people at Real World Ltd, Nelson and his team prepared a storyboard of the disc.

Having to translate rough video cuts between NTSC and PAL ▶ 203 *was a bit of a problem—the video capture boards used for the prototype required NTSC input, and most of the source material was in PAL format.*

All materials are owned either by Peter Gabriel and his companies or by Steve Nelson and Brilliant Media, so license rights were much less of a problem than they would be in most cases. Nelson is working in this case under the same arrangement as a record producer.

Production:
Testing and production were integrated in three major cycles. The initial production process involved shooting all new video, digitizing all the materials, writing text, creating graphics, and finally assembling all pieces for testing. The team then cycled through at least three major tests, with time in between to correct problems and redo any materials. At all stages Nelson's team pressed test CD-ROMs to check performance.

Again, the transatlantic nature of this project created slight logistical problems. Brilliant Media and Real World Ltd are using DAT tapes to transfer materials back and forth.

Testing:
Testing was integrated into the production process, as discussed above. Nelson hired a professional QA consultant to do thorough testing. Brilliant Media personnel also contributed to testing. User testing was conducted at early stages to make sure the interface and content ideas were sound and exciting.

Distribution:
Retail channels, computer stores, and record stores via a major distributor. An arrangement to bundle the CD-ROM with a major hardware manufacturer is in the works.

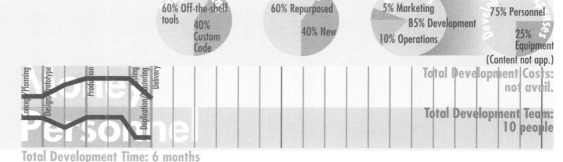

60% Off-the-shelf tools / 40% Custom Code

60% Repurposed / 40% New

5% Marketing / 85% Development / 10% Operations

75% Personnel / 25% Equipment

(Content not app.)

Total Development Costs: not avail.

Total Development Team: 10 people

Total Development Time: 6 months

New technologies are continually arriving on the scene. More frequently now than in the past, these technologies are more evolutionary rather than revolutionary and can be supported with little additional effort. An example is the series of Power Macintosh™ computers recently introduced by Apple Computer. Although these computers are powered by a new RISC-based chip set called PowerPC, they behave exactly like any other Macintosh—only faster.

Delivery Platforms

The **delivery platform** is the equipment potential audiences will use to receive delivery media and interact with a multimedia product. Sometimes it is the same as the development platform on which the project was created. Most multimedia developers choose a delivery platform and a delivery media and then select the platform that has the best tools to generate a product for the delivery platform. A few consider the decision of which platform to develop for as secondary. They believe developing durable digital content with the best development environment will allow them to leverage the content on the platforms of choice. In reality, the situation is likely a combination of both. Incomplete production tools will limit the potential for a product but an insufficient market may not support its development in the first place.

Talking about delivery platforms, though, does not give the whole story. The general computer type alone does not assure adequate multimedia capabilities. It is the set of hardware and software components and capabilities

that allow a product to use a full range of multimedia options. In many cases, platform manufacturers have created product lines that are more suitable for multimedia purposes. The Apple Macintosh Color Classic is an example. It has built-in sound and color, comes with QuickTime, and has a processor fast enough for most multimedia demands.

The technical plan should note target system specifications down to the models and necessary components. Evaluate and select the hardware before committing to prototype and production. In the design of a product, most developers allow for capabilities that are available at the moment. In some cases, they may support a technology that is in the beta-phase at the time of development and launch their product in conjunction with the release of the new technology. Planning on technical capabilities outside of this range can be a risky, if not foolish, strategy.

Processors

The speed of the **processor** will make a big difference in the interactivity that is possible. The processors that can adequately support multimedia capabilities include the Motorola 68020, 68030, and 68040, the Intel 386 and 486, RISC-based chips and many others.

Monitors

The type of **monitor** can make some features possible but not all multimedia products need color support. The Voyager Expanded Books series has found success on the Apple PowerBook computers with 1-bit displays. The nature of the products in the series and the convenience of the PowerBook makes color an expendable option. Types and issues with monitors include black-and-white (monochrome), 8-bit grayscale, 8-bit or 24-bit color, resolution, screen size, multiple screens, and projection capabilities.

Sound Capabilities

A few studies have shown that **sound quality** can often be more important than the quality of the display. Some platforms can support sound right out of the box, others need additional boards. The issues in sound include the

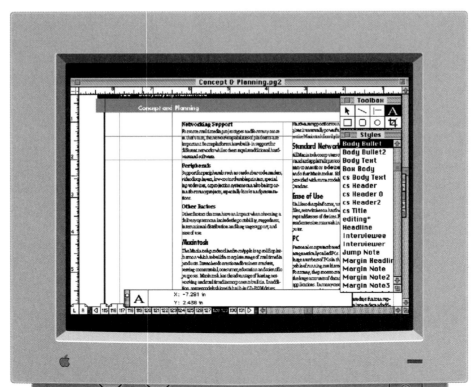

sample size ▶ 191 (8-bit and 16-bit) and the **sampling rate** ▶ 191 (11kHz, 22kHz, and 44kHz). **Speakers** also make a big difference in the quality of the playback. To support **MIDI** ▶ 155, 193 sequences and CD-quality sound, external hardware and additional software is often needed.

Storage Support

Media types such as images, sound, and video can take up huge amounts of storage. Most computers ship with hard drives in sizes that are adequate for most productivity uses but may not be as adequate for playing some multimedia products. As the price of hard drives continues to drop, many new platforms are shipping with much larger drives. Support for external storage devices such as other hard drives, CD-ROM drives, and cartridge drives should also be a consideration. Some platforms make it easier than others to attach these peripheral storage devices.

Networking Support

For some multimedia project types and for many more in the future, the network capabilities of platforms are important. Some platforms have built-in support for different networks while others require additional hardware and software.

Peripherals

Support for peripherals such as card or bar code readers, videodisc players, low-cost or durable printers, special input devices, or projection systems can also be important for many projects, especially kiosks and presentations.

Other Factors

Other factors that can have an impact when choosing a delivery system can include the portability, ruggedness, international distribution and language support, and ease of use.

Macintosh

The Macintosh product line from Apple is a prolific platform on which to build a complete range of multimedia

products. It reaches domestic and business markets, serving commercial, consumer, education, and scientific purposes. Macintosh has the advantage of having networking and multimedia components built in. In addition, most modular Macintosh computers are now shipping with built-in CD-ROM drive options. The Macintosh Classic provides a monochrome display and sells for under $1,000, and is a delivery system suitable for non-video multimedia projects. Higher end machines like the Quadra models support color and have a very capable 68040 processor. These models are great for any multimedia project, especially large projects like kiosks, multimedia databases, and interactive movies.

A Few of the Features of the Macintosh Include:

Standard Interface The standard graphical interface based on a desktop metaphor gives users a powerful footing for learning and using multiple applications.

Standard Imaging Model and Displays The display architecture of the Macintosh system is designed so that images can appear on any model, black-and-white or color, without the need for conversion software.

Standard Audio Hardware support for sound and microphone input gives it unusually powerful sound capabilities across the entire Macintosh product line.

Standard Networking All Macintosh computers can communicate via Apple's standard AppleTalk protocol. This allows simple and easy connections to devices such as printers, modems, and other Macintosh computers. Ethernet capabilities are also provided with some models including high-end Macintosh Quadra computers.

Ease of Use Unlike other platforms, users do not have to edit system files, set switches on hardware boards, or compare interrupt addresses of devices. Most also do not have to read extensive manuals in order to operate the computer.

Consistently, the advice of expert multimedia developers is to get the best affordable tools. Cheap tools are just not worth lost labor cost and poor quality results. Think about simple ways to improve a system. Good microphones are one of the ways to get good recordings. Additional RAM or VRAM or a larger hard drive can save days when measured over the time it takes to create a project.

New computer models are not only providing integrated multimedia capabilities, some are providing two-way communication capabilities. Examples are new Macintosh models from Apple Computer with AV technologies. These Macintosh computers have a telecommunications architecture for sending and receiving data, fax, and voice telephony, video-in and video-out capabilities, and speech recognition and text-to-speech features.

To help users take advantage of the new features of the AV computers, Apple has developed a full-color high-resolution computer display with integrated audio and video capabilities. The Apple AudioVision 14 Display has built-in high-quality speakers optimized for CD-quality audio playback and near-field listening, and an integrated uni-directional microphone for recording speech, or driving voice macros using PlainTalk technology. The AudioVision 14 has connectors for ADB and audio in/out and can be used with the new AV computers as well as with other Macintosh computers.

PC

Personal computers based on the Intel family of CPUs are generically called PCs. Although there are incredibly large numbers of PCs in the marketplace, most are incapable of running multimedia software and hardware. For many, the processors are not fast enough to support the huge amounts of data common in most multimedia applications. In many cases, additional cards are needed to support graphics, sound, and video.

Some PC models are shipping these days that can support multimedia without additional upgrades and add-on devices. The **Multimedia PC** (MPC) is a standard set by Microsoft for OEMs to build a multimedia-compliant personal computer. An MPC runs Multimedia for Windows software and has CD-ROM, sound, and a minimal processing speed to run digital video.

Cross-Platform Delivery

Many developers plan on supporting multiple platforms. Some develop a product simultaneously for multiple platforms while others release first on one platform and then "port" to the others after success on the initial platform. **Cross-platform delivery** strategies can be based on custom engines and tools or third party components. Developing a large set of proprietary tools that allow the delivery of multimedia products on multiple platforms can be costly, but some developers have done this. A strategy used by many and becoming more popular is to use an authoring engine that has players for other platforms (or authoring engines with very similar capabilities) and storing the media element in standard formats such as TIFF or as QuickTime movies.

Delivery Technologies

Technologies that are related to the delivery media and platform can have a huge importance in whether a project or design approach is feasible. These technologies can either be add-on boards, software in the form of system or third-party extensions, or both. In particular,

I want to emphasize how important it is to have the installed equipment be the same as the development equipment. Small unreported changes can be frustrating and take a long time to fix in expensive hardware installations when you discover them too late. One way to avoid the problem is to warehouse equipment.

— *Glenn Corey, Apple Computer, Inc.*

Personal Digital Assistants *(PDAs) are small, personal, and highly portable computers. The Apple Newton is an example. Unlike most computers used for productivity work today, the primary use of a PDA is as a personal communicator.*

For mass-market products, the single most important component is the development environment. The delivery piece of the puzzle is much easier than the development piece. The widget that they use to view it, whether it is a phone, a CD, handheld, or hooked into their TVs is completely irrelevant. To be able to show the value added and the compelling use of the medium, there must be tools to help create really good content that people will want to do things with.

— *Barry Schuler, President, Medior*

video playback and **compression technologies** ▶ 208 can make the difference between a useful product and a compelling one. See the video segment in Production for more information.

Development Platforms

The **development platform** is the equipment used to design and produce a multimedia project. It is not necessarily the same caliber or even platform used for delivery. Often, development platforms are much more powerful. This saves time producing a product but can easily lead to the creation of a product too sophisticated or demanding for the intended delivery equipment. Developers should measure all performance by the *delivery* platform and not the *development* platform.

A point made by many developers is that the platform is not as important as the tools on the platform. In other words, the best development platform is the platform with the best tools. Many MPC developers using Windows find that the Macintosh is the better multimedia production station for most multimedia projects. Macintosh animators sometimes turn to other machines to construct high-end animations. Cross platform development is becoming increasingly common.

Future Technologies

Communications, computers, and content are converging to use common technologies. This is the driving force behind new platforms, new components, and new capabilities. It can be tempting to use these platforms, components, and capabilities when developing a new product or version of a product. Deciding to use unreleased technology is risky. The risk is less pronounced the less a product hinges on the technology.

A number of steps can be taken to decrease the risks. One of the steps is as simple as getting on beta programs for a technology. Developing products without sufficient access to the technologies is dangerous. Creating different scenarios and then developing responses to those scenarios can help supply the other steps. For example, playing out a scenario that has the ship date for a new component slipping six months can lead to putting in milestones to decide whether to go ahead or to use the existing technology. Some technologies are fairly safe bets; others are risky. A project team should remain open to the ones that stand a good chance of becoming widely used, but they should realize that the general consumer market moves much more slowly in response to new technologies than the developer market.

Digital Signal Processors

The **digital signal processor** (DSP) has many unique media processing characteristics. It can be used to perform compression and decompression of data streams and for image and sound processing. DSPs can obtain the highest level of sound playback and can exceed CD stereo sound chips. They are being used in new systems to generate **binaural sound** ▶ 154 (3D audio). Computers with DSPs can operate music synthesizers with the proper conversion software, meaning that MIDI playback can come for free with a DSP computer architecture.

Interactive Television

A popular technology under investigation is **interactive television**, a kind of two-way television system. This technology can be found at present in pilot programs performed by broadcasting, cable, or telecommunications companies. Some notable projects are the Time-Warner experiment in Queens, NY, the VIACOM project in Castro Valley, CA, or the GTE trial in Cerritos, CA. Each project is experimenting with a wide range of technologies and services such as unique interactive remote controllers, targeted advertising, interactive game shows and television listings, and electronic yellow page services. Different elements of technologies and services change as the pilots continue. What the final form will look like and when or if they will make it to mass-market distribution is anybody's guess.

CD Video

Another component technology to study is the emerging **CD-Video** standards that are related to videodisc technology. A number of vendors are bidding to use various combinations of hardware with a movie format to deliver digital video. Traditionally, videodisc has been used to deliver most video in multimedia projects, especially in kiosks and educational projects. Although videodisc is a sensible way to show random accessible video, the media itself is large, the seek times are long, and the equipment configuration is complicated. CD

Video may prove to be a much better way to integrate the display as well as be cheaper to produce.

Virtual Reality

Virtual reality gives the user an interactive 3D experience by surrounding the user with a moving simulated world. These systems are extremely expensive, the applications are currently limited, and up to now virtual reality has met with limited commercial success. Related technologies originating from virtual reality are remote location interfaces that permit the operation of robotic and sensory devices from a distance. One of the restrictions of virtual reality is having to put on gloves and glasses. In response to this, a branch of virtual reality called **immersion technology** proposes systems that work with large projected displays and motion detectors. Simple motion detectors react to presence and location information. Musicians have used these in MIDI performances where mallets hit imaginary instruments.

*One promise of digital multimedia is to provide alternate interpretations in media that are different from the original media. The simplest example of this type of **transcoding** between media types is converting speech to text or text to speech. The technical issues are enormous but the utility is clear. Directions could be presented pictorially or spoken depending on the situation at the time. Notes could be typed in or dictated to a computer. The results of a test could be shown numerically in a table, graphed as a picture, animated, presented as a movie, or presented as music. The Media Lab at MIT has pioneered a number of theories about transcoding, deducing theoretically that any medium can be transcoded to another.*

Other Delivery Platforms

IBM's Personal System/2 *product line must be upgraded with sound boards and CD-ROMs but they are good machines to run OS/2 which features IBM's Multimedia Presentation Manager on top of the AVI multimedia extensions.*

IBM's Ultimedia *machines have the equipment and sufficient performance needed to run multimedia. They come with audio boards and a CD-ROM and can run OS/2 using the IBM multimedia extensions.*

NeXT's NeXTSTEP *operating system is targeted at corporate installations creating custom applications. The software runs on its own discontinued hardware as well as on some configurations of Intel 80486-based machines and above.*

Nintendo *and* ***Sega*** *have huge player markets for interactive games. The development environment is extremely technical, and in Nintendo's case, they control many of the business relations concerning developers. Storage and reusability of data is also a limiting factor.*

Tandy's Video Information System (VIS) *is a small device that is based on Microsoft's Modular Windows, a downsized version of Windows. Modular Windows omits the Program Manager interface, fonts, multitasking, and supports remote control interfaces.*

The ***Sony Multimedia CD (MMCD)*** *is a small market player that requires a Windows development environment.*

The ***CD-I*** *market, pioneered by Philips and SONY, has a controlled development environment and, at the moment, relatively limited distribution.*

Silicon Graphics computers *run in a UNIX environment and provide high-end graphics capabilities. The Silicon Graphics' Iris, Indigo, and Crimson workstations are particularly good at doing computation for QuickTime and animation rendering.*

Sun *and other* ***UNIX workstations*** *have a few authoring tools but lack many of the standard production tools available on the more common multimedia platforms.*

Amiga *has a devoted market of graphics enthusiasts, partly the result of a unique hardware and software product called Video Toaster that can be used for online video editing and generating computer graphics.*

3DO *is a company that licenses technology to hardware manufacturers creating interactive multimedia players.*

Early Visualization

Research on the idea and on the market and the creation of a good plan will not go far if the elements can not be communicated effectively to others. The way to communicate early ideas and concepts, especially to someone who is new to the technology, is to provide some type of visualization of the project. **Early visu-alization** is a way of clarifying abstract concepts and kindling a client's imagination about the project. It can complement a written proposal and put a team in a better situation to receive funding or internal approval for resources.

Descriptive words can create powerful visions but words alone cannot capture the multi-faceted experience of

Interview: Rosalyn Bugg

Rosalyn Bugg is a CD-I (Compact Disc-Interactive) producer in the Fantasy Factory Games Group at Philips Interactive Media of America (PIMA). Her educational background is in television and film production, and her professional experience includes studio and field program production, writing, and project coordination. At PIMA, she was working as the facilities coordinator when she seized an opportunity to produce Jazz Giants, a CD-I title in Philips' "Jukebox" series of interactive music compilations.

Explain Philips' Jukebox concept.
"Jukebox" was already a genre at Philips and I tried to apply my experience of TV and film to the work I was doing. When Jazz Giants began, the original proposal was for a 90 minute disc, with artists spanning the spectrum of jazz from the early 1920s through the 1980s. I took the TV angle which immediately asks, "Where is my hook? Who am I going after with this thing?" I did background research on the jazz culture and the musicians and it seemed that the richest period of music was 1945 to 1965. I narrowed the original list down to only those musicians who worked between that period. Then I did more research to get a strong feel for how the thing should look and what it should say.

Where did you do research?
I interviewed people and read as many books as possible on the subject. I looked at the period and at the people who were working in the period. I decided that the target dates were between 1945 and 1965. Now I can build a structure, I thought. I made up a bunch of cards on a board as I did when working for talk shows in television.

When you work on a TV talk show, there's usually a big board on the wall. This board tells who is doing what on what day. If somebody or something drops out, you can take the card out and you know you have a hole to fill. You know you've got to put somebody else up there.

So I made a big board filled with all of the musicians who could be on the board. I was also limited to using only those who were in the Polygram catalog because it is easier for us to get the rights. Luckily Verve, which is owned by Polygram, was a very important jazz label. I made a big board filled with people and said OK, these are all the people that could be in. I organized them by status, then started cutting and pasting.

How did you decide on what to choose?
The criteria for Jazz Giants were:

- *Were they popular between 1945 and 1965?*
- *Was the recording between 1945 and 1965?*
- *What instrument do they play?*
- *What is their status within jazz community?*
- *And an even bigger issue, how long is the song?*

The Jukeboxes are basically slide shows. I set a time limit, between two and five minutes, with the understanding that it's easy to lose someone's interest in the show if it's any longer than that. Because of this criteria, some of the prominent artists got bumped because their songs were too long. The longest song on the disc is about 4 minutes and 45 seconds and the shortest is just over 2 minutes.

So you set these constraints to make life easier?
Yes, it definitely makes life easier. I knew what I wanted. What I wanted was something that looked elegant, reflected the period, and showed the history of people we were talking about.

The CD-I is laid out in a timeline. I called it "From Big Band to Bossa Nova." It includes artists such as Count Basie, Lester Young, Max Roach, Lionel Hampton, Sarah Vaughn, and Stan Getz. It's being sold wherever CD-I players are sold.

What accounts for the different approaches among producers?
The approaches are different because the producers are different and the environments in which you work are different. You have to trust your own gut. I set the constraints because it gave me a vision of what the whole thing was going to look like. If you do one thing one way and another thing another way, you don't know what will happen at the end of it. You have to have a theme overriding everything. For me, I chose the criteria that told me how the product would look.

I've had to mediate between the engineers and the artists. Everybody wants something out of this. Everyone puts a lot of their heart, their soul, their time, their effort into these projects. Everyone wants their vision to be used. And you have to try to get their vision as well as Joe's vision and Jeannie's vision and your executive producer's vision in. You have to make everybody think and feel that what they are working on is a part of them.

Once you become committed to a vision, how willing are you to change it?
I have to be flexible to a point. You have to measure the effect your stubbornness or lack of stubbornness is going to have. It's always a matter of checks and balances, of cause and effect. It's saying, "All right, I have an idea of what it will look like. What's going to happen if I stick with this? What's the worst case? What's the best case?" And then you stay with your decision.

What are your biggest challenges as a producer?
Being balanced is one and keeping your eye on the prize, the final end product that everyone can be proud of. It's learning when to force the issue and when to mediate, when to let someone else run with an idea and when to let go, and when to realize that your initial concept might not be the best one. The other challenge is trying to get the movie you see in your head, or in my head, onto the disc. I see projects in terms of visuals, of how they look in addition to how they work. If multimedia is going to work effectively, it's going to have to remember who it's competing with.

multimedia. The best early visualization tool is a **proof of concept** or simple prototype that illustrates the basic look and feel of a product. This type of prototype does not have to be elaborate, but it should capture the attention of people who may be involved with the project. The visualization could also be an earlier example of a similar work taken from a project team's digital portfolio. Steve Nelson of the multimedia firm Brilliant Media attests that his prototype of an interactive music title opened doors for him with musicians, publishers, and potential sponsors.

Evaluate Whether You're Ready for the Next Step

At the end of this stage, a well-formed project plan should exist. In the case of custom projects, a **proposal** may need to be written, presented to the client, and then signed. It is important not to proceed too far into a custom project without some type of formal agreement. If more exploration is needed, then consider making arrangements with the client to have them pay for the additional exploration.

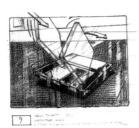

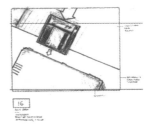
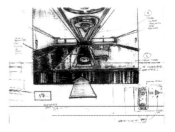

If an early prototype is not feasible, it may be possible to show sketches or diagrams of the relationships among media elements and interactions. To illustrate sequences and interrelationships of images and events, a rough **storyboard** ▶ 136 can be effective. Some computer tools provide effective and inexpensive ways to create these storyboards or some other visual depiction to show to people. These tools include desktop presentation applications, image processing and video editing software, animation programs, some authoring tools, or any other type of software that will help convey the experience of the project.

Try not to get too discouraged by unsettling information learned in this stage. Market data can be wrong. Something not technically feasible now may be feasible in a year. Content that is expensive to license now may not be in the future. Most issues are likely to change dramatically in the coming months and years. Consider restating a project to do what is possible now, keeping in mind what may be possible in the future.

When the idea, finances, people, resources, and work environment are in place for the remaining stages and when the delivery media and platform, and production platform are resolved, the project team can then move on to the design and prototype stage.

One of the most important elements in dealing with a client is to manage the expectations effectively. Make sure that any piece of content, feature, or element shown to a client can be included in a product or at least outline the conditions that those elements hinge on.

Concept and Planning Tips

- Take care of items well before you think you need to.
- Keep the audience in mind when forming your concept.
- If you're going to do a project, then do it. If not, put it away and move on.
- Clients and investors may not be able to visualize a project as well as you can. You may have to develop something that expressly shows them.
- Ask stupid questions.
- Find out what you don't know.
- Start the licensing and permissions process early.
- Think big.

Design and Prototype

Design and Prototype

One of the secrets of the team of inventors working with Thomas Edison was that they generated thousands of prototypes. The idea for the light bulb was simple. It was their process of making plenty of models and then selecting the best ones that made the distinction. This method is similar to what goes on in the design and prototype stage of many multimedia projects.

Too many project managers think that there is too little time and money to spend on prototyping and move too quickly to production before they've adequately thought out their needs.

... it's awfully hard to be pious about the printed word when the National Enquirer uses the same medium as Shakespeare. Brilliance has always coexisted quite comfortably with trash in any genre, and the same is already true of interactive media. There are plenty of bad titles out there, and the unfortunate pioneers who are buying them find they're chock full of gratuitous button clicking, disco music, and flashing video. A good interactive title chooses the best information from all the media at its disposal and combines them into something indefinable yet powerful.

— Denise Caruso, former editor of Digital Media (now at Friday Holdings), in Utne Reader, Jan/Feb 1993

At first glance, the prototype and production stages seem the same. Both involve creating and editing content for interactive use on the screen. But while **production** steps emphasize repetition, automation, fine quality, consistency, and volume output, **prototyping** emphasizes exploration, rough quality, trial runs, and evolving standards. Many of the same processes and techniques are used in both stages, but prototyping helps a team make decisions that will simplify and improve production processes.

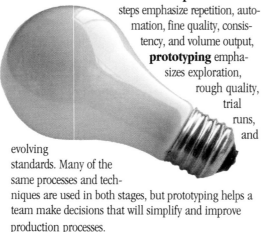

The design and prototype stage is also a time for refining the **project plan** ▶ 67 after determining accurate times for completing tasks. The project manager should keep track of progress and communicate any changes in responsibilities, constraints, or expectations to everyone on the team and, if applicable, to the client. In addition, this stage tests the appropriateness of the technology as well as the dynamics of the team.

Design is the deliberate creation of a shape and structure that embodies a concept. The industrial designer Victor Papanek defines design as "the conscious effort to impose meaningful order." To prove that a design can work is the purpose of a prototype. A **prototype** is a working model of the conceptual design. You may have already used a simple prototype to help other people visualize your concept earlier in the planning stage. In the design stage, the prototype grows in importance as it becomes a kind of "multimedia drawing

board." Designers use it to try out ideas about interface design, image resolution, or optimization schemes. Working within constraints of time and budget, they evaluate, discard, keep, and reshape designs again and again until the right model is attained. This **iterative** routine eventually yields the final form and the specifications used in production.

Designing for multimedia integrates the challenges inherent in each medium. Text, audio, and video each have different design conventions, standards, and vocabularies. Multimedia product development requires the integration of different media into an appropriate balance. Equally as important, multimedia brings with it another challenge for developers—the design for **interaction** ▶ 67. Although audiences respond to or learn from other media such as stories, songs, or films, they can directly interact with multimedia.

Kickoff Meeting

A positive way to begin the design and prototype stage is to gather everyone involved with the project to discuss the project direction and plan. This gathering is referred to as a "**kickoff meeting.**" Depending on the project, a kickoff meeting can be an informal living room discussion among ad hoc team members or a structured meeting in a corporate board room. The kickoff meeting, in a sense, is like telling a patient what is going to happen before, during, and after an operation. It reiterates goals, roles, expectations, and strategies from the beginning of design to the end of testing and beyond. It also serves to unite the team, often only a core group of key players, in a spirit of mutual understanding and commitment. Whether the project is for a custom application or commercial product, all must agree on the project details before committing time, energy, and resources to a project.

For custom projects, the kickoff meeting is an opportunity to introduce the client to the individuals who will help build the product. The purpose of this is to emphasize the team effort needed for development and to assure the client of the competence of the individuals involved. Depending on the size and scope of the project, the representatives at the kickoff meeting should include the **project manager** ▶ 16, 66 as well as any **artists**, **designers**, **testers**, **writers**, **animators**, **videographers**, or other staff members who are available to participate in the meeting.

Clarifying Expectations and Understandings

Clarifying **expectations** ▶ 78 and **goals** ▶ 93 in the kickoff meeting is a group activity. Try to find an environment conducive to discussion. Have a way of recording ideas for all to see such as a whiteboard or similar visual aid. Use the project plan to help guide the progression of the meeting. Walk through each part, explain the topics, invite questions, and explore answers. Have clients explain each point in their own words to confirm mutual understanding. Discrepancies—especially concerning deliverables and expectations—must be clarified before development work can proceed. The meeting should be directed toward specific closure of issues.

Multimedia project developers tell war stories of the problems encountered because of work that proceeded on assumption without clear mutual understanding of all involved parties. Problems can arise from misunderstandings of seemingly simple things. There will be a tendency to say "let's see how it flies later" or "we'll cross that bridge when we get there" when confronted with an unresolved part of a project. It is important to erase these ambiguities before they cause problems later.

Working Content

A prototype illustrates a design or an aspect of a design. It is *not* a finished product. The amount of content needed for prototyping is usually a fraction of what will be used in production. **Working content** ▶ 101 can be anything that represents the content to be used in the final product such as text excerpts, sound samples, or video clips.

The amount of working content depends on the reason behind the prototype. An interaction designer who

wants to test several designs for navigational paths may be able to work with dummy illustrations in the prototypes until the flow is right. An interface designer may want to test video clips for appropriate digitization quality before choosing the footage for production. An illustrator may want to compare how different background colors affect the presentation of an engineering schematic. Prototyping shapes the product from different angles. One angle may be technical, another may be design, and still another content.

To assemble working content, a project team needs to review and organize what is already available. Content may not always be readily accessible, though. For example, a client may request a multimedia database front-end and specify that mainframe data to be used without arranging for database access, security clearance, user accounts, or other items the project team needs for designing. The project manager needs to be aware of all content requirements and make sure that content is accessible to the team.

Taking stock of existing content will reveal whether there is enough to start prototyping. "Enough" content is that which covers every intended use of media for the final product. If an interactive game will feature sound, animation, graphics, and video then the prototype should include samples of each medium and demonstrate their interaction. Testing several different samples of each medium is necessary so that each possibility can be compared. To make assumptions about the effect of any one medium without prototyping may create surprises when it comes time for production. At the same time, it is possible to have too much material. The **content expert** ▶ 20, 99 may be faced with catalogs upon catalogs of historical film footage to select from for a project. At this stage, the expert just needs to make a decision and move on.

Content Organization and Audience Review

Arranging content effectively can be difficult without grasping a project's concept and visualizing the user's experience. Multimedia projects that have no meaningful purpose are easy to spot. They are the kiosks that no one uses and the shrink-wrapped boxes that do not move from the store shelves. Revisit the concepts and messages as well as the audiences and purposes identified in the concept and planning stage.

A big goal in a kickoff meeting is to move the focus from the people to the ideas of the project. If you can't accomplish this, bickering typically ensues.

— Kristina Hooper-Woolsey, Distinguished Scientist, Apple Computer

Something that I look for in an associate is a certain amount of misunderstanding of what I'm trying to do. Not a fundamental misunderstanding; just minor misunderstandings here and there. When someone doesn't quite completely understand what you want from them, or when they didn't quite hear what you told them to do, or when the tape is bad, or when their own fantasies start coming through, I often wind up liking what comes out of it all better than I liked my original idea. Then if you take what the first person who misunderstood you did, and you give that to someone else and tell them to make it more like how they know you would want it, that's good, too. If people never misunderstand you, and if they do everything exactly the way you tell them to, they're just transmitters of your ideas, and you get bored with that. But when you work with people who misunderstand you, instead of getting transmissions you get transmutations, and that's much more interesting in the long run. I like the people who work for me to have their own ideas about things so they don't bore me, but then I like them to be enough like me to keep me company.

— Andy Warhol

Design Goals

The design of a prototype should embody the project's **concept ▶ 90**, **purpose ▶ 93**, and **messages ▶ 94**. It is these ideas that guide the design through several iterations. A good design team can generate dozens of design choices as they search for the right one. Good design is usually invisible. Users do not always notice when projects are well-designed (especially with respect to interface and interaction) because the best products operate seamlessly without drawing attention away from the content.

Bad design, on the other hand, is more obvious. Almost anyone can point out everyday items that annoy or frustrate—the victim of poor design. In multimedia, design goes beyond the static presentation. **Interactivity** creates a new experience that, like anything new, invites exploration. The prettiest interface in the world will not help badly designed interaction.

When designing, be willing to move beyond the familiar ways of seeing and doing. The filmmaker and actor Orson Welles said he never understood why any filmmaker would study his films. The issue, he said, is to make a movie—*your* movie, about *your* world. Multimedia developer John Borden has an extensive background in film yet advises others to maintain a fresh perspective and not cling to preconceived notions of how things should work or be accomplished.

Simplicity

The content and interface work together to create an interactive experience. As long as content is presented clearly, it can be as complex as necessary to communicate whatever messages are intended. The interface and interaction, however, should not only be **clear**, they should be **simple**. Too many choices and too many things to remember will only confuse and alienate users. Multimedia that bombards the user with multiple colors, images, sounds, and options without maintaining the purpose will eventually be ignored. In multimedia, less is often more.

Consistency

Strive for a **consistent** design. A consistent design throughout is easy to follow and builds trust with the user. Imagine driving in a city where red sometimes means "go" and sometimes means "stop." Even Wonderland made some sense to Alice once she learned that everything was *consistently* the opposite of what she expected. Simple and consistent design paves the way for understanding and interaction.

Engagement

Multimedia should invite the user to **participate**. It should engage the user. In a sense, the user is having a **conversation** with the multimedia piece. The design should make it easy for the user to have this conversation. A conversation could be based on something as simple as making a selection and receiving a reply or as complex as exploring a city.

Depth

Reward curiosity by designing depth into a multimedia project when you can afford it and when this is your aim. Make sure people can explore more than one level of information, but only if they choose to do so. Most people enjoy exploring and discovering new paths.

Fun

Designing for fun depends on the audience. An architect might enjoy a structural puzzle; a musician might like to play with new sounds. In designing a fun experience, a designer should consider simple issues like use of time. If a title includes animation sequences that take too many seconds to load, only a few people will have enough patience to continue using the product.

Affordability

Finally, a successful design takes into account what a typical user can afford to buy. Different audience segments have different amounts they are willing to spend on a given product. A goal of **market research ▶ 106** should be to gauge affordability. A goal of design should be to accommodate what is possible within a given price. The design may make production easy or hard, an important point when looking at something produced on a periodic basis such as an electronic magazine.

Shaping the Design

Many design ideas can spring from a single concept. A travel guide to a city, for example, can appear as a map, narrative explanation, videotaped tour, handbook, or a combination of these. Shaping each possible design involves generating and exploring a bounty of ideas about the nature, purpose, and structure of information. The ideas to generate when designing a travel guide involve why people would use it, how they would use it, and how it would look. A travel guide for business people might include a listing of places to have "power breakfasts" while a travel guide for Japanese visitors might include audible pronunciations of English words.

Some multimedia designers look at people's participation with media and computers as being hot or cool. Designers can set the "throttle" to be any speed they like.

Hot *The user is physically interactive. This is generally true of quick-paced, high resolution, loud experiences that demand a lot of the user. Perception and involvement are hot.*

Cool *The user is not engaged in physical interaction but mental interaction is high. Cool experiences are not "cold" but cool in the sense that jazz is cool. These let the user breath, are generally quieter, less stressful, and slower paced. Interpretation and abstraction are cool.*

A game designer asked his neighborhood kids, average age 11, what they thought made a game "fun." Without taking their eyes off the screen during an intense round of Super Mario, one kid said, "Good graphics." Another said, "It's gotta be challenging. It can't let me win too easily." Another said simply, "I don't know. It's just gotta be fun, you know?"

It's easy to become enamored of what you can do, but it's often hard to face the limitations of what must be done. You need to be aware of how design may affect performance.

— Abbe Don, Artist and Interface Designer

Brainstorming

Shaping the design for a multimedia project begins with an outpouring of ideas and creative exploration of possibilities. The real strength of development is in collaboration, and this begins with brainstorming. **Brainstorming** is a dynamic process of generating ideas without judgment or constraint. The purpose of brainstorming is to open the spigot of creativity for everyone involved in the project: managers, artists, production staff, potential users, and client representatives, (if there are any). A good brainstorming session results in a collection of ideas and solutions that become the basis for designs and their prototypes. The ultimate objective of this exercise is to come up with a workable visualization of the design for the information and the interface.

A brainstorming session can take place in a coffee shop or in a conference room. Everyone involved in the project can contribute something, be it technical tips, design ideas, content, or procedural suggestions. The point of brainstorming is to tap into everyone's bank of ideas and solutions about a particular topic. No idea is bad or irrelevant and everyone should feel free to contribute. Some of the best product ideas seem foolish or silly in brainstorming. It helps to "seed" a brainstorming session by focusing on one topic for a particular session. For example, one session could be devoted to generating ideas about content sources. Another could develop ideas for navigation. Yet another could focus on interface design. Someone who has a clear vision of the concept often acts as session coordinator and records ideas as they develop.

There are several tools for recording ideas during brainstorming sessions. A **whiteboard** is a popular tool because it is portable, reusable, and easily viewed by a group. Other tools for capturing ideas are **blackboards**, **flip charts**, or individual pieces of **paper** that are later collected and recorded. **Videotaping** is another tool for recording brainstorming sessions. All in all, people work with the media they are most comfortable with to capture ideas that will build information about the concept and design of the project.

Information Design

Solving communication needs is an essential design task for any product. **Information design** ▶ 32 addresses ways to organize and present information in a meaningful and useful form. It includes the information in all media (whether textual, aural, or visual) and, to some degree their interaction. Where **graphic design** ▶ 24 is primarily concerned with creating a beautiful visual arrangement of information, information design is concerned with creating a clear, accurate, and meaningful arrangement of information. This is not to say that graphic design and information design are necessarily at odds. In the best case, information can be both attractive *and* meaningful, and succeed from both standpoints.

Information design can affect the color, layout, sequence, and styles of any media, but it is most concerned with the organization of all elements in an entire product. The organization affects the communication of those elements. For example, reorganizing all of the words in a dictionary by order of everyday use instead of alphabetical order would change how a user might search for words or make associations.

Visual dictionaries use pictures and scenes to allow users to find a word for something they can identify by sight. A thesaurus groups words by similar or opposing meanings. Each solution solves a particular need.

In his book *Information Anxiety,* Richard Saul Wurman identifies five general ways to organize any information:

- Alphabetically
- By time
- By location (either geographic or something more relevant)
- Along a continuum or magnitude
- By category

When balanced with an appealing interface, information design can be used to create a powerful use of multimedia.

More great ideas happen by complete accident than by trying to think of great ideas.
— Brooks Cole, President, Brooks Communication Design

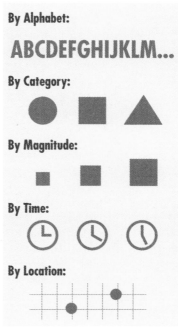

By Alphabet:

ABCDEFGHIJKLM...

By Category:

By Magnitude:

By Time:

By Location:

Alphabet

An example of organizing data alphabetically is a telephone directory or Rolodex file. Alphabetical organizations have no inherent meaning but most people who speak Roman-based languages are more than familiar with this sequence of letters. However, the **alphabet** does not necessarily translate into other languages. Users who speak Asian, Semitic, or Cyrillic languages may be unfamiliar with "an alphabet" and thus unable to find things.

Time

Organizing by **time** can be effective in relating events to each other. Train schedules and theater listings do this because this is the most important aspect of their use. A timeline might be the navigation method for a multimedia piece depicting the evolution of a species. Time is a particularly useful organization because just about every culture on earth shares a common method of measuring time. In fact, the international time standard is active in nearly every spot throughout the world (although somewhat confusingly in Southern Asia and along the north coast of South America).

Location

Ordering information by **location** is a common form of presenting spatial relationships and is particularly effective when such relationships are part of the message. Maps are obvious examples of organizations by location. A less obvious example is a medical book that starts at the top of the body (the head) and works its way down to the toes (the thigh bone's connected to the knee bone...). A multimedia piece about automobiles, for example, might explain each component and major subassembly when users click on that component from a detailed illustration of a car. The illustration essentially forms a "Table of Contents" for the product.

Continuum

Continuums or magnitudes can be anything with two opposing parameters. Number systems like the Dewey Decimal system, used to catalog books in a library, are continuums where major ideas are represented with a number from 0 to 999; minor ideas are divisions from the major represented by a decimal number from .000001 to .999999. Magnitude can be from "best to worst," "least to most," or "biggest to smallest" or vice versa. A multimedia title about movies might be organized from highest to lowest revenues or highest to lowest budget. A game might be organized by levels of difficulty.

Category

Finally, content can be organized by **category**. Categories can be obvious or unexpected. They should be chosen to reveal something about the content itself. How content is grouped or separated speaks for the purpose and understandings its creators intend to communicate. Newspapers, for example, are often organized by categories such as Business, Entertainment, Sports, Food, Books, and Classifieds.

Multiple Organizations

A product should have a single, clearly understood organization, but sub-organizations are often necessary. The **organizations** and arrangements of sections may also be different. A cookbook could be organized alphabetically by cuisine, with recipes within each cuisine ordered by level of difficulty. Or, the types of cuisine could be organized geographically, with each cuisine's recipe further organized by type of ingredient. Different ways of organizing information can be combined, depending on the nature of the content and the intent of the project.

Indexes

There is almost always one primary organization (and possibly finer organizations within this) but it may be helpful to include alternate organizations in the form of **indexes** ▶ 162, 181. An A-Z index is a common alternate organization for many books. An index of illustrations, footnotes, or maps are other examples. Indexes can be ordered by location, category, alphabet, time, or magnitude. The Roles and Projects sections at the beginning of this book are a way of accessing the rest of the book from specific perspectives on roles and projects.

Users have different needs and interests. One user might want to search for a particular movie or sound that was seen or heard while using a product. Perhaps there should be an easy way to find only examples of sounds. Review the section on Text for ideas on multiple criteria for searching text. Sometimes, more than one or two indexes can be powerful supplements to the principal organization.

Hypertext

Hypertext can pose a particular problem depending on the degree of links within a project. How do you organize a product when the user can jump from anywhere to anywhere? And how do you make the relationships visible when they are ubiquitous? The answer is probably to choose one primary organization that is clearly represented to users and leave some visual cues about passages through this organization. Hypertext **jumps** ▶ 145, 162 can be interwoven for

While the alphabet is just as much an organization by continuum as a number system, it is such a common and understood one (in Western culture, at least), that it is pulled out as a separate method.

The best way to organize information is the way that most easily reveals what you want to communicate.
— Richard Saul Wurman, "Hat Racks for Understanding," Design Quarterly, 145

user convenience but not to the point where the user becomes trapped in "no-man's land." Organize a product in a way that expresses the intentions for the content. Consider including secondary and tertiary organizations and multiple ways of accessing this content.

Information Design Tools

When organizing information, certain tools lend themwselves well to certain functions. A map or diagram might be useful to depict interaction or relationships of different elements. Outlines describe order and sequence well. Information maps informatively describe elements and their connections, especially when the connections outnumber the connecting points. (An information map is a web or tree that shows all the elements and connections between them.)

In film, theater, or video production an effective tool for visualization is a **storyboard** ▶ 136. A storyboard is an illustrated scene-by-scene plan for telling a story and for indicating the balance of visual and aural elements in each scene. Storyboards, by nature, are organized by time since that is the unifying component. In many ways the experience of multimedia is like that of film or theater, meaning that several forces are at play in creating a rich experience. A storyboard, therefore, can be a useful tool for describing the multiple "tracks" that work together to create a multimedia experience.

Another useful tool for designers is a **notebook** to capture design ideas for future reference and to communicate them with others as necessary. A glimpse into a designer's notebook might reveal pencil sketches of screen designs, rough outlines of navigational paths, quick studies of animated characters, phone numbers of possible recording studios, or anything that represents the flood of thoughts-in-process that are inevitable in any design process.

Interface Design

Interface design ▶ 97 is very much like information design but its domain is mainly screen display and interactivity with computers and electronic devices. Many of the same organizational concerns apply but there are some additional ones that deal with specific media and with specific interaction in an electronic environment. Interface design encompasses everything a user sees, touches, hears, and interacts with. While many project managers, programmers, and interface designers define interface design as a primarily visual exercise dealing mostly with screen, button, and icon design, its scope extends to include all visual components

as well as audio elements and, most importantly, interaction and navigation.

The interface design orients the user to the experience or message of the project. Paradoxically, the best interface is one that is *transparent* to the user, meaning that it does not distract from the purpose and message of the experience. A transparent interface is one that is so subtle and quiet that users do not perceive an interface at all. Elements of the interface range from screen layout and color selection to modes of interaction such as a touch screen, keyboard, joystick, or voice control.

Principles of Interface Design

Interface design presents a challenge of balancing different traditions of communication to create a meaningful and understandable experience for people. The first question an interface designer should ask is, "What is the experience people should have?" **Defining the experience defines the interface design.** If the experience is a conversation, the interface should draw from the conventions of human conversation. If the experience is that of a journey, the interface should give a person the means to orient and explore. A good interface respects human intelligence and faculties without getting in the way of understanding. A poor or non-intuitive interface continually reminds people that they are working with a machine.

Each medium has a tradition of experience and a history of how people relate to it. Reading a book may seem like a passive experience but people do more than just read the words. They underline them, dog-ear pages, scribble notes in the margins, look up words in a dictionary, drop the book accidentally in the tub, and lend them to friends. One of the challenges of interface design is to allow the user as much control of the environment as possible.

The Apple *Human Interface Guidelines* present principles of the Apple Desktop Interface and the particular specifications of standard interface elements. These guidelines can be interwoven with the design conventions of other media such as literature, music, video, and film.

Metaphors

A metaphor allows someone to understand and **experience** one kind of interaction in terms of another more familiar kind. Use **metaphors** based on real-world experience and make them clear so that users have a set of expectations to apply to the computer environment. Carefully craft a visual, aural, and behavioral environment to support the metaphor. Build a stable and consistent world for the metaphor. Even an interactive game that takes place on the distant planet *Devargas* should give the player a way to find their way around.

Graphic elements such as typeface, color, style, and spacing help convey the intent of the basic information but they cannot create order, information, or quality where there is none to begin with. Graphic elements add most to the communication intent when they work with, and not in place of, the overall structure.

Here is interactive design in a nutshell. Nobody wants to read a manual. Nobody wants to wait. Everybody wants to be in control. When I design a product I want to make it accessible. I want you to forget about the computer so that you're absorbed in the environment of the game or reading product. And I think that learning should be fun. The challenge is to tie all of those pieces together into a compelling environment that involves you, and where you leave it feeling you've got something.
— Mark Schlichting, Creator and Designer of Brøderbund's Living Books

Sometimes structuring the interface in a metaphor can clarify the interaction. One might present information about a city with a street map interface. An interactive program to teach research skills to young people might use the metaphor of an archeological excavation,

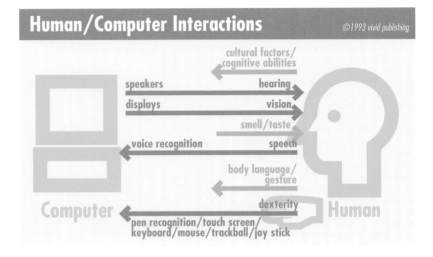

Human/Computer Interactions ©1993 vivid publishing

The most important thing I learned [doing interfaces for animals] is that if you want to do a quality job, do not assume anything about the user. Make sure that during the design phase there is a dialog going between the designer and the user or someone who understands the user. This is much easier to remember when you have engineers like us designing for a gorilla, but when a human designs for another human, it's too easy to assume that the user is you!

The second important thing I learned is that you don't get a second chance. If a user interface does not work right the first time, you stand a high chance of losing the user. They won't come back for a second try. Ron Cohn [a researcher at the Gorilla Foundation] served as Koko's tester and made sure that the system we delivered was extremely responsive to Koko's inputs. Any delays in button hilighting and audio feedback would break the cause-effect relationship we were trying to establish.

— Mike Clark, project manager on a project to design a computer for Koko the gorilla

complete with maps, excavation "tools," "finds," and perhaps a local guide. Organizing the interaction around a metaphor can only be useful if the metaphor is familiar, stable, and consistent. Misusing a metaphor can range from being corny to irritating to unusable.

Direct Manipulation

People want to feel that they are in charge of the computer's activities. They expect their physical actions to have physical results and want their tools to provide feedback. Objects and their properties should be movable. This is especially true of multimedia programs which invite interaction.

See-and-Point
(instead of remember-and-type)

People select actions from alternatives presented on the screen. They rely on recognition, not recall; they should not have to remember anything the computer already commands. A multimedia program that requires a complex manual for the users may not last long. If people understand *what* has to be done, they can usually figure out *how* to do it. For example, if someone wants to quit a program, they will try the obvious first (such as the word QUIT or an EXIT sign) and then explore other options to get the desired result.

Consistency

Effective applications are both consistent within themselves and consistent with one another. People feel centered when they can rely on familiar ways to get things done. With consistent design a person is more likely to take chances on exploration. An icon that indicates "return to screen one" displayed on every screen is reassuring as long as it works consistently. As soon as the icon freezes or brings the person to a screen other than the one expected, that person's faith in the system is shaken.

WYSIWYG
(What You See Is What You Get)

Implement the **metaphor** as realistically as possible. There should be no secrets from the user, no abstract commands that only promise unpredictable results.

User-Initiated Actions

The person, not the computer, initiates and controls all actions. People learn best when they are actively engaged. This is different from the more traditional model, in which the computer acts and the user responds with a limited set of options.

Feedback and Dialog

People appreciate immediate feedback on the progress of an operation. Communication should be brief, direct, and expressed in terms of the user's point of view.

Forgiveness

Users make mistakes; forgive them. Forgiveness means letting users do anything reasonable, letting them know they won't break anything, and allowing them to explore all territory. All actions should be reversible—let users know about any that are not.

Perceived Stability

People feel comfortable in a computer environment that remains understandable and familiar rather than one that changes randomly. Consistent graphic elements provide visual stability; a finite set of objects and actions to perform on them provide conceptual stability.

Aesthetic Integrity

Visually confusing or unattractive displays detract from the effectiveness of human-computer interactions. Avoid clutter. Simplify representation to what is essential for the user to know, hiding the rest. Messes are acceptable only if the user makes them—multimedia applications are not allowed this freedom. The user should be able to control the style and individuality of the experience.

90/10 Functionality

User operations performed often (90% of the time) should be very simple while operations performed infrequently (10% of the time) can be more difficult if necessary. Dangerous operations such as erasing all files should be difficult to do, preventing inadvertent triggering.

Perspective

The **perspective** ▶ 146, 160 or voice conveyed in a work of art, literature, film, or multimedia affects the user's experience. Using first, second, or third person perspectives can change and reshape a story. Since multimedia invites interaction, perspective is largely a matter of audience participation. The **first person** perspective lets the individual user make selections to navigate in the multimedia experience. Successful interactive games immerse the person in the first person experience. **Second person** perspective can engage the user in a participatory experience like a conversation. **Third person** perspectives can convey objectivity and detachment, causing them to appear more credible or official.

Point of View

A **point of view** ▶ 103 in an interactive design can describe a character's experience to the user. It can enliven content by providing perspective, context, and character. Points of view have inherent biases, however, that can influence the information communicated or the way the user understands it. Because of these biases, consider balancing any point of view with an opposing viewpoint. This approach can not only add context to a point of view but enrich its meaning and interpretation.

With a zoologist as content expert, popular writer Douglas Adams is documenting extinct species on a CD-ROM called *Last Chance to See....* The CD-ROM is done with great simplicity integrating pictures, text, and voice. Midway through the text, Richard Dawkins, author of *The Blind Watchmaker* and *The Selfish Gene*, intrudes with counterpoints, explaining how nature eliminates species.

Multiple points of view can be an important feature for training or educational products, reinforcing the idea that there is more than one way to present and interpret information. In one example of a medical project for families expecting a child, the point of view of the mother, father, the nurse, and the doctor can be shown at any point before, during, and after labor and delivery. Such an approach provides a wide opportunity for someone to selectively learn from both the medical professionals' and patients' knowledge and advice about the birth experience.

Agents

In everyday terms, an agent is a force that carries out a specific action. A travel agent designs a trip itinerary. An acting agent promotes his client's acting career. An **agent** ▶ 41 in interface design is a feature that guides the user through interaction by interpreting conditions in the computer and providing knowledge or direction. Some interface designers choose to anthropomorphize agents, that is, give them personalities. The agent in Apple's *Knowledge Navigator* video appears as a human-like personal servant. However, such an extended metaphor is not necessary. An agent can just as easily be an animated neutral creature like Zak in the *Macmillan's Multimedia Dictionary for Children.* An agent's manifestation does not change its function.

An amusing example of a search agent appears in Wim Wenders' film *Until the End of the World.* The agent is portrayed as an animated talking bear called the "Bounty Bear" who performs the complex task of searching multiple networks to identify and locate missing persons. While the computer agent searches algorithmically in memory, the animated agent searches on-screen streets, buildings, and sewers until a match is found.

The advantages of including agents are that they relieve the user of having to perform extensive or repetitive tasks such as writing elaborate database queries or sifting through mounds of information. Agents can provide focused metaphors to simplify processes for a user. If a project has some complex dynamics, it may be unrealistic to expect users to train themselves to understand them. Instead, an agent may be able to handle tasks with only a small amount of information from the user, freeing the user from these responsibilities. Users should be able to "deactivate" the agent to bypass its helpfulness and, in effect, "shut it up."

The decision to personify the agent depends on the nature of the project and the intended audience. Just like people, multimedia agents with the wrong "personalities" can irritate, bore, or even alienate users. The right personality, however, can be very powerful. An animated character might speak more universally as an agent than would a human actor. A friendly character may be more appropriate to some novice or nervous users. The design team needs to validate the use and design of agents by user-testing them in the design phase.

Guides

A lot of confusion exists in interface design between the roles and features of an **agent** and those of a **guide**. Often in multimedia projects, point of view is personified by

How well the user understood and utilized the Visual Almanac was dependent on the language we used to name and describe its elements. The problem was that we were dealing with new ideas, needing to be presented in new ways. Even the language we used to describe things was unique. Words like "nuggets," "goodies," and "building blocks" cropped up as we attempted to label these new concepts.

Any good interface team should include a writer to help define and refine its terminology. The vocabulary has to be consistent, clear, and helpful in communicating to the user.

— Kristee Rosendahl, Visual Almanac Technical Report, Apple Computer, Inc.

Some recommended but rarely seen features of multimedia CD-ROM interfaces are:

- *Ability to export and print text files of "articles" or the text track of a movie.*
- *Extremely low-memory features that write to a hard drive to note where a particular user has been and left bookmarks and to allow a new session to begin where a user has left off in a previous session.*
- *Automated dial-in for product registration, more information, or technical support on a product provided that a modem is connected.*

— Christine Perey

Some computer systems feature artificial intelligence capabilities in the form of agents. An agent is a feature with unique resources, special knowledge, or functions that acts on behalf of the user. Some agents can follow specified rules that describe how to retrieve information or coordinate resources. Agents embody certain features or mechanisms and can perform these tasks independently of a user's control, often giving the impression of a dedicated servant.

characters that respond to queries or impart knowledge. These characters can be called agents (among other things) but function more as **guides**. Guides generally have knowledge to share and only do so when triggered by the user. Agents, however, are more like collaborators or aides. They have structured but modifiable capabilities that act on data or perform specific functions in the background of a project. An example of an agent might be a facility that grabs news items from an online news database responding to changing conditions and inputs. Guides are less dynamic and often relate information from a unique perspective. They do not work without a user's knowledge and the user cannot change their behavior or response. (Examples of guides are Apple's *Guides 3.0* research projects.) Some online help systems provide guides that the user can invoke at will to learn more about specific functionalities or features. It can be reassuring for a user to know that the guide is there if needed.

Navigation

Moving through a landscape requires a means of **orientation** and **navigation** ▶ 141, 162, 165. Here users may deduce direction when given clues that match their intuition. For example, how do people find their way through a forest? They can rely on signs or phenomena such as the angle of the sun, the footprints of animals, or the slope of a hill. They can use a map or compass. They can follow the sound of laughter or the flicker of light toward a campsite. An interface should provide different clues for navigation—for moving forward, backward, and around, as well as for exploring.

How a user navigates depends on the level of interactivity in the multimedia program. In a simple linear presentation, the navigation path is forward or backward; the user hardly needs more than the ability to move in either direction and perhaps bypass screens to return "home."

Interview: Michael Arent

Michael Arent, formerly an interface designer in Apple's Human Interface Group and now at Pacific Bell, has specialized in designing interfaces for multimedia elements.

What are the biggest concerns in interface design for multimedia?

- *The need for ever better applications/titles creation and development tools.*
- *Better scalability and transferability of interfaces across platforms.*
- *Developing better processes and techniques for allowing the end user to participate in the design of multimedia products.*
- *Making sure multimedia "glitz" doesn't overwhelm the basic objective of the application.*

What are the biggest misconceptions about interface design?

- *That interfaces can be slapped on late in the development process rather than something that is planned and integrated from the beginning.*
- *That guidelines are the formulae for creating good design.*
- *That one person can adequately do the human interface design, testing, and implementation.*
- *That interface design is only software.*

What is a good approach to developing an interface? What are the steps, the process and the sequence?

1. *User studies — understanding who the end users are.*
2. *Design (ideation, sketching, storyboarding, etc.).*
3. *Build (prototype and simulation building).*
4. *Test for usability and evaluate.*
5. *Iterative design and testing until the interface is suitable.*

What should developers look for in an interface designer?

- *Designers that can work in multidisciplinary team situations.*
- *Ideally, a small interface team that can adequately carry out a user-centered, participatory approach to design and implementation using the process described above.*
- *Designers who understand implementation issues and how to deal with their constraints in the design.*

Direct manipulation and metaphors are a few of the interface buzzwords of the past, what are some of the techniques and issues we'll see developed in the future?

Techniques:

- *Interoperability and cross platform consistency: the ability (the dream?) for software and their interfaces to run, look and feel as consistently as possible on different types of computers; e.g., Macs, PCs, UNIX machines, etc.*
- *Ubiquitous communications and information retrieval: communications and retrieval anywhere, anytime.*
- *Adaptive systems ▶ 51, 95 and interfaces: systems and interfaces that seem to intelligently adapt themselves to the user by noticing patterns of interaction or responding to user idiosyncrasies or desires according to expectations. For example, a device that can sense where you are in the geographic world and have navigation information about that part of the world readily available for you.*
- *Usage scalability: operating systems and applications that can naturally scale up, down or across in terms of user physical/mental capabilities, I/O, resolution, color, processing power, usage affordances, etc. An example would be a map navigation application that can scale from a hand-held touchscreen-based, monochromatic device to a mouse-based, full color desktop system with large display.*
- *Sentient interfaces: interfaces that allow interaction across the range of human senses.*
- *Delegative interaction: (see below)*

Issues:

- *More sociological and ethical issues centered around security, intrusiveness, privacy, etc.: the use of certain colors, graphical symbols, certain forms of representation, methods of communication, etc. may be offensive to some cultures or, on the other hand, may enhance communications across cultures. For example, the realistic*

Programs with complex paths are more difficult to navigate and should employ tactics to prevent the user from getting lost. The interface designer and programmer must work closely together to create an environment that makes sense to the user. Include ways for users to orient themselves in the digital terrain they are traveling. For example, tagging sections with **unique colors**, **backgrounds**, **icons**, or **sounds** helps give the user footing in a jungle of hypermedia. Or the designer might provide a set of screen maps which specify territories. The programmer might calculate sequential positions to produce different forms of feedback depending on the order chosen. Other aspects and elements of navigation include the use of consistent terminology, links, and search mechanisms.

Even with hypermedia in which a user can follow several leads of interaction, navigation should follow a structure. As systems grow increasingly complex, so does the challenge of building manageable navigation. The interaction (and, indeed, the interface) should always be clear. Whiz-bang features will not save an interface that is too complex or inconsistent to use. User testing will give the best indication of which features and interface elements are performing well, which need more work, and which should be eliminated.

One rule of thumb is that **the user should not have to go through more than three "hops"** from the initial request to the desired result. Another is to **make sure that users always know where they are**. If the branching for information takes too long or is too deep, the user loses footing, if not patience. Still another is that users should be able to **reverse any action**. If a user clicks to go directly to one place, they should not have difficulty returning to the previous place.

I like to think of interaction design as the primary tool for experience design.
— Kristina Hooper-Woolsey, Distinguished Scientist, Apple Computer, Inc.

One component to good navigation has nothing to do with links, indices, or jumps It is the consistent placement of labels and headlines that describe the hierarchy and position of a particular screen in the whole product.

representation of the human figure as well as inappropriate display of the human body is offensive to Islamic cultures. As communications become more ubiquitous and multimedia and multiple modalities become easier to use, these issues will become more prominent.

As electronic technologies (especially multimedia) and telephone and TV broadcast systems more and more converge, security/privacy, and intrusiveness, etc., will become bigger issues. Imagine an electronic multimedia consumer product catalog that builds a profile of you every time you order a product and customizes its advertising to you based on that profile. Does that scare you? Well it happens today on Prodigy. I recommend reading Marshall McLuhan's and Camille Paglia's writings—especially Camille Paglia's interview, "This Is A Naked Lady" in the premiere issue of Wired *magazine.*

- *Capability of tools to simulate advanced technologies: It is very difficult to get the current prototyping tools to adequately and rapidly simulate such technologies as voice recognition, pen recognition, client/server relationships, collaborative computing, VR/telepresence, etc. Today it requires designers to build time-consuming, robust implementations to see how this stuff should work, which doesn't leave much time for the necessary design iterations.*
- *Interfaces that allow user control and/or adaptation techniques to achieve the correct mixtures of interaction techniques and modalities, such as direct manipulation, delegation, etc. through voice, touch, pen, etc.: Today's interfaces are primarily interacted with via direct manipulation. Often, delegation (passing off) of tasks via voice commands, agent processes, etc. is more appropriate, for example, manipulating virtual 3D objects in a complex scene. Often, many interfaces could be drastically improved by allowing a good mixture of direct manipulation and delegation either through redundancy or user preferences.*

How do you represent interaction concepts and solutions to others on the project team and clients?
- *Role playing scenarios*
- *Use of 'blank models' (if appropriate)*
- *Storyboards*
- *Interactive prototypes*
- *Video task/usage simulations (à la Apple's Knowledge Navigator tape)*

Is there an ideal interface? If so, what are its characteristics: Virtual Reality? Conversation? Personal Interaction?
- *The ideal interface is the one that has been designed with deep understanding of users and their needs.*
- *The best interfaces will result from a design process in which end users have had substantive participation.*
- *An important component in designing ideal interfaces is having good tools that will allow designers to rapidly simulate, test, evaluate and iterate the design. These tools should be easily extensible and have enough flexibility to allow designers to incorporate or experiment with any techniques and technologies that will most effectively result in an appropriate design.*
- *Tools that allow adequate automation in the transfer from design to implementation.*

What is underappreciated about interface design?
- *It is more of an art than a science, and consequently can't be performed by simply following rules.*
- *It takes a lot longer than people think, but doesn't have to take as long as people fear.*

Presenting a map of a system can be a powerful way to orient users. A two-dimensional flow chart or map can describe the navigation system for most products. These should include all of the major places to go. A three-dimensional model might illustrate how more complex systems are organized. (Ideally, three-dimensional maps should be viewable from different perspectives).

Most early storyboards at this stage only detail one area of a project. Creating full storyboards may be an inadequate use of resources and time because of design changes and iterations common in most projects.

Users need to "navigate" the content. They need to be able to answer at any point in time: Where am I? Where have I come from? Where can I go? How do I know what I can interact with? Where are the hot spots?
—S. Joy Mountford, Manager, Apple Design Center

Bookmarks

Some users may need to mark their place in a project. **Bookmarks** can indicate where a user left off last. They can be useful in training applications where users may need to stop and resume their training over several sessions. Markers of some kind can allow users to reference pages that held particular interest for them. One of the challenges is to make these elements easy to search for and access. Another is determining how users can mark these passages and what is needed to do so (with a pointing device or special editing mode, for example).

Group Interactions

Presenting multimedia to large groups can offer several opportunities for interaction. For example, people in an auditorium could view a multimedia program in which only one person, the presenter, controls the flow of the presentation. A more ambitious design might allow each person in the entire group to interact with the program, as with a group voting system. Of course, this would require extra processing, but it could develop shared experiences.

Storyboards

Brainstorming and preliminary design activities should generate several designs—all of which could be the basis for a prototype. The project team should evaluate each possible direction and choose one that best embodies the purpose of the project and the audience experience. If necessary, as many as three different directions can be chosen and presented but only one should be approved for further development.

A **storyboard ▶ 122** is an illustrated scene-by-scene plan for telling a story. Many developers use a storyboard to represent the first stage of a **conceptual design** because it is a clear way to represent actions, images, and narration unfolding over time. It also translates easily into directions for the prototype team. Although draft versions of the storyboard may have already been used, the process of developing a toryboard to represent the final design is a more thorough effort.

The interface designer, scriptwriter, and graphic artist create the storyboard so that it represents each significant frame in detail and maps the important actions. It is a list of sorts that indicates all of the necessary elements for the prototype such as characters, animation sequences, dialogs, music and sound, and maps of the content. The detailed storyboard provides information that allows the project manager to fine-tune the original estimates of the time and cost of project tasks.

Approving the Storyboard

The final storyboard is a specification for all team members that defines the prototype and ultimately the product. For a project to run smoothly, everyone must agree on the content and direction before actual prototyping begins. In custom projects, **clients ▶ 12, 81** should sign-off on storyboards. If the client requests revisions, the project manager needs to measure the impact of the changes. If the changes are big enough to throw the project off course or off schedule, renegotiating the content, schedule, and fees may be necessary. It is not uncommon for projects to reach this stage and go back to the beginning of concept and planning because of changed expectations.

Prototype

The great sculptor Auguste Rodin would fashion a small clay maquette or preliminary model of a statue before committing the time, materials, and people to execute the full scale form in bronze. By doing so he was able to shape his vision and communicate its form so that his team of workers would have no question about how the final piece would look. The preliminary prototype became the model for production and many of the same techniques and processes were used to create both the prototype and the final product. In multimedia development, the purpose of the prototype is essentially the same—to give shape to the ideas presented in the approved storyboard and to pioneer the techniques for production. Prototyping is a time of **experimentation** in which the project team explores the technology, tools, and methods to determine what will work best for the final product.

Interface designers, programmers, content experts, and select artists are needed to work on the prototype. The emphasis is on experimentation and creation, not mass production. Later, in production, more people can be brought together to bring the product to completion based on the model specified in the prototype. Exploring new technology and new ideas brings opportunities for innovation but also raises the question, "Will it work in the real world?" What works in a prototype does not always transfer to a product—at least not without some effort. For example, a prototype of an interface that includes speech-to-text conversion may be incredibly exciting on the high-end machine used for development but may be impractical on the low-end computer intended to be the delivery platform.

Because the prototype is only a slice of the whole product, it is important that it is representative of the best ideas and most impressive capabilities of the product. Make sure that at least one of each element and type of interaction is included in the prototype. Only a fraction of these ideas and features can be shown in most demonstrations of the prototype, but this means that the elements most important to the particular audience can be displayed with more depth and exploration.

Balancing Quality, Time, and Cost

Ideally, the prototype should reflect the highest level of quality in the shortest amount of time at the lowest possible cost but this goal is unrealistic. **Prototyping is a constant balance between three factors—quality, time, and cost.** It is up to the project team, led by the project manager, to define the parameters of each. The permutations are endless. For example, a beautiful but intricate 3D animation may take up too much disk space and take too long to produce to be practical. A professional illustrator who produces stunning 24-bit graphics may charge fees that exceed the budget. Richly-worded but lengthy blocks of text may diminish the fast pacing intended for the project. It is better that such realities be discovered earlier through prototyping rather than later in production.

The **quality of the media** used during prototyping varies with the purpose of the prototype. If the prototype primarily serves to illustrate the design for interaction, then it may not be necessary to include high-quality illustrations, sound samples, and video clips. Inserting placeholders or temporary elements is a useful way to shape the overall design flow. Some sound engineers use audio placeholders when matching sounds to scripts to establish synchronization and to discern the general effect a piece will have. Later, the sounds are mixed and "sweetened" (removing noise or adding consistent ambient sound) for production.

If a prototype focuses on the effect of using a specific element such as animation or video, then it is not enough to work with rough estimates or quick shots. It is important to explore the different ranges of such aspects as lighting, camera angles, and framing so that the best approach and the cost of executing it can be determined before production begins.

Prototype Methodologies

A methodology is a way of structuring the exploration of a design. Different methodologies exist for multimedia prototyping. A prototype can be constructed in a depth-first or breadth-first manner. It can grow through a series of design studies or be represented in simulations. A design can also evolve in a series of rapid prototypes in which the user is an active participant in the design process.

Depth-First

A **depth-first** or "slice" approach focuses on a particular function or area of the overall project and explores it completely before moving on to other areas. An example of the depth-first approach to prototyping was used in the development of the *Macmillan's Multimedia Dictionary for Children.* The project team decided to begin with the letter *A* to examine every possible issue and concern for designing an interactive dictionary for children. Everything from interface design to animation to navigational path was explored in depth, but only for the letter *A.* By constraining the prototype to one letter, the project team could test different elements such as sound synchronization, animation sequences, and accuracy of text. From this they could fix errors and create an appealing interface that paved the way for producing the remaining letters of the alphabet. In this case, the depth-first approach was a complete project in its own right although on a much smaller scale. The depth-first approach is useful for any project that includes recurring instances of a similar structure.

Another example of the use of the depth-first approach is in the creation of *ADAM,* an interactive guide to human anatomy. With *ADAM,* a person can follow the steps a surgeon would take to explore and identify the different layers of the human body, starting with the outer skin and "cutting away" to the bone. Says *Adam* program designer Dan Backus, "We started with the feet and are working up to the head. We are now at the midsection." Each area of the body is researched and represented in depth before the next area is explored. With *ADAM,* the depth-first approach applies to prototyping *and* production. The product is being released in installments as each anatomical area is completed.

Breadth-First

Another way to approach prototyping is the **breadth-first** or partitioning approach. The breadth-first approach blocks out the scheme for the entire project before presenting deep detail. The designer using a breadth-first approach sketches a "big picture" of the project and gradually fills in details. The filmmaker Francis Ford Coppola created a rough videotaped version of *Bram Stoker's Dracula* before committing final scenes to film. Doing this helped him visualize continuity and make decisions more quickly than with viewing separate daily rushes. Multimedia development benefits from breadth-first study because it helps plan the design for interactivity and establish continuity of a project. Glenn Corey of Apple Computer, Inc. makes use of the breadth-first approach when designing interactive videodiscs. He uses HyperCard to prototype the interaction without including detailed illustrations or animations.

Prototyping is an iterative process of dynamic exploration—of trying, shaping, testing, and reshaping.

Put a time limit on prototyping. Design has a tendency to extend beyond a schedule because of the desire to do better and better things.

Iterate your designs as many times as possible by prototyping and gathering user feedback.
—S. Joy Mountford, Manager, Apple Design Center

Case Study: We Make Memories/Share With Me a Story

We Make Memories is a HyperCard/videodisc project that simulates the way Abbe Don's great-grandmother told stories as she weaved in and out of the past and present, the old country and America, English and Yiddish. It also captures the way family history was constructed and passed down to Abbe from her great-grandmother, grandmother, and mother. The interface uses a timeline of family photographs from 1890 to 1990 that enables users to move through time and hear stories from the perspectives of the different generations.

Share With Me a Story is a companion piece developed in response to viewers who often told Abbe their own family stories after seeing We Make Memories. Share With Me a Story enables users to participate in the personal storytelling process by scanning a photo, adding a caption, and telling a story. Their contributions are added to an evolving portrait of a community. Users can also view the stories of their co-contributors.

Project Type:
Interactive Art

Hardware Used:
We Make Memories uses a Macintosh II and 13in. monitor, a Pioneer 4200 LaserDisc player and a 13in. NTSC video monitor.

Share With Me a Story uses a Macintosh IIci or better, 13in. Monitor, a 400MB hard drive, a modified scanner, MacRecorder, and an external microphone.

Software Used:
HyperCard

Team Members and Roles:
We Make Memories: 1 primary member (Abbe Don) and support from numerous people along the way. Andres Edwards did camerawork on the interviews with Abbe. Joe Rosen created the main title graphics and fade-ins on the videodisc. Tim Oren wrote the search engine.

Share With Me a Story: 1 primary member (Abbe Don); Nathan Shedroff produced the on-screen icons and the signage for the first museum installation.

Concept and Planning

We Make Memories started as a three-page prose poem Abbe created after her great-grandmother passed away. It became the organizing thread of an interactive family history project. Abbe originally envisioned a twelve-card electronic book with images and text on each card as well as additional materials called up with "hot buttons." She felt that her original concept, however, relied too heavily on a traditional book layout.

Design and Prototype

For her first real prototype, Abbe used interactive video tape controlled by a HyperCard stack. These media because were readily accessible to her. Again, she felt that this prototype was "boring and stiff" and still looked too much like a book. It had none of the qualities of the experience she intended her audience to have and certainly didn't convey the experience she had listening to her great-grandmother.

After a three month hiatus, she began another prototype and redesigned the interface. Although it was still book-like, she moved the four images of herself, her mother, her grandmother and her great-grandmother to the four corners of the screen, so that they were always available. She decided that the story was wonderful already and didn't need extra gimmicks to dress it up, that in fact, it should remain a linear story. This

enhanced the four different perspectives and integrated the stories in a more "video-like" interface. This new arrangement both simplified the experience and made it more powerful.

Production

Abbe then launched into video and audio production to prepare the content. She both transcribed audio recordings of interviews and transferred them to 3/4" videotape for integration onto the videodisc. She quickly learned that her assumption of each person having an equal amount of storytelling on the videodisc wouldn't work. The audio recordings of her great-grandmother and grandmother's alone filled the space available. She decided to use the best of the stories from each perspective which leaned heavily toward her great-grandmother and grandmother. After doing this, common themes emerged and she cross-referenced all of the content by these themes.

Testing

Next, Abbe created a "check videodisc." She still felt that the interface was stiff and looked for a way of creating a more fluid experience. After playing with desks full of family pictures, she created a collage that combined the montage of family storied with the four portraits. She created a linear scrolling timeline (in decade sections) that provided a fluid representation of the time between each person's generation. She quickly realized, however, that to make this work in HyperCard, she would need to create 500 separate cards by hand with tedious, subtle changes to create the illusion of one continuous timeline. She hacked together a script that would automate this process and the visual component to the interface was complete.

Next, she asked Tim Oren for help in developing the search algorithm that determined which video or studio clip to play when. They ended up with a sophisticated system that would choose only segments not previous played from the chosen perspective and topics that related to the timeline segment visible. If these segments had already been played, the system would cleverly choose other segments that related first by topic and then by time. This relationship was more arbitrary and represented more accurately the experience of listening to her great-grandmother tell stories that would span time and topics throughout the conversation.

Only then did Abbe feel that she had completed her envisioned concept.

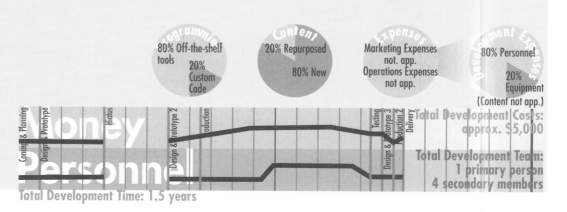

Programming 80% Off-the-shelf tools 20% Custom Code

Content 20% Repurposed 80% New

Expenses Marketing Expenses not. app. Operations Expenses not app.

Development Expenses 80% Personnel 20% Equipment (Content not app.)

Money **Personnel**

Concept & Planning · Design & Prototype · Hiatus · Design & Prototype 2 · Production · Testing · Design & Prototype 3 · Production 2 · Delivery

Total Development Time: 1.5 years

Total Development Costs: approx. $5,000

Total Development Team: 1 primary person 4 secondary members

Then, when he is satisfied with the flow, he copies the design into Macromedia Director and proceeds to fill in detailed sound, animation, and video.

Design Studies

Another way to approach prototyping is to construct a series of design studies. A **design study** is a focused study or experiment that explores a particular design problem on a small scale. The study can be a formal endeavor that involves the entire team or a one-on-one run-through conducted by the interface designer and the videographer. The purpose of a design study is to provide a realistic idea of how a specific aspect of the system may affect the final outcome. A single design study, for example, can help determine whether video clips or single frames would be more effective for a particular project. Another design study might test users' reactions to foreground and background colors. Another might resolve a question about using a video-disc or QuickTime movies. Design studies help uncover potential problems with production, implementation, and even team dynamics before heavy investments are made in time, effort, and money.

Simulation

A **simulation** is a type of prototyping that fully illustrates some aspect of the product design without full functionality. Simulations illustrate the "look and feel" of a product but do not offer depth. The advantage of a simulation is that it captures the imagination of the project team and client as it depicts the essence of the design. A good simulation can be an effective "buy-off" tool because it demonstrates the promise of the product to other people, especially the client. Simulations are useful to show the effect of multimedia to those who have minimal experience with it, such as new clients or traditional artists who are unfamiliar with digital technologies.

The danger of a simulation is that it can raise expectations that the final product may be unable to meet. Before showing any simulation to a client, the project manager should consult with the project team members to guarantee that any magic displayed in the simulation is something they are capable of accomplishing in the final product.

Prototyping Tools

Because prototyping is a dynamic, iterative process of trying, testing, and retrying ideas, prototyping tools should enable rapid turnaround of ideas and solutions. It is also not always necessary to use the same tools for prototyping as for development. Some development tools may be too unwieldy or low-level to use for rapid prototyping while many prototyping

tools may be too slow or incapable to be delivery tools. Separate prototyping tools can be used to prototype navigation, interaction, and interface and to lay in content. Care must be taken, however, to avoid implementing features not possible with the chosen delivery tools.

The prototyping tools selected for a project depend on the amount of **programming** ▶ 32, 208 expertise available. An expert programmer might be able to write a custom tool geared specifically to a project. If programming expertise is unavailable, another option is to use a standard authoring tool. Some authoring tools are really toolkits that provide ready-to-use templates and simple controls for arranging elements into a standard configuration. Although the tools have the advantages of speed and relative ease of use, they may not allow much originality in the features, interface, or screen design. Other authoring tools are construction sets with a scripting language that allows the interaction to be customized. These offer a much higher degree of control but are more difficult to use and will probably require programming knowledge.

Tools and Engines

A multimedia project needs some basic tools to organize content, to build an interface, and to structure the sequence of interaction for the user. Most projects are built either from a proprietary and custom-built engine or from one of the many shrink-wrapped authoring tools on the market. For example, the Brøderbund Living Books are all built on top of their own custom engine. The CD-ROM game *Total Distortion* is made principally from the authoring tool Macromedia Director. Custom engines and authoring tools each have their own advantages.

Custom Engines

A **custom engine** is often developed with a specific purpose or need in mind. This can include building an engine for a family of products, providing support for multi-platform products, integrating special features, or optimizing performance for specific content types or delivery media. Some custom-built engines are built on top of existing authoring tools but others, especially those used for interactive games, are developed from scratch and require months of specialized software programming. Ambitious engines are sometimes made to provide everything for the product. They have items such as proprietary video compression, sound processing, or memory management. An example is the *Sherlock Holmes* series of CD-ROMs which provides exact control of features like lip-synched video.

Participatory design is when potential users work directly with project designers and artists to build a product or prototype. The design team and group of users work together to generate ideas, test their execution, give feedback, and revise a design repeatedly until a working model is achieved. Users may not know what they want until they see it. Rapid prototyping in this manner gives them information to make decisions. Participatory design is useful for projects that will help people carry out specific functions such as diagnostic or maintenance tasks.

One advantage of participatory design is acceptance. If the intended audience has a hand in designing and building a project, they are more likely to use and promote it. The challenge of participatory design is maintaining the project scope. Potential users may want to include features that are not realistic within established constraints of time, budget, and technical feasibility. Another possibility is that so many people may contribute to the project that it lacks overall consistency.

Developing a custom engine takes serious resources and commitment.

The same authoring tool can be used for both prototyping and production, different authoring tools can be used for each stage, or an authoring tool can be used for prototyping and then a custom-built engine developed for production.

Most engines that do not use an existing authoring tool as a foundation are built on top of an operating system and use standard multimedia extensions for that platform. These fully proprietary engines are rarely designed for full system compatibility. In addition, they usually have a difficult time sharing data with other programs because of the many specialized programming skills required to add these capabilities. Creating a custom engine may also mean having to support new **platform models** ▶ 118, operating systems, and other components. Custom engines definitely require more testing to ensure compatibility with all possible hardware and software configurations. They are also likely to be much more costly and troublesome than using "off-the-shelf" authoring tools.

For best performance, a programmer might write a custom application in a standard programming environment. This process is comparable to writing more traditional software for computers. Such custom programs use the programming resources available to the computer platform to access its operating system commands. They require computer language tools, editors, compilers, and other development tools.

Authoring Tools

A multimedia **authoring tool** is a general purpose program that lets designers create an interface to navigate multiple media and choreograph content. Although authoring tools have a lot in common with each other, each one seems to have a special focus. They all handle media types to a differing degree, provide different kinds of interface tools, and are built and programmed in different ways. If you find an authoring tool that does everything you need for a project, you are fortunate. Authoring tools today are generally designed to build interfaces and organize content using three different metaphors—cards and stacks, icons and diagrams, and time and sequences.

Cards and Stacks

Some authoring tools are suited to be presented as a series of cards in stacks or as pages in books. They have many cards, pages, or screens filled with text and graphics. HyperCard and SuperCard, for example, are particularly good for projects that have large numbers of screens with repetitive elements. Backgrounds in these programs allow common elements to remain unchanged and manage memory better within tight memory constraints.

Icons and Diagrams

Some tools present an overview of all content and programming as a diagram and look more like an electronic erector set. Authorware from Marcromedia is a good example of this type of metaphor. Each element

Future object-oriented development systems promise to simplify the mixing of established tools. Several companies are now developing such object-oriented operating systems. This should help developers build large scale multimedia engines more rapidly.

appears as an icon and represents objects like a screen or menu. When an icon is selected, dialog boxes are filled in to give it special properties, and then laid out with other iconic objects and connected by lines to show order and dependency. These tools work best when projects are made of a large number of different parts and require continual detailed management. These tools, however, may not be ideal for projects that require substantial visual changes or require careful synchronization of media. They do provide a general routine for organizing and building large projects such as institutional courseware.

Time and Sequences

Other tools are essentially time-oriented and act more like drawing or animation programs by providing synchronization of content elements. Macromedia Director with its animation-based environment is an example of an authoring tool in this category. Projects built with a time-oriented tool manage media objects in detail. These objects are dynamically triggered at certain points in time on a presentation stage.

Researching Authoring Tools

A good authoring tool will offer certain features that are useful in building multimedia projects. Some are simple while others have more industrial strength elements. Industrial strength systems are needed for large projects, fast performance, and handling large volumes of content with many individual elements. Authoring tools are evolving as the multimedia industry grows and are becoming increasingly powerful. Look at both the old and new tools to find the right mix for the needs of your project.

Ease of Use

The ability to quickly build and modify an interface and to add content of any media type is a powerful capability that can reduce design and production schedules and budgets tremendously. Many authoring tools today are highly visual making them easier to operate than having to write scripts and perform other time-consuming tasks. Many improvements can still be made, though.

Interface Tools

The ability to graphically create and modify elements such as buttons, fields, menus, graphics objects, and timing controls is important for rapidly constructing interfaces. Toolkits for building and connecting interface elements should be as simple, visual, and as unconstrained as possible.

Transitions

Blending screens or media through the use of fades, cuts, dissolves, wipes, and other effects helps create a better flow of content. **Transitions** can be colorful and subtle (Macromedia Director) or fairly simple (HyperCard or SuperCard).

Navigation

Navigation ▶ **134, 165** tools such as links, branching, screen movement, and support for building maps and overviews is helpful. Links let you move between any part of the built content. Some let the user make any relationship through links or mark any area to return to at any time with bookmarks. Program branching is another way to move around built content. Overviews and maps are usually custom built, but are sometimes automatically provided by some tools.

Search Engines

Search engines ▶ **162** are the hidden magic of some systems. The size, speed, and capabilities differ. HyperCard has fast text searching but can only work with limited sizes of text in fields. Some authoring tools do not have text searching capabilities and require custom programming to add them.

Media Support

Support for text, graphics, photos, sound, animation, and video such as **QuickTime** ▶ **153, 208** as well as **color-support** is one of the first features to look at. Almost all provide an ability to create type and graphics in place. Authoring tools are adding the ability to compose and edit some of these media with special tools. Developing content in place is a useful time-saving feature in prototyping. Sometimes the content quality is good enough for production although specialized content tools and artists are more commonly used in production. Timing controls for **synchronization**, event handling, and precise triggering of events are important for sound and video work.

Cross-Platform Capabilities

Decisions about supporting different delivery platforms can have a big impact on deciding what authoring tool or authoring tools to use. Some developers use tools that work on multiple platforms while others use different tools that operate similarly. There are also tools that support cross-platform playback but support authoring on only one.

Playback Environment

If a product is planned for mass-market distribution, it may be wise to use an authoring tool that provides playback capabilities outside of the full authoring environment. This makes it easier and less expensive for users to use a product because they will not have to purchase the authoring tool in order to run the product. SuperCard is an example of an authoring tool that has stand-alone playback capabilities.

Development Tools

Tools such as editors, debuggers, file format support, system extensions, links to the operating system, and automation tools help complete a robust product. Developers often need these tools to resolve technical problems, create custom scripts, or develop automated production tools. Use of macro utilities can save hours and hours of time for some repetitive production processes.

Efficiency

Efficient use of computer resources is another measure of a good authoring tool. Issues like screen redisplay, memory management, speed of operation, and automatic storage compression should be examined. Getting the screen to repaint when an object is moved across the screen is not always done well.

Scripting Languages

Most authoring tools have **scripting languages** ▶ **208** that give greater control for creating interactions and adding unique features. A scripting language can be a very powerful feature. But though it may appear easy to learn and use, it can be difficult to create useful and efficient scripts. An experienced programmer who is familiar with the chosen tool may be mandatory for some projects. Experience teaches programmers how to write efficient scripts that run faster and with more stability. They often bring with them scripts and solutions developed for past projects that can be instantly applied to a project's needs. In these situations, it may be necessary make a licensing arrangement with the programmer to secure rights to use the code in a product.

Some of the authoring systems do not expressly support new media like animation or video. A **customized authoring tool** is enhanced or extended typically on the Macintosh by adding XCMDs (pronounced "ex command"). An XCMD is an external command specially programmed to add functionality to an existing program. XCMDs are either bundled by a tool vendor or created by a programmer. Sometimes new XCMDs or system extensions that support new media types or formats can be cumbersome and may interfere with other features within the tool. Even when these media are supported, how well they implement technologies like scalable fonts or color palettes may vary and need comprehensive functional testing.

Logistic Management Tools

Many developers mention the need for expanded capabilities to help organize content elements, record versions, and calculate storage limits. These tools are usually stand-alone or are found in the larger more expensive systems such as the Media Manager component of Authorware. At the moment, many developers create their own systems using spreadsheets and other tools.

HyperCard 2.2, a significant new release from Apple Computer, provides increased power, functionality and flexibility. It integrates AppleScript which allows users to automate repetitive tasks by launching and controlling data with over 100 scriptable applications. It provides 24-bit color support using ColorTools, allowing users to apply color to buttons, fields, backgrounds, and cards, as well as import and resize color PICT images. New features let users create double-clickable applications which can be distributed free of royalty fees, incorporate QuickTime movies using the QuickTime Tools stack, and using WorldScript support, create multilingual titles for large international markets.

Picking the Right Tool

Be sure to explore the capabilities of each tool before committing a project to using it. Look for ease of production, a comprehensive scripting language, the ability to handle all media types well, and a way to provide enhanced functions. Look at projects that are similar to yours and find out what tools have been used. Some are terrific for two-dimensional animated styles of interaction. Others are not very rich in features but operate across different platforms. The prototype stage is a time to explore the limits of an authoring tool and work through any logistics necessary for it to perform as needed. Keep in mind that these tools change constantly. Closely watch their developments and evolution. A tool that does not meet your needs for a current project may be better suited for the next one.

Case Study: Lockheed Waste Management

Description:
Lockheed Missiles and Space Company in Sunnyvale, CA created a multimedia presentation to address the needs of its Photographic Waste Management Group to illustrate the procedures and issues involving hazardous chemical disposal. The presentation informs upper management on the regulations of regulatory agencies, orients employees about photographic waste procedures, and proves to inspectors the steps Lockheed takes to ensure compliance with regulations. In addition, the project represented an investigation of the multimedia technology by incorporating examples of the various media types.

Project Type:
Presentation and Communication

Development Hardware:
3 Macintosh IIci computers with 200 MB hard disks, Silicon Graphic Iris workstations, RasterOps 364 digitizing card, Apple OneScanner™, Apple CD SC®, LaserWriter® II NT

Delivery Hardware:
Macintosh IIci with 200 MB drive

Software Used:
QuickTime, MacroMind Director, Swivel 3D Professional

Team Members and Roles:
project manager; content expert; creative director; animation artist; programmers

Funding:
Corporate overhead for new technology research

Price:
Not for sale

Contact:
Bob Price
Lockheed Waste Management
Sunnyvale, CA

Management:
Co-managed with Apple Computer, Inc. to investigate and provide technology transfer of multimedia practices and procedures.

Concept and Planning:
Lockheed wanted to explore multimedia as a business tool to build an information database. The Lockheed project team discovered that there were many myths and conjecture about what multimedia could or would do for corporations but few actual case histories. The project team contacted the Apple Integrated Systems Group, now called ISG, who provided a lot of background material on what other corporations were doing.

Lockheed's Photographic Waste Management group requested a multimedia presentation to illustrate its regulatory compliance procedures. About a month was spent researching and analyzing the project requirements.

Design and Prototype:
After contracting with Apple Computer to investigate the technology, the Lockheed project team reviewed sample applications provided by Apple and decided on a design and interface before beginning development.

Content acquisition required the most time and effort (six months) in that numerous corporate and governmental sources had to be researched and coordinated to define the regulatory procedures that would be presented in the project. It was a challenge to build links between different analog sources such as documents, video, and audio and the corporate groups responsible for maintaining them.

Production:
Production did not begin until all content was acquired. The Lockheed project team spent about a month learning production tools. Another month was devoted to creating and digitizing original content including video, animations, illustrations, and text. Programming was done concurrently by Apple personnel and took about 2-3 weeks.

Testing:
The Apple and Lockheed joint team spent about two weeks testing the product.

Installation/Delivery:
A single 200 MB drive is dedicated to the Photographic Waste Management organization. The original program is being used by Lockheed's Advanced Projects Lab to describe and demonstrate capabilities in producing interactive multimedia products.

The project had been routinely used by Photographic Waste Management executives to demonstrate regulatory practices. It also has been extremely successful in providing insight to the process of producing multimedia projects. Lockheed is discussing future plans for the use of multimedia technology but no definite projects have been set.

Programming: 80% Off-the-shelf tools, 20% Custom Code

Content: 100% New

Expenses: Marketing Expenses not. app. Operations Expenses not app.

Development Expenses: 30% Personnel, 10% Equipment, 60% Content

Money
Personnel

Delivery

Total Development Costs: not avail.

Total Development Team: 9 people

Total Development Time: 9 months

Manufacturers generally require a license for products created with their authoring tool. Sometimes a royalty fee on each product sold is required. These fees need to be a component of any project budget and marketing plan.

Authorware

Authorware from Macromedia is an industrial-strength diagram-based authoring tool. It uses an icon and diagram approach to laying out all interface objects. Authorware is also designed to be cross-platform. It is good for sequencing and managing large numbers of screens and it has been used on computer-based training and large projects. Special volume license arrangements must be made with Macromedia.

Macromedia Director

Macromedia Director from Macromedia is a capable and pervasive animation-based authoring tools for the Macintosh. It excels at providing animation of graphic objects, managing color palettes, color transitions, and provides some level of media synchronization. Scripting is required to control object behavior, branching, and the appearance of text. The Director scripting language, Lingo, is used for event control and object behavior. Macromedia sells a runtime player that allows a Director file to run on any computer Director supports.

Expanded Books Toolkit

The Expanded Book Toolkit is from The Voyager Company and is used internally for creating their line of Expanded Books. This toolkit requires HyperCard and is used to create titles within this environment. The toolkit is best for text-intensive, linear books, especially those repurposed from the print publishing world. It runs well on PowerBook computers. All media such as sound, animation, and video can be added to toolkit but within a fixed format and interface. Its searching and navigation tools are useful features.

HyperCard

HyperCard is in wide use and uses a card and stack metaphor on which text fields, user buttons, and graphics are built. HyperCard has a rapid text search mechanism making it attractive for any project that requires linked text. It does not support color or video directly but uses XCMDs to handle these media.

The HyperCard scripting language, HyperTalk, is powerful and fairly easy to read and learn. It has become the model for most other product-scripting languages.

HyperCard is an inexpensive product suitable for a variety of projects. Finished commercial HyperCard projects require a license from Apple Computer. HyperCard may be integrated with AppleScript™, a general purpose language that can provide communication between all Macintosh applications and the operating system.

Plus

Plus from Spin- naker Software is a card-based authoring tool similar to HyperCard and SuperCard. It runs in color and has object graphics and database fields. It has the unique advantage of being one of the few tools that runs on both the Macintosh and Windows platforms.

SuperCard

SuperCard from Aldus Corporation is much like a color version of Hyper-Card. It aims at providing a superset of HyperCard's capabilities and offers a high degree of compatibility when converting HyperCard stacks into SuperCard projects. It supports color well and includes a scripting language, SuperTalk, that has many elements of HyperTalk. Unlike most other tools that require a "runtime player," SuperCard projects can be built as stand-alone applications that do not require SuperCard to run.

ToolBook

ToolBook from Asymetrix Corporation is similar to HyperCard in many ways but it runs on the Windows platform. It includes built-in support for color and a wide library of .DLL commands, the Windows equivalent to XCMDs. Some developers have used tools to port from HyperCard stacks to the ToolBook format but these may not be 100% accurate. ToolBook has a scripting language that is very similar to HyperTalk. Like the others, it supports the modern media like CD-ROMs and videodisc players.

Next generation authoring tools are quickly adopting visual and object-oriented programming paradigms in order to provide more natural and more powerful mechanisms for creating multimedia products. These new tools enable designers and content producers to create multimedia products themselves, without having to learn complex scripting languages. An example of this type of development environment is the Apple Media Kit, which contains the Apple Media Tool and the Apple Media Tool Programming Environment.

Designers can use the Apple Media Tool and its direct manipulation interface to quickly assemble media elements and add interactivity. The second part of the kit, the programming environment, is a fully object-oriented language and application framework. Programmers can use this environment to further customize and extend projects created with the tool. The Apple Media Kit will also provide a direct path to ScriptX™, the object-oriented language from Kaleida Labs, Inc.

Many people ascribe attributes of objectivity or official status to text. Just writing down a thought tends to give it more prominence to most people. This effect can be used to gain respect or attention from some readers, but it can be misused just as easily.

Programming

Until tools become more universally standardized and easier to use, programming expertise will be almost mandatory for effective prototyping. Available tools are simply not at the "just add water" stage of usability yet, although they are moving in that direction. Many developers end up designing their own tools or customize existing tools to attain the results they desire.

If a conventional authoring program is used, the programmer must write "**scripts**" ▶ **209** in the authoring language that are interpreted by the authoring program. Scripts have lists of "**handlers**" ▶ **210** or procedures that perform specialized tasks. HyperTalk is an example of a scripting language.

This button handler is a HyperTalk script for navigating forward when a mouse is clicked in a card-based system:

```
on mouseUp
    visual effect wipe left fast
        if the commandKey is down
            then go last card of this background
        else go next
end mouseUp
```

Programming expertise also comes into play in situations other than creating or tailoring a multimedia engine or optimizing performance. Special programming might be needed to access mainframe databases, for example. A savvy programmer can devise ways to access and format data for use in multimedia. For example, in creating an interactive map for a building in San Francisco, the multimedia firm Spatial Data Architects created custom procedures to extract items such as building layouts, forms, wiring diagrams, and furniture inventory records from a client's mainframe computer. They devised a scheme to generate information maps from the data. The underlying data structure, reflected in the interface design, pictured the floors of the building, the furnishings, electrical and telecommunications wire boxes, and employee room assignments. The project is configured for different uses to disclose more information, depending on the user. Company managers, for example have full access to lease information, property lists, and maintenance reports. Human resource managers can plan employee reallocations and redistribute furnishing and equipment. Building managers have access to architectural specifications, telecommunications and electrical wiring diagrams as well as maintenance records.

Text

The printed word can be an expressive medium, giving emotion to a thought and life to an idea. **Text** ▶ **177** is ideal for conveying detailed information or describing abstract phenomena that have no visual or aural component, such as feelings. But large amounts of text or poorly organized text may bore users. Text is easy to generate but it is not necessarily easy to generate well. Like all media, if text is not interesting, exciting, or engaging, it either will not be read or will turn a user's opinion against a project.

Unlike most other media, text can be searched efficiently by a computer. Text is also very portable in raw form across different computers and platforms. This is because text is one of the oldest media computers have used. Images, sound, and especially video are relatively new to computers.

Text may take more forms than written prose. Text includes numbers and mathematical formulas, instructions, outlines, indexes, or databased information. Each of these forms may require special handling and formatting. **Databases** may require careful coordination between the form data is stored in and the form required for access, processing, or presentation. If a client is providing data from a database, be sure that the format required and the nature of the data is clearly understood by the client and the project team.

Repetition

Repetition can be a powerful way to communicate ideas. Some users respond better to reading text while others respond better to sounds or images. Regardless of preference, the combination of different media can reinforce ideas more effectively than a single medium. Text can reinforce the meaning and messages of photographs, illustrations, sounds, music, animations, or video. **Captions**, **titles**, **short explanations**, or **headlines** can quickly explain the point of a particular illustration without detracting from its influence. Pictures or illustrations without captions often raise unanswered questions.

Readers vary in their expertise with **grammar** and **vocabulary**. Some people are more comfortable and experienced with gathering information from written forms of media such as books and newspapers than they are with watching television or listening to the radio. Others prefer to skim over blocks of text and instead concentrate on pictures or broadcasts. Text in a multimedia piece does not stand alone. It needs to reach the intended audience and work well with other media.

Localization

While text offers great advantages in economy and detail, it is one of the least portable media to communicate to other **cultures** ▶ 96. While pictures and sounds may not be as deep or elaborate as text, they tend to be more universally understood when used in other cultures. If readers are not familiar with the language or use of language, text is a much less useful medium. Literal translation is only the first step to convey written ideas from one language or culture to another. Truly localizing text requires adjusting vocabularies, grammar, and connotation to convey different slang, expectations, and meanings of other cultures.

Chunking

Text is inherently a linear medium—ideas are communicated word by word until the concept is developed, whether at the end of a paragraph or the end of a story. Large amounts of text may require indexes, searching capabilities, and possibly even hypertext functions. These functions can allow users to traverse text to find the information most important to them. Many kinds of text, however, can be **chunked** into concise paragraphs that fully communicate a single concept and help simplify navigation. Reference works like dictionaries and encyclopedias can be made more understandable and accessible when topics are chunked. Chunking is a useful principle to follow when designing text for a multimedia application because it presents text in a compact form that can be easily moved and arranged to achieve a balance with other media.

Hypertext

Hypertext features allow users to **jump** ▶ 130, 162 between different segments or chunks or compare two paragraphs or excerpts concurrently. Hypertext features can be added to text once it is written, formatted, or built into the very nature of a project. Some products allow users to click on words to perform searches for similar or related words or topics. Others let users jump from passages to glossaries, bibliographies, or footnotes. The essential idea is to allow users to move through text at their own pace so that they can access information relevant to them and bypass information not interesting to them. Hypermedia extends the same concepts to all media—sounds or videos, for example, that users can jump between.

Accommodating User Input

Projects that allow or require users to add their own information should address how users are to do this. Do they require a keyboard? Does the interface allow users to select text from a pre-generated list with a finger or pointing device? Readily available options can alleviate the need for a keyboard but may be too cumbersome for a lot of text.

Repurposing Existing Text

When repurposing existing text, consider how to get the text into the form needed. If the text already exists in a digital form, it may be a simple task to translate or port it to the correct development platform in the right form. Beware that some translation methods may strip formatting or punctuation from existing text. For more information on the mechanics of preparing text for use in a multimedia project, see the Text section in the Production chapter.

If text is not already in digital form, there are two primary avenues to convert it into digital form. The first is to **retype** it (or hire a professional typist or word processor) using a word processing application. The other is to use a **scanner** ▶ 188 to create a digital image of the page and **OCR** ▶ 178 (Optical Character Recognition) software to convert the image into text in editable form. Good OCR applications are now about 98% accurate most cases but some have problems converting certain typefaces and type sizes. If you plan to convert existing text using the latter method, be sure to test the software, scanner, and process on a sample of the text you will be converting.

Voice recordings such as taped interviews are time-consuming to **transcribe** ▶ 178 into written form. It can take about 4 hours to accurately transcribe an hour of recorded speech. Special transcription machines can be rented or purchased to ease the process or transcribers can be hired. Some special machines can transcribe simple spoken text into written text, but such machines are expensive, not very accurate, and limited in their capability at this time.

Most existing media, including text, are owned or **copyrighted** by the author, originator, or designated representative and it is therefore advised to obtain licensing permission before incorporating the material into a product.

Generating New Text

Besides eliminating the need for permissions, writing new text may be the most effective way to communicate the ideas and information necessary for a particular project. Most developers are careful to create all text on computers. This practice can save time and resources by eliminating the need to convert text to a digital form at a later stage.

A good writer will be able to prepare samples in different styles to convey versatility with tone and voice. These samples should be evaluated and used to communicate to the writer the style expected for the project.

Writing for multimedia projects is similar to writing for print-based products, with the following special considerations:

- *Continuity and flow is more critical since text is usually split onto separate screens. This can make reading more disjointed and requires extra consideration for starting and ending paragraphs.*

- *Screen size and resolutions usually necessitate larger type in smaller spaces than in print. Writing must often be terse and to the point to fit into such tight quarters.*

- *Text should balance and complement other content elements. All objects on a screen should work together. This requires cooperation of all content experts and artists.*

Helpful Style Manuals

American Medical Association Manual of Style (ed 8)

AP Style Manual

The Chicago Manual of Style (ed 14)

Copyediting: A Practical Guide (ed 2)

The Elements of Style

The New York Times Manual of Style and Usage

The Elements of Editing: A Modern Guide for Editors and Journalists

Words into Type (ed 3)

Some helpful questions to ask about any media element:

- *Is its use gratuitous?*
- *Does it match the style of the piece?*
- *Is it the principal medium?*
- *If it is time-based, can it be stopped or replayed easily?*
- *Does it describe what it is supposed to do?*
- *Is it self-explanatory?*

Research

Information may need to be **researched** for a particular project. If much research is required or if the research is particularly difficult, it may be more efficient to hire a **professional researcher ▶ 22** than someone unfamiliar with research tools or techniques. Perceived cost savings should be weighed against any potential loss of time or valuable information. Many professional **research consultants** and firms specialize in finding obscure information fast and effectively. These firms, however, vary widely in their efficiency and prices. Be sure to describe in detail the information you are seeking and be sure you clearly understand the fees involved. **Libraries** can be a great source if the information needed is commonly available. Some libraries even provide limited information search services for people who telephone during the service's operating hours.

All facts should be checked for **accuracy**. While this seems like a small detail, it may take a considerable amount of time and resources to do well. It may also be critical to the project that the information is timely. For example, a medical encyclopedia that incorrectly describes an illness or treatment will damage credibility and have potential legal repercussions.

Editing

All text needs to be edited for style as well as **grammar** and **punctuation**. Good text **editors** are rare and valuable resources. They must understand the content and style of a project as well as its purpose and messages. They ensure that their edits enhance the text and maintain its effectiveness. Most of all, they need to understand the importance of balancing text with other elements in a multimedia presentation.

Tone and Perspective

Well-written text usually has a distinct tone. **Tone** can range from formal, technical, or terse to casual, comfortable, or even "chatty." The perspective or voice of the writing is another component. Readers react differently to text written from different **perspectives ▶ 133**, from a first, second, or third person voice. The correct voice for a particular project is determined by its purpose and intended audience. A project meant to command attention and authority should be written in a style that does just that. One that tries to remain "objective" may have no discernible personality but will still have a particular style even if it is downplayed. Text for a project that attempts to make users comfortable or evoke personal answers may need to be written with a comfortable, casual style that allows users to almost "hear" the writer speaking the words.

Think about or even test how users react to text conveying different tones or voices. While the writing styles of James Joyce, Jack Kerouac, or Henry Rollins might evoke flowing streams of vivid images, emotions, and thoughts, they would be inappropriate in conveying concise instructions or brief descriptions. Be sure that the writing style chosen for a project is consistent with the project's goals.

Legibility

Text is traditionally difficult to read on a screen, but there are many elements that can make it easier to read. The **resolution** of most computer displays makes small print barely discernible. Even **larger type** loses much of its character and detail—especially with color monitors which are not as sharp as monochrome ones. Choose a clear **typeface ▶ 183** and size that users can easily read.

Legibility is also influenced by letter case. **Lowercase** letters help readers distinguish words more easily than do all uppercase letters. ALL-**UPPERCASE** LETTERS TEND TO LOOK ALIKE TO THE READER. If you need to emphasize a word, phrase, or sentence, experiment with different sizes, fonts, or weights and test their effects on viewers.

Special effects or **color choice** can also improve text legibility. A title that is overlaid on an complex image can be made more distinct with 3D **drop shadows** or a contrasting color, for example. Again, it is a good idea to experiment with different text designs and test each one before settling on a final look. Look at titles on television for ideas.

Graphics, Illustrations, and Photographs

Illustrations, **diagrams**, **charts**, **maps**, and **photographs** are familiar forms for presenting certain types of information. Screen graphics are used to integrate all media into a cohesive visual appearance for a project. Visual media are usually used as examples and supporting data but can many times be the predominant feature. Some products require little or no text to present information.

Graphics, illustrations, and photographs are often better media for conveying a lot of information in a little space. Photographs and illustrations are especially useful for communicating **emotion** and **feeling**. Charts, diagrams, tables, and maps are well-suited for presenting **detailed, exact information**. Many readers and users, though, may not be as well-trained to discern meaning from visually presented information as they are from text. As a result, the use of any visual elements in a product should be viewed from the audience's perspective, and not the design team's.

Because visual media are often not as precise as text, their meanings can be more portable across cultures. This portability is especially evident with **icons** used in international signage. Almost every airport uses symbols instead of text to direct and explain various aspects and functions of the airport. While there are still cultural variations to be aware of with visual media, these media may be more reliable and need less **localization** ▶ 96.

Consumers are exposed to visual media constantly from television, magazines, and books and expect a high level of quality. While this level is not yet attainable in terms of resolution (print media are roughly 2400dpi while electronic media can only attain between 72-100dpi), it should be comparable in terms of style. Historically, computer illustrations and graphics have been able to succeed with very low quality and creativity compared to print media, but consumer standards for multimedia are much higher. It is probable that you may need to use qualified professionals for illustrations and photographs and not amateurs.

During prototyping, visual examples are often blocked out in screens instead of generated to a highly finished level. Low-resolution samples or simple rectangles are used as placeholders until the finished pieces are completed in prototyping or production. The prototype allows the project to be visualized before all the pieces are complete.

Graphics

The domain of graphics includes **typography**, **layout**, **screen design**, and **graphic style**. Graphic designers familiar with design in print products are able to handle these same issues for multimedia products. They must, however, acquaint themselves with the limitations and possibilities inherent in electronic media.

Typography

Typography concerns the aspects of text that make it legible and expressive. Typeface, size, weight, and layout all affect how text conveys information. **Typefaces** have distinct names such as Helvetica, Palatino, or Futura. **Size** is traditionally measured by points, for example, 12 point Times Roman or 24 point Bodoni. **Weight** is an indicator of optical prominence, that is, how "heavy" the letter appears, as when it is **bold.** **Layout** is the design of text into an appealing and legible arrangement on paper or the screen.

Be aware that screen resolutions hinder the **legibility** of small type and the detail in typefaces. Even at larger sizes, however, much of the detail that is standard in print media is lost in electronic media. Each typeface has a different **optical weight** that makes it appear darker or lighter. This optical weight can affect the legibility and ambiance of text. Choose a typeface, size, and weight that is easy to read but that still allows some expression to be apparent. An unreadable but expressive typeface is not as useful as a legible but plain one.

Serif Font
Sans-Serif Font

Typefaces are generally placed into three general categories—serif, sans-serif, and decorative. The letters of serif typefaces have little "handles" at the ends which increase their legibility. (By the way, the text of this book is set in a serif typeface called Garamond.) **Serif** typefaces, however, tend to lose their screen legibility if they are too small or if the screen resolution is too low. **Sans-serif** typefaces are literally "without serifs" and can appear more modern or contemporary than serif typefaces. Generally, sans-serif typefaces are more legible on even the lowest resolution screens. **Decorative** typefaces may or may not have serifs. They are generally more expressive and less utilitarian than either serif and sans-serif faces and are usually used at large point sizes. Used appropriately, decorative typefaces can enhance the meaning and feeling of the text. Used inappropriately, they can detract from style and legibility.

Layout

Layout concerns the positioning of text, specifically paragraphs, on the screen. **Column widths** and **lengths**, **leading** (the space between lines of text), **letter spacing**, **rivers**, **widows**, and **orphans** all affect the readability and professional appearance of the text. Few multimedia authoring systems have adequate layout controls although most can be made to accommodate most designs.

Column widths affect legibility by allowing a reader to return to the beginning of the next line easily. Lines of text that are too long or spaced too closely together are difficult to read fluidly. **Rivers** are formed when text is block-justified (set to line up evenly on both left and right sides). Rivers are lines of spaces that form vertically through a paragraph and direct the eye away from the horizontal line of text. The easiest and most

Each typeface is a story in its own right—with some dating back four hundred years and others just a year or two. Many are named after their designers, among these Garamond, Baskerville, and Caslon.

fool-proof alignment for text is to set it flush left so that all lines start against a common edge on the left. Flush right text (where all lines align on the right edge) is more difficult to read because the lines do not begin in a common place.

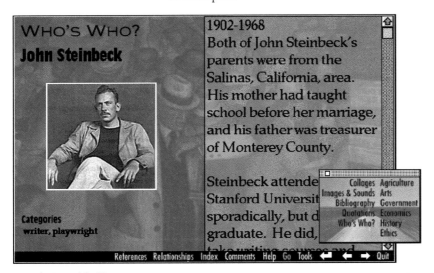

Layout for Voices of the 30s

Layouts effect navigation and understanding. The right layout not only organizes elements but presents them within a specific context and relationship.

Orphans are single lines of text that end a paragraph from a previous column or screen. These lines should be somehow rejoined to the previous paragraph during layout either by lengthening the column height or pushing two or more lines of text to the next screen. Similarly, **widows** are single words that fall by themselves on the last line of a paragraph. Like orphans, widows can be visually disturbing. Try editing the text or changing the letter spacing to make room for the additional word or move more words to the last line to keep the widow company.

Screen Text
Anti-aliased Text

Related, but non-essential information can be included on screens to provide context or contrasting viewpoints. Such information in the form of text, illustrations, or photographs can be set to the edge of a screen in the same way that **pull-quotes**, **footnotes**, and **illustrations** are set in the **margins** of printed books and magazines. It is helpful to look to printed media for ideas about screen design although it is important to remember that they are two different environments.

Anti-Aliased Text

Text on a computer is bit-mapped and usually hard-edged. Anti-aliasing text can make it more legible at larger sizes. **Anti-aliasing** ▶ 182 is a technique performed by many image manipulation applications that softens edges by producing colors between the type and the background. This technique at the moment can only be done for text as an illustration. In most cases it will no longer be searchable, editable text. Anti-aliasing is a good solution for headlines and navigational text, but poor for text that users need to edit, search, or select.

Grids

Grids are common elements that help graphic designers quickly lay out elements. They can help produce a much more professional look to screen designs. One look at a product where text screen graphics or buttons move slightly from screen to screen is all it takes to show how disconcerting inconsistent placement can be. Grids specify where to align text, photos, illustrations, or other elements and help maintain consistent places for headlines and controls. This consistency can be crucial for users to find their place in a project.

The overall appearance of the screens is an important element for organizing and displaying content. Screen layout can separate elements and media into self-contained units or integrate them into a cohesive whole. It is difficult with most authoring tools to format illustrations, graphics, photos, video, and controls in the ways possible with print production tools. **Wrapping text** around an illustration or video segment may be a lot of work, but the integration of elements that can result may be worth the effort. "Breaking the frame" formed by text and grids can often produce a more lively and active screen design.

Also, consider displaying video without the standard rectangular border that is common with television. With the help of image processing tools, video can be displayed in any shape or be made to appear floating over text and other screen elements.

Pacing

Pacing is another feature of graphic design. It is a very subtle attempt to visually control the speed at which a user moves through content. Some designs include a lot of **white space** around objects on a screen. Sparse screens with only one or two elements on each may establish a slower pace that places more prominence on each element. In contrast, other designs can fill the screen with many elements that can imply a faster pace with less emphasis placed on individual elements.

Content elements and screen designs can set up a rhythm for moving through a project. Like all other aspects, this rhythm should reflect the purpose and messages of the project decided upon previously.

Information Hierarchies

Decide what the most important information on a screen is and make it the most **prominent**. The emphasis could be on the content such as text, animation, or video but more likely will be on headlines, navigation elements, or controls. The second most important element should be the next most prominent. One way to test prominence is by squinting at a screen until it is blurred. What catches the eye first? That is the most prominent object. The first, second, third, and fourth "scans" should reflect your decisions on the hierarchy of importance among content and screen elements.

Styles

Lastly, graphics can portray different **styles**, one of which may be appropriate for your product. Design can be traditional, formal, casual, active, futuristic, historic, modern, loud, quiet, utilitarian or express other styles. The style your project presents should relate to the audience it communicates to and the purpose and messages of the project. A good graphic designer can understand a project's goals and develop a unique style that is appropriate.

Illustrations

Illustrations such as **charts**, **diagrams**, **graphs**, **maps**, **time lines**, or **icons** can convey information or be purely decorative. Each type of illustration has its own concerns. Like photographs, decorative illustrations can add depth and emotion to a project. They can project a style that is easily recognized, but they should meet audience expectations of quality. Styles should also be compatible with other content elements and overall project goals. Information graphics such as charts should be legible and meaningful. People are not as adept at reading information in these forms but these can be much more efficient at displaying data.

Using illustrations is often better than using photographs. Illustrations can replace photographs for sensitive or questionable content. Medical illustrations, for example, are usually easier to read and less disturbing than photographs of surgical procedures or internal organs.

Illustrations can be found in **clip-art collections** or created especially for a project by a professional illustrator. While there are many clip-art collections offering a wide variety of images in different **styles** such as people, animals, objects, computers, business, or religious images, they may not be appropriate for your needs. Professional illustrators usually specialize in spe-

cific styles and subjects such as cartoon-like portraits, engravings, or realistic machinery. Illustrators can show you a portfolio of their work with which you can judge their capabilities. Most illustrators work in traditional media which can be scanned into a computer but some

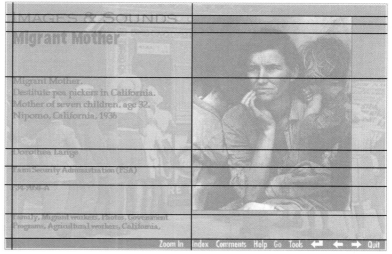

Grid for Voices of the 30s

are proficient with electronic tools and create their work in digital form from the start.

The use of any existing work will require licenses or permission from the copyright owner. Works in the **public domain** can be used without any permissions but may not fit your needs. Many developers are building whole projects around public-domain artwork. Storybook Software, for example, searches for the best public-domain children's books from the turn of the century and builds beautiful and thoughtfully designed multimedia versions that carefully introduce color, sound, and animations without impeding a book's original style or character.

Graphs and Charts

Graphs and **charts** can accurately communicate data only if they are carefully designed. Unfortunately, they are often "dolled up" with unnecessary decoration that can mask the real data and confuse readers. When including graphs or charts, clearly state the parameters and dimensions represented. Use relative measurements, provide indications of average or unusual conditions or data, and point out the direction of improvement.

Diagrams

Diagrams usually combine text, data, and some form of visual element whether an illustration, photograph or animation. They are especially useful for pointing out detail or meaning in an existing image or object. Diagrams can help the user navigate between an object and its related commentary.

Grids can help align and arrange elements on a screen in a clear manner.

In ADAM the decision was made to use illustrations of human bodies instead of videos or photographs. Our investors are doctors. They are all of the same mind that the illustration, from a learning standpoint, is a much better image to work from than the real thing. You can't tell from the real thing what a nerve is. The nerve really isn't bright yellow, but in the illustration it is and it is much more easy to identify.

— Dan Backus, Programmer of ADAM, an interactive human anatomy system

Most cartographic maps are oriented with the north at the top of the page. Different orientations can bring new relationships to light but at the risk of bewildering audiences used to standard orientations. Projection refers to the scheme used to display three-dimensional information in a two-dimensional space. In small scale maps (maps of countries and the world, as opposed to cities and regions) the choice of projection can greatly alter the meaning and display of information.

Maps

Geographic **maps** are common but frequently misunderstood illustrations. The **projection** or two-dimensional graphic representation and the directional orientation can be critical for legibility. Above the equator, for example, readers expect maps to orient north at the top of the page and may not even recognize common landmarks if the orientation or projection is unusual. **Cartography**, the study and design of maps, is a meticulous science of organization and accurate presentation of geographic data.

Accuracy and **level of detail** may be relative. Subway maps, for instance, seldom need to portray accurate geographic features since they run underground. Simplified lines are frequently as useful and often more memorable that accurate graphic representations. For the same reasons, choose a level of detail that is appropriate for the information to be

Families of icons that function together should relate in **style**. If an icon designed as part of one family is to be used in a different family, it may need to be redesigned to fit into the new family.

Color

Color on computers is substantially different from color in print media. There are many more colors possible on computer displays but the technology and capabilities in a given platform or model often impose constraints. Computers use an **RGB** (Red, Green, Blue) **color model** and lower-end systems use color palettes to manage colors. Computers have **color depths**, also called **bit-depths**, that restrict the amount of colors they can show at any given time. One-bit displays can only show black and white, while grayscale displays can show 254 shades of gray in addition to black and white. The color standard for Macintosh computers is 8-bit color which allows 256

Icons courtesy Brooks Communication Design

presented. Screen resolution does not allow much legible detail so pick only the points of interests, features, and labels necessary to orient a user and communicate the information.

Maps need not be only geographic. Information can easily be organized and communicated in map form for many subjects such as maps of the human body, an automobile, a process, or a game. The same issues of orientation, projection, accuracy, and level of detail apply, however.

Icons

Icons are special symbols that are used to identify places, things, or attributes. If designed carefully, icons can be easily understood by people from different cultures. Different **cultures**, however, may hold different meanings for a visual symbol. For example, an icon of a cow that in the United States might indicate a source of food may very well cause offense in India where cows are sacred symbols.

The visible color gamut (the range of colors the eye can see) includes more colors than the RGB gamut used to show color on monitors. The gamuts that can be printed with premixed inks (Pantone colors) or with process inks (CMYK) are even more limited.

Icons often work best as **symbols** and not exact, realistic representations of objects. Their abstracted meaning is what communicates to the greatest number of people across varied experiences. The effectiveness of icons needs to be tested by users. If an icon must be explained repeatedly, it probably needs to be redesigned. In some cases, reinforcing an icon with text can eliminate ambiguity.

colors to be shown at once. These colors can be any 256 from millions of possible colors. (Most systems have a resident **palette** of 256 standard colors that display faster than other colors.) Less standard are 24-bit color displays which can show over 16 million colors at once but may slow performance. Be sure that the colors used in illustrations and other screen visuals conform to the possibilities of the intended delivery platform and models.

As a general rule, images should work in **black and white** before they are rendered in color. In other words, a black and white visual should have sufficient contrast to be legible without the addition of color. Because human eyes "see" contrast before they register color, contrast is a more important characteristic of images than color. Also, try not to rely on highly **saturated** (bright) colors for large objects or backgrounds. Colors that are too bright or harsh can be hard on eyes and look garish or amateurish.

Often, color can have meaning when it is used to color-code information. **Color-coding** can help label, distinguish, or relate objects or elements. For example, a project with color-coded sections can be an effective way for users to help determine their position in an application. Color-coding can also reinforce relationships such the progression from red to blue to illustrate the continuum from hot to cold. Refer to the bibliography and the Apple *Human Interface Guidelines* for more detailed explanations of color issues in design.

Photographs

Photographs ▶ 185 are a powerful and evocative media. They can evoke emotional responses. Audiences are experienced with photography from magazines and television and have high expectations of quality and composition. Good photography is an effective balance between **focus**, **exposure**, **lighting**, **subject matter**, **composition**, and **effects**. Photographs are not as well suited for detailed data because viewers usually notice the overall composition or subject before the details. **Captions** can help users discern detail and fine points intended to be communicated with photographs.

Subject matter can vary from still-life objects to portraits to landscapes and beyond. Photographic styles also vary, although some styles that rely on small detail or subtle effects may not translate well to the computer screen. For example, an 11x14 in. high-quality color photographic print of a crowd scene in New York's Times Square may lose much of its effect and clarity if displayed in an 8-bit 160x120-pixel window.

Photograph Quality

The quality of photographs varies with the **focus**, **exposure**, **lighting**, **background**, and **color balance**. While most of these attributes can be corrected or modified with image manipulation applications, the better the quality is of the photograph when shot and digitized, the less work, time, and money will be necessary to prepare the photograph for use in a project.

Photos can be taken in a variety of formats such as 35mm transparencies or prints. Although the **formats** all offer similar photographic quality, they differ in their ease of use with **scanning equipment** ▶ 188. Flatbed scanners, for example, cannot usually accommodate slides or transparencies. Choosing a format that is compatible and easy to use with available scanning equipment will save long-term time and effort.

Repurposing Existing Photographs

Some projects may be built around existing photographs or photo series. Rick Smolan's interactive CD-ROM *From Alice to Ocean* is a good example. A few years ago, some of Smolan's photographs were featured in a *National Geographic* magazine article about one woman's adventurous trek with camels across the Australian outback. The rest of the photographs were archived. Smolan had the idea to repurpose the photos into a new form: an interactive story of the woman's journey across the Australian outback. The result

was a combination hardbound book and CD-ROM set that featured the photographs accompanied by music, audio, and video commentary and related subject matter. *From Alice to Ocean* demonstrates how photographs originally used in print media can be reused in a digital form.

I Photograph to Remember is another compelling example of repurposing photographic content. It is a simple, CD-ROM photoessay about the life and death of photographer Pedro Meyer's parents. The photographer himself provides voice-over narration in English and Spanish that is accompanied by piano. It uses the strengths of both the photographic content and the interactive medium to the best effect.

Ethical Considerations

Because photography is such a persuasive medium, it implies an especially strong responsibility to use it wisely. Lately, the ethical use of photographs has become a popular issue because of some well-publicized misuses of the technology. Pay close attention to the purpose of the project and the messages it embodies. If the project is meant to be a historical database, the photos should be prepared for screen display with an intent to preserve their authenticity. Try to respect the original intent of photographers for their photos.

If you use a copyrighted photograph, be sure the license agreement clearly states what you can and cannot do with the photograph. If you take your own photos, be sure to obtain all necessary model releases from people who will be in the photo.

Photographers usually specialize in specific styles of photographs and subject areas. Good photographers are more versatile than their portfolios may portray, but not all photographers are interested in general purpose photography and may prefer to keep to their specialties. Also, unique genres like aerial photography or pets may require photographers with special knowledge or experience.

Photo CD is an great way to scan photos for use on a computer. Kodak offers Photo CD processing through many standard photo finishing stores. Photo CD scanning can accommodate slides, prints, or transparencies and is an inexpensive process especially if you do not already own or have access to a scanner.

Interview: Wayne Williams

Wayne Williams is the president of Wayne Williams Photography in Los Angeles. What he is most known for are the many celebrities he has photographed. He has done covers for Redbook, The Ladies Home Journal, Popular Mechanics, and TV Guide. He has clients at Fox Studios and Disney and has spent time working at Euro-Disneyland doing work for them.

In this interview he discusses the challenges and advantages a photographer encounters when working within the digital domain. "There's a dramatic learning curve you take when you get into [digital technology]. Unless you have someone to guide you, you can bounce around and get ripped off."

As a professional photographer, what do you think about the current trends in technology?

What has happened over the years is that photographers have become technicians. They used to be true creative forces in the industry; people would come up to them as if they were gods and ask them "We want you to come up with an idea." Photographers have become documenters of a client's image and have lost much of their creative control. They've given it away. The Macintosh will allow them to get the control back, if they choose to take it.

Because we will probably find more people reading magazines and looking at pictures on **personal digital assistants** ▶ 120 or laptop computers than on paper, CD-ROM is the first step in that direction. Photographers must be able to work with the new digital media.

Have you worked with digital cameras?

Digital in terms of photographic cameras is in two realms right now. One is the sort of video image we see from an inexpensive digital camera like the Canon XapShot. Then there's the Kodak Digital Camera System (DCS). You can get an 8x10 output using a disublimation printer with the Kodak DCS. You can get a fairly good match with film. Digital photography has difficulty picking up highlights and shadow areas, though. The digital camera disrupts the area with pinks and turquoise colors that should have definition. That is a very telltale sign of digital photography. The advantage, of course, is the turnaround speed. You can plug a digital camera into a PowerBook with a modem attached and send it anywhere in the world in a matter of seconds. For most newspaper and magazine prints you'll do very well with it. For anyone who needs to have photographs right away, it's worthwhile.

For CD-ROMs, because you're not displaying the images very large, digital photographs are good. The downside is that you only get so much information during a photo session; during a regular shoot I would do five to ten 35mm rolls on a setup. Multiple 36 shots by 10 rolls and that's a lot for one shoot. With a digital camera, though, I can take only 50 shots in a row. I can't use the camera unless I download the information to my Mac. This takes time.

There are other digital devices. They will do high resolution images, but they are intended for studio use. It costs $20-30,000 for a Rollei digital camera, for example.

What would you recommend to photographers who are interested in multimedia?

Stop spending money on cameras and start spending money on learning about computers. Take classes at places like the American Film Institute or any place that teaches [Adobe] PhotoShop and start to learn. Multimedia will be the next boom market for anyone who is visually driven. If you don't do it in the next two years you will be left behind.

The multimedia market will explode. Whether it will stay in CD-ROM or not is anybody's guess. If you can create the software or create content like video, sound, or graphics in other media and know how to put together a story and tell it effectively, you will be in a new business.

How will it be different from traditional photography?

It will be very different because the traditional photographer will become a production house. If a photographer is an advertising photographer, he is essentially a producer, director, and cameraman to get one still image that is requested by an ad agency. With that same talent, the photographer can create a disk and tell a story with a number of images,

and he is going to be expanding his creative potential immensely and given more control. I think that photographers are getting farther and farther away from controlling their destiny, unless they step into the computer world.

What have you invested in?

I work with an Apple Quadra, SuperMac monitors, one and two gigabyte hard drives, tape DAT drives, magneto-optical drives, Syquest removable cartridges, pen tablets, and PhotoShop. Many of my friends have asked my advice on how to set up computer systems. I help them get going. One of them is a successful photographer who was losing jobs to other photographers who were linked up to art directors who had computers. He figured out a way to go out, shoot the subject indoors, go out to a scenic location, and combine the two digitally. This has cut his costs tremendously and given him an edge.

Will the digital darkroom replace the chemical darkroom?

Many photographers now don't have darkrooms they use regularly. Instead, they use labs or a printer. Many clients just want the prints because they can process it themselves. Printmaking is becoming a fine art. And that fine art, with an Iris workstation, color printer, and other forms of archival will put traditional printers out of business.

How has the nature of taking photographs changed for you?

I do a lot of high level portraiture for executives and for celebrities. They often have the same old concerns about retouching and cleaning up images to look better. There's a degree I'm willing to take them to which is fair and appropriate, but there's a limit I won't exceed. I photographed an executive for a studio who was concerned about her appearance. There were some shots in which her face and energy were great but her eyes weren't right. I could take the image from a shot where her eyes were great and mix that with a face shot that was better. The computer allows me to do this.

It's really no different from a photo session with making a group photo look good by combining the best of different pictures. This has been going on for decades, except now the photographer has direct control over it. Before, the client would go to a service bureau or other retouching service.

The photographer has a better eye. The photographer has been working with light and understands depth and shadow and concept and texture much better for his photographs than a technician who sits at a machine. The photographer has never been able to control those tools until now. The advent of PhotoShop and Mac graphics have enabled photographers to have control once again.

Many photographers have been away from direct control for so long that they are afraid to step back in. It's too big for them. They may spend thirty to fifty thousand dollars on camera equipment to get started in their business. Now, someone can come along and say, "The next time you're going to spend that money, don't buy cameras, buy a computer." There's a whole new learning curve involved. Those who dive into it, those who get involved, those who understand it are going to quadruple the type of money they have been making and they are going to get their creative control back. Before, they have been giving it away to other people.

Time-Based Media

Some media elements such as **music**, **animation**, and **video** are expressed over a duration of time and can be described as time-based media. Other media elements such as text, illustrations, and photographs are static and can be described as still media. Balancing different time-based media with still media to create a cohesive experience is one of the most powerful and challenging tasks of developing interactive multimedia.

Traditional time-based media cannot move beyond the linear sequence. You can't "jump" to the middle of a videotape without moving through the previous sequence, for example. Multimedia applications can present time-based media in traditional linear sequences as well as in a nonlinear fashion that lets the user control sequence and duration. Users can choose to play a song or movie sequence from beginning to end or decide to experiment. They can play the sequence fast or slow (change the time), play it in reverse (reverse time), or jump between different parts of the sequence at random (change sequence).

Mixing time-based media with other media raises issues of **synchronization ▶ 194, 205** and **composition**. For example, lyrical text can be synchronized with music, music can be matched with an animation, or subtitled text can arranged to match dialog in a motion picture. Narration or music can be central to a motion picture's story. Sergei Eisenstein, for example, describes how he designed his film *Alexander Nevsky* with the music of Pudovkin. He details how frames of film match lines of music and how movement in film sequences match movement in the melody.

Making artistic decisions about time-based media involves not only structuring the media elements themselves but also developing a sense of the dynamic presentation in which timing, pacing, and duration of different media are balanced to create a cohesive experience.

Sound

Sound can be more than just background music. Voice actors can narrate passages; music can be the focus of a title. Distinct sounds can even carry meaning that communicates. Researchers at MIT's Media Lab have found sound to be more important than once thought—even in visual media. In tests with identical televisions, unknowing test subjects consistently choose the television with the best sound system as having the superior picture.

Sound should be considered as more than just an add-on to enhance a visual element. "Audio is underestimated in multimedia," says professional sound engineer Jim McKee. "Look at how it has helped film and television. Sound provides another whole level of communication. It gives the author a direct line of communication through dialog and narration, an emotional palette for music, and an enriched palette for effects and design elements."

Generic Sounds

Effective sounds can attract users from across the room and draw them into a project. Sounds in the interface can alert users of problems or opportunities, mask transitions, acknowledge user actions, convey information, and divert attention from other processes. Also, consider how sounds can widen the audience for a particular product. Visually impaired users can benefit from recorded narratives of written text and children whose non-text skills are normally ignored can participate in ways that are not possible with traditional text-only products.

For example, a research project by Paramount's Media Kitchen explored how to teach 7th and 8th graders how to become better storytellers. The project, *Finding Your Voice*, made extensive use of sound and video to intentionally draw in students who usually perform poorly because of their lack of good reading and writing skills. While the project is not anti-text, one of its purposes was to be non-text so that it could appeal to a wider audience and help develop frequently forgotten or neglected skills.

Sound Quality

Sound can be of different quality levels and still be understandable. For example, compare the sound quality of CD-Audio, television, and telephone, or **stereo** and **monophonic ▶ 191**. While CD-quality stereo music is impressive and appropriate in many cases, low-quality monophonic sound can be easier to produce and accomplish the same purpose of communication. During prototyping, test all sounds at different levels of quality to determine what is adequate for your purposes. Remember that the higher the fidelity or trueness to real-world sound, the more storage space the sound data will require. For voice, interface, and ambient sounds, lower fidelities may be adequate. Make sure that users can turn sounds off if they choose and that the project still makes sense without sounds or music.

My litmus test for a kiosk is that I can stop a text/video presentation easily if I don't want to watch, listen, or read. It is amazing how few kiosks pass this test.

— Kristina Hooper-Woolsey, Distinguished Scientist, Apple Computer, Inc.

QuickTime from Apple is a multi-platform video format that provides a standard interface for controlling movie playback and a suite of media compressors and decompressors to optimize performance and economize storage space.

A QuickTime movie can contain a set of synchronized tracks (each for a specific medium). The most common tracks in QuickTime movies are:

- *Video, animation, still picture sequences (any kind of moving visuals)*
- *Sound*
- *Text (closed-captioning, for example)*

Special tracks can also be added for other data. Think of a QuickTime movie as a universal container for dynamic media that marches along, triggering and synchronizing any media element or event that is stored in the movie format. A QuickTime movie could be a conventional video, a presentation slide show, a dynamic bar chart of data, or a graph of laboratory data over time.

The QuickTime file format is called a MooV file on Macintosh computers and .MOV under Windows. Movies can be represented on the desktop with a single "poster frame" or with "previews" which play a small thumbnail clip of the movie.

Literacy is too often defined in terms of textual reading and writing skills. Visual, aural, and motor skills are just as important. People experience and develop skills with sounds before they learn to read or write. Sound offers an opportunity to tap into these experiences.

Experienced multimedia project managers hire professional sound designers from the motion picture or radio industries because these people have great experience with a range of sound types. Also, they tend to be experienced at meeting high expectations of quality.

Sound Effects

Sound effects ▶ 194 can provide humorous or serious punctuation to events and content in a project, but use them wisely and sparingly. Products full of sound bites can often frustrate or annoy the user. Experiment with different effects and choose those that capture the mood or trigger the reaction you desire. Again, experienced sound engineers can save a lot of time in exploring and refining soundscapes.

Sound Morphing

Like visual morphing, **sound morphing** combines two or more sound objects to create a blend with elements of each. This effect is rather new and unusual but can be appropriate if used carefully. For example, words in a poem can be morphed to give them an onomatopoetic effect that sounds like what they describe. The phrase "water drips and drops" can be morphed with sounds of water dripping to color the phrase with the sound.

Interface Sounds

Often, well-chosen sounds can verify or reinforce user actions. Sounds can alert the user to new conditions or convey information. In this case, sound engineers should work closely with interface designers to develop meaningful sounds that enhance the interface. Interface sounds can range from the original *Speak-n-Spell's* enthusiastic voice saying "Outstanding!" to subtle background music that indicates a specific section of a multimedia guidebook. Good interface sounds can delight or assist the user.

Binaural Sound

Advanced sound equipment is capable of producing three-dimensional sound called **binaural sound** ▶ 121. Binaural sound techniques can subtly change sounds to make them seem to move around in space. A user usually requires headphones to listen to binaural sound although it can be played to a limited degree with stereo speakers. Many music albums make creative use of 3D sound for special effects. 3D sound can enhance interactive games, music, film, and artwork but it may be unnecessary for most other uses at this time.

Sound Prototyping

For all sounds, voice recordings, and music, be sure to plan and budget the number, duration, and cost of sound segments. Schedule studio time well in advance

The future for the use of music in interactive games is wide open. Before CD-ROM, most game music suffered; the result of sound limitations and few musicians who knew how to program. Now we can record vocalists and acoustic or electric instruments in traditional ways, giving developers a better chance of getting the music they want.

— Dezsö Molnár, free-lance music producer for interactive games

and carefully explain to musicians and sound engineers your needs as well as the purpose and nature of your project. Background information on the project such as storyboards and screenshots can help them understand what you need. Unless you are experienced with sound engineering, very often these professionals will know what you need better than you will.

For the purpose of prototyping with placeholders, low-fidelity sound can be acceptable unless you are specifically testing different levels of sound quality. Sometimes, a "thumper track" or drum rhythm is used to establish a placeholder for background music or ambient sounds. It is used to set the pace for video tracks and guide the interaction design. (The sound equivalent of text's Lorem Ipsum.) This can later be filled in when the final music is finished.

Music

Music can be an emotional and alluring enhancement to a project. It can be used for ambient background sounds or be a prominent focal point of a project. Voyager's Beethoven CD-ROM, for example, is a music education product that allows users to explore *Beethoven's Symphony No. 9* by giving them control over displaying the commentary and playing the music. In this case, music forms the principal subject matter and is not just an addition or enhancement.

Background Music

Background music is most often used as an enhancement to other content. Because more and more personal computers have acceptable sound capabilities, background music is becoming more prevalent. The model for music in many multimedia projects is how music is used in filmmaking. Sweeping, engaging music has long been used in movies to draw in and affect the audience. More and more multimedia products and especially games are using continuous movie-quality background music to create richer, more exciting environments.

Background or ambient music can also divert attention from other processes. Sounds are often used in products to fill-in dead time while the product is loading other data. Instead of a lack of activity or action on the screen, background music can keep a user's interest piqued. Ambient sound can also be used as a navigational cue. Different areas of a project can have different background music or ambient sounds. While this is a subtle factor, it can be an apparent or even subconscious reinforcement to navigation. Movies and television series, most notably *Star Trek: The Next Generation*, use this technique to great effect.

Repurposing existing music

Existing music can be repurposed for use in multimedia projects but it may not be easy to obtain rights of use. Recording companies may not be familiar with multimedia products and may try to treat multimedia licensing negotiations as they would other established music contracts. Although some major recording studios are inventing new ways to address licensing for multimedia, obtaining permission for use of material remains a challenge.

Leave plenty of time to negotiate **licensing arrangements** and some money in the project budget. It may be easier and less costly to hire studio **musicians** ▶ 26 to create new music for a project than to use existing music owned by someone else. Musicians and **sound engineers** generally contract on a project basis, but ownership rights for the finished music vary from project to project. Make sure you understand exactly what you are buying, how you can use it, and for how long you can use it.

MIDI

MIDI ▶ 48, 193 (Musical Instrument Digital Interface) is a real-time music control and network protocol connecting digital music instruments and computers for musical performance, recording, and playback. A MIDI instrument is a **synthesizer** built on a **DSP** ▶ 121 (digital signal processor) that allows for both MIDI input and output. All messages running on the MIDI network can be stored in digital form on a computer disk and translated into electronic music notation. A single MIDI network runs a synchronous timing pulse and all the control information for up to 16 separate MIDI synthesizers.

A MIDI synthesizer as an output device can create the sounds of many conventional instruments such as drums, pianos, violins, trumpets, electric guitars, choirs, and industrial machines. Although most synthesizers can simulate hundreds of different instrumental sounds, only 127 of those sounds can be designated per synthesizer. The instruments are designated by programming a special patch table.

MIDI synthesizers vary in the quality and richness of the synthesized sound. For example, a high-end synthesizer will produce distinct notes and resonances over different octaves whereas a less expensive synthesizer will be less likely to reproduce such nuances. MIDI matches keyboard and percussive sounds well but is not as true-to-life with horn or string instruments. If voice is used, it needs to be recorded and stored as sampled data separately and then synchronized with MIDI.

Because it stores musical information as binary code and not sampled waveform data, MIDI is very efficient in storage. Ten minutes of 44kHz sound may require 100MB on a CD but only 100KB on MIDI, representing a 1000-to-1 storage advantage. Although MIDI is very efficient in terms of storage space, its use means that every user must have a MIDI synthesizer or DSP attached to their computer. This limitation may be acceptable for a niche market, but is not likely for the general consumer market for a few years to come.

Voice

Of all sounds, the human **voice** ▶ 192 is probably the most absorbing. Humans are subtly conditioned from birth to pay attention to others talking. Compared to text, speech can add character and point of view to multimedia content. A familiar exercise for actors has them express the same phrase tirelessly to explore range of character. "I'm so happy you are here" could be stressed, paused, inflected, and intoned in many different ways to project different emotions. The tempo combined with the arts of rhetoric can provide completely different interpretations of the same material. Actors whose voices will be heard in a multimedia project should understand the goals of the project so that the appropriate image can be conveyed.

MIDI can control an entire multimedia exhibit with multiple audio-visual devices through a software extension called MIDI Show Control (MSC). MSC can control such stage elements as lighting, sound devices, sets, video machines, slide machines, projectors, fog machines, and pyrotechnic devices. MSC can cue and start devices that are synchronized with the MIDI clock.

Accents are an important consideration when localizing products. Pay attention to regional as well as continental accents. English audiences can discern a Scottish accent from an Irish accent from an Australian accent, much as someone from Chicago can pick out an accent from Boston or New York.

How to Listen to Sound Demos

What to listen for in a sound engineer's demo tape:

- Is the intended message conveyed clearly? For example, if the piece is meant to be a narration, is the voice clear and distinct from the music or is it buried by the music? Are soloists clear? Are music and sound effects well chosen to support the theme? Not every presentation benefits from a loud disco beat.

- Are the variations in loudness of the component sounds appropriate to the message? A good engineer will work with music and other sounds appropriately and not push faders up and down simply for effect. For example, if a horn blasts suddenly for no reason, that's not appropriate and it detracts from the message. If a guitar fades up to emphasize a transition or the music fades down to accommodate a voice, that would be appropriate. Background music and effects should support the message, not compete with it for your attention.

- Are all the frequencies in the audio range represented in a balanced way? Are there bass frequencies, very high frequencies, and various ranges of mid frequencies present? The balance of frequencies doesn't always have to be uniform, but over the run of the mix, all of the frequencies should be present. Even if there's a prominent instrument like a harpsichord or a flute that may not have any low notes, a good engineer can do things to make the sound fuller and more interesting.

- Is the noise level low? Is the tape free of distortion? Does the sound material have life and liveliness as opposed to being compressed in one loudness range? These criteria let you know that the engineer operates the equipment correctly. If so, the engineer will optimize the signal to noise ratio and won't overuse a compressor, which is one of the most common gadgets people process audio with. (A compressor is an automatic loudness control. When the signal is low, it turns up the gain. When it is too high, it turns it down automatically. But if everything is the same loudness, nothing will be clear.)

—Craig Connally, President of Neotek, a Chicago manufacturer of professional audio mixing consoles for film, television, and broadcast

The use of voice in computer systems can be frustrating for the user who has no opportunity to interact. Such an experience is common with people who call movie theaters for a specific show time only to be forced to listen to a long recorded message of all times for all movies that day. Voice in a multimedia application should provide information concisely and clearly. The user should be able to bypass the voice or interrupt it and move on to another point of interest.

Text-to-Speech Processing

At this time, **text-to-speech processing** offers a workable but not always aesthetic or natural solution for generating voice. Synthesizing speech as needed rather than storing sampled voice data may save disk space, but the quality may not meet requirements for a particular project. Synthesized speech tends to sound tinny, artificial, and robot-like. Subtle cues like intonation, pauses, and pitch are often lost altogether.

Interview: Jim McKee

Jim McKee is a founder and sound designer for Earwax Productions, an audio production company. Jim and his two partners are all classically trained musicians with music degrees. They put their group and studio together to realize composition and realize their craft. Faced with the difficulty of making a living as composers, Jim found a niche creating sound designs for theater. One of the early theater groups McKee hooked up with was Antenna Theater, headed by Chris Hardman. In this interactive theater, the audience wears headphones and manipulates props to become involved in the performance with the actors. The audience is told to do things, move things, react in certain ways on the audio tape. He did more and more sound design for theaters such as General Magic Theater but then began doing work with film and video along with some research. Earwax Productions developed sound designs for a number of projects at the Apple Multimedia Lab in 1987.

What is sound design for multimedia computers?

What you have here in the box is a little proscenium, a little theater, with its own set of rules, expectations, and limitations, just as you have lights, props, sets, and accoutrements to theater. The elements that we generally deal with range from design in terms of architecture, navigation, and territory within the software mostly doing sound effects. Our expertise is in sound and music, but we are involved in other areas of multimedia like animation. We've been involved long enough with interactive multimedia to usually give good suggestions at an early point in a project. I usually get involved on the design end with what the thing will look and feel like. Specifically with sound, the things that I have been working with lately are quite elaborate. Sound production has definite areas that can be treated almost like a language with its own purpose and structure. Other sound production is more subjective and must evoke emotion like music. In between the absolute and the emotional you have a mixture of these.

What are the components to sound design?

One way of looking at sound tasks in multimedia is to think of an axis with music on one end and speech and narration on the other. Music and sound effects are in between. These activities operate with a foreground and background sound design as well a response time considering both the machine and the user. The machine needs to respond to confirm to the user certain things; the sound needs to be able to respond at a certain rate. If you put yourself at the foreground, with a mouse click you want to be able to get an audio response or to be able to get some other action. This is a kind of "stage front" which calls your attention the most. This is also like film, where narration and dialogue is handled by one department, music by another, and sound effects by another. The sound effects department is subdivided into hard effects and background. If you could imagine yourself in a restaurant with a crowd. background is the certain sounds that might be the general conversation level, general dining sounds in the room. If a waiter served your meal, the dish placed on the table would have a certain sound to it, a hard effect. All of these elements are married together in the final mix. Depending on how the person mixes it, the narration, dialog, music, effect, background will put the viewer at a different point of view. These are the basic elements. Depending on the computer, you get a certain range of control and fidelity.

What special considerations do you make for the audience?

Timing and fidelity are platform dependent. User confirmation feedback is becoming more characteristic, almost iconic at both a machine and user level. There is a vocabulary of sound that must match the platform limits. If you look at sound in feedback it can be useful or annoying. This is a

problem in pen-based systems we're looking at now. I can't say much about it. But you can look at Kid-Pix to get an idea of useful and creative sound feedback for children.

The psycho-ergonomic aspects of sound are now becoming important with the evolution of new computers. There is a lot to consider when you are dealing with a little speaker on the side of a computer that has a loud fan blowing. Are you going to take this and reproduce it on bigger speakers or sub-woofers, or play it through a THX theater system? The delivery of your sound has to be a consideration. If I'm producing something for a large public museum, I need to know what kind of speakers are going to be used. How are those speakers going to be placed within the kiosk? What is the level of the ambient noise in the surrounding area? Are we going to be broadcasting this in a space where the sound may be turned down? Is it going to be an annoyance? The danger of being intrusive to the listener depends on how those sounds have been designed and stylized. You may want to have different character sets that express the same functions but in a different manner. You might have a "hey dude" set, the "quiet office" set, or "exploded game" set to be used with headphones for your sound world.

You cannot always use recorded sound for an effect. My job is to provide something that has a psychological effect on the viewer, and doesn't pull itself out as a sound effect, but creates a tension or some emotion behind an image.

How?

With most of the projects the task is to create a sound design that is continuous. In one interactive environment simulation that had six locations, you could visit such things as a fish market, or a power plant. We did a hypershoot with six environments on two CDs. We created 2-second bridges. When you went to any of these places you heard a hard transition. You knew you were going to the fish market. Also, when you were visiting an environment, there was a general background sound—like the barking of fish market sellers, or power line hum and alarms. This levitated the user experience by providing dynamic continuous sound.

Is audio overlooked in multimedia design?

Audio is underestimated. Look what it has done for other media. Look where it is going and how it has helped film and television. It is a whole other level of communication. Sound provides the author a direct line of communication through dialog and narration. It provides them an emotional palette for music and an enriched palette with effects and design elements. Ultimately it broadens the limitations of a computer experience.

Only very sophisticated systems are able to produce speech that sounds vaguely human. Text-to-speech processing usually requires special system software that may not be compatible or available for the delivery platform or computer model in your target audience. Nevertheless, text-to-speech processing is a technology worth watching.

Voice Recognition

Another possible use of sound is to allow users to control a product with their own voiced instructions. Voice recognition requires special equipment and software. A **microphone** ▶ 191 is needed to capture the user's voice that is then processed and interpreted by complex hardware and software. Voice recognition is not yet a solution for consumer applications but may be appropriate for specialized projects for training, simulations, or kiosks.

Voice Prototyping

Experiment with different **voice actors**, **ages**, **genders**, **accents**, and **intonations**. Be sure to choose final voice stylings that reflect the content, the audience, and the project's purpose which in turn should be communicated clearly to the voice talent. **Scripts** must be written for each voice clip needed. Voice talent should have ample time to **rehearse**. Anybody's voice can be used as a placeholder during the prototyping phase, but final specifications for speech must be established before production begins.

Animation

Animations ▶ 195 are moving images used to show objects in motion or to illustrate a process. Although they have a long history in the movie industry, animations are a lot more than cute, anthropomorphized cartoon animals. They can describe **two-dimensional** (2D) or **three-dimensional** (3D) objects, processes, or phenomena in ways not possible in the "real world."

Like illustrations, animations may be better suited than video for portraying sensitive or complex events. For example, showing a car part assembly process in animation provides a clearer, more focused view than videotaping the process with all of the other parts and associated dirt and grime in the way. Animations can describe events or processes that cannot be easily videotaped such as global networks, biochemical processes, or prehistoric ecological systems.

Brøderbund's children's book *Arthur's Teacher Trouble* is a noted exception to the point above. It uses hundreds of small, wonderfully creative animations merely to add fun to the story. Almost everything on any page of the book will do something if selected by the user. There are many inventive events that enliven the product and make it more fun for both children and adults. Still, none of these animations are gratuitous because the purpose of the product is to be fun and silly and a wonderful place to explore.

Good animations require talent, appropriate tools, and sufficient equipment. Depending on the desired quality and length, an animation can be expensive and time-consuming. Ten seconds of a complex 3D animation can take hours to process on a dedicated computer, for example. Animations that have no purpose and are little more than "eye candy" are expensive luxuries for any project. Even the best animation cannot mask deficiencies such as problems with the interface that should be corrected instead of masked.

Overly long animations can also be boring to users. Simply giving users control over starting, stopping, or changing animations can correct this problem. For some processes, it may be useful for users to view the animation in reverse. User testing can help uncover weaknesses in animation but it may be necessary to develop animations to a reasonable degree in order to test their use sufficiently.

Animation Quality

Many of the animations shown at conferences and on television are produced on high-end workstations with specialized software. In the film industry, platforms like Silicon Graphic computers are very popular because of their immense power and processing speeds. Many high-end animations, however, can be brought to the Macintosh or most other platforms because of standard file formats. It is common to build models and objects on personal computers and have them rendered on more powerful workstations. Once finished, the final renderings can then be transferred back to the personal computer for use in a multimedia product. Let the animator judge the complexity of animations and whether more powerful computers would help in the rendering process.

Animation Styles

Styles of animation can vary as much as illustration styles. Any illustration can be transformed into an animation by moving it or its elements. Animations can be cartoon-like, photorealistic, or anything in between. Animators and illustrators can help explore variations and possibilities, but like all elements the style approved must

When recording sounds for a multimedia project, aim for the highest quality possible. A good standard to follow is **44kHz** and **16-bit stereo**. Use the best quality equipment you can obtain, even if it means renting instead of purchasing it. Paying extra for professional sound expertise will bring returns in the high-quality sound that will play well even on the lowest-end delivery setup.

Music from artists such as Joni Mitchell, Ice-T, Graham Nash, and David Crosby, Ted Nugent, Linda Ronstadt, Jesus & Mary Chain, and James Taylor is now available to multimedia developers looking to add some legal, quality sound to their next title.

For $300, Warner Special Products (the licensing agency for the Time Warner Music Group) will license up to 30 seconds of music (only) to CD-I and CD-ROM title developers. To do so, you call Warner Special Products at 818/569-0500 and talk to a service rep who walks you through the procedure. Signing the contract obligates you to send the company a final product that it can clock against the sample you've chosen.

— Janice Maloney, Digital Media: A Seybold Report, October 12, 1992

Like many artists and specialists, animators often work as consultants on a freelance basis. They usually specialize in one form of animation or another because the tools and many of the processes used are very different. The best way to find an animator is to ask others in the industry for recommendations. Professional organizations like SIGGRAPH may have directories or other resources.

be consistent with other content elements and with the purpose of the project.

Animation Technologies

There are two common ways to create animations. In the first, motion is simulated by rapidly stepping through slightly different complete images one at a time, as with **flip-books**. In the second, objects move independently from the background and other objects. Each object may have its own constraints and behaviors and move through different positions and backgrounds. This method is similar to traditional **cartoon cel animations** in which characters appear to move across a separate background. This technique can be used for both 2D and 3D animation. "**Fly-throughs**," a technique that allows users to move within animated 3D structures are a version of this technique. **Virtual reality** ▶ **121** is another example of this type of animation. Direct movement and control of objects allow more flexibility but require more processing.

Animators use a variety of tools including modeling, animation, and rendering applications. These tools differ in their capabilities and degree of appropriateness for certain jobs. **Modeling** applications are used to create 3D objects and environments. There are at least four levels of rendering precision, with each level requiring increased processing power and time. The lowest level is a simple **wire-frame** model which shows the lines of every object's basic construction against a plain background. Wire-frame drawings are frequently cluttered with lines that are not necessary to describe a specific view. For this reason, the next level of **hidden-line** views suppress extraneous lines to draw simpler and more understandable scenes. Objects in hidden-line views appear solid and are thus easier to distinguish. The next level of rendering is **solid modeling** in which shade, shadow, and color are added. Solid modeling can add a great deal of "realism" and be more easily understood. Modeled objects tend to look more finished and complete. The last level is **realistic rendering** which can add more realistic light sources, multiple light sources, reflection, and texture mapping.

Interview: Lucia Grossberger Morales

As an artist who has "collaborated" with computers since 1979, Lucia Grossberger Morales' current work includes interactive shrines that invite the viewer to experience facts and fantasy of the artist's Bolivian-American heritage.

As an artist, what is your relationship with the computer?
When working with a computer, one realizes that the computer has logic. I always keep that in mind. I always ask, "How can the computer do this type of effect most easily?" I find it useful to know the way bits and bytes and everything work together. And I have an understanding of the hardware structure of the computer—not at the engineering level—but enough to understand how it works. So I know which methods of animation might work best.

The more you know it, the more elegant the effects you can get from it. You should understand what pixels, bits, RGB, and NTSC are and what they do. Know the difference between additive color and subtractive color.

There are two levels of knowing, the first being the basic understanding of the computer's behavior, of "that is the way it works." The second is being able to really change and alter the tool. The more an artist knows, the better he or she can use the medium. It comes down to knowing your tools. You do not have to know how a brush is made, but you had better know how it works. The computer is a collaborator, not just a tool. It is a meta-tool. It is more than a brush or stylus.

What fascinates me about computers is their ability to process logical operations. The computer produces quick effects. The computer will let us do things with animation that were never done before, and computer animation will become very different from traditional animation.

How would you compare traditional and computer animation?
The computer has a mathematical base that enables it to interpret, reformulate, and recalculate numerical forms, so it can alter and modify images. It can represent mathematical extrapolations, even when it is being used to create "traditional" frame-by-frame animation.

Thus, the computer will allow you to extend your ability as an animator. All the information is stored in digital form. The computer becomes an intelligent canvas. For example, you can do a fade-in several ways on the computer, and very easily. The computer follows an algorithm to move bits around to create the effect. The same effect would be hard to do manually, and not nearly as easy to change.

Talk about some of your work.
La Abuelita is a piece I began five years ago to capture the story about my Bolivian grandmother. I kept working on animations to get them right. About a year ago I started to work on the interactivity of the piece. This was a lot of work; the animations had to work well together. I am trying to come up with visual metaphors to help the viewer move through different areas. On the main track, one learns about my grandmother. Other tracks lead to stories about Bolivia: the political scene, the workers, etc. Each area has a different identifying style. I am still in the process of showing the piece to people and I am still working on it.

My early experiments with computer animation taught me a lot about balance. Normally, a still image is balanced in a single moment of time. An animated image is balanced over a period of time. I do not think of one frame at a time. I always keep the whole sequence in mind. Just as our eye needs to find satisfaction in balance in an individual frame, it also needs to find it through time.

Anyone working with the computer in a creative way does not generally know that much about what a computer can do. So it is really important that we have a playful attitude.

Animation applications usually allow only two-dimensional animation to be constructed and controlled. While drawn or rendered objects and backgrounds can appear to be three-dimensional, they can only be moved up, down, or across a screen. Animation programs, however, have many features that help automate the movements, including abilities to do "betweening" or filling in movements from start and stop points.

Animation Prototyping

During prototyping, it is probably not necessary to render all animations to their ultimate levels of quality. One or two highly finished examples are probably enough. The rest can be rendered in much less detail and used as placeholders for more finished versions that will be completed in the production stage.

Try to project the amount, length, and complexity of all animations by experimenting with a few samples. Determine the level of rendering quality sufficient for prototyping purposes. Animators will need the production list and storyboards to estimate production and rendering times and to state equipment needs. Also, be sure to account for the space needed to store these animations on the delivery medium. Animations can take up a lot of space and may eclipse space budgeted for other content.

full of nuances and details that often must be addressed with high quality production.

Because of its portability and almost universal everyday acceptance, video can be especially good for capturing personal information in interviews. Documentaries incorporate video to describe theories, present evidence, and support conclusions. Video can be used to teach by example and show processes that are difficult to describe in text. Video can also be used to communicate to a wider audience than text or speech can reach. Depending on the subject matter, video can more easily cross **linguistic** and **cultural boundaries** ▶ 96. It can also be an effective means of communicating to hearing or learning impaired people.

When using actors to convey information in video form it is important to understand the knowledge and background of the audience. A good **actor** can enhance the content of a piece but an actor whose **style**, **language**, and **attitude** are not right for the audience might hinder credibility and acceptance.

Repurposing Existing Video

Depending on the nature of the project, there are many sources for existing film and video such as university film archives, public libraries, or client materials. Most

Video

Video ▶ 30, 199 is fast becoming the celebrated medium of multimedia, in part because it is the newest medium to be available for use on personal computers. People are familiar with video through movies and television and expect similar levels of production values. These demands, though, will vary with the application, project, and subject matter. Video has an innate ability to attract, engross, and persuade people. Video images can be emotional, evocative, and powerful. Used ineffectively or inappropriately, however, they can also be gratuitous and dull.

The use of motion pictures and video can have revolutionary and social implications, as evidenced by the videotape of the Rodney King incident or Abraham Zapruder's footage of the assassination of John F. Kennedy. However, video can be a complex medium

video must be edited to match the purpose of the product. If a product is not adding significant features such as commentary or interactive control to existing content, the chances of its success are slim. Users may be more inclined to watch a training seminar on videotape than on their computer if the computer version offers little or no additional content or control.

An example of repurposing existing content with added control and new content is the *Life Story* CD-ROM from WINGS for Learning. This product began as a research project in Apple's Multimedia Lab and takes its point of departure from a BBC-produced movie about the discovery of DNA structure. The movie is divided into segments that portray various issues and steps that led to the discovery. Students can either watch the movie in one continuous sequence or stop at any time and explore different issues. *Life Story* makes use of all media types to elaborate on the concepts

Some people choose to be innocent, not contaminated by past history or criticism. I was one of those people. For 15 or 20 years of my filmmaking career I knew nothing about the past. Only later did I realize how much I missed by not knowing the inventory of conventions. By all means, we've got to break the prison house of cinematic language. We have to break conventions. But I would recommend knowing about tradition, not to accept it or believe in it but to be deliberate in choosing whether or not we follow it. If one wants to be free and fly, one has to be aware of the past.

— Bob Bell, Director of the Multimedia Studies Program, San Francisco State University

Navigable Movies provide a means for capturing views of an object or an environment in a way that allows a user to freely examine its details. These movies provide a simple form of "telepresence" in that the user's experience is of manipulating a virtual object for purposes of inspection or of gazing around a virtual space for purposes of observation. Some fertile applications for this idea are:

- *The construction of a "virtual museum," whereby navigable movies of the rooms in a museum (real or synthetic) can capture the contents of the rooms while still providing the user a sense of place. Such a set of movies offers limited access to a place that is otherwise remote, inaccessible, or imaginary.*

- *The construction of a catalog of objects that a user can inspect, perhaps a catalog of artifacts contained in a virtual museum. This allows a user to inspect objects that are too fragile, precious, or nonexistent to be handled.*

- *The capturing of the interiors of homes or other properties by a real estate agent, for later display to prospective customers. A database of such movies can be collected to provide a richer catalog than that afforded by still photographs.*

— Mitchell Yawitz, Kaleida Labs, Inc.

behind the technology and processes shown in the movie. The movie contributes its narrative and dramatic characteristics, while the additional content contributes control, interactivity, and context.

Generating New Video

Original footage can be shot with either **film** or **videotape**. While 35mm film traditionally offers greater clarity and color quality than video, it can require more expensive equipment and expertise for production and post-production. Before it can be digitized for computer use, film is usually developed and transferred to videotape via a special post-production process. A special process also exists for converting film to videodisc format. Both processes are usually completed by professional production agencies.

For most purposes, however, video offers both less expense and faster results. Video does not require developing, and videotape is reusable. Most **video digitizing boards** ▶ 205 for personal computers supply common connectors for **video cameras** and recorders, allowing a faster turnaround time to create a clip. In addition, video offers immediate viewing so that all shots can be checked for adequacy.

Film and video have different **frame rates** (the number of frames or images that display in one second). The film standard is 24 frames per second, while the video standard is 30 frames per second. Translating film to video can affect the quality of the image due to the conversion in frame rates. Although professional post-production agencies may be needed to translate film into video, almost anyone can digitize video directly into a computer with any of the numerous digitizing cards available. Video digitizing cards are on an extremely fast track of technological development and vary in quality, performance, capabilities, and price.

Working well with video requires an awareness of other media types and disciplines. Like a still photographer, a videographer should understand **lighting**, **focus**, **exposure**, and **composition** ▶ 185. The importance of good quality sound in video should also be acknowledged. And as with theater or film, video involves coordination of the script, actors, setting, and movement. Consult with professionals or people well-versed in the art and technology of video and other media to determine your needs in all of these areas.

Video Styles

Like all media, video can have many different styles which should be explored and determined in the prototype stage *before* production starts. Professional videographers and video editors can suggest the equipment, resources, and time needed to achieve certain

styles such as documentary, corporate, informal, fast-paced, or personal. Nonprofessionals who wish to shoot their own video should decide whether the style that results from limited equipment and expertise is adequate for the purposes of the project.

Certain **styles** can be obtained by applying **special effects**, a useful way to enhance video footage that otherwise may be in poor or ordinary condition. Adding color tints or borders can add interest to a low-resolution video image. **Rotoscoping,** for example, is a technique of converting video into outline drawings that can appear as animations. **Morphing** is an effect that creates the impression of one or more images being transformed into another. For example, a fish can appear to transform into a sailboat, or one person can "morph" into someone else. Special effects can create unusual and appealing sequences but run the risk of creating "eye candy" unless they enhance the meaning or experience of the video content.

Video Technologies

The most important and enabling components of video software are the **compression and decompression formulas** ▶ 206 used. These formulas are referred to as **codecs** and are the key to the ability of personal computers to display video at acceptable quality. **QuickTime** ▶ 153, 208, for example, includes at least five compressors, each specializing in a different type of image (one each for photographs, animations, and sounds and two for video). While QuickTime is compatible with other platforms such as Windows and Silicon Graphics, most video technologies for personal computers are not as portable—Microsoft's Video for Windows, for example.

Be sure that the video technology used is compatible with your project's target platforms and each platform model. Again, experienced video engineers can help determine the best technologies and specifications for now and hopefully in the future.

Video Prototyping

Videographers and editors will need a list of production tasks and storyboards to estimate production times and equipment needs. Several items should be determined, such as the amount, length, and complexity of each video clip and the level of quality sufficient for prototyping purposes. Estimates can be calculated from measuring the effort and time required to produce sample clips of varying complexities.

Video takes up the most amount of data per second of any other medium and can quickly consume a videodisc or CD-ROM. It is therefore important to calculate the space needed to store the video on the delivery

Interview: Nicole Leduc

How did you become a videographer?

My educational background includes degrees in communications and television production. I spent almost 12 years in middle management in different corporations. As a manager, I gave many presentations and concentrated on new product marketing strategies. To convince upper management of the value of our market research and proposed strategies, I arranged to videotape the consumer interviews we were doing and incorporated the videos into our presentations. We had the traditional overhead transparencies and popped in the video at the appropriate times. It was a simple form of multimedia.

Eventually I left the corporate managerial world and formed my own videography company with a colleague. My company produces corporate videos and presentations for major clients in the San Francisco Bay Area.

Do you work independently?

Yes, but I subcontract to other groups. A lot of people do this. I hire people to do elements of production and they are very skilled. I will generally hire an editor for special jobs that require detailed work and patience. Otherwise, I prefer to do the editing myself. I prefer to work with people who are experienced, who have done media production for many years, and who know the different and best ways to do something.

For example, on a typical video shoot I need to have at least one very good camera person and one very good sound person, both of whom know how to set up lighting. That's minimum. If it's a two-camera shoot, I would need two cameramen, one sound engineer, and one person who's doing the sound recording on the floor. They need split-second timing, nerves of steel, and quick reflexes—especially for live production shoots.

Has your business background helped with your current work?

If you're not a creative filmmaker and want to make a living with videography, you need some knowledge base that will help you leverage your skills. You have to be able to talk to your clients in their own language so they understand that you understand their business. If they are sure of your knowledge, they are more inclined to give you a media contract. If you don't have the rapport, they won't trust you. For the client to feel good and let you have free reign, you have to understand the client's business.

Almost all of the work I do is informational in content. Making an informational video is like putting together a presentation, a presentation that is necessarily linear. Once it is in video form you can't do more with the piece except re-edit it. Some clients ask me to create extracts from large video presentations, often four or five from one tape. Video production takes time. If my clients had the means to select the clips, digitize them as QuickTime movies, and retrieve them from a database, they would be able to create their own presentations from the original video we had created for them.

What they need is the video equivalent for HyperCard. People need tools that will help them take in available information in video format and play with it. But even with such a tool, a lot of people are not trained editors. They do not always have an eye for editing or working in a time-based medium. It's not a skill that happens overnight. Editing is a craft.

Please explain "an eye for editing."

It's the ability to pare away the fuzziness to get to the main thought or story. A good editor can find the common threads that make the sequence seamless and helps the listener parse it effortlessly. When someone is looking at one of my videos, they should never be aware they are looking at a video. They are listening to a story. That is what I aim for when doing a video or presentation. It's important to fit the different elements together so that there is no break or disruption or sudden shifts in thought.

How can existing video footage be used effectively in an organization?

Most companies have tons of video footage and a latent demand to use it. Unfortunately, people don't have the simple tools they need to get the video into a format they can easily manipulate. Even if the video were digitized, a lot of people don't have the experience or the computer software to manipulate the images correctly. People must turn to specialized production companies that have a lot of equipment to prepare the videos. Even then it is still usually in a linear format because the production companies do not have the software tools yet to easily create interactive forms.

There are three huge problems with repurposing video: getting it in to a computer, manipulating it once it is in, and finding some way of maintaining and cataloging it.

What about nonprofessionals who want to shoot video?

Videography is like film in many respects. There are so many nuances to be aware of. If you want to have a beautiful image you have to have it lit beautifully, you need good camera people, you need to know the kind of camera that will give you the effects you want, and you need to know how to edit the production. You have to know your equipment and your people. That is why you hire really good, expert people.

For most purposes, though, it may be more important to capture the information or event in a timely manner with whatever equipment you can obtain. It's not hard to obtain a good image, as long as you have good color saturation and enough light and the image is in focus. It is important to make sure the color balance is accurate, although it is sometimes hard with fluorescent lights to do so. I started using Hi8 tape as an alternative to BetaCam SP or 3/4 in., and I'm pleased with it so far. Hi8 has a big drawback: it is not physically durable during the editing process. If I use Hi8, I transfer it to a 3/4 in. master before I edit.

Quality also depends on the level of expectation. With shows such as America's Funniest Home Videos or the simulated police stories, people have gotten almost used to the fact that they are not going to see perfect images. Look at the Rodney King videotape or MTV or I Witness Video. What we are finding out is that if the informational content is striking enough, people will want to see it.

It's important with QuickTime movies to capture the essence of the information you want to present. Because of disk space constraints, video clips should be selected carefully before they are digitized for use with QuickTime. The audience will see enough of the image and hear enough of the audio to get an idea of what's going on, even if the images and audio have been compressed. The message, though, must be clear.

Nicole Leduc is a videographer and president of Leduc Communications in Cupertino, CA. Drawing on her extensive experience in business management, Leduc specializes in producing high-end videos for corporate market research studies.

Incorporating editorial links in a multimedia product is much the same as preparing the index for a book. The content for both has to be laid out before the links or index can be generated.

*Most **search mechanisms** operate solely on text, although some multimedia databases provide visual search mechanisms such as key word entries and thumbnail views. Other types of search mechanisms for time-based and spatially organized information are being explored by developers and researchers in a variety of fields. Searching, filtering, and providing new views or relationships of information are powerful tools to help users customize the information to their needs. Keep abreast of developments in this area and look for new ways to give them these empowering capabilities.*

*Think about pre-building **indexes** before finalizing the content list in order to build in storage space in the product for the indexes.*

platform and to choose a compression scheme. For example, typical video compression ratios between 4:1 and 10:1 allow a CD-ROM to hold about 30 minutes of quarter screen movie.

Integration

The integration stage of prototyping is the time to review and assemble the pieces of the project so that they function as a whole. Once all of the separate content pieces reach an acceptable quality, check them off the list and give them to the person responsible for incorporating them into the prototype. The amount of actual **storage space** taken by the content pieces should be compared with the projected estimates for the remainder of the project. If content pieces prepared to production standards are larger than planned, all of the final pieces may not fit onto the delivery medium. It is better to learn about such limitations in the prototype stage rather than be taken by surprise at the end of production.

How the pieces are integrated varies with different authoring environments. Text, illustrations, and sometimes sounds can be copied and pasted into appropriate places in the prototype. Animations and movies, however, do not sit *in* the product itself but are called up from disk and played on demand. Each clip must be somehow linked to the main program, a task that may require some custom scripting. Depending on the linking mechanism of a particular authoring tool, it may be necessary to change or rebuild the links if the movie or animation files are moved from their original locations.

Plugging in the parts is not the end of the prototyping stage. Several additional steps may be necessary to ensure a smooth product. Depending on the interface and interaction design, it may be necessary to establish links, generate indexes, and activate navigation controls within the product.

Links

A **link** ▶ 130 is a connection between two media elements. There are a few different kinds and permutations of links. One distinction is between editorial and free links. **Editorial links** are connections established by the project team that connect items felt to be significant. Not all items are linked to all other items and many items may have no links at all. These links are editorial decisions made to enhance the understanding of a particular topic at a particular point.

Free links, however, relate any like item to any other like item. Free links may be an automatic function of the authoring engine. For example, selecting the word

computer in the text of a project with free links might bring up a list of every other occurrence of *computer* in the project and allow the user to jump to any of them. An editorial link, however, might only list a few possible connections that the designers felt elaborated on the specific topic of computers at that point. Targets and destinations are usually determined by the editor although automatic methods may exist or be built for a particular authoring environment.

Editorial links can also be one-way or two-way. **One-way links** allow a user to jump to a connecting point without returning while **two-way links** allow users to return from where they first jumped.

Search Mechanisms

Many authoring environments provide built-in search capabilities for identifying keywords and building indexes and links. HyperCard, for example, provides a robust text searching engine that can be accessed easily at any time while using a HyperCard stack. Faster text searching and data filtering, however, may be custom-built while the product is in the production stage. For example, a list of all illustrations in a project is easy to prepare and quicker to display for a user than generating the same list on the fly at the time it is requested.

The task of a **search engine** ▶ 141 is to locate where particular words or phrases occur in a text. A search engine can help users hunt for items they recall by content or topic but not by name. Instructions given to a search engine are called a query. The user forms a query by entering words to specify the sought-after information. Without an index, all text would have to be searched thoroughly for the specific words in the query. This can take an extremely long time on a CD-ROM filled with text. If these indexes are pre-built, the search engine can look for queries in this index instead which is a much quicker process.

Most search engines permit **Boolean searches** which are queries that use the Boolean operators AND, OR, and NOT to control what will be found. Although Boolean operators are powerful parameters, they can confuse users who are not practiced with Boolean logic. Boolean searching in an authoring environment may require a custom interface that masks the complexity of its use.

When searching and building lists of links or content, it is often best to allow a user to see this list as it is being compiled and cancel the search process whenever necessary because these processes may take time to complete. Features like *Find Next* may save time and frustration for many users. Also, allowing users to save and manipulate old queries can be valuable. Consider allowing users to **filter** lists for specific kinds of content. For example, users may remember an illustration or animation they saw although they cannot remember its name. Providing a list of all content with controls to filter for animations would narrow the search.

Programming

The primary role of the **programmer** ▶ 32, 208 of an interactive prototype is to combine pieces of content with a basic interactive design that makes sense to users. A secondary role is to ensure that the program is consistent and efficient so that it can be easily understood, tested, and maintained by others who will be later using the program. Not all projects will need custom programming, but many of the authoring tools or the design requirements of a project may make it necessary for some.

Programming for interactivity can be **procedure-based**, meaning that it follows the basic flow of input, processing, and output. A flowchart is a useful visual tool for presenting the basic process flow, the path of interaction, and the appearance of media elements in a program. Each step in the flowchart could identify some action taken by the user or the system. Some steps require decisions, again made either by the user or the programmer. Many repetitive processes can be organized into subroutines which are small, self-contained pieces of the overall program that increase programming efficiency.

An alternative to procedure-based programming is **object-oriented programming** which describes events in terms of independent objects and their relationships with each other. Objects have their own **scripts** ▶ 209 or methods that describe how they interact with data or other objects. Object-oriented programming offers the advantage of flexibility because objects can be changed independently without usually affecting other objects.

Programming Software

General shrink-wrapped software tools can reduce the need for extensive programming. Some **authoring systems** ▶ 139 give the developer a visual depiction of the flow of all the screens and materials for a project. Programming for such tools involves little more than sequencing screens in a diagrammatic form, opening up the units, and designating their look. Such tools have been used to develop large bodies of educational material for corporations or schools with a minimum of programming resources.

Sometimes tools provide a limited set of interface options that may put severe design constraints on a

Programming Guidelines

Simplicity
Even for the most low level data structures and algorithms, the best choice is often the simplest. Developers and researchers can spend untold hours optimizing an approach from a theoretical viewpoint when in reality the conditions are not the same as originally assumed or the performance differences are so minor as to be unnoticeable. (Of course, Einstein once said, "A theory should be as simple as possible but no simpler.")

Implementation Issues
An advantage of simplicity is that it makes implementation easier. In software development, the largest feasible system is often determined by the point at which details are forgotten and new bugs are created as fast as details are remembered and old bugs fixed.

Time/Size Tradeoffs
Many data structures and algorithms can have different permutations depending on the relative costs of memory versus CPU cycles. Prototyping quick solutions can help determine the right approach when confronted with the trade-off between storing intermediate or end results or recalculating the information each time.

product. Or perhaps a tool does not have a text search mechanism. Specialized subroutines can sometimes be added to programs. In most Macintosh software, these specialized subroutines are called external commands (XCMDs). Some commonly used commands can be found in catalogs or resources provided by developer programs. Others can be written by programmers under contract. The Voyager Company's Expanded Books series uses a library of specially built XCMDs which extend many functions of HyperCard.

User Testing

The role of **user testing** is to ensure that a project satisfies the basic elements that contribute to a rich multimedia experience. These elements include interface, navigation, usefulness, and appeal. Results from well-conducted user tests can be a surprise for many multimedia developers, most of whom, unlike the testers, understand the product inside and out. User feedback is a valuable element in the prototype process where ideas are spawned, tried, tested, and discarded or improved in an ongoing loop. For example, an interactive game that has an innovative navigational design but a boring interface will probably not last long on the market if it is meant for ten-year-old boys.

A multimedia project is a multisensory experience for the user. Many elements of the experience cannot be predicted because they vary from person to person and from group to group. Therefore, user testing must take into account the audience who will most likely use the product but at the same time not leave out the possibility for other types of users.

Graphical programming environments are becoming more popular on some platforms. At the moment, many of these concern themselves primarily with the creation and design of interface elements along with relationships between them. The promise is that these environments will evolve to allow more control over abstract elements of software, making knowledge of programming language syntax and logic less necessary.

User testing is an ongoing process throughout the design and prototype stage. Individual content elements can be tested outside the domain of a prototype. Others can be tested with very rough prototypes.

Case Study: Theseus Cervical Cytology Multimedia Package

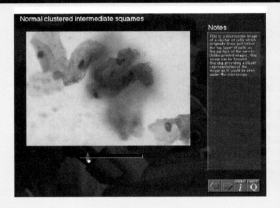

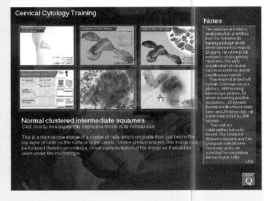

Description:

Theseus is a hypermedia image database/training tool for use in the medical arena. The first course to be developed with Theseus was the Cervical Cytology Multimedia Package, designed to assist in the first year training of Cervical Screening Lab assistants who are responsible for examining cervical smears for incidence of cancer and other conditions that may require treatment. The package features over 3,500 microscopic images, video clips, and interactive exercises for cytology technologists. The collection of core reference materials forms a "media base" that is hyperconnected by 200 instructional lessons.

Eventually, the Cervical Cytology course will be stored with other Theseus multimedia courses at Liverpool John Moores University's Aldham Robarts Learning Resource Centre, now under construction. The Centre is intended to house up to 400 networked multimedia workstations by the end of 1994. The ultimate goal of the center is to create a large database of multimedia entities that teachers can use like a slide library to create interactive lectures and courses and that students can use to create multimedia essays.

Project Type:
Multimedia Database

Development Hardware:
Macintosh IIci 20Mb RAM, 520MB HD, Canon Hi8 videocamera, ScreenMachine digital video board, Olympus microscope and Panasonic camera with mount, Sony recordable LaserDisc System

Deliver Hardware:
Macintosh IIci w/ 8MB RAM and 160MB hard disk, Sony LaserDisc player, ScreenMachine digital video board

Software Used:
MacroMind Director, SuperCard, QuickTime, Adobe PhotoShop, FileMaker Pro

Team Members and Roles:
2 Consultant Cytology Pathologists, 1 Multimedia Producer (Roy Stringer), 2 Video Production Crew members, 1 Project Manager, 1 Project Coordinator, 1 Consultant Gynecological Surgeon, 1 Cytology Lab Technician, 1 Graphic Artist. 10 total, only 2 full time.

Funding:
Department of Employment (Training Initiative Fund)

Contact:
Roy Stringer
Interactive Designs Ltd.

Management:
The Open Learning Department of the Liverpool John Moores University facilitated and managed the project, including the managing of finances.

Concept and Planning:
Brainstorming and project analysis included regular weekly meetings of 4-5 hours each over a 3-month period with the entire team. The first meeting included an in-depth discussion to answer the demands of training cytology technologists.

Design and Prototype:
Several prototypes with QuickTime were completed to determine image and design requirements.

Production:
It was essential that the consultant pathologists have complete control over microscope image recording to ensure color fidelity, appropriate content, and database accuracy. This required setting up a hi-specification microscope, broadcast spec' video camera with microscope mount, and Sony recordable LaserDisc system. A lengthy process of quality testing was carried out to ensure the best image quality. Considerable training was provided to the pathologists who were entirely unfamiliar with either the Macintosh computer or video technologies.

Testing:
Arrangements have been made for testing the first version in Liverpool John Moores University, the University of Nujmegen, and the Birmingham Regional Cytology Training School when it is ready at the end of March 1993. Testing will be concerned with software robustness and with the integrity of the teaching materials.

Distribution:
Initially to Regional Training Schools on LaserDisc and 160MB hard drive. Later, when CD-ROM version is finished, by CD-ROM and over FDDI within the University's LAN.

Programming
20% Off-the-shelf tools
80% Custom Code

Content
2% Repurposed
98% New

Expenses
5% Marketing
75 % Development
20% Operations

Development Expenses
70% Personnel
30% Equipment
(Content not app.)

Money
Personnel

Total Development Time: 15 months

Total Development Costs: approx. $150,000

Total Development Team: 10 people

Interface Testing

Interface testing improves the chances of the project being accepted and used after it is produced. The caveat to user interface design and testing is that it can go on forever. There will always be ways to improve a design to best meet the needs and desires of an audience—indeed of several audiences. Set limits to the iterative cycles of testing and design by working from the stated purpose and goals of the project. For some projects, it may be possible to choose a simple approach for hard-to-resolve issues, putting further refinement off to future releases.

If at all possible, involve members of the intended audience to test different interface prototypes. A good example of interface testing is provided by Dr. Alan Shelton, a Los Angeles ophthalmologist who experimented with an interactive kiosk in his office to educate his patients about surgical procedures. The Macintosh-based kiosk incorporated color QuickTime movies of eye surgery techniques displayed in 160x120-pixel windows. He soon realized that his vision-impaired patients were having difficulty discerning any of the procedures. Dr. Shelton has taken this knowledge and made use of improved display technology to re-scale the movies to a larger size.

Interface testing involves balancing user needs with current technical feasibility. Sometimes, technical and budgetary constraints can impose an economy of design that may actually create a more effective interface. Designers who wish to develop a project using 24-bit color full-motion video but find that they must deliver on an 8-bit color platform may need to forget the fireworks and concentrate on more effective and possibly simpler solutions. Limitations force a design team to look at the purpose and ask, "What does the user absolutely need to create an interesting and useful experience?" Testing the interface will help sort out the glitz from the real substance, although in some cases the show may be the intended substance. Many developers have found through user testing that simple interfaces are often more effective and that technology should never get in the way of the message.

Special Considerations

Special market requirements should be taken into account during user interface testing. For example, how easy is it for a motion-impaired individual to trigger an option from screen to screen? Are there too many keystrokes or mouse-clicks required for different actions? Is there a way for hearing-impaired users to raise the volume? Is there a simple way to turn the sound off?

International markets pose special challenges for localization testing because expectations and prefer-

ences differ from culture to culture. If your product is meant to be used by people from different cultures, make sure you adequately test these people's reactions to your project. Localization is the process of readying a product for specific national or cultural markets. Not only must words be translated correctly, they must be spelled, pronounced, and used in the right context. For example, the "Grandma" in Brøderbund's *Just Grandma and Me* is presented differently for each language translation to accurately reflect specific cultural norms and expectations. Ignoring international concerns can bring results that are humorous in some cases and disastrous in others.

Another example of a lesson learned through cross-cultural user interface testing is that of a multimedia developer and his team who had designed and installed a public information kiosk featuring a touch-screen interface. The kiosk was placed in an area frequented by tourists. Weeks after the installation the developer learned that the kiosk was being used frequently by everyone except Japanese visitors. Was there something wrong with the display? Was the information incorrect? It was not until an acquaintance informed the developer that most Japanese people were extremely conscious of maintaining personal hygiene and that touching a screen that had been already touched by others was considered distasteful. Tissues were provided next to the kiosk and it was discovered that Japanese visitors were inclined to use a touch screen if they could clean it before and after use. "I never would have known that because I'm not Japanese!" claimed the developer.

Navigation Testing

Be sure to test the product's navigational features. Wayfinding techniques should be effective. A **sign**, **sound cue**, **color scheme**, or **backdrop** should contribute to a sense of place or heading in a product. A **navigation system** ▶ 134 that meets the design specifications may still be too difficult for an audience to use. If testing reveals that users grow confused, lose their way, or ask for help then the navigation elements probably need to be revised.

Even if the interface and navigation system tests well, the ultimate test of success is whether the project is appealing and useful to people. Much of this information is expressed in subjective statements such as "It was fun," or "Now I understand the concept much better than when I read about it." Degrees of appeal and usefulness, though, depend on the audience and the purpose of the project. In fact, one of the biggest questions among K-12 educators who want to bring multimedia into the classroom is how to make learning appealing and fun. One way to test effectiveness is to observe how

During the first installation of TPTV, we constantly watched people use it. we videotaped them saying to each other, "Wait, wait, wait...it's doing something." Or people would say, "So now what do I do?" That told us we weren't giving enough feedback. Setting up TPTV in a public place was a good way to test. We didn't have to find some sort of sample group.
— Abbe Don, Artist and Interface Designer

Recommended Apple Computer Interface Design Steps:

1. *Identify and meet your user*
2. *Write a scenario (A Day in the Life Of . . .)*
3. *Sketch steps as a rough storyboard*
4. *Construct a system map*
5. *Build a flipbook prototype*
6. *Solicit user feedback*
7. *Redesign interface using user results*
8. *Gather more user feedback*
9. *Refine and develop prototypes*
10. *Code, after interface designed*
11. *Iterate as many times as possible*

— S. Joy Mountford, Manager, Apple Design Center

Never be the sole tester of your own code. Invite members of the target audience to do the testing, and watch them carefully without guiding or interfering. Many developers and designers have an overwhelming tendency to grab the mouse and say, "No, here's how you do it." Videotaping users' reactions and comments as they try to navigate on their own can produce some startling discoveries about the effectiveness or ineffectiveness of a design.

The prototype team should understand and communicate how much more production work is not covered by the prototype. This is the "mirage" of the prototype. There may be dozens of unrealized screens, rough sound recordings, or missing transitions. For any potential client, the manager should show the prototype in the context of the initial proposal and explain what is needed for production.

eager students are to interact with a project and ask them later to discuss or demonstrate what they have learned. Flight simulators are examples of interactive products that were first used for industrial training purposes. Aviation companies would train prospective pilots in simulations of take-off, flight, and landing procedures. The game-like interface proved to be so appealing and useful that it is now available to consumers who want to "play" pilot.

Fine-Tuning the Prototype

When tested, a prototype may reveal major problems that will need redesign. These may include issues such as performance of search mechanisms or insufficient room on the delivery media. The prototype team must then address these problems with new or modified solutions and build a new prototype for testing. It is risky to proceed with the next stage under the belief that "necessary changes" can be made once production begins. Major problems often only get worse.

Functional Testing

The prototype must be tested for performance and capability on the intended delivery medium and equipment. Functional testing is an important time to check the validity of the **design specifications** ▶ 173. Once production work has begun, changes to specifications can wreak havoc with schedule and budgets. Test that the prototype functions as intended on the slowest platform in your target market. Video and audio quality especially suffer on slower equipment. All media features and interaction must function within performance goals or else be redesigned.

Test on differently sized screens and at different color depths. Do screens become illegible in black and white, grayscale, or 8 bit-color? Are parts of the project cut off by 9-inch or 12-inch screens? If so the art work may need to be redesigned. If the project is designed to use specific equipment such as an 8-bit 13-inch color monitor, be sure that these requirements are stated on packaging and in documentation and advertisements.

Creating a CD-ROM check disc is an intermediary step when pressing CD-ROMs. A check disc contains the data in the same form as a pressed CD-ROM and serves as a way to test a prototype or to test a production version before going on to mastering and production. (A master is a component created for and used in the replication process.)

If your project requires equipment not standard on all computers, for example, CD-ROM drives, large screen monitors, video compression cards, or DSPs and MIDI conversion software, be sure to test it with a variety of manufacturers. Because a product works with one manufacturer's drive or card does not mean it will work the same with all models that your client or customer may have.

Optimization

Optimization ▶ 232 is the process of improving the performance and storage configuration of a project. Optimization techniques should begin to be explored and decided in the prototype stage before production begins. All optimization depends on having access to the delivery platform specified, which means having the exact platform CPU with the actual amount of memory stated in the product specification. The precise CD-ROM, network, hard drive, or storage access device needs to be acquired for testing. Too often, developers test performance on high-performance development workstations which have completely different timing and interaction characteristics.

Make sure that the complete audio-visual requirements are optimized for the correct delivery environment. Sound optimized on a computer rigged up to a stereo sound system will be completely different from sound optimized for a stand-alone computer.

Each platform and model has its own level of performance. The measurement for speed of processing data is called the transfer rate. Each delivery medium has a transfer rate. For example, a CD-ROM drive's data rate (150-300 KB/sec) is much lower than a hard drive (1-3 MB/sec). Test the prototype at the specific data rates of all components.

Space on computers is always at a premium. Even CD-ROMs fill up fast if sound or video is included in a project. Examine the prototype elements carefully to estimate how big the finished product will be. It may be that the pieces planned will take more room than is available on the delivery medium specified. Compressing images, sounds, and video may be possible with the authoring system being used but do not wait till the end of the project to find out. Some smaller products that ship on one or two diskettes use a decompression utility to assemble the working program on a user's hard disk.

The size-time tradeoff is a typical optimization decision. Prototypes can be implemented differently depending on the speed of the computer, the amount of available memory, the capacity and speed of the disk, and the speed of data transfer on the data bus.

Testing the Delivery Medium

It is a good idea to test the delivery medium with the final prototype. This step can uncover problems in performance, interface, programming, and access. Whether the delivery medium is a locked diskette, videodisc, or CD-ROM, at least one **check disc** ▶ 111, **232** or "one-off" should be made for functional

testing. This disk is a first attempt of compiling all the pieces into a working prototype.

A check disc or one-off is a CD-R (write-once CD-ROM) produced in-house or by a premastering service. It contains the data in the same form as a pressed CD-ROM. A check disc is useful not only for testing the delivery medium and running through the preparation and premastering process in a less strenuous situation, but it also provides a convenient way to retain a functioning demo. Storage space can be at such a premium during development that project teams often throw out old demos. This practice can leave little to show at impromptu demo situations that often present themselves during development.

Product Specifications and Standards

Testing every content, interface, and interaction element will help develop product specifications for each type of media and each aspect of the product. A **product specification** is a complete list of features drawn up by the manager or the client. The list should cover type and amount of content, interface characteristics, and level of interaction. The list includes the expectations for the production staff and also provides material for marketing and promotion.

The standards for each media type used in the project should be derived from the prototype. It should be very clear before going into production what image, sound, animation, and video quality and styles are expected or what performance can be relied on. The specification should cover all aspects of the interface, including all interaction.

In addition to providing a model for media standards, the prototype will show what user interface and interaction standards should be followed for production. The examples in the prototype should show all ranges of the look of the production and how it should feel.

Task Chart

The tasks of the prototype offer a preview of production. The **task chart** from the proposal can now be re-evaluated for production based on the experiences that produced the prototype. The plan should show each task fixed with team members, materials, resources, time, and cost estimates. The collection of these tasks should form a picture of what is needed to complete the project.

Evaluate Whether You're Ready for the Next Step

It is tempting to continue refining the design, changing screen colors to improve the look or revising code to increase efficiency. In any project there will always be room for improvement, but at what point does the design and prototype stage end and production begin? The decision to freeze the design for production is influenced by factors such as schedule, finances, patience, and expectations.

A good point of reference is the original project proposal document that conveyed expectations and specifications. If the design meets the basic expectations and specifications it should be ready for production. A checkpoint meeting involving the project team and client can be conducted to obtain final approval of the design. Once production standards are in place, the project can then move on to production.

All of us failed to match our dream of perfection. So I rate us on the basis of our splendid failure to do the impossible. In my opinion, if I could write all my work again, I am convinced that I would do it better, which is the healthiest condition for an artist. That's why he keeps on working, trying again; he believes each time that this time he will bring it off. Of course he won't, which is why this condition is healthy. Once he did it, once he matched the work to the image, the dream, nothing would remain....

— William Faulkner

Design and Prototype Tips

- It is much easier to make changes in the prototype stage than in the production stage.

- A design on paper is not enough. Most multimedia products require a working prototype or model for everyone to understand.

- Keep a notebook for you and your team during prototype. Use it to make sketching variations, lay out calculations, and record test settings, and refer back to it when necessary.

- Don't spend a large amount of money until you know exactly what you are going to build.

- As exciting and fun as multimedia computers may be to design and play with, treat them as production tools.

- Don't get so attached to an idea or technique that you lose sight of the project's purpose.

- Allow team members creative autonomy but figure out ways for them to work together.

- User-test early and often. Don't show the testers how to use the product. Let them try to figure it out on their own.

Production

Production

Michelangelo once described the process of sculpting as "freeing the man who is inside the marble." Ideas remain locked in abstraction if no one carves the stone and brings the complete form into the world — creates a full and real experience fit for an audience.

Prototyping defines a product's design as well as the procedures to use in its formation. The final design should be "frozen" before production begins. If it is still unclear or undecided, then the time is probably not right to begin production.

Simply stated, the goal of production is to **build and finish the project**. "To finish" can mean to complete a CD-ROM title for distribution, to create and install a custom kiosk, or to fulfill whatever final requirements appear in the proposal, such as providing ancillary training materials.

At first glance, the prototype and production stages seem the same. Both involve creating and editing content for the screen. But while prototyping emphasizes exploration, rough quality, and trial runs, production emphasizes repetition, automation, fine quality, and consistency. Many of the same processes and techniques will be used in both stages but prototyping creates standards and specifications that should be used for all media in the production stage.

Production Methods

In some cases, the same **authoring engine ▶ 139** or prototyping environment can be used for both prototyping and production. For example, HyperCard might have been used to prototype an electronic book or multimedia database. If the production tool and delivery engine is also HyperCard, then the original prototype might simply need to be "filled out." Usually, a programmer will need to optimize the code and create a refined version which can then be given to the production team for integrating the text, graphics, or other media elements.

If the prototype and production tools are different, a programmer or team of programmers will use the model provided by the prototype to create the engine using the production tools. In both cases, the programming team should create a finished and optimized model before others begin integrating and duplicating elements. Otherwise, once the model is built, making a change to scripts or code may require repeating that change many times throughout the project.

Some authoring tools that can be purchased on the market are essentially someone else's engine that they sell. Provided you have the necessary programming capabilities or have access to them, there is no reason why you cannot build your own engine. You can leverage this engine across multiple projects and even market it to others, provided you understand the extra investment in time and money this typically entails.

Another production method allows the production team to work with a smaller, faster editor for attaching and integrating elements. An **editor** is a smart template or form built in the chosen authoring system for the sole purpose of placing and laying out elements. Actions performed in an editor can create scripts that would otherwise have to be created endlessly by a programmer or content integrator. This technique can greatly speed up and simplify the process of content integration. In addition, any number of editors can be used at once, splitting the project into manageable sections that can be produced independently by different members of the production team.

Once an editor is filled out, an **instantiation engine ▶ 211** can be created to build the project using the structure provided by the editor. The resulting piece is the integrated project within the delivery engine. The working of the editors and instantiation engine is similar to a database publishing model. The editors place the content in structured form and then the instantiation engine in a sense plays the role of the input filters and page layout application. The end result in database publishing is a book or catalog. The end result in multimedia authoring is a set of content within an interactive viewer or delivery engine.

An engine's value is in automating repetitive processes in an optimized way. It takes a skilled programmer to build an editor and instantiation engine system but the benefits in speed and organization may be well worth the time.

Organizing the Production Schedule

One of the challenges in organizing production of a multimedia project, or any project for that matter, is to specify all the tasks and interdependencies. This includes listing all tasks involved with generating, integrating, and testing content and interaction. The prototyping phase should have provided information about the length of time and amount of effort needed to produce the different pieces. The project manager needs to use this knowledge to extrapolate and create **estimates ▶ 68** for each task in complete form.

Planning tasks and interdependencies requires juggling time, resources, and personnel. For example, if it takes 20 minutes for one person to digitize and enhance one photograph, what would it take to produce 300 photographs? A simple answer might be one person working 100 hours. But if that 20 minutes was for an experienced digitizer and the production person is not as skilled, then the estimate would be inaccurate. Too many times, a project manager will calculate the time for a task using values provided by experienced prototypers and then hire lower-priced, and, often, slower and less experienced personnel to complete the production. This type of ambitious forecasting can cause a project to miss production milestones from the start.

Adding additional people to speed up the process is not always an answer. Some tasks may depend on others being performed first. Knowing and scheduling these interdependencies will help reduce the amount of idle time for any of the team members. For example, images may need to be produced before accompanying text can be written. They will certainly need to be produced before layout and integration. If more people are added, then they will likely require more equipment, training, and supervision. Is there enough money and time budgeted for this? Also, if the primary person for a task gets sick, is there someone who can finish the job? A project manager must plan for these possibilities, making decisions on a daily basis to move the project ahead. Organizing the production schedule requires planning for the best and worst case scenarios for each task in a network of dependencies.

Milestones

Project managers should organize work schedules so that the entire project can be divided into manageable tasks, tasks that a group can complete in a reasonable time. Arranging manageable sections and setting achievable **milestones** helps both morale and control. Without attainable goals, projects can lose direction.

Production cycles can weaken the efficiency of procedures and people. Long production cycles with few "breaks" can lead to disheartened, stressed workers, and substandard work. The project manager needs to assess the scope of work and set milestones that will break up the long stretch of work to be done. Milestones keep the project team focused and prevents "surprises" at the end of the project. Achievement of several interim milestones is more psychologically rewarding than moving slowly toward a distant finish line. Focusing on attaining milestones improves efficiency and morale among team members.

Organizing Production Personnel

Each production task or responsibility in a multimedia project has an role associated with it. The project manager should assemble these **responsibilities** into logical collections and then assign a **role** to them. These roles can then be assigned to new or existing team members. The same person can perform several roles or several people share the same role. This delegation is especially important when team members are dependent on one another to complete tasks or if there is the potential for overlapping responsibilities. Defining who has the authority over what domains can reduce confusion and conflict when two people's jobs interconnect.

Every professional learns standards of **quality** from their own experience. An editor spots faulty writing and suggests improvements. A graphic designer judges color fidelity. A sound engineer winces at low-fidelity recordings. Professionals have levels of distinction that are beyond the eyes and ears of non-professionals. They can help determine the overall production values for a project by combining their expertise with a knowledge of the limits of the technology and the objectives of the product design.

At the same time, coordinating talented people can be a challenging situation. Professionals and non-professionals alike need to understand the production standards for the *current project*, not one they may have worked on previously. Creative people can often be strong-willed, in part because they often have to withstand criticism in order to step outside the boundaries of convention. Allowing them freedom to produce great work and yet have their styles match the other media elements requires upfront communications and expectations.

The reality of production is that many people may be needed for the tasks involved. Adding new people takes coordination and the need to understand the objectives of production and the many subtle elements in a project. The project manager should work with the artists and engineers on the production team to establish production standards for everything from equipment use to naming conventions to grammatical preferences. Standards can be as simple as a list of do's and don'ts and as complex as a corporate style guide covering all media types.

Used extensively in the publishing industry, a **style guide ▶ 146** is a compilation of detailed, project-specific information for the preparation and evaluation of media. For example, a style guide for text can specify requirements for punctuation, grammatical conventions,

Project management software is a good tool for managing projects that have more than a few people. These types of applications can illustrate dependencies between tasks and people and help validate or invalidate a production schedule.

Don't forget to calculate training time into the production process. Even the most experienced artist will need to come up to speed on a project before hitting peak effectiveness.

A popular saying in software engineering is that if it takes 3 people one year to design software, it will take 6 people two years to do the same thing.

Style guides can be either online or in print but should exist somewhere convenient for constant reference by artists, engineers, and managers.

Without managed organization and communication, production can be a baptism by fire for the beginning multimedia development team. Extensive and unorganized production jobs can drain both resources and morale. Project managers play a key role, but all project members should see themselves as collaborators in maintaining organization and communication.

Before production begins, be sure to budget time and resources for the following:
- *The number of screens*
- *The level of screen complexity*
- *The number of links among screens*
- *Any transitions*
- *Animation complexity*
- *QuickTime movies per minutes of digitization time*
- *Testing time times the number of screens and elements*
- *The number of check disks*
— Tyler Peppel, Arborescence

use of jargon, and other text concerns such as whether *online* should have a hyphen *(on-line)* or not. The more advanced style guides provide writing samples, illustrations, and templates. Style guides are not just for text, however. Style guides for all media elements can explain standards for preparing and evaluating video, sound, illustrations, and animation. For example, the video production staff should agree upon or develop a guide for resolution standards, digitizing rates, studio management policy, lighting, compression rates and processing sequences. Style guides are a result of the lessons learned in prototyping and allow everyone on the team to produce work that is consistent.

Bringing new people into the group may detract from efficiency, especially if they are not familiar with multimedia production issues or project specific ones. When introducing new people into the project team, the project manager should **acquaint professionals with the multimedia production issues that affect their area of expertise.** A traditional animator may not be familiar with the specific animation tool chosen for the project. This person should be given a chance to learn the tool either through classroom instruction or by them playing with the tool— whichever suits their personality and the project budget. Glenn Corey of Apple Computer recommends spending a day with video professionals before a shoot to familiarize them with the nature of digital production techniques. He believes it is well worth the extra time and expense to familiarize professionals this way. Artists and production staff need to know about equipment schedules, and standards before they launch into production.

Production Meetings

One way to improve communication among team members, and possibly with clients, is to hold regular meetings that feature project status, problems, concerns, and reports. Team members must feel free to speak up about problems and resolve them before it becomes too late to do so. If people always answer that everything is on schedule even when things may not be for fear of their jobs, then these problems may not surface until late in the project.

Before production begins, many project team have a **production kickoff meeting** which includes a review of the project plan, a review of the final prototype, and a report of testing results. The purpose of the production kickoff meeting is to reiterate each aspect of the project and clarify expectations. To proceed with production without ensuring that all involved—the team members and the client—**have a clear understanding of the goals** is almost a sure way for

problems to appear later. Product release is not the time to find out that the client wanted the company promotional kiosk to include images of the CEO officiating at charity functions. An unaddressed expectation or a misunderstood goal is bound to disappoint, if not alienate someone, whether it is a user or a client.

If the project involves a client, the project manager should organize additional **checkpoint meetings** with the client and the project team to report progress and communicate concerns. Checkpoint meetings are incentives to hit milestones and reassure the client. No one likes surprises, especially clients. If problems or snags have arisen, be upfront and show them you have taken steps so that these situations will not happen again. Even if everything is progressing according to plan, there is no substitute for human interaction.

Organizing Production Resources

Production resources are the tools and equipment needed to produce content for integration with the entire project. Occasionally these tools can be used in production, but in many cases this is not possible. A production tool needs to fulfill different requirements of quality, performance, capacity, and flexibility. These requirements can be met with "off the shelf" tools, custom tools, or a combination. Production tools should be able to accommodate increased volume without demonstrating a drop in performance. If the project will be ported to other platforms, the production tool should facilitate conversion through its features or other utilities.

General off-the-shelf **shrink-wrapped** software tools can reduce the need for extensive programming. Some shrink-wrapped **authoring systems** give the developer a visual depiction of the flow of all the screens and materials for a project. Programming for such tools involves little more than sequencing screens in a diagrammatic form, opening up the units, and designating their look. Such tools have been used to develop large bodies of educational material for corporations or schools with a minimum of programming resources.

Although some software tools are easy enough to learn and provide a high level of functionality, they are only capable of so much. Many developers choose to create their own **custom tools** and engines to optimize the building of a product. Programmers also design production tools to perform repetitive media placement tasks, check errors, resolve version changes, track the status of different elements, or automate building of the final product. Such tools may speed the production process but increase the time needed to develop and test them. Custom tools can pay for themselves if the time spent designing them improves product reliability and reduces production time on future projects.

In production, any tool that saves time is greeted with great enthusiasm. The project programmer should try to **automate routine processes** ▶ 226 when possible. Examples of such processes are checking file formats and names and verifying compression ratios. The key advantages to automated routines are consistency and speed. Tools such as programmable command key sequences can help reduce time and effort for routine processes. The production manager needs to make sure that team members have all the resources they need and understand the tools fully.

Equipment

Another major resource consideration is the hardware needed to generate, modify, integrate, and test content. These equipment needs include everything from cameras, microphones, tripods, and lights, to video digitizing boards, digitizing pads, and storage devices. The project manager should estimate the equipment needs and come up with plans to get them. Some project teams have a designated "mechanic" on board who is responsible for obtaining, installing, coordinating, and maintaining equipment.

One thing to consider when planning equipment purchases is **availability**. This industry is growing so rapidly that supplies of more powerful (and usually more popular) equipment can be scarce. You may be better off paying a premium for equipment in stock rather that purchasing equipment that might take time for delivery.

Because of the ongoing evolution of technology, some developers prefer to lease equipment. **Leasing** ▶ 79 equipment does not bind a development effort to a technology that may soon be inadequate or outdated. Many computer and audio/video equipment dealers lease equipment often with variable options. Leasing can also have certain tax advantages over purchasing but consult an accountant or equipment dealer to understand what these might be.

Buying used equipment is a consideration when the equipment is sure to meet specific needs. Reconditioned storage drives, for example, are less expensive than new ones and usually carry a warranty.

Maintenance

Most project teams designate someone who performs routine equipment maintenance such as checking cable quality, cleaning disks, monitoring memory usage, and anticipating warranty expirations. Even more important than the hardware, however, can be the software usage. Running multiple versions of system software, extensions, and applications can cause untold problems and frustration. Synchronizing all development machines can reduce the number of incompatibilities and glitches. This is especially true with software applications in beta-form, which may have different file formats than their shipping counterparts.

File Formats

One consideration needed early is the choice of **file formats** to use as standards. Not all authoring tools support all file types. Therefore, the file formats chosen for text, images, sounds, and movies must be compatible with the tools used on the project. For example, large files that are not used daily can reside in compressed format on the disk. Text files that move from one tool to another can be stored in simple ASCII format. Be aware that file formats perform differently. For example, PICT is the standard Macintosh image format and is native to the Macintosh. Saving images as PICTs can mean a noticeable speed increase over other image formats on a Macintosh. File formats also vary greatly in file size—even for the same data.

The reality of production is that it is very labor intensive.
— Sandra Mueller, Production Manager, Voyager Expanded Books

One of the more important things is to integrate everyone's language into an overall language that everyone can then understand. You have videographers that have a language, graphic designers, programmers. Each has their own jargon and vision. It's essential that everyone is able to communicate to everyone else.
— Donald Brenner, Multimedia Programmer

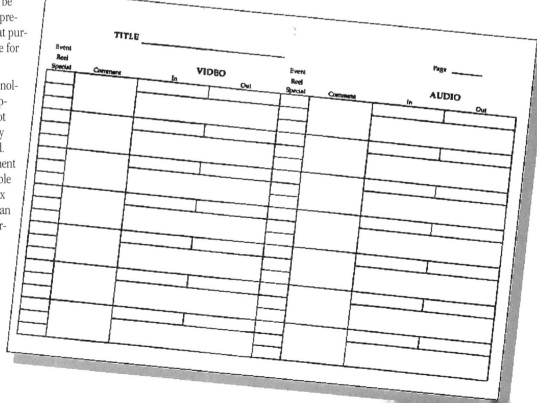

Naming Conventions

Naming conventions ▶ 211 are systematic and meaningful labels given to files and media content. Naming conventions facilitate use, storage, and retrieval. The name can tell the production staff the file's contents, revision history, source, format, and other details relevant to the project. Well-thought naming strategies add continuity to a team's work before and after production—a factor that can make reuse of the data much easier.

If production calls for retrieval under different operating systems, an important issue is using **multi-platform names**. A file name that demands a three-letter extension appended to a name of no more than eight characters, as on DOS platforms, poses a challenge to creating a clear naming scheme. For example, some platforms cannot use colons (:), dashes (-), or spaces ( ) in file names. Beware of system limitations when developing cross-platform content. Duplicating files under different names can be a logistical nightmare.

An important thing to understand before naming files is how team members will use the files in their work. Although each project has unique requirements, below are some naming strategies that work for some developers.

Indicate the File Type

Designating a file's **type** by using an extension such as *.eps* and *.tiff* may be necessary for some operating systems and can be helpful when organizing a large number of different file types. It can also help distinguish between files with the same name but stored as different file types. Many developers, for example, use various file types for scanning and storing images but save them as 8-bit system palette PICTs for final integration. This difference might be reflected in the file name. For example, *Rock_Formation.tiff* and *Rock_Formation.pict*. Even if the system displays a unique icon for the file type, this may not be reflected in list views and dialog boxes.

Refer to the Source

Naming digital files with a reference to the **source** of the original version can be useful for multimedia projects. For example, names for **step files** (still images) taken from a videodisc might contain an extension or prefix with a step code reference to the disc location of the image. The images might reside on the disc as *EiffelTower.159a* or *314.MountFuji.night*. Similarly, photographs scanned from rolls of film might be referenced by photo shoot number (A), roll number (3), and frame number (20) as in *A.003.20.restaurant*. Sounds, movies, and images digitized from video or audio tape might be named with the counter or time code readings and the source tape number for quicker identification: *A02:00:20:46_02:02:04:53.interview*, for example.

Identify the Creator

Another naming strategy might include an extension that includes the **creator** or editor's name or department such as *Timeline1960s.chris* or *Notebook3.teamone*.

Organization and Storage Schemes

Naming conventions are usually not enough to manage content effectively. A **multimedia cataloger** can be useful in tracking content elements. At minimum, use a spreadsheet or even a word processor to track element status. A multimedia cataloger, however, will make this much easier because it can do much of the work automatically. If using a spreadsheet or word processor, each project member must take the time to log in elements. The record can then be used to track all materials and supply reports that can determine aggregate file sizes, show available resources, or describe the method for reconstructing an item. Because multimedia projects typically generate so many diverse elements, multimedia catalogers may be more useful than a general database tool.

Version Control

Production is a repeating cycle of changes, revisions, and fine tuning. As cycles repeat and as more people contribute to different parts of the project, the volume and versions of content items rapidly increase. Such complexity demands some method of control and identification. The project manager must establish and

---

Even if you are using a media cataloging utility during production, don't assume that naming conventions and organization schemes are not necessary. Names allow for a lot more options than merely finding and identifying. Good naming and organization strategies are essential for version control and communication between team members.

Sample Logistics Database Record

A sample record description from a logistics database might cover:

- *Computer file name*
- *Full name*
- *Source material*
- *Licensing/copyright status*
- *Time of creation, how it was digitized, by what application tools/version, and at what settings*
- *Where stored and in what file format*
- *Size in bytes, duration of clips*
- *Order of consecutive transformations such as image processing filters*
- *Where image or resource appears in the system*
- *Revision history to identify the version number*
- *Keywords—these will help locate lost files more easily*
- *Process for compressing and decompressing*

enforce a system of controlling versions to synchronize revisions and identify the most current pieces. **Version control ▶ 217** can help track errors and ensure functional integrity. It also helps maintain some sanity among the team members, who should always be working with the current version of any element.

Content Archiving

Another logistics consideration is the **storage of master data**, sometimes called assets, which is the source material before digitization, cropping, enhancing, or editing. Master data includes film, videotape, manuals, audio cassettes, and existing computer files. Keeping source material in its original form can be less costly than keeping digitized versions on disk. However, there are cost effective options for maintaining first-pass digitized data. One option is to create **one-off CD-ROM discs ▶ 111** for the sole purpose of archiving master data such as video clips that have already been digitized. Creating a one-off is less expensive and more durable than maintaining data on hard disks that are in constant use. **Photo CD ▶ 153, 188** is a similar, cost-effective process for storing digitized images of photographs.

Backup schedules are critical! Making consistent backups is like buying life insurance for the project. Regularly scheduled backups will make it easier to go back to previous versions to reconstruct an object in the event of a mistake or accident. Popular backup media include cartridges for smaller numbers of files and more frequently changed data, CD-R discs for archiving video, sound and other data-intensive media, and DAT tapes for networks (these hold over a gigabyte per tape and facilitate automated and remote backups of large drives, servers, and networks).

It is essential that all team members backup their work regularly (this can mean daily) and that the project manager enforces these backups.

Repurposing Source Materials

Source materials are any items that contain images, sound, video, or information that can be used in a multimedia product. A project for a client may involve conversion of existing materials such as company tutorials, videotapes of speeches or events, file drawers of audio lecture tapes, magnetic tapes of digital data, drawers of product concept illustrations, banks of slides, and other items. **Repurposing ▶ 101** these data sources for multimedia content production includes digitizing, cleaning up, correcting, and storing the source materials. Whenever possible try to work from digital source materials.

The process of repurposing materials demands a labor-intensive effort to digitize and process the different elements. Each media conversion process involves calibration of the various conversion devices across the sample range and variety of materials. Repurposing existing materials is usually an exercise in compromises. The source materials are usually not in digital form and often lose much of their quality in the process of digitizing them. Some of this loss can be compensated for and corrected, however.

Existing source materials may not be exactly what is needed. For example, the prototype might call for video clips of lecturers against a particular, constant background from the waist up and lit in a particular way for latter processing and removal of the background. The existing video available from the client, however, may only provide a few of the individuals needed, against different backgrounds and only as close-ups from the neck up. Either new video must be shot, if time and budget allow, or the prototype must be redesigned. Organizing and evaluating content in the Design and Prototype stage is important for this reason.

Generating New Content

Multimedia production concentrates on generating and integrating content with an interaction engine. Digital data, however, creates opportunities for later reuse beyond the scope of the project. The video clips, sound effects, animation sequences, text documents, and other content items that are collected and digitized for the current project can be used again for other projects. **Durable content should be of the highest possible quality in order to be reused.** Although content for a kiosk may need only screen resolution now, if it is repurposed for broadcast or HDTV transmission later, it will need to have much higher resolution. Preparing content so that it can be scaled to accommodate different and emerging technologies is a way of building "digital assets" that could save production time and create more opportunities in the future. Tyler Peppel of Arborescence sums it up well by saying, "Digital data stays; technologies come and go."

Content production can involve creating new materials or converting existing materials into digital form. Either way, **good content comes from good source material**. Every effort should be made to obtain the best quality source material for content. Existing video should be of the highest resolution possible; audio should be crisp; artwork should be camera-ready. Existing materials are prone to degradation from generation

Many multimedia service bureaus will "press" a one-off CD-ROM (CD-R) disc with your data for under $250. Costs and turn-around times vary. As these services become more common, the prices should drop. One-offs can be good ways to archive production files, prototypes, and demos.

No matter what the medium, capture content in the highest quality and resolution affordable and archive it digitally.

Multimedia production is 2% inspiration and 98% digitization.

Case Study: Voices of the 30s

Description:

Voices of the 30s *is an interactive CD-ROM journey through the images, sights, and sounds of the Depression Era. It is rich with historical photographs, video clips, commentary, and activities that are both exciting and educational. The CD-ROM provides an explorable multimedia database about the history and artifacts of the 1930s. In about 500MB of space it provides extensive material including over 400 images, movies, and sounds. It also indexes, summarizes, and references over 200 books.*

Project Type:

Interactive Learning

Development Hardware:

Macintosh IIfx, Macintosh Quadra 950, Macintosh LCII for testing, 1 gigabyte hard drives, optical drives, VideoSpigot, color flatbed scanner

Delivery Hardware:

Macintosh LC and above, CD-ROM, 4MB RAM

Software Used:

QuickTime, HyperCard 2.1 with colorized HyperCard and QuickTime XCMDs. Adobe Photoshop for all images. Adobe Premiere for movies and sound mixing. SuperCard for color prototyping.

Team Members and Roles:

Lisa Paul of WINGS for Learning, Business Manager; Kristina Hooper-Woolsey of Apple Computer, Executive Producer; Abbe Don, Producer (she also redesigned and reprogrammed the interaction scheme); Pat Hanlon and Bob Campbell, Content Experts and Editors; Nathan Shedroff, Interface and Graphic Designer; Jim Cottle, Digitizer; toward the end of the project, others were added including Cindy Rink, Editor; Steve Willis, Programmer; Kevin Barrack, Andy Armstrong, and Donna Kemper, Production Assistants and Testers.

Funding:

Joint funding by Apple Computer and WINGS for Learning. Apple supplied funds for initial personnel costs and facilitated the use of equipment and operations in the early phases of the project. WINGS for Learning assumed responsibilities for final production, programming, marketing, distribution, and content acquisition.

Voices of the 30s *has its roots in an ambitious multimedia project called Grapevine that was created and developed over six years by high school teacher Pat Hanlon and librarian Bob Campbell to teach John Steinbeck's* The Grapes of Wrath *to high school students. With the help of Kristina Hooper-Woolsey of the now-disbanded Apple Multimedia Lab, the Grapevine project evolved over the years as an example of computer-assisted education and helped shape new technologies such as videodisc, HyperCard, color imaging, and QuickTime. In 1992, the project was prepared to be sold as a public product in a joint effort between Apple Computer, Inc. and WINGS for Learning. Voices of the 30s is not only interactive but adaptive, allowing students to add material to the project. With a special feature called "Route Maker" anyone can create a list of pages that can be shown like a slide show with the "Route Player" feature.*

Concept and Planning:

The productization of Voices of the 30s raised issues about designing for classroom and computer interaction. The interaction design was restructured maintaining the original version's metaphor of the road but organizing the content into two general categories, Resources and Activities, each of which contain several subcategories. Some original features, such as the Collages section, could not be maintained in the CD-ROM version because they posed design and production problems.

Design and Prototype:

Interface designer Nathan Shedroff redesigned the interface to give it a professional look and feel, make the navigation scheme more apparent, and capture the spirit of the Depression era. His attention to details such as appropriate font choice and color schemes helped create the mood that Voices of the 30s was to invoke.

Adding color and using QuickTime while still maintaining good performance levels posed a challenge. During prototyping, it was found that using the 256 System Color Palette with a diffusion dither provided overall consistency, good color, and good CD-ROM performance. The result of the design and prototype stage were twenty prototype cards that were used to illustrate the basic interaction design and "look and feel" of the product.

Another special feature discovered during protoype was on-the-fly text searching. Almost any text can be searched by clicking on it. Any matching text on later screens is then immediately brought forward.

Production:

Licensing of material presented a special challenge, an issue that was not apparent when the project was used only in the classroom. The project is based on a wealth of public domain source material which is readily obtained.

There was one major redesign after the production phase started which changed the background image of one stack. The extra effort to make the change from a solid black background to a photograph involved modifying more than 300 images but resulted in a more appealing appearance.

Testing:

The testing consisted not only of testing the engine but of proofing all the quotes and references in the materials.

Distribution:

WINGS for Learning will market the material primarily in educational and art channels.

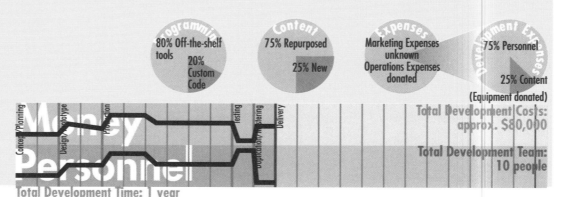

Programming: 80% Off-the-shelf tools, 20% Custom Code

Content: 75% Repurposed, 25% New

Expenses: Marketing Expenses unknown, Operations Expenses donated

Development Expenses: 75% Personnel, 25% Content (Equipment donated)

Total Development Costs: approx. $80,000

Total Development Team: 10 people

Money / Personnel

Total Development Time: 1 year

loss; that is, they are often copies of copies of the originals. Photocopies of photocopies, VHS format "dupes" of Betacam master videotapes, and audio cassettes of radio broadcasts are all examples of diminished-quality sources. If possible, work from the original masters. When working with inferior quality materials, it may be possible to enhance them with software programs, for example, to use an image processing program to despeckle grainy photographs, using special filters in the program. Any methods for enhancing such materials should have been developed during the prototype stage and made part of the production specifications.

Some very old works like original manuscripts, letters, old photographs or drawings, old film or audio tapes might need to be restored. **Restoration** requires the permission of the owner and is usually handled by a conservator or technical specialist of the art and the period. Restoration of official or sensitive images, sounds, or video should be left to the direction of qualified content experts in the appropriate field.

Expert artists in each of the media realms will be able to perform miracles with neglected content elements, but do not expect too much. Some materials are just beyond repair and should be left out if not in good condition.

Content Verification

During production, **content experts** ▶ **20, 99** work with artists to provide and check the accuracy of materials. They assist in interviews and general research of the **subject matter**. While these experts need not be present at every step of production, it is often necessary for them to review progress and finished work. Do not leave all of the fact checking and content verification until the end of production. There may not be adequate time left for changes or corrections if needed.

Text Production

Writing New Text

A **writer** creates text while an **editor** ▶ **22** helps compose the outline and corrects wording and style issues. Both usually use **word processing** software. An **outline** should be developed before any work is started. This outline does not need to be detailed to the *nth* degree. In fact, it should leave some room for the writer to maneuver within. Some projects get by with a one-page outline, while others require as long as ten page outlines. The correct length for an outline will depend on the needs of the project and the relationship

and understanding of those involved. As long as everyone feels informed and sure about their responsibilities, the outline can describe just the elemental structure.

Text is written in successive **drafts**. The creation of the text can parallel the prototype approaches with its bread-first and depth-first methodologies. The more common approach is breadth-first, or in other words, covering all the major ideas and sections to some level of degree. The draft is commonly called the **first draft**. It does not need correct grammar and spelling of proper names, although it will help anyone reading the text. (It should at least be spell-checked if done on a computer.) Polishing text can be time-consuming and may not be warranted if the text is likely to change dramatically. Covering all the major topics makes it possible to address any missing sections. While it is not too late to add a few new topics, any major changes or reorganization may take the text production dramatically off schedule. It can also be a good idea to expand a sample section or chapter in a polished form so that editors and other team members can acquaint themselves with what to expect.

Second drafts commonly are completed manuscripts lacking only final polish and consistency. Style and voice should be represented accurately. The things to edit for at this stage should only be spelling, grammar, word choice, and facts and figures. This last step is especially important. Often, inaccurate or misleading information is passed on from source to source. If each references the same initial source, however, the information could easily be wrong. Always check the data, ideally from first-hand information.

The last draft is called the **final draft**. In reality, there are often more than three drafts depending on the amount of text and the duration of the project. With practice and experience, however, writers and editors can reduce the number of iterations to an efficient number. This last draft should include all corrections from spelling to fact checking. In any project, there will almost always be something missed such as a misspelled word or name, an out-of-date fact or theory, or an incorrect price or phone number. The duty of the writers and editors is to leave enough time to catch everything they can but at some point, the text must be integrated with the other elements. Anything that slips through the cracks can be addressed during content testing.

A writer or editor might suggest type styles and formats but these are often the decisions of the graphic designer. This is an example where proper delineation of authority can reduce disagreements or "turf wars."

Sometimes slightly damaged or low quality content can add a historic flair to a product. For example, the pop and crackle of a music recording from the 1920s may sound more appropriate than a processed and enhanced version that sounds too "new" or too "clean."

During research and composition, it is important to record the sources of information to make fact checking easier by others. Information that cannot be verified may have to be stricken at the last minute.

To learn more about text as a medium and what types of issues to explore in its use, see the Text section in Design and Prototype.

Effective writing is effective communication.

Style Guide Issues for Text
- *Naming conventions*
- *Content-specific terminology*
- *Gender-specific words or phrases*
- *Use of hyphens*
- *Use of commas, semi-colons, colons, and em-dashes*
- *Jargon to omit*
- *Use of smart quotes and apostrophes*
- *Appearance of names, titles, dates, and phone numbers*
- *Appearance of bibliographic information*

Writing Equipment

When using a computer, writers and editors should work with large and easy-to-read **displays**. Large screens are helpful for seeing the scope of a "page" and a second screen can be handy for editing or referring to a dictionary or thesaurus. The **keyboard** should be strong and able to sustain the writer's top writing speed without dropping characters.

Portable computers are great writing machines because they can be used in many situations for writing and note-taking, such as presentations and interviews. **Tape recorders** are good for capturing thoughts or conversation, but transcribing text is very time consuming.

Grammar checkers and **spelling checkers** are available from many software publishers. Most word processors include spelling checkers and some now include grammar checkers but it is possible to buy separate checkers that work with most word processors. There are two important points to remember. The first is to **use these tools**. Many writers are in such a hurry to meet a deadline that they never bother to use the spelling checker. This can aggravate an editor to no end and slowly destroy a working relationship. An editor's job is not to correct spelling but to check for style and text flow and to catch grammar and spelling problems that have slipped past the writer. The second is that grammar checkers only search for common mistakes and may not catch everything. They are not substitutes for a human editor with experience, vision, and judgment.

Repurposing Text

Many times, existing text can come in digital formats. If this is the case, translation to the format and development platform needed can be relatively easy. Any translation utility should be able to convert between the files you have and the ones you need, although some text characteristics like bold, italics, and underlines may drop out, depending on the source and target formats. Text is the easiest medium to translate across formats and platforms.

Optical Character Recognition

If the text is not in digital form, it will need to be either retyped, a lengthy and time-consuming process, or scanned and converted with **optical character recognition** (OCR) software. For short lengths of text, retyping may actually be the less expensive and faster but for large amounts of text, consider using an OCR utility.

Optical character recognition utilities work by analyzing a scanned or digitized picture of a page of text and matching the characters it can recognize with ones it understands. These utilities will create a file with the converted text and can be up to 98% accurate. Most have trouble with certain typefaces and sizes. Be sure that scan settings like resolution and brightness are optimized for the OCR utility's optimal performance. Most OCR utilities will work with standard image formats like PICT or TIFF and should therefore allow any scanner to be used to digitize the printed text.

Accuracy is important. While 98% sounds fine enough, it is tedious to reread all text to check for missed characters. 98% accuracy means that 2 out of every 100 characters will be wrong. Since there are over 250 characters in this paragraph, the amount of errors and additional work can add up.

In general, one person can scan and convert 30-40 pages in an hour depending on the density of text on the page. That person may need another four hours to check the accuracy of these pages. Always run spelling and grammar checkers first once the text has been converted. This will find most of the mistranslated characters.

Transcription

Transcribing recorded speech to text is another tedious process. There are very few, if any, affordable utilities that do this automatically. It may be best to give this work to a transcription service if the budget and schedule allow. Otherwise, a standard word processor, a tape player, and a lot of time are all that are necessary. Depending on the speaker, a person can transcribe about 15 minutes of speech per hour.

Translation

If text needs to be **translated** to support a multilingual audience, plan on the time and resources necessary to do this. Also, if screen space is at a premium, remember that many languages (especially German) will take more characters to say the same thing as other languages. Some languages also read right to left or up and down instead of left to right like most Western languages.

Because text translation involves more than merely substituting words, it may take more time than expected and be expensive. Be sure to get a translator who is familiar with the audience for the project. When text is translated, it must be rewritten with idioms and phrases that are understandable to a native speaker of that audience. It is important that the translator understands the project goals as well as the audience in order to choose appropriate translations. For example, a multimedia kiosk that represents a company at an international conference may require more formal language than an electronic magazine about global pop culture.

Translators can be found in business or phone directories or through friends and colleagues. Be sure to use qualified, careful, and sensitive translators who are experienced with writing. Just because a person knows another language—even if they are a native speaker of that language—does not guarantee that their translation will be accurate or appropriate.

Interview: Domenic Stansberry

As a writer, how did you become involved in multimedia?

Most of my experience as a writer has been in fiction, journalism, and documentary film. I have advanced degrees in writing and literature and was a visiting writer at the University of Idaho. I came to multimedia because of a long-standing love of storytelling through film, especially documentary film. I also write articles about multimedia for magazines such as NewMedia.

I became involved with developing a program about AIDS awareness with the Bay Area Video Coalition. The work I did involved a kind of scripting that is special to multimedia.

Explain.

It seems that the role of the writer in multimedia changes from project to project. The creative person is not necessarily the writer. The writer is the implementor of ideas that have already been thought of by a director or producer. It's different from being a novelist who is at the core of the creative process. If you are a documentary filmmaker, you are also at the core. But if you write for multimedia, you are one of a larger team of people. What will happen to your work is even more alteration than when you are writing for film.

On the AIDS Awareness project, I worked with someone who was an instructional designer whose attitude was different from mine. I was concerned with putting together dramatizations that showed the health messages we wanted to convey. Her focus was on presenting information in a manual for a certain audience who would go through certain exercises and be quizzed at the end. Blending her approach with my storytelling background plus trying to do what the producer wanted was a challenge. What I laid down for the story and character development stayed in the end product but came out in a different way.

I'm working now with the Mill Valley Film Group on a documentary about the North Beach Italian neighborhood of San Francisco, to be part of a larger series about San Francisco's ethnic neighborhoods. We want to involve a multimedia person from the beginning so that we can plan for an eventual interactive educational program that can be put in the public library. It could be something that high school kids could use to learn about their ethnic cultures. The filmmakers I know seem to be thinking ahead to multimedia with their projects.

How is the documentary process different from interactive?

The documentary film process involves looking for as much information as possible and then observing what themes or main ideas come to the surface. Once you find your theme, you use it as a prism for the direction of the film. Designing for interactivity requires that you already have some notion of what the goal of the project is. This affects what you shoot and how you think about it.

You mentioned storytelling as being important.

People who tell the stories are the ones who need to be working with multimedia. The storyteller doesn't have to be a writer. Is someone who uses HyperCard a writer?

What about hypertext?

There are not that many interactive hypertext novels that are well written. You jump around, you go back and forth, and you have to read text on a computer screen which isn't the most joyous experience in the world. The novels are similar in form and intent to the post modern novels of the '60s by authors like Thomas Pynchon, for example. The death of the novel is not a new concept; it was popular in the '60s along with the "literature of exhaustion." Some authors, like Greg Roach with The Madness of Roland, are incorporating different media including QuickTime into their interactive novels.

What advice do you have for someone who wants to write for multimedia?

There are different things that are useful for a writer to know. For example, one should know how to write an audio/visual script, which is a video technique. A writer should be able to put together a treatment or proposal. He or she should know how to write different things for different occasions. If you want to be a writer in multimedia and you want to maintain some control over your work, you need to familiarize yourself with as much of the entire process as possible.

What roles will the writer play?

One role will be to simply copyfit words to the screen design. Copyfitting reminds me of the task of the headline writer, who must come up with a descriptive headline in a given number of characters to match the page layout. The headline must attract the reader to pursue the text.

Another role will be that of a researcher, someone who finds background information about a topic. The researcher would decide what's relevant and then rewrite the copy.

Without a doubt, there's a role for the writer in the funding process, because a well-written proposal gets you in the door. The proposal contains the inception of the creative process. From there, if you know things about scripting, and about how to write dialog, you can be much more involved in the creative process than you would otherwise.

As the technology develops so that it is more accessible to everyone, the writer will be someone who can put together graphics with text to create a statement. In truth, people are not that interested in text in multimedia. They want to move to the next image. The goal of the whole production determines the extent of the writing.

Domenic Stansberry, a writer for the Mill Valley Film Group in Marin, teaches the course "Writing for Multimedia" in the Multimedia Studies Program at San Francisco State University.

Case Study: Voyager Expanded Books

Description:
Voyager Expanded Books are digital versions of original paper books to be read on Apple PowerBook computers. The Expanded Books series combines the experience of reading traditional books with computer-based capabilities such as variable type size, customized word searches and indexes, on-screen pop-up annotations and footnotes, and the "ability to read in bed without the light on." The Voyager Company has published more than 40 titles since January 1992, including Douglas Adams' Hitchhiker's Guide to the Galaxy, Michael Crichton's Jurassic Park, Susan Faludi's Backlash, and Herman Melville's Moby Dick. To produce a large number of Expanded Book titles, Voyager created the Expanded Book Toolkit which is marketed as a separate product.

Project Type:
Electronic Book

Development Hardware:
Macintosh IIsi, PowerBook, Hewlett Packard IIC ScanJet

Delivery Software:
Specifically designed for Apple PowerBook computers or any Macintosh computer with a hard drive and large display.

Software Used:
Voyager Expanded Book Toolkit with HyperCard 2.1, Caere's Omnipage Pro OCR program, Microsoft Word 5.0, MacWrite II

Team Members and Roles:
Sandra Mueller is the product manager for all expanded book titles. The team for each book includes an assigned producer and graphic artist. The artist also designs the packaging and promotional materials for the title. Staffing requirements include editing, writing, proofreading, and scanning. Production team members share duties of scanning, clean-up, formatting, proofing, and testing.

THE COMPLETE ANNOTATED ALICE

LEWIS CARROLL

Introduction and Notes by MARTIN GARDNER

Content Rights:
The content is licensed from the copyright holder.

Price:
$19.95-$24.95

Contact:
Sandra Mueller
The Voyager Company
Santa Monica, CA

Management:
A production team is assigned to each book. One person acts as "producer, overseer, and editor," says Mueller.

Concept and Planning:
The concept of each book depends on the author. Voyager tries to preserve the author's original intent. For example, some authors do not want sound added to the text of their writing. Acquiring content rights and actual content is often challenging and time consuming, a process that sometimes takes weeks.

Design and Prototype:
The design goal of Expanded Books is to create a suitable reading environment in digital electronic form. Familiar practices such as page-turning, index searching, and chapter layout are carried over, yet the reader has more choices. For example, readers can select 12 or 18 point typeface size. A black and white, horizontal format was designed to accommodate the PowerBook.

HyperCard was chosen because of its linking abilities, but the special requirements of the book metaphor made custom programming necessary. For example, special code was written to allow "flowing"

of the source text into HyperCard in a page format. The custom tools that were created to simplify the design and production of Expanded Books evolved into the Expanded Books Toolkit, which Voyager uses in-house and also markets.

Production:
The bulk of the effort is in text production. This involves "feeding" the scanner (30-50 pages/per hour can be scanned), "cleaning up" the scanned images, establishing and enforcing filing standards, and constantly checking for accuracy. The last stage for non-fiction books is indexing, a time-consuming task. "The reality of professional production is that it is labor intensive," says Mueller.

Testing:
Testing occurs in two stages before the product is released. At least two testers are assigned to the task. The first stage involves a complete screen proofing of the book and, depending on the book, takes about two to seven days. Any changes or corrections are made and everything—grammar, spelling, formatting, image quality, and links—is tested according to test scripts.

HyperCard's requirement to have unique links always uncovers inconsistencies within the book. "One name can be spelled different ways throughout an entire book, but you might never catch it with traditional proofing methods," says Mueller. "The digital magnifying glass of truth" fleshes out inconsistencies in spelling, hyphenation, and content, says Mueller.

Mastering and Duplication:
From 3000 to 5000 covers are printed at once for a title. Diskettes are duplicated about 100 at a time in case there are last minute corrections or additions such as catalog updates.

Distribution:
Expanded books are marketed at trade shows, online services such as CompuServe, and press reviews and are distributed through traditional book, computer, and education channels such as bookstores, computer stores, direct mail strategies, and catalogs.

Programming
99% Off-the-shelf tools
1% Custom Code*

Content
99% Repurposed
1% New

Expenses
Marketing Expenses not. avail.
Operations Expenses not avail.

Development Expenses
Personnel Expenses not avail.
Content Expenses not avail.
Equipment Expenses not avail.

*Any additional tools needed are incorporated into future Toolkit versions.

Money
Delivery
Personnel

Total Development Costs: not avail.

Total Development Team: 5 people per book

Total Development Time: 2-3 weeks (Fiction), 3-5 weeks (Non-Fiction) per 400page book

Indexing

Many word processors will allow **indexes** ▶ **130** and **tables of contents** to be automatically indexed but few authoring systems offer these capabilities. All indexing must be done once all pieces are integrated and signed-off. It should be one of the last steps because any changes to the content may require regeneration of the index. A skilled programmer may be able to automate some of this process, but an editor, content expert, or creative director's judgment is often required to decide what words are indexed and how. This is true for any cross-referencing or hyper-links as well. While a programmer can build a tool to search for words and their locations, it is rare that every occurrence of a word is relevant. Usually, an editor or content expert will need to review the elements and index and decide which connections and references are important.

Professional Text

The publishing industry uses characters that distinguish professional from amateur publishing. These include "**smart**" or "**curly**" quotes and **apostrophes** instead of the common straight characters created by a typewriter. **Double spaces** at the beginning of a new sentence are also not used unless the typeface specified has fixed-width characters (which is rare in print publishing, but may be more common on some computer platforms). If the type styles specified for a project have variable width characters, double spaces should not be used.

SGML

Standard Generalized Markup Language (SGML) is a generic tagging scheme for describing text-based, structured documents. It is actually a meta-language for developing other languages and type definitions. It is a sophisticated way of notating the text, styles, and structure of a document in a standard way. An SGML parser can then filter this text and reformat it for a particular need on-the-fly. This allows text to be encoded and stored in a standard way and reused in different ways by building a parser that translates the notation into the form needed. Storing text in SGML notation may take more time and training for writers and editors, but may allow text to be more easily stored and reused for other purposes. This can also make the text more platform independent and more viable as technology changes rapidly. It is, however, only to be used by developers and publishers who are committing to its support for a long duration and should not be undertaken lightly. Not all page layout applications and only a few, if any, word processors support SGML so research your tools carefully if SGML is an issue.

Graphic Production

Before production begins, the graphics team should have already created or been supplied working layouts of screen designs and production specifications for all graphical elements. The production team now needs to create the images and illustrations for the project, finalize the elements for integration, and then lay them out.

Producing Illustrations

Because there are many types and styles of illustration, the exact process and tools may vary. Regardless, all will have to function within the same basic limitations of the screen—namely resolution, size, and color. Each illustrator will have their own way of working. Some work exclusively on the computer, some exclusively on paper, and some a mixture of both. Illustrations created entirely on the computer will be more easy to use and archive, at least until paper-based illustrations are converted into digital form. Computer-generated illustrations may also offer advantages of color consistency and resolution.

Paint Tools

Paint tools are computer applications that manipulate the individual **pixels** on screen to form images. This is fundamentally different from drawing tools, which manipulate graphic objects to form images. Some image manipulation tools can be used but these may not have features specific to the creation of illustrations. These can include special drawing and painting tools, effects, and better type controls.

Draw Tools

Draw tools allow images to be composed of **graphic objects**. Because these applications understand these objects as geometric entities instead of pixels on a canvas, the objects can be changed much more easily than with paint tools. This makes updates and changes easier but may limit the types and styles of illustrations. Most draw applications are designed for creating charts, diagrams, and illustrations for printed output and may not provide enough granularity to create adequate illustrations for the screen.

Draw tools can be used to create certain illustrations and then designers can take a screenshot of the illustration to translate it into a pixel version. This image can then be edited with a paint tool or image manipulation application to impart finer details. This arrangement will be more difficult to track but may offer the right combination of tools and features to create the intended look.

To learn more about illustration and graphics as media and what types of issues to explore in their use, see the Illustration section in Design and Prototype.

Anti-Aliased Type

Because a computer's screen has a much lower resolution than print materials, type is usually "pixelated" and awkward looking, making it much more difficult to read. **Anti-aliasing** ▶ 148 type in an illustration can make it more legible and more beautiful. Anti-aliasing involves mediating the edge around a character with colors that are a combination of the character color and the background color. This produces a slightly fuzzy edge that can help define detail better.

Anti-aliased type, however, will be a picture and no longer machine-readable text. There are no authoring systems that currently anti-alias text "on-the-fly" keeping text as text (which is why this subject is in the illustration section). All require that type be anti-aliased and stored as imported graphics.

Interview: Kenneth Jones

Ken Jones is a traditionally-trained illustrator whose work has appeared in numerous multimedia kiosks produced by the San Francisco-based firm Spatial Data Architects.

As an illustrator, what kind of work do you do?
I do whatever needs to be done that cannot be done on the computer. Recently I did work for a trade show kiosk. The project manager and animator would ask me to do such things as draw a landscape, a person, or a desert. Whatever was needed for the scenario they were building. It's basically old-fashioned illustration, something you would do with any book. Since we were working within a tight time frame (five days) to complete the piece, it was a matter of making the artwork as camera-ready as possible so we wouldn't waste time on camera manipulations. The illustrations needed to be ready to scan and use.

How did you become an illustrator?
I grew up in an artist's workshop. My mother was an artist and writer, and one of my brothers became an artist. I learned a lot about artistic media from my brother. We would mix our own egg tempera and stretch canvasses. I learned how different pigments and oils would set at different rates.

I kept my own notebooks of images and ideas. I learned by observing, doing, and reading books in the library. I looked at many photographic reproductions of paintings, because there were no major art museums in the small Oklahoma town I grew up in. When I eventually learned that there were original Van Gogh paintings in nearby Little Rock, Arkansas, I wanted to see them because I was interested in seeing how thick the brush strokes were. You can't get the feeling of thick brush strokes from looking at a photographic reproduction.

Still, if you grow up as I did looking at the books of the old paintings, you become a part of them and they become a part of you.

What is your view of the computer as an artist's tool?
It depends on your point of view. The poet John Ciardi said that there's no such thing as a negative work of art, that there's no such thing as a negative poem. If you say something, someone is listening. If you look at it from that point of view, there is the human soul and many avenues of expression for the soul. Everything is material, everything is grist for the mill, everything is useful. Then there's the McLuhanesque argument that man's tools are extensions of himself, but the tools alter his perception. It's a twofold process. By being a traditional artist, I'm humanizing the medium. On the other hand, the computer medium is bringing me face to face with what we are becoming through our tools. It's an infinite series of mirrors.

What was it like when you first started working with digital tools?
I am still learning. It's a process that can go on forever. I still draw with traditional media. The photographer Man Ray used the phrase "as stupid as a painter." The painter who only draws what he sees is, in a sense, stupid. It's easy to do that with computer tools, capture what you see. We must go beyond that.

I was raised in the old tradition, going way back to when I was a four year old playing with crayons and thinking that if I enjoy it that much, it must be good. There's no way I can dispense with the tools I've grown up with. They're part of my training. Sometimes they're useful, sometimes they're not. It all depends on the job at hand.

Do you play with tools on the computer?
I do a little bit of that. I feel a bit like a Cro-Magnon man who's been thrown into 2001, because there's such a great deal there to work with. It's overwhelming. It's also overwhelming to have 40 television channels and only 24 hours in a day. What choices do you make? What is the point of making a choice? It gets very cosmic when you think about it.

How do you feel when you see your work in an animation in a kiosk?
It's always nice to see your name in lights. That's one of the nice things of being a child of this century; you can have your own personal magic lantern.

Do digital tools change traditional aesthetics of illustration?
Of course. You have a hard time separating what's happening right now from the potentiality of the tool. For example, at MACWORLD 1993 in San Francisco there was a package that claimed to eliminate the "jaggies." The technology that introduced the jaggies eventually evolved to eliminate the problem. You can criticize the current tools but future enhancements will correct the problems.

What advice do you have for people who want to work with multimedia?
Have fun.

What are the tools of your trade?
Colored pencil for painterly effects, occasionally a bic pen, a flair pen, generally a simple palette. The animator on my team puts my images into motion or incorporates my backgrounds using computer tools like MacroMind Director and Adobe PhotoShop.

If you're an artist or talented person you can make something out of anything. It's the artist, not the tools. You can be a terrible artist with the thousand dollar sable brush and nothing will happen. You can know as much as you want to know. You can learn as much as you want to learn. It's up to you.

Most image manipulation applications and many paint tools will automatically anti-alias type on request. Because draw applications are not pixel-based, most will have this capability.

Repurposing Illustrations

Like photographs, illustrations scanned into a computer will lose some **fine detail** and **dynamic range**—especially when converted to the screen resolution of most delivery platforms (around 72-100dpi). This will cause the illustration to have a higher contrast than the paper original. It may be a good idea to design the illustrations in black and white before adding color to insure that the color and detail are readable once digitized.

A computer's display is capable of producing many more colors than can be printed or created with physical media such as paints or colored pencils. This means that scanned color illustrations may look dull next to other screen elements. **Image manipulation applications** allow the saturation and brightness of these scans to be changed to compensate for this difference.

Illustration Equipment

While many illustrators will already be familiar with traditional tools like paints, colored pencils, chalk, or other physical media, they may not be as experienced with electronic tools like scanners and paint software. A little time spent experimenting with these tools can make a big difference in the quality of the finished illustrations.

Pressure Sensitive Tablets

Pressure sensitive tablets can be more comfortable to use when creating paint-type illustrations. These tablets include a stylus, often times a wireless one, that moves the on-screen pointer for all tools and serves as a replacement for a mouse. It works much like a pen or pencil and thus may be more familiar to many users. Many software applications—including most paint, draw, and image manipulation applications—support pressure sensitive tablets so that both pressure and location determine the tool behavior. This allows illustrators to produce variable width lines, as in traditional calligraphy, instead of the more rigid and regular ones produced with non-pressure sensitive input devices.

Graphics

Graphic designers ▶ 24 define the type and layout of the elements on screen. This involves the visual arrangement of all pieces of the project. Graphics standards like typeface and size, color palettes, and screen grids should be set after the prototype is approved.

Fonts

A **font** refers to the style of type used on a computer. The term comes from the print publishing industry where it referred to a particular size of a particular typeface. On computers, it is usually interchangeable with the word *typeface*. Different fonts render the characters of the alphabet in different styles and each conveys a different mood or tone. Helvetica®, for instance, seems efficient and utilitarian to many designers and readers while Caslon seems more traditional and "bookish." Personal preferences are not easily determined or communicated, but a good book on type can explain the nuances of typography much better than this short section can.

More important than style oftentimes is a typeface's **legibility** ▶ 146. Both **size** and **style** make a difference in the legibility of text on screen. Many fonts are designed for printed communication and so they may not be as appropriate for the screen. Others are designed specifically for computer screens and have hand-tuned screen fonts.

Remember to choose a type size that is readable in the environment where the project will be presented. For electronic books or magazines that will be used primarily by one person on a personal computer, smaller sizes may suffice. For presentations seen by many people at once, however, larger type sizes will be needed. This is because the screen may be projected onto a larger screen and viewed from afar.

Another issue is font rendering across **platforms** ▶ 118. Various platforms may handle fonts in different ways. There are also several font formats so care must be taken that the exact typeface and size appears correctly on each platform. This involves either choosing standard fonts that users will have installed in their systems, or building the fonts used into the project so that type will appear correctly even if users do not have the fonts installed.

New technologies may reduce many of the issues in this area. One includes Multiple Master typefaces from Adobe Systems which automatically adjust to different optical sizes, widths, and weights. One caveat with using these types of technologies is not to rely on technologies that may not be present in a user's computer. For more controllable or definable configurations like those in presentations or kiosks, these technologies may be well suited.

Any fonts other than native system fonts included with the project will likely need to be licensed from the creator or distributor of the font. Unless font technologies that convert printer-based fonts into screen representations are used, only screen fonts may need licensing. Contact the typeface vendors to discuss licensing arrangements.

Although pictures in catalogs, magazines, and coffee table books appear more colorful than computer-based photos and illustrations, the vividness is often the result of the paper stock, resolution, and production values more than it is the color qualities of the ink. The range of colors possible with inks are a subset of the range of computer-monitor colors which is a subset of the range of visible colors.

Display Text

Display text is a term from the print-publishing industry that refers to the use of highly decorative typefaces for **titles** and **headlines**. These elements may be appropriate for the style and tone of a project—especially one dealing with a particular historical subject—but should be used sparingly as they will be harder to read. For example, a product about Haight-Ashbury in the 1960s may convey the style of the period with psychedelic type styles that were common on street posters then.

Screenshots

Screenshots of various applications or other electronic products are often used in catalogs and interactive sales products as well as for documentation and brochures for all electronic projects. There are many utilities that allow pictures of the screens to be taken including the cursor, menubars, and menus if desired.

Case Study: Australia Post Stamp Designer

Description:
The Australia Post Stamp Designer is a fun, interactive kiosk that lets users of all ages design stamps. Commissioned by the Australia Post, it demonstrates the process of designing stamps using a direct manipulation touch screen interface. Several choices of stamps are offered for manipulation of graphic elements and coloring. Two kiosks are installed at a museum for stamp collectors in Melbourne, Australia.

Project Type:
Kiosk

Development Hardware:
Macintosh IIfx, Macintosh IIci

Delivery Hardware:
Macintosh IIsi, 13in. color monitor

Software Used:
MacroMind Director, Adobe Photoshop, Aldus Freehand

Team Members and Roles:
Peter Mitchell, direction, programming and interface design; Scott McNeilage, project management; Rob Wellington, computer graphics and interface; Andrew Bruckshaw, testing and debugging

Funding:
Client funds

Price:
Customized versions available.

Contact:
Jim Passmore
Australia Post, Philatelic Section
Phone (Intl + 613) 204-7718

Peter Mitchell
Big Animated Digital Productions
Glebe
N.S.W., Australia

Concept and Planning:
With Big Animated Digital's input, the client developed the concept and provided black-and-white artwork, in Aldus Freehand format, of popular stamp designs. Basic guidelines were specified but otherwise free rein was allowed to BAD for creative development. Ample time (ten weeks) was allowed for development.

Design and Prototype:
Three weeks were spent in designing the interface and writing code. During this time, all black-and-white artwork was separated into layers and colorized to produce six versions of each art piece.

Production:
Two weeks were spent refining code and graphics. The XCMD "flush event" was found to be important for touch screen kiosk. Some research was dedicated to finding the optimal memory configuration for performance.

Testing:
One week was spent on bug testing and debugging code.

Delivery:
Two kiosks were installed at the museum.

Programming
100% Custom Code

Content
50% Repurposed
50% New

Expenses
1% Marketing
10% Operations
89% Development

Development Expenses
88% Personnel
12% Equipment
(Content not app.)

Total Development Costs:
not avail.

Total Development Team:
4 people

Total Development Time: 16 weeks

Photograph Production

All photographic specifications should have been completed during the Design and Prototyping stage. Production **photographers ▶ 25, 151** and **image manipulation artists** should understand these specifications before setting out to create or modify photographs. Shooting photographs for multimedia products is similar to many other types of photography.

One prominent piece of advice mentioned by many developers is to take great pictures. While image manipulation applications can be used to correct just about any problem from color balance to composition, these corrections take time and require skilled team members. The better and more consistent the initial images, the less work that will be required to prepare them for use.

Composition

Composition is the arrangement of the objects and/or people in a picture. The edges of the pictures are abrupt and form a frame that sets the objects on a type of stage. Good compositions are arrangements of objects, people, and even landscapes that are balanced and interesting. Balance need not be symmetrical, but must ensure that the photograph does not leave the impression that something is missing. See the Resources section for recommended books on photography. These will describe composition and other photographic concepts much more thoroughly.

The **long shot** is a composition whose subject is far away from the camera. Usually, this shot establishes the context and background of a subject. Landscapes are usually long shots as are some dramatic portraits. The **medium shot** is a composition that places the subject in the mid-ground between foreground and background elements. Often, the subject fills the frame in a medium shot.

The **close-up** is used to focus on a particular part of the subject. In portraits, a close-up usually has the head and shoulders filling the frame. A close-up is a much more personal view of a subject—especially a person. This can be used to create a sense of involvement with or relation to the subject in the viewer. The **extreme close-up** focuses on a small detail of the subject; for example an eye of an animal or the keys on a keyboard. It is used to establish a sense of intimacy with the subject. In photo essays and video, it is important to vary shots to keep the viewer's interest piqued. Too many shots at the same range can get tiring and uninteresting.

Many photographs for multimedia projects are simply of objects. These are often shot for cataloging or for illustrations that accompany text. If this is the case, composition is less important.

Exposure, Aperture, Focus, and Lighting

Exposure is the amount of time the camera's shutter stays open. **Aperture** is the size of the opening that allows light into a camera. **Focus** is the adjustment of the camera lens to sharpen the image detail. **Lighting** refers to the amount, position, and color of light sources that affect the scene. All four of these factors are related and impact each other. Strong lighting, for instance, will require a smaller aperture (the f-stop number on the camera lens) which may narrow the field of focus and require a shorter exposure. Changing any one of these four factors will require adjusting the others. Automatic cameras handle these adjustments for the photographer but do not allow as much control over the picture. Many photographers turn these automatic features off for critical shots.

Good photography books can describe in detail how to use exposure, focus, and lighting to best effect but be aware of the changes that will occur when digitizing for the screen. Because the dynamic range will decrease (the number of grays or colors in the photograph) and because the contrast will be heightened, some of the fine detail may be lost. It is best to shoot uncomplicated, simply lit pictures that have even lighting and balanced focus. These will digitize with better results than pictures with tricky or bizarre effects. Complex photographs will need more time and skill when scanning and converting.

Any photography should **use at least two light sources** that are color neutral. If you cannot get professional lights, sometimes called lamps, the next best source is usually to shoot outside in the sun. The sun at noon time is usually the best, but you may need to shoot

To learn more about photography as a medium and what types of issues to explore in its use, see the Photography section in Design and Prototype.

When shooting in low light, widen the aperture. Focus is also more critical under these conditions because the depth of field is less.

Long Shot

Medium Shot

Close-Up

Extreme Close-

*When composing a picture, pay attention to the positive and negative space formed by the subject and background. The **positive space** is the subject itself and the **negative space** is everything else. These should feel balanced.*

*Natural light varies tremendously. The sun can cast **warm** or **cool light**, harsh or soft throughout the day. Light color and brightness will vary between shade and shadow, in overcast or cloudy weather, in direct sunlight, at noon, at dusk, or at dawn.*

When photographing a television or monitor screen, the exposure will need to be more than 1/25 second to avoid any separating lines between interleaved frame signals. It is best to shoot at or near 1/10 second in these cases, but adjust the aperture accordingly for these longer exposures so that the scene isn't washed out by too much light. In the case of an image on a computer screen, it is always best to use a screen capture utility instead of taking photographs.

When shooting a subject against a backdrop, have the subject stand 5 feet or more from the backdrop so that the shadow falls onto the floor and not onto the backdrop. This will create a cleaner background, making it easier to drop out when superimposing over another image.

A background that curves into the floor can create a smoother, more even background that hides any seam between horizontal and vertical surfaces.

in the shade if the light is too high-contrast or bright. Shooting outside will also require fast work to keep all the shots consistent as the sun moves across the sky, if consistency is an issue.

Using more than one light source helps to avoid bright spots, loss of detail on the unlit side of an object, and shadows. The main light source is called a **key light**. This is usually positioned in front and to the side of the subject. The second light source is usually positioned on the other side of the subject but still to the front. This is called the **fill light** and is usually not as bright as the key light. The fill light is meant to add light and detail to the shade side of the subject but not so much that the key light no longer provides the primary light. Sometimes, a **backlight** is added to illuminate the edges of the subject and wash out the background.

Any of these lights can be either direct or reflected. A **reflector** can be any reflective board such as a white board, piece of paper, or anything fairly light. Professional photographers sometimes use special umbrellas to bounce light. Hold the reflector up to the subject, out of the camera's view, to bounce light into the darkened area. This will show more detail in shaded areas and can be especially important when shooting portraits.

Spot lights can be used to direct strong lighting on a subject but avoid washing-out the features by using too much light. Many times, photographers use diffusers in front of lights to soften the light coming from them. A diffuser will not only soften the light but spread out its range. Frosted glass or plastic, sheer fabric, or even tracing paper can act as diffusers.

Gels and **filters** are common in traditional photography to add special effects to pictures. With multimedia photography, it is usually best to perform these effects using an image manipulation program. There are many more filters and effects that can be accomplished in the computer both faster and easier than in traditional photography.

Color

The **color** ▶ 150 in photographs is profoundly affected by the color of the light source as well as the color of surrounding objects. For example, a white object next to a red one on a white background will have a red coloring on the side nearest the red object. This is because light bounces off objects and picks up the color of those objects. White is an especially reflective color and will be susceptible to picking up colors in its environment. Also, the light from a light source will pick up color from anything it passes through, for example, a window, lens, lampshade, or filter. This is one reason why

professional photographers use special quartz bulbs that are color balanced for even, neutral light.

What is known as **warm light** is the kind of light that comes directly from the sun in the early morning or late afternoon. Warm light tends to be yellowish and higher contrast, casting more distinct shadows and showing more detail in objects. **Cool light** is the light cast in the early morning or late afternoon looking away from the sun. Cool light can be very blue and casts a softer light that shows less detail and has a somewhat fuzzy or hazy quality. Humans do not usually notice this difference much because our eyes automatically adjust to these conditions. Photographs, though, will pick up these differences. For this reason, professional photographers use controlled lights in a studio to be sure that the light they are seeing is color neutral.

Backgrounds

Backgrounds should reflect the subject matter and style of the photographs. Choose backgrounds that will not clash or distract from the objects of main interest. When shooting photos of people, be sure there is nothing in the background that might look odd once the photo is taken. In particular, anything directly behind the person, sticking out above or to their side, might look like it is growing out of them in the finished photograph. For example, a picture of a CEO in her office lobby might have a ficus tree in the background that looks as if it is growing out of her head. Most people would not notice this in real life because of depth perception and motion cues, but once the picture is taken and the moment frozen, it will be more noticeable.

When shooting simple objects—especially when these are meant to be **superimposed** ▶ 156 into a scene or another photograph—be sure that the background is simple and consistent. The more even the background lighting and color, the more easily it can be deleted or dropped out in the final composition. Many times, a photographer will shoot objects against a blue screen or another odd color so that this color can be dropped out or "keyed" more easily in image manipulation programs.

Cameras and Lenses

Any **camera** can be used to capture pictures but some are better than others. Single-lens reflex cameras that allow control over everything from focus to f-stop are good for professionals or those who know something about photography. **Automatic cameras**, however, are perfectly acceptable for pictures that do not require special lighting or other circumstances. Even **disposable box cameras** perform well for simple photography.

A **wide-angle lens** captures a larger field of view. If you cannot get back far enough, this lens may work well. The disadvantage of a wide-angle lens is that it distorts images. With close-up portraits it will make noses and other features appear to stick out. A **telephoto lens** brings objects far-away closer. It has an effect of flattening images out. Portraits are more "dignified" with a telephoto lens. A telephoto lens, though, has a narrow field of view, focusing on the subject but not picking up the surrounding environment. It also cuts out a lot of light and cannot be used for dark scenes. A **macro lens** brings the view very close to a subject. It is ideal for photographing detail or small objects because it allows the camera to focus within a few inches of the subject. The disadvantage of a macro lens is that the area that stays in focus, the "depth of field," is very short.

Focus and composition are probably more important for creating good simple pictures than lighting, exposure, and aperture. A simple camera will allow anyone to take good photographs and concentrate on the composition and subject matter. Truly spectacular pictures, however, will require more sophisticated equipment in the hands of a skilled professional. These differences depend on the style and needs of the project.

Film

The film used for photography can greatly affect the picture quality. When using automatic or disposable cameras, stick to simple daylight film. Be sure to match film with the exposure setting on your camera or ask someone in a photo store for the correct film to use. Higher numbers capture the light faster and are better for shooting moving objects. These tend to be grainier, although once scanned and prepared for the screen, the difference is negligible. Lower numbers will need more time to expose and will capture better detail, but will also require a steady tripod so that the camera does not move while the lens is open.

Daylight film is suited for shooting outdoors and will produce a slightly yellowish/warm cast when used with indoor lighting. **Tungsten film** is specially balanced to capture color accurately in indoor and studio lighting. If used outside with natural light, it will produce an overall bluish cast. **Infrared film** can be used to create special effects or in low-light and no-light situations. Infrared film will "see" light from an infrared bulb and is able to penetrate fog, mist, and haze. It produces special coloring effects.

Tripods and Monopods

Any repetitive photography of objects, or any pictures of moving objects, will likely require a tripod or monopod to stabilize the camera and prevent it from moving while the picture is exposed. The camera must be held rock-steady for the split-second the shutter is open. Tripods are specially designed to be stable in a variety of settings, but anything stable at the moment will suffice. If a tripod is not available, try leaning against a wall or large object or sitting on a chair or the floor to prevent yourself from moving while taking a picture.

A monopod is a one-legged tripod used when walking around and taking pictures casually. The one leg will distribute the majority of weight to the ground and reduce the number of axes the camera can move within. This can stabilize the camera sufficiently while allowing better and quicker portability than a tripod.

Repurposing Photographs

Existing images can be obtained from almost anywhere, depending on the project and subject matter. Often, a **client** will already have related images that may or may not need re-touching. **Content experts** ▶ 20, 99 may also be good sources for images or information on existing images.

Stock Photo Houses and Photo Services

Stock photo houses and **photo services** provide a wide variety of images for use in different kinds of projects. These organizations have libraries of thousands of images of varying subjects and in many styles. The difficulty with these libraries is usually not whether the photo needed is in the library or not but if it can be found. These photographs can be expensive and may have severe limitations on the type or amount of use. Many are available only for one-time or for noncommercial use. Depending on the use, prices can

A studio will provide the greatest control over lighting and subject allowing more consistent composition. On location, remember to bring everything that could possibly be needed. Also get signed model releases for any people photographed. It may be difficult, if not impossible, to get these later.

A copy stand can be used to photograph large amounts of printed materials or small objects. A copy stand is a stand or table with lights and a tripod that allows consistent and even lighting, focus, and perspective.

Digital cameras automatically digitize and store pictures. For example, Apple Computer's QuickTake 100 is a point-and-shoot digital camera that captures 24-bit color images for use on Macintosh and Windows computers. It connects to the computer through a modem or printer port and captures both standard resolution images (320 by 240 pixel) and high resolution images (640 by 480 pixel). In internal memory it can store 32 standard resolution photos, 8 high resolution photos, or a combination of each. These types of cameras can save time and money when capturing photographic images for multimedia projects.

Black Star, Magnum, The Image Bank, Comstock, and Sygma Photo News are all well-known stock photo houses. Local outlets can be found in the Yellow Pages, a professional photographer's directory, or by asking in a photography store.

The Picture Network International (PNI) in Arlington, VA has an online service for subscribers to search and retrieve photos from its vast library as well as from libraries of several other stock photography houses.

Scanner resolution is measured in dots per inch (dpi). This refers to the amount of pixels or dots that fit within one linear inch.

Many models of each type of scanner can digitize images in color although the degree of color quality and accuracy varies. Although many color discrepancies can be corrected with image manipulation software, it is always easier to work with artwork that has been scanned under the best possible conditions.

range from $150 to $1500 each. Be as descriptive as possible when requesting images.

Some stock photo services are now online, allowing picture previews to be browsed over the phone lines. Many of these charge a subscription fee as well as a per photo fee.

The Library of Congress is a great source of images in the public domain. These are also inexpensive, usually only covering the price of the photograph copy. The collections in this library are vast but only cover certain types of photos typically relating to the United States, its history, and its events. It may also be difficult to find a source of reproductions from which to search without sending someone in person to Washington, D.C.

Photo Clip-Art

Many companies now sell photographs already scanned and archived onto CD-ROMs for reasonable prices. Like stock photo houses, many have licensing limitations on use and may be expensive. More and more CD-ROMs, however, are becoming available that have unlimited use at affordable prices. While most photo stock houses enforce high quality standards, photo clip-art CD-ROMs can range from excellent to poor. Try to see samples beforehand before purchasing to be sure that these CD-ROMs will meet your needs.

Scanning Photographs

A **scanner** is a device that converts an image into digital form. Some scanners scan in color and some only in grayscale. Some are capable of high resolutions of 1000 dpi or more, although the average is 300 dpi. Most computer screens are only 72–100 dpi—well within the resolution of most scanners.

All scanners, no matter what type, tend to reduce dynamic range, heighten contrast, and dull colors. This can be corrected, but you may want to exaggerate these in the original shots or choose different shots altogether.

Be sure to **oversample.** This is the process of scanning an image at the highest possible resolution. While an image may only be used at a set size and resolution, if it is scanned at a higher resolution than needed, it can be used for other purposes if the project content is changed or repurposed. Archiving oversampled images gives the content greater flexibility and opportunities.

Be sure to test scan a few different images to determine the best brightness, contrast, and resolution settings. Clean both the source material and scanner thoroughly before scanning to insure the best results. Most scanner software will allow images to be cropped, rotated, and manipulated to some degree. It is usually quickest, however, to scan and save the images and manipulate them in an image manipulation application.

Flat-Bed Scanners

Flatbed scanners work much like photocopiers in that a bar of light passes under a flat plate of glass to read the image. These multi-purpose machines are ideal for digitizing artwork and sketches into a computer where they can be modified, cleaned up, or enhanced with software. Resolution capabilities for flatbed scanners range from 300dpi to 600dpi. Since screens are generally 72dpi, this resolution is more than adequate for multimedia. Most flat-bed scanners can scan a legal size piece of paper but some can scan even larger areas.

Hand Scanners

Hand scanners work similarly to flatbed scanners but are small enough to fit in a hand. The hand scanner is moved over the image and scans at resolutions comparable to those of flatbeds. Hand scanners are generally much less expensive than flatbeds but they are more limited in the width of the piece that can be scanned and the control the user has over the scan quality. As a result, hand scanners are not as well-suited for multimedia use.

Slide Scanners

Slide scanners are used for 35mm slides. Some are also capable of scanning 4x5in. and 8x10in. transparencies. They generally cost more than the average flat-bed scanner and are capable of higher resolutions ranging from 600dpi to 1000dpi.

Drum Scanners

Drum scanners are used for high-end publishing and have resolutions that can reach up to 3000dpi. Drum scanners are very expensive and are used primarily to create high-quality documentation or packaging.

Photo CD

Photo CD ▶ 153 is a CD-ROM format and service from Kodak. It uses a **multi-session CD-ROM Bridge disc format** and works in most CD-ROM drives provided the attached computer has special software.

Photo CDs are an efficient way to have images scanned in color and archived automatically. The scanning technology used by Kodak produces well-balanced color and fine detail. This makes it an ideal alternative over scanning photographs by hand. The price of each image ranges between $1.50 to $2.00 depending on the amount of images scanned at a time. While Photo CDs can have data written to them in multiple sessions (so that more images can be added to the same disc later), only newer CD-ROM drives can read these multiple sessions. The older drives will be able to read the first session but not the later ones. Be sure to ask that all images be scanned in a *single session* if you are having different rolls of film digitized onto a new disc and have only a single session drive.

Color Matching Systems

Some scanners and systems include **color matching software**. These are most needed when scanning and manipulating images for print publishing. Because multimedia projects will appear on a low-resolution computer or television monitor, it is usually less important to invest in a color matching system. It is still important to test a few images on the final delivery platform to be sure that colors and picture quality do not change appreciably. If it does, adjust the scanning and manipulation settings to insure that images displayed in the final project are of the best quality possible.

Photographic File Formats

Decide early on which **file formats** ▶ 173 will be used to store and manipulate images. Tagged Image File Format (TIFF), PICT, and Encapsulated PostScript (EPS) are all popular formats. Because PICT is the native file format on the Macintosh, PICT files are usually smaller and faster to display. EPS files are used extensively in print publishing but are usually larger and slower files to display. They are also not supported by many authoring systems. Programmers and designers can help determine which file formats are best for a chosen authoring environment.

Manipulating Photographs
Image Manipulation Software

Image processing or manipulation software is used to "clean-up" images, enhance them and add special effects. At the minimum, this software will allow an image to be cropped, scaled, rotated, and adjusted for contract and brightness. Most offer features that allow images to be collaged together to form entirely new pictures. **Color** programs will allow the color balance to be enhanced and conversion between various color formats. **Grayscale** images can be colored by hand, for example.

Some photographers are already familiar with these tools and are comfortable with them, while others avoid them. Many people specialize in image enhancement even if they are not photographers themselves.

These applications are well developed and offer a vast array of features for digital editing. It is usually a better strategy to manipulate and edit pictures in a computer rather than in a camera. Many effects and adjustments

Image Formats

File sizes for 640 x 480 pixel images at different color depths (qualities):

"True" color	24-bit	16 million colors	921K
System color	8-bit	256 colors	300K
Grayscale	8-bit	256 shades of gray	300K
Black and White	1-bit	black and white	38K

can be made with finer control and immediate feedback than through a viewfinder. Using the "undo" and "redo" capabilities in most applications, designers can quickly compare an image after a transformation with the image immediately before. Once manipulated, these programs can save an image in the precise format needed by the authoring environment. This may include changing the **color depth**, **color palette**, and **file size**.

Special Effects

Many **special effects** can be added to photos and images with image manipulation software. Special filters allow images or sections of an image to be twirled, squeezed, rippled, distorted, despeckled, and diffused, among others. A graphic designer, illustrator, or photographer can perform any multiple transformations in many combinations to achieve a desired effect.

Photoediting is forbidden in some circumstances. Documentaries and some educational projects may bar any editing or changing of photographs besides possibly adjusting contrast and brightness levels. Be sure to address the issue of changing photos with the client and any content experts in the Design and Prototype phase.

Photo CD

Most photography stores that develop film will be able to send any photos out for processing as a Photo CD. Photo CDs can be made from negative or slide film and can hold slightly over 100 photos in five resolutions per disc. Call Kodak at 800/235-6325 (CD-KODAK) to find the nearest Photo CD finisher near you.

The five resolutions stored for each picture in pixels are:
("Base" stands for the resolution for television.)

BASE/16	128x192
BASE/4	256x384
BASE	512x768
4 BASE	1024x1536
16 BASE	2048x 3072

Photo Compression

The same image will vary in size depending on its resolution and bit depth. For example, an 8-bit color image will be about a third the size of an equally sized 24-bit image. Images can be compressed for archiving but often not for use in a project. Photo CDs use their own form of compression but most authoring systems do not support compressed image file formats. One way around this is to use the QuickTime image compression **codec**.

The **QuickTime Photo codec** implements the **JPEG** ▶ 153, 208 (Joint Photographers Experts Group) compression scheme for high-quality still image compression. JPEG is designed to compress full-color images and typically gives compression ratios in the range of 10:1 to 25:1 with no visible picture degradation.

Compression time will vary according to a computer's CPU and could take many seconds. Be sure to test decompression time when using compressed images to be sure that the user is not frustrated with an inactive product.

Sound Production

To learn more about sound as a medium and what types of issues to explore in its use, see the Sound section in Design and Prototype.

One of the fundamental issues for recording any type of sound is to **capture the highest quality possible**. This insures more flexible source content for archiving and processing. Thoroughly testing the sound levels at the time of recording will help keep the quality high. Once sounds are captured, they must be converted to digital format, if they were captured with analog equipment, "cleaned-up," and stored for integration into the final project.

Recording New Sounds

*Record some "**room color**" or local ambient sound in addition to recording narration or dialog. Ambient sound can be added to create continuity between separate recordings or through edited cuts.*

Producing sound in-house or with assistance from a sound engineer or sound studio can give the cleanest and most appropriate digital materials. This will also sidestep many of the copyright issues that can occur with

2 seconds of Miles Davis playing

repurposed audio. Traditional sound engineers can be huge assets when trying to generate good recordings and most are generally familiar with digital technology. They may not be as familiar with multimedia, though, and might benefit from having some extra time to learn how their work will be used.

It is often difficult to hear any audio problems such as background noise and distortion while recording. During playback, however, problems will be much more noticeable—especially with high-fidelity playback such as CD-Audio. A skilled audio engineer will be able to notice any problems and correct them during the recording to get as high a quality as possible.

Generally, getting good **acoustics** requires selecting the right placement of microphones and conducting rehearsals and sound checks. A **sound check** is the only way to truly test the quality of a recording session. Place the microphone as close to possible to the subject or subjects and adjust the sound levels accordingly. This helps reduce background noise and minimize echoes. Throughout a recording session or sessions, the microphone should be at the same distance from the subject to retain consistent sound characteristics. Special microphones can be used that pick up directed sounds from farther away, but these are tricky to operate and should be left to professionals.

Like photo studios, **sound studios** provide the best control over ambient noise and recording level. The walls of a studio are specifically designed to dampen noise and prevent it from reverberating back into the room. Sound studios may also have equipment that allows multiple tracks of sound to be recorded at once and mixed with other previously recorded sounds.

When sound recordings are made, be sure to leave blank recorded time at the beginning and ending of the recording to make editing easier. Also, logging recording times and descriptions will make it easier to find and edit different sources. Be sure the log includes the start and stop times of the segment, a short description of the recording, and the number of the tape or the place where the recording is stored.

Sound Quality

There is a wide spectrum of sound quality available on computer platforms. Most computers are capable of fairly good sound quality. Even the lowest-end computers are usually capable of at least 8-bit 11kHz sound playback, which is better than telephone quality. Highest qualities may require special sound cards but these levels are more than what most projects need. Computers that have **digital sound processing chips (DSPs)** ▶ 121, 155 built-in or on external boards can process and output CD-quality sound but these capabilities are not widespread in the general consumer market.

The sound quality appropriate for a project will be most naturally determined by the capabilities of the target delivery platform. Using DSPs to provide a high level of sound quality may be a consideration for a kiosk or presentation, but is probably not advisable at the moment for consumer products. The delivery platforms should have been determined during the Concept and Planning phase, while the sound standards should have been decided during Design and Prototype.

Stereo vs. Monophonic Sound

Stereo sound provides data in two different channels: left and right. Often the sound in each channel is essentially the same with the two channels providing a depth to music that monophonic sound does not have. Sometimes, different sounds or instruments are recorded only to one channel or with special **spatial mixing** equipment to simulate the effect that it is emanating from a specific place in an environment.

Monophonic sound includes only one channel. When played through stereo speakers, this one channel is either played through one speaker of the two or through both. In this later case, the sound will be "flatter" than a stereo recording through the same speakers. It is always best to record sound in stereo but deciding whether to process it as stereo and include it in a project should be determined by the target delivery platform.

Digital sound consists of "samples" taken at discrete intervals. Digital sound quality is measured in terms of the sample size and the sampling rate. The **sampling rate** refers to number of the samples per second, expressed in kilohertz (kHz). The common sampling rates are 11kHz, 22kHz, and 44kHz. The higher the sampling rate, the higher the sound quality. The **sample size** is the size in bits that are used to quantify the signal. Sample sizes are either 8-bit or 16-bit. The larger the sample size, the more "steps" that can be represented within the dynamic range of sound. CD-Audio has a 16-bit sample size and a 44kHz sampling rate (actually its 44.1kHz). Sound volume is measured in **decibels** (dBs) which are logarithmic. This means that the difference between 20dBs is not twice as loud as 10dBs but ten times as loud.

Audio CDs use a special format for recording and playing sound called the **Red Book** ▶ 48, 110 standard. This format describes how sound information should be stored on audio CDs. (Sound can also be stored on Mixed-Mode CD-ROMs.) Red Book audio provides two channels of 44kHz sound. CD-Audio disks contain both the digital sound and the time code for the sound measured at 75 frames a second. A computer has software

Sound Formats

Delivery	KB/min	Sampling Rate (kHz)	Sample Size (bits)	Number of Channels	Consumer Level
Binaural	17280	48	24	2	HDCD/DAT
CD Stereo	10560	44	16	2	CD quality
High-end Macintosh Stereo	5280	22	16	2	FM quality
Best Macintosh Stereo	2640	22	8	2	television
Best Macintosh Mono	1320	22	8	1	television
Low-end Macintosh Mono	660	11	8	1	television
Telephone-quality	n/a	4	analog	1	telephone

drivers that allow you to access the time code from the CD-Audio (or CD-ROM) player to find a particular song or sound fragment. The time code can be used for synchronizing music with other events.

Sound Equipment

Microphone

Microphones are the most important pieces of equipment for recording any kind of sound. Too often developers use substandard microphones and are disappointed with the quality of the recording. Microphones vary greatly in price and quality. Be sure to use one that can handle the dynamic range required. Some microphones are **unidirectional**, which means that they tend to record sounds from one direction and filter out sounds from other directions. **Shotgun microphones** are unidirectional but they will pick up ambient sounds to a lesser degree. Unidirectional microphones should be used when necessary, as is the case when the microphone cannot be moved close enough to the sound source.

A **lavaliere** microphone clips onto a person's lapel or shirt. These are usually small and unobtrusive and record quite well since they are so close to the speaker's mouth. **Wireless microphones** may seem like a convenient idea but they are expensive and can produce poor sound due to radio interference. It is usually best to use to use microphones with attached cables and get them as close as possible to the sound source. Also, be sure to use high-quality cable and secure it from foot traffic.

Sound Recorders

A variety of recording devices are available for recording sound. These include audio cassette recorders and **Digital Audio Tape** (DAT) recorders. Record in digital format if at all possible.

Two mistakes often made in recording sound are using an on-camera microphone and having the microphone too far away from the subject. Ambient room sound generally dominates these recordings. Monitor sound quality throughout a recording and not just at the beginning.

The human ear can hear frequencies between 16Hz and 16,000Hz. The lowest sounds include low rumbles while the highest ones are high-pitched squeaks. As humans age, the range narrows, most noticeably in the lower frequencies. The pain threshhold of most humans is around 120dB, but again, age imparts differences in the range.

To find good microphones, visit an audio-visual equipment supplier instead of a consumer electronics store and make sure the entire system uses good quality shielded cable.

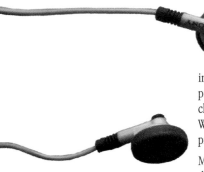

The American Federation of Television and Radio Artists (AFTRA) in New York and the Screen Actors Guild (SAG) in Hollywood are good sources for finding vocal artists. AFTRA can be reached at 212/523-0800 and SAG at 213/465-4600.

A good sound engineer can clean up and enhance voice recordings dramatically. They can remove any "ums" and "ers" from speech and tighten up or space out the "dead space" between words in much the same way that an image processor touches up a photograph.

This prevents the need for re-digitizing and the loss of quality that often accompanies it. Use whatever format is most convenient and whatever equipment is most accessible. While most portable and pocket recorders offer reasonably quality for later transcriptions, only a few will be acceptable for recording actual sound source material.

Sound Digitizers

A **sound digitizer** is a combination of hardware and software that digitizes sound from a microphone, tape, CD, television, or other sound source. Any sound that is not recorded in a digital format originally must be digitized to be used on a computer. Some computers include sound recording and digitizing equipment as part of standard equipment but it may have a single channel and be capable of only 8-bit, 11kHz quality. While this may be acceptable for voice recording, it is probably not good enough for music.

Most **sound digitizing boards** come with software that allows sound to be recorded and edited. Some of these digital-sound processing applications allow more features for sound editing and manipulating than others. A few offer the ability to produce elaborate special effects like smoothing, reverberation, echo, and reverse waveforms.

Recording New Vocals

Voice production begins by having a **scriptwriter** prepare a cue sheet and **voice talent** rehearse and read the materials. When choosing a voice artist, consider not only the speaker's voice qualities like **diction** and **attitude**, but keep in mind what the product needs to appeal to its audience. The **gender**, **age**, and **accent** ▶ 96 of a voice artist may have an effect. The difference of a man or woman speaker can be very important relative to the intended audience. It may be possible to provide multiple recordings of the same passage performed by different speakers.

Good voice artists are capable of speaking in many different styles. These can be confident, aggressive, friendly, assertive, honest, apathetic, dynamic, mature, sensitive, educated, enthusiastic, overbearing, pretentious, timid, boring, or sexy. Voice quality can also be described as high pitched, throaty, expressionless, soft, tired, mumbling, whiny, nasal, loud, breathy, childish, fast, clipped, slow, solemn, tense, resonant, crackly, shrill, or whiny. Be sure to communicate the stylistic needs of the vocal recording to the voice artist and choose an artist that is capable and comfortable with that style.

A scriptwriter should prepare a **script** of any vocal work no matter how short. This practice will ensure that no vocals are forgotten and that each is communicated clearly to the vocal artist. Any longer **narration** will probably need to be directed with cues. Vocal artists should be directed to leave spaces between statements so that editors can clip segments more easily if necessary. Run-on speech is difficult to edit.

Some general things to beware when recording vocals:

- **Thoroughly rehearse the script** and speak *to* the imaginary audience and not *at* them. It can be difficult to speak to an anonymous audience but lack of meaning or intent will undoubtedly be heard in the recording.

- **Avoid monotone speaking** and emphasize appropriate words and phrases. Raise and lower you voice naturally when speaking. Listening to test recordings and experimenting with different exaggerations will help clarify how much emphasis is needed and where. Listen to newscasters or radio announcers. Their dynamic range can vary dramatically.

- **Remember to breath evenly** and speak through your mouth. This will make speech sound more natural and even.

Recording New Music

Music can be more than just an afterthought to a product. It can be the central focus or a rich accompaniment that enriches other content. Films have used soundtracks to establish mood and emotion as well as location. These are usually more integral than merely background music. Soundtracks can often punctuate action and provide continuity between sections.

The size of the music production effort is determined by the number of compositions, their length, and level of quality. Music can be used in a multimedia project in many ways:

- Composing and producing original theme music for a project, such as a game, kiosk, or presentation.

- Performing music that will be the main focus of a product (as opposed to background music), such as an interactive music title.

- Composing MIDI tracks for live performances.

When designing for music, establish what kind of music is needed and how many musicians it will take to perform or record it. Musicians, like other artists, will need to know how the music is to be used, and who the audience is, to tailor their performance appropriately.

Musicians can be found from a variety of resources. Professional musicians can be reached through performing arts organizations, symphonies, and agents. Recording studios will often recommend musicians. Colleges and universities can be excellent sources for competent musicians at reasonable prices. Asking friends or other developers can often uncover successful contacts.

MIDI

MIDI ▶ 155 (Musical Instrumental Interface) is a standard format for communicating sound information between electronic instruments and computers. MIDI files are not sampled sounds like on audio cassette tapes or CDs. They contain instructions for reproducing sounds. MIDI can indicate what pitches to play at what durations. This encoding scheme makes MIDI files much smaller than recorded sound files but requires more sophisticated equipment for recording and playback.

Any computer will need both a hardware **MIDI interface** and software to process and communicate MIDI information. This software usually includes a MIDI synthesizer that can replay the MIDI information. The synthesizer is capable of recreating the sounds associated with different instruments, such as a drum, keyboard, flute, or guitar.

MIDI allows instruments to simulate other instruments. In fact, any MIDI instrument can be used as a **sampler** or input device for MIDI instructions to be played on any other MIDI device. These instruments include MIDI flutes, guitars, drums, keyboard, and even voice interfaces so that musicians or singers can create MIDI instructions with the instrument they feel most comfortable with.

A **sequencer** is used to mix and change MIDI instructions to create complex music or interactions between different instruments. Once a sequencer orders and arranges the music, a synthesizer can be used to play the composition.

Many musicians have experience with MIDI instruments. Whether MIDI is a technology worth exploring for a particular project is something that should be determined by its design specification. To play MIDI files, a synthesizer will need to be present. This means that MIDI files may not be appropriate for a consumer product unless the software includes one. For projects with controlled environments such as kiosks and presentations, for example, MIDI may be an appropriate choice.

Repurposing Existing Sounds

Many sources of speech, music, and sound effects already exist. A majority of these speech recordings are of historically important speeches or radio and TV broadcasts. These recordings are available on audio tape, diskette, and CD-ROM. The quality is usually better and more consistent than some clip-art or clip-video libraries but the limitations upon their use and their cost will vary. Some sound publishers—especially record companies—may have strict policies on usage and charge large licensing fees. Recently, some companies have created exceptions to this rule by recognizing the possibilities of multimedia and reducing both the fees and the licensing procedures.

Be sure to obtain the necessary rights to use any sounds not recorded by the project team or furnished by the client. Recordings whose copyright protection has expired will be in the public domain. The rights to the music and lyrics in a song are often separate from the particular recording. Even if a song's copyright has expired, a newer recording of it is likely to be under copyright. Tracking down copyright owners can be difficult and should be started early to give enough

For an address of the publisher of music you want to license, contact:

American Society of Composers, Authors, and Publishers (ASCAP)
New York, NY 212/621-6000

Broadcast Music, Inc. (BMI)
New York, NY 212/586-2000
Los Angeles, CA 310/659-9109

MIDI is often used for live musical performances that combine live music, prerecorded MIDI sequences, prerecorded music and lighting effects. MIDI functions as the lingua franca between the various equipment, triggering different actions when called upon to do so. MIDI is also used to coordinate timing between different instruments.

Different MIDI synthesizers may produce different sounds because the ranges of instruments may be in different orders. "Patch tables" may need to be configured to map one system to another. Even when everything is in synch, one synthesizer may produce a horn with a long decay while another may be short, so the composition will sound different from machine to machine. MIDI files themselves are transportable but it may take some tinkering to match system performance exactly. A new mode of MIDI called General MIDI attempts to reduce this variation and provide synthesizer-independent capabilities.

Folly artists originated in the early days of radio programs and are specialists in creating sounds from common objects. For example, crinkling cellophane can be used to simulate fire and shaking and warbling large sheets of aluminum can sound like thunder.

Many sound effects are available on audio-tape or CD-ROM and are usually license-free.

Lip-synching should not vary more than 33 milliseconds from the visual track to appear accurate. (There are 1000 milliseconds in a second.)

Music Storage Comparison

22kHz stereo music	5,280 KB / minute
44kHz stereo (CD-quality) music	10,560 KB /minute
44+kHz stereo/polyphonic MIDI	50 KB /minute

time to secure the rights. Also, know what you want beforehand. Rights to perform music can be possible to obtain usually for an amount far less than a complete recording.

There are libraries of license-free sounds and music on tape and CD-ROM. These can be found through mail-order catalogs and professional sound stores and magazines. Sound studios can recommend which recordings are appropriate and how to acquire them.

Sound Post-Production

Sound processing allows digital sound to be edited and mixed with little loss in quality. Sound recordings can be enhanced with **special effects** like filtering, reverse, or echo. Sound processing may be simple (if the recording is clean) or complex (if the source is of poor quality). Many times, recordings are long, making it necessary to edit less important parts from interesting material. To add continuity between cuts, ambient sound from the environment the recording was made can be inserted so that the cuts are less apparent. A good sound engineer can clean up and enhance sound dramatically. Sound engineers can also easily remove the "ums" and "ers" from speech.

Sound editing software allows many sounds to be combined, much like video editing applications. This allows separate sounds to be combined into a more complex soundtrack. For example, a recording of a conversation that is supposed to occur on a busy sidewalk can be created from a recording of the conversation in a studio and a recording of ambient noises from the street.

Often, sounds will need to be synchronized with other elements. While most of this is in the domain of element integration and under control of the programmer or creative director, some explicit sound synchronization can still be necessary. **Lip-synching**, or in other words, matching a voice track to a visual track may be necessary. **Time codes** ▶ 205 are usually used for this type of synchronization. If lip-synching or any other synchronization is planned, be sure to use recording equipment that records a time code or have it added later. This will make the synchronization process much easier.

Sound Effects

Sound effects include the addition of special sounds to punctuate certain events, such as the sound of a page in a book turning when the user moves to the next screen, or the processing of recorded music and voice to take on special characteristics. Realistic sounds like barking dogs, falling rain, or chirping birds can give character to otherwise silent actions. These sounds generally reinforce the action taken by a user or represent a sense of place, but they should relate to the event as well as the subject matter of the project.

Many times the sound used to represent a natural sound is not actually the real sound. Film makers often substitute sounds made with odd objects that may sound more "realistic" than the actual object. For example, the sound of horses trotting in the street may actually be made by slapping wooden blocks on a block of tile. Sounds for fires, water, gunfire, and car crashes are often designed by sound engineers to sound more realistic than the actual sounds.

Other sound processing can include combining or *shading* music or voice recordings with other sounds to give them a poetic effect. For example, a speech about a famous battle might be processed with a low-volume recording of a battle so that the words themselves take on the tones of the battle. This can be tricky and should be handled subtly for best effect.

Sound Engineers

Designing sound transitions from screen to screen requires careful composition. A good sound engineer thinks sonically, as opposed to visually or numerically, and can create a continuous sound design. Films typically handle these transitions very well with subtle cues and cuts that help communicate a story and create a rich atmosphere.

Animation Production

Animations ▶ 28, 157 are moving illustrations and most of the rules and techniques of illustration and graphics apply to animations, with the addition of elements that concern time and motion. And, animators, like illustrators, have their own styles and ways of working. Even to create similar animations, two different animators will likely approach them from two different ways.

The rough prototype in the Prototype stage establishes the kind of characters, scenes, or models to be animated along with their color schemes, lighting, style, mood, and textures. Before production begins, estimates and a schedule of the development time for the animations should be complete.

Animations can sometimes be the most time-consuming and complex content in a project. While shooting video involves balancing and organizing many disparate details, it is essentially recording existing objects and actions. Animation, on the other hand, must deal with many of the same details but creates all objects and action from scratch. The expense of digital animation is essentially the software and labor. No special equipment is needed beyond a CPU, although fast computers will make a big difference in the production time. Building and rendering animations—especially for 3D—are intensive tasks for computers. Personal computers may not be adequate for high-quality, photorealistic, or complex rendering. Many animators use workstations with much more performance to reduce the processing time.

Because animation is so time-consuming to produce, it is imperative to thoroughly sketch and **storyboard** animations before building them. This will let creative directors, project managers, or other team members critique and approve concepts before making large investments of time.

Final animation sequences are usually compressed or saved as QuickTime movies. This compression allows them to be optimized for the performance of the delivery platform and media. Animations can be built from scratch on the computer or with any kind of digitized materials. Depending on the style, **sprites** or objects that move in an animation can be scanned from photographs, line art, or sketches, built from graphic drawing or painting software, or digitized from video sources. Almost anything can be used in an animation, which means that the digitizing processes in the sound, video, and graphics sections of this chapter are also applicable to animation.

While traditional film animations are usually played at either 12 or 24 frames per second, animations may be created at just about any frame rate, depending on the effect desired. **Stop-motion animation** such as claymation and animations for music videos experiment with a variety of different frame rates in the constant quest for new styles.

2D Animation

2D animation is more than just cartooning; 2D animations can be of any style. Frequently, animations in presentations look more graphic or illustrative and rarely use characters or cartoons. **Cartoons**, however, are a familiar form of animation to many users.

Be careful not to use single-pixel width lines in 2D animations. These types of lines may not reproduce correctly when compressed or converted into a movie format. Because television formats like NTSC are **interlaced**, these lines will be especially bad when transferred to video tape or played on a television monitor.

2D animation tools produce animations in two fundamentally different ways: frame by frame and object-oriented. **Frame-by-frame animation** is little more than high-tech page flipping just like a flipbook. This can be easier to produce in some cases but usually takes more time and storage space to play. **Object-oriented animation** tools are more popular because they allow separated objects to be defined and manipulated independently of other objects, backgrounds, or other scene elements.

Object-oriented animation tools often follow a movie or theater metaphor, defining different cast members within a score. **Cast members** are any object used in a scene. These can be characters, objects, props, or backgrounds. Cast members can usually only be moved within a scene and not transformed. Any differences in a cast member's shape or expression must be represented as a separate cast member. Some animation tools allow video clips to be used as cast members. A **score** is a matrix of frames with representations of cast members and their movements over time. Scores can quickly become complex and difficult to decipher when many cast members interact within the same frames.

Staging

Staging involves designing every aspect of a scene, including the props, backgrounds, cast members, camera position, lighting, movement, and color. Small details like shadows or secondary action add depth and interest to an animation as well as complexity and time. While these details are important, it is equally important that secondary actions and effects do not upstage primary actions and messages. Staging is essentially described by storyboards. Staging can be as complex or simple as required to satisfy the needs of the project.

To learn more about animation as a medium and what types of issues to explore in its use, see the Animation section in Design and Prototype.

The widening use of animations can quickly cause animation styles or effects to become outdated or cliché. An example is the "spinning logo" which opens many presentations.

Animation is often an illusion, especially in 2D. It is not always necessary to render each object in fine detail or even to design realistic movement. Sometimes, an animation can perform better and look believable in motion even if the pieces, when slowed-down or viewed separately, look less believable.

Ways to mess up an animation are easy. For example, complete the animation without going over it in storyboard format with the client. You can waste hours, days, or even weeks this way. Second, don't have a project manager to stay on top of details. That way you can have an excuse not to meet the client's deadline. Third, work like you know how to solve everything; self-sufficient in every aspect. I try not to act as though I know a lot about this business. That way I'm constantly learning.

— Kathleen Egge, Art Director,
***vivid** studios*

The 2D animator pays great attention to screen behavior. What's up, down, right, left, makes a difference. 2D computer screen interfaces are mechanical and boring. The basis for 2D animation is to bring things to life.
— *Chuck Clanton, Animator*

Animation Tools

2D animation tools and applications can be either frame-based or object-oriented. Some, like MacroMind Director from Macromedia, are full authoring tools, while others are meant for creating animations to be used in other authoring environments. Some animation tools are meant to plug into and supplement other tools.

ADDmotion 2.0 from Motion Works, for example, is meant to be used with HyperCard to provide color and animation capabilities not possible within current versions of HyperCard.

Most object-oriented animation tools allow sound elements to be synchronized with the animation in the animation scores. Many also include **scripting**

Case Study: IslandTrapper Product Demonstration Disk

Description:
Island Graphics Corporation of San Rafael, CA, produces software for color desktop prepress, desktop publishing, and presentation graphics. To explain and promote its product IslandTrapper, the company commissioned Brooks Communication Design to create an interactive demonstration disk for distribution to new and existing customers. The disk also explains trapping, a term used in professional printing that refers to the control of color balance.

Project Type:
Presentation and Communication

Development Hardware:
Macintosh IIfx, 13in. color monitor, scanner, cartridge drive

Delivery Hardware:
Any Macintosh computer with a color display

Software Used:
MacroMind Director, Adobe PhotoShop, Adobe Illustrator

Team Members and Roles:
Brooks Cole, Art Director and Animator; Syndee Collison, Storyboarding; Brandy Bartosh, Business Manager; Terry Schussler, Specialist in MacroMedia Lingo programming and interactive multimedia design

Price:
Not Applicable

Contacts:
Island Graphics San Rafael, CA

Brooks Communication Design San Francisco, CA

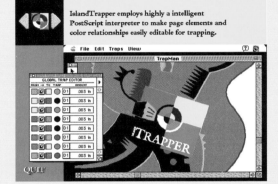

IslandTrapper employs highly a intelligent PostScript interpreter to make page elements and color relationships easily editable for trapping.

Management:
A core team of two people developed the concept and initial design. A business manager was hired to schedule and manage processes and activities. During production, a programming specialist was hired to complete the project. This arrangement illustrates a "virtual corporation" where people with different skills contribute as needed at different points of project development.

Concept and Planning:
Island Graphics wanted to emphasize three key points about IslandTrapper:

1. What trapping is.

2. How IslandTrapper works.

3. The product's ease of use and innovative user interface.

Brooks Communication Design spent about one month with the client to determine the concept and plan the initial design. Island Graphics prepared a basic storyboard. Brooks Communication Design added illustrations and animations to add a "creative look and feel" to the basic concept, spending about two weeks to enhance the client's storyboard.

Design and Prototype:
It took about 24 hours to create a limited-screen prototype for client buyoff of the design and interface. Illustrator Steve Lyons created a highly stylized character known as "Trap Man" to bring consistency to the message and interface.

The major design limitation was size: the entire piece had to fit on one 800K floppy disk. This constraint influenced decisions about image resolution and size. File compression would be an inevitable necessity.

Production:
The production stage lasted about two months. Says business manager Brandy Bartosh, "Prototyping and production are similar; one is always tweaking and improving the interface, with a highlight here and a button click there." Brooks Cole created most of the animation and illustrations, and a programming specialist created the design for interaction. Labor-intensive but necessary tasks such as scanning were shared by all, depending on the availability of equipment and people.

Testing:
Quality assurance was important at every step of development. Modules were tested as they were created. One full day was dedicated to testing the product thoroughly before it was handed off to the client.

Mastering/Duplication:
A master diskette was given to Island Graphics Marketing department which coordinated duplication and distribution.

Distribution:
Island Graphics distributes 800K floppy diskettes through the mail and at trade shows. The disk was also presented in a kiosk at a trade show.

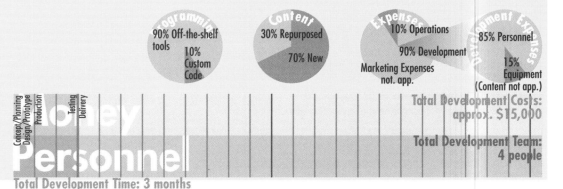

90% Off-the-shelf tools / 10% Custom Code

30% Repurposed / 70% New

10% Operations / 90% Development / Marketing Expenses not. app.

85% Personnel / 15% Equipment (Content not app.)

Total Development Costs: approx. $15,000

Total Development Team: 4 people

Concept/Planning / Design/Prototype / Production / Testing / Delivery

Money Personnel

Total Development Time: 3 months

languages that allow object or user actions to trigger other actions. These can be used to create interactive animations that play differently depending on a user's control.

Title Animation

Title animation is a form of 2D and sometimes 3D animation for text. Films usually use some form of animation for the opening and closing credits. These can be as simple as text scrolling up the screen or as complicated as moving, shimmying type characters interacting with each other and with other objects on the screen. Doris Day movies from the 1950s and the recent movie, *Naked Lunch*, use title animations in creative ways. Almost everyone who saw the movie *Star Wars* remembers the opening text scrolling back into space away from the viewer. Title animations from movies and television shows can be good sources of ideas. Music videos sometimes offer creative type effects as well.

2D and 3D animations tools can all be used for creating interesting title effects. The complexity of the title design will determine the type of tools necessary. Highly-rendered, three-dimensional text will require 3D animation tools, while flat or cartooned type can use 2D software.

2½ D Animation

There are some animation applications that allow simple 3D effects to be created from 2D artwork. These are not true 3D animation tools but can extrude shapes to add depth and then render them with a variety of effects. Type illustrators and animators are examples of these applications. These specifically extrude text in a number of different typestyles. Color and sometimes lighting can be applied to create more complex styles and the final animation or illustration can be output to another animation tool for combining with other animations.

3D Animation

3D animation is much more than just a third dimension added to 2D animation. 3D applications are typically much more sophisticated and complex in the way they approach building and rendering objects and scenes. Simply scanning in sketches or other artwork and making them move is difficult or impossible with most 3D tools. 3D animations require detailed descriptions of 3D objects, a process called **modeling**, before they can be **animated** and **rendered**. Once the animations are complete, they can be saved as movie or animation files or stepped-out directly to videotape.

Modeling

The first step is to build each object in 3D space. Some applications allow the construction of objects by **extruding** 2D objects into a block shape, **lathing** or spinning a 2D object into a solid 3D object, or by **combining** pre-made 3D objects from a library.

More advanced modelers are called **spline modelers**. These allow more complex 3D shapes to be built and manipulated point by point. Curves are usually built and rendered better with spline modelers. These can select and move a single point or surface for fine-tuning subtle shapes. Advanced modelers use **quadratic curves** to control even more subtle shapes in three dimensions. These are usually found on workstations in high-end CAD systems.

Animating

Once the models are built, a piece of software called an **animator** (sometimes combined with a renderer or modeler) does the remaining work. This step is where the motion for the models are defined. The interactions between the various objects, camera angles, lighting, and other elements over time are defined and run through in rehearsal. These steps are similar to the staging details described in 2D animation. Because rendering takes so much time, animations should work correctly at this stage before going to the rendering stage.

Rendering

Once the models and scenes are built and animated, they can be rendered in a variety of different qualities. Some of the simpler and faster techniques are used to test the models and animation while they are being designed. The high-quality techniques require much more processing time, which in some cases can amount to days. These techniques are commonly saved for final output.

The lowest-quality technique is called wire-frame animation. **Wire-frame animation** renders the edges of objects. This is actually the mode used by most modeling programs for working. Most modeling programs have the facility to create wire-frame models with hidden lines. **Hidden-line animation** draws only the object edges that are visible and not the ones that are hidden behind solid objects. The calculations are a bit more complex for this technique but the result is more legible and understandable scenes.

The next level of rendering quality is solid modeling. **Solid modeling** or **Gouraud shading** not only hides any hidden lines, but fills the space between lines with color. Usually, very simple shading is calculated with this technique. The objects and shading will definitely have a "computerized" look, but it will be easier to judge the quality of the final scene once it is rendered. Solid modeling is often used as a proofing stage for 3D animations.

Phong shading is a slight modification of Gouraud shading that calculates more realistic shading around an object. Phong shading usually calculates cast shadows and more even steps of shading around an object's

The whole cast of models for an average one minute animation may take 3-5 days to build.

Special 3D modeling cameras can photograph and semi-automatically build a 3D image of a person to use as a model in an animation program.

*The behavior of cartoon animation has its own rules, its own physics. Viewers may not explicitly recognize these, but they respond to them unconsciously. **Cartoon physics** govern character behavior and may be different for some characters or cartoons. For example, when some characters run off the edge of a cliff, they only fall when they look down. Conservation of volume is another rule of cartoon physics. When a character squashes vertically it bulges out horizontally. When it stretches horizontally it contracts vertically. This squishiness adds to the endearing nature of cartoon characters.*

One minute of ray-traced animation at 480-600 pixels and 30 frames per second may take 50 hours to render and 200-300MB of storage space. Film-quality rendering (2000x3000 pixels) may take up 1 gigabyte just for four seconds.

surface. Shading for curved objects is especially enhanced. Solid modeling may also be **anti-aliased** to remove jagged edges and replace them with smoother ones. This can be a simple but powerful difference.

The next level of quality is ray tracing. **Ray tracing** is a complex rendering technique that calculates the values, intensities, and directions of rays of light bouncing off objects. Ray tracing takes considerably more time than wire-frame or solid modeling techniques. Each ray of light is calculated as it enters and reacts with objects. Theoretical light beams pick up the color and characteristics of objects based on their reflection, texture, pattern, and color specifications. Ray-traced scenes can look almost photorealistic. Textures and patterns wrapping convincingly around objects, reflective surfaces like chrome, and transparent solids like glass are all rendered to reflect the light sources and other objects around them.

The highest-quality technique currently available is radiosity. **Radiosity** is much like ray-tracing but includes atmospheric qualities as well. Images and animations rendered with radiosity can look photoreal if built properly. Radiosity allows a better sense of mood to be portrayed in an animation. This technique requires incredibly powerful systems to calculate large, complex scenes and may take days to render.

It is not always necessary to use high-quality renderers. Depending on a project's requirements, simple Gouraud or Phong shading may suffice. Be realistic about the render requirements for animation and test samples before deciding on the final rendering specifications.

Before beginning a rendering, review once more the entire animation in wire-frame and render a few **snapshots** of the sequence to final quality. Use these to get final approval from clients or project managers.

This will be the last chance to make any adjustments before the arduous task of rendering is complete. Any problems may require re-rendering the entire sequence.

Some systems and software allow the rendering of complex animation to be spread over many computers on a network. This can accelerate the rendering process. Another option is to use a more powerful workstation.

Morphing

It involves the combining of two images or objects so that it appears that one transforms into the other. It is a common special effect that may become cliché in a short while. **Morphing** ▶ 206 is described in the video special effects section of this chapter.

Animation Compression

Animations are usually compressed in some form to optimize space and playback performance. There are a number of compressors available to compress animations stored in PICS format. (PICS is a common animation file format on Macintosh computers.) PICS compressors are usually spatial compressors and not temporal compressors. **Spatial compressors** ▶ 207 are able to compress single frames of animation. Large runs of colors and little detail will compress to higher ratios with spatial compressors than lots of detail in a frame. **Temporal compressors** compress differences between frames. Little movement and long time lags will compress to higher compression ratios with temporal compressors than detailed movement occurring frequently. Compression ratios for PICS compressors usually range between 2:1 and 5:1, depending on the detail in the frames.

The **QuickTime Animation codec** uses both lossy and lossless, spatial and temporal compression routines. Compression ratios for the QuickTime Animation codec range between 5:1 and 15:1 depending on the detail in the frames. It is usually better than the video codecs for fine detail, especially one pixel-lines, although the compression ratios will not be as high. This codec will save the animation as a QuickTime movie that can be played from any authoring tool that supports QuickTime or Apple's MoviePlayer™ utility. The Animation codec supports playback of images at up to 30 frames per second at full-screen resolutions. Like the PICS compressors, the compression ratios, and thus the playback performance, are highly dependent on the type of images in a scene. Large runs of color, less detail, and less movement will produce higher compression ratios.

Texture and Environmental Mapping

*A **texture map** can resemble anything you might encounter in nature like gravel on a sidewalk or a brick wall or rice paper. These can be brought into the 3D environment in the form of digitized pictures or your own computer art. The 3D object receives a texture map via "projection"—like a slide being projected onto a wall or table or wrapped around a sphere. The texture, in a sense, adds a pattern or detail to the surface. A reflection map, on the other hand, adds reflectivity and gives the illusion of the material the object is made out of such as highly polished marble, plastic, metal, or glass.*

*An **environmental map** is a **reflection map** of a real environment wrapped around an object. The 3D object reflects the universe in which it lives, i.e. the polished ball bearing sees the room and table it sits on. Both texture and reflection maps can also be assigned a **bump map** which embosses a surface relief on the texture or reflection based on light and dark values. Usually, I use all these types of maps in a typical animation. And there are other techniques to use. You can tweak the amount of transparency, decide if the object casts shadows, adjust lighting values, etc. An animator has a lot of options and plenty of room for experimentation.*

— Cody Harrington, Animator, Cody Film

Animation Across Platforms

Animations can be played on different platforms in a few different formats. MacroMind Director has a Windows player available that will play Director files on Windows-compatible PCs. QuickTime animations can also be played on a Windows-compatible PC with Apple's QuickTime player.

Color equivalencies between platforms may be a limiting factor. Colors are managed differently through the values set in the computer's **color map** or **color palette** ▶ 150. Most Macintosh animations are built for 8-bit color and although the Macintosh has a default system palette, it can configure itself to any 8-bit color palette. Most Macintosh computers with color monitors are capable of 8-bit color at the minimum. Windows machines, however, can vary greatly in color capabilities. While the MPC specification defines 8-bit color as standard, most Windows and DOS PCs with color monitors only have 4-bit color. It is usually safe to build animations for the Windows platform with a 4-bit color palette, but be sure to use the exact 16 colors defined in the VGA system palette for best results.

Video Production

Before production can start, a production list of all video segments should be finalized and be accompanied by approved video production **specifications**. This is usually supported by a copy of the project's **storyboard** as well as the prototype so that videographers, actors, and engineers can share the same vision of the final product.

Estimate the time, costs, equipment, and talent required to complete all video shots on the production list. Each video clip must be storyboarded and scriptwriters should script any **dialog** or **action**. The locations and subjects of the segments may require scheduling, along with renting production studios and hiring freelance engineers. The video producer may need to arrange all these resources. **Audio synchronization** and **time code** needs will also need to be addressed.

Shooting new video is frequently necessary because video may not exist for the shots needed. It is also a good way to avoid licensing and copyright issues but video is a complex medium that requires coordination, detail, and quality. Video production combines the details of sound recording and design, those of photography (especially lighting and composition) with the aspect of motion and transitions.

Video production, from planning to digitization, integration, and compression, is time-consuming and expensive.

It can take weeks and cost thousands of dollars. The cost of video can be drastically reduced by being organized and by using resources wisely.

The amount of videotape required for shooting can exceed the calculated time for finished footage by quite a bit. Since finished video is edited down considerably from source footage, typically three to ten times as much video can be shot than is used.

The three major phases of video production are **pre-production**, which includes scriptwriting, location and talent scouting, and planning; **production**, which includes filming, directing, sound recording, stage and prop managing, lighting, and acting; and **post-production**, which includes video editing, sound editing, synchronization, mixing, and special effects.

Preproduction for New Video

Once the needed materials are planned and the talent and locations arranged, a production team should become familiar with the **storyboard** ▶ 123, 136, **prototype** ▶ 136, and **script**. Each video clip should be storyboarded in detail in order to plan materials, equipment, talent and prop needs. It is advisable to plan the most difficult shots first. The most complex shots may require more resources than all of the other shots combined. These resources can include multiple cameras, location sound units, and many actors, stagehands, and engineers.

Assembling a Crew

Scriptwriters are commonly responsible for generating dialog while **illustrators** and **designers** create storyboards for all to follow. The **director** is not only responsible for directing the action while the cameras

To learn more about video as a medium and what types of issues to explore in its use, see the Video section in Design and Prototype.

Shooting video includes many of the same considerations as shooting photographs. It is a good idea to read the section in this chapter on photography to familiarize yourself with these issues in depth.

Video production is frequently subcontracted to video production companies. One of the project team members takes the role of producer and works out the details with the director at the video production company.

Many freelance professionals prefer to use their own equipment. This is especially true for videographers, photographers, and sound professionals but can apply to writers and illustrators as well.

*When videotaping a scene in which a television or computer monitor is on, use a **video signal synchronizing utility** to align the refresh rate of the monitor or display with the record rate of the video camera. Not synchronizing the display will produce distracting scan lines to appear on the monitor when recorded.*

are rolling, but also for the organization and smooth running of the entire production unit. A simple crew might contain only one camera person who doubles as the director, one lighting person, a sound technician, and the actors. A complex crew may have many of each, plus stagehands, prop coordinators, recorders to log shots and keep on schedule, and others.

Multimedia developers have discovered it is important to have a **"digital screen test."** Although done in prototyping, the screen test is especially important for actors to see how video is used in the multimedia prototype. Everyone, however, needs to see the tests and prototype because lighting, acting, and camera work are often different when making multimedia projects because of screen resolutions, playback sizes, and other technical and design considerations.

Producing New Video

Shooting video is the process of recording the shots needed to complete the storyboard. Often, this means shooting multiple "takes" with slight variations to ensure enough good working material for editing. It is rare that shots can be completed flawlessly in one take because there are so many factors that must perform well. Some movie studios now hire separate film crews to shoot a series of shots for subsequent uses, including use in multimedia products. This can include views from various heights and perspectives of every room and every possible entrance. While this is tedious, repetitive work, it is far less costly than rebuilding a set to recreate a needed shot.

There is no reason why each shot must be recorded in the sequence they appear in the final video composition. It is often easier to shoot similar scenes with the same actors or sets at once, whether they appear together in time or not. Shooting out of order requires planning these shots and their sequence carefully. It also entails noting the types and number of shots needed in each scene—for example, two close-ups, a reaction shot, and four long shots from opposing angles. A well-planned shot list serves as both a guide and checklist.

A **slate** that identifies the scene number and take number should appear at the beginning (and sometimes the end) of each scene. This will make it easier to find the best take and identify scenes once the video is digitized. A slate can be as elaborate as a professional electronic display or pieces of paper. Record a **pre-roll** and a **post-roll** of at least 5 seconds before and after the action in a scene. This will make the video easier to edit. Also, use short tapes or only portions of tapes. The cost of the time it takes to rewind and fast

forward can be more expensive than the cost of extra cassettes. Also, try not to jam scenes onto every last inch of tape.

Camera Angle

The building blocks of video-making are camera angle, composition, and continuity. The **camera angle** is the position of the camera and the view it captures. The story requirements will help suggest which angles to take. Camera angles establish a **frame** and gives the audience a **point of view**. The frame is an area that covers the players, the setting, and the action for a particular period of time in the story. All action in a scene should take place within the frame. Provide enough "elbow room" for actors to move around within. Actors need to be aware when a scene is a "tight shot" so they know that they have little room to maneuver.

An entire story often cannot be told from a single shot. A **sequence** of shots is needed. Each shot tells its particular part of the story in the time it is given. As the story develops, camera angles will shift viewpoint from one actor to another. Even interviews often use sequences shifting between the interviewer and the interviewee.

Camera angles with an even horizon are traditional because they match our sense of gravity and our experience with nature. Tilting the camera to shoot at odd angles produces a psychologically unsettling feeling which may or may not be appropriate. The Batman television series made great use of these odd angles—shots in a criminal's hideout were always at odd, unsettling angles.

Rule of Thirds

Many photographers and videographers use a **rule of thirds** when composing frames. They mentally divide the frame into nine even rectangles and align the main action at one of the four intersections of this imaginary "leading lines." This rule can help create good, simple results when time or creativity does not allow more adventurous shots.

Camera Movement

As in photography, **focus** is of paramount importance. Most video cameras autofocus because action is too difficult to focus manually while controlling other parameters of a shot, such as different types of camera movements.

Panning is when the camera stays stationary but turns horizontally to follow the action. When not using a tripod, plant your feet firmly where they should be at the end of the pan and then twist to the beginning of the pan. When the action starts, you will be moving to a more stable position and produce a smoother pan. **Tilting** is when the camera stays stationary but tilts up or down to follow action (such as filming the height of a skyscraper from the bottom up). As with panning, plan the shot to end in the most comfortable position. **Zooming** is when the camera stays stationary but changes depth to fill the frame with more or less detail. Most video cameras include a built-in zoom feature. When panning, tilting, or zooming, first focus on the spot at the end of the maneuver and then move backward through the motion to the start of the shot. This ensures that the focus is correct throughout the shot, and especially at the end.

The motions of each video shot have names to distinguish them. They include tracking, dollying, tilting, and panning. It is advisable to always start and end with still (non-moving) pictures. **Tracking** is usually when the camera moves horizontally with the action. Tracking can describe moving the camera vertically called **craning**, but this is rare and more difficult to do. **Dollying** is when the camera moves forward or backward with the action as in following the actors in front as they walk. Both tracking and dollying require some sort of moving platform, called a dolly, to create smooth, stable movement. While professional studios have specially constructed platforms on train-like tracks, almost anything can be a dolly. It is usually easier to have one person control the camera and another to control the dolly.

Always practice a shot first to be sure that everything is planned correctly. This includes camera movements as well as actors' actions. **Tripods** will help stabilize any camera motion. When using a tripod is not possible, try leaning against a wall or large object or sitting in a chair or on the ground. Any position that will limit camera movement will help. If standing, try holding the camera in one hand with the other firmly beneath it, with both elbows propped tightly against the abdomen. This will form a small pyramid and create a more stable position for filming with less chance of camera shaking.

Move more slowly than you think is necessary and lead the action with the frame. When viewing video as opposed to shooting it, there is always more to look at. Moving too fast will make the finished piece seem awkward and rushed. **Leading the frame** refers to panning to keep more space in front of the actors then behind them. This gives the actors space to "move into" from the standpoint of the frame.

While it is possible to combine panning, tilting, zooming, tracking, or dollying movements, it is best to keep the combinations simple—in other words, no more than two at a time. Also, it is better to shoot discrete motions and cut to different views or motions rather than repeating or reversing the same motions. For example, avoid "watering the lawn" or panning back and forth in the same shot like a lawn sprinkler.

Primary Shots

There are three general frame compositions used: the long shot, the medium shot and the close-up. **Long shots** establish a set context and are generally recommended to begin most scenes. This is often referred to as an **establishing shot** because it fills the frame with a landscape and establishes the scope of the story. Establishing shots show relationships between things. (Using titles at the beginning of scenes can also help to establish context when detail is not easily discernible.) Remember that computer and television screens are small. Epic, far away views are great in cinema but the resolution of a small screen often fails to provide the fine detail needed to make these work on a computer or television. **Medium shots** generally fill the frame with the actors from head to toe. Medium shots are best for "stage business" and general action. **Close-ups** fill the frame with a face or an object of specific interest. Close-ups are especially used for dialog and reaction shots and have strong emotional power. Other shots include the **extreme long shot**, used in epic scenes and not usually appropriate for video, and the **extreme close-up**, used for small details of people and objects.

A change of angle horizontally of at least 45° in between shots will help develop the scene and create variety. Also, shots should not move more than one step between long, medium, and close-up shots.

Secondary Shots

Each of the primary shots described earlier can be used for purposes other than establishing primary action. They can be used to establish secondary or related action as well as context. For example, a **reaction shot** is usually used in a conversation to momentarily show the listener's reaction to the speaker. This can be a close-up of another person or a medium shot of an audience. Reaction shots usually involve capturing a facial expression or body movement. In action sequences, these might continue the motion or the results of one person's action on another.

Different points of view can be shown to balance dramatic tension. The reverse cut-away or reverse-angle shot is one of the most effective devices to shift alternate points of view. A **reverse-angle** shot looks at the subject from the opposite direction from the shot that

Panning

Tilting

Zooming

A common mistake made in beginning camera work is excess camera motion. Professional camera people move with the slightest touch. Limit camera motion by using a tripod and keep in mind the viewing tolerance of the audience. The human eye senses motion even before it determines shape. Be still and let the story move. If the camera must move, then it should do so for a reason.

Dollying

Craneing

Tracking

Travel Axis

preceded it. **Reverse cut-aways** show a scene from the reverse perspective. For example, in a scene where a motorcyclist is being chased by a car, one shot might view the scene ahead of the motorcyclist with the motorcycle in the foreground and the car in the backgrounds, both speeding toward the camera. A cut to a shot from behind the car driver's shoulder of the motorcycle speeding ahead would be a reverse cut-away. Because the scene must match the action (the backgrounds must be consistent, for instance), reverse cut-aways can be expensive and time-consuming to produce.

Shots of action and movement usually involve some form of **travel axis**. This is the imaginary line that directs or results from the movement. When planning shots, be wary of this travel axis. For continuity, it is usually best when changing camera angles or shots to stay on the same side of the travel axis. This well help the viewer understand the action. Crossing this axis usually makes a scene confusing and inconsistent.

Another axis, the **action axis**, is generated from the eye contact between the actors. The eyes carry the energy of any scene and makes the action axis a powerful element in video. To make a speaker and audience appear as if they are speaking to each other, shoot them on the same side of this action axis. Imagine filming a tennis game with two stationary cameras. If one is focused on the left side of the court and the other on the right side of the court (and both on the same side of the action axis), by cutting the shots of the match, the viewer can understand the relationship of the two players. If the cameras were on opposite sides of the court (and the action axis), the ball would always appear to be entering the frame on one side, regardless of the player. This can be confusing to viewers.

Another fine detail of shooting is to have **clean entrances and exits**. This means that a shot entering or leaving a scene should pan or zoom into the scene and exit it from a static shot without action. This will be less jarring to the viewer and establish the scene more easily. It is not necessary to do this for every shot but it helps for the first and last shots of a scene.

Subjective and Objective Viewpoints

An occasionally used shooting style is the **subjective camera angle**. These take the viewpoint of one of the actors, as if the story were told in first person. It is often used in horror stories and dream sequences.

Most camera scenes are filmed from **objective camera angles**. Objective angles are distant views of the entire field of action, not taking any specific point of view, not letting any subject upstage the others. Actors

should not look at or acknowledge the camera in objective scenes unless the product storyboards specifically calls for it.

Continuity

Multiple takes require **continuity** to achieve consistency, flow, and credibility. Good continuity always requires a plan. Since a camera can go anywhere at anytime, some sense must be made of the time and space of continuity. If you show action going from left to right, continue having subjects enter frame-left and exit frame-right in order to develop the movement. Reversing angles will tend to confuse the audience.

Scenes shot out of sequence or takes that are separated in time can cause great continuity problems. It may make sense to put one person only in charge of continuity to track subtle details that change. These details must be checked before the scene is shot to make sure they match other takes. The most common error in continuity is failing to recreate the exact dramatic mood, looks, and action. But little details are important. For example, the sun might be bright in take one but overhead clouds in another take will destroy any sense of continuity. Water glasses on the table may have been consumed, so the levels must be refilled. A pen in hand in one take needs to be in the same hand, held the same way in the next. Candles may have burned during the time between takes and need replacing.

The simplest way to achieve continuity is to overlap the action of successive takes. This means the action at the end of one take is then repeated at the beginning of the next take. This technique is especially necessary if there is no script.

Lighting

See the Photography section in this chapter for more information on **lighting** ▶ 186. Generally, it is safe to keep the sun at your back when shooting outdoors. Many photographers advise not to shoot during bright daylight since shadows are harsh and colors often wash out.

Production Equipment
Video Cameras

One key to great videography is having great equipment. Most often this means a great **video camera**. At a minimum, use Hi8 or S-VHS formats. These offer near-professional resolution and color quality in a compact form and can record up to 120 minutes in length per video cassette. Hi8 and S-VHS scan more data than is necessary for both broadcast and computer display. This allows the quality to remain high even after digitization and signal degradation.

In contrast, consumer 8mm video equipment has a weak signal, and poor color and resolution levels that are up to neither broadcast nor computer standards. They can be adequate for small studies or **video sketches**, or for the "home-made look," but once they are digitized and processed they may not be adequate for final video. At the high-end are bulky professional cameras which record component color in short 20 or 30 minute formats. Betacam is the preferred format for professional video camerawork but these systems correspondingly are more expensive.

When choosing a camera, look for great optics, quiet running, and good color balance. **Optics** are judged by how well the camera records in low light, details in long shots, and quality of focus at the corners of the frame, both in close-ups and long shots. **Color balance** is the ability to record colors accurately. As with a still camera for photography, features are not the most important aspect. Some are convenient, like white balance and zoom, while others may be frivolous. Most video editing and transitions can be done on a computer or in a studio so these features are not needed in the camera.

Sound Equipment

Many producers think that the worst problem with video is **audio ▶ 76, 194**. In making a decision about video, remember that audio carries as much power and emphasis as video in a multimedia experience. The microphone in a camera will not be adequate most of the time. Invest in a great microphone. See the Sound section in this chapter for detailed information.

Object Cameras

Special **object cameras** will film small objects in a programmed sequence from all sides (360° horizontally and 270° vertically). These are essential for building scenes that describe every view of an object and for creating **navigable movies ▶ 186** in which users can navigate around objects and scenes from different vantage points. These object cameras are rare and expensive but are invaluable when this particular effect is needed. Some object cameras can be configured to capture an environment looking out from a particular point with the same range or motion. These are ideal for capturing a spectacular view from a lookout-point or other vistas from every angle.

Repurposing Existing Video

Sources for existing video are still few but the options are slowly getting better. Clients may already have usable video on tape that is appropriate for a project. This will also sidestep the issues of copyright and licensing. Other sources include video and film libraries, the Library of Congress, some video production houses, and clip-video CD-ROMs. Any of these may have video that meets a project's needs but the licensing and use limitations, as well as the issue of royalties, can be prohibitive. More and more clip-video CD-ROMs are offering license-free video, but much of this video may not meet the quality of subject matter needs of a particular project. Be sure to investigate licensing issues early since this process is often long and arduous.

Post-Production

Once the video is captured on tape, it will need to be edited and digitized before it can be used by a computer. One alternative is to edit the videotape with traditional tools and digitize it once it is in final form; the other is to digitize all video and edit it with digital editing tools. The best alternative for a particular project will be determined by the type of editing necessary, the budget, and the tools and personnel available. Experienced video engineers can help determine which alternative is best.

Many times video editing is sub-contracted to a video production house and managed by the creative director of a project. More experienced production teams can

"Prosumer" is a word that describes semi-professional level equipment sold to consumers. Hi-8 camcorders and certain sound equipment fall into this category. A prosumer device is not quite as sophisticated as true, professional gear but it is more advanced than what was once considered typical consumer equipment.

Video Tape Formats:

Format	Scan lines
8mm	240
VHS (Video Home System)	260
S-VHS and Hi8	400
1/2 inch Betamax	480
Component video	480
NTSC	525
PAL/SECAM	625

For live production, consider working with at least two cameras. Two cameras can capture dialog and interaction of actors more easily than one—especially in interviews. They will capture a better variety of shots and will be able to respond more quickly to serendipitous events.

The WPA Film Library sells a unique collection of still video images and film clips ranging from the 1890s through the 1980s. Film clips sell for approximately $20 per second. Contact the WPA Film Library in Illinois at 800/777-2223.

Video Standards

There are three worldwide standards for video and they are not compatible with each other. NTSC (National Television Standards Committee) is used in the U.S. and Japan, PAL (Phase Alteration by Line) is used in the U.K., Germany, China, and Australia, while SECAM (Système Electronique pour Coleur Avec Mémorie) is used in France, and the Soviet Republics. SECAM and PAL have slightly higher-resolution formats and SECAM is not compatible with black and white receivers. New, higher-quality broadcast standards are being developed called HDTV (High-Definition TeleVision).

Crude synchronization between sound and video used to be provided by clapping a board while both the sound and video tape was rolling. Later, the visual frame where the clap appears and the sound of the clap were lined up. Today, synchronization is often handled with a time code.

digitize and edit their own video but this can be a costly and time-consuming venture and should be planned before shooting begins.

On-Line vs. Off-Line Systems

Video can be edited either on-line or off-line. **On-line editing** refers to computer-based editing systems and **off-line editing** refers to traditional analog video editing systems. Either type of system can be either lin-

ear or non-linear. A **linear editing system** is a traditional arrangement of playback and recording equipment that assembles video clips one after another. These allow working with only two clips at a time. **Non-linear editing systems** arrange many clips of different types together and allow many clips to be moved, changed, and manipulated at once. Adobe Premiere is an example of an on-line, non-linear editing system.

Case Study: Ultrasound Equipment Acceptance Testing

Description:
This project was designed by a team of medical professionals to teach test procedures for specialized ultrasound devices. The project was first presented at the Fall 1992 annual meeting of the Radiological Society of North America. The purpose was "to produce something that would illustrate the potential of simple tools for education," says Dr. Tessler.

Project Type:
Interactive Education

Development Hardware:
Macintosh IIfx, RasterOps Color Board, 8mm Sony camcorder, commercial ultrasound equipment.

Delivery Hardware:
Macintosh Quadra 700, although project will play on any Macintosh computer capable of playing color QuickTime movies.

Software Used:
HyperCard, QuickTime, Adobe Premiere, and Adobe PhotoShop

Team Members and Roles:
Dr. Carolyn Kimme-Smith, Content Developer and Tester; Dr. Franklin Tessler, Videotaping and HyperCard programming; Peter Marx, Initial HyperCard design and programming.

Funding:
Personal investment of time and equipment.

Price:
Not for sale but available to anyone who requests it.

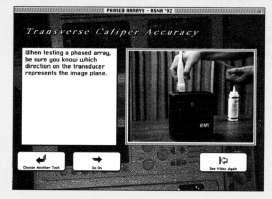

Contact:
Dr. Franklin Tessler, Assistant Professor
Department of Radiological Sciences
UCLA School of Medicine
Los Angeles, CA

Management:
Cooperative work among medical professionals from UCLA.

Concept and Planning:
Dr. Kimme-Smith and Dr. Tessler had often discussed the idea of developing Macintosh-based training. An opportunity to present such a training tool at a Radiological Society of North America conference gave impetus for development. Dr. Kimme-Smith suggested a module to train ultrasound specialists about test procedures for phased array transducers. These transducers must be checked when they are first acquired from the manufacturer and periodically when they are used over time. The concept was discussed and finalized in a matter of days.

Design and Prototype:
Dr. Kimme-Smith designed tests to verify transducer operation. The tests and image sequences were identified. A simple interface that included a digitized background photograph of an ultrasound machine was designed in Adobe PhotoShop for display in HyperCard.

Production:
Once content and design were settled, taping of the content took less than a day. Programming required a few days. "It didn't take very long to produce this piece and it didn't require a lot of high end equipment," says Dr. Tessler. "I was trying to show that with HyperCard, a standard camcorder, a commercially available ultrasound machine, and a Macintosh, one can produce a good, usable application."

To illustrate how to use the transducer tests, Dr. Tessler used a consumer-level 8mm camcorder to videotape some of the manipulations used in the tests. He also obtained video images directly from the ultrasound equipment (most ultrasound machines have direct video output capabilities). The procedural sequences and the ultrasound images were digitized with a RasterOps digitizing card and edited in Adobe Premiere. Because ultrasound images often have low frame rates, they play back especially well in QuickTime.

Many of the same techniques were used to produce ultrasound images in the Medicine Room of the interactive CD-ROM The Virtual Museum.

Testing:
Simple functional testing was performed by the team.

Delivery:
Installed in the medical laboratory and used in a class lab environment

Programming
80% Off-the-shelf tools
20% Custom Code

Content
100% New

Expenses
Marketing Expenses not. app.
Operations Expenses not app.

Development Expenses
60% Personnel
40% Equipment
(Content not app.)

Total Development Costs: not avail.

Total Development Team: 3 people

Delivery

Money
Personnel

Total Development Time: 3 weeks

Digitizing Video

After video is shot, it can be brought into the computer through a digitizing process. All computers require digitizing hardware and software to digitize video clips. Very few computers have this hardware built in, so most require a video digitizing board. **Video digitizing boards** vary greatly in quality, speed, and capabilities. Some can only digitize small windows of video at a few frames per second, while more powerful but more expensive boards can capture full-frame (640 x 480 pixels) video at 30 frames per second, the acknowledged standard for broadcast quality. Video boards can capture video from just about any video source, provided that both the board and the source share a common connector. A **videodisc** or **video cassette recorder** (VCR), for example, can attach to a digitizing board via a standard RCA jack. Some camcorders include the newer **composite video** jack as well as the standard RCA video and audio jacks. This is a plug that is becoming more popular for high-quality computer video editing because the camera outputs the video in computer-readable format instead of as an NTSC signal. Not all boards digitize sound as well as video. Audio may need to be digitized with separate hardware and software and resynchronized in the editing software.

Most video digitizing boards are able to capture video from NTSC sources and many are able to capture video from PAL or SECAM sources (two standards used internationally). Many video digitizing boards will allow edited video to be output to video tape or straight to a television screen. These boards can be used to output high-quality full-frame presentations as well as capture video.

Time Code

Time code ▶ 194 is a reference recorded alongside video or audio in professional equipment. This reference provides precise synchronization points with other video and audio. The standard time code used in the professional audio, video, and film industries is **SMPTE time code.** SMPTE time code, short for Society of Motion Pictures and Television Engineers, stamps each frame of media with the hour, minute, second, and frame number. SMPTE code is one way to help synchronize the 30 frames per second of video with the 24 frames per second of film. For example, the SMPTE code 01:23:34:29 represents one hour, twenty three minutes, thirty four seconds and the 29th frame of a clip.

Editing Video On-Line

Once digitized, the video can be imported with other media elements into an editing application. These programs are usually time-based which means they organize media clips in multiple tracks over time. Most allow transitions and effects to manipulate these clips as

they cut to each other. Most video editing applications can import many different file formats, but it is necessary to determine which formats are best and have production personnel save final work into these formats.

Because digital video consumes so much space, it is imperative to plan storage and archiving solutions ahead of time. For many projects, a gigabyte drive is considered minimal storage capacity for working with video, while archiving finished and source video will require optical drives, DAT tapes, or one-off CD-ROMs (CD-Rs).

Editing Video Off-Line

Post-production houses may use off-line editing systems to compile video. Traditional, off-line editing may be faster and offer better quality for full-frame, broadcast quality video. Experienced video engineers are familiar with these tools and may be able to edit and prep video clips faster and less expensively with these traditional tools. Off-line and linear editing systems, however, will

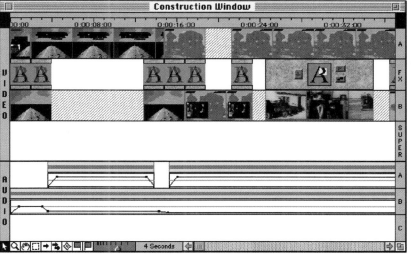

not allow as much flexibility and will require seasoned engineers to perform the video post-production.

It is especially important to develop an **edit decision list** that describes the clips to be edited, the sequence they should be put in, and the location of them on tape. It is a good idea to create an edit decision list for any video editing, whether on-line or off-line, but it will be mandatory for communicating with video professionals at a post-production house.

A video production house will usually create a **rough-cut** that includes the correct editing in the correct sequence but in rough form and quality. Once approved, the **final cut** is produced to final production standards. This saves time if changes need to be made to the rough-cut and eliminates some repetition of work.

SMPTE is not the only kind of time code in use. Some consumer video equipment use their own type of time code which may not be compatible with SMPTE time code.

Some video digitizing software is capable of copying video from computer-controlled videodisc and video tape players in successive passes. This allows more video data to be gathered for each video clip than could be captured in one pass.

Screenshot of Adobe Premiere

Videodisc players often lose their ability to track because of dust that accumulates on pick-up heads. Maintenance personnel can be trained to clean the pick-up head without having to send the player out.

After a few copies, videotape degrades, colors shift out of register, red becomes streaky, and images blur, smear, and develop halos. You have to preserve master tapes and work sparingly with original sources. Repeatedly using a tape stretches it, causing such artifacts as dropped frames or the appearance of white roll bars.

A small list of today's filters or effects include:

- Twirl
- Emboss
- Bend
- Explode
- Watercolor
- Posterize
- Spherize
- Image blur
- Sharpen

Special effects

Special effects can add special drama, humor, or excitement to a video clip. A variety of techniques and filters can be used to enhance a shot in unlimited ways. Special effects filters can twirl or distort shots, exaggerate colors, or simulate special circumstances such as dream sequences. Most video editing systems and software offer many different filters for effects, which can usually be combined to create even more complex effects. It is a good idea, however, to be conservative when using special effects so that the meaning and content of the video is not upstaged by the effect itself.

Photo of a sample Edit Decision List

Types of wipes can include circular, contracting, swinging, rolling, angular, linear, and spinning. They can appear to open or close as an iris, star, flame, keyhole, heart, or any other shape. Wipe patterns may be continuous or broken into several shapes in the frame such as a series of bands opening a scene like a venetian blind. Wipes add a narrative style that may have specific meaning to a particular subject matter, but they are more subjective than other transitions, and should be reserved to elicit specific reactions from the viewer.

A three-minute 160x120-pixel movie with 22kHz sound creates a file approximately 16MB in size.

Superimposing Images

Superimposing involves the placement of one image into another, with selected portions of the first image "dropping out" to reveal the second image. This technique has the effect of appearing as if the first image was part of the second one all along. Using a color key or **chromakey** means that the subject in the first image is shot against a neutral or unique solid color, keying this color to disappear when the two images are combined. This effect can be used to combine objects from different shots. It is tricky to do seamlessly and depends on having good-quality original shots. For example, if a person walking in front of a blue background is superimposed over a picture of a park trail, the lighting and sizing may be off just enough to make the shot look fake. On the other hand, if both shots are planned carefully, they may be superimposed so well that most viewers will never question if the person was ever in the park.

Morphing

Morphing is a special effect that transforms one object into another. Morphing software provides filters that distort and combine each image to form interim images

that are combinations of both. These interim transformations make it seem as if the first object and person is transforming into the second object or person.

Morphing is becoming more common in movies and television shows and can be a stunning effect when not overused.

Transitions

Movement between media sequences and media types is important. A raw cut can often create an unintended jarring effect. Good transitions are hardly ever noticed but bad ones are readily apparent. Almost all movies and television use a variety of transitions to create different emotional relationships between media clips. The vocabulary of transitions applies to all time-based material, sound as well as video. One key to video and audio transitions is that they should track the event being depicted. The length of the transition should match the dramatic tempo. Often transitions are used to cue different types of navigation. Different types of transitions may represent different types of jumps or different sections within a project.

The four most common transitions are fades, dissolves, wipes, and cuts. A **fade** is a transition between an image and a black screen. A **fade-in** allows the image to emerge from black, while a **fade-out** darkens the image until it is completely black. A **dissolve** is a cross-fade from one image into another. Dissolves are blends in which both images inhabit the same space for a brief period of time. Dissolves are effective for linking scenes or storylines through a short jump in time. The dissolve is often used in movies, for example, to soften a scene transition. A **wipe** is a transition in which one image pushes another off the screen, either from the left or right side (**wipe-left** and **wipe-right**). A **cut** is a straight replacement of one image to another without any transformations between. Cuts can often be jarring to a viewer and should be used only when a sudden transition or contrast is called for.

Video Compression

Compression is a means of encoding data in a special format to conserve space. One advantage is that it allows more data to be placed on a delivery medium. Another advantage of compression is that it can improve the time it takes to transfer data between computers or from the media into memory.

The right compressor to choose depends on the storage media and delivery system. For example, since CD-ROMs have fairly low data transfer rates, video will need to be compressed for a low data rate. The **transfer rate ▶ 109** refers to the amount of data required to play video for the duration of the clip. Different storage media are capable of different data transfer rates which means that the trade-offs between the data rate and the time to decompress may have to be weighed on an individual basis. The level of quality that is possible given the data rates and the decompression times is another consideration.

Compression Characteristics

Compression schemes can be either lossy or lossless. **Lossless** compression preserves all of the original data. These schemes are appropriate for situations where data integrity is a primary importance. Software instructions and text data are examples where all information must be preserved. **Lossy** compression drops data or degrades the quality according to the compression setting. With lossy compression, data is actually lost and cannot be recovered but the compression ratios are usually far greater than lossless schemes. Lossy schemes attempt to remove information the viewer is apt not to notice (dropping visual information before audio), but if the compression settings are too restrictive, the picture quality may become too poor.

There are four main characteristics by which you can judge compression algorithms— **compression ratio**, **image quality**, **compression/decompression speed**, and **spatial/temporal compression**.

The **compression ratio** is a comparison of the storage space for the compressed data with that of the uncompressed data. This ratio gives an indication of how much compression is achieved for a particular image, sound, or video clip. Most compression algorithms allow a range of compression ratios with the exact ratio depending on the complexity of the content. For example, a highly detailed image of a crowd at a football game may yield a very small compression ratio, whereas an image of a pure blue sky may yield a very high compression ratio.

The compression ratio typically affects the **image quality**. Generally, the higher the compression ratio, the poorer the quality of the resulting image. This trade-off between compression ratio and picture quality is an important consideration.

Compression and **decompression speed** represent the times required to encode and decode data, respectively. Compression/decompression speed depends on the efficiency and speed of the compression/decompression algorithm, or **codec**. Some codecs take a long time to compress even a little data. This will affect how fast the production team can work, so

consider this when planning the production for a project. Some codecs are **symmetric**, which means that it takes the same amount of time to compress as to decompress. Other codecs are **asymmetric**. This means that compression and decompression times are not the same. Asymmetric codecs may take a very long time to compress data but they decompress and "play" much more quickly.

Spatial compression is used to remove information from within a single frame of picture or video. The frame is analyzed and compressed independently of the other frames. **Temporal compression**, however, analyzes the changes between one frame and the next and only records the changes. For video with little detail or movement, the changes between individual frames is low and the compression ratio can be very high. But for video with lots of minute changes throughout the frame, compression may make little difference.

Compression Limits

Finely detailed video or high fidelity audio may perform poorly on lower-end computers. Such performance may not permit the kind of fluid presentation that is required for some uses.

For active and "live" multimedia, like a teleconference or videophone, the compression and decompression times may stifle real-time interaction and destroy any sense of spontaneity. When using decompressed imagery, avoid finely timed interactions because the performance of the playback equipment may not be able to deliver the elements within the time expected. Again, test all elements before finalizing production specifications.

Each transition has its own data rate associated with it when in a digital video format. Cuts, for example, use less data than a cross-dissolve. Data-intensive transitions may be a problem in movies made for less-powerful computers. If a computer cannot process the frames fast enough, it will drop some out, which may degrade the quality of the movie. It may be better to redesign the edits to use less intensive transitions. Prototyping should determine the appropriate transition styles to use.

Older CD-ROMs have a minimum data transfer rate of 150KB/sec while newer ones can handle 300 KB/sec.

Hardware compressors often require the same hardware to be used for both compression and decompression. This may be acceptable for kiosks or presentations where the delivery platform equipment is controllable but will not be acceptable for consumer products until hardware compressors become more standardized.

Version 2.0 of QuickTime supports larger video images at faster frame rates. It also creates an infrastructure for development and delivery of interactive television applications through MPEG support and network enhancements. There is also enhanced support for closed-captioning and custom, multiple data tracks like text and MIDI.

QuickTime for Windows Developer Kit (a hybrid CD-ROM) includes a set of Windows Dynamic Linked Libraries (DLLs) to provide playback and control of QuickTime movies on PC platforms. It also supports Windows MCI (Media Control Interface) and OLE (Object Linking & Embedding), Visual BASIC, and Visual C++.

Video Compression Technologies
QuickTime

QuickTime ▶ **153** is a video format from Apple that provides a standard multi-platform multimedia movie format, a suite of media compressors and decompressors to optimize throughput and storage space, multi-platform tools to make and playback movies, and a movie display and control interface standard. Apple has released a version of QuickTime that works with Windows. QuickTime is used extensively in multimedia for most time-based animations and movies. It is also commonly used for still-image slide presentations.

QuickTime provides two dynamic software codecs for video, a **video compressor** and a **compact video compressor**. These compressors are designed to compress and decompress data for playing video on any reasonable performance color-capable Macintosh or Windows computer. Compression ratios for the QuickTime Video Compressor codec can vary between 5:1 and 8:1. Compression ratios for the Compact Video codec can vary between 5:1 and 25:1. Both use lossy compression schemes.

Video for Windows (VfW)

Microsoft's **Video for Windows** is extension software similar to QuickTime. It uses a file format called Audio Video Interleaved (AVI) that alternates blocks of video and audio. Microsoft has also written a special set of drivers for the Intel DVI boards to run under Windows.

JPEG

JPEG (Joint Photographers Experts Group) is an international compression standard for encoding high-quality still-images encodes. JPEG compression ratios generally fall between 10:1 and 25:1. Higher compression ratios are possible but image quality can suffer noticeably. The Photo Compressor in QuickTime implements a JPEG algorithm. JPEG can be implemented in either hardware or software.

Motion JPEG is a variation of JPEG that allows for sequences of JPEG images to be compressed. The advantage of Motion JPEG over MPEG is that no interframe or transition compression takes place, making it quicker and easier to move randomly through a sequence of images. This is because MPEG requires computation to reconstruct individual frames. The disadvantage of Motion JPEG is that it takes up two to three times more space than an equivalent MPEG video stream. Motion JPEG has no facility to handle sound either.

MPEG

Like JPEG, the **MPEG** (Motion Picture Experts Group) standard was developed jointly by the Consultative Committee, International Telegraph and Telephone and the ISO, two standards-setting bodies. MPEG encodes motion picture images by compressing space within and between frames. MPEG compression ratios range from 50:1 to 200:1. As a result, up to 72 minutes of VHS-quality video can be stored on a CD-ROM. MPEG also synchronizes compressed sound with the compressed video. MPEG compression is too demanding to be performed in software and so special boards are needed. The cost of these boards are over $1000 but are expected to drop to under $500 in mid-1994.

DVI

Digital Video Interactive (DVI) is a chip set from Intel that was developed in conjunction with IBM for compressing and decompressing video and audio. The DVI software requires this special hardware. Like Apple's Compact Video codec for QuickTime, DVI is asymmetric. This means that while compression takes a long time, decompression is very fast. Although technically efficient, the DVI card is proprietary. Its limited display format, cost, and proprietary movie format make it appropriate for a closed set of custom applications. The competitor to DVI is the MPEG card, which is technically more ambitious and more standard.

Programming Production

When production starts, all **interface** and **interaction design** should already be completed. Interface designers may help create and critique details of elements like icons, but the principles of interaction and interface elements should have already been established in the Design and Prototype stage.

Programmers ▶ **32** typically know computers intimately and often take on technical responsibilities other than programming. These include mastering CD-ROMs, configuring kiosks and networks, converting projects and data across platforms, and other technical tasks.

Programming Basics

Most multimedia projects are developed with high-level scripting languages. Some are even built using simple iconic languages. **Higher-level languages** are more commonly used for development because they offer quicker and sometimes more stable development. These are often interpreted languages which means that the computer processes the instructions on the fly. This eliminates the need for compilers, but may be slower than compiled instructions. Interpreted languages allow programmers to test as they go, instead of compiling code and then running it to see if it works.

Developing a project using C++ or in assembly language is not that common but may be chosen in some cases. A few interactive game developers, for example, create assembly language routines to improve performance in critical areas. This lower level programming can be very complex and often takes months to develop what many may consider to be simple features. This code needs to be tested on numerous machines, with many types of peripherals, and several versions of system software to ensure usability.

Objects

Objects can mean different things in different operating systems and authoring tools. Essentially they are logically related actions and data. In some cases, objects have onscreen representations such as buttons, cards, sprites, or movies. Most of the authoring systems have pre-defined objects but do not allow programmers to define new objects unlike many object-oriented programming environments. Objects provide a powerful way to conceptualize and control data and its interaction with other data.

Scripts

Scripts are programs that are written in an authoring system's native language. Scripts are typically written in logical groups of commands and together form a **handler**. Scripts control how objects respond when a user interacts with them or when other things in the program environment change. Scripting languages are normally based on easy-to-remember English terms but can be as powerful as other "regular" programming languages like C and Pascal. Some common scripting languages are HyperTalk (HyperCard), Lingo (Director), and SuperTalk (SuperCard).

Interview: Sally Ann Applin

What makes a good interface?

It depends on its application, whether you're looking at it from art or from education or wanting to teach or make an impact. An interface is a collaboration between the function of the technology, of the platform, of the software that you're using, what the client wants, the kind of content, and your team of programmers, interface designers, graphic designers, writers, and editors. It's important to hide the computer from the user. What you are showing is more important than the machine you are showing it on. The guiding questions should be "What is the goal?" and "What do we want to communicate?"

You have to pick who you are designing for. If you are designing a multimedia piece that will be in a museum environment or a kiosk in a public space you have to understand that people may not know computer interface conventions. However, if you're designing a CD-ROM project for people who are using the Macintosh, you can rely on a lot of the constructs of Macintosh interface design. Although you might not want to, because the standard Macintosh interface may not map well to the content you intend to communicate.

TV is an important part of all of our lives. It is one of the things that gives us instant feedback. We hit the remote, it changes channels. We hit, the volume goes down; we hit, the volume goes up. We can control the TV and it responds immediately. There's a danger with multimedia design if you can't get your video up to speed in terms of acceptable frame rate, transitions, or synchronization with other media. TV is a standard we need to pay attention to as we design new media. Multimedia not only has to match TV in speed and flexibility, it has to provide something better and deeper for the user.

How did you become an interface designer?

I made jumps with what I knew. I realized that multimedia would let me try out different experimental interfaces. I talked to people in the interface design industry. I'd go to trade shows and chat with anybody

who would give me the time of day. I passed out resumes trying to get into the industry by selling myself with, "Look, I've done project coordination at a museum design company. I'm good at coordinating little pieces of projects, if that's what you need." It got me a job as a project manager but I soon realized that I needed to go back to school to get the experience I needed to design interfaces. When you're working all the time, even if you have keys to the office and the tools are there, you're exhausted. You've worked 9-to-9 and you don't have time to play with tools.

I didn't know there was a job called Interface Design when I started my search. Some people who think they want to get into multimedia may find they are interested only in marketing it, not developing it. Others may not even know multimedia exists.

You should document your work. Keep records of what you did and when you did it. When I interviewed at Apple I had a "multimedia portfolio" of models, mockups, and photos. I've seen great portfolios on disk or videotape. We hired an animator who had a video of his work and it was great. Also, try to find out ahead of time what kind of product or project you'll be working on and create a sample geared to that need. Make sure the sample can be played on the interviewer's platform.

If you had to hire an interface designer, what would you look for?

It depends on what I needed it for. I would look for someone with good skills. Someone who can understand a need and apply it, take a design, layout, or sketch and work with others to put functionality behind it so that it can go out and be shown and tested. Also, if you're looking for work you need to explain where you stand passionately. With the Virtual Museum, I loved what I was doing. I would look for someone who felt the same passion for his or her work.

Sally Ann Applin is a Human Interface Designer with the Personal Interactive Electronics Division at Apple Computer, Inc. As a member of Apple's Media Technology's Virtual Museum project team, she was responsible for conceptual, interface, and graphic design as well as artwork and some scripting. Much of her direct museum experience comes from her contribution as a researcher, writer, and project coordinator at West Office/Design Associates, a museum design firm in San Francisco, CA. Her education includes a master's degree in Interactive Telecommunications and an undergraduate degree in Conceptual Design.

Messages

Messages are pieces of information sent from one process or object to another that signals an event to process or an action to take. Most operating systems send continual messages about the cursor location and keyboard actions to active applications. In the case of most multimedia products, these messages are received by the authoring system. They are then routed to the appropriate object within the authoring engine. For example, when a mouse is clicked over a graphic object or button on the screen, several messages are sent to the object's script to perform some action. In this example, the events registered may be:

1. The mouse enters the location of the object (mouseEnter),
2. The mouse is depressed over the object (mouseDown),
3. The mouse button is released over the object (mouseUp).

Messages can also be sent by objects to themselves or to other objects in response to any action or condition. For example, any one of these events above could send a message that triggers the execution of an **external command** (XCMD).

If you're trying to do something cutting edge with new technology then you can multiply your time estimates as much as you want but it will always take a little longer than that. Five trivial features will turn out to be impossible and five impossible features will turn out to be trivial.

— Ken Laws, Multimedia Programmer

Some event messages are sent specifically by the authoring system. MacroMind Director, for instance, sends an event message when a movie starts and ends. The language guide for each authoring system typically lists event messages that are generated by the product.

Handlers

A **handler** is a self-contained part of a program that performs specific tasks when triggered. Handlers might be scripted to play an animation sequence, look up a picture in a database, or even send a credit card authorization request. When a user or program event messages a handler such as a *mouseUp*, for example, the script that responds to it is called an **event handler**. A **programmer-defined handler** is identical to an event handler except that the message that triggers it is initiated by a script that was written by a programmer— not triggered by a user or program event. This triggering message is always sent from another handler. One handler can receive a message from any number of other objects and it will still operate in the same way. This framework can be valuable, because modifying one handler's behavior ensures that the change occurs no matter which other handler messages it. A **programmer-defined function** is somewhat different. A handler sends data to a function, the

Interview: Dan Backus

Dan Backus has spent the last year working as project director of ADAM, the interactive guide to human anatomy. He discusses some of the programming issues involved in the project as well as his concern for **adaptive systems** ▶ 51, 95 in which content can be added.

How did you program for interactivity?
One of the things we agreed upon was to make the content highly intelligent, highly interactive. If the user touched something, it would be displayed. We used pixel-level recognition. In order to get that level of interactivity, we had to build special tools.

What we had to do as programmers was to give people the ability to navigate up and down through the content. We [also] gave them the ability to produce additional content, and after capturing an image or QuickTime movie, to be able to bring it into either HyperCard or MacroMind Director. The concept is that you navigate back and forth where you can create multimedia from a database of content. We've tried to simplify this kind of programming by providing good tools like good page turners and automatic dissolves. It allows users a quick and easy way to produce multimedia without being multimedia developers. They can bring content into their projects and link it to other related material. It's not just a question of anatomy. It's what one does with anatomy, the kinds of relationships that can be made. What we found students doing frequently was highlighting portions of anatomy for later reference.

We encourage people who want to produce higher level multimedia from our package to learn SuperCard or HyperCard. If one knows a little scripting, they can modify the content—of course, not the original database.

What were some of the programming challenges?
We started with the foot and worked our way up. As soon as the foot was complete, marketing would come back asking for more functionality. There are things we left out because there was no time.

Another programming decision we made was to use an 8-bit system palette to counteract the problems of a custom palette. The artwork was done in Adobe PhotoShop from scanned-in images. It was originally designed to run on a 16-inch monitor. One of the challenges we had was to create an interface that would work with different monitors.

Why didn't you use a real body?
In ADAM, the decision was made to use illustrations of human bodies instead of videos or photographs. Our investors are doctors. They are all of the same mind that the illustration from a learning standpoint is a much better image to work from than the real thing. You can't tell from the real thing what the nerve is. The nerve isn't really bright yellow but in the illustration it is and it is much easier to identify.

What was the cost and how long did this project take?
The real cost is in content produced by four medical illustrators. It took a year and a half to make it…. In the production process, the computer is unforgiving, especially for an artist who is unfamiliar. We built tools that would do error checking at the end of the day. We have spent almost as much time on the tools as on the scripting to create the interface itself.

function manipulates it, and then returns the new values or some result to the handler that called it. For example, a function might be called to convert Fahrenheit degrees to Centigrade. By understanding and using the three types of handlers, a programmer can accomplish the majority of customization tasks.

Externals

Scripting languages do not always support every command that a programmer might need. Most authoring systems allow for the addition of self-contained pieces of code developed in another language to be attached to a project. These externals, often referred to as **XCMDs** ▶ 226, **XFNCs**, or **Xobjects**, allows more sophisticated and unique instructions to be called upon by the authoring environment.

For example, HyperCard uses an XCMD to show color pictures or QuickTime movies which are not able to be shown otherwise. A Director project might send data to an Xobject module to be processed and sent back. While these are not features of the scripting language, they are fairly simple to access.

Programming for Automation

Multimedia programmers should not be restrained only to tasks directly related to features of the project. Many successful programmers, when exposed to other roles in the development process, introduce automation methods that save thousands of dollars in time and even create new opportunities. For instance a programmer in San Francisco developed an application that names and renames all files in a folder with the click of one button. The development time for creating this tool was 2 hours. The time saved was easily 40 hours in the first project. This tool has since been used to strip file endings off the end of movies as well as other tedious renaming. When the number of files increases with multiple versions, the time saved quickly adds up. The same tool could be used to rename files so that they are copied over to a one-off disc in a specific order to increase CD-ROM response performance. This tool could then rename the files back to the original names after they have been copied.

Editors

An **editor** ▶ 170 is another media preparation tool that assists a team in the creation of content. An editor can be custom built for one project or can be built for many projects. Editors are often visually similar to the final project, but they have built in features for things like storyboarding ideas, importing graphics or movies, and displaying grids for proper alignment of objects. They may also contain utility programs that automatically create indexes or navigation elements.

Instantiation Engines

An **instantiation engine** ▶ 170 is a script that automatically creates linked media objects based on data, rules, and templates. These are typically custom built to convert an exported flat file from a database program and automate the population of data or other elements into a project. For example, a FileMaker® database of contacts may need to be built into a multimedia project with a new screen for each person. The instantiation engine might analyze each record and build a new appropriate card for each individual. It may also build new cards for each region and populate that card with the name of the individual and a pointer to the related card.

Instantiation engines require that a programmer build template interface elements, such as one screen for each project part. By using a "read file" command or Xobject in the scripting language, a programmer can program the project to replicate a new card for each occurrence of data. The same method can be used to import a related picture from another source and place it on the record.

General Scripting Tips
Naming Conventions

Naming conventions ▶ 174 are important not only to managing files and archives, but also to multimedia authoring. Handlers can be written to analyze the name of the object that generated a message and allow a program to react specially to different objects with certain names or types of names. By thinking out the naming conventions of objects in a multimedia project in advance, a programmer can change attributes of all objects with that name. For example, you may have a button on 1000 cards in a 2000 card stack, and need to change its color, size, location, script, or some other attribute. By searching for all of the buttons with a name beginning with AA, you can alter as many attributes as necessary. This could save hundreds or thousands of hours of tedious, repetitive work.

Documenting Your Code

Many successful producers will ask to look inside a program at the scripts to see how well things are documented. It is a good idea to write explicit comments in your scripts and handlers explaining the use of variables, functions, Xobjects, etc. This can become a lifesaver when a bug needs to be fixed or when reusing part of your code for another project. It also helps when another programmer is brought on to help write or debug code. The documented code will help other programmers figure out what is happening where.

Tools can be quickly built to rename thousands of buttons or pictures, change colors, resize objects, or perform other functions. Using a simple macro program like QuicKeys from CE Software, artists can program complex key sequences to respond to one keystroke. One firm in San Francisco used QuicKeys to replace all of the sound resources in over 100 MacroMind Director movies in 1 hour and 15 minutes. The task would have taken 10 hours using traditional methods.

Typical fine tuning activities include:
- *Adjusting memory caches to optimize operation*
- *Pre-loading images at interaction points*
- *Adjusting timing of feedback events*
- *Adjust synchronization of sound and image*
- *Balancing color and contrast levels*
- *Adjusting sound volume levels*
- *Disabling debugging tools that might interrupt actions*

There are many different packaging options available for CD-ROM distribution. These range from simple transparent sleeves to plastic "jewel-boxes," cardboard fold-out panels, and "eco-paks." Some use more plastic than others and all offer their own combination of size, durability, and complexity. Check with your CD-ROM manufacturer to review the various options and prices.

Production Integration

Integrating content elements is usually the programmer's responsibility. It is also the project manager's responsibility to make sure that no content is forgotten or missing. The **final storage size** and **performance characteristics** of delivery media must be taken into account as the product begins the integration stage. It is entirely possible to create more content than can fit onto the delivery medium, especially for products created for diskettes. Sometimes, production artists "go wild" and collect and produce more movies, animations, sounds, and images than can fit even on a CD-ROM. If this happens, some of the content may need editing or cutting. For a diskette-based product, it may be possible to license a compression utility and deliver the product in a self-decompressing form that can copy to a user's hard drive to be used.

Final checks should be made on all content and code. This can include checking for viruses, optimizing data rates, compressing files, disabling testing and debugging scripts, and deleting code for unused features. It is also important to arrange windows and icons within them in the most obvious and usable fashion for a user.

Resources, file and application icons, and content media should be checked to make sure that they function in all bit-depths and work with all monitor sizes. See the testing chapter for more information.

Documentation

Some form of **documentation** ▶ 24, 223, 254 is almost always needed—even for a kiosk or presentation. The amount and type of documentation will depend on the product and its audience. Sometimes, simple instructions will suffice as with a kiosk or interactive art installation. Other times, detailed manuals and workbooks may be necessary, as with authoring tools or interactive education. Documentation can include **quick reference cards**, **registration cards**, **manuals**, **tutorials**, **guides**, **workbooks**, **online help**, **training materials**, and **teacher's guides**.

Documentation is much more difficult and time-consuming than you may think. Leave plenty of time and hire qualified and experienced people to compose the documentation. Too often, developers try to pro-

duce documentation on the side while doing other tasks. In most cases when this is done, the product either ships late or ships with incomplete documentation. Top-notch software companies spend a lot of time and money to create exceptional, clear, and understandable documentation.

Marketing and **sales people** ▶ 18, 85, 241 may also need materials like screenshots and brochures to help them sell and pre-sell products. These may include demo disks and presentations to conferences, trade shows, and distributors. These materials should be planned so they do not take needed resources from other responsibilities at critical times.

Product Packaging

Packaging for a consumer product may include the documentation, brochures, registration cards, labels, and the box or package that holds all of the pieces together. Many publishers shrink-wrap the final package to ensure that nothing falls out during transport or delivery.

Most product packaging requirements need to be decided. The design of each piece of the packaging must be completed and production and printing may need to start in order to meet distribution deadlines. Many graphic designers have packaging experience. While packaging companies often offer design services, they may be a better source for pricing and option information, but not original design ideas (some packaging companies, however, offer exceptional design services).

If the product will be delivered on **CD-ROM** ▶ 109, the disc manufacturer will be able to describe the options and associated costs available for screen printing onto the media. **Videodiscs** ▶ 112 and **diskettes** ▶ 113 may require labels which can be produced by the manufacturer or by independent label printers. Be sure to ask in what form the label or printing department needs to have artwork.

There are many different cases now available for delivering CD-ROMs. The traditional plastic "**jewel case**" is only one of many designs now available. All include a way to hold at least one disc, but some have multiple fold-out panels for printing instructions, information or holding booklets. Some jewel cases can actually hold two CD-ROMs. The costs vary for each of these options.

Ecological Considerations

Some CD-ROM cases are designed to use less plastic and, therefore, be more ecologically friendly. It can be both a cost-saving approach and a good marketing strategy to choose materials that are as environmentally safe as possible. While there are conflicting opinions about which materials are best and why, most experts agree that using as few materials as possible always helps. This means designing packages to take up as little space as possible and using no more materials than necessary. This may translate into using smaller boxes or using the manual or other documentation as the box.

Market Considerations

Different packaging is sometimes required for different markets. This is certainly true for international markets and is sometimes practiced in regional markets as well. **Registration cards** ▶ 256 can be used to track users and user profiles.

Evaluate Whether You're Ready for the Next Step

The end of the production cycle is often a difficult point to identify. Project team members may be experiencing emotions ranging from "more work could be done" to "let's just ship this thing and get it over with." An experienced project manager, along with team members who have worked on long projects, can be a big help in determining when to end the production phase. They will know when to wrap things up and ship the product and when to keep going. Inexperienced teams may release a product before it is finished or, on the other hand, continually refine the features and content with little justification or plan. The skill in going to the next step is knowing where to draw the line and keeping the team focused on the goals set forth previously.

Production Tips

- Don't begin production if the design is not resolved.
- Limit the amount of redesign performed in production.
- Create clear production specifications and standards.
- Communicate often. Uncover tasks that are falling short early enough in the process to allow for resources to be shifted or alternatives taken.
- Share tricks and shortcuts with team members.
- Obtain high-quality digital sources. The quality will likely degrade in later mixes, edits, and modifications.

Testing

Testing

The multimedia experience is a journey through a landscape that has its own design, guideposts, and customs. Testing is a way of walking in the user's shoes before the user does to make sure the experience is complete, using as a map the specifications in the project plan or proposal.

Multimedia products are a careful balance of complex interdependent parts. As a result, good testing tracks many items and relationships such as navigation elements, color specifications, sound clips, hardware incompatibilities, operating system conflicts, and multiple delivery platforms. Testing is a way of making sure that many complex elements will perform as promised.

In concept and planning, testing means checking assumptions about technology and markets. During design and prototyping, user testing represents a willingness to meet user's needs and abilities and requires repeatedly discarding what does not work and trying again for something that does. Later, during production, testing fills the role of keeping a project on target as it helps the team identify and remove errors so that it lessens their impact on other team members. After production, the formal testing stage strives to eliminate all errors and discrepancies before it reaches the client or customer. Good testing reflects a concern for the people who will ultimately experience the project. Ultimately, it is an investment in the continued success of the product and the team that produced it.

The greater the degree of testing, the greater the degree of certainty that a multimedia project will succeed in creating the intended experience. Almost every creative development process involves some form of testing. For example, filmmakers test for continuity between shots, checking such details as making sure water in glasses is at the same levels or hats are worn at the same angle. They also may try out different movie endings with test audiences before final release. Book or magazine editors will edit several drafts and revisions of a manuscript until it is acceptable for print. Software producers test features and functionality to discover and fix errors or

"bugs" and other problems before releasing a product. Developers owe it to their users to test the product no matter how simple they believe it to be. Even the most ambitious user will walk away feeling let down or even angered by a product that has obvious errors or is too difficult to use.

Multimedia Testing Issues

Multimedia development with its quick and frequent changes to code or design requires a flexible and **iterative** approach to testing. Testing should occur throughout a project. This "test as you go" philosophy has been mentioned by many multimedia developers. Testing is a process that has recurring loops and checkpoints all geared towards raising the quality and acceptability of the project. Testing that occurs only at the end of production may reveal an interface that is too confusing or problems that are too serious to fix before the scheduled release date.

Scheduling and Budgeting for Testing

Experienced project teams make it a point to build adequate time and money for testing into the project plan or contract. They try not to run the risk of chipping into the production time and budget to accomplish this responsibility. (Many large projects actually have separate testing contracts.) Experienced teams also know enough not to fool themselves into believing that things will work the first time. Plans that do not account for testing are almost always modified to include it somewhere down the line.

Testing Approach

Multimedia testing uses elements of software testing, with many additions to accommodate the different tools, practices, interfaces, and content issues in multimedia. This approach includes **user testing** and **functional**

Unfortunately, testing can be a rather expensive exercise. If you are a very small company and you estimate a job, you might say, "It's going to take us three weeks to do that, with this many people. We will start here, and I reckon that's it." You think you are within the profit margin and everything will be fine. That's the theory. What happens is that if you design it but don't test it and leave it with the client, you will soon find out that all of the problems you never thought of are there as soon as the project is installed. People will say, "This thing is not working right. Come and fix it." Before you know it, fixing the problem starts eating into your budget and your profit. You've got to plan for and allow for testing.

— Peter Mitchell, Big Animated Digital Productions

testing. User testing makes sure the interface and navigation are appropriate for the intended audience. (User testing is much more emphasized in multimedia than it is in software development.) Functional testing ensures that the features and capabilities of the product work as intended. A third type of testing, called **content testing,** has its foundation in the publishing, film, and music world. Content testing checks the text, illustrations, movies, sounds, and other content elements to make sure the material is accurate and consistent. (What is "accurate" depends on the medium, the information presented, and the purpose of the information.)

When to Test

In the **concept and planning** stage, testing involves challenging assumptions about product elements and the audience. Testing here may take the form of market or technological research. In the **prototype ▶ 136** stage, testing is part of the design process. **Design studies ▶ 139** are useful tools to test alternative design issues such as determining whether video clips or still images are more effective. Once a tentative production model is determined, user testing plays a big role in assessing the suitability of the model. A final production model implies that the interface is well-established and that the conceptual design is complete and integrated. The results of this stage become the foundation for the production stage.

Alpha-Testing

Near the end of the **production** stage, testing begins to take a more structured form with tracking, test scripts, and formal processes. The software industry tests a newly assembled product in-house, referring to this stage as **alpha-testing**. The objective of alpha-testing is to ensure functionality, that is, to make sure that the system does not crash, screens do not freeze up, all navigation works, and buttons and screen elements perform as they should—in other words, that it works as designed. Any problems or bugs encountered in alpha-testing are usually tracked, prioritized, and fixed in a series of versions that culminates, hopefully, with a system that is robust enough for extended use. (Keeping track of all previously reported problems and testing them again is often referred to as **regression testing**.)

The software industry labels each **version ▶ 174** of a product in order to track problems with different renditions. Shipping versions are usually labeled with numbers such as 1.0, 3.1, or 7.0, where major releases are indicated by whole numbers and minor releases by fractional parts. Version numbers help a testing team know where to look when trying to fix a problem.

Beta-Testing

In the software industry, once production is complete, another concentrated testing effort occurs—often referred to as **beta-testing.** At this time, features should be set and major bugs fixed. The focus should be on completing the project for distribution. The results from beta-testing help developers and marketing personnel fine-tune the product before installation or delivery.

For mass-market products, most software developers solicit potential customers to become **beta-testers**. A beta-tester is an outside party that has agreed to test a preliminary version of a product and report back with problems and comments. Beta-testers are commonly rewarded for their efforts with free or discounted copies of the shipping product or another suitable reward. Depending on the sophistication of the software and the size of the market, the number of beta-testers can vary between a handful or a few hundred or thousand. Microsoft and IBM have each conducted beta-tests for software products in which tens of thousands of users participated. (Most multimedia projects will not run into these types of numbers.) Getting the product out of the development lab and into the hands of actual users before it ships will uncover a number of unforeseen problems. The number of testers used for any particular project should take into account the sophistication and variation of the audience as well as the resources required for managing beta-testers. The number should also include a fair estimate for unresponsive beta-testers (testers that receive beta copies but never respond with any feedback). Depending on the size of the program and how well it is run, the amount of unresponsive testers can range from 20% to 60%.

As with alpha-testing, test results should be collected and problems reported and prioritized. The last thing in the world a project team should see during beta-testing is a "show stopper," that is, a problem that is so serious that it prevents release of the product. Hopefully, serious problems are caught in alpha-testing or, better yet, addressed in the design and prototype stage. The objective of beta-testing is to create a stable and consistent product. If customers, clients, or articles in the press mention any **bugs**, glitches, missing or incorrect content, or any other problem related to the shipping product's use, then the beta-testing was not thorough enough. Granted, it is almost impossible to get all errors out of a product, but the goal of beta-testing is to track down and correct as many as possible.

Producing and testing multimedia content is not the same as creating traditional software. It's probably closer to producing a movie or television program. First we worked on paper—storyboarding and scripting the production. Then we created an interactive storyboard on the computer that we tested with kids. Next we recorded voiceovers and music. The final step was putting all the pieces together and creating finished graphics for every screen. At this stage, we tested the "look and feel" again with a group of preschoolers, before we assembled the final product.

The last stage of testing, referred to as beta-testing in the software industry, was done by parents and their families at home with their own computers. We also used in-house professional testers to perform our own tests before we shipped the final product.

— Bill Rollinson, T/Maker

At the end, a lot of developers are too tired to see if the product works. They're broke. They just want to get it out the door. But you have to test. Not testing causes a lot of products to fail. Someone conceptually thought the product would work and sold that bill of goods to a lot of people. When it comes out, it may not have the same effect.

— Mark Schlichting, Brøderbund

Case Study: EyeLearn

Description:

To reinforce his patients' education about different ophthamological conditions, Dr. Alan Shelton created EyeLearn, an interactive program that explains six common ocular diseases and related surgical procedures. In addition to textual and audio explanations, EyeLearn includes time-lapse visualizations that illustrate post-operative healing and gradual loss of vision.

Development Hardware:

Macintosh IIfx, SuperMac Technology's VideoSpigot board and Digital Film card, Photo CD, 24" monitor, flatbed scanner

Delivery Hardware:

Macintosh IIsi, 13in. color monitor

Software Used:

Special Delivery by Interactive Media, QuickTime, Adobe Premiere, Adobe PhotoShop, After Effects by The Company of Science & Arts, HyperCard

Price:

Not for sale

Contact:

Dr. Alan Shelton
Moore-White Medical Center
Los Angeles, CA

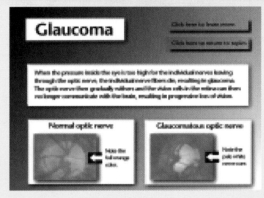

Management:

Dr. Shelton worked alone in his "off-duty" hours from his medical practice.

Concept and Planning:

In the course of his practice, Dr. Shelton observed that many patients had difficulty recalling details from previous office consultations, or that they would be hesitant about proceeding with required surgery. To reinforce his patients' understanding, Shelton devised EyeLearn, which he regards as "another member" of his clinical team. An important feature of EyeLearn is visualization, which Dr. Shelton believes "is the most powerful way to teach people." He decided to present information on six common eye diseases: glaucoma, cataract, diabetic retinopathy, macular degeneration, pterygium, and vitreous disease.

Design and Prototype:

The needs of eye patients created design constraints such as high contrast displays, large fonts, and simple color schemes. Text was displayed simply as black on white or white on black, because most patients had trouble discerning letters with gradient fills.

Animated visualizations were particularly effective to illustrate progressive processes such as deterioration of vision due to glaucoma or postoperative healing after pterygium (a corneal disorder) surgery.

The early prototype of EyeLearn was done with low-resolution 160x120-pixel QuickTime movies to determine how the movements and transitions should be. Because 160x120 windows are difficult to discern, he

rendered the images again at higher resolution. He digitized QuickTime movies at five different frame rates to determine acceptable quality. The interface was designed in PhotoShop. Shelton also experimented with Kodak's DCS (Digital Camera System), Photo CD, and scanned images to determine quality.

In designing the different sections, Shelton wanted to give the patient a frame of reference about each disease before they saw an animated visualization. In the glaucoma section, for example, the patient would first learn about how pressure damages the nerve and see anatomically what happens to the eye. "What's normal and what's abnormal is shown," says Shelton. "People can't see what's wrong with them unless you show it."

Production:

Shelton created all content from patient data and original photographs and videos. He used After Effects to composite images for animation in Adobe Premiere and Special Delivery to integrate the different media to create the final product.

To demonstrate visual field changes over time due to glaucoma, Shelton used data from a series of visual field tests, which monitor a patient's peripheral vision. The patient's test response points were printed out, scanned into the computer, and then processed in Adobe PhotoShop to produce a black and white or grayscale image. Shelton scanned in each image and used After Effects to make a movie showing the dissolving visual field on a white background. He then composited the movie over a still image of a rainbow. "The rainbow picture was taken on our vacation to Hawaii," says Shelton. "It just happened that the angle of the rainbow corresponds to the angle the visual field loss takes in a person with glaucoma." In reality, visual changes from glaucoma happen over a period of two to three years, and "obviously a person isn't going to sit still and watch a rainbow for two years." The effect of the visualization, though, is convincing.

Testing:

Dr. Shelton met with patients one on one to obtain direct feedback about the effectiveness of EyeLearn. He made changes to improve visibility and navigation, for example, changing color schemes or text size.

Programming
100% Off-the-shelf tools

Content
100% New

Expenses
2% Operations
98% Development
Marketing Expenses not. app.

Development Expenses
70% Personnel
30% Equipment
(Content not app.)

Total Development Costs: approx. $100,000

Total Development Team: 1 person

Money Delivery
Personnel
Total Development Time: 6 months

When to Stop Testing

Testing results should always be compared to the product specifications in the project plan or proposal. The features and interaction can be observed and evaluated in a series of "go/no-go" steps. Either the project works at every level as designed or it does not. In most cases, the schedule slips until everything works. In the instances where a product ships with problems, everyone involved usually sleeps a little less restfully, waiting and wondering if the next day will bring an unfavorable review or a call from a disgruntled customer.

Without a project plan or clear objective, testing can lead to adding new features or changing features on the fly so that the project never ends. Testing should be performed again and again until the result is "right," but if there is no definition of what is "right," there may be no end to testing. This point cannot be emphasized enough. It is important to draw a line in the sand and say that any feature on one side of the line needs to get finished and tested completely before the product ships. Any feature on the other side gets removed or put into another version. Without this line, the project features continue to grow and the initial purposes and goals get subverted or changed without conscious thought. The later in the schedule that this line is drawn, the more chance the project will fail. Again, the product plan or proposal should be used to set these lines.

What to Test

Very simply, test what is important to the success of the project. Every project's scope is different, of course, but there are common elements throughout. For example, a simple sequential desktop presentation to explain personnel policies may need no more testing than to check that it flows smoothly and displays the correct images in the right sequence. On the other hand, a multimedia kiosk that provides pharmaceutical information to the public would be subject to strict content testing to ensure accurate information. Or consider an interactive adventure game. If a twelve year-old walks away from it bored after only a few tries, that is a sign that more user testing is needed.

The three major areas of testing include **user testing**, **functional testing**, and **content testing**. Other areas include to test include documentation and training materials.

User Testing

User testing ▶ 163 should be done before production starts. Making changes to the interface and interaction become almost impossible once the content is incorporated. User testing after production is complete should be for the sole purpose of making cosmetic changes. These kinds of tests might include such details as making sure buttons are aligned or menus and button titles have consistent capitalization. In other words, all elements of the interface are **consistent** ▶ 142.

Consistency can mean anything from a consistent navigation scheme to consistent locations of common screen elements, from consistent terminology to consistent icon styles. Ideally, most of these issues are addressed beforehand. Navigation, for example, and all other elements of the interaction should be designed during prototyping and be in place before content is placed in the product.

Making sure all standards and guidelines have been followed correctly can be critical to the image and perception of the product. Some products in emerging markets manage to survive despite inconsistencies and quirkiness in the interface, but this is rare. Inconsistent products in an established market never have a chance. Users maynnot be able to recognize that lack of consistency is the problem but they will definitely know there is a problem. They may not be able to come right out and say something like, "The product suffers from a lack of consistency in its navigation model, naming conventions, and screen elements." Instead, they will use words like "quirky," "ugly," "dumb," and "weird" in their descriptions about the product.

Functional Testing

Functional testing ▶ 166 is a method of verifying requirements that are stated in the project proposal. It is also known as "testing to spec" because the specification maps each part of the system as it relates to the whole. This aspect of testing follows the approach used in software development because many of the issues addressed are the same as those found in producing a software application. The areas of functional testing include **unit testing**, **integration testing**, **media testing**, **stress testing**, **configuration testing**, and **environment testing**. Refer to the project proposal or design document to identify the complete list of functions to be tested.

The problems likely to be uncovered can range from minor cosmetic ones such as a button that does not have an action associated with it or a link that takes you to an incorrect content file. Larger problems may be something like an unexplained tendency to crash after 10 minutes of use. The challenge is not just to notice problems but to locate and fix these problems as soon as possible. Tests serve multiple functions. The first is that they provide a comprehensive check of most of the variables in the course of using a product. The second is

When testing a CD-ROM one-off, be sure every file can be opened.

The big challenge in testing is to find ways to test before a product is done and is fully working—when one can still make functional changes.

— Kristina Hooper-Woolsey, Distinguished Scientist, Apple Computer

Testing is not some sort of black box...some voodoo that happens at the end of a project. It's pretty systematic and absolutely necessary to the success of a product. A project could look beautiful but if every time you press a button you get a script error, or it goes to the wrong place, or it crashes, then all of that beautiful work you've done is for nothing. It is the one bug that people remember. They don't remember all of the good stuff.

— Bob Eddings, Manager of Testing, Claris Corporation

You need good solid testing, because you don't want to recall 100,000 CDs because of a few stupid bugs. You test as you go and you have to do a lot of it. One way to do it is you can build and test sections that are really tight, a kind of a block by block building. If you move the bottom block, it is all going to fall down. But if you think ahead and build it so that any one block can be edited without destroying everything else, then you can have sections that you know are completely solid many months before you ever release the product. Usually what happens at the end is that you are testing not the entire thing, not every little nitty gritty thing, but testing to make sure that it all hangs together.

— Joe Sparks, Game Designer, Pop Rocket

Functional Testing Checklist

- Program loads and runs successfully
- Program terminates successfully
- All navigation links function
- All input controls function (keys, touch screen, mouse, etc.)
- All output controls function (displays, printers, speakers, etc.)
- All arrow keys function where appropriate
- All menu key equivalents function
- Acceptable levels of performance on multiple configurations
- Time-based content can be interrupted
- Unexpected input entries are handled
- Unavailable fonts and other resources are handled
- Unavailable peripherals/ extensions are handled
- Incorrect monitors and bit-depths are handled
- Low memory conditions handled
- No adverse reactions with other projects or applications that are running
- Icons, prompts, and terminology match
- Correct help screens and balloon help for each element and object
- If using a card-based engine, check for unlocked fields except where desired
- The About Box has the correct names, version numbers, and dates

that they do it in such a way as to help locate the area where the problem resides as quickly as possible. Many software developers have horror stories of problems that took days or months to locate because they never had a clear idea of where the problem was in the first place. The more custom development in a project, the more this issue may be a problem.

Unit Testing

One of the earliest ways to test multimedia projects is to test the pieces as they are being developed and then integrate the finished pieces into the whole. This focus on the unit isolates a specific area of functionality. Software developers often refer to this as **unit testing**. It is useful for making sure the smallest portion is working before moving on to larger pieces. Game designers frequently test parts of their "worlds" as units. Another example is to isolate an animation sequence to make sure it works as proposed under different color systems or through different entry routes. Many developers do this before testing it with other components such as text, sound, or video. Throwing all the elements together and then testing can sometimes make locating a problem next to impossible.

One of the major units in a multimedia product is the **engine ▶ 139,211**, the mechanism that directs the flow of information and interaction of the product. If a product has an engine that functions poorly, the messages and content will probably be lost on the audience. An engine should be tested before content is incorporated. An unstable engine can hamper productivity when people begin integrating content. The amount of testing involved depends on how much of the engine is custom-built. Ones that are developed entirely or partially in-house will likely need more testing than ones built from authoring tools.

One of the principal areas of an engine is the navigation scheme. This part should be tested over and over to make sure that each action triggers the correct steps. An engine might also include complicated indexing to retrieve data from a database or search mechanisms to let users find their way around a system. Testing all the possible cases or variations on a small subset of data can be faster than using the finished set of all data.

Integration Testing

A multimedia project is more than the sum of its parts. A balanced integration makes the product sing and dance. **Integration testing ▶ 212** commonly takes place whenever units are connected. Timing is one area that often cannot be tested as a unit. An automatic

screen sequence may work fine for dummy screens but when movies and sounds are integrated, the timing between screens may be too fast and interrupt the sound or picture sequences. (The prototype should use appropriately sized images, sounds, and movies to prevent any surprises late in development.)

Media Testing

The functionality of the selected media must also be tested. For example, **media testing** a CD-ROM for an electronic book should ensure that all files can be opened, that all indices work as designed, that nothing attempts to write to the CD-ROM, and that data links are correct. In the case of videodisc, make sure that the media is properly indexed and can be referenced by the application. Even if the data is included on the disc, if the application cannot get to it, it means having to remake the videodisc.

Media testing also means continually testing throughout the development process to make sure the software and the content elements will fit on a CD-ROM, diskette, or other delivery media used. Make sure you know how much room you have before going to mastering. Some delivery media have substantially less storage space available when formatted than when unformatted. Some developers use in-house hard drives to store the image before mastering. These may have less capacity than the CD-ROM and so the storage should be tied to the hard drive capacity and not the CD-ROM.

Stress Testing

Stress testing or failure testing ensures that integrity of the product remains intact under extreme conditions. For example, if the multimedia project is on a network, how many users can be active at once without experiencing a slow response time? How does this performance compare to times of light activity? If the project is an interactive database front-end, how complicated can queries be before the system bogs down? What happens if the plug is pulled out and plugged back in while the program is running? (A realistic possibility with an interactive presentation.) If the product adds each user's contribution to a database, how long will it be before storage space is used up? Testing simple cases on a few problems is helpful. But having more people test for longer periods of time can increase the amount of data or the number of interactions exponentially. This situation is a key challenge when developing large-scale **multimedia databases.** Finally, if a multimedia system does fail, are there procedures to restore operation? Self-running systems like kiosks should recover automatically.

One way to look for extreme conditions is to deliberately introduce errors and difficulties that will force the product to fail. For example, what happens if too many options are selected at once? What if users choose options or actions that seem "silly" or "stupid"? Failure testing allows you to respond to problems and warn users about potentially harmful actions. If such problems or weaknesses are identified early they can be overcome by adding preventive code or establishing recovery procedures. Such testing can help you produce nearly error-free products.

Ideally, unexpected conditions should be anticipated in the design phase and uncovered in the production stage. Trying to add protection or recovery mechanisms at the last minute can add days or weeks to the schedule, increase the risk of other problems occurring, and possibly reduce the product's performance. A product that works perfectly under normal conditions may fail in unusual situations. To make a product robust enough to survive real-world use, be prepared for all situations — usual and unusual.

Configuration Testing

Still another type of functional testing is **configuration testing** which tests the product on various groups of computers, attached devices, and software arrangements. A multimedia presentation that runs smoothly on a high-end machine is likely to run differently on a system with slower processor, but *how much* differently? Without testing, it is hard to know if distributing the product for less powerful platforms is even feasible. Another example is the response time between CD-ROM and disk-based content. The CD-ROM will likely be slower, but to what degree and to what effect? This variation might mean the difference between an interesting product and a marginal one when moved from hard drive to CD-ROM.

Many developers target low-end equipment as a minimum delivery configuration. These **low-end configurations** usually have large customer bases but may require optimizing portions of a product. Since many developers use high-end platforms for development, there is a danger in failing to optimize every necessary part of the system. While testing low-end machines at the beginning of a project may show appropriate performance, after many changes are made and additional features or preventive measures added, the performance on low-end machines may no longer be acceptable. Not having low-end machines on hand to test the product repeatedly can create the false assumption that the product will run on these machines.

One challenge to successful configuration testing is keeping up with technological changes as different models of equipment become available in the market. Although different equipment vendors claim to have identical device drivers, there can be enough variation in performance to warrant testing each piece of equipment and its driver in a project configuration.

Differences are particularly evident with CD-ROM drives and videodisc players. Videodisc players may vary in **access time ▶ 109** (the time it takes the player to switch tracks while searching for data on the disc). Such differences can alter the performance of a new configuration, often in surprising or annoying ways. Clicking on an icon to call up an image may instead force the user to wait at a blank screen for seconds while the player finds the video frames. Sound effects may no longer be synchronized with their animations, giving the same impression as a poorly dubbed foreign movie. Testing each configuration will provide information about timing differences that can be factored into the program for each device. This practice will help maintain smooth audio and video transitions.

Configuration testing should not be limited solely to hardware configurations. Older **operating systems** and **extensions** should be tested as well as any that may be in beta form (if it is possible to get them). Even if some versions or extensions are not supported in the shipping product it is still a good idea to test them. If a customer calls up complaining of similar symptoms, it will be easier to diagnose the problem. It may even be possible to alert the user with a dialog box instead of either failing to launch or crashing.

Environment Testing

One last element of functional testing concerns the environment in which a multimedia project is installed and used. For example, a kiosk placed in an office lobby may play music to attract users. The continuous music, however, may irritate or distract a receptionist or security guard who sits near the kiosk. The **environment testing ▶ 99** in this case would be to accommodate the user *and* the receptionist or guard. One possible solution is to install headphones at the kiosk. (Many times, the sound is simply turned off by people who work in the area, preventing users from getting the full experience. Sometimes the exhibit is just unplugged.)

Almost every project has a special environment to test. With a multimedia presentation, the equipment should be tested at the site of the presentation. This practice can reveal problems like not enough power strips or the need for an adapter to hook into the sound system.

Environment testing is not limited solely to hardware. Not having on hand the necessary system version, extensions, or decompression utility have delayed or prevented many demos and presentations. Place these elements on the delivery media along with the multimedia piece. Set up on-site beforehand or walk through a complete scenario in-house on completely blank equipment.

Case Study: Total Distortion

Description:
Total Distortion is delivered on CD-ROM, billed as a "music video adventure game." The player is set in the role of an adventurous music video producer of the future who travels to strange dimensions in search of new material.

Project Type:
Interactive Game

Development Hardware:
Macintosh IIfx, Macintosh Quadra 900, Macintosh IIci, Macintosh IIcx, Audiomedia cards by Digidesign Inc., VideoSpigot board by SuperMac Technology

Delivery Hardware:
Any Macintosh computer with color capabilities and CD-ROM player

Software Used:
Adobe Photoshop, Adobe Premiere, Swivel 3D Professional, Macromedia Three-D, MacroMind Director, OpCode Systems' Studio Vision

Funding:
Private

Price:
$99

Distributor:
North America: Electronic Arts

Contact:
Joe Sparks
Pop Rocket
San Francisco, CA

Concept and Planning:
Planning was an ongoing activity for this project. The product concept evolved over time. The development team had to be flexible in developing ideas.

"After you settle on the initial idea for a product, take this little test. Sit down and try to make an realistic ad for the product. What points would you highlight? What screenshots would you show? Think of the activities. How would you convince the user that this product is really cool? Why would someone really want to have this product? This will help focus the concept and sharpen your goals throughout development," comments Joe Sparks.

Design and Prototype:
During the prototype a lot of music, animation, and 3D modeling was tested. Each feature had to complement the game and they could not override the user's fun. The design goal was to make well-rounded experiences and avoid experiences that became limiting and monotonous. They tried to plan six or seven interesting and likable things to do that were common and would be repeated by the user frequently throughout the game, such as talking to characters, browsing around animations, or 3D navigation. One thing they learned was to identify what made their product fun and to focus on that part of the game first. Sometimes the things you wanted to do and the things they could actually do were two very different things.

Production:
To make an elaborate multimedia project for CD-ROM, one that contains thousands of images, sounds, scripts, and more, they had to become librarians. They learned to develop consistent ways of naming things. For example, they would label all of the dialogue components using the first two letters of the character's name followed by a number.

Keeping artwork consistent across a big 3D world with thousands of images was very difficult. The artwork went through many stages before it became "final" and ready to be integrated into the product. The first stage was 3D modeling and texture creation. Next, the models were animated and then rendered as 24-bit PICTs with an alpha channel. Each PICT file went through a PhotoShop processing stage. From here, Joe created cropped and masked sprites and backgrounds. Each image had to be dithered to 8-bit and registered properly as Director sprites. All of these files had to be kept around until the end because the developers might have to return to a scene and modify or add new material to the artwork.

Testing:
Joe finds it helpful to imagine what it would be like to see Total Distortion for the first time. Since he does production, planning, and business, he has a lot of freedom and this is important to him.

He did a lot of testing along the way. A key technique was to build and test sections as they were developed—block by block. "If you move the bottom block of a structure it will fall down. But if you think ahead and build it so that any one block can be edited without destroying everything else and it still holds together, then you have sections that are completely solid many months before releasing the product."

Distribution:
They shopped around for a publisher, making first contact at trade shows. "If you can go to a publisher, demonstrate that you have a product and show it's on the way and that it's neat. That's the number one thing you can do. There's nothing else more powerful." Finalizing the deal took many meetings but not as many as their first product.

Joe found that 3.5 % of the retail price per unit is about what you can expect for a SEGA or Super Nintendo title. He finds that with a PC title publisher you can expect about 7.5% or 8.5%.

Programming
50% Off-the-shelf tools
50% Custom Code

Content
100% New

Expenses
30% Marketing
65% Development
5% Operations

Development Expenses
65% Personnel
35% Equipment
(Content not app.)

Total Development Costs:
approx. $250,000

Total Development Team:
3 people

Money
Personnel
Total Development Time: 14 months

Making sure users are comfortable with the audio and video display equipment can make the difference between a successful presentation and an awkward experience.

Functional testing may not eliminate all surprises that come when a multimedia project is sent to live in the real world of the intended delivery platform, but it can substantially reduce the number, intensity, and cost of many avoidable problems.

Content Testing

The purpose of **content testing** is to make sure the materials in the multimedia product are accurate. The goal of content testing to prevent errors ranging from transposed letters to inaccurate subject matter. **Content experts** ▶ 20, 99 are used for much of this testing because they can rely on their expertise to check facts and the presentation of the information. These can be subject consultants, client representatives, or educators. They work with members of the project team at key points to add their insight and critical eye. Illustrations, audio, video, and any other elements need to be checked for correctness (content is not the exclusive domain of text). For example, an option to view a Model 200 turbo-widget should not present an illustration of a Model 100. Likewise, a voice-over from Winston Churchill or Harry S. Truman should list the right year.

The role that **proofreading** plays is easy to underestimate during development with all the other types of activities going on. But once the product is in distribution, seemingly small errors like misspelled words, typos, mispronunciations, and incorrect grammar can distract users from the content and damage a product's credibility. Proper names and **trademarks** should be verified. Clients financing a project will bristle to see their company or product name misspelled or logo displayed incorrectly. Some companies have exact policies to make sure their trademarks are used properly. With forethought, this issue can be resolved in a fairly systematic manner. Usually companies have standards manuals or some formalized documents that describe possible and proper usage of logos, symbols, and trademarks. Ask for these "corporate identity" books from any commonly referenced companies so you can prepare these elements correctly. (Do this early.)

Content Testers

As in consistency testing, finding people to look over the content with an eye towards accuracy is not all that difficult. Many people have the innate ability to spot spelling mistakes by just glancing at a page or screen. A content expert should know the material well and be

acquainted with the product's purpose and audience. Finding qualified people to do content testing is not so much the problem as is getting them to cover **all** the material **more than once**. Content testers should be used effectively. Even experts have a hard time concentrating on 300MB of text, graphics, sound, and video upon seeing it for the fourth time. Limiting an editing pass to specifically look for adherence to a style guide will probably pick up details that might have been missed if the editor was required to also correct content, punctuation, facts, and trademarks at the same time. All testers need to feel that their suggestions and efforts are being addressed. Ignoring their concerns or skipping their edits without explanation can disgruntle an editor and cause them edit less thoroughly in the future.

Ideally, most of the proofing should be done when the material is in its easiest form to edit. For text, this means before the text is "poured" into the template or engine. Editing with a good word processor with spelling and grammar checkers can be more effective than flipping through screens presented by an authoring tool. For all media, especially graphic or time-based media, the production stage is the appropriate place to seriously proof for content. Reworking or replacing illustrations, photos, sounds, or video is much more difficult and time-consuming after the production is finished.

Regardless of how carefully the production team integrates the content, testing and proofing can make the difference between an award-winning product and an acceptable one. And as with functional testing, a product is only as good as its last testing stage. When the project team feels the content has been tested for the final time, it means that one more iteration should still be done.

Collateral Materials

A multimedia project is usually accompanied by some form of **documentation** ▶ 212, 223. This may be **workbooks** for training sessions or **marketing materials** that describe system requirements and capabilities. Or it may be instructions that briefly explain how to install the product and use the major functions. Many training and educational products contain **teacher notes**, **workbooks**, **manuals**, or **tutorials**. These must also be tested for accuracy because they are valuable resources and contribute to the overall use of the product. Useful, well-tested documentation can offset later service responsibilities.

Illustrations and screenshots should reflect the features and appearances of the *shipping* product and not earlier versions. Element names and locations must be correct. The documentation should not contain references to content or features that are not in the final product.

Content Testing Checklist

- Correct content of text, graphics, sound, animation, and video
- Correct licensing and copyright information
- Correct versions of materials
- Correct dates and numbers
- Correct trademarks and logos
- Correct entries in index
- Appropriate production values for sound and movies
- Images, photos, and diagrams matched to text
- Correct credits for materials (if included)
- Correct aspect ratio for pictures and movies
- Correct headers and comments in script including version number and copyright notices

A problem with editing illustrations, photos, sound, animations, or movies after production is complete may be getting ahold of the people that performed the original work. If they are free-lance workers, they may be working on other jobs or otherwise unavailable.

Collateral Testing Checklist

- Installation steps are clear and correct
- Text, graphics, dialog, and animation and video stills match the electronic versions
- Icons, prompts, and terminology match
- Messages in dialog boxes match
- Positions of windows and panels in screenshots are the same
- Times of operations are correct if included

A big challenge in preparing collateral materials is producing them in concert with ongoing development. Late changes in an interface or feature set can seriously delay getting documentation out on time.

Market Testing

Market testing ▶ 17,107 is not the ultimate measure of success but it can provide a clear view of the sales tactics to use. This type of testing can be done toward the end of production and before distribution to find out how much the targeted audience likes the content and design. Often, market tests provide insight into the validity of the market model or about potentially new markets. They can also identify improvements for future versions.

Some industries rely on market testing of quasi-finished products in order to fine-tune the finished piece. For better or worse, some movie endings have been changed after an initial ending received unfavorable reviews from test audiences. Ideally, most script issues should be handled in the design stage but some elements, like a movie ending, need to exist in the context of the entire product in order to be adequately reviewed.

Creating a Test Plan

A **test plan** is usually started at the beginning of a project. It is reviewed and refined as more details are known about the project such as its schedule and features and the delivery media and platform. A good test plan contains structure in the form of listing all the elements to test and the types of tests to run. It outlines the way problems are to be reported and fixed. It locates the resources and people and manages them through the testing phase. One of the more important items to formalize is an end point, a point when testing is considered complete. This point is usually determined by the feature set listed in the latest version of the project plan. Without a solid idea of what to test, it is hard to know when testing is done.

Test Scripts

The tests to run and the problems to look for will be different from project to project. The complete body of tests profile all possible uses of the product and look at many of the areas discussed earlier. One or more **test scripts** can be written for testers to make sure these areas are covered. A test script is a formal description of a single test. It presents a specific sequence of events that can be repeated by someone else at a later point or in another location. One type of script can be a step-by-step description that walks through every feature in a prescribed order. Each line states a specific action to take. This type of test is versatile because it can be run throughout the testing phase, on different platforms, and under different configurations. It makes sure all the features work consistently at the most basic level. When some fixes occasionally propagate errors to other areas, this simple and routine step-by-step test may catch these as a matter of course.

Sample Outline for Test Plan & Testing Certification

Statement of Certification
  Certification
  Production Run Verification (for Master)
  Signatures

Information Distribution List
  Bug Reports

Test Team Members
  Functional & Content Testing
  Compability Testing

Product Release Description
  Description of Product
  System Requirements
    CPUs
    Monitors
    Memory
    Drives
    Operating System Software & Drivers

Verified Systems and Equipment
  Hardware
    CPUs
    Memory Configurations
    Monitors
    Peripherals
    Printers
  Software
    Operating System Software & Drivers

Appendices
Test Results
  Testing Methodology
  Checklist
  Automated Tools
  Mastering & Final Checklist
Closed (and Deferred Bug Reports, if any)
  Summary
Known Problems in Final Product
  Summary
  System Software & Driver Incompatibilities
  Hardware Incompatibilities
  Peripheral Incompatibilities

A test script can also be a description of a process to act out, a function to try, or a problem to solve. In working through the script, testers may notice errors, bottlenecks, problems with the interface, or inconsistencies. This type of test closely simulates how a user might use the product. Too often testers casually work through a few areas and move on to something else giving a cursory pass to the product. Asking them to use the product in a real-world situation may uncover problems that only occur in complex situations.

Regardless of the form test scripts take, they focus on reproducible steps and give testers direction so their efforts are put to good use.

Recording Test Results

Reliably compiling and tracking test results and fixes to problems can make testing a much easier process, especially when many people are involved. What may start out as a well-meant, "quick and dirty" fix may in fact cause new and mysterious errors later on. Having a way to track changes and new errors is essential for keeping a project's testing phase from getting out of hand.

A good test plan includes a **standard form** for reporting errors. The form does not have to be elaborate. A good form will at least capture the most critical information. This includes who did the testing, the version of the product, what type of machine and system the test was run on, the nature of the problem, and the steps that led up to the problem. Without this basic information, untold hours can be spent fixing a problem that has already been fixed or looking for the solution in the wrong place. For example, a problem that could be traced to a network might not be found at first because the network was not mentioned in the bug report. Another example is a problem that gets ignored because it was thought to be fixed in an earlier version. Listing the version of the product in the bug report would have indicated to the testing team that the problem had not been fixed after all.

The **test form** to be used by testers can be developed on paper or created for use with e-mail. It should have room to list:

- Person who identified the problem
- Contact information—phone number, e-mail address
- Date and time of discovery
- Version of the product
- Platform, system, extensions, peripherals, and inits
- A description of the problem, step-by-step if possible
- Whether it is repeatable with the steps listed above

It is also helpful to ask for any collateral material about a problem such as screenshots of error conditions, debug logs, videotaped sessions with users—anything that will clarify and illustrate the nature of a problem to those in charge of fixing it.

After receiving these reports, a testing group usually creates a record to track the problem. Reports that are similar are often combined into one tracking record.

Recording information on problems helps in evaluating the progress of testing as well as in eliminating time spent chasing problems that have already been fixed. Regardless of the types of forms used or whether databases or spreadsheets are brought in, a way to track problems and their resolution can help keep project development on track.

Testing Hints

A few general guidelines can help to catch as many errors as possible and make the testing process run more effectively for all involved. One of these is to introduce **variation** into some of the tests to look at elements from new angles. Just as a search grid goes over the same area twice but from different angles, the testing of a multimedia product can introduce a similar amount of variation. For example, instead of having content experts or editors always start from the beginning of the material and go to the end, it might be effective to have them start at the end and progress to the beginning a few times. This ordering may catch problems that testers would normally miss because they either run out of time or become too tired to cover materials in later sections.

Another guideline in testing is to **narrow the focus** in test scripts during different editing passes. Just as it is easier to pick up mistakes in a violin section of an orchestra by having an ear isolate these instruments, it may also be easier to spot problems in the interface, navigation, or content if testers are testing for these

Information to track for a bug report:
- Identification number
- Assignment of priority
- Status (open, closed, pending, or delayed)
- Corresponding report or reports
- Person responsible for fix
- Date of completion
- Description of solution
- Supporting illustrations or documentation
- Comments

Apple's Third-Party Compatibility Test Lab

The Third-Party Lab was created to encourage the exchange of compatibility and integration test data on Apple's new and enhanced Macintosh products and commercial third-party products, to share the latest compatibility testing resources, and to strengthen testing partnerships with Apple Partners and Associates (in particular with third-party Quality Assurance personnel).

This lab is open by appointment to Apple Partners and Apple Associates who are developing commercial products for the Macintosh. Developers may book a solo session or work with other developers to do joint application testing, for one or two day sessions. No fee is charged, but developers are required to share test data on a confidential basis.

The lab features over 30 Macintosh CPU configurations, with multiple versions of system software. International system software and keyboards are available, as are a wide variety of Apple and third-party products including monitors, hard drives, printers, plotters, and scanners. For more information, please call 408-862-7175.

It takes a special discipline to turn innocuous or bewildering errors into useful reports that increase the chances of finding and resolving problems. Value testers who have this ability are a valuable asset.

elements one at a time. Testers usually have neither the time to spend nor the knowledge of the product to catch everything in one sitting. Limiting tests to one or two elements may tune out enough noise to spot problems that might otherwise have been missed.

A third idea to keep is mind is to **use testers effectively** by giving clear guidelines for tests, responding to bug reports and edits, and passing out new versions judiciously. Nothing frustrates a tester more than to see a new version every three days or to see problems or edits unchanged from version to version. Testers should not be viewed as chess pieces to move around or sacrifice at will. Like any team member, testers need communication, motivation, and consideration.

Automating the Process

Testing can be streamlined by automating routine processes such as error correction or format checking. This streamlining requires in-depth knowledge of the tools and platforms. Some existing macro utilities may be useful, but more elaborate test tools can sometimes be scripted by a programmer.

To automate some of the testing process, make a list of routine actions such as checking navigation paths, properties of fields, naming conventions, and other "housekeeping" tasks. Build or acquire tools to automate their processing. Many developers write their own utilities to filter and format information or automatically integrate content into an engine. Explore the capabilities of existing products and create testing tools that perform such iterative tasks as checking for locked fields in HyperCard or ensuring that screen elements are consistently positioned. Helpful tools such as XCMDs for HyperCard are available from online forums, developer programs, user groups, and electronic magazines. Apple's developer program regularly distributes useful information and tools on CD-ROM.

Two of the caveats in building tools for development or testing are that they should be cost-effective and transferable to other projects, if at all possible. In other words, the time and cost it takes to develop the tools should be recouped in time and money saved in testing. Tools should not be developed unless estimates of their capabilities and development time are based on solid evidence rather than vague possibilities.

Resources for Testing

Although the degree of testing varies at different points in the development process, it is important to be as consistent as possible with the equipment and configurations used within a test cycle. It is also important to obtain a sample of each designated delivery platform and

run the same tests on each. Memory requirements, operating system versions, caching status, color display settings, and other options should be checked before testing a product so that discrepancies can be isolated. An ideal testing environment is a laboratory where dedicated equipment is set aside specifically for testing and experimentation. Some platform manufacturers including Apple have labs available for testing various platform and system configurations.

Most companies do not have the luxury of this type of set-up and so other alternatives or creative strategies need to be explored. Other developers and friends may have a wide variety of machines available for an afternoon or evening. Some dealers may also have different configurations, and a close relationship with one or two may provide access to needed machines. A beta-test program is another way to get exposure to a variety of machines and configurations. (Remember to have testers note the type of machine, system, extensions, and other details that may have an impact on the product.)

Finding People to Perform Testing

By the time this final test stage comes around, developers know their products in minute detail. They know the backroads, mud ditches, mad dogs, muggers, and dead ends as well as the local color, landmarks, scenic paths, secret gardens, and fun places to go. Developers have set ways of approaching the product that are burned into their neurons. Users have none of this knowledge and no pre-determined reflexes. Getting new faces in front of a product during the test phase may be one of the more critical parts of testing. Even without a test plan or a formal way to report errors, testing a project with people other than those who developed it will shake out a good number of the bugs and problems.

Testing Supervisor

A testing supervisor is a needed role in a multimedia project. Ideally, this person should understand the project but have enough distance to maintain a clear user perspective. Larger companies usually hire a manager whose sole job is to oversee testing. Smaller companies often have the project manager fill the role. The relationship between developing and testing is similar to the checks and balances between writing and editing. Having different people or teams play these roles lessens the chances that problems are overlooked or ignored.

A testing supervisor should have the authority to determine which tests to run and what fixes to make. The person who oversees testing should be in close contact with the development team, so that he or she can understand the scope of problems and help devise and implement effective solutions.

Testers

Finding good people to perform testing is just as important as finding people to produce text, illustrations, video, and other parts of a multimedia piece. Depending on the stage of development, it may be necessary to go outside the organization to find and hire testers. Larger companies have entire staffs of people devoted to testing products. Smaller teams may need to be resourceful to find people to test.

A good tester is someone who is conscientious and who is not afraid to question the capabilities of a system. They will also give an accurate sense of the stability of the project. A difficult part of testing is listening carefully to this feedback with an open mind. But it may be better to hear criticism from a few testers than it would be to hear complaints from a few hundred customers. Also, for every one tester who speaks up, there are likely to be another five or ten who feel the same way but do not take the time to say anything.

Finding testers without having to hire them may not be difficult but may require a little planning. **Potential users** with a need for a product can be good testers because they are usually not enamored with the technology. They will look for the heart of the product's purpose and usefulness. **User groups** (there are many for different platforms and tools) are also valuable sources of interested and enthusiastic participants, as are local schools and universities if these students represent the audience of the product. Friends and relatives can also help for some types of testing. They may require a little more coaching but given the proper guidance of what to look for, a 12 year-old cousin or a 65 year-old grandmother might give as good insight from a personal point of view.

Invite testers to add their criticism and comments so they can help plan the next release of the product. More importantly, make it a point to recognize and reward testers for their hard work. Pizza parties, t-shirts, and other special gifts, along with letters of appreciation, are common but effective rewards.

Evaluating Test Results

Once testing information has been gathered, organizing it in different ways can provide a useful picture of the state of the project. Organizing errors by **severity** will form a priority ranking of all errors. A number of severe problems means that the product has far to go before it is complete. Just a few cosmetic changes means that, barring any bugs being introduced along with fixes, the project should soon be ready to move to the next phase. Organizing the errors by the **date** reported may also

give an indication of the stability of a product. More errors reported later in the testing process than in the beginning may mean that more thorough testing is being done or it may mean that some of the fixes are introducing new errors.

Organizing the errors by **category** of problem may bring to light a number of related problems. This ordering may reveal the need to reevaluate the underlying architecture instead of handling the problems by applying topical fixes. Organizing errors by category will also let the people in the production team know where their skills are needed most.

While work in the production phase of a project can be reasonably estimated, fixing problems or reworking materials is less empirical. Expecting a team member to drop current work to redo a handful of illustrations and photos or fix some bugs may not be unreasonable if the work can be completed in a few hours or even an evening. Redoing animations or rewriting a text indexing scheme might be more of a problem because of the time and concentration required. Organizing errors by category can give a more complete picture of the amount of work needed and can maximize the time team members spend fixing errors. Waiting a few days to fix several at a time may be more efficient than fixing a new problem every other day.

Slipping the Schedule

In many cases, it becomes necessary to slip the schedule. Test results can help determine when and how to make that decision. Sometimes it is a benefit to keep the schedule firm in order to get maximum effort out of everyone involved in the project. Staying up all night a few times may be a small price to pay for shipping a project on time.

At the same time, some problems cannot be cured in a few nights. These "show stoppers" require a clearer view than can be summoned forth at 3:00 AM, two days before the project is scheduled to ship. Most project teams that run into this situation have a good idea that something is wrong. Some try to sweep it under the rug and hope it will go away.

The situation is not unlike the stages of grief, with its own versions of denial, anger, and acceptance. Many developers first deny a problem and continue to act as if the product will be released as planned. The intended miracles never happen and the release date gets postponed again and again. Next comes anger and the search for someone to blame, causing pain for many. Finally, the reality of the situation sinks in and

Testers are the champions of the user.
— Bob Eddings, Manager of Testing, Claris Corporation

I know how my programs work because I write the code. I know that if I hold down the option and command key and click and drag I'll be able to do a special function, but unless I tell somebody that, it will not be very obvious. The only way to tell if something truly works or not is don't let the programmer test it, don't let the designer test it, and don't let the designer's family test it.

Find somebody who is going to be a typical user, put them in front of it, and videotape how they work with the product in the testing session. Then afterwards, look at the tape. There's an overwhelming desire that happens to programmers. If they see somebody who cannot use their program, they take the mouse out of their hand and say, "This is how it works."

Unfortunately, the programmer is usually not present all the time in the real world when these situations come up again and again.

— Peter Mitchell, Big Animated Digital Productions

*The final version of a product is commonly referred to as the **golden master**.*

acceptance takes over, hopefully bringing with it clear-thinking and options for resolution. Experienced developers and managers learn how to spot these situations early or, failing that, move to a quicker resolution.

A few options that can be taken include:

Ignore the problem – And play Russian roulette with the press and the market. Some companies will ship the product as it is and prepare an immediate release that fixes the problem. While this move may work for existing products with a large market share, it often ends up leaving a bad impression of the product or version.

Take out the offending feature – This move may quickly solve the problem but at the possible expense of having a product that does not match the documentation or, worse, the contract with the client or publisher. Users or the press may also remember the feature from demos or prerelease versions and view the removal as a sort of "bait and switch" technique, promising a feature and then going back on the promise.

Invent a workaround – This solution lessens the problem by providing an alternate way to achieve the intended result. Workarounds are considered temporary. Subsequent releases should provide a correction.

Redesign the system – This approach may be the right one but it will certainly set the schedule back. It may also disappoint the client or cause the product to miss an important launch date.

Evaluate Whether You're Ready for the Next Step

The decision to end testing is not always a simple one. The "bug list" will likely show some items that may not be problems but they may still need attention. Testers might say things like, "I like the way it works but it would be great if it did this...," or "Works great but all the other products I've seen work like this...." A lot of these comments may indicate that the planning was not careful enough at earlier stages. On the other hand, every project gets these types of reports. One challenge is to get feedback as early as possible so that changes are easy to accommodate. Another challenge is to decide which ones are important to address and which ones are not.

Consider adding new features or changes to later releases or future products. Only in the most severe cases should major additions be made during the testing phase. Many developers believe the decision to do this should rest on whether or not a project will succeed or fail without the desired changes. When all the changes have been integrated into the content and the final test is complete, the product is then submitted to the client, publisher, duplicator, or disc manufacturer.

Testing Tips

- **Test as you go.**
- **Testing is part of the development process and should be integrated with design, programming, and content production.**
- **Set aside explicit time and budget for testing in the project plan.**
- **Consider a separate contract for testing on larger projects.**
- **Know when to stop testing.**
- **Find tools that help automate routine testing.**
- **Know the behavior of the delivery platforms.**
- **Don't be the only one to test your own code or design.**
- **Have editors, experts, or teachers review the content.**
- **Listen carefully to testers.**
- **Reward the people testing the product.**

Mastering, Duplication, and Distribution

Mastering, Duplication, & Distribution

Once the project team considers a multimedia product finished, it travels a path that places it, or a copy of it, in the hands of a client or customer. Before it gets to this stage, the product must be placed in a form suitable for delivery. For mass-market products, this commonly includes mastering, duplication, and packaging. Along the way, the product may change hands from publisher to distributor to reseller to customer. As a product makes its way along this path, marketing, sales, and distribution strategies can play a big role in its success or failure in the marketplace.

Many multimedia developers sell their product or give exclusive distribution licenses to publishers and affiliated labels. This allows them to concentrate on producing other products instead of managing distribution and support issues.

Emergence of earlier technologies followed a distribution lifecycle: from early adopters to a broader technology-buying base, to the mass market. With multimedia, we are jumping from early adopters (via mail order) directly to the mass-market channels and consumers. This jump pressures the multimedia industry to succeed in a very short time or risk being dismissed as a viable consumer category.

But at this point, the channels have the power to make, break, or simply delay not just a product, but an entire category of products. This can prevent a category from finding its market in a timeframe that allows a reasonable return on investment for its pioneers.

—Joanna (Joey) Tamer, President, SOS Inc., in "CD-ROM Titles Distribution," Digital Media: A Seybold Report, October 12, 1992. Joanna has specialized in distribution strategies for new media developers, publishers, distributors, retailers, and hardware manufacturers since 1990. She is based in Venice, CA.

Marketing, sales, and distribution are often used interchangeably but each has important differences. Marketing builds an awareness of a product, sales handles individual purchases, and distribution delivers products to customers. The path, or channel, from developer to customer represents the distribution strategy. Sales occur at the junctions in the chain, the places where product and payment change hands. The direction and extent of the chain is created, controlled, and influenced by the marketing strategy.

The distribution of multimedia products is constantly changing because of new products, new distribution models, and competition between publishers, distributors, and resellers. Just as products face competition at a feature level, they also face competition at a distribution level. **A product will not sell, no matter how much better it rivals a competitor's, if customers do not know about it, cannot find it, or will not pay the price listed**.

Importance of Distribution

Developers have a tendency to underestimate the value of distribution. They take the view that good products will always succeed. They are seduced by the value they place on a product, not the value that customers place on the product. They also have little understanding of the value of distribution. Water is more valuable in the desert than at the river's edge. That difference is added by the **distribution channel ▶ 18**. More experienced developers and publishers place as much, if not more, emphasis on marketing and distribution than on the creation of the product.

In addition to underestimating the value of distribution, some developers also underestimate the cost of distribution. Many will attach a retail price assuming that the entire revenue goes to themselves, forgetting that

distributors, retailers, and others in the chain each take a substantial margin off the retail price. A developer/publisher may only receive only 40-55% of the retail price of a product. If they sell directly they will receive all of the retail price, but there are costs to this strategy as well. A developer or publisher deciding to handle their own distribution, or in other words, **self-publish**, needs to know as much about distribution, marketing, and sales as they do about interface design, scripting, and QuickTime.

Preparation of Physical Media

Before a product can be handed off to a client or sold to distributors or customers, it must be prepared for release and possibly replicated in volume. The common delivery media for custom projects are diskette, hard drive, or cartridge. The primary delivery media for mass market multimedia products are diskette, videodisc, and CD-ROM.

Custom Preparation and Delivery

A **custom project ▶ 81** often has a narrower scope of preparation and delivery from the mass-market product. The limited or one-time nature of a custom product often simplifies or omits some printing, duplication, and packaging steps. A set of diskettes or a cartridge along with a backup copy plus the documentation materials may be the extent of the delivery for an in-house presentation or trade show kiosk.

Wherever possible, a production company should strive to do the installation on-site and ensure that the project is in running order. Handing over disks along with an invoice and leaving the set up to the client may result in the final payment, but at a cost of future business.

Shows and Conferences

Include one complete backup system plus on-site support and replacement. Have contingencies thought through in case of equipment failure, system problems, or other occurrences.

In the case of a multimedia **presentation** to be shown to an audience, the installation should occur well before the scheduled time in order to resolve any equipment or configuration problems that may arise. Never assume a presentation will work the first time without testing it on the delivery equipment beforehand. Besides equipment failures or incompatibilities, video projection, audio equipment, or room lighting may need adjusting or repositioning to suit the nature of the content or improve the quality of the presentation.

Ongoing Projects (Multimedia Databases or Kiosks)

If existing systems are in use, plan a smooth transition so that work patterns are not disrupted and operations are preserved if there are problems with the new system. Updates and service contracts may be a part of the contract as well. Mechanisms and delivery media for updates will differ according to the project and its complexity. A point of sale kiosk for a store showing products and their uses may need seasonal or yearly updates. Other kiosks may need updates on a monthly or even daily schedule.

When producing **multimedia databases** ▶ 40 or **kiosks** ▶ 36, include the set-up costs in the initial contract if set-up is an issue. A day or two of installation can cut into a project's profit. In the case of a kiosk, the idea is to present a finished and working booth to the client. The presentation of the finished piece should be as professional as possible. Any set-up equipment and materials should be out of sight and the display and keyboard should be clean. The hand-off should include the instructions for operation and support and repair procedures and contacts.

Products for Duplication

Some custom projects such as demos or advertisements may be distributed to a large number of people. The steps for these products are the same as many mass market products and include mastering, duplication, and packaging. Depending on the client, they may or may not need help in the with these steps.

Mass Market Preparation and Delivery

The nature of a mass market product implies the manufacture of multiple copies of the product. Some firms try to handle some of the initial preparation steps. Most, though, use outside firms to handle output and printing, **diskette** duplication, or **CD-ROM** ▶ 109 disc manufacture. Assembling components, shrink-wrapping, and shipping directly to customers are also issues in packaging. The final result is a shrink-wrapped product that is fit for delivery to a distributor and purchase by a customer.

The major steps in the printing, disk duplication, and CD-ROM manufacturing processes include preparation, mastering, duplication, and assembly. Some stages include some form of sign-off between client and developer, or developer and CD-ROM manufacturer. Sign-offs are not just formalities; they are essential to ensure that a product is acceptable in its final form. Months of hard work can be undone by not checking for viruses or by missing errors on one-offs from premastering services. Problems such as these may not ruin a product's chance in the marketplace, however they can still place a serious drain on resources.

Preparation (Step 1)

The **preparation** stage places all product elements and any dependent system components in the appropriate state for initial use. For printing materials, preparation can include making color separation files using digital pre-press software. For electronic products, this includes steps such as placing the files in the right directories and having the windows and icons appear in the appropriate places.

Getting the client to "test" the CD-ROM one off before you go to duplication is critical. It's also a good idea to have the client buy-off on the CD one-off before going to the press—even if you have only made "minor" changes since the last one-off, or since they tested the hard drive master. Paying twice for duplicating 1000 or more CD-ROMs really cuts into your profit margin.

— Trish Mayers, Production Manager, Magnum Design

The steps in CD-ROM manufacturing:

- Image creation
- Premastering (data-formatting)
- Mastering
- Duplication
- Assembly

Don't rush the process of creating a CD-ROM. If you aren't really prepared to write the disc—maybe you didn't get to test one last thing because you were up until 5am debugging something else—then don't. Test that one last thing really well before you write it. Chances are you'll regret it if you don't.

— Trish Mayers, Production Manager, Magnum Design

In CD-ROM preparation, the preparation step includes organizing and optimizing the data and premastering. Premastering takes data stored on tape, hard drive, or other media and adds synchronization, header, and error-correction information to create a software version of the digital image that will eventually be placed on a CD-ROM.

Most developers use a separate hard drive called a **master** or **staging drive** to store the data before premastering. They then ship the drive or a copy of the data on tape, cartridge, or CD-R to a premastering service or directly to the disc manufacturer. (Some applications do premastering but most are expensive and may be too difficult for most developers to use.) The premastering process creates a **one-off disc ▶ 111, 180** which is then tested rigorously. The one-off is the last step before the process moves to mastering and duplication. If there is anything wrong on the one-off disk, it needs to be spotted and corrected (and then premastered again) or else it will appear on the pressed CD-ROM.

CD-ROM Optimization

The speed of a CD-ROM can be sluggish when compared to a hard drive (a hard drive is 10-20 times faster). While the speed is still sufficient for just about anything but uncompressed, full-screen, full-motion color video, all CD-ROM applications should take some steps to optimize CD-ROM performance. Apple's *CD-ROM Handbook* contains a comprehensive listing of steps to take but a few of the important points are listed below.

Organize Files Efficiently

First, if you have many small files, organize them in a way that makes it easy for both the user and the computer to work. Avoid burying important files six or seven folders from the root level of the file system, and conversely, avoid putting 1,000 files into a single folder or at the root level. Also, place the most commonly accessed files at the beginning of the CD-ROM to reduce the seek time. When creating the image on the master drive, do

not copy the files over in one big bunch. Copy the main files first and any files that are critical to your interface or are linked to an introductory movie or animation.

Use Absolute Filenames if Possible

Take full advantage of the static nature of CD-ROM. Consider using absolute filenames in your application if they are to be run only on the disc. An **absolute filename** has the **direct path** to where the file is located and makes no assumptions about where a file is located. (If you do this, you should provide a mechanism to enable users to change the location of your applications and data should they decide to copy them to a hard drive.) One method for doing this is hard-coding only default pathnames and prompting the user if the files the user needs are not found in the default locations. Save the resulting choices to a preferences file on the hard drive.

Precompute Common Tables and Indices

Once you have the master hard drive organized, look for opportunities to precompute and store information to speed up your application. Take advantage of the large space available on a CD-ROM—using extra space here can be less expensive than using CPU cycles during runtime. Building indexes to accelerate searches will take space but can improve performance.

Look for Specific Areas to Improve

The best method for gaining speed on a CD-ROM is to thoroughly test the entire contents on different machine configurations and note the areas that slow down. Make changes and then go back and test it again to make sure you have not missed anything. Different layouts, default memory configurations, and pathnames can produce different results, especially for HyperCard stacks. If possible, test the hard drive as a locked volume on a file server or on a CD-ROM simulator which may be available at your local disc mastering company. These tests will give

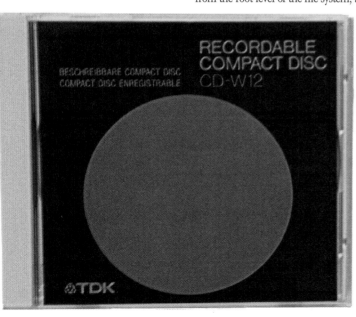

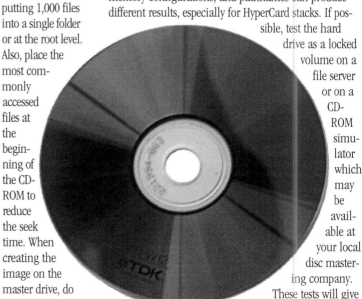

a more accurate reflection of how the final CD-ROM should perform rather than testing on a local hard drive.

Defragment and Zero the Boot Block

Finally, before you master the CD-ROM, optimize the hard drive that you will use for the premastering process. You can either use a third-party defragmentation program (be sure to back up your disk first) or even better, copy the entire contents to a freshly formatted hard drive. This process guarantees that your files are written and will be read contiguously on the disk. Also, rebuild the **desktop resource file** so that the Finder finds files optimally. When you finish this process, unmount the hard drive and use a disk editor to **zero the boot blocks** on the hard drive. This final process speeds the time it takes the CD-ROM to mount and also ensures that it is not mistaken for a boot volume.

CD-ROM Premastering

In CD-ROM creation, a premastering step is required to make a low level conversion of computer data to create a CD-ROM compliant image. The input disk image which holds application programs, data files, index files, filenames, and directories must be expanded to add CD-ROM level addressing and error detection and correction. A 2048 byte sector of user data expands to 2352 bytes by the time this conversion is complete. Some developers make their own premastered files, although it is common to use a service. To premaster a CD-ROM, you will need a formatting program to create and the image file on a hard drive. Some formatters come with CD-ROM simulators. CD-ROM simulators run on a hard drive and can be used to simulate and test the behavior of CD-ROM. Since the hard drive simulates access and transfer times that match real CD-ROM drive rates, full behavior is simulated. These simulators can be used to catch problems such as trying to write to the CD-ROM, a problem that might not be noticed when the image is on a hard drive.

Developers are now able to record their own premastered files with recordable CD systems and send CD-Rs to disc manufacturers. Both 9-track and 8mm tape is also popular. A 2400 foot 9-track tape can only store about 140MB of data, requiring five reels to fill a disc. For the same job, a small 8mm tape can hold 2.5-5GB of data. This avoids reel changes, sequence errors, and reduces overhead by allowing unattended operation. Whether you record your own or use a premastering service depends on how often you make them, whether you have the time, and how many discs you will need during the course of the project.

Mastering (Step 2)

Before mass production begins, a master is a made. A **master** is a copy of the source material in final form to replicate raw delivery media. In the case of diskettes, a master is a diskette that gets loaded into a machine that reads the entire digital image into memory and rapidly writes the data image onto a new disk. Developers often create master diskettes themselves.

In the case of a CD-ROM, a master is created using laser technology and photosensitive material. After inspection, the silvered surface of the master is electroplated with a nickel shell. The nickel copy is called the **father** and can be used for low volume production or to create a family of nickel stampers. For the latter case, electroplating is used to create several **mothers** which in turn are used to create several **sons**. These sons, or negative masters, are used as stampers in mass duplication.

Duplication (Step 3)

Duplication is the process of making multiple copies from a master (or a copy of the master). For a CD-ROM, it is the process of molding replicas from the stamper. The making of the copies may seem like a routine process but it requires sophisticated machinery on the part of the printer, duplicator, or disc manufacturer. Just as computers and similar equipment comprise the physical assets of a multimedia developer, the printing presses, disk duplicators, and CD-ROM molding equipment comprise the physical assets of the printer, duplicator, or manufacturer.

Assembly (Step 4)

For CD-ROM packages, the **assembly** may be as simple as inserting the liner notes and shrink-wrapping the jewel box. In cases of more traditional software-like packaging, many disk duplicators have services that will label the disks, assemble the other components such as inserts, manuals, stickers, boxes, and registration cards, and shrink-wrap the package. Small developers may choose to do these tasks in-house at least initially to save costs, but the costs are usually nominal. Most publishers have them handled by the duplicators or disc manufacturers.

Costs

The costs for printing, duplicating diskettes, and manufacturing CD-ROMs will vary greatly. The costs for making CD-ROMs, especially, are rapidly decreasing. Roughly, the cost for producing a CD-ROM includes a premastering charge of $150-500 and a mastering charge of $800-3000. Duplication charges range between $1.25-2.00 a disc. (Add $.35 for jewel box, inserting liner notes, and shrink-wrapping.) Same day pressing may double the standard rate. Minimum quantities may be as little as 50 in some cases, 200 in others.

How CD-ROM duplication works:

Molten plastic is squeezed into a disc-shaped mold containing the stamper. High pressure forces the hot plastic to fill the mold and flow around every bump in the stamper. The plastic cools rapidly and solidifies, locking in details. The mold opens to release the freshly pressed disc, clamps shut, and does it again. A reflective mirror of aluminum is coated onto the dimpled side of the polycarbonate. A thin coat of tough acrylic lacquer is then added on top of the aluminum. The product label is silk-screened onto the lacquer and the CD-ROM is ready.

Presses can make about 600 discs an hour.

CD-ROM labels are printed using photo-silkscreen as opposed to a magazine which is printed by offset lithography. Photo-silkscreening places limits on elements such as character size and half-tone dot resolution. Make sure the people handling the graphics talk directly to the CD-ROM manufacturer.

A printer, duplicator, or disc manufacturer will need exact specifications in order to give an estimate or make a bid. For a CD-ROM manufacturer, this includes number of colors on the label, jewel box type, liner notes, serialization, premastering, and other services. Ask for a pricing sheet if one is available. For a printer this will include paper size and stock, binding, colors, bleeds, inserts, and other elements.

For printed materials, the cost commonly includes the cost to a service bureau to create negatives or paper positives plus the cost for the printer. (Some high-end copiers can take digital input directly, eliminating the need for negatives.) The cost of the negatives will vary according to the relationship with the service bureau, the number of negatives (or positives), and the number of colors (one piece per color). Output prices can range between $8-20 a page. Prices for printing are impossible to give because of the wide variation in binding, folds, colors, inks, paper stocks, page sizes, and other elements. Have a good idea of what you want or find examples that are similar and ask what they cost to print. Do this early.

CD-ROM Packaging Checklist

Liner notes/Inserts
- *Are there inlay cards or cover booklets?*
- *Are the liner notes to spec and will they allow automatic insertion?*
- *Have they been tested in a jewel box?*
- *Are they packaged separately and clearly marked?*
- *When will they arrive? (1-2 weeks before is common)*

Label Design
- *Do you have the label specs? (color-separated film positives, emulsion side up is common)*
- *How many colors? (2 is standard)*
- *When will the artwork arrive? (3-5 days before is common)*

Serialization
- *Should the discs be serialized?*
- *If so, what are the starting and ending numbers?*
- *Should the cartons be marked?*
- *Do you need a record of where the numbers were sent?*

Jewel Box
- *Should it be provided by the manufacturer?*
- *If not, will it fit the tolerances for automatic insertion of CD-ROMs and liner notes?*

Input Data
- *What type of media will the image arrive on?*
- *9-track or 8mm tape, cartridge, hard drive, CD-R (write-once CD)?*
- *When will it arrive?*

Logistics
- *How should the packages be shipped?*
- *Where should they be shipped?*
- *Ship directly to customers or mailing house?*
- *— compiled from materials and information provided by Disc Manufacturing, Inc., 800/433-DISC*

Choosing a Printer, Diskette Duplicator, or Disc Manufacturer

Working with a printer, duplicator, or disc manufacturer has many of the same nuances as the relationship between multimedia developers and their client. On one side is an expert in the language and lore of a process and on the other is a person or group that needs something done quickly and expertly. The best ingredients for working in these areas are knowledge, clear direction, and a high level of trust. Researching several firms, asking dumb questions, and reiterating expectations and obligations will help prevent misunderstandings and make the process smoother. Many printers, duplicators, and disc manufacturers operate from their trade assumptions when elements are not explicitly called out. Covering every item in detail (and confirming it in writing) is always recommended.

Researching Vendors

Know What You Want
Knowing the specifications for the components in the packaging ahead of time will make a big difference in getting prices, making schedules, and knowing dependencies.

Other Developers
Ask other developers to provide a list of names, costs, and evaluations of vendors they have experience with and recommend.

Suppliers
For printing, service bureaus and paper companies may be able to provide names of reputable printers. Label-makers may be able to provide a list of diskette duplicators. For CD-ROM, premastering companies, special jewel box providers, or others in the chain can be great resources.

Samples/References
Ask for samples of previous work. Ask for a list of clients and references and follow through with inquiries.

Questioning Vendors

Schedule and Lead Time
Most disc manufacturers can turn around discs quickly—some even offer same-day service. For optimal pricing and to plan for contingencies, though, anticipate a 3 week turnaround. If they handle printing the liner notes and designing the disc label, allow

a couple more weeks. Call a month before starting the process to schedule time. Smaller and less complex jobs will need less lead time.

Most printers have busy schedules and need several weeks, if not months, to schedule jobs. Not scheduling print time far in advance can put a big kink in the duplication schedule.

Quantities and Cost

The size of jobs a firm typically handles will directly affect the price. Large-run firms will charge more for small-run jobs while other firms may be better suited for these. A printer, duplicator, or disc manufacturer will need exact specifications in order to give an estimate or make a bid. For a CD-ROM manufacturer, this includes input data format, disc label composition, jewel box type, and liner notes. For a printer this will include paper size and stock, binding, colors, bleeds, inserts, and other elements.

Cost Breakpoints

Ask about quantities that may make a difference in the price. For example, price breakpoints for CD-ROMs may be at 200, 500, 1000, or 10,000 units. For a printer, paper sizes, number of pages, or other elements may give lower costs per unit. On the other hand, beware of being seduced by breakpoints and ordering more than may be wise. The turn-around time for reprinting is often quick, providing that materials are available.

Necessary Materials and Formats

Ask them what materials they need to do their job and when. For CD-ROM production, the disc manufacturer may need the disc label artwork, special disc holders, and liner notes up to two weeks before disc production begins. They may prefer the input data to be on 9-track or 8mm tape, removable cartridge, hard drive, CD-R, or IBM punch cards (just kidding). Service bureaus may need some of the fonts or applications used.

Packaging

Many disk duplicators will label, assemble other components, and shrink-wrap supporting materials to create the finished package. These extra costs are usually far less than performing these steps in-house when comparing time, materials, labor, and warehouse space. (CD-ROM manufacturers label as part of the production process. Most will allow more intricate label designs, insert liner notes, and shrink-wrap **jewel boxes** ▶ 136 for additional but nominal charges.)

Available Options/Costs

Ask for suggestions on lowering the cost, speeding up the process, or increasing the quality and appearance. Ask them what other developers are doing and what is appropriate. Are there demand-printing strategies? Are there environmentally safer options? Learning from an expert is much easier than learning from a book or, worse, learning from mistakes.

Special Handling

Special considerations can increase the price or delay the delivery. This may include placing a serial number on diskettes, CD-ROMs, or manuals, packaging in certain quantities or configurations, or other items out of the ordinary.

Rush Charges

Know about extra charges beforehand so that they can be factored into a decision if a need arises. The charge for same-day CD-ROM pressing may be double the normal charge.

Delivery

Ask about types and cost of delivery. Most will ship in a variety of configurations including overnight service. Because of the weight, shipping thousands of CD-ROMs by overnight air may be expensive so plan ahead.

Fulfillment

Fulfillment commonly means warehousing inventory, filling orders, and shipping directly to distributors and resellers. Some duplicators or manufacturers provide fulfillment services. Others just ship to outside fulfillment services. The prices, shipping rates, and convenience of a fulfillment service may be more efficient than performing these duties in-house.

Provide a printer, duplicator, or CD-ROM manufacturer with a contact person and give lots of contact information so that they can be contacted at any time, anywhere throughout the process.

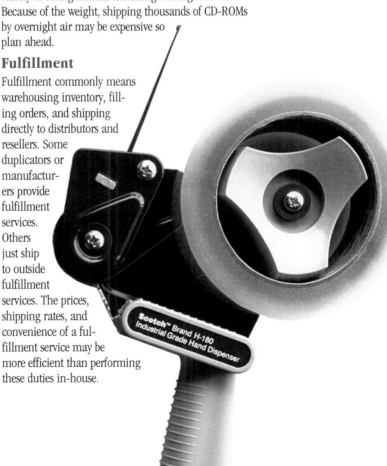

*A **publisher** is the company that is responsible for funding, creating, and selling products. A **distributor** is the person or company that the publisher sells to directly. A **reseller** is a store or company that often buys from distributors and then sells to customers. **Customers** are the end-users of a product, the people the product was designed for and who will own and use it.*

Publishers may buy a product or line of products outright or pay production fees, advances, royalties, or any combination. The amounts and rates vary according to projects, titles, and publishers and finding industry figures can be difficult, especially in a dynamic and varied industry such as multimedia.

Things that interest a publisher about a developer:
- *Previous products*
- *Previous successful products*
- *A product that is about to ship*
- *A product that is shipping*
- *A product that matches their catalog*
- *A product that complements their catalog*
- *A product that can be leveraged into more products*

Distribution Options

Ideally, developers and production houses should know how they plan to distribute a product before production, or even design, begins. Relationships with publishers or affiliated labels or marketing plans for self-publishing should be in the works early so that everyone involved has the same expectations. The resources needed and dependencies involved in a competent distribution strategy are often underestimated. Any person or firm creating a product with intentions to eventually sell it to customers needs to seriously consider the distribution options before proceeding down the development path.

The wrong distribution strategy can limit the success of a product in the marketplace or, on the other hand, compromise the vision of the product.

The three primary options for a multimedia product are publishers, affiliated labels, and self-publishing.

Publishers

A **publisher** ▶ 12, 60, 72 is any company that is responsible for producing a finished work and placing it in the hands of distributors and customers. Publishers coordinate printing, duplication, and packaging as well as marketing, distribution, and support. Any company that puts out a CD-ROM title, book, magazine, audio CD, newspaper, or movie under their own name is commonly viewed as the publisher. A list of publishers can be generated by looking through CD-ROM, multimedia, and software catalogs and magazines and attending trade shows.

Publishers generally look for finished or well-developed materials that appeal to their existing audience or to audiences they see as valuable. Some publishers will accept and fund well-formed proposals. Others may develop the proposals themselves and solicit them to production houses. The type of publisher may vary with each multimedia project. For example, Electronic Arts is known for publishing interactive games, WINGS For Learning markets educational software, and The Voyager Company publishes film videodiscs, interactive music titles, and electronic books. Some concentrate on a single market while others have broader catalogs.

The specifics of the contract and the quality of the relationship between a publisher and developer will determine the ownership of the product and the amount of influence a publisher will exercise in the creative aspect of a project. Conflicts can arise between a publisher and the developer over different visions of a product and its market.

Approaching a publisher at the right time is an important consideration. Any concept, prototype, or product should be well-developed and its presentation rehearsed before presenting it to a publisher. Expecting the publisher to assist in helping refine a product is not unreasonable, but a developer needs to provide as much structure ahead of time as possible. A developer also needs to think through many of the issues in this type of relationship before any serious talks occur. The nature of a publisher/developer relationship may not be for everybody.

Affiliated Label Programs

An **affiliated label program** is a distribution option that fits between signing a product over to a publisher and deciding to self-publish. An affiliated label program is an arrangement with an established publisher to exclusively market and distribute another publisher's products. A few publishers that have affiliated label programs include Brøderbund, Electronic Arts, Sony, and Compton's NewMedia. This relationship with affiliates may or may not be limited by a period of time.

In this type of arrangement, the affiliate typically creates, replicates, and packages a product. The main publisher carries it in their channels as if they had published it. An affiliated label is a hybrid approach between publishing and self-publishing with obligations and responsibilities ranging between the two spectrums.

Entering an affiliated label program may fit small companies that do not have the resources to develop their own distribution channels but want to retain more control of their product. Some developers become affiliates and then leave the programs after a few years to manage their own distribution. Others leave and move to other publishers' programs. Maxis Software, publisher of *Sim City* and other simulations, recently left Brøderbund's affiliated label program in March 1993 to set up its own distribution channels. The relationship began in 1989. At the time of this announcement, Brøderbund also announced that it had acquired exclusive one-year North American distribution rights from three publisher's, one of which had recently left the affiliated label program of another publisher.

Self-Publishing

Self-publishing ▶ 72 is a term commonly used to describe a developer or production house that handles its own distribution. One advantage of this avenue is that complete control of the entire product, from concept to sales, lies in the hands of the originator. A disadvantage is that complete control of the entire product, from concept to sales, lies in the hands of the originator. It is a choice that carries with it as many risks and responsibilities as it does rewards. Besides developing the product, the responsibilities include finding funds to manufacture and market the product, as well as managing marketing, distribution, sales, and support. Other responsibilities include handling foreign distribution, customer orders and inquiries, and inventory.

In a mature market, marketing and distribution costs often meet or exceed the total development costs of a product. In the software industry, support costs are often also as large. Emerging markets may not have such large marketing, distribution, and support costs, but they may still be substantial.

Researching Publishers

Before a developer talks to a publisher, they should do some research so they know beforehand if the publisher is an appropriate one to be talking to. Some publishers may not be right either because of incompatible product lines, markets, or corporate cultures. Knowing the right questions to ask will also help move things forward and result in a smoother agreement, if one is to be made.

Publisher Affiliates, Products, and Sales

This information will give a good indication of the resources and capabilities of a publisher. They can help a developer know if their product will fit into the publisher's market, and if the publisher is marketing to the audiences the developer has targeted. A company with excellent general consumer channels may not be appropriate for an interactive educational title.

Industry Royalty Rates, Advances, and Production Fees

Knowing what is possible provides a central point to start from in negotiations. Variables such as the publisher, project type, and reputation of the developer can have a big influence on the particulars in an agreement. Friends that have similar products may provide some information.

Duplication and Packaging Charges

By knowing the cost of goods, the final retail price and working backwards, a developer can put the production fee, advance, and royalty rate into better perspective. (The information may likely show that the publisher's margin is not as large as originally thought.)

Distribution Channels

The right **distribution channels** ▶ 18 are not always obvious—especially in a varied industry such as multimedia. When personal computers first came out, there were no established channels. The earliest computers were sold person-to-person at hobby clubs and trade shows. Computer stores did not exist and had to develop. Since then, there have been a number of twists and turns in how computers and software are sold, moving from small computer shops to large chains and, finally, to mail-order catalogs and superstores. Video-cassettes went through a similar transformation. On the other hand, audio CDs use the same outlets as the preceding technology, LPs. CDs have simply replaced records in the store bins. The point is, the channel of distribution that may be the best for a new product may or may not already exist. Some channels may have to be invented right along with the product itself. With multimedia, the issue is amplified. Multimedia is not just one product, it is many products and in many different forms. This reality makes the distribution channels one of the more undefined elements in multimedia.

Goals

The goal of distribution is not only to generate high revenues, but to build future business with satisfied customers, distributors, and resellers. This can only be done by being perceptive of the needs of everyone in the channel and not just the end-user. The responsibility for promoting and selling a product lies in the hands of the publisher and not the distributor, as some developers have a tendency to believe. One of the items distributors often want to know is how the developer or publisher plans to promote the product. Distributors and retailers will only sell what people want and will not "push" a product that has no record of sales or success.

Several publishers have affiliated label programs that provide exclusive distribution channels for multimedia products developed by other publishers. The affiliates typically retain full ownership to the product but give exclusive marketing rights to the main publisher. Agreements can be for one or two years, indefinitely, or any other time-period agreeable to both parties.

Potential advantages offered by affiliated labels:

- *Handling of orders and receivables*
- *Extensive direct mail and catalog options*
- *Distribution into education and government*
- *Distribution world-wide*
- *Representation for bundling arrangements*
- *Assistance in determining program content, pricing, and packaging*
- *Assistance in promotion at trade shows and exhibitions*

Distribution decisions when self-publishing:

- *What price?*
- *What quantity?*
- *What channels? Direct mail? Mail-order?*
- *What distributors and what type of discount?*
- *What type of packaging?*
- *Where to print and replicate?*
- *Where to advertise and how often?*
- *What to say in press releases and where to send?*
- *How to handle support?*

Case Study: Greg LeMond's Bicycle Adventure

eden
interactive

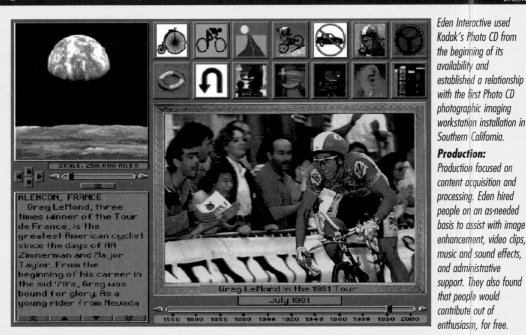

Eden Interactive used Kodak's Photo CD from the beginning of its availability and established a relationship with the first Photo CD photographic imaging workstation installation in Southern California.

Production:
Production focused on content acquisition and processing. Eden hired people on an as-needed basis to assist with image enhancement, video clips, music and sound effects, and administrative support. They also found that people would contribute out of enthusiasm, for free.

Description:
Greg LeMond's Bicycle Adventure is an interactive multimedia computer voyage through the world of bicycling. The product covers different topics about cycling including history, racing, mountain biking, environmental impact, people, and equipment. It includes more than 200 still images, 13 video clips, music, and sounds.

Project Type:
Interactive Book

Development Hardware:
Macintosh Quadra 950, 486/66s, Photo CD, Radius VideoVision display board, scanner

Delivery Hardware:
IBM 286 or compatibles and above and Macintosh Plus computers and above

Software Used:
Knowledge Adventure's Interactive Book Engine; Adobe PhotoShop, Adobe Premiere, and Adobe Type Manager; Aldus PhotoStyler, Equilibrium's deBabelizer; Caere OmniPage Pro.

Team Members and Roles:
Minoo Saboori and Matthew London, primary developers; Tom Fiene, imaging, video clips, and sound processing.

Funding:
Complete bootstrap: personal savings and credit cards, loans.

Price:
$79.99

Contacts:
Minoo Saboori and Matthew London
Eden Interactive
San Francisco, CA

Concept and Planning:
Operating as a bootstrap team, Saboori and London searched for an authoring tool that would enable them to begin development of their ideas quickly and reach the widest possible audience. They chose the interactive book toolkit by Knowledge Adventure chiefly because of its proprietary compression technology, appealing interface, and playback capability on 286-based machines, which promised the widest audience base. "We believe that multimedia does not have to equal CD-ROM," says Saboori.

Eden Interactive invested in high-end development tools, often at the expense of operations and personal pursuits.

Design and Prototype:
The Knowledge Adventure toolkit provided a shell that allowed the Eden team to focus on content acquisition and preparation. Eden obtained permission and won support from world-class bicycle racer Greg LeMond to use his name in affiliation with their piece on the world of bicycling.

Testing:
Testing was ongoing and occurred with production.

Mastering and Duplication:
Eden works with a premiere turnkey manufacturing and fulfillment firm who maintains inventory, processes orders, and ships product.

Distribution:
Eden chose to target the existing installed base of PC and Macintosh owners as well as CD-ROM owners. The product is distributed on diskettes and occupies 8MB of disk space. A CD-ROM version is also available. The product is marketed through press reviews, trade shows, word of mouth, and some advertising and can be found in both traditional and new outlets.

Programming: 100% Off-the-shelf tools

Content: 50% Repurposed / 50% New

Expenses: Marketing Expenses not. avail. / Operations Expenses not avail.

Development Expenses: 20% Personnel / 80% Equipment / (Content not avail.)

Total Development Costs: approx. $120,000

Total Development Team: 5 people

Money / Personnel

Concept/Planning / Design/Prototype / Production & Testing / Duplication/Mastering / Delivery

Total Development Time: 9 months

Tradeoffs

Typically, the lower the price of a product the greater the number of channels. A turnkey multimedia authoring system may require a **direct sales force** ▶ 45 because of the higher level of commitment involved in a purchase. A shrink-wrapped multimedia title may use mail-order catalogs and distributors for initial sales as well as direct mail for upgrades and new products. One of the difficulties when using multiple channels is trying to keep all the channels satisfied. Selling directly at a price less than what resellers offer may cause resellers to stop carrying the product. Balancing multiple channels effectively takes experience and skill.

Channels

Channels can be distributors, mail-order catalogs, direct mail strategies, small and large retail dealers, super-stores, bundling arrangements, and special sales. Education and government are also special types of channels. These categories, though, are not so orderly in the real world. The lines between and among channels, publishers, and even hardware manufacturers are rapidly shifting. Most people in the industry will agree this situation produces both confusion as well as opportunity.

Mail-Order Catalogs

Mail-Order catalogs provide a channel by which customers can order and receive products through the mail. Many exist outside of computer-related domains, such as business executive catalogs containing books, software, and multimedia products for executives. Even some hardware manufacturers have catalogs. For example, Dell Computer, one of the largest mail-order PC computer manufacturers, has an extensive catalog featuring many popular third-party software applications and peripherals.

Mail order is effective in reaching customers who already are familiar with a market and its technology. Many small businesses and home users order through mail-order catalogs because of the low-cost and quick delivery. (Many catalogs offer inexpensive overnight delivery.)

Many publishers deal directly with catalogs. Because of their high volume, many mail-order catalogs are able to get steep discounts from publishers and in turn pass those on to customers. Selling through mail order can be an attractive option because of the high volume and high visibility. People that have a sudden need to buy a product often go to the catalogs to make the purchase. If a product is not in the catalog then they may either postpone the purchase or buy a product that is similar. A disadvantage is that large discounts can cut into profit margins and cause problems with distributors and resellers with smaller discounts.

Distributors

Distributors ▶ 11, 62 like Ingram Micro coordinate the distribution and sale of a product to retail stores and other resellers. Established distributors can offer extensive experience with retail issues and established relationships with many outlets. Most distributors carry a large number of products. Ingram Micro handles more than 13,000 items from more than 650 vendors (300 of which have a Macintosh product). They receive more than 100 new products a month.

The elements that interest a distributor about a product are not all technical. Distributors are looking for products that will sell, not necessarily ones that just look great. They are also looking for products that have proven track records.

To know the book industry's distribution model is not to understand the models of software, consumer electronics, audio, or video. To be a major player in the audio mass market does not prepare you for the attitudes of the computer industry about its "intellectual property."

To be an author without knowledge of retail channels is to be powerless to negotiate a publishing deal that supports your future efforts and livelihood. These conflicts of style and culture across industries are not minor and can have a serious impact on the way deals are struck, margins are won or lost, and success in any particular channel is achieved.

The planning of our course—as author, publisher, and distributor—must be informed by extensive knowledge of all targeted channels (software, consumer electronics, audio, video, and books) and the current hard realities of mass market retailing.

— Joanna Tamer, SOS Inc., "CD-ROM Titles Distribution," Digital Media: A Seybold Report, *October 12, 1992.*

It is important not to view the distributor as the final sale. Developers with this view tend to expect the distributor to generate channel and user demand; they structure their businesses without focusing on creating the necessary pull and product exposure needed to generate demand. This is a mistake, given what the distributor's role is. The key is to remember that the final sale is a transaction between the reseller and the user, and the developer must play a role at every level.

— Barry Evleth and Jeff Davis, Ingram Micro, "Understanding Distribution Realities," Apple Direct, *October 1992*

Items of Interest to a Distributor

Current Track Record
- *Existing market demand for a product*
- *Penetration in two or more reseller channels*
- *Ongoing relationships with dealers and resellers in more than one geographic region*
- *Proven end-user acceptance of the product*

Business Considerations
- *Market size, perceived value*
- *Current marketing budget*
- *Marketing fit with distributor*
- *Industry positioning and reputation*

- *Support required*
- *Price vs. Competition*
- *Gross margin and estimated monthly volume*

Technical Considerations
- *Features and benefits*
- *Ease of set-up, understanding, and use*
- *Competitive products*
- *Customer appeal*
- *Packaging quality*
- *Documentation*
- *Overall performance*

Retailers

Retailers include small retail stores, large chains, and superstores. **Small retailers** base many decisions and requests for products on individual reactions. They usually deal with distributors and have no formal means for communicating directly with developers. Customers often do business at small stores where they have built up a personal relationship. Working closely with a few small stores in an area can be a help for small publishers with new products because the direct feedback from customers and store owners can be put to use analyzing the product, its market, and effectiveness. Feedback only from distributors and large chains can be incomplete about customer reactions. (Is it the price? Is it the packaging? Is the product too complicated?)

Large chains offer the power of mass exposure to a product and the affiliation with the store name. Large chains may have well-trained and knowledgeable sales forces. Working closely with these stores can help refine a marketing and pricing strategy. (Some stores may have computerized inventory and tracking systems allowing them to measure demand elasticity with minor changes in price.) Success in large regional chains can also provide the track record that distributors often look for before carrying a product.

In the last several years, **superstores** such as CompUSA have emerged as a powerful channel. The characteristics of these warehouse-like stores include low prices and less service. Customers are typically on their own as much as they are when purchasing through mail-order.

Education and Government Markets

Educational ▶ 45 and government channels typically need a direct sales force knowledgeable in the habits and regulations of governmental and institutional purchases. Many states have strict content and purchasing guidelines for K-12 materials. Ignorance of these can disqualify a publisher from further consideration. Sales cycles are also usually longer as well as support requirements. Some school systems may require that a product remain available at a guaranteed price for several years.

Selling to the **government** can be equally as challenging and distinct as the educational market. Products may have to support officially-sanctioned file formats. Products may also have to run on a variety of nonstandard platforms. Guaranteed availability, price, and support may also be an issue.

Content-Specific Channels

Content-specific stores include any outlet that sells products related in content. Content-specific outlets can include book, music, video, and toy stores. For example, some bookstores are now carrying titles from Voyager's Expanded Book Series. Music and audio stores are possible avenues for interactive music and film related titles, and toy stores are great outlets for interactive games. Challenges when using these channels include identifying the appropriate platforms and configurations and then

Distributing through mail-order catalogs may not always be what it seems. The pictures in the catalogs and their order and prominence are often paid for by the product manufacturers as advertising fees.

We concentrate on the things we do and know well, which are content creation and tools. We would rather leave the things we don't know that much about, such as manufacturing, to companies that do.

As for selecting distribution channels, we realized that there is a glut of products in the software channel. We are a content-driven company. There are people who are interested in bikes who shop at computer stores, but there are also computer owners who shop at bike shops. We decided to go after the content-specific user to break ground in those channels. We wanted to forge our own channels such as bike retailers, direct mail, and mailing lists for bicycle-related events.

— Minoo Saboori, Eden Interactive

Tried-and-True Ways to Turn Off a Distributor

Submit a me-too product before you've generated sufficient market demand

Unless your product is on the cutting edge, the distributor is looking for an established sales record and existing relationships with customers. Without demand, it is difficult for the distributor to move a product off of its shelves, which does no one any good.

Send a brown-bagged product

Sending a product before its packaging is complete is an unmistakable sign that the product isn't already on the market. Also, the distributor is looking at your product's market appeal as a whole, not just its technical merits—and that includes how effective the packaging is.

Focus on how big the distributors opening order will be.

From the distributor's viewpoint, developers that dwell on how big the opening order will be betray their misunderstanding of what a distributor's role is. A better topic for discussion is what the product's long-term success will be. The distributor's job is to ascertain what level of stock will be required to fill its customers needs; its buyers are expected to have the right amount of stock needed to fill the demand, and will work with the developer to create the proper flow of product.

—Barry Evleth and Jeff Davis, Ingram Micro, "Understanding Distribution Realities," Apple Direct, October 1992

clearly labeling those supported on the packaging. Ease of installation and ease of use issues for a product are also more critical the farther the product is removed from traditional computer outlets.

Direct Mail

Direct mail is a promotional method of contacting potential customers through the mail, special delivery, or online services. Tools of direct mail are catalogs, brochures, letters, postcards, coupons, or special announcements. An emerging tool is the **unlockable CD-ROM** that contains products that can be purchased over the phone and enabled with a special license number.

One big advantage with direct mail is that it allows experimentation with different market segments at a relatively low cost (compared, for example, to magazine advertising). Direct mail addresses potential customers through more personal communications channels. This enables a company to tailor its approach to specific market segments and use the response, or lack of response, to focus on the more promising markets. The literature should be professionally prepared and the steps for the recipient should be apparent. The costs of direct mail are the costs of material design, printing, and postage as well as the cost of labor and mailing lists.

Mailing lists can be purchased from marketing services, magazines, user groups, and other publishers. (Publishers and catalogers in other industries often sell or trade lists among themselves.) Costs vary with the number of names and the accuracy and depth of the list. Many mailing lists are copyrighted and unauthorized use can result in penalties or legal action.

Bundling

Bundling is an arrangement to have a product included with the purchase of another product. This can provide an important image-boost if the bundler is a reputable company. These relationships are usually limited in duration. They can be between hardware manufacturers and publishers or publishers with complimentary products.

Special Sales

Special sales can be an effective way of moving large amounts of inventory to a specific channel or end-user. For example, large sales to a corporate customer for in-house training or corporate gifts justify as special sales. Another example might be a magazine that offers a bonus for subscribing. Although, it is common for consumer magazines to offer audio CDs, books, and other gifts, multimedia or computer magazines may offer diskette or CD-ROM products as subscription bonuses. The discounts on special sales are often large because of the volume and/or exposure.

Marketing

Marketing at the delivery end involves establishing, promoting, and maintaining an identity for a product so it can be sold more effectively. Marketing must find the right customers, get information to them, and work with distributors, resellers and sales forces to put the product in their hands. Marketing for custom or mass market multimedia audiences differs in scope but the objective is the same—to motivate the audience to want a product.

Custom marketing is an extension of **customer service**. It includes promotional activities that smooth the process of delivery and installation. Since the sale has already been made by way of a contract beforehand, the role of marketing in this case is to enhance the image of the production company's work and services. A constant flow of information to the client on progress of the project is one element. Another element is to slightly exceed expectations either by delivering a project early or producing more than contracted. The goal is to leave a lasting impression of quality, professionalism, and excellence. This will help generate future business with the client and with anyone who sees the client's project and takes the time to inquire who did the work.

Mass marketing is the act of creating a large-scale public identity for your product and company. The purpose of marketing is to set the stage for sales. Mass marketing is part science and part art. It demands an ability to effectively analyze factors such as promotion, pricing, and timing and their relationship to sales. It also draws on intuition and inspiration in decisions that will bring a strategic selling advantage. The components that help marketing people communicate about a product include public relations, promotion, and advertising.

Public Relations

Public relations ▶ 11 is an extremely effective way of getting information to the public about a company and its products. Examples of active public relations are **press releases**, **press kits**, and participation in industry-specific events such as **trade shows**. They can also include creative approaches such as donating samples of a children's interactive educational title to grade schools. Publishing an article in a journal about new multimedia tools and content products for learning anatomy is another example. A more passive form of public relations is the perception people get from talking to employees and contractors. People working for a company should know about relevant issues before the general public does. If employees are finding out about internal events from outside sources, it can be an indication of a poorly run company.

This section covers only a few of the tools of the marketing role. The resources section contains a list of good books for understanding the more formidable questions about marketing.

*The **Software Publishers Association** publishes a guide on software channel marketing and distribution strategy entitled the U.S. Software Channel Marketing and Distribution Guide. The guide provides advice on product differentiation and positioning in the channel, dozens of cost-saving tips for motivating resellers, boilerplate contracts and checklists for negotiating them, and detailed company case studies of what works and what doesn't. The cost is $199 for SPA members, $299 for non-members. Call the SPA at 202/452-1600 ext. 336 for more information.*

Press Release

A **press release** ▶ 136 is as formal announcement about a company or product that is sent to press contacts to include in their publications. An announcement about a company might be a management change, a financial report, or any other business activity worth mentioning. An announcement about a product might lists its benefits, features, availability, and cost.

All press releases should have a **title**, a news byline giving a one to two sentence **summary** of the release, **contact information** for further information, a body describing the information, and summaries about the companies involved. The press release should look professional and credible, and by all means, be legible and understandable. It is a tool for sharing information, not listing every feature. Do not overwrite or over-hype the product. Editors prefer text they can use without any editing or rewording. Also, use high quality printing and leave plenty of space between the text lines in the press release to make it easier to read.

Do not send a disabled or beta version to the press. Any materials they receive should be professionally prepared. If a product is included, they should have full use of its capabilities.

Consider including a few slides or pictures of the product and its screenshots as well as the packaging. High quality magazines will want color slides or transparencies while newspapers and other magazines or journals may use black-and-white photos. Savvy magazines may request screenshots or artwork in digital form. Also consider including a demonstration disk or copy of the product (provided the recipients have access to the necessary equipment). A **demo disk** should reflect well on the product. If it is too limiting or in any way frustrating to use, leave it out. These additions to a press release comprise a **press kit**.

Although press releases can be sent out en masse to publications, it is always a plus to build personal relationships with press contacts to increase the chances of publication. (Knowing people in the press can also be a valuable source of feedback about a product or industry.) Keep press releases and press kits on hand for distribution at seminars, trade shows, user meetings, and other forums where information may be requested. They should be updated frequently to reflect changes in the product and the shifts in potential markets.

The disadvantages of a press release is the lack of control over the probability and timeliness of appearance. Each time a press release crosses the desk of a person in the press, it is a solid bet that there are at least 10-20 others there as well. Another risk is that a disk included in a press kit may not run or may run poorly on an editor's machine. It can be harder to undo a wrong impression than it is to generate a good one.

Promotion

Promotions are techniques used to induce sales of a product at or near the point of purchase. Examples include handing out free samples and demo disks, giving retailers materials to help them make a sale, and offering spiffs, payments, or rewards given by the publisher to internal or external sales people who sell the product. The use of promotions can stimulate product sales, but their use should be thought through carefully. How they are used can reflect well or poorly on the company and affect the long term perceptions of a product and company. In addition, promotions should enhance advertising and other efforts to sell the product.

N S   R E L E A S E

ts: Jessica Switzer, Public Relations Manager, (415) 382-4568
Kathleen Burke, Public Relations Coordinator, (415) 382-4567

Brøderbund

IMMEDIATE RELEASE:

Arthur the Talking Aardvark Debuts on the Mac

NOVATO, CA (October 28, 1992) — Brøderbund Software, Inc. (NASDAQ:BROD) today released Arthur's Teacher Trouble™, an interactive, animated book on CD-ROM (compact disc, read-only-memory). The newest release in Brøderbund's Living Books® series, Arthur's Teacher Trouble is based on the best-seller by Marc Brown and is intended for children ages 6-10.

"We recognize that the home consumer needs a compelling reason to buy a CD-ROM drive. Now we've given them one more reason," explains John Baker, Brøderbund's vice president of product development for educational and entertainment products. Just Grandma and Me, the first Living Book released for

Case Study: *HyperBole* Magazine

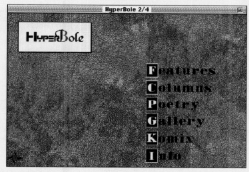

Concept and Planning:
The magazine was Art Director Greg Roach's idea to explore the potential of digital media in the arts. Roach continues to pioneer the interactive novel format in order to "remove the blinders from traditional ways of reading novels and stories," says staff member Halle Eavelyn. "The way we do stories is that we don't say 'That's never been done before. We can't do it.' We say instead, 'That's never been done before. How can we do it?'"

Planning for an issue begins right after an issue is released. The team determines content within a week and assigns tasks. Most of the content is created by staff members although outside contributions are considered. Each person works alone to complete the assigned tasks within six weeks or so.

Design and Prototype:
The design of the magazine is constantly evolving with each issue. There is a basic template but new sections are added in response to audience requests. Comics, stories, poetry, and artwork are presented

in a hyperlinked labyrinth of creativity. Some of the stories and ideas that begin in the magazine evolve into other projects. For example, the novel The Madness of Roland began as a series of magazine installations. Another item that was featured in a magazine issue grew into an award-winning QuickTime movie. The staff members see the magazine as a good forum for storyboarding and prototyping ideas that will evolve into other forms.

Production:
Each person completes tasks as assigned. Sometimes new content is accepted but made "interactive." Despite self-extracting archive, space is always a concern. Material must be limited to what can fit on three diskettes. Sound is always the first to be deleted for the sake of space, then animation or graphics.

Testing:
Readers provide ongoing suggestions and comments. The HyperBole staff also constantly asks people, "What do you think of the magazine? What can we do better?"

Mastering/Duplication:
All duplication of diskettes is done by HyperBole staff members and is not sent out. HyperBole once hired a distribution subscription service but was dissatisfied with their subscription handling service. By assuming responsibility for duplication, distribution, and customer contact, *HyperBole* has increased its subscription renewal rate.

Distribution:
Hyperbole magazine is not marketed directly. Publicity is gained through written press reviews and trade show exhibits. Currently the magazine is distributed with another HyperBole product, the interactive novel The Madness of Roland.

Description:
HyperBole is an electronic magazine that is dedicated to publishing original works of interactive fiction, art, and literature to explore the potential of the digital domain. The magazine is distributed quarterly on diskettes in both black and white and color versions.

Project Type:
Interactive Magazine

Development Hardware:
Macintosh LC and Quadra, Wacom Digitizing Tablet, scanner

Delivery Hardware:
Black and white and color versions are available for different Macintosh models. Will add PC based versions in 1993

Software Used:
HyperCard, Adobe PhotoShop, Painter, MacroMind Director, soon to convert to Authorware Pro

Team Members and Roles:
Greg Roach, Artistic Director (also winner of QuickTime Film Festival, 1992 and 1993); Halle Eavelyn, Director of Marketing and Evangelism; Paul Hiaumet, Fiction Editor; George Jacobs, Staff Writer; Mark Arend, Software Engineer

Funding:
Labor of love, subscriptions, reassignment of other HyperBole Studios production funds

Price:
$60/year black-and-white
$75/year color

Contact:
HyperBole Studios
Houston, TX

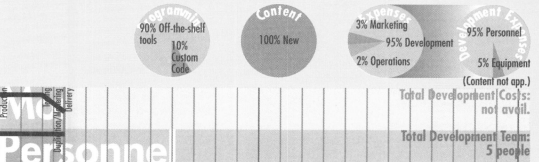

Total Development Time: 1-3 months per issue

The reason to advertise in computer magazines as opposed to general interest magazines is to reach computer buyers. People read computer magazines in order to make buying decisions—they don't read Business Week or Fortune or Forbes to make buying decisions. Computer magazines are one of the most important resources buyers have; it provides them with comprehensive product reviews, details of technology trends, and product availability. In order to maximize every ad dollar spent, it's best to go where the buyers go.

The purpose of advertising is manifold—branding, marketshare, mindshare, and sales. A common misconception inexperienced developers have is that they don't need to advertise. They think they have a better mousetrap and often they do. But they expect everyone to know about it, which isn't always the case. Another misconception is that they believe running a full-page ad once is going to get them immediate sales. They blow their whole budget and when the floodgates don't open, they give up and think that advertising doesn't work. Advertising is a long process and to really get results, it's best done very consistently.

— Jackie Caldwell, Advertising Sales

Three principal types of promotions are consumer offers, trade deals, and sales force incentives. All of these typically have a limited duration of time.

Consumer offers are enticements such as free samples, demo disks, or coupons. Some multimedia companies may offer a coupon for purchase of a similar or related product or a discount on the cost of a training class. The option may be bound to the return of a registration card to retain the name for future mailings.

Trade deals take place between the manufacturer and a distributor or retailer. A manufacturer may offer a special deal such as a free unit for every ten units that are sold. Or they may offer retailers a free display unit if they purchase more then a certain number of units at a time. The numbers and sophistication will vary depending on the product and the channel.

Sales force promotions are typically between the manufacturer and a sales force. It could be their own sales force or distributor sales forces. The manufacturer may offer a prize for top-sellers in the form of a free weekend vacation or a television or video camera. These promotions can be effective but also very expensive.

Advertising

Advertising is a means of promotion through purchasing magazine ad space or radio or television air time. Advertising rates vary with size, placement, and duration of the ad and the status of the advertising vehicle. One advantage of paid advertising is that it

---

Editors: Five Ways to Turn Them On or Off

Five Ways to Turn Them Off:

1. Use bait & switch tactics

The envelope says one thing and the contents are something else entirely.

2. Don't edit the press release

Spelling errors, grammatical errors, and typographical errors in a press release are terrible. It's especially bad if your product is a spell checker and you have bad spelling, a grammar checker and you have poor grammar, or a typeface and you don't use smart quotes. Believe it or not, I see these a couple of times a week.

3. Photocopy press releases

Do not send an editor a photocopied press release. Editors have to read so much stuff that if a press release isn't easy to read, their job becomes more difficult. Editors are very aware of what is laser-printed quality or better. Also, if you have to photocopy the press release, editors assume that the product itself is not quite ready for the professional world.

4. Leave poor phone messages

If you're a public relations firm, state your name, firm, client, and your client's product. Leave a phone number. Leave it twice in fact, and speak it slowly. If the product's new, leave a short description. Your message is often forwarded based on this information. Shorter messages work better than longer ones and don't leave multiple messages in one day unless you've already received some response back.

5. Have a pretentious attitude

Never make fun of your competitor's products. If someone asks you to compare your product to a competitor's product, don't assume they like the other product better. More likely they just understand the other product better and want a clear idea of how your product differs. It helps to explain your product by comparing it and contrasting it to something the editor already knows.

Five Ways to Turn Them On:

1. Know your product

Don't bother to represent or promote anything you don't understand. Editors develop a sixth sense about whether or not they're talking to someone who can actually give them the information they need. If they ask you a question which you can't answer, call them back later with the correct information or a technical person they can contact directly.

2. Be flexible

Each editor has a different working situation and set of needs. Offer as many different ways to get your information across as possible. There are many kinds of meetings, demos, telephone conference calls, and visits. Offer evaluation copies of the product, photographs and slides, sample documents, technical specifications, promotional materials, copies of articles, and charts of any kind. If an editor needs multiple copies of a product, it's often for a good reason. An editor naturally writes more about a product they use than one they have simply examined, seen, or read about.

3. Leave lots of contact info

If an editor cares enough about what they read to want to contact you, make this as easy as possible. Include your name and telephone number, an assistant or someone else they can call if you aren't there, a fax number, a business card, and every e-mail address you have on as many networks as you can.

4. Show consideration for an editor's time

Editors can handle x number of pieces of mail, x number of pieces of e-mail, x number of faxes, x number of Federal Express packages, x number of phone calls, and x number of demos or meetings in a day. At this time, I can personally handle with some level of attention: mail=20, e-mail=30, faxes=3, Fed Ex=5, and demos=2 per day. It doesn't work when a caller gets me on the phone to say "I sent you a press release which you should have received by now and I wanted to see if you had any questions." If you need to do this, send a fax instead.

5. Send information at the right time

Don't expect editors to publish a review of a product when its still in production. They may mention future versions and list new elements but usually only for products with good track records from established companies.

— Rick Reynolds, Technology Director, Publish Magazine

guarantees placement in the medium of choice at a known time. This can be useful for strategically timing special announcements about the product. Some disadvantages include the risk of ineffective ad placement at a high one-time cost and an exposure that is limited to the audience of the medium.

Different magazines provide access to different audiences. Initially, many multimedia products are likely to be advertised in computer magazines. As multimedia titles and technology gain acceptance in the general consumer market, advertisements will likely appear in content-specific magazines instead of just multimedia or computer specific ones.

Advertising is a powerful and informative medium for communicating a message to consumers but its costs can mount rapidly. Added to this is that its effect may not be noticeable at first. Advertisements often need time and repetition to have any effect. They also need reinforcements from press articles, reviews, and personal references.

Sales

A company's success in selling is a major factor in its success as a company. **Selling** ▶ 18, 83, 85 is the signing of an agreement, the preparation before, and the results afterward. It can be likened to the speakers of a stereo system. No matter how sophisticated the sound system is, cheap speakers produce cheap sound and no speakers produce no sound.

Developers often underestimate the difficulty of selling. They compare the creation of a product to climbing a mountain. The summit or apex of the mountain represents the completion of the product. The route up the side may be influenced by weather conditions and other elements, but the success or failure of the climb is directly attributable to the mountain climbers tools, skill, and perseverance. Sales people and marketing people rarely see their job as climbing a mountain. First, sales and marketing never ends (unless the product gets pulled off the market). Individual sales may have a finite duration, but a sales person's job is re-born every quarter when their quota is set back to zero. A second difference is that outside influences (namely a client or customer) play much more of a role in the success or failure of a sales person's job. Too much perseverance in pursuit of a sale or

too much information too soon can intimidate and turn a customer away.

Selling Goals and Strategies

The selling process moves through several stages with the success or failure of the process commonly represented by obtaining a purchase order or check. It is a cyclical process of bringing clients into sales situations, closing deals, getting repeat business, and receiving referrals. It consists of goals, strategies, meetings, milestones, presentations, and purchase orders.

Everybody in a project is involved, to some extent, in sales. If you want to find out the problems in a product, you usually just have to ask the development team. They will often spend one minute talking about the good things in the product and 20 minutes talking about the bad things.

A **goal** could be a contract for building a multimedia database or the sale to a distributor of shrink-wrapped CD-ROM packages. Good sales people start with a goal and then work backwards. If the goal is a purchase order or check, they need to know who approves the purchase and who signs the purchase order. The sales person can eventually work all the way back to making the first phone call and setting up the first meeting.

Working backwards will help decide the strategy. A **strategy** should not be confused with tactics. A strategy is a plan for identifying prospects and knowing what makes them want to distribute a product. **Tactics** are approaches such as telephone calls, meetings, or product demonstrations. The most distinguishing characteristic of a strategy is that it is a plan with goals and milestones and a sales person's effectiveness can be measured by how they achieve these goals.

Selling: A Devalued Skill

Selling is a devalued skill. It's considered beneath anyone with an MBA's training. Marketing, on the other hand, is somehow "clean," something professional business people aspire to. If you go to a cocktail party and you're asked what you do for a living, and you reply, "I'm a salesman," people look at you like you've got crumbs on your shirt. Tell them you're a marketing director, however, and they say, "How interesting." One has become a high-status occupation and the other something most people don't want to get their hands dirty doing....Selling is fundamental. It is impossible to go out and sell a product you don't believe in, particularly if, as CEO, you're directly responsible for the quality of the product. Again and again, American business breaks that direct-feedback loop by divorcing responsibility for making the product from the responsibility for selling it.
— *James Koch, President, Boston Beer Co., "Portrait of the CEO as Salesman," Inc. magazine, March 1988*

Selling Process

Research

Before a sales person begins to approach a prospect, they usually do research on the people or company involved. Much of this can be done at a local public library. Recent magazine articles about the company can give information such as company goals, executive histories, and financial status. The process is simpler if selling to public companies because the Securities Exchange Commission mandates the preparation of quarterly and annual reports. Getting information on a private company can be much more difficult to obtain. The press, product information, and company advertising are all good sources. (Some companies such as distributors may produce guides on how to do business with them.) Good research allows the sales person to ask more informed questions and understand the motivations of the prospective client better.

Qualifying

One of the prime responsibilities when researching as well as in initial meetings is to qualify the account. **Qualifying** ▶ 82 means determining if a prospect has the resources, authority, and desire to make a purchase in a reasonable time frame. Qualifying accounts helps determine how and where a sales person should spend their time. Spending time talking to a distributor who does not carry other multimedia products may not be a wise use of time. Spending it on a superstore actively pursuing titles, however, can be. Good qualifying questions are, "Do you have the money in your budget right now for this project?" or, "Are you actively pursuing titles?" If they are not ready to purchase, then ask when they will be, and make a note to get back in touch then. Qualifying questions may seem hard hitting but they

can be a valuable tool in trying to figure out which ten prospects in two hundred should get attention.

Meetings, Presentations, and Negotiations

Once a prospect has been identified, the process then begins to move towards its goal. This is where tactics come in. Tactics are not the shady techniques often associated with sales people. They are the tools that sales people use to show the capabilities of a product and its viability in the marketplace. They include product demonstrations, phone conversation, supporting materials, and sales calls. There is a balance in this step in moving towards the goal but trying not to scare the customer away. This can happen by giving too much information, approaching them before a product is in a suitable condition, or generally, just trying too hard.

Support

An existing account can be a sales person's best source of referrals, references, and repeat business. Supporting a client means following through with obligations. A sales person should make sure the product is delivered on time and make sure the support organization is doing their job. A sure way to fail is for the sales person to disappear once an agreement is made.

Sales Tools

Sales Calls

A **sales call** is a face-to-face meeting with a prospect. A typical sales call can be a product demonstration or a meeting to discuss issues. They are usually initiated by the sales person at the convenience of the prospect. There may be many calls in a sales process, but each should be treated with care and planning. The sales person should know what commitments they want and how they plan to get

*Every meeting should have a next step that moves the sales process forward. The **next step** signals the right to participate or proceed in the sales process. Try not to leave a client with just "Think about it and get back to me." Before a meeting adjourns, each side should know its action items, and agree on the time and form of the next contact. Not having these elements ends the meeting with lots of ambiguity and little commitment. A sales agreement represents a large commitment for each party and any step that brings the two sides closer together makes an agreement all that much easier.*

Five Ways To Chase Away a Client

1. Talk too much.
It is critical to listen to a client and not just spew forth prepared information.

2. Oppose a client's intentions.
A client should be respected. You will get further in sales if you solve their problems as opposed to trying to change their intentions.

3. Set expectations too high.
No matter how wonderful a product or presentation may be, if the client expects more, the experience will be a let down.

4. Be insistent.
When things are not working, take some time off from the account. Chances are you are missing something really important. Learn to say and hear, "No."

5. Be inconsistent.
If one day you say one thing and the next day you say another, your credibility will disappear rapidly. Even if things are changing, let the client know something is happening. Customers rarely enjoy surprises.

Interview: Joe Sparks

How do you know which people to talk to —the ones who are potential decision-makers? Who do you show your software to? Everybody?

Well, that is pretty easy. The main thing is to hang out. If you're serious about this industry you'll go to MACWORLDs, multimedia expos—small and large. You go hang out at the booths and places where these people appear. Read the magazines. Read interviews with all these people. See them on panels in trade shows. If you're serious about it, stay close to the industry and you know who's who. If you do not know anything, you have to call up and say, "I have this great demo for a software product and I am shopping around for a publisher. Who evaluates software like this?" You can find somebody, set up a meeting with them, and they will call together two or three of their colleagues. If you go in there and do an impressive demo, the next time you go there they will have fifteen or even thirty people there to see it, and it won't take long to pique their interest. The main thing is to not give in just because they're interested. You want to go to four or five other publishers.

Really shop around?

Oh yeah, absolutely. The first deal you are going to get from anybody is going to be absolutely bad. I could probably describe it more harshly. It is not the fault of any one publisher; this is just the way it is. They're going to try anything and it seems to be international. We have talked with many people in Japan and all around and have been to Tokyo twice and have gotten proposals and plans from distributors and companies, large and small. It seems that the larger the company is, the worse the things they will try. It is almost like a test, "If you can pass this test we will continue. We're going to see just how smart you are." They will always try to get you for nothing.

An analogy is music brought out by a recording company. The artist gets 3% and they get the other 97. The musician has stars in his eyes about becoming famous and everything.

Right. Believe it or not 3.5% is about the deal you can expect someone to offer you for a Sega or Super Nintendo. I have seen this again and again; the bigger the market or even the bigger the market perception, they will want to give the developer a lot less money for a PC title. Expect about 7.5% or 8.5% of the retail price per unit if you try to find a publisher for it. You will find out right away how badly they want you if they are willing to come back after you say, "Well, this deal doesn't sound right." That's why we went the way we did. We set up a corporation here in San Francisco and are trying to keep control of all of our products, as independently as possible. There are lots of ways of working with other companies without selling your soul or without completely giving everything away. It always takes more work but it also pays off a lot more.

We know that for these products, there is a market now. Everyone speculates about multimedia but if you produce a good product, you have a market right now. Your title can make a million dollars a year if you have a good one. You just have to get that product out. That is the tough part. Actually enduring this whole development stretch, if you are trying to do it on your own, is the tough part. I would advise anyone to at least try and go part of the way. Then go all the way if you can, because you are always going to get a better deal if you are already part of the way. The publisher does not feel that this is a total risk since you have done a lot of the work on your own and actually funded this thing to get to a certain part, even if it is just by yourself or two or three people.

How do you do PR? How do you do package design?

We usually do package design in-house although we sometimes work with other designers. Personally, I feel that we should use as much of the graphics that are in the product on the package design so people can see what they are getting. We have a lot of faith in our graphics and we want to put those on the cover. We want to put our graphics on the cover. There are so many opportunities—we are finding out more and more.

There is such a big business out there in software distribution. There are distributors large and small, mail-order houses, co-op houses, retailers, ads in the local newspaper, regional stores like ComputerWare. There are tons of outlets and channels to go through and you have to make a lot of important decisions along the way because there are so many things that you can do right and wrong. You have to come up with a plan of what you are going to do and just go through it. What we are doing is to try to really hit as many places as possible. This is why we decided to sign with Electronic Arts. We are going to be in the CompUSAs, Sears, Montgomery Wards, and all the major retail outlets and also mail-order catalogs.

There are ads that you can do. Once you start getting involved with these guys you start finding out all these mail-order catalogs— everyone is paying for those little positions out there: MacWAREHOUSEs and MacConnections and those people —they are not so much in it to sell a product as to sell ads. Like advertisers, you pay thousands of dollars to have your little picture in that ad that goes into so many people's homes and also stuck in MACWORLD and MacUser. It is very expensive and they get incredible business. Every month or every week they are selling every little picture. It is a thousand dollars here, two thousand there, for hundreds and hundreds if not thousands of products and so their business is mostly in advertising. Here is the danger with that. They will shave your product down to nothing because they are making money in advertising and that is OK, if they only make a couple of dollars on your product it is OK. But then we shaved it down a couple of dollars in our own retail market, to get more people our way and it is just crazy. You have to be very careful when you are dealing with that plan. Your pricing must carefully anticipate all those things.

There is a lot of good stuff you can do no matter how big you are— one thing you can do is get on America Online; you can get on CompuServe; you can hang around the game boards; you can upload screen shots; you can talk to all the guys personally; meet with customers—all this kind of stuff to just get the word out and get people to know you. Trade shows are incredibly important. A lot of money goes into these things and you see so many people. You will meet people that will affect your life for years to come. You will meet people, you will make contacts, you will meet distributors, all your potential customers, they will tell you things to your face. "I really hated that," or "I really liked that!" You will be seen, you will do demos, so you have to go to the trade shows as much as you can— all the important trade shows.

Joe Sparks is an interactive game designer and runs a multimedia game design company, Pop Rocket in San Francisco.

Any meeting with outside personnel should have a pre-determined set of goals. The goals can be to get more information, to measure the level of interest, to impress, or to gain respect. If more than one person is representing an organization, all those attending should know what these goals are.

them before a meeting (or phone call or product demonstration, for that matter). One bad impression can leave doubts that may be difficult to overcome.

The purposes of a sales call are to **obtain information** and **get commitments**. Good questions and patient listening can provide a clear understanding of the direction, motivations, and hesitations of the other party. A good sales person lets the customer do the talking, prompting them with thoughtful questions that call for more than just yes or no answers. These should be searching questions that stir conversations. A sales person selling interactive music titles to a distributor could ask either, "Do you sell interactive music titles?" or, "How do you feel about the multimedia products you currently carry?" The first question might provide a yes or a no. The second question would start an entire conversation. These types of questions gather a lot of information and help the customer explain their business and their needs.

A second class of questions helps keep the process on a converging course, narrowing the gap between the two parties. Answers to questions such as "Do you agree?" or "Are you interested?" quickly lets sales people know when matters are taking a divergent course and helps them move it back to safer ground.

Some form of evaluation should take place after a sales call. The sales person or team should think about what could have gone better and what the next steps should be. This type of evaluation will refine the skills of the sales person or team and make the process more cohesive.

Product Demonstrations

A sales tool that illustrates a product's potential is the product demonstration. An effective demonstration of multimedia involves both the presenter and the multimedia product working together to tell a story. When listening to a good story, an audience is more receptive and eager to hear every twist and turn. The basis for a good demonstration is good planning, rehearsal, and preparation. Begin by writing a plot with a script that runs the audience through a story in which features and benefits are places to visit. Write it out, step by step, scene by scene retracing the steps a user would take to solve a problem or craft an experience.

Rehearse the demo several times. The purpose is to feel comfortable enough with the actions and steps in the demo to be able to concentrate on the reactions of the audience. It is easy to get lost in a demo especially when you try to do something not planned for. Common as well as uncommon questions should also

Questions a sales persons should ask after a meeting:
- *Did we do what we set out to do?*
- *What could we have done better?*
- *What's the next step?*

Ten Tips for a Demonstration

1. Respect the audience.
They are respecting you by showing up.

2. Provide a quiet and comfortable environment.
Fewer disturbances will make the flow of information go smoother.

3. Make sure everyone can see and hear.

4. Take notes.
This is so as to not forget action items or critical concerns of audience members.

5. Stick to the agenda.
Digressions usually lead to no one remembering what happened.

6. Be patient.
The product you are very familiar with is extremely foreign to the people you are demonstrating it to.

7. Beware the "Show Everything Demo."
This type of demo consists of a blitz of information in a monotone voice with few benefits explained and no client interaction.

8. Point out benefits, not just features.

9. Make it seem effortless.
Products that demo poorly will be seen as more difficult to use.

10. Interact with the audience as individuals.
Face them. Make eye contact. Acknowledge good questions.

be rehearsed. The demo suffers when the presenter has to say, "I'm not sure." Memorable demos share certain characteristics.

Short—Most demos should not take longer than 20 minutes (with ten more minutes for questions and answers). Respect the time constraints of the audience. A demo is quick and enticing, not an in-depth expedition.

Simple—A good demo is easy to follow with no more than three or four key themes. The demo should show enough to entice and not so much that it bewilders.

Deep—At the same time, a good demo offers depth and substance. Show that the content is credible and not just a light and color show.

Direct—Show the most important and unique features and save the detail for the product brochure. Overwhelming an audience with too much information will ensure that they remember little of it.

Interactive—A good demo should be scripted but not canned. Ideally, the presenter should be able to gauge an audience and modify the demo by adding or passing scripted sections based on audience response, interest, and expectations.

Finding Sales Managers and Sales People

Recruiting sales personnel can be a tricky task. If the company is looking for a **sales manager** ▶ 18, look for the ones who have built successful sales teams. It is not so important that the sales manager have the best sales skills, but they should have the ability and aptitude to recruit, select, hire, and train successful sales people.

Sales people ▶ 19 should have good sales records and a proven ability to build quality relationships while generating better than average results. Good sales people should have excellent rapport with people and fit well into an organization. Sales people who do not fit in will be a problem no matter how good they are. Two things to really look for in sales people is ego and insight. A strong ego gives a sales person the desire to achieve and overcome the rejection they will encounter every day. Insight lets them understand a client's position. Once a sales person understands a situation, they can then evaluate options and select the best alternatives for the client and the company.

Managing and Supporting Sales People

Sales people are a diverse lot who need a great deal of freedom in operation as well as clear guidelines of company procedure and goals in arranging agreements. In addition, organizations should provide product, company, and industry information to sales people specifically designed to help them do their jobs. Sales people spend much of their energy on understanding people and their motivations. Expecting sales people to understand nuances and complexities of a product or market from the eyes of a developer, designer, or marketing person is asking them to devote their most precious resource—time—to an activity best left to someone else.

Good sales professionals are always looking for ways to improve their sales skills. Effective sales programs reimburse enthusiastic sales people with training courses and books in sales and other fields such as finance and marketing.

Tips for shipping equipment:

1. *Ship several days in advance. (If it is to a trade show, storage may be included in the bill so take advantage of it.)*

2. *Before the event, verify that the packages have arrived. (Have them read off unique shipping numbers placed on the boxes and their condition.)*

3. *Only use shipping services that have tracking systems.*

4. *Insure all equipment for the full value of its cost.*

5. *Ask about limits and policies in the event of loss or damage.*

Distribution Tips

- The right distribution channels are not always obvious.
- When deciding whether to self-publish, seriously consider the distribution and support costs.
- Know the distribution channels that are possible and build solid relationships that will grow.
- Get the product into the hands of the user as inexpensively and effectively as possible.
- Everyone on a project team should know at least a little about marketing and sales.
- Don't look back. If the first deal doesn't work out so well, make things right on future projects.

Follow-Up

Follow-Up

The corporate kiosk has been installed in the company's lobby. The demo disk has been delivered to the client. The interactive children's book has finally reached the software store's shelf. The electronic magazine is in the mail. What's the next step?

Like the god Janus who opened doors to new beginnings by seeing both the past and the future, members of a project can gather lasting insights by looking back on the project, and build new opportunities by looking forward. While the shipment or delivery of a product marks the end of development in formal terms, other less formal endings should occur to leave the production effort on a good note. At the same time, steps can be taken to help support a project as it moves into the marketplace. These can include areas such as maintenance, support and training as well as customer relations, product feedback, and looking in new directions. These new directions include ways to capitalize on past efforts through **repurposing material**, planning **upgrades**, or launching **special programs** to invite continued customer participation.

Except for wrapping up development, publishers usually handle the follow-up stage. These steps can sometimes require a large amount of resources and an infrastructure within a company to handle them. Developers and production houses should consider these seriously before deciding to self-publish.

Development Wrap-up

Finishing the technical end of a product is much different than finishing the emotional end. Handing master disks to a duplication house or to a client usually marks the technical end of a project. At the same time, this step does not mark the end of emotional commitment. Just as a kickoff meeting acts as a ritual to mark the start of development, some form of ritual should mark the end. In software development, the occasion is usually marked by a "shipping party." For small firms, this can mean a dinner or an open house at the office. For larger firms, the company may stop work in the afternoon for a party or a picnic. Some book publishers recognize authors by hosting a "book party." This can be a well-publicized affair or a small intimate dinner. Hollywood has the traditional film opening to mark the end of production and the beginning of distribution.

One multimedia production company in San Francisco makes it a point upon completion of a project to rent a limo and take the project team out for a night on the town. Whatever the form of the ritual, the purpose is to bring the development phase to a formal close and give recognition to the people involved.

Related to this idea is recognizing people indirectly involved in a project. This can include people who provided funding, initial ideas, or content. It can also include people who did testing, editing, or any of a number of informal activities that make up a project. The amount of recognition can range from a simple note of thanks, project T-shirt, or a copy of the product. Since many people, both inside and outside the company, may not see the press clippings or the letters from customers, consider relaying this information to people on a periodic basis. This can create a family of supporters whose good words, involvement, and support can help promote the product by word of mouth.

Revisiting the Project

One area often overlooked after a product has shipped is to **determine the actual schedule ▶ 66 and costs** associated with a project and compare them against the original estimates. One mistake that is possible is to use the *estimates* from previous projects instead of the *actual figures*. Sometimes developers may not know the actual numbers because no one took the time to calculate them. Other times, the real figures may be known but too painful to acknowledge. Realizing that a $20,000 multimedia project had $5,000 in non-reimbursible production expenses not budgeted for is a bitter pill to swallow. The only lesson here may be to include a reimbursible expense clause for future projects. Ignorance or conscious denial may be less painful in the short term, but only at the cost of repeating the same mistakes.

Another area that can help future projects is to meet with members of the team and ask how the process could be improved. The creative director may not realize the extent to which the creative talent was set back due to the constant updates and changes made to production standards. The production manager may not have realized that user testing near the end of production instead of during prototype caused the product to slip two months. An informal discussion with the team a week after the project will give more ways to improve the process rather than doing it three months later at the onset of another project.

Maintenance

Regardless of the type of project or the complexity, almost all products will need some form of maintenance, training, and support. **Maintenance** refers to managing the operation and use of a product once it has been developed and is in distribution. Training and support programs are customer-focused efforts. Training helps increase the awareness and enjoyment of a product; support resolves any problems that may result from its use or interaction with other products or equipment.

Preventive Maintenance

A **preventive maintenance** strategy anticipates conditions or changes that can cause problems later. It may be far less expensive from a publisher's viewpoint to have customers use on-line help or read an instruction card than it is to answer a telephone help-line or e-mail query. Simple things like instructions on a kiosk explaining how to adjust the sound can prevent later support problems. Defensive maintenance reacts to problems; preventive maintenance eliminates or diminishes them before they affect customers.

The best way to prevent problems is by proper product design and testing. Designing with unusual circumstances in mind or testing on multiple configurations can point out specific areas of concerns in time to correct them. Some issues cannot be anticipated before a product is released. When users add new hardware and software it can change how a product works. Whenever major new hardware models appear, developers should check to make sure that all product features still work. A list of all the compatible and incompatible hardware and software components and configurations should be readily available to any person who may come into contact with a customer or distributor. Not having a ready answer for an inquiry can mean a lost sale or a frustrated customer. For example, the developer of a videodisc project should keep on hand a list of compatible videodisc players. The publisher of a CD-ROM title should list compatible CD-ROM players and operating systems and the correct multimedia extensions. System requirements and compatible equipment should be clearly stated for the buyer on the packaging or the point of delivery.

Defensive Maintenance

Defensive maintenance is providing support and feedback when problems occur. If a kiosk freezes at the main screen, if a navigational structure sends the user into digital limbo, or if there are glaring errors in content, then something needs to be done.

One solution is to provide a maintenance upgrade that fixes the problem. The most vulnerable component of a multimedia system is its software. While content is relatively stable, software reliability fluctuates with system conditions and usage. Changes in software such as operating systems, multimedia extensions, or authoring tools can affect the way a product works and cause it to run haphazardly or not at all. A development team is far better off if these cases can be anticipated before they affect the customer. Many times, these issues cannot be addressed by careful design and scripting. For example, a new multimedia extension may alter the color palette of an animation. The only response in these cases may be to notify users, explaining the problem and the ways to work around it. Sending out a new version of the product may be necessary as well. Directing letters to people who have returned registration cards and press releases are two ways to notify customers. This approach can be more cost effective and image enhancing for a company than having the press uncover problems or requiring on customers to call or write.

Thinking ahead can prevent mad scrambles to solve problems. Glenn Corey, former lead designer at Lumen, now at Apple, regularly purchases all the equipment he needs for a kiosk installation ahead of time, making sure to order at least one spare machine. (Many equipment suppliers will warehouse the equipment until it is needed.) This guarantees that the finished project will perform on the same equipment it was developed for. Months of constant use can stress videodisc players, increasing the risk of failure. The time to **repair** a videodisc player can be weeks and too much downtime can ruin a public exhibit. Replacing failed equipment with spare equipment keeps an exhibit running constantly while the damaged machine is sent for repairs. The foresight of ordering spare equipment and providing replacement instructions and resources at the installation site can be the difference between a smoothly running multimedia installation and an inoperative one.

Training

Training ▶ 66 is focused on teaching an audience about the purpose and use of a product. Training equips users to be self-sufficient with a product. It can reduce their need and your expense in supporting the product.

Crutchfield Corporation, a premier catalog retailer of car stereos, telephones, and other electronic equipment, goes one step further in its preventive maintenance strategies. Not only does it list in its catalog the car stereos that fit each car model but it also includes in each order, free of charge, special wiring, brackets, and installation instructions specific to the customer's car model. This level of service and proactive support saves time and money for both the customer and retailer and dramatically increases the likelihood of repeat business.

Some projects will not require training other than including simple **installation** ▶ **98, 231** instructions or steps for basic operation such as loading a CD-ROM. Small instructional details and reminders are common for multimedia titles and are inexpensive to include in the packaging. Training programs, however, should match the complexity of the subject. A demo disk may require nothing more than a single walk-through to illustrate controls. A multimedia database that lets students create, maintain, and retrieve content may require extensive training for both teachers and students. A successful training strategy allows people to learn at their own pace through their own experience with the system. On-line help and manuals can be useful when they work this way.

Planning for Training and Support

Clients are usually responsible for providing training and support unless a clause in a contract specifically includes these services. Regardless of who is responsible for them, they should be planned for at the outset of the business contract. Not addressing these issues or underestimating the obligation can quickly turn a profitable piece of work into a costly embarrassment. Some installations of kiosks and other presentations break down and are never fixed because someone at the site cannot operate the computer. Support responsibility should be clearly outlined before an installation goes in or a product is handed over. Training materials should be provided that specifically addresses problem scenarios. In addition, the client should be given the name of an individual or department to contact in case any problems cannot be resolved on-site. Good relations with clients and prompt handling of client problems can boost your reputation and the likelihood of future business.

Other Training Possibilities

Some products may require levels of training that go beyond manuals or on-line information. More personal forms of training may be needed such as having people on hand who can instruct others, or holding courses or arranging conferences. Many multimedia network and database projects, education products, and multimedia authoring tools need some form of instruction for people to assemble new content. Each user may not have the time, knowledge, or motivation to use electronic or printed training materials. One solution is to identify **key users** and provide them with tools to instruct others. These may be the people responsible for keeping the system running or the content current. A company can provide specific materials such as teacher's guides and administration manuals or hold seminars for more direct contact.

Documentation

The ideal condition for any designer is to create a product that is so easy to operate that no additional sources of information are needed. Most products, though, never achieve this condition and usually need some form of **instructions** ▶ **23, 212, 223** either in electronic or printed form. Although these materials commonly appear in the form of text and diagrams in Help panels and in manuals, the possibility of providing them in multimedia form should not be overlooked. Movies or voice annotation in installation or trouble-shooting procedures can be a highly informative. They work to instruct an audience short of providing someone in person.

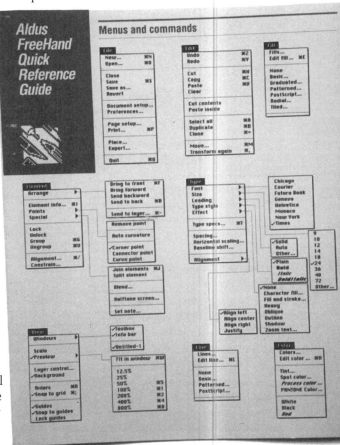

Regardless of the form of support materials, they should try to always reach the average audience, people unfamiliar with technology and jargon. Sections may address the advanced user but the majority of instructions and training materials should communicate in a common-sense manner. Instructions fail when they assume too much knowledge about terms, products, and procedures involved in the process. For example, some buyers may be unfamiliar with CD-ROM installation procedures. To minimize their anxiety, a simple instruction sheet showing how to use the CD-ROM, and how to hook up external speakers, will prevent problems that might otherwise make a customer want to throw the computer out the window.

Some manuals go further than just how to use a product, they describe how to use it well with examples, ideas, and background concepts. They also try to address common problems and misconceptions. For example, a developer who creates an interactive children's story can include information for teachers on ways to design curricula around such stories. The depth and amount of materials provided should be weighed against their cost-effectiveness, but everyone gains when customers use products to their fullest capabilities.

Customer Relations

Support

Support is commonly defined as providing assistance to customers and clients in response to specific problems and inquiries. Most multimedia titles will not need much support and if they do, the support is usually pro-

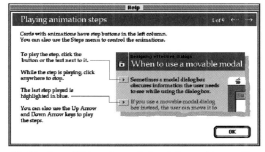

vided by the publisher. One solution is to provide a section in the on-line help or in the manual to address common problems. This section should be the first place a customer looks in response to a problem or question.

Many software companies provide some form of phone support for customers with questions about products. Some provide this support free while others charge a fee through the use of 900 numbers or credit cards. The policies and motivations differ from firm to firm. Some firms like WordPerfect Corporation have won many fans because of their free no-questions-asked support policies and their helpful response to problems outside of their domain. Others view their support operations as profit centers, generating additional revenues aside from the sale of the software products.

If a company decides to provide phone support, it should be done with prior thought and planning. Many inexperienced developers are surprised by the amount of resources needed to support products, particularly in the tools and software areas. This oversight can deplete

profits and reduce available time spent for new products. Phone number and support policies can appear prominently in documentation, although some companies discourage calls by placing numbers and policies only in select places. A toll-free 800 number or a 900 number may be a worthwhile option to pursue. Competing long-distance carriers offer affordable rates and services for all sizes of businesses including start-ups and small firms. The cost of a single line 800 number usually consists of a one-time installation charge, a monthly fee, and a per-minute charge tied to telephone use.

Many software companies track calls and solutions with databases or special software to help respond to customers more quickly and to eliminate spending time solving known problems. Companies sometimes provide access to these problem logs by directly distributing them to customers or by placing them on computer archives where customers can download them at their cost and expense.

Other support programs use bulletin board systems (BBSs) to maintain inexpensive contact with users who have modems and communications software. These systems require a computer system and skilled people to install and manage them. One advantage of a BBS is that users can usually send and receive documents along with their messages. A company can create its own BBS or rent space on a popular service like AppleLink, America Online, or CompuServe.

Measuring Product Acceptance

One of the activities that can be important once a product has been delivered to a client or has entered the channel is to measure any increase of the acceptance of the product. If the project is a one-time effort in which the delivery concludes the contract with the client, then nothing more than a review meeting may be necessary to get their opinion of the project.

Measuring **market acceptance** for **mass-market products** is a larger effort, mainly due to the size of distribution and the diversity of the market. Different methods for measuring how the market perceives a product are mail-back **registration cards**, **direct customer contact**, **press reviews**, and **sales statistics**. Some questions to ask in this process are: Who buys the product? How did they hear about it? How can the product be improved? Is the price right? Is the product what customers expected it to be? How does it compare to the competition?

Our approach to the text [in the Visual Almanac Companion] was based on the realization that many people receiving the Visual Almanac would not know what multimedia is or recognize its potential. This printed piece was the place to talk about some of the philosophical and pedagogical underpinnings of the project. We also wanted to let people in behind the scenes of a work in progress.

— Kristee Rosendahl with Nancy Hechinger, Visual Almanac Technical Report, Apple Computer

The aim is to reduce the support needs for your products. Anything you can do to reduce your customers' problems, whether providing better manuals, a better interface, online help, eliminating copy-protection, or a combination of any of these will more than pay for itself in reduced staff and equipment to help users with problems.

*Information to consider
including on a registration
card:*

- *Name*
- *Title*
- *Company*
- *Address*
- *Phone number*
- *E-mail/link address*
- *Type and size of business*
- *Types and numbers of computers*
- *Types of operating systems*
- *Types and numbers of CD-ROMs,
  videodiscs, etc.*
- *Network configuration*
- *Where they purchased the product*
- *How they heard about it*
- *What magazines they read*

Registration Cards & Direct Feedback

Mail-back **registration cards** included with a product invite customers to provide information about themselves and their opinions of the product. The information from these cards provides publishers with one of the best ways to learn about their market. The cards can serve several purposes. They can provide names for a mailing list for upgrade notices or other product announcements. They can provide feedback on the success of various distribution channels or advertising campaigns. They can even identify a market segment different from the ones currently targeted. Contacting these registered users directly can also provide information to help improve future versions or create new products.

Press Reviews and Sales Statistics

Other sources of information about market acceptance are **press reviews** and **sales statistics**. Press reviews can provide details about a product from a more objective viewpoint by comparisons to competitive products. Contacts in distribution channels can provide sales statistics on a product and its competition. Retail salespeople can comment on how well a product is selling in a store or how customers respond to the product. They can also give a better picture of seasonal sales cycles and the sales performance relative to the competition.

Increasing a Product's Appeal

All of this information helps management and salespeople better match the product to likely buyers. Lessons learned while measuring the acceptance of a product help shape the strategy for increasing its appeal. For example, one strategy is to differentiate a product from other products by highlighting its unique features or lower cost. Another possibility is to modify the promotion method relative to the distribution strategy. A large number of registration cards from a particular market segment may indicate a group not previously considered. Appealing to select markets with direct mail or targeted advertising may provide a better return than more general advertising approaches.

A new version of a multimedia product might support additional content, more languages, or new hardware models and software extensions.

Maintaining Customer Relations

Many companies put a lot of emphasis and resources on **customer service**. This can be done through prompt responses to customer queries, special offers, newsletters, design contests, and showcasing customer work in publications or advertisements. Any indication that a company values its customers will help generate favorable recommendations and create opportunities for future sales.

Pursuing Additional Opportunities

Successful products often create secondary opportunities for products and services bringing with them additional room for sales growth. These **after-market** products and services include updated or extended editions of the content, reuse of the material in a different publishing medium, or creation of companion products.

New Versions or Upgrades

Almost every successful product has room to expand and improve. Often, the life and usability of a product can be extended by releasing new **versions** or **upgrades**. Many software developers once viewed producing new versions as a task that prevented them from working on other products. They often charged only enough to cover duplication and mailing charges. Now, many see new versions and upgrades as a valuable source of revenue, pricing upgrades at up to one-third of the retail price. In the motion picture industry, some films are re-released in an uncut or re-edited version. A version of *Blade Runner*, featuring additional footage and a subtle change in tone, was released in 1992, 10 years after the first release. Popular books are reprinted with new sections, different photographs, more recent examples, and other additions. The content of some books like reference materials, atlases, and travel and buying guides requires that new versions are published every other year or so. These updates appeal as much to new audiences as they do to previous audiences.

In producing subsequent versions of a multimedia product, the new versions should fix any problems in earlier versions as well as take advantage of new technology wherever possible. For example, a re-release of a title can now contain video clips and use the latest QuickTime compression algorithms available. This assumes, however, that a significant portion of the intended market has the necessary software extensions installed.

Families or Series

Another option is to create new products that form a **family** of related products. These spin-offs can capitalize on both the development and marketing investment of the initial product. For example, the success of the game *Where in the World is Carmen Sandiego?* from Brøderbund led to related games: *Where in Time is Carmen Sandiego?*, *Where in the USA is Carmen Sandiego?*, and *Where in History is Carmen Sandiego?*, as well as a popular television game show for kids. A title covering a certain period in history or musical form may have a corollary to other periods and forms. The design and interaction may be the same for future titles with only the content changed. A look at the TV, film, and book publishing industry provides numerous examples of spin-offs, sequels, and series that preserve storylines and characters. In fact, game companies are incorporating footage from first-run films into spin-off games.

Repurposing Work

Tools

There are many ways to **repurpose** ▶ 98 existing content or program elements once a product is finished. The engine for a product can be used for other titles or can be developed and sold as a separate development product. For example, The Voyager Company uses and licenses its Expanded Book Toolkit developed for producing their own electronic books. Pieces of the production tools can be packaged and sold to other developers as time-saving tools. Tiger Media licenses tools for creating images that can be moved across platforms. The danger in these activities is not recognizing the support and documentation that may be needed for these toolkits. Selling a few thousand copies of toolkits may not be worth the effort when compared to the amount of support needed or the drain in resources from producing content titles.

Content

Content elements in multimedia titles can be separated and licensed for other uses. Someone may wish to create a printed book or audio tape of a successful multimedia title. Another developer may be interested in using some of the illustrations or movies in a new way. Also, consider the possibilities that any characters created in the product may be suitable for a television show, movie, cartoon, or comic book. Some portions of a work may be included in compilations or reproduced as serials. The music industry often produces "best of" recordings and sampler CDs of a number of different artists. The magazine industry often publishes sections of books called serials. Not only does this repurposing of the original content provide a direct source of revenue but it also provides additional exposure to other audiences who may become new customers. The multimedia versions of these options may not be established at this time but that should not stop a publisher from exploring them.

Domestic distribution of movies alone will not make enough money. Related product lines and ancillary products are the extra marketing potential for a movie. Multimedia is a huge example where ancillary products can be created. Coppola's movie Dracula employed a second film unit for interactive purposes. For example, an instruction might be start at point A, track forward, go to right. Start at point A again, track forward and go to left. All the variations that will be needed for interactive computer-based products. Start where the source is and create a series of objects: a multimedia library with video shots for potential interaction. The multimedia computer will provide ancillary, secondary distribution.

— Scott Billups, Film and Video Director, Viz-Net

Follow-Up Tips

- **Consider support costs at the beginning of a project.**
- **Mark the end of a project with a celebration.**
- **Never forget your installed base of customers.**
- **Include great documentation or quick reference cards.**
- **Be available for customers.**
- **Solicit honest feedback.**
- **Explore new opportunities.**
- **Explore repurposing content & tools.**
- **Consider a series or family of products.**
- **Plan for new versions or upgrades.**

Resources

Resources

Books

Animation

Animation From Script to Screen
Shamus Culhane
St. Martin's Press, 1988, New York, NY
General introduction to 2D animation procedures.

Disney Animation—The Illusion of Life
Frank Thomas & Ollie Johnson
Abbeville Press, 1981, New York, NY
A coffee table book of grand illustrations with a great section covering many of the principles of 2D animation.

QuickTime Handbook
David L. Drucker & Michael D. Murie
Hayden Books, 1992, Carmel, IN
How to make movies on the Macintosh. Covers QuickTime, video capturing and editing, sound, animations, formats, and distribution.

Arts, General

Art and Visual Perception— A Psychology of the Creative Eye
Rudolf Arnheim, University of California, 1954, Berkeley, CA
A primer on the principles of psychology operating with visual elements. Useful for designers.

Art as Experience
John Dewey
Capricorn Books, 1954, New York, NY
Thinker's book discussing ideas about experience and action. The chapter "The Common Substance of the Arts" applies pragmatic thought to all digital media.

Christian and Oriental Philosophy of Art
Ananda Coomaraswamy
Dover Publications, 1956, New York, NY
Multicultural and multihistoric issues of exhibition, inspiration, and the value of art, craft, and society.

CD-ROM

Apple CD-ROM Handbook
Joel Nagy
Addison-Wesley, 1992, Reading, MA
Well written book covering all phases of CD-ROM production.

Breaking Through
Apple Computer, Inc., 1993 Cupertino, CA
A technical companion to the Apple CD-ROM Handbook.

CD-ROM Buyer's Guide & Handbook
Paul T. Nicholls, Ph.D
Pemberton Press Inc. 1993, Wilton, CT
A clear and useful guide to CD-ROM publishing from the publishers of CD-ROM Professional magazine.

The CD-ROM Directory
TPFL Publishing, Washington, DC
International annual directory of company information, CD-ROM titles, electronic books, hardware, software, conferences and exhibitions, and journals and books.

CD-ROM Yearbook, 1989-1990
Oberlin and Cox
Microsoft Press, 1989, Redmond, WA
Updates CD-ROM volumes to include CD-ROM/XA.

Red Book CD-ROM Specification, CEI IEC 908
Yellow Book CD-ROM Specification, ISO 10149:1989
Specification for ISO 9660
American National Standards Institute
1430 Broadway, New York, NY 10018
212/642-4900
The key specifications for CD-standards. Red Book defines CD-Audio, Yellow Book defines CD-ROM, and ISO 9660 defines computer information that is found on CD-ROM.

Green Book CD-ROM Specification
American CD-I Association
11111 Santa Monica, Suite 750, Los Angeles, CA 90025
213/444-6619
The specification for the CD-I standard.

Computers, General

Communications, Computers, and Networks
Michael Dertouzous, Editor
Scientific American, September 1991
Tremendous resource of articles by key individuals describing underlying technologies of the immediate future.

Understanding Computers
Nathan Shedroff, J. Sterling Hutto & Ken Fromm
Sybex, 1992, Alameda, CA
A four-color, highly graphical book on computers that has sections on Uses, Components, Technology, and Buying and Selling. The perfect book for the novice or intermediate computer users.

Computers, Macintosh

Danny Goodman's Macintosh Handbook
Danny Goodman
Bantam Books, 1992, New York, NY
Comprehensive book on System 7 and the Macintosh based on an information design layout.

New Inside Macintosh (15 volumes)
Apple Computer
Addison-Wesley, 1992-1993, Reading, MA
Documents tools and resources in the Macintosh system software.

Design, General

A Primer of Visual Literacy
Donis A. Dondis
MIT Press, 1973, Cambridge, MA
Ideas and elements of graphic design such as form, layout, movement, type, grids makes this recommended reading for illustrators, animators, and graphic and interface designers.

Film and Video

The Book of Video Photography
David Cheshire
Alfred Knopf, 1990, New York, NY
A highly visual book on every aspect of video movie-making including equipment, lighting, capturing a subject, editing, sound, and special techniques.

Film Technique and Film Acting
V.I. Pudovkin
Bonanza Books, 1959, New York, NY
A good book for anyone with a film image in mind, especially editors, videographers, and film-makers.

The Film Sense by Sergei Eisenstein
Jay Leyda, Editor
Harcourt Brace, & World, Inc., 1942, New York, NY
Motion picture analysis and lessons. Good for videographers, and film producers, and editors.

The Five C's Of Cinematography
Joseph V. Mascelli
Cine/Grafic Publications, 1965, Hollywood, CA
Comprehensive information useful for film making. A little dated, though.

Video Lighting & Special Effects
J. Caruso & M. Arthur
Prentice Hall, 1990 , New Jersey
Knowledgeable production book on the subject.

Games

**"Lessons from Computer Game Design"
from The Art of Human-Computer Interface
Design**
Chris Crawford
Addison-Wesley, 1991, Reading, MA
*Chris has many thoughtful things to say about game
design.*

Hypermedia

Mapping Hypertext
Robert E. Horn
Lexington Institute, 1989, Lexington, MA
*A book on hypertext with some basic ideas on infor-
mation mapping technique. Goes hand in hand
with Wurman's work on information design and
Tufte's aesthetic analysis of thematic mapping.*

Information Design

Hats
Richard Saul Wurman
Design Quarterly 145
MIT Press, 1989, Cambridge, MA
*Brief issue on information design
delightfully written.*

Information Anxiety
Richard Saul Wurman
Doubleday, 1989, New York, NY
*If you are interested in the design of information,
this book will help you sort out the meaningful from
the meaningless. It offers valuable insight into organizations of information, although the book can, at
times, produce a little anxiety itself.*

**Notes on Graphic Design and
Visual Communication**
Greg Berryman
William Kaufmann, Inc., 1984, Los Altos, CA
*A wonderfully simple resource giving thumbnail
rules for graphic art design. Highly recommended
for graphic designers and illustrators.*

Symbol Sourcebook
Henry Dreyfus
McGraw-Hill, 1972, New York, NY
*An excellent source of information about the power
and meaning of symbols. Includes information on
the history and development of symbols and what
distinguishes good symbols from bad ones.*

**The Visual Display of Quantitative
Information**
Edward R. Tufte
Graphics Press, 1983, Chesire, CT
*Superb book explaining and illustrating basic prin-
ciples of graphic illustration, thematic mapping and
good information design. By the author of Envision-
ing Information, 1990.*

Interface Design

Computers as Theater
Brenda Laurel
Addison-Wesley, 1991, Reading, MA
*An advanced aesthetic philosophy and observations
on the design of virtual reality and modern interfaces is developed. This book literally transcribes the
principles of Aristotle's On Poetics as a basis for
interactive design.*

**The Art of Human-Computer Interface
Design**
Brenda Laurel, Editor
Addison-Wesley, 1991, Reading, MA
*Articles by many writers covering most elements of
the interface discipline.*

The Design of Everyday Things
Donald A. Norman
Doubleday, 1988, New York, NY
*An introduction to some basic principles of user-
centered design based on a study of the obvious and
the ordinary.*

Macintosh Human Interface Guidelines
Apple Computer, Inc.
Addison-Wesley, 1992, Reading, MA
*This book consists of guidelines for Macintosh Com-
puters plus color capabilities, open architecture and
enhanced system software.*

Making It Macintosh
Apple Computer, Inc., 1993, Cupertino, CA
*This CD-ROM interactively demonstrates the inter-
face design practices discussed in the book Macintosh Human Interface Guidelines*

Tog on Interface
Bruce Tognazzini
Addison-Wesley, 1992, Reading, MA
*Good running commentary and general lessons on
computer interface design.*

Understanding Comics
Scott McCloud
Kitchen Sink Press, 1993, Northampton, MA
*Elements of visual communication (e.g., use of
icons) found in comic books.*

Management and Marketing

Bionomics
Michael Rothschild
Henry Holt and Company, 1990, New York, NY
*A great book with wonderful new thoughts about
how to view business. Excellent insight on innova-
tion and technology.*

Changing The Game: The New Way to Sell
Larry Wilson
Simon & Schuster, 1987, New York, NY
*Revolutionary book about how to sell and run a
business. Covers all issues and sets the stage for a
powerful sales program.*

The High-Tech Marketing Companion
Apple Computer, Inc. 1989-1993
Addison-Wesley, 1993, Reading, MA
*Expert advice on marketing to Macintosh and other
PC users.*

Marketing in Emerging Companies
Robert Davis & F. Gordon Smith
Addison-Wesley, 1984, Reading, MA
*An instructive and comprehensive text that applies
aspects of traditional marketing to emerging
companies.*

Multimedia Law Handbook
Ladera Press, 1994, Menlo Park, CA
A practical guide for developers and publishers.

Multimedia Markets
John C. Gale
Information Workstation Group, 1991, Alexandria, VA
*A thick research manual for industrial market
planning for multimedia. Call703/548-9320 for
more direct information.*

Relationship Marketing
Regis McKenna
Addison-Wesley, 1991, Reading, MA
*Powerful text on understanding the why and how of
real marketing. Great for beginners to get off on the
right foot and inspirational for more experienced
marketing or sales people.*

**Shared Minds: The New Technologies of
Collaboration**
Michael Schrage
Random House, 1990, New York, NY
*Good book about technology and collaboration by
syndicated columnist Michael Schrage. An insight
into collaboration which can many times be more
powerful than the technology involved.*

Strategic Selling
Robert Miller & Stephen Heiman
William Morrow and Company, 1985, New York, NY
*Excellent text for the salespeople in the organization
and not a bad read for all other members of the
company. Everybody is a salesperson at one time or
another.*

Multimedia

CyberArts: Exploring Art and Technology
Linda Jacobson, Editor
Miller Freeman, 1992, San Francisco, CA
*A well-edited series of articles from the individual
speakers at the CyberArts forums. A great modern
resource covering subjects like binaural sound, new
computer art, and music.*

The Desktop Multimedia Bible
Jeff Burger
Addison-Wesley, 1993, Reading, MA
*A comprehensive sourcebook that provides concise
information on the background technologies, major
components, and creative application of all the
associated media in multimedia projects.*

Digital Harmony – On the Complementarity of Music and Visual Art
John Whitney
Kingsport Press, 1980, Kingsport TN
A thoughtful book exploring the relationships between abstraction in music and visual art through examples of electronic music and computer animation.

Multimedia: Making It Work
Tay Vaughan
Osborne McGraw-Hill, 1993, Berkeley, CA
A sensible and straightforward handbook written by a multimedia professional. Covers issues from choosing sound boards to selecting CDs, from picking the best fonts to selecting the right software.

Multimedia Power Tools
Peter Jerram and Michael Gosney
Random House, 1993, New York, NY
A book/CD-ROM package assembled by professionals in the field. It is an interactive reference guide and toolkit that surveys multimedia tools and technologies and provides essential advice on creating multimedia.

Technologies for the 21st Century: ON MULTIMEDIA
Martin Greenberger
Voyager Company, 1990, Santa Monica, CA
Classic roundtable discussion on the implications of multimedia.

The Medium is the Massage: An Inventory of Effects
Marshall McLuhan and Quentin Fiore
Bantam Books, 1967, New York, NY
Interesting book that shows how media transforms society. Introduces many stimulating ideas about experience, sense ratios, and media as extensions of the mind and body.

Que's Macintosh Multimedia Handbook
Tony Bove and Cheryl Rhodes
Que Corporation, 1990, Carmel, IN
Step-by-step applications and examples specifically created for producing multimedia products on Macintosh computers.

Understanding Media
Marshall McLuhan
Signet Paperback, 1964, New York, NY
Probing look at the effects of many media types and technologies in modern and past societies.

Music & Sound

The Art of Music Licensing
Al and Bob Kohn, Editors
Prentice Hall Law & Business, Englewood Cliffs, NJ
A 1000-page guide on granting licenses and obtaining permissions to use music.

MIDI for Musicians
Craig Anderton
AMSCO/Music Sales Corp., 1986, New York, NY
Basic book on MIDI issues.

The Musician's Home Recording Handbook
Ted Greenwald
Miller Freeman/GPI Books, 1992, San Francisco, CA
Many common issues of acoustics, recording, and recording are covered.

Synthesizer Basics
Brent Hurtig, Editor
Hal Leonard Publishing, 1988, Milwaukee, WI

Photography/Image Manipulation

The Photographer's Handbook, Third Edition
John Hedgecoe
Alfred A. Knopf, 1992, New York, NY
A complete reference manual of photographic techniques, procedures, equipment, and style. Full of illustrations, examples, and comparison photos.

The Photographer's Source – A Complete Catalogue
Henry Horenstein
Simon and Schuster, 1989, New York, NY
A good resource book about serious photography.

Presentation

How to Prepare, Stage, and Deliver Winning Presentations
Thomas Leech
AMACON, 1982, New York, NY
A well written, complete book on the art and science of presentation. Good conceptual material on the process of forming and building communication for audiences.

Online Forums

comp.multimedia
Newsgroup on the Internet featuring discussions of hardware, software, conferences and seminars.

MMDEVX
To subscribe, send the following command to:
Mail-Server@knex.mind.org
SUBSCRIBE MMDEVX FirstName LastName
Mailing list for people interested in crossplatform multimedia development tools in general and Apple Media Kit (AMK) and Kaleida ScriptX in particular.

Morph OnLine
By modem: 510/238-4544. For login information:
Info@morph.com
Provided by Morph's Outpost on the Digital Frontier, the technical magazine for multimedia developers, this free BBS features forums on interactive development issues and provides a place to hang out on the Information Superhighway.

Multimedia Products Directory
Send mail to DEVSUPPORT or
DEVSUPPORT@APPLELINK.APPLE.COM
An Applelink directory of Apple-compatible, third-party hardware and software for multimedia creation and playback.

Multimedia Services Directory
Send mail to DEVSUPPORT or
DEVSUPPORT@APPLELINK.APPLE.COM
Applelink directory of multimedia service providers.

Periodicals

Apple StartingLine
Quarterly, Apple Computer, Inc.
Cupertino, CA
Apple Computer's marketing communications catalog specifically designed for Apple resellers and employees. It contains videos, advertising materials, logoed merchandise, and literature to help market, promote, and sell Apple products. Authorized Apple resellers may contact StartingLine by sending AppleLink to STARTINGLINE.

AV Video
Bi-Monthly, Montage Publishing, White Plains, NY
914/328-9157
For production and presentation technology enthusiasts.

BMUG Newsletter
Semi-Yearly, BMUG Inc., Berkeley, CA
510/549-BMUG
Part newsletter and part book. An eclectic, informative, and useful book about Macintosh products and technology and other computer related topics.

Byte
Monthly, MacGraw-Hill, Inc., Peterborough, NH
800/257-9402
A comprehensive monthly magazine about computer technology in the workstation and personal computing area. It provides an extensive amount of technical detail on platforms, operating systems, applications, and peripherals.

CD-ROM Professional
Bi-Monthly, Pemberton Press Inc., Wilton, CT
800/248-8466
A useful collection of articles and checklists for mastering, producing and evaluating CD-ROM and CD-ROM related materials.

CD-ROM World
Monthly, Mecklermedia, Westport, CT
203/226-6967
Buyers guides, title reviews, and trends in technology for CD-ROM users.

Communications of the ACM
Monthly, Association for Computing Machinery,
New York, NY
800/342-6626
The leading magazine in computing technology, ethics, theory, and academic research.

Converge
Bi-monthly, Multi-Facet Communications, Inc.,
Sunnyvale, CA
800/274-5116
An independent newsletter that provides information about QuickTime system software and related media integration products.

Desktop Video World
Bi-Monthly, TechMedia or IDG Communications
Publishing, Peterborough, NH
603/924-0100
Essential digital video product reviews, updates and technology trends.

Electronic Musician
Monthly, Act III Publishing, Emeryville, CA
800/888-5139
Reviews, buyers guides, tips and techniques for the digital musician.

Digital Media: A Seybold Report
Monthly, Seybold Publications, Media, PA
800/325-3830
This perodical keeps readers informed with good background reports of the issues and players in the digital world. An extremely valuable resource for business managers and product planners.

Electronic Entertainment
Monthly, Infotainment World, San Mateo, CA
415/349-4300
Information on multimedia titles and hardware heavily weighted towards the game industry.

Electronic Media
Weekly, Crain Communications, Chicago, IL
800/678-9595
Information on the television and cable industries with emphasis on business and government issues.

ID Magazine
Bi-monthly, Magazine Publications, L.P., New York, NY
800/284-3728
Visually arresting magazine that addresses the art, culture, and business of creating objects and images. ID explores design's role in society as a link between ideas, form, aesthetics, and commerce.

Imaging
Monthly, Telecom Library, New York, NY
800/999-0345
Practical advice and straight-forward information on the tools and process of working with images and text on a computer.

MacUser
Monthly, Ziff-Davis Publishing, Foster City, CA
800/627-2247
A magazine for Macintosh users that relies heavily on product comparisons and how-to articles.

MacWEEK
Weekly, Ziff-Davis Publishing, New York, NY
609/786-8230
A timely resource for developments and trends in the Macintosh industry. MacWEEK specializes in keeping the Macintosh business community informed on late-breaking news and rumors of upcoming products.

Macworld
Monthly, Macworld Communications
San Francisco, CA 800/288-6848
A useful resource for product information for the Macintosh platform.

Mondo 2000
Quarterly, MONDO 2000, Berkeley, CA
510/845-9018
Wild mix of technology, art, and cyberpunk lifestyle.

Morph's Outpost
Monthly, Morph's Outpost, Inc., Orinda, CA
510/238-4545
Dedicated to serving the technical, business, and creative needs of the interactive multimedia developer community.

Multimedia Monitor
Monthly, Future Systems, Falls Church, VA
800/323-3472
Good newsletter on multimedia business and technology issues.

Multimedia Week
Weekly, Phillips Business Information, Potomac, MD
800/777-5015
Short information newsletter full of late-breaking events of the industry.

Multimedia World
Monthly, PC World Communications, Inc.
San Francisco, CA 415/281-8650
Multimedia news, reviews and how-to tips.

NewMedia
Monthly, Hypermedia Communications, Inc.
San Mateo, CA 415/573-5170
A prominent magazine for multimedia technology for desktop computer users. It contains information on processes, resources, and products as well as insightful articles, interviews, and editorials.

PC WEEK
Weekly, Ziff/Davis, Riverton, NJ
609/786-8230
A timely trade resource for products, developments, trends, and news items in the personal computer industry.

PHOTO Electronic Imaging
Monthly, PPA Publications & Events, Atlanta, GA
404/522-8600
Information on integrating photography, electronic imaging, and computer graphics.

Publish
Monthly, Integrated Media, Inc., San Francisco, CA
800/274-5116
Useful information on computer technology, processes, and design mostly directed to the desktop publishing industry but with increasing emphasis on electronic publishing.

The Red Herring
Monthly, Flipside Communications, Inc.
Redwood City, CA 415/853-6853
Covers technology, finance and investment.

Upside
Monthly, Upside Publishing Company, Foster City, CA
619/745-2809
Information on people, companies, trends, and future developments in technology written for business executives and managers.

Variety
Weekly, Variety, Los Angeles, CA
800/323-4345
A must-read for anyone in the entertainment industry. Information about movies, television, cable, and multimedia as it applies to entertainment.

Videography
Monthly, P.S.N. Publications, New York, NY
212/779-1919
A trade magazine for videographers with good articles on digital video production.

Wired
Monthly, Wired USA, San Francisco, CA
800/SO-WIRED, *subscriptions@wired.com*
A well-produced consumer magazine for the digital generation. Self-labeled as "A Vanity Fair for Propeller Heads."

The World of Macintosh Multimedia
Quarterly, Redgate Communications Corp.
Vero Beach, FL 407/231-6904
An independent journal encompassing multimedia product reviews, descriptions and listings including production tools, peripherals and CD-ROM titles.

Pamphlets

Compact Disc Terminology
Introduction to ISO 9660
Integrating Mixed Mode CD-ROM
Disc Manufacturing, Inc., Wilmington, DE
800/433-DISC
Well-written illustrated technical guides to many elements of CD-ROM technology and production.

An Introduction to Digital Color Prepress, Volumes One and Two
AGFA Corporation, 1990, Mt. Prospect, IL
800/395-7007
These two great volumes explain the intricate details and concerns of color print publishing. Must-haves for anyone doing complex color publishing.

Organizations and Foundations

American Society of Authors, Composers, and Publishers (ASCAP)
New York, NY
212/621-6000
A content-licensing source.

Apple Multimedia Program (AMP)
1 Infinite Loop, MS 303-2D
Cupertino, CA 95014
408/974-4897
This program is designed for multimedia developers—including title developers, production service companies, VARs, systems integrators, content owners, and other groups that want to keep up with Apple's plans in the multimedia industry.

Apple Programmers and Developers Association (APDA)
P.O. Box 319, Buffalo, NY 14207-0319
U.S. 800/282-2732
Canada 800/637-0029
International AppleLink APDA 716/871-6555
A source for Apple developer information and tools.

Association of Computing Machinery
SigCHI (Computer-Human Interaction)
SigGRAPH (Computer Graphics)
1515 Broadway, 17th Floor, New York, NY 10036
212/869-7440
Ongoing meetings of professional and academic individuals to advance the knowledge of interface and multimedia uses of computers.

Audio Engineering Society
60 East 42nd Street, New York, NY 10165
212/661-8528
Technical association for audio professionals and music engineers. They also cover issues like licensing and royalties.

Broadcast Music, Inc. (BMI)
New York, NY 212/586-2000
Los Angeles, CA 310/659-9109
A content-licensing source.

Electronic Frontier Foundation (EFF)
1001 G ST NW, Ste 950E, Washington, DC 20001
202/347-5400
Association leading the dialogue on social, legal, and political issues of multimedia computing.

IMA Intellectual Property Task Force
1 Fifth Street, Cambridge, MA 02141
617/864-6606
In charge of figuring out appropriate legal and business models for the multimedia industry.

Interactive Multimedia Association
3 Church Circle, Suite 800, Annapolis, MD 21401-1933
410/626-1380

International Interactive Communications Society (IICS)
14657 SW Teal Blvd. Suite 119, Beavertown, OR 97007
503/579-4427
Organization of individuals concerned with issues of interface and multimedia design.

International MIDI Association
23634 Emelita Street, Woodland Hills, CA 91367
818/598-0088
Distribute MIDI specifications.

Multimedia Development Group (MDG)
2601 Mariposa Street, San Francisco, CA 94110
415/553-2300
A non-profit trade association providing information about business, technology, tools and professional services to the multimedia community.

Multimedia PC (MPC) Marketing Council
1730 M Street NW, Suite 700, Washington, D.C. 20036
202/452-1600
Promotes and issues the Microsoft MPC standard.

National Computer Graphics Association
2722 Merilee Drive , Fairfax, VA 22031
703/698-9600

Software Publishers Association
1730 M Street NW, Suite 700 , Washington, D.C. 20036
202/452-1600
Organization of computer vendors who occasionally develop multimedia policies.

United States Office of Copywriting
202/707-3000

YLEM: Artists Using Science & Technology
PO Box 749 , Orinda, CA 94563
415/856-9593
Organization of creative multimedia artists.

Market Research Firms

Dataquest
1290 Ridder Park Drive, San Jose, CA 95131
408/437-8000

Digital Information Group
51 Bank Street, Stamford, CT 06901
203/348-2751

DISK/TREND
1925 Landings Drive, Mountain View, CA 94043
415/961-6209

Electronic Industries Association
Marketing Services Research Center
2001 Pennsylvania Ave. NW
Washington, DC 20006-1813
202/457-8739

Freeman Associates, Inc.
311 East Carillo Street, Santa Barbara, CA 93101
805/963-3853

InfoTech
P.O. Box 150, Woodstock, VT 05091-0150
802/457-1037

INTECO Corporation
110 Richards Ave., Norwalk, CT 06854
203/866-4400

In-Stat
7418 East Helm Drive, Scottsdale, AZ 85260-2418
602/483-4455

LINK Resources Corporation
79 Fifth Avenue, New York, NY 10003
212/627-1500

Market Data Retrieval
16 Progress Drive, Shelton, CT 06484
800/333-8802

Market Vision
326 Pacheco Ave., Ste. 200, Santa Cruz, CA 95062
408/426-4400

Dr. Paul Nichols, Pelican Island Information
P.O. Box 24004, London, ON Canada N6H 5C4
519/679-9107

Quality Education Data
1600 Broadway, 12th Floor, Denver, CO 80202-4912
800/525-5811

T.H.E. Journal
150 El Camino Real, Ste. 112, Tustin, CA 92680-3670
714/730-4011

TPFL Publishing
1301 Twentieth Street NW, Ste. 702, Washington, DC 20036
202/296-6009

Training and Schools

American Film Institute
Los Angeles, CA
213/856-7664
People who want to make multimedia titles often attend this affordable and talented school. Reinventing Hollywood is part of their charter.

Apple Developer University
Send e-mail to DEVUNIV or
DEVUNIV@APPLELINK.APPLE.COM
Provides expert instruction for all levels of Macintosh programmers.

Apple Training Providers Directory
Send e-mail to DEVSUPPORT or
DEVSUPPORT@APPLELINK.APPLE.COM
Nationwide network of training providers on Applelink.

Center for Creative Imaging
Camden, ME
800/428-7400
Innovative art and learning facility.

Multimedia Training Library
Send e-mail to DEVSUPPORT or
DEVSUPPORT@APPLELINK.APPLE.COM
Worldwide database of multimedia training providers on Applelink.

New Media Centers Program
415/329-1316
Nationwide program based on a new model that fosters the widespread integration of interactive media in teaching, learning, and communicating. Founders include Adobe Systems, Inc., Apple Computer, Inc., FWB Inc., Macromedia, Prentice Hall, Sony Electronics Inc., and SuperMac Technology, Inc.

San Francisco State University Extended Education
San Francisco, CA
415/904-7700
Offers a Multimedia Studies Program that provides hands-on design, production, and writing experience. Also includes instruction on multimedia marketing and promoting.

Conferences

January

Consumer Electronics Show
Electronics Industries Association
Las Vegas, NV
202/457-4900

MACWORLD
Mitch Hall Associates
San Francisco, CA
617/361-2001

MILIA
Midem Organization
Cannes, France
212/689-4220

February

DEMO
InfoWorld Editorial Events
Indian Wells, CA
415/312-0545

Digital Hollywood
American Expositions
212/226-4141

MACWORLD Tokyo
World Expo Corporation
Tokyo, Japan
508/879-6700

SALT
Society for Applied Learning
Orlando, FL
800/457-6812

Virtual Reality International
Meckler, Ltd.
London, UK
44-071-976-0405

March

Electronic Books International
Meckler, Ltd.
London, UK
US 203/226-6967, Europe 44/071-976-0405

FOSE's CD-ROM Conference
National Trade Productions, Inc.
Washington, DC
800/638-8510

InterMedia
Reed Exhibition
San Jose, CA
203/352-8240

International Quicktime and Multimedia Conference
MACWORLD/Sumeria
San Francisco, CA
415/904-0800

National Association of Broadcasters (NAB)
Las Vegas, NV
202/429-5346

Seybold Boston
Seybold Seminars
Boston, MA
310/457-8500

Software Development and Business Software Solutions
CM Ventures Inc.
San Jose, CA
415/905-2784

April

Electronic Entertainment Expo
Knowledge Industries Publications
Atlanta, GA
914/328-9157

ImageWorld
Meckler, Ltd.
Chicago, IL
US 203/226-6967, Europe 44/071-976-0405

Multimedia Expo
American Expositions
New York, NY
212/226-4141

Multimedia Expo East/Digital Video
New York, NY
212/226-4983

New Media Expo
The Interface Group
Los Angeles, CA
617/449-6600

May

Apple Worldwide Developer Conference
Apple Computer, Inc.
San Jose, CA
408/974-4897

COMDEX Summer
The Interface Group
Atlanta, GA
617/449-6600

Computer Animation
Secretariat: CUI
Geneva, Switzerland
41/22-705-7769

Interactive
Ziff Institute
800/34-TRAIN

MACWORLD
Washington D.C.
508/872-8237

Multimedia
Multimedia Exposition and Forum
Toronto, Canada
800/888-7564

Multimedia
National Educational Film & Video Festival
Oakland, CA
510/465-6885

Virtual Reality
Meckler, Ltd.
San Jose, CA
800/632-5537

June

AMI
Association for Multi-Image International
New Orleans, LA
813/960-1692

Art Teco
Morph's Outpost, Inc.
San Francisco, CA
800/GO-MORPH

Computer Graphics International
Michael Gigante
Melbourne, Australia
61/3-282-2463

Consumer Electronics Show Summer
Electronic Industries Association
Chicago, IL
202/457-4900

Digital World
Seybold Seminars
Los Angeles, CA
310/457-8500

IICS Annual Conference
IICS
Anaheim,CA
503/579-4427

Interactive
Ziff Institute
San Jose, CA
617/252-5187

Interactive Media Festival Awards
Cunningham Communications & Seybold Seminars
Anaheim, CA
800/573-1212

Multimedia Conference and Exhibition
Blenheim Group PLD
London, UK
44-81-742-2828

NECC
National Education Computing Conference
Boston, MA
503/346-4414

Technology & Issues
Sumeria
Yosemite, CA
415/904-0811

VISCOMM
United Digital Artists
San Francisco, CA
212/777-7200

July

ACM SIGGRAPH
SIGGRAPH
Ontario, FL
312/644-6610

Interact
Interactive Services Assoc.
Boston
301/495-4955

MACWORLD
Singapore
508/872-8237

August

MACWORLD
Mitch Hall Associates
Boston, MA
617/361-2001

SALT Conference/Interactive Multimedia
Society for Applied Learning
Washington, DC
800/457-6812

Software Development and Business Software Solutions
CM Ventures, Inc.
Boston, MA
415/905-2784

September

Agenda
InfoWorld Editorial Events
Scottsdale, AZ
415/312-0545

Electronic Book Fair
Sumeria
San Francisco, CA
415/904-0811

Electronic Books
Mecklermedia
New York, NY
800/632-5537

ImageWorld New York
Knowledge Industry Publications
New York, NY
800/800-5474

Macromedia Developers Conference
Reed Exhibition Companies
San Francisco, CA
203/352-8296

MACWORLD Expo Berlin
Frankfurt, Germany
49/61-51-26121

Multimedia Expo/Digital Video
American Expositions
San Francisco, CA
212/226-4141

Seybold San Francisco
Seybold Seminars
San Francisco, CA
310/457-8500

October

CD-ROM Expo
Mitch Hall Associates
Boston, MA
617/361-2001

MACWORLD
Auckland, New Zealand
508/872-8237

MACWORLD
Aedile Enterprises, Inc.
Toronto, Canada
416/620-1078

Multimedia Expo
American Expositions, Inc.
San Jose, CA
212/226-4141

Smart Media
Knowledge Industry Publications
New York, NY
800/800-5474

TIME Europe/CD-ROM Europe
Lowndes Exhibition Organizers Ltd.
London, UK
44/0-733-394-304

November

COMDEX/Fall
The Interface Group
Las Vegas, NV
617/449-6600

European Multimedia and CD-ROM Conference
Claire Menadue
Wiesbaden, Germany
49/211-55-62-81

MACWORLD
Hong Kong
508/872-8237

NICOGRAPH
Nippon Computer Graphics Association
Tokyo, Japan
81/3-3233-3475

Virtual Reality
Meckler, Ltd.
New York, NY
800/632-5537

December

Personal Computer Outlook
Burlingame, CA
212/696-9793

ImageWorld West
Knowledge Industry Publications
San Jose, CA
800/800-5474

Text Software

Dictionaries/Thesauruses:

American Heritage Electronic Dictionary
Writing Tools Group, Inc.
800/523-3520

WordFinder Plus
Microlytics
800/828-6293

Grammar Checkers:

Correct Grammar
Correct Writing
Writing Tools Group, Inc.
800/523-3520

Editorial Advisor
Petroglyph, Inc.
415/979-0588

Grammatik Mac
Reference Software
415/541-0222

Indexing Tools:

HyperKRS HyperIndexer
Knowledge Set Corporation
800/456-0469

OCR Software:

Accutext 3.0
Xerox Imaging Systems
800/248-6550

OmniPage 3.0
OmniPage Direct
OmniPage Professional
Caere Corporation
408/395-7000

Read-It! OCR
Olduvai Corporation
800/548-5151

TextPert 3.5
CTA Corporation
203/786-5828

TypeReader
ExperVision
800/732-3897

Outliner:

More 3.1
Symantec
800/441-7234

Text to Speech:

Soliloquy
Sound Bytes
Emerson & Stern Associates, Inc.
619/457-2526

Word Processors:

ExpertWriter
Expert Software
800/759-2562

MacWrite Pro 1.5
Claris Corporation
408/727-8227

Word
Microsoft Corporation
206/882-8080

WordPerfect 3.0
WordPerfect Corporation
801/451-5151

WriteNow 3.0
T/Maker
415/962-0195

Scriptwriting Software:

Scriptor 4.0
Screenplay Systems
818/843-6557

Text Hardware

OCR Scanners:

see Scanners under Photography Hardware

Graphics Software

Graphic/Drawing Software:

Canvas 3.5
Deneba Software
305/596-5644

CricketDraw III
Computer Associates
800/225-5224

Freehand 3.1
Aldus Corporation
206/622-5500

Illustrator 3.2
Adobe Systems, Inc.
415/961-4400

Intellidraw
Aldus Corporation Consumer Division
619/695-6956

MacDraw Pro 1.5
MacDraw II 1.1
Claris Corporation
800/334-3535

Streamline 2.2
Adobe Systems, Inc.
415/961-4400

SuperPaint 3.0
Aldus Corporation Consumer Division
619/695-6956

Typography:

Adobe Type Library
Adobe Systems, Inc.
800/833-6687

Fluent Laser Fonts Library 2
Casady & Green, Inc.
408/624-8716
800/359-4920

Fontographer
Altsys Corporation
214/680-2060

LetraStudio
Letraset
201/845-6100

TypeStyler 2.0
Brøderbund Software, Inc.
415/492-3200

Illustration Software

Paint Software:

MacPaint 2.0
Claris Corporation
800/334-3535

Monet
Delta Tao
408/730-9336

Oasis
Time Arts, Inc.
800/959-0509

Painter 1.5
Sketcher 1.0
Fractal Design Corporation
408/688-8800

PixelPaint
Supermac Technology
408/245-2202

Studio/8 2.0
Studio/32 1.2
Electronic Arts
800/245-4525

UltraPaint 1.0.5
Deneba Software
305/596-5644

2D Illustration Software:

JAG II
Ray Dream, Inc.
415/960-0765

Smoothie
Pierce Software
408/244-6554

3D Illustration Software:

addDepth
Ray Dream, Inc.
415/960-0765

Dimensions
Adobe Systems, Inc.
800/833-6687

StrataType 3d
Strata Inc.
801/628-5218

Typestry
Pixar
510/236-4000

Clip Art Illustrations:

ArtDisk Collection
D.V. Franks

Backgrounds for Multimedia Volume 1
Backgrounds for Multimedia Volume 2
Marble & Granite
Artbeats
800/444-9392

ClickArt
T/Maker
415/962-0195

Clip Art Masterpieces
Wayzata Technology
800/735-7321

Cliptures
MacGallery
Dream Maker Software
303/762-1001

DeskTop Art Collection
Dynamic Graphics
800/255-8800

Digi-Art Collection
Image Club Graphics
800/661-9410

Images with Impact!
3G Graphics, Inc.
800/456-0234

Educorp Clip-Art CD-ROM
Educorp
800/843-9497

MapArt
Cartesia Software
800/334-4291

StrataTextures
Strata Inc.
800/869-6855

WetPaint Collection
Dubl-Click Software
800/266-9525

Wraptures
Form and Function
800/843-9497

Illustration Hardware

Drawing Tablet:

Wacom ADB Digitizer
Wacom
201/265-4226

Photography Software

Compression Software:

Colorsqueeze
Eastman Kodak Company
800/233-1650

ImpressIt
Radius, Inc.
408/434-1010

Clip Art Photographs:

CD Stock
Mirror Technologies
800/654-5294

Classic Art
G&G Designs/Communications
619/431-7400

Clip Art Masterpieces Volume 1
PhotoBank
Wayzata Technology, Inc.
800/735-7321
218/326-0597

Digital Photography Volumes
Comstock
800/225-2727

Cantrall's Photos on Disc
Gazelle Technologies World Travel Series
Educorp
800/843-9497

Folio 1 Print Pub
D'Pix
800/238-3749

PhotoDisc Volumes
PhotoDisc
800/528-3472

Royalty Free Series
The Multimedia Library
800/362-4978

Stock Workbook CD
Scott & Daughters
800/547-2688

The Westlight Sampler
Westlight
800/872-7872

Image Manipulation Software:

ColorStudio 1.5
Fractal Design Corporation
408/688-8800

Digital Darkroom
Aldus Corporation Consumer Division
619/558-6000

Enhance 2.0
MicroFrontier, Inc.
515/270-8109

ImageAssistant
Caere Corporation
408/395-7000
800/535-7226

PhotoShop 2.5
Adobe Systems, Inc.
800/833-6687

Gallery Effects 1.5
Volume 1: Classic Art
Volume 2: Classic Art
Gallery Effects: Texture Art
Aldus Corporation Consumer Division
619/695-6956

Filters/Special Effects:

Lightning Effects 2.5
Spectral Innovations, Inc.
408/955-0366

Kai's Power Tools 2.0
HSC Software
310/392-8441

Multimedia Catalogers:

CompassPoint
Northpint Software
313/543-1770

Digital Album
GTE ImageSpan
510/416-0150

Fetch
Aldus Corporation
206/622-5500

ImageAccess
Nikon Electronic Imaging
800/645-6678

Media Cataloger
Interactive Media Corporation
415/948-0745

Media Tree
Tulip Software
508/475-8711

Sensicon Mediabase
Intelligent Systems Design
206/869-5501

Screen Capture:

Capture 4.0
Mainstay
805/484-9400

CameraMan 2.0
Vision Software International
408/748-8411

Exposure Pro 1.0.2
ScreenShot 1.2
Baseline Publishing Company
901/682-9676

Image Grabber 3.0
Sabstian Software
206/865-9343

Scanning Software:

Ofoto 2.0
Light Source, Inc.
800/231-7226

File Format Translation:

deBabelizer
Equilibrium
415/332-4343

Fast Eddie 2.0
Paradigm Concepts
505/888-0112

Photography Hardware

Digital Still Cameras:

Canon RC-250, 360, 570
Canon USA, Inc.
516/488-6100

FotoMan
Logitech, Inc.
510/795-8500

QuickTake 100
Apple Computer, Inc.
408/996-1010

Hand Scanners, Color:

Animas True-Color Hand-Held Scanner
Animus
714/590-3334

Hand Scanners, Gray:

LightningScan 400, Compact, Pro 256
Thunderware, Inc.
510/254-6581

ScanMan
Logitech, Inc.
415/795-8500

Typist Plus Graphics
Caere Corporation
800/535-7226

Scanners, Color

Color OneScanner
Apple Computer, Inc.
408/996-1010

Focus Color Scanner
Agfa Division, Mile Inc.
201/440-2500

HP ScanJet IIc
Hewlett-Packard
800/752-0900

JX-320, JX-450
Sharp Electronics Corporation
201/529-9594

Personal Color Scanner
Howtek
603/882-5200

ScanMaker IIXE, 45t, 4000, 600ZS
Microtek Lab, Inc.
213/321-2121

UC1200S, UC630
UMAX Technologies, Inc.
800/562-0311

Scanners, Grayscale:

HP Scanjet IIp
Hewlett-Packard
800/752-0900

Focus S600 GS/S800 GS/S800 GSE
Agfa Division, Mile Inc.
201/440-2500

OneScanner
Apple Computer, Inc.
408/996-1010

ScanMaker 660GS, Model 32
Microtek Lab, Inc.
213/321-2121

Slide Scanners:

Eikonix 1435 Slide Scanner
Eikonix
617/275-3232

Kodak Professional RFS 2035 Film Scanner
Eastman Kodak Company
800/242-2424

Leafscan
Leaf Systems
508/460-8300

ScanMaker 1850S
Microtek Lab, Inc.
213/321-2121

Image Manipulation Accellerators:

Thunderstorm, Thunderstorm Pro
Supermac Technology
408/561-6100
800/541-7680

Animation Software

2D Animation:

ADDmotion 2.0
Motion Works Inc.
604/685-9975

Animation Stand
Linker Systems Inc.
714/552-1904

interFACE
Bright Star Technology
206/451-3697

MacroMind Director 4.0
Macromedia, Inc.
415/252-2000

2D Clip Animation:

Animation Clips
Media In Motion
415/621-0707

AniMedia
Animatics
800/665-3898

IllusionArt
IllusionArt
510/839-9580

3D Animation:

Crystal Desktop Animator 4.21
CrystalGraphics, Inc.
800/349-0700

Dimensions
Visual Information Development
818/918-8834

ElectricImage 2.0
Electric Image, Inc.
818/577-1627

Fractal Terrain Modeler
Strata Inc.
800/869-6885

Infini-D 2.0
Specular International Ltd.
800/433-7732

MacRenderman
Showplace with MacRenderman
Pixar
800/888-9856

Macromedia Three-D
MacroModel
ModelShop II
Swivel 3D Professional
SwivelMan
Macromedia, Inc.
800/288-47970

PROmotion 1.0
Motion Works, Inc.
604/685-9975

Ray Dream Designer 2.0
Ray Dream, Inc.
415/960-0765

Sketch 1.5
Alias Research, Inc.
800/447-2542

StrataVision 3d 2.0
Strata Inc.
800/869-6855

Super3D 2.5
Aldus Corporation Consumer Division
619/695-6956

Virtus Voyager Professional
Virtus Voyager Executive
Virtus Walkthrough Pro
Virtus Corporation
800/847-8871

3D ClipModels:

3-D Object Library
Viewpoint
801/224-2222

Acuris ClipModel Libraries
Acuris, Inc.
415/329-1920

StrataClip 3d
StrataShapes
StrataTextures
Strata Inc.
800/869-6855

Utilities:

CD-I Animation Stack
Optimage Interactive Services Co.
515/225-7000

Sound Software

Music Software:

Alchemy
Encore
Master Tracks Pro 5
MusicTime
TurboTrax
Passport Designs, Inc.
415/726-0280

Audioshop 1.1
EZ Vision
Galaxy Plus Editiors
Galaxy—The Universal Librarian
Max
Vision
Studio Vision 1.5
Opcode Systems, Inc.
415/856-3333

ConcertWare+ Version 4
ConcertWare+MIDI Version 5.2.2
ConcertWave+Music
Great Wave Software
408/438-1990

Deck
Sound Designer II
Turbosynth
Digidesign, Inc.
415/688-0600

Deluxe Music Construction Set 2.5
DeluxeRecorder
Electronic Arts
415/571-7171

Digital Performer
Performer Version 4.01
Mark of the Unicorn, Inc.
617/576-2760

DMP7Pro
DX11 Pro, DX7 11 Pro
FB Pro
TX1Z Pro, TX802 Pro
Digital Music Services
741/951-1159

MIDI ClipSounds:

AudioClips
Sound Source Limited
805/494-9996

A Zillion Sounds
BeachWare
619/492-9529

Bogas Sound Effects Disk
Bogas Productions
415/592-5129

The Best of MIDI Connection
The Best of Sound Bytes
Metatec Corp./Nautilus
800/637-3472

Clip Audio
The Publishing Factory, Inc.
800/835-5547

Clip Tunes
Digidesign, Inc.
800/688-0600

Desktop Sounds
Optical Media International
800/347-2664

Grooves
Media Design Interactive
(UK) 44-252-737630

Hollywood Film Music Library
The Hollywood Film Music Library
818/985-9997

Killer Tracks Music Library
Killer Tracks
800/877-0078

Royalty Free Series
The Multimedia Library
800/362-4978

SoundFX
Hologlyph
303/422-9082

Sound Hardware

Microphones:

F-99LT, F-VX50 Dynamic Stereo Microphones
Sony Corporation of America, Inc.
800/352-7669

MIDI Interfaces:

Apple MIDI Interface
Apple Computer, Inc.
408/996-1010

MacNexus
JLCooper Electronics
310/306-4131

Studio 3, Studio 5, Studio Plus Two
Opcode Systems, Inc.
415/856-3333

Sound Digitizers:

AudioMedia
Digidesign, Inc.
415/327-8811

MacRecorder
Macromedia, Inc.
415/252-2000

**Voice Impact
Voice Impact Pro
Voice Record 2.0**
Articulate Systems, Inc.
800/443-7077

Speaker Systems:

AppleDesign Powered Speakers II
Apple Computer, Inc.
408/996-1010

Bose RoomMate Computer Monitor
Bose
800/444-2673

MacSpeaker
Persona Technologies, Inc.
415/871-6000

**SRS-38, SRS-58, SRS-88 Active Speakers
IFS-20K Infrared Speakers**
Sony Corporation of America, Inc.
800/352-7669

Video Software

Video Editing:

HSC VideoWare
HSC Software
310/392-8441

Premiere 3.0
Adobe Systems, Inc.
800/833-6687

QuickTime Starter Kit
Apple Computer, Inc.
408/996-1010

VideoFusion
VideoFusion, Ltd.
419/891-1090

VideoScript
Truevision, Inc.
800/522-8783

VidSynth
Cybernetic Arts
408/248-0377

Screen Recorders:

Spectator
Baseline Publishing, Inc.
901/682-9676

ClipVideo:

AdClips Volume One
Mediacom, Inc.
804/794-0700

Clip Media
Macromedia, Inc.
415/252-2000

ClipTime
ATG, Inc.
410/781-4200

Clip Video
The Publishing Factory, Inc.
800/835-5547

Clip*Video*Art "Animation Effects"
Freemyers Design
916/533-9365

Media Clip-Art
Medial Clip-Art Inc
609/795-5993

Royalty Free Series
The Multimedia Library
800/362-4978

The WPA Film Library
708/385-8528

Video Hardware

Computer Controlled Video Decks:

EVO-9650
Vdeck Hi8
Sony Corporation of America, Inc.
800/352-7669

PC-VCR
NEC Technologies
800/562-5200

Camcorders:

Canon UC1 8mm
H850 Hi8 Stereo 8mm
Canon USA, Inc.
516/488-6100

CCD-TR81 Hi8
Sony Corporation of America, Inc.
800/352-7669

Touch Screen Displays:

Mac Snap-On
MicroTouch Systems, Inc.
508/964-9900

Monitor Mouse For Macintosh
Elographics, Inc.
615/482-4100

MouseTouch
Information Strategies, Inc.
214/234-0176

TouchWindow
Edmark Corporation
206/556-8484

Touch Monitor
Information Strategies
214/234-0176

TouchStar
Troll Technology
805/295-0770

Video Digitizing Cards:

ColorSnap 32+
Computer Friends, Inc.
503/626-2291

ComputerEyes/Pro
ComputerEyes/RT
Digital Vision, Inc.
617/329-5400

DigitalFilm
VideoSpigot
VideoSpigot Pro
SuperMac Technology
408/245-2202

DigiVideo Color
Wardco Holdings
408/366-6903

Kodak Professional DCS 200 Digital Camera
Eastman Kodak Company
800/242-2424

Morph 1.5
Gryphon Software
619/536-8815

NuVista + Videographics Card
Truevision
317/841-0332

VideoTime
RasterOps Corporation
408/562-4200

VideoVision
Radius, Inc.
800/227-2795

Video Accelerators:

NuMedia
Spectral Innovations
408/955-0366

RenderEdge
StarTech
619/749-4383

Videodisc Players:

LaserDisc Players
Pioneer Communications
201/327-6400

Video Production Systems:

Avid Media Composer
Avid Technology, Inc.
508/640-6789

After Effects
Company of Science & Art (CoSA)
401/831-2675

Apple Professional Video Production Solution
Apple Computer, Inc.
408/996-1010

Video F/X

Digital F/X
415/961-2800

Programming Software

Authoring Tools:

Action! 1.0
Authorware Professional
Director 3.1
Macromind Media Maker 1.5
Macromedia, Inc.
415/252-2000

Aegis Showcase F/X
Aegis Development
213/42-1227

Apple Media Authoring Solution
Apple Computer, Inc.
408/996-1010

HyperCard 2.5
Claris Corporation
408/987-7000

LINX Lite
LINX Industrial
LINX Test Factory
Warren-Forthought
409/849-1278

MediaText
WINGS for Learning/Sunburst
800/321-7511

MovieWorks
Interactive Solutions, Inc.
415/377-0136

PACo Producer 2.0
The Company of Science & Art (CoSA)
401/831-2672

Passport Producer
Passport Designs, Inc.
415/726-0280

Serius Multimedia
Serius Corporation
801/261-7900

Special Delivery
Interactive Media Corporation
415/946-0745

Spinnaker Plus
Spinnaker
617/494-1200

SuperCard 1.6
Aldus Corporation Consumer Division
619/695-6956

The Expanded Book Toolkit
The Voyager CD Audio Toolkit
The Voyager Videodisc Toolkit
The Voyager Company
310/451-1383

The Textbook Toolbox
Chemeketa Community College
503/399-8390

Production Tools:

QuicKeys
CE Software
515/224-1995

Multiplatform Conversion Tools:

Convert It!
Homeward
Heizer Software
800/888-7667

Player
Macromedia, Inc.
415/252-2000

Interview and Case Study Index

Interviews

Case Studies

Index /Glossary

Symbols

2D animation ▶ 28, 157, 195
2½ D animation ▶ 197
3D animation ▶ 29, 157, 197
3D navigation ▶ 222
3DO ▶ 121
8-bit color ▶ 118, 150, 165
Representing colors using 8-bits. An 8-bit monitor is capable of displaying 256 colors at the same time.

24-bit color ▶ 118, 150, 165
Representing colors using 24-bits. A 24-bit monitor is capable of displaying over 16 million different colors at the same time.

800 numbers ▶ 255
900 numbers ▶ 255

A

accelerator card
A card or board that can be placed into a computer to improve the performance of the CPU.

accents ▶ 192
access time ▶ 41, 110
The time it takes to search, retrieve, and return data from computer media. Video tape takes minutes, videodisc takes a few seconds, CD-ROM under 350 milliseconds, hard disk 10-20 milliseconds, and memory microseconds.

acquisition
The process of transferring data from analog to digital form; specifically video material. Also referred to as capturing.

action axis ▶ 202
actors ▶ 30, 152
ADAM ▶ 137, 149
Adams, Douglas ▶ 133
adaptive interaction ▶ 4, 51, 95, 134, 176
Adobe Premiere ▶ 205
Adobe Systems, Inc. ▶ 183
Adobe Type Manager ▶ 183
ADPCM
(Adaptive Differential Pulse Code Modulation) An audio encoding and compression standard.

advertising ▶ 23, 52, 244, 256

affiliated label ▶ 12, 18, 49, 236
A distribution option where publisher provides marketing and distribution for a product developed by a production company. The ownership of the product typically remains in the hands of the producer.

affordability ▶ 128
age ▶ 11, 96, 106, 192
agents ▶ 41, 133, 134
Aldus Fetch ▶ 40, 57
Aldus Persuasion ▶ 55, 57
Allen, Rebecca ▶ 50
alpha-test ▶ 217
The first formal testing period for a software or multimedia product that tests correctness and general functionality. Followed by a beta-testing.

ambient sounds ▶ 27, 98, 155, 190, 194
American CD-I Association ▶ 110
American Federation of Television and Radio Artist (AFTRA) ▶ 192
Amiga ▶ 121
analog
Any physical system indexed, controlled, or represented by continuously variable physical quantities, typically electrically based. A digital system, by contrast, uses discrete representations.

AND Communications ▶ 93, 103
animation compression ▶ 198
animation ▶ 28, 123, 153, 157, 195, 222
A sequence of illustrations that give the illusion of motion. The two basic branches of animation are 2D and 3D animation.

animator
An artist that produces animations, commonly on a computer using animation software.

Animatrix ▶ 94
ANSI ▶ 110
anthropomorphization ▶ 133
anti-aliasing ▶ 82, 148, 198
A process of blurring a jagged line to give the appearance of a smooth line.

Antman, Michael ▶ 75
aperture ▶ 185
Apple Computer, Inc. ▶ 2, 43, 67, 76, 81, 92, 94, 108, 118, 119, 127, 134, 137, 172, 209, 219, 255
Apple Desktop Seminar Toolkit ▶ 43
Apple *Human Interface Guidelines* ▶ 131, 151

Apple *Localization Guidelines* ▶ 97
Apple Multimedia Lab ▶ 92, 176
Apple Programmers and Developers Association (APDA) ▶ 97
Apple Third-Party Compatibility Test Lab ▶ 226
Apple Worldwide Multimedia ▶ 7
application
A software program that performs a specific task such as page layout, word-processing, or illustration.

Applin, Sally Ann ▶ 209
Arborescence ▶ 38, 62, 99, 172, 175
The Architecture of Catastrophic Change ▶ 51
Arent, Michael ▶ 134
Arthur's Teacher Trouble ▶ 34, 157
ASCII
(American Standard Code for Information Interchange) A widely used convention for encoding characters using 8-bit pieces of data.

aspect ratio
The ratio of the width to height of an image or screen generally expressed as a fraction. Consumer television has a 4:3 aspect ratio. Images will become distorted if forced into a different aspect ratio during enlargement, reduction, or transfers.

assembly language ▶ 209
asset
An original source or a high-quality digital content element.

asymmetric compression ▶ 207
attraction loop ▶ 38
audience ▶ 13, 25, 55, 61, 94, 107, 128, 159, 217
Audio Video Interleaved ▶ 208
(AVI) A file format for digital video under Microsoft Windows.

audio ▶ 3, 30, 98, 119, 153, 190
The medium of sound. In multimedia, this includes voice, music, sound effects, and ambient sound.

audio synchronization ▶ 199
authoring tool ▶ 33, 43, 58, 91, 108, 123, 140, 144, 148, 163, 170, 172, 253
A tool that provides much of the framework for creating electronic books or presentations.

authors ▶ 62, 64, 66
Authorware ▶ 143
automation ▶ 135, 173

B

backgrounds ▶ 151, 186
backlight ▶ 186
backup schedules ▶ 175
Backus, Dan ▶ 137, 149, 210
bandwidth ▶ 116
The capacity of an analog or digital signal transmission or network.

bartering ▶ 83
beta-testing ▶ 217, 226
A second and final testing period for a product usually done by actual users in real-world situations. Follows alpha-testing.

Big Animated Digital Productions (BAD) ▶ 184, 216, 228
Billups, Scott ▶ 75, 128, 257
binary
A system with only two possible states such as on or off, 1 or 0, high or low.

binaural sound ▶ 121, 154
Sound specially recorded and played that gives a listener a three dimensional audio perception.

bit depth ▶ 150
The number of bits used to represent black and white, grayscale or color values. Common bit depths are 1, 4, 8, and 24.

bitmap
Images or fonts that are described as pixels. A bitmap can contain grayscale tones or colors but is commonly used to describe black-and-white images.

Black Star ▶ 188
bookmarks ▶ 136
boot blocks ▶ 233
Borovoy, Roger ▶ 73
Bounty Bear ▶ 133
brainstorming ▶ 117, 129, 136
Brenner, Donald ▶ 173
Brilliant Media ▶ 117, 123
Broderbund ▶ 34, 96, 98, 131, 157, 217, 236, 257
budgets ▶ 14, 16, 60, 67, 154, 166, 216
bug ▶ 217
A problem or incompatibility in hardware or software.

Bugg, Rosalyn ▶ 122
bulletin board systems (BBSs) ▶ 108, 255
bump map ▶ 198
bundling ▶ 239, 241
business management ▶ 14, 60
business model ▶ 62, 63
business plan ▶ 61
byte
A measure of data equal to eight bits.

C

C++ ▶ 209
Caldwell, Jackie ▶ 244
California Academy of Sciences ▶ 38, 62
camcorder
A small consumer video camera typically recording an NTSC signal and using either VHS or 8mm tape.

camera angles ▶ 200
cameras ▶ 30, 152, 186, 189, 203
Camplejohn, Doug ▶ 116
captions ▶ 151
cards ▶ 140
Carlzon, Jan ▶ 62
cartography ▶ 150
cartoons ▶ 24, 195, 197
cartridge ▶ 108, 114, 119
A form of removable computer storage that typically has high volume and is transportable, typically measured at 40 and 80MB.

Caruso, Denise ▶ 22, 126
cash flow ▶ 14, 74
cast members ▶ 195
casual multimedia ▶ 5, 92
CAV ▶ 113
(Constant Angular Velocity) A videodisc storage and playback standard where the drive spins at a fixed rate which is optimal for time synchronization and access, as opposed to CLV.

CD+G ▶ 111
CD+MIDI ▶ 111
CD-Audio ▶ 26, 48, 52, 154, 191
Commonly called a CD. A format for storing audio music in digital form that is used for the CDs found in music stores. All audio compact discs will play in any audio compact disc player. (The specification for CD-Audio is known as the Red Book.)

CD-I ▶ 111, 122, 157
(Compact Disc-Interactive) A compact disc storage format similar to CD-ROM requiring a television and intended for the consumer electronics market. CD-I discs play only in special players with a specific operating system called CD-RTOS. (The specification for CD-I is known as the Green Book.)

CD-R ▶ 108, 111, 175, 232
CD-ROM ▶ 35, 49, 63, 103, 106, 108, 119, 133, 152, 157, 162, 166, 175, 188, 207, 212, 220, 232
(Compact Disc-Read-Only Memory) A format for storing computer data or compressed audio or video data on a compact disc in a digital form. (The specification for CD-ROM is known as the Yellow Book.) Often used to refer to a compact disc that contains computer data in a read-only format. They have space for about 650 MB of data and track information.

CD-ROM formats ▶ 108
CD-ROM labels ▶ 233
CD-ROM/XA ▶ 49, 110
(Compact Disc-Read-Only Memory/Extended Architecture) An extension of the original CD-ROM standard which adds the capability for interleaving data to enhance real-time playback of time-based data. Closely related to CD-I but intended for use with computer systems.

CD-Video ▶ 121
CD-WO ▶ 111
CDTV ▶ 111
cel animation ▶ 30
charter ▶ 60
charts ▶ 24, 146, 149, 181
check disc
See one-off.

chromakey ▶ 206
The technique of laying one image in the space of another when selecting colors.

chunking ▶ 145
Claris Corporation ▶ 219, 227
Clark, Mike ▶ 132
classifying products ▶ 85
Cleese, John ▶ 66
client ▶ 12, 39, 65, 70, 81, 83, 91, 94, 127, 136, 161, 230, 246, 254
A person or company that specifies and funds a multimedia project for a production house.

clip-art ▶ 149
clip-photography ▶ 188
clip-video ▶ 203
close-ups ▶ 185, 201
CLV ▶ 113
(Constant Linear Velocity) A videodisc storage and playback standard where the drive changes its speed to optimize storage.

co-creation ▶ 51
Coates, George ▶ 50, 51, 74
codec ▶ 160, 190, 207
(Derived from compressor/decompressor) A hardware chip or software algorithm that compresses or decompresses data.

Cole, Brooks ▶ 57, 76
collateral materials ▶ 223
color ▶ 24, 32, 97, 131, 150, 186, 189
color balance ▶ 151, 185, 203
color correction

Any method such as masking, dot-etching, screening, or scanning used to improve color rendition.

color depth ▶ 150, 189
color palette ▶ 189, 199
color-coding ▶ 151
column widths ▶ 147
commissions ▶ 64
commodity products ▶ 85
Commodore ▶ 111
composite video ▶ 205

A complete video signal used in transmission of conventional television and consumer camcorders rather than professional component color systems.

composition ▶ 151, 160, 185

A method of accumulating separately rendered video, graphics, animations, backgrounds, and sounds into a single final track.

compression ▶ 108, 207

Encoding a file, image, sound, or movie with a special algorithm to reduce space requirements for storage or transmission. Compression may be done with either software or hardware.

compression ratio

A measure of the efficiency of compression expressed as the ratio of the original size of the data to its compressed size.

Compton's NewMedia ▶ 236
Comstock ▶ 188
concept ▶ 90, 93, 128, 136
configuration testing ▶ 219, 221
Connally, Craig ▶ 155
consistency ▶ 128, 132, 134, 219
consultants ▶ 14, 62, 92
consumers ▶ 10, 47, 85, 106, 110, 119
content ▶ 11, 20, 63, 83, 101, 107, 136

The information, media, or story used in a multimedia product to educate, entertain, communicate, or in any way affect an audience.

content expert ▶ 20, 48, 63, 99, 127, 133, 136, 187, 223

An authority in a multimedia project typically specializing in one subject or media area.

content testing ▶ 217, 219, 223
continuity ▶ 145, 202, 216
continuous tone

A photographic image that contains gradient tones from black to white.

continuum ▶ 130
contracts ▶ 12, 14, 25, 70, 81

Legal documents that establish an agreement between two or more parties.

contractors ▶ 14, 64
cool light ▶ 186
copy editor ▶ 23
copy stand ▶ 187
copyright ▶ 12, 26, 60, 83, 101, 145, 190

The right of ownership to an original work of art. Automatically granted to the creator but transferable to another party by law or by contractual agreements.

Corey, Glenn ▶ 81, 108, 119, 137, 172, 253
corporate training ▶ 42, 91
costs ▶ 67, 72, 137, 233
Couey, Anna ▶ 51
CPU

(Central Processing Unit) The actual computer processor that performs computations. New custom variety ASIC and RISC CPUs are being made for new special purpose computers.

craning ▶ 201
creative directors ▶ 17, 64, 101
credits ▶ 12, 83
Crichton, Michael ▶ 101
crop

A process used in editing images and video that removes or obscures portions of the frame.

cross-platform ▶ 120

A strategy or method to develop media or software to run on more than one multimedia player or computer.

cross-referencing ▶ 181
Crutchfield Corporation ▶ 253
cue sheet ▶ 192
cultural issues ▶ 11, 97, 150, 159
cursor

A symbol on a computer screen that acts as a pointer for some action taking place.

custom projects ▶ 10, 64, 91, 108, 127, 136, 230
custom tools ▶ 37, 139, 173
customers ▶ 108, 241, 256
cut ▶ 206

Editing term that refers to a piece of sound, video, or film media that is abruptly followed by another piece of media. When experienced the media seems to jump.

CyberArt ▶ 27, 51

General term referring to computer art of the 1990's derived from cybernetics which is the study of man-machine interfaces.

CyberSoft ▶ 47

D

D'Cuckoo ▶ 49
DAC

(Digital to Analog Convert) A device that reads digital sound data and converts it to sound waves that can be played out of a speaker.

Darryn, Chris ▶ 21
DAT ▶ 108, 115, 175, 191

(Digital Audio Tape) A delivery medium used for high definition sound recording and computer file backup. DAT has better time synchronizing quality than analog tape.

database ▶ 41, 144

An organized set of data within a file or set of files in a prescribed format that can be accessed with structured routines for storage and retrieval.

Davis, Jeff ▶ 239, 240
daylight film ▶ 187
DCS

(Desktop Color Separation) A file format for encoding images as five files: four EPS files (one for each CMYK layer) and one PICT preview file.

DeBevoise, Allen ▶ 93
decompression ▶ 117, 207

Restoring a file or image from its compressed form to its original format.

decorative type ▶ 147
default

A value, action, or setting that a computer system assumes unless the user gives an explicit instruction to the contrary.

defensive maintenance ▶ 253
defragmentation ▶ 233
deliverables ▶ 12, 82
delivery ▶ 63, 108, 231, 235
delivery media ▶ 53, 108, 230
delivery platforms ▶ 53, 118
demo disks ▶ 52, 91, 242
demographics ▶ 18, 122
demonstrations ▶ 248
The Desert Music ▶ 51
Desert Storm: The War in the Persian Gulf ▶ 36, 90
design goals ▶ 128
design specifications ▶ 166
design study ▶ 139, 217

Using a small prototype for a multimedia project to test certain ideas.

designers ▶ 80, 101, 127, 199
desktop publishing

Use of a computer system that provides the ability to produce publication-quality documents.

developer programs ▶ 108, 226
development environment ▶ 63, 108, 119

development tools ▶ 57, 134
diagrams ▶ 24, 140, 146, 149, 181
dialog box
A window that offers choices and settings for attributes that becomes visible only when the application requires instructions from the user.

diction ▶ 192
differentiation ▶ 85, 107
Digital Audio Tape (DAT) ▶ 115, 191
Digital Media ▶ 11, 22, 106, 126, 157
digital
The representation of a signal by a set of discrete numerically values. Commonly represented on a computer in binary form.

digital awareness ▶ 76
digital cameras ▶ 152, 187
digital sound processors (DSPs) ▶ 121, 155, 166, 190
A chip that is specialized for working with digital sound. It can convert analog sound waves into digital form and then perform various operations on the data.

digitizer
Any multimedia device that records media to a computer disk in digital form. There are sound, video, and image digitizers.

direct mail ▶ 239, 241, 256
direct manipulation ▶ 132, 135
direct sales force ▶ 239
disabilities ▶ 11, 97
Disc Manufacturing, Inc. ▶ 48, 234
disc
A plate of optical or magnetic material used to store data in digital form.

disk array ▶ 114
diskette ▶ 46, 52, 108, 109, 113, 166, 212
A transportable, light weight diskette that has a flexible disk encased in either a flexible or a rigid plastic case. Commonly called a floppy disk.

display text ▶ 184
editors ▶ 22, 23, 146, 170, 177, 211
dissolve ▶ 206
Media editing term that refers to overlapping two pieces of media to make a transition from one to the other. A dissolve is usually the fading out of one overlaid on the fading up of the other.

distribution channels ▶ 11, 18, 35, 47, 51, 57, 62, 230, 237
distributor ▶ 2, 11, 62, 85, 107, 239, 247
A company that carries and supplies a product to retailers and end-users.

dithering

A way of assigning colors to pixels in order to simulate a color unavailable in a particular output device.

documentation ▶ 23, 24, 57, 212, 223, 254
dollying ▶ 201
Don, Abbe ▶ 51, 83, 128, 165
dpi
(Dots Per Inch) A measure of resolution or detail used for monitors, printers, and other pixel-based devices.

drafts ▶ 177, 216
drawing tools ▶ 25, 181
Computer applications that lets a user create images using combinations of rectangles, ovals, lines, and other geometric shapes.

drive
A computer disk or CD-ROM disc device that accepts, reads, and in most cases, writes data to a disc or diskette. Can refer to a hard drive, floppy drive, CD-ROM drive, cartridge drive, or other.

drop shadows ▶ 146
drum scanners ▶ 188
duplication ▶ 230, 233
DVI ▶ 208
(Digital Video Interactive) A chip set, pioneered by RCA, developed and marketed by Intel, that provides real-time decompression full-motion video from a hard disk or CD-ROM.

dynamic range, sound ▶ 183

E

e-mail
(electronic mail) The process of sending and receiving messages with computers. Messages may be sent and stored for later retrieval.

early-adopters ▶ 106
People who buy and use early technology in new markets.

Eavelyn, Halle ▶ 62
Eddings, Bob ▶ 219, 227
Eden Interactive ▶ 80, 106, 238, 240
Edison Brothers Entertainment ▶ 47
Edison, Thomas ▶ 126
edit decision list ▶ 31, 206
(EDL) A format describing all the editing information about video and sound media for final assembly editing.

editing ▶ 64, 146
editorial links ▶ 162
education ▶ 2, 106, 119, 240
edutainment ▶ 46

Media products that serve both education and entertainment purposes.

effects ▶ 151
Egge, Kathleen ▶ 195
Electronic Arts ▶ 236
electronic books ▶ 34, 91
electronic magazines ▶ 36, 52, 91, 226
Em, David ▶ 50
emersion technology ▶ 121
employees ▶ 10, 14, 76
end-user
The final user of a product. If a client commissions a kiosk, it is the people that ultimately use the system who are the end-users.

engine
In multimedia this refers to the basic software shell that controls interaction and displays content.

Englander, Roger ▶ 48
environment ▶ 55, 98, 219, 221
environmental concerns ▶ 52
environmental map ▶ 198
EPS ▶ 186
(Encapsulated PostScript) A format for importing and exporting PostScript™ language files among applications. An EPS file can contain any combination of text, graphics, and images.

equipment ▶ 106, 173
estimates ▶ 68, 91, 252
Ethernet ▶ 37, 116, 119
A widely used protocol of networking high-speed transmission cables and software used to transfer data between computers.

event handlers ▶ 211
Evleth, Barry ▶ 239
executive producers ▶ 16, 64
Exotic Japan ▶ 20, 93, 99
expandability ▶ 95
expectations ▶ 127, 167
exposure ▶ 151, 160, 185
extreme close-up ▶ 185, 201
extreme long shot ▶ 201
EyeLearn ▶ 218

F

fade-in ▶ 206
A gradual transition from one static media to a moving scene. In video, fade-in from black is most common. In audio, fade-in from silence or ambient sound.

fade-out ▶ 206
A gradual transition from one media to a static one. In

video, fade-out to black is most common. In audio, fade-out to silence or ambient sound.

failure testing ▶ 221
Faulkner, William ▶ 167
FDDI ▶ 116
(Fiber Distributed Data Interface) Network standard for high speed high bandwidth traffic on an optical network.

field
An NTSC video signal is divided into interleaved two fields.

file
A set of data created with an application and stored on a computer by name.

file format ▶ 57, 173
The name and standard specification for the storage of a particular kind of data. TIFF, EPS, WKS are file formats.

file server
A remote and common disk storage connected to computers by a network that manages the sharing of common data and applications.

file type ▶ 174
A code that identifies a particular file format.

fill light ▶ 186
film ▶ 160, 187
film archives ▶ 159
film recorder
A computer-controlled output device that generates images independent of what appears on the screen. The film recorder driver sends a series of instructions that tell the recorder how to draw the final image on the film.

filters ▶ 186, 206
Software algorithms or devices that modify audio or visual signals to create special effects.

final draft ▶ 177
finances ▶ 16, 65, 71, 167
Finding Your Voice ▶ 153
first person ▶ 133
fixed-priced contracts ▶ 69
flash RAM ▶ 115
flatbed scanner ▶ 151, 188
A device that works in a manner similar to a photocopy machine with original art positioned face down on a glass plate. Instead of replicating the image, the image is scanned or placed into a digital form. The scanner is commonly controlled through software running on a computer.

floptical ▶ 115
fly-throughs ▶ 158

focus ▶ 151, 160, 185, 187
focus groups ▶ 12, 106
folly artists ▶ 194
font
A complete set of characters in one design, size, and style. In traditional typography usage, a font may be restricted to a particular size and style or may comprise multiple sizes and styles of a type face design. See typeface.

font substitution
A replacement of a requested but unavailable font by another usually similar font. The replacement decision can be handled automatically by an operating system or application or propagated to the user through a dialog box.

fps
Frames per second.

frame ▶ 160
A single unit of media data. In NTSC video, a frame is a measure of the two fields that make up 1/30th of a second.

frame grabber
A device that converts a screen's worth of analog video signal into a digital form.

framework ▶ 61
Franklin, Marjorie ▶ 50
free links ▶ 162
frequency
The number of times a sound wave oscillates measured in Hertz or cycles per second.

From Alice to Ocean ▶ 34, 151
front-end
The visual interface to a software application commonly used in reference to database implementations.

fulfillment ▶ 235
A service provided by a printer, duplicator, or disc manufacturer that can entail warehousing inventory, processing orders, and shipping to customers.

full-motion
Used to describe video that moves at 24 to 30 frames per second, a rate fast enough give the eye the perception of continuous motion.

functional testing ▶ 166, 216, 219

 G

game cartridges ▶ 46
gender ▶ 96, 97, 106, 192
generalization ▶ 97, 98
genlock

A process of synchronizing video and computer signals with a hardware board.

gigabyte
(GB) A unit of computer memory equal to 1024 megabytes (1,073,741,824 bytes).

golden master ▶ 228
Gourard shading
A rendering algorithm that averages the color and illumination of each corner of a polygonal shape. It renders faster than Phong shading and is more realistic than flat shading.

government ▶ 240
grammar ▶ 144, 146, 178
grants ▶ 72
graphic design ▶ 32, 129, 146
graphic designers ▶ 32, 136, 183, 212
graphs ▶ 149
grayscale ▶ 118, 189
Using levels of gray as opposed to just black and white.

Green Book ▶ 111
Refers to the specification documents for the CD-I format.

Greg LeMond's Bicycle Adventure ▶ 106, 238
grids ▶ 148
group interaction ▶ 136
groupware
Software that allows several people working on the same tasks to better interact and work together.

guides ▶ 133, 212

 H

Habitat ▶ 50
halftone
The use of dots of various sizes in one color, or combining dots in two colors, to simulate a color value that is not available.

hand scanners ▶ 188
handlers ▶ 210
hard drive ▶ 108, 114, 119
A disk drive containing one or more disc platters for storing data. Characterized by moderate to high volume and extremely fast access times. Also commonly referred to as a hard disk.

Harrington, Cody ▶ 198
HDTV ▶ 114, 175, 203
(High Definition TV) A variable standard essentially based on doubling the scan rate of conventional television and displayed in a new 16:9 aspect ratio that is more like a movie screen.

Video format using standard 8mm video tape originated by SONY. Higher in resolution to camcorder 8mm and of the same quality as S-VHS.

An organizational structure for presenting information where text, graphics, and other media are associated in a dynamic and navigable form.

I

A graphic or pictographic symbol used to represent an abstract or concrete object or process.

Any picture drawn to depict a subject.

An technique in animation where frames are rendered by interpolating between two key frames.

in-point
The beginning point of a piece of media that is selected for editing.

A form of design directed at making information clear and understandable as opposed to merely visually attractive or information intensive. An approach to arranging data into a meaningful organization.

A place where multimedia projects are set up for long term or public use, requiring special equipment and security. Usually kiosks are said to be installations.

A branch of interface design referring to the feel and operation of multimedia.

interactive
Software that responds quickly to certain choices and commands a user makes.

The ability for separate applications to communicate data and instructions between themselves.

Designing the interaction and visual display of content and elements for electronic products with an eye towards intuitive understanding and ease of use.

The practice of sector-by-sector alternation between data types within files on a CD-ROM disc. Interleaving permits different types of data to be routed to different hardware or software as a file is playing.

(Integrated Services Digital Network) A digital network architecture that allows for simultaneous digital voice and data transmission currently being installed by telephone carriers worldwide.

ISO
(International Standards Organization.) An active worldwide body which develops, promotes, and establishes standards and protocols for data communications and storage. They have established international CD-ROM, compression, and character encoding standards.

An international standard for CD-ROM file structure. Files on a disc organized according to this structure can be recognized by any computer that understands this format. Sometimes called the High Sierra format.

italic
A type style that is designed to reflect some elements of handwritten script. Italic typefaces slope to the right.

J

A clear, hinged polystyrene case commonly used for compact disc storage.

joint venture
A relationship of two or more business partners who collectively research, develop, or market a technology, product, or service.

(Joint Photographers Experts Group) A set of standard ISO protocols for compressing and decompressing still digital images. It can be implemented in either software or hardware.

K

A key frame in an animation that is used to guide subsequent action or interpolation from another key frame.

kilobyte
(K) A unit of computer memory equal to 1,024 bytes (2 to the 10th power).

kiosk ▷ 38, 52, 63, 91, 98, 153, 165, 209, 221, 231
An installation of multiple media for public use.

Knowledge Navigator ▷ 133, 135
Koch, James ▷ 245
Kodak ▷ 188
Krause, Kai ▷ 100

L

labels ▷ 18, 135, 233
LAN
(Local Area Network) A network that generally connects a group of computers for communicating and transmitting data and sharing printers and other similar types of resources.

languages ▷ 11, 97, 210
Last Chance to See... ▷ 133
lathing ▷ 197
Laurel, Brenda ▷ 95
lavaliere, microphone ▷ 191
Laws, Ken ▷ 210
layout ▷ 24, 32, 147
LD-ROM ▷ 113
The Learning Company ▷ 46
leasing ▷ 80, 173
legal issues ▷ 23, 65
legal professionals ▷ 15, 70, 81
legibility ▷ 146, 183
Letter from a Birmingham Jail ▷ 93, 103
libraries ▷ 146
Library of Congress ▷ 188, 203
licensing ▷ 14, 21, 26, 62, 81, 85, 97, 101, 155
Life Story ▷ 160
Life Through Time ▷ 38
LIFEMap ▷ 38, 62
light source ▷ 186
An algorithmic or programmatic device that gives the appearance of light from a particular angle and intensity in a 3D model, showing reflections, color shadings, and shadows. Multiple light sources can be applied to an image.

lighting ▷ 30, 51, 98, 151, 160, 185, 200, 202
linear editing system ▷ 205
links ▷ 162
lip-synching ▷ 194
Living Books ▷ 34
local area networks ▷ 116
localization ▷ 96, 145, 147
London, Matthew ▷ 238
long shots ▷ 185, 201

lossless ▷ 207
Refers to compression and decompression algorithms that result in reconstructed images that have no degradation in picture quality. Commonly takes longer and provides a smaller compression ratio than lossy algorithms.

lossy ▷ 207
Refers to compression and decompression algorithms that produce reconstructed images containing less information than the original source. In many cases, the difference is unnoticeable but successive lossy compressions may degrade image quality. Typically faster and offering better compression ratios than lossless algorithms.

lowercase ▷ 146
LucasFilms ▷ 50
Ludwig van Beethoven: Symphony No. 9 CD Companion ▷ 22, 50, 99
Lumen Productions ▷ 253
Lunicus ▷ 47

M

Macintosh ▷ 4, 10, 98, 110
Macmillan's Multimedia Dictionary for Children ▷ 97, 133, 137
macro lens ▷ 187
macro utilities ▷ 226
MacroMind Director ▷ 55, 143, 196
MacUser ▷ 38
The Magic Flute ▷ 48
magnetic-optical ▷ 109, 114
(MO) Small optical disks that can be rewritten.

mail-order catalogs ▷ 51, 194, 239
mailing lists ▷ 241
maintenance ▷ 13, 39, 64, 253
managers ▷ 60, 64, 129
Mandala ▷ 50
manuals ▷ 212, 255
maps ▷ 24, 149, 150
market research ▷ 11, 39, 87, 106, 107, 109, 123, 239
market segments ▷ 86, 106, 236
market testing ▷ 224, 255
marketing ▷ 18, 65, 85, 212, 223, 241
Martin, Bob ▷ 189
mask
A special graphic area on which nothing can be imaged.

mass-market products ▷ 64, 91, 108, 120, 230, 255
master
A CD-ROM mold, diskette, audio or video tape, or other

image used to make copies. Mastering is the process of producing that image.

mastering ▷ 109, 230
A step during the process to replicate compact discs.

Maxis Software ▷ 236
Mayers, Trish ▷ 231, 232
McChesney, Brooks ▷ 60
McCormack, Ann ▷ 44
McKee, Jim ▷ 26, 153, 156
McLuhan, Marshall ▷ 103, 135
media testing ▷ 219, 220
Medior ▷ 4, 102, 120
The Medium Is the Massage ▷ 103
medium shots ▷ 185, 201
meetings ▷ 126, 172, 246
megabyte
(MB) A unit of computer memory equal to about a million bytes, exactly 1,048,576 bytes.

messages ▷ 18, 94, 101, 128, 210
metaphors ▷ 131, 132
Meyer, Pedro ▷ 52
microphones ▷ 27, 119, 157, 191
Microsoft ▷ 2, 110, 120, 221
MIDI ▷ 27, 48, 51, 119, 122, 155, 166, 193
(Musical Instrument Digital Interface) A communications standard for representing time-based data for the generation of digital music. It runs on a digital network connecting instruments and computers. MIDI is event-based and can be interpreted by both software and hardware MIDI devices.

MiniDisc ▷ 114
mission statement ▷ 60
Mitchell, Peter ▷ 83, 184, 216, 228
Mixed Mode CD-ROM ▷ 110
A CD-ROM disc which contains data and audio tracks in the compact disc audio Red Book format.

mixer
An audio or video board that is used to mix multiple signals into one.

model releases ▷ 15
modeler ▷ 29, 158, 197
The creation of basic wireframe forms in the animation process.

modem
A device that allows a computer to transmit data over phone lines to and from other computers.

monitors ▷ 118, 186
monochrome
A display that uses only two color values most commonly black and white.

monophonic ▷ 154, 191
monopod ▷ 187

monospaced
A type style in which all characters take up the same amount of horizontal space, an i is as wide as an M. Monospaced fonts are commonly found in typewritten material and in early computer displays.

morphing ▶ 160, 198, 206
A transition by shape of one scene or object into another.

Morris, Marney ▶ 94
Motion JPEG ▶ 208
Mountford, S. Joy ▶ 2, 93, 136, 137
movie
A QuickTime file that contains moving images and/or sound.

movie studio model ▶ 6, 64
MPC ▶ 120, 199
(Multimedia PC) A trademark specifying a minimal multimedia computer standard introduced by Microsoft and Tandy. It specifies an Intel-based CPU with a CD-ROM player, sound board, and speakers.

MPEG ▶ 208
(Motion Picture Experts Group) A set of standard protocols for compressing and decompressing digital video and sound.

Mueller, Sandra ▶ 173
multi-platform strategies ▶ 139, 174
multi-session ▶ 112, 188
Multimedia Week ▶ 106
multimedia
Combining text, graphics, sound, animation, video, or other media into a product or presentation.

multimedia databases ▶ 40, 91, 220, 231
multimedia newsletters ▶ 106, 108
Multiple Master ▶ 183
musicians ▶ 26, 155, 193

N

naming conventions ▶ 101, 171, 211
narration ▶ 192
natural language ▶ 41, 97
Nautilus ▶ 37
navigable movies ▶ 160, 203
navigation ▶ 32, 134, 141, 163, 165, 219, 220
Controls that allow a user to move around a product as well as elements that provide spatial cues.

negative space ▶ 185
negotiations ▶ 83, 246
Nelson, Steve ▶ 117, 123
Nelson, Ted ▶ 90
network ▶ 41, 107, 116, 119

A collection of connected computers that share resources and data.

NewMedia **magazine** ▶ 11
News Navigator ▶ 37
Newsweek Interactive ▶ 36
NeXTSTEP ▶ 121
NeXTWORLD **magazine** ▶ 244
Nintendo ▶ 2, 46, 106, 121
non-linear editing systems ▶ 205
notebook ▶ 131
NTSC ▶ 113, 117, 195, 203, 205
A television transmission standard that supports 30 frames per second established by the National Television Standards Committee and used in the United States, Canada, and Japan.

O

object cameras ▶ 203
object-oriented animation ▶ 195
object-oriented databases ▶ 41
object-oriented programming ▶ 163, 209
An approach that views distinct software components and data types as modular elements.

objective camera angles ▶ 202
off-line editing ▶ 205
one-off ▶ 112, 166, 175, 232
A writable compact disc used for testing CD-ROM production. One-offs contain an actual CD-ROM image and can play in CD-ROM drives. Used interchangeably with proof disc.

one-way links ▶ 162
online facilities ▶ 52, 205, 212, 255
operating system ▶ 41, 59, 253
Software running in a computer that contains all general instructions to manage processes, memory, communications, and other system level responsibilities.

optical character recognition ▶ 35, 145, 178
(OCR) A process of converting scanned images of text into digitally-based character information.

optical disc
Storage medium that is transportable, high volume, and light weight. It uses a magneto-optical disc encased in a rigid plastic case.

optical weight ▶ 147
optics ▶ 203
optimization ▶ 166, 232
Techniques used near the end of prototype or production stages to improve the performance of a product.

Orange Book ▶ 111
orientation ▶ 134
orphans ▶ 148
OS/2 ▶ 110, 121
The Other Side of Town ▶ 50
out-point
The ending point of a piece of time-based media that is selected for editing. The in-point and out-point specify an editing cut of a fixed duration.

outlines ▶ 144, 177
oversample ▶ 188

P

pacing ▶ 148
package design ▶ 80, 247
packaging ▶ 26, 37, 212, 230, 233, 235, 242
page-layout application
A class of computer software that allows the user to arrange text and graphic images more creatively than word processors.

paint software ▶ 181
Computer applications that let the user create images by manipulating individual pixels on the screen.

PAL ▶ 117, 203, 205
(Phase Alternation Line) A color video broadcast standard that supports 25 frames per second; used in China and many European nations including England and Germany. It offers slightly better resolution and color than the NTSC standard used in the US.

palette ▶ 150
A collection of colors or shades available to a graphics system or program.

panning ▶ 201
Swinging a camera slowly, typically from one side of a scene to another. Usually accomplished with a tripod for smooth transitions.

Paramount's Media Kitchen ▶ 153
participatory design ▶ 11
passive interaction ▶ 95
patch tables ▶ 193
PCM
(Pulse Code Modulation) Audio compression standard usually used for analog voice compression.

pen recognition ▶ 135
Peppel, Tyler ▶ 172, 175
Perey, Christine ▶ 67
peripheral
A piece of hardware connected to a computer that gives a computer certain external capabilities.

A high quality shading technique that calculates a color for each pixel in a 3D model. It cannot, however, render more advanced lighting effects such as transparency or reflection.

An image file format and color standard conforming to Kodak's specifications for CD photo finishing. It stores about 100 pictures and is recorded on CD-ROM/XA discs.

Exactingly real presentation or imaging of a scene by a computer. The rendering of the scene pays attention to light, reflection, texture, shadow, and other visual details.

A standard data format in which many Macintosh illustrations are encoded. PICT data can be created, displayed on a screen, and printed by routines incorporated in the Macintosh system.

pixel
(Picture Element) The smallest unit within an image or on a screen that can be assigned a color value.

placeholder
The technique of putting working media in place until finished media can be produced.

player
A small computer or device that plays back multimedia.

point size
A measurement of height, from the top of the ascender to a fixed depth below the descender. There are 72 points in an inch, so 36 point type occupies about 1/2 inch and 18 point type about 1/4 of an inch.

Short for post-production house. A place where media is edited and special effects are added, typically for film, video, and sound production.

Processing of video or sound data after it has been captured by a post house.

A CD-ROM or videodisc production step in which all the individual files are combined into a single large file for a mastering machine.

presentation software
Computer software that helps users create presentations including output to slides and transparencies. Usually given by a speaker, but they can be made to be self-running.

A person who assembles financing and production resources and takes responsibility for making a multimedia title.

The work phase in a multimedia project that comes after prototyping.

proportional spacing
Fonts where some characters take up more horizontal space than others. They are easier to read and look

more like traditional typesetting than monospaced fonts.

A written document stating an intent to produce product or perform a service.

protocol
A set of rules that governs the way information is exchanged between processes or machines, commonly referring to networks.

The inventive phase in a multimedia project that comes after concept and planning and explores many possible designs.

A company in the business of making copies of a media and in some cases distributing it. Multimedia publishers typically produce CD-ROMs from authors and creative production companies.

A system extension developed by Apple Computer, Inc. that displays video and animation on Macintosh computers and under Windows without additional video hardware. It gives developers a common set of routines for manipulating, compressing, and synchronizing moving images and sound in real-time.

R

radiosity
A photorealistic rendering technique where the light energy reflected from various objects in a scene is painted.

RAM ▶ 119
(Random Access Memory) Principal memory used by a computer in which data and instructions are momentarily used. Most RAM memory chips do not preserve the data when the power is turned off.

raster display
A raster image is divided into scan lines. Each line consists of a series of dots from a thin section of the final image. The pattern of dots corresponds to a bit pattern in memory.

raw data
Uncompressed video or audio data.

ray tracing ▶ 198
A sophisticated 3D rendering algorithm that traces rays of light as they bounce off objects. It can add effects such as transparency, true reflection, light refraction, and shadows.

reaction shot ▶ 201
Reactor ▶ 46
Reader Rabbit ▶ 44
recording studios ▶ 27, 193
Red Book ▶ 48, 110, 191
The CD-Audio format developed by Philips and Sony, used to record sound for conventional stereo CD.

reflection map ▶ 198
reflector ▶ 186
registration cards ▶ 212, 255, 256
reimbursible costs ▶ 69, 82
Reiser, Beverly ▶ 50
rendering ▶ 197
The final stage of painting the image in the creation of a 3D image blending of various light sources and surface textures.

repetition ▶ 144
replication
A part of compact disc manufacturing following mastering that includes the pressing of discs. Also a part of diskette duplication.

repurpose ▶ 62, 101, 252, 257
A term referring to the reuse of content. Commonly used when taking existing print or film products and putting them to digital uses.

request for proposal ▶ 12, 82
(RFP) A formal document issued by a client to a group of contractors requesting work to be done.

research ▶ 104, 146, 246
researchers ▶ 20, 23, 32, 99, 146
resolution ▶ 118, 145, 146, 147
The granularity of a display or image typically indicated by a dots per inch measurement. Apparent resolution can be increased by allowing the dot to have a wider color range.

retailers ▶ 11, 239
reuse ▶ 98
reverse cut-aways ▶ 202
reverse-angle ▶ 202
RGB ▶ 150
(Red, Green, and Blue) A model for defining color within a computer system which assigns values to the percentage of the three primary colors of light which make up a color.

rich text format
(RTF) A data format consisting of text with font, formatting, and other properties which determine its look. RTF often serves as an intermediate step in the process of converting from one document type to another.

Richmond, Wendy ▶ 97
RISC
(Reduced Instruction Set Computer) A fast and efficient CPU design.

rivers ▶ 147
Rock Ridge ▶ 111
role ▶ 6, 67, 69, 74
A set of logically related responsibilities performed by a member of a project team.

Rollinson, Bill ▶ 107, 109, 217
ROM
(Read Only Memory) A stable, permanent or semi-permanent type of memory which stores key data used by a computer. It can only be read and is not erased when the power is turned off.

Rosendahl, Kristee ▶ 133, 255
rotoscoping ▶ 160
rough-cut ▶ 206
royalties ▶ 12, 15, 64, 74, 82, 86, 237
Payment made to an artist by a publisher taken from the percentage of gross or net revenues from a product.

rule of thirds ▶ 200

S

S-VHS ▶ 202
Video format using standard 1/2 inch video tape. Higher in resolution to consumer VHS and of the same quality as Hi-8.

Saboori, Minoo ▶ 238, 240
sales ▶ 18, 64, 65, 85, 98, 245, 246
sales people ▶ 19, 212, 249
sample size ▶ 118, 191
sampling
A process by which analog audio signals are put into

digital form. A sample is a snapshot of sound pressure at one instant in time. Samples are taken quickly enough so that their replay in sequence gives the impression of actual sound.

sampling rate ▶ 119, 191
The frequency in which sampling occurs during digital audio recording. The higher the sampling rate, the greater the rate of pitches accurately recorded.

sans-serif ▶ 147
Sarnoff, Jill ▶ 104
scalable
Property of being able to take a finished product or transmission to a number of different receivers of differing quality. New digital broadcast standards are designed to scale to receivers of different color and resolution.

scanner ▶ 24, 28, 145, 183, 188, 197
Any graphical input device that converts printed matter into digital data.

schedule ▶ 16, 67, 68, 166, 167, 227, 234
Schlichting, Mark ▶ 96, 98, 131, 217
Schrage, Michael ▶ 66
Schuler, Barry ▶ 4, 63, 102, 120
Screen Actors Guild (SAG) ▶ 192
screen size ▶ 118, 145
screenshots ▶ 184, 242
script
In multimedia, a script can mean a storyboard, computer commands written in a scripting language, or exact speech and action for production of audio, video, or film.

scripting languages ▶ 32, 141, 163, 196, 209, 211
scriptwriter ▶ 136, 144, 157, 192, 199
SCSI
(Small Computer System Interface, pronounced scuzzy) An industry-standard interface between computers and peripheral device controllers.

search mechanisms ▶ 141, 162
SECAM ▶ 203, 205
(Sequential Couleur a Memoire) A television standard that supports 25 frames per second; developed by the French, and used in 20 countries, including France.

second person ▶ 133
secondary shots ▶ 201
security ▶ 98, 134
Sega ▶ 2, 46, 111, 121
self-funding ▶ 72
self-publishing ▶ 35, 230, 236
sequencer
A digital machine that records, mixes, and plays back MIDI tracks. Other synthesizers hook up to a sequencer.

Williams, Wayne ▶ 152
Windows ▶ 110, 121, 221
WINGS for Learning ▶ 44, 90, 160, 176, 236
Winnick, Gary ▶ 50
Winter, Robert ▶ 22, 48, 50
wipes ▶ 206
Wired ▶ 61, 135
wire-frame ▶ 158, 197
A computer animation technique of modeling a three dimensional object with a line segment prior to rendering it.

wireless microphones ▶ 191
word processing ▶ 177
Manipulating words and text on a computer screen to create a letter, memo, or report.

WordPerfect Corporation ▶ 255
work environments ▶ 65
working content ▶ 127

WORM drive ▶ 115
(Write Once, Read Many) A disc drive that allows information to be written only once by the user but read many times.

WPA Film Library ▶ 21, 203
writers ▶ 22, 30, 127, 177
Wurman, Richard Saul ▶ 129, 130

X

XCMD ▶ 141, 210, 211
Short for external command. It is a command written in a computer language other than HyperTalk but made available to HyperCard to extend its built-in command set.

XFNC ▶ 211
Xobjects ▶ 211

Y

Yawitz, Mitchell ▶ 160
Yellow Book ▶ 49, 110
Refers to the specification documents for the original CD-ROM format developed by Philips and Sony.

Yokokura, Nikki ▶ 22, 93

Z

Ziff-Davis Publishing Company ▶ 38
zooming ▶ 201
Special transition or picture effect that brings something closer in view or further away by moving the perspective.

Notes

Notes